郑功成　【德】沃尔夫冈·舒尔茨 / 著

全球社会保障与经济发展关系：
回顾与展望

GLOBAL
SOCIAL SECURITY AND
ECONOMIC DEVELOPMENT:
RETROSPECT AND PROSPECT

中国劳动社会保障出版社

图书在版编目（CIP）数据

全球社会保障与经济发展关系：回顾与展望＝Global Social Security and Economic Development: Retrospect and Prospect: 汉文、英文／郑功成，（德）沃尔夫冈·舒尔茨（Wolfgang Scholz）著. -- 北京：中国劳动社会保障出版社，2019

ISBN 978-7-5167-4179-5

Ⅰ.①全… Ⅱ.①郑… ②沃… Ⅲ.①社会保障-关系-世界经济-经济发展-研究-汉、英 Ⅳ.①D57

中国版本图书馆CIP数据核字（2019）第183868号

中国劳动社会保障出版社出版发行

（北京市惠新东街1号　邮政编码：100029）

*

中国铁道出版社印刷厂印刷装订　新华书店经销
787毫米×1092毫米　16开本　31.75印张　548千字
2019年9月第1版　2019年9月第1次印刷
定价：128.00元

读者服务部电话：（010）64929211/84209101/64921644
营销中心电话：（010）64962347
出版社网址：http://www.class.com.cn

版权专有　　侵权必究

如有印装差错，请与本社联系调换：（010）81211666
我社将与版权执法机关配合，大力打击盗印、销售和使用盗版图书活动，敬请广大读者协助举报，经查实将给予举报者奖励。
举报电话：（010）64954652

前　言

本报告是中国社会保障学会（CAOSS）、国际劳工组织（ILO）、德国艾伯特基金会（FES）三方合作研究项目的成果。中国社会保障学会是中国社会保障及相关领域专家学者组成的全国性学术团体，它以公平、正义、共享为自己的核心价值取向，致力于推动中国社会保障体系建设和促进社会保障领域的全球合作与交流。国际劳工组织在全球致力于促进社会正义，促进女性和男性获得体面和生产性劳动的机会。它通过涉及187个国家的政府、劳动者和雇主组织的三方架构，采纳和促进国际劳工标准和工作中的权利、普遍和有效的社会保护制度，并推动改进与工作有关议题的社会对话。艾伯特基金会是德国的非营利性组织，致力于促进社会公正、可持续发展和国际合作。

作为国际劳工组织亚太工作论文系列的一部分，本报告聚焦于社会保障与经济发展之间的关系，旨在分享知识、推动全球特别是发展中国家有关社会保障制度发展的讨论。

社会保障被广泛认为是减少贫困和预防个体整个生命周期中脆弱性的主要手段。同时，有效社会保障的经济效应在各种情境下已被证明是积极的，使其成为任何现代社会不可替代的制度安排。2012年通过的国际劳工组织《第202号建议书　关于国家社会保护底线的建议书》以及社会保障议题在"2030年可持续发展议程"中的突出角色均反映出这一共识：社会保障作为人权和尊严问题的必要性。

全球社会日益认识到，社会保障在塑造各国经济发展方面发挥着作用。经济增长为充足的社会保障待遇给付奠定了物质基础，而社会保障制度则有助于稳定经济，甚至往往刺激经济增长。尽管社会保障具有固有的稳定功能，但社会保障对经济增长的影响及两者间的关系是复杂的，也是有争议的。不同的体系和制度项目在特定的情况下可能会产生不同的效果。剖析社会保障与经济增长之间的复杂关系，将有助于改善各国制度，以及最大限度地发挥积极的协同作用。

如今，大多数国家都建立了以国家立法为基础的社会保障制度，尽管在许多情况下，这些制度只覆盖少数国民。从欧洲引入社会保障到新兴国家（最突出的是中国）近期的发展，本报告深入探讨了过去一个世纪的全球经验，这些经验显示了社会保障扩张与经济发展之间总体积极的关系。

本报告对中国、美国、英国、德国、法国、北欧国家、日本和韩国的社会保障与经济发展之间的关系进行了评估。此外，它围绕中国社会保障制度的演变及其在中国近期社会经济转型中的作用提供了深入透彻的见解。基于中国的经验，本报告认为，当社会保障很好地适应国家的社会和经济结构时，可以产生积极的直接和间接生产力效应；反之亦然，积极的经济发展可以促进社会保障的发展。

本项研究缘起于中国社会保障学会、国际劳工组织、艾伯特基金会的一个基本共识：在当前发生深刻结构变化和全球不稳定的背景下，社会保障是可持续发展不可或缺的部分。经济增长旨在通过充足的社会保障更多地惠及民生，而社会保障制度在促进经济发展方面发挥着积极作用。

我们希望，本报告将有助于更好地理解上述复杂的关系，并阐明社会保障制度作为可持续发展和转型进程中之不可或缺要素的重要性。

Tomoko Nishimoto

Assistant Director-General and Regional Director for Asia and the Pacific

国际劳工组织助理总干事兼亚太局局长

致　谢

本报告是中国社会保障学会、国际劳工组织、德国艾伯特基金会共同努力的成果。执行摘要、第1.1节、第2.2节、第3章和第4章由中国社会保障学会会长、中国人民大学教授郑功成撰写。国际劳工组织高级顾问Wolfgang Scholz先生负责撰写第1.2节和第2.1节。浙江大学何文炯教授和中国社会科学院华颖博士参与撰写第3.1节。报告的其他部分由郑功成、Wolfgang Scholz和华颖共同完成。

作者特别感谢中国社会保障学会名誉会长、原国务委员、全国人大常委会副委员长华建敏先生在本项目启动会上发表的卓越见解。作者对中国社会科学院欧洲研究所前所长周弘教授、中山大学申曙光教授、中国人民大学杨立雄教授、中国人民大学鲁全副教授参与研讨所做出的贡献表示感谢。作者也非常感谢国别报告作者的贡献，包括美国北卡罗来纳大学John D. Stephens教授、英国约克大学John Hudson教授、德国卡塞尔大学Wolfgang Schroeder教授、法国经济与社会研究中心Pierre Concialdi研究员、南丹麦大学Klaus Petersen教授、日本政策研究大学院大学Taichi Ono教授、韩国中央大学Kim Yeon-Myung教授。

作者还要感谢下列专家对报告的讨论和各时期版本所做出的宝贵贡献：国际劳工组织亚太局高级社会保护专家Nuno Cunha先生、国际劳工组织中国和蒙古局项目官员李青宜女士、德国艾伯特基金会北京代表处前驻中国代表Christoph Pohlman先生、国际社会保障协会社会保障高级专家朱玉坤先生。本报告的早期版本也在各种高级别会议和研讨会上发表，作者感谢与会者们的意见和建议，他们包括伦敦经济学院 Athar Hussain 教授、巴黎第一大学 Francis Kessler 教授、南京大学林闽钢教授、日本女子大学沈洁教授、成均馆大学 Hong Kyung-Zoon 教授。作者还要感谢参与了整个研究项目的国际劳工组织中国和蒙古局前任局长 Tim De Meyer 先生、国际劳工组织社会保障部社会政策部门负责人 Christina Behrendt 先生、国际劳工组织亚太局区域经济和社会分析部门负责人兼高级经济学家 Sara Elder 的评论和反馈意见。

还要特别说明的是，何文炯教授、华颖博士不仅参与了本报告第 3.1 节的写作，而且参与了全过程讨论。华颖博士更是自始至终承担着联络各国做者和将报告从中文翻译成英文、英文翻译成中文的任务，为本报告的完成做出了独特的贡献。

报告简介

  本报告从历史视角和全球层面全面阐释了经济和社会保障发展的相互作用，在展示西半球丰富的社会保障政策文献和观点的同时，弥补了对中国通过积极发展社会保障及相关制度，支持其令人印象深刻的经济发展方面之相关研究的不足。本报告认为，全球化对贸易和增长的积极影响——由始于1978年中国的改革开放所引发的——为中国社会保障改革与体系建设提供了发展良机，而由政府主导的扩张性社会保障政策又对中国经济改革与发展产生了积极影响，因此中国的经验值得全球政策制定者重视。相较而言，西方同期整固了其社会保障制度，包括通过国家紧缩和私有化手段，后来在紧缩加剧的背景下，助长了经济停滞、失业和日益严重的贫困现象。社会政策制定者宜重新考虑主流社会政策方法。本报告希望能够证明，社会保障与经济发展可以良性互动并实现共同发展，这不仅是西半球国家验证过了的历史经验，而且是中国近几十年来一直在验证的经验。

执行摘要

自2008年美国次贷危机爆发以来,全球经济陷入发展低谷,社会保障[1]成了政策层面与学界普遍日益关注的讨论焦点。如何理解并正确处理社会保障与经济发展的关系,已成为国际社会的重大议题。

2012年国际劳工大会通过的《第202号建议书 关于国家社会保护底线的建议书》重申社会保障是一项人权,并敦促各国发展社会保障制度。2015年9月,联合国193个成员国在纽约举行的联合国可持续发展峰会上正式通过了17项可持续发展目标(SDGs)。

本报告归纳了对社会保障与经济发展关系的理论思考,分析了经济思潮与实践模式的范式变化给社会保障带来的当前和未来挑战。在澄清一些认识误区的基础上,本报告从历史的视角总结社会保障与经济发展的关系,并寻求能够实现两者之间良性互动与共同发展之路。

报告的核心观点如下:

1. 从历史上看,社会保障对美国和欧洲大陆等不同国家和地区的社会经济和政治发展具有重要意义。虽然社会保障起初主要是作为一种应对政治危机或经济危机的治理机制,但后来社会保障也有助于促进体制转型。人们认识到,可以且应该在危机应对之外的情况下运用社会保障。事实上,许多国家的经验

---

[1] 本报告使用了"社会保障"这一术语,该术语与国际劳工组织界定和通常使用的"社会保护"基本一致。在本报告中,两个术语根据语境需要交替使用。

已经证明，在"正常"（非危机）情况下，社会保障可以作为一种具有社会效益和经济生产力的政策工具。因此，社会保障制度的设计必须使其得到利益相关方的信任，并在两种情况下都很好地运行。

一个多世纪以来，治理良好的社会保障化解了社会矛盾、增进了国家认同、弥补了市场失灵，有助于稳定甚至往往还能刺激经济增长。近二三十年来，中低收入国家越发意识到建立社会保障体系的重要性，这是建立社会保护制度百年历史的最新篇章（ILO，2017）。中国是这一发展中的先锋。目前，尽管大多数国家已经制定了以国家立法为基础的社会保护制度，但这些制度在许多情况下只覆盖少数人口。尽管取得了值得称道的进展，但仍然存在巨大差距，特别是在亚洲和非洲的部分地区（ILO，2017）。

随着联合国的成立，社会保障成为一项人权[1]。因此，人们普遍认为，社会保障不仅是应对人们临时收入损失的潜在有效的反危机治理工具，更是一系列人权和应享权利。当然，如果没有物质支持，权利和资格则易大打折扣。因此，应当重视社会保障与经济协同发展的政策。在现代国家，社会保障与经济发展是政治和社会经济实践的基石，两者相互依存、不可分割。必须多加注意，以使得两者相得益彰，实现最大程度的积极互动（Scholz，2015）。

2. 有关社会保障对经济增长的影响的国际讨论较为复杂，并不总能达成一致意见。总体而言，人们认为如果一国的社会保障体系具备充足的财政规模，则社会保障体系能对生产（国内生产总值）和就业、劳动生产率、劳动力市场参与、收入分配和国际贸易等产生影响（Scholz，2015）。争论的具体结果往往取决于所考虑的社会保障体系的设计，例如，是更倾向于俾斯麦模式还是贝弗里奇模式，或者两者兼具的混合型模式。

为学者专家们所普遍接受的结论是，俾斯麦模式的社会保障制度更以生产

---

[1] 享有社会保障的人权载于《世界人权宣言》（1948年）、《经济、社会、文化权利国际公约》（1966年），以及联合国其他主要人权文书以及国际劳工组织的标准中。

率为导向，而贝弗里奇模式则倾向于实现社会公平。随着社会经济的发展，兼具俾斯麦模式和贝弗里奇模式特征的混合型模式越加常见，未来，社会保障制度将很有可能更加具有混合性。

3. 在现代社会，社会保障往往是一个结构复杂、财务综合全面的系统，占据一国国内生产总值的25%～30%以上，其中1/3或超过1/3的社会保障收入来自政府（公共部门），是一个以现金发放与服务提供为形式的收入保障制度体系，伴随在个人生命周期的不同阶段。[1]

尽管社会保障具有内在的稳定属性，然而在大约二三十年前，社会保障及其在国民经济中的作用进入了重要的调整期。这在很大程度上源于1989年后"华盛顿共识"的国际传播（Williamson，2002）、中国逐步深入的改革开放以及随后越发激烈的全球化竞争。

在西方，许多国家决定通过抑制成本来应对随之而来的挑战，包括人口老龄化、财政负债及其对劳动力市场的复杂影响。自2008年次贷危机以来，许多国家更是采取了财政紧缩政策。因缺乏适宜的经济政策和财政政策，数十年来具有指导性的西方福利国家转入退却态势。

4. 原则上，全球化为一些国家提供了契机，使这些国家实施以出口导向达成高增长的暂时发展战略，并同时发展和加强社会保障。[2] 然而，在发展中国家，特别是在巴西、俄罗斯、印度、中国和南非（即金砖国家）之中，主要是中国成功抓住了经济转型的机遇（包括通过出口导向型贸易政策），在这一进程中，社会保障制度的快速发展发挥着重要的支持性作用。

这些（暂时）快速发展的国家（主要是金砖国家）都采取措施改善社

---

[1] 在本报告中，社会保障包括儿童和家庭福利、生育福利、失业保障、工伤保障、疾病津贴、老年保障、残障保障、遗属津贴、健康保障和教育福利。

[2] 对这一论述的解读必须谨慎，本报告无法就此进行充分解释。在全球层面，贸易顺差国家需要贸易逆差国家作为对应国，因为从逻辑上讲，全球贸易是平衡的。换言之，20世纪90年代开始的出口导向型战略依赖于（主要是）美国准备接受这种赤字。

保障制度，目的是使全体人民得以分享全球化的果实，而非只让小部分人独享。国际劳工组织通过开展社会保障技术合作等方式提醒世界各国：经济发展的根本目标是提高人民福祉。国际劳工组织第202号建议书的批准和可持续发展目标的通过表明，社会保障在国际议程中变得更加稳固。

我们在西方国家看到了社会保障紧缩，但同时在某些地区（如东南亚国家联盟成员国）看到社会保障有了更大空间，就如同在中国和其他金砖国家所观察到的类似发展方向。这表明社会保障存在不同方向发展趋势，这是多方参与者复杂互动的结果。

5. 在此背景下，各国必须设法重塑其包括社会保障在内的福利政策，以使得其社会得以继续（或转而）适应全球化带来的新情况。为此，西方国家及相关发展中国家应当重新考虑其现有紧缩的社会政策，并寻求代之以旨在加强收入保障和缩小收入差距的政策；应当通过加强社会保障免除人们日益增长的后顾之忧。

构建更加积极的社会保障制度并赋予其与时俱进的自我调节、不断优化的功能，应当成为21世纪各国社会保障制度发展的正确取向（郑功成，2017a）。中国在调整其社会保障制度以使其适应成功的经济转型，并有助于释放长期保有的增长潜力方面是一个典型的例子。然而，中国每年的社会支出只占其GDP的约13%[1]，仅相当于欧洲相对社会支出水平的一半。这说明尽管中国取得了很大成就，但初次分配仍然存在不公。

因此，中国应当进一步系统性地扩大与发展中的经济能力相适应的社会保障体系，即使仅出于为应对经济发展挑战做准备的考虑。采取这样的政策也有

---

[1] 中国社会保障总支出的统计口径，主要包括财政性社会保障支出、公共卫生支出、国民教育支出和社会保险支出等。其中，财政性社会保障支出包括社会救助支出、保障性住房支出、社会保险项目财政补贴、残疾人与老年人的福利津贴等；社会保险支出包括养老金、医疗保险基金及工伤保险、失业保险、生育保险支出；国民教育支出包括义务教育支出和幼儿教育、残疾人教育、职业教育支出及高等教育中的补助支出。该数字与国际劳工组织（2017年）的估算不同，后者不包括医疗卫生支出。

助于中国成功地从出口导向型向内需驱动型的经济增长模式转变。与此同时，还应该加强教育体系和教育福利、就业措施和住房政策，而最重要的是要稳步提高工资水平，尤其是低收入劳动者的工资水平。

6. 对包括中国在内的许多国家而言，人口老龄化被视作提高了社会成本，对国际竞争力有负面影响，从而阻碍国家经济发展。然而，这种担忧似乎忽略了事实上全球几乎所有区域的人口都在经历老龄化，即所有区域都面临老龄化相关成本的扩张。因此，（至少在 G20 国家之间）应当努力达成国际协议，将那些因人口老龄化引致的、不可避免的额外社会成本置于国际竞争的议程之外。这将使各国得以更有效地推行旨在减贫的社会政策，包括预防老年贫困。如若不然，今后老年贫困将成为全球日益严峻的问题。

7. 在当代社会保障政策讨论中，中国有着引人瞩目的地位。这是因为中国的社会保障发展可称得上是重要范例：合理利用包括社会保障在内的制度安排，协调和引导体制转型，以此开启强劲的增长。中国成功地采取了一种综合性的策略，使经济改革和问题导向的社会保障变革相辅相成，在社会保障改革释放了经济增长潜力的同时，这种增长反过来也促进了社会保障制度的发展，总体上实现了良性循环。

这种策略得以成功的深层原因之一在于，它为改善民生（作为改革结果）提供了持续的制度保障；不仅保障未来，也保障当下。尽管中国新型社会保障制度改革还在不断深化之中，新制度的定型还需要通过更为科学的顶层设计才能走向完善，但已经取得的巨大进展，应当对世界各发展中国家的社会保障与经济发展的有效结合具有重要的启示。从国际视角看，中国（的改革经验）之所以使人印象深刻，与其说是因为所采取的政策措施内容（毕竟中国政府采用的是人们所熟知的方式：覆盖全民的养老保险和医疗保险，辅之以失业津贴和最低收入保障），不如说是制度建立与实施的速度之快。

8. 社会保障是应对危机负面影响，或更广泛地说，促进系统转型的有效治理工具。然而，这些情况并不是设计社会保障制度的标准情况，也不应只在这些情况下使用社会保障。相反，社会保障应该在正常（非危机）条件下发挥社会效力和促进经济生产力发展。社会保障体系设计须使其在危机和正常情况下都能够很好地运作。为此，应考虑不同方面和各种工具。理解不同社会保障项目的社会经济功能，是合理设计社会保障制度并在实践中最大限度发挥其社会功能和经济功能之先决条件。然而需要强调的是，社会保障不应该被视为实现政治或经济目标的手段，而是实现体面生活和人类尊严的重要方式。

在这一背景下，许多国家的社会保障制度正面临着以下挑战：

● 必须克服过去新自由主义的泛滥（如必须再次强化劳工权利），再次促进社会保障隐性和显性的生产力效应。

● 必须提高劳动报酬。将那些因老龄化引致的社会保障成本置于国际竞争议题之外，以促进国家落实反贫困政策。

● 必须减少收入和财富不平等（包括通过税收和社会保障立法中的更多再分配因素），以增强国内需求。

● 在数字经济加快发展的背景下，社会保障应当增强适应性，不仅确保社会保障的财务基础，而且应该覆盖数字经济带来的各种新就业形式的劳动者。

● 必须提供更加公平的优质受教育机会，以确保人口素质不断提升。

● 必须加强社会保障以应对世界人口的持续增长、环境问题，以及其他全球性挑战，包括污染、淡水短缺、气候变化等。

社会保障无法独力解决上述问题。鉴于社会保障对社会经济的影响，它是人们（和政府）获得必要时间以寻求可行解决方案的不可或缺的前提条件（ILO，2017）。

9. 全球经济发展与社会保障正面临着诸多挑战：经济全球化与区域竞争、

人口老龄化、人口流动、社会结构变化、科学和信息技术的进步以及由此带来的新业态、非标准形式就业与生活方式的改变等。

尽管这些变化对社会保障可能具有各种影响，但却远未影响其维持社会功能和经济功能的基本适应性与有效能力。世界各国必须积极而稳健地应对上述挑战与变化，因此需要在众多政策领域中寻求新的平衡。应当积极地使用社会保障政策以寻求解决方案，而不是将其作为国际竞争中调整成本的狭隘工具。同时，根据社会保障的性质，既不应当让其扮演经济政策的角色，也不应将经济政策失败的责任转嫁给社会保障。

特别是在最近一轮全球金融与经济危机期间，多边国际组织就社会保障的重要性达成一定程度的协议。即使未就具体模式和支出水平达成共识，国际货币基金组织和世界银行等机构在某种程度上也就社会保障的重要性达成了一致。例如，国际货币基金组织独立评估办公室在一份报告中指出："过去十年来，国际货币基金组织加强了对社会保护的关注，因为社会保护应对了全球金融危机的后果，解决了人们对粮食和燃料价格冲击所带来影响的担忧，缓解了对低收入群体和最脆弱群体的更广泛的压力。因此，国际货币基金组织已经超越了传统的'以财政为中心'的做法，认识到社会保护由于社会和政治稳定考量等更广泛的原因而具有宏观上的重要性"（IMF，2017b）。世界银行和国际劳工组织主导的"全民社会保护全球伙伴关系"于 2016 年启动。这表明世界银行意识到社会保护在应对贫困和正在加剧的收入不平等方面的重要性 (World Bank and ILO，2016)。

10. 坚守社会保障基本原则（如国际劳工组织公约与建议书所规定的），构建健全的、多层次化的社会保障体系，可在面临各类危机时最大限度地减少制度失灵。为了改善并保持社会保障的服务功能，宜持续优化现代化社会保障机构内外部工作流程，包括借助信息技术等手段。这将增强社会保障相对于私营部门竞争者的吸引力。

21世纪的社会保障与经济发展均需要继续创新思维，并与时俱进地调整相关制度安排，而社会保障必须成为缴费者与待遇领取者的坚定保障。因此，实现社会保障与经济发展之间的良性互动和共同发展应当成为所有利益相关者的准则，且应当避免社会保障沦为短视政策、既有商业利益的附属品。

在这方面，中国改革开放以来的发展实践虽然不能说是非常完美，但它确实是当今世界社会保障与经济发展相得益彰的典型案例。

如果一国的社会保障制度能够适应社会和经济结构，则可以产生非常积极的直接和间接生产力效应；同时，经济增长对于社会保障的扩张至关重要。德国、美国、英国和北欧国家等（社会）支出较高的一些国家的长期经验表明，通过社会保障等方式提升人力资本积累、提高劳动生产率，不会对经济发展产生负面影响。日本、韩国在20世纪下半叶的经济腾飞与社会保障制度的建立是同步进行的，这也是很好的例证。

在当代世界，将经济下滑归咎于管理良好的福利制度并无科学依据。这种错误的认识，不仅会损害社会保障制度的健康发展，而且不利于寻求经济增长的积极途径。

本报告旨在细致地探讨和强调社会保障与经济发展的这种关联。

关于作者

郑功成，全国人大常委会委员、中国社会保障学会会长、中国人民大学教授。他长期从事社会保障、劳动就业等研究，多项政策研究成果为中国社会保障改革与立法提供了重要的理论背景与决策参考。

沃夫冈·舒尔茨（Wolfgang Scholz），国际劳工组织高级顾问，日内瓦国际劳工局社会保障部前社会保障顾问。他在国家级社会保障规划、国际（联合国）级别社会政策咨询方面具有丰富的经验。

声明：文章、研究报告和其他稿件中表达的观点的责任完全在于作者，出版并不构成国际劳工组织对其中所表达的观点或提及的任何产品、过程或地理名称的背书。

主要缩写表

ASEAN	东南亚国家联盟
CAOSS	中国社会保障学会,北京
CNY	人民币(元)
ESSPROS	欧洲综合社会保护统计系统
EU	欧盟
EUROSTAT	欧盟统计局
FES	弗里德里希·艾伯特基金会
GDP	国内生产总值
ILO	国际劳工组织
ISSA	国际社会保障协会
MHRSS	中华人民共和国人力资源和社会保障部
OECD	经济合作与发展组织
SNA	国民账户体系
UN	联合国
US	美国

说明:①货币符号 $ 表示美元。

②"大陆"表示不含英国和爱尔兰的欧洲大陆。

③北欧国家指丹麦、芬兰、冰岛、挪威、瑞典及其相关领土。

目 录

1 引言 ··· 01
  1.1 研究背景 ··· 01
    1.1.1 背景 ··· 01
    1.1.2 研究目的与内容 ··· 04
  1.2 社会保障与经济发展关系的理论假设 ················· 06
    1.2.1 社会保障传统介绍 ····································· 09
    1.2.2 社会保障的利与弊 ····································· 11
    1.2.3 对社会保障的正面论证 ····························· 13
    1.2.4 作为初次收入再分配工具的社会保障 ········ 16
    1.2.5 社会保障制度设计和经济表现 ·················· 20
2 国际视野下的社会保障和经济发展：历史经验和当代挑战 ··· 24
  2.1 全球范围内社会保障与经济发展的历史经验 ········ 24
    2.1.1 遥远的过去：现代社会保障的先驱与发展动因 ··· 25
    2.1.2 19 世纪：英国、德国和罗马教廷 ················ 26
    2.1.3 20 世纪：两次世界大战期间的社会保障 ······ 29
    2.1.4 20 世纪：第二次世界大战后走向全球的社会保障 ··· 32
    2.1.5 第二次世界大战后西方国家社会保障的发展 ······ 33
    2.1.6 1989 年之后东欧、中亚及世界其他地区社会保障的发展 ·· 55

2.2 全球社会保障与经济发展面临的新挑战 ………………………… 57
    2.2.1 经济发展与社会保障关系背后的发展理念出现
          分歧 ……………………………………………………… 57
    2.2.2 全球化进程具有不确定性 ……………………………… 59
    2.2.3 人口老龄化快速发展对经济社会影响深远 ………… 60
    2.2.4 新技术革命对传统产业的冲击与新业态的常态化 … 62
    2.2.5 福利刚性增长与财务可持续性的矛盾 ……………… 63

3 社会保障与经济发展：中国的案例 …………………………… 65
  3.1 中国社会保障制度促进经济发展的历史经验 ……………… 66
    3.1.1 中国 40 年取得的经济发展成就 ……………………… 66
    3.1.2 中国社会保障改革与发展取得的成就 ……………… 71
    3.1.3 社会保障对中国经济发展的贡献 …………………… 96
    3.1.4 中国处理经济发展与社会保障关系的经验 …………113
  3.2 主要社会经济挑战和政策建议 …………………………………120
    3.2.1 中国面临的主要挑战 ……………………………………120
    3.2.2 对中国政府的政策建议 …………………………………124

4 总结 …………………………………………………………………130
  4.1 全球经济发展与社会保障关系的基本历史经验和理论
      共识 ……………………………………………………………130
  4.2 结论和对各国的政策建议 ……………………………………134

附件 1 社会保障的定义 …………………………………………………139

附件 2 附表 ………………………………………………………………143

参考文献 ……………………………………………………………………150

附录：国别报告 ……………………………………………………………167

德国经济发展与社会保障体系建设：历史经验与未来方案 …167

英国社会保障与经济关系的演变：从福利国家到竞争国家? …180

法国的经济发展与社会保障：以20世纪80年代中期为
　　转折点 …………………………………………………204

北欧国家经济发展和社会保障之间的动态关系——为福利
　　而增长还是为增长而福利? ………………………………230

比较视野中的美国：福利国家与经济发展 ……………………239

日本社会保障的历史发展与当前问题 …………………………253

韩国的经验：没有福利制度的经济增长局限 …………………264

图表目录

表 格 目 录

表 1　部分国家社会保障的首次立法年份与经济发展水平 … 28

表 2　2006—2017年中国基本医疗保险参保人数 …………… 84

表 3　2000—2017年中国城乡最低生活保障基本情况 ……… 91

表 4　2007—2017年中国公共预算支出表 …………………… 115

表 5　1978—2017年中国卫生费用支出结构表 ……………… 116

表 A1　1978—2017年中国GDP总量与人均GDP ………… 143

表 A2　1978—2017年中国基本养老保险参保人数历年
变化情况 …………………………………………… 143

表 A3　1998—2017年中国基本养老保险基金累计结余 …… 144

表 A4　1978—2017年中国基本养老保险参保人数 ………… 145

表 A5　2001—2017年中国基本养老保险基金人均支出
变化情况 …………………………………………… 147

表 A6　1985—2017年中国农村贫困线、贫困人口和
贫困发生率 ………………………………………… 148

图 目 录

图 1　1900 年以前至 2010 年以后对社会保护项目进行全国性立法的国家占比，按政策领域分列 ………… 32

图 2　1978—2017 年中国 GDP 总量与人均 GDP …………… 68

图 3　1978—2017 年中国就业结构发展变化图（按产业划分） ………… 68

图 4　1978—2017 年中国产业结构发展变化图 …………… 69

图 5　1978—2017 年中国城镇化率发展变化图 …………… 70

图 6　1980—2017 年中国城乡居民家庭恩格尔系数 ………… 70

图 7　1998—2017 年基本养老保险参保人数历年变化情况 … 77

图 8　2009—2017 年基本养老保险基金人均支出变化情况 … 78

图 9　2000—2017 年基本医疗保险人均基金支出变化情况 … 85

图 10　1985—2017 年农村贫困线和贫困发生率 …………… 90

图 11　2005—2017 年职工基本养老保险人均基金支出增长情况 ………… 102

图 12　1998—2017 年基本养老保险基金累计结余 ………… 103

专 栏 目 录

专栏 1　研究进程 ………… 05

专栏 2　如何界定社会保障以及一些含义 ………… 07

专栏 3　什么是初次收入？ ………… 17

专栏 4　中国社会保障制度体系框架 ………… 73

专栏 5　养老金支出占 GDP 比重的决定因素 …………………… 81

专栏 6　中国农村扶贫开发：加强消除贫困的措施 ………… 90

专栏 7　中国的住房保障改革与发展——从去福利化到

　　　　重归社会保障体系 ……………………………………108

1 引 言

1.1 研究背景

1.1.1 背景

我们已经处在一个全球化深度交融的大变革时代。大变革势头不可阻挡、不可逆转,各种文化的、制度的、技术的文明在比较与鉴别中相互交融,工业化、信息化、现代化进程明显加快,带来的是全球政治和经济格局的重构和全球治理的更大可能性,最终将实现人类文明发展的升华。大时代带来了深刻影响,世界进入了深刻的社会经济结构调整期。20 世纪 80 年代以来中国和其他一些发展中国家的快速发展,更加证明了全球化对人类社会发展进步有积极的促进作用。然而,保护主义倾向、收入差距扩大、贫困的加剧以及由此带来的普通民众不满情绪蔓延,表明进一步的全球化需要从构建人类命运共同体并促进社会公正原则出发(郑功成,2017b)。

2008 年美国次贷危机触发世界经济陷入发展低谷,全球主要经济体都面临新的挑战。不仅美国与欧洲的经济发展未见曙光、日本深陷经济低潮,新兴经济体(如巴西、俄罗斯、印度、中国)的经济增速也都出现下滑,部分国家甚至出现了经济负增长。2008 年以后,一些国家以福利削减——通常被称为"紧缩"的一揽子财政紧缩政策的一部分——作为应对手段,但遭到民众的普遍抵制。

在欠发达国家和发达国家,这场危机都直接或间接地触发了收入和财富鸿沟的进一步严重扩大。在收入金字塔顶层的人很少，同时处于底层的人数众多。这导致饥饿、移民、经济脆弱和政治不稳定——又进一步削弱了区域经济基础，从而削弱了国家维持和扩大有效社会保障的能力。一些有着健全社会保障制度的国家面临着削减福利开支的压力。[1] 2016 年，全球范围内掀起支出紧缩的狂潮，预计至少持续到 2020 年。2018 年，124 个国家（其中 81 个为发展中国家）将调整其支出水平，并徘徊在此水平上至 2020 年（ILO，2017）。

与此同时，一些国家迈向另一个发展方向，即通过对制度的结构调整来扭转之前的改革，化解社会保障个人化和市场化的风险，并支持其福利体系长期可持续。在社会保障和经济同时快速发展方面，中国是一个较为典型的例子（见第 3 章）。而在南亚、非洲的大多数欠发达国家和最不发达国家中，迄今只有有限的社会救助政策和税收筹资的福利，或是覆盖面有限的社会保险。例如，在数据可得的大多数非洲国家中，只有不到 30% 的人享有社会保障（ILO，2017）。

在此背景下，发达国家需要继续帮助这些区域发展有意义的社会保障并缩小不平等，包括通过"南北转移"（"南"指欠发达国家，"北"指发达国家）。同时必须明确说明的是，仅靠社会保障不能解决这些发展中国家的问题。因为如果没有健全的初次收入分配，将国民收入产出的成果公平分配给生产者，则用于社会保障筹资的收入基础便过于薄弱。

构建一个不让任何人掉队、消除一切形式和表现的贫困的世界，是全球最大的挑战，是实现可持续发展必不可少的要求，也是"2030 年可持续发展议程"的核心。这些原则也体现在中国国家主席习近平近年反复倡导的构建"人类命运共同体"的主张中。[2]

---

1 关于术语的问题和使用，见专栏 2 和附件 1。

2 中国国家主席习近平所倡导的构建人类命运共同体主张与联合国的价值观一致，也呼应了 2030 年可持续发展目标。2012 年 11 月，中国共产党第十八次全国代表大会报告中首次提出"人类命运共同体"的概念之后，习近平主席在国内外多个重要场合提出并阐述构建人类命运共同体。中国奉行共享发展新理念，倡导构建人类命运共同体，这和全球最新发展趋势一致。

历史证明，实现经济增长与发展福利制度的双重目标是任何一个国家在经济和社会发展过程中都无法回避的。19世纪末社会保险制度在欧洲大陆的出现，极大地缓和了劳资矛盾，为现代资本主义的发展提供了最重要的动力；1935年美国的《社会保障法》不仅于经济危机中挽救了美国，而且有效地维护了美国的长期繁荣；20世纪40年代英国的福利国家设计，增进了对社会团结的共识，创造了新的就业岗位，从而有利于经济增长方式的转型；日本、韩国在20世纪下半叶的经济腾飞与社会保障制度的建立是同步进行的。

20世纪80年代，部分国家在社会保障领域借助市场机制的改革和基金积累制养老金的引入，在一定程度上有助于积累资本，但通常也损害了社会保障的再分配功能。在过去10多年中，阿根廷、匈牙利等国重建公共性质的团结养老金，增强养老保险制度的再分配性。这些一再表明个人化与市场化改革取向对收入再分配的削弱已经导致了巨大的政治风险与社会风险。进入21世纪后，中国的社会保障获得了全面发展，巴西等国也采取了类似的政策策略。

尽管在评估社会保障与经济增长的关系方面付出了努力，但围绕不同观点的讨论远未结束，尚需要更多的证据和评估。[1] 近一个多世纪的全球发展实践，总体上呈现的是社会保障制度的扩张与经济发展的正相关关系。然而，在过去30年间，政治与经济精英在这方面的国际共识有所减弱。近年来则伴随全球化进程中可观测到的不平等现象的加剧及其导致的不良社会经济现象日益显性化而有所回归（参见第2.1节）。[2]

---

[1] 部分经济学家认为，福利制度是经济衰退的罪魁祸首，或更宽泛地说，福利制度抑制了生产力。其他人则持不同意见，尤其是在持续的不良发展态势下，他们认为不平等是政治与经济危机的重要导火索和驱动因素，因此，公共支出和社会保护可以且应该在推动各国经济复苏中发挥重要作用（Cingano，2014）。

[2] 尽管在全球辩论中存在着分歧，但即使是国际货币基金组织和经合组织等机构发布的研究结论，也指出不平等造成的负面影响，即弱化再分配不仅会损害社会公正，也会阻碍经济发展（IMF，2015；Cingano，2014）。

1.1.2 研究目的与内容

社会保障和经济发展紧密交织，构成了同一社会经济现实的要素。因此，不应任由将两者对立起来的错误思潮来支配可能导致不良后果的政策措施。相反，社会保障和经济发展是同一枚硬币的两面，应该从整体的角度进行分析。要在澄清社会保障与经济发展的历史逻辑及相互关系的基础上，谋求并促进那些已经证明能够实现两者之间良性互动的合理、可靠和富有成效的方式。这并不意味着忽视或掩盖企业利益和个人通过社会化组织的保障机制获得保护的诉求之间存在的不可避免的固有冲突。只有开诚布公地正视这种冲突，才能找到解决方案。它可能对特定经济体的生产力产生或大或小的影响，这取决于具体的制度模式（见第 1.2.5 小节）。

本报告的目的，是以全球社会保障制度与经济发展的关系为核心议题，通过对中国和一些有着成熟社会保障制度的国家的观察与研究，为全面、正确地理解社会保障与经济发展的关系提供科学的理论依据，并寻求新时代背景下的社会保障可持续发展之路。

本报告包括如下四个部分：

（1）全球范围内社会保障与经济发展的历史经验与趋势。这包括社会保障发展与经济增长的关系，以及社会保障投入减少与经济危机之间的关系。

（2）对社会保障与经济发展之间关系以及不同社会保障模式对经济发展的影响的理论解释。

（3）先行国家社会保障与经济发展的历史实践，以及在新经济形势下协调社会保障与经济发展的政策措施。

（4）中国社会保障与经济发展的历史经验、现实挑战与趋势。

本报告具有与当前全球转型相关联的重要意义。一方面，本报告旨在促进理性认识社会保障在人类社会发展进程中所肩负的历史使命与现实责任，提出确立公平取向、覆盖全民、权责清晰、保障适度、可持续的社会保障建设方案，避免短视的改革抉择（郑功成，2016a）。另一方面，本报告为世界了解中国、德国、英国、法国、北欧国家、美国、日本、韩国的社会保障与经济发展提供了最新的评估。本报告希望为全面、客观地了解中国社会保障制度在经济社会全面转型的背景下的发展进程及其积极作用提供一个权威来源。

一个能够为13亿多人口提供稳定的、不断发展的社会保障并有助于国民经济持续发展的中国特色社会保障制度，可以为世界各国重塑自己的社会保障制度提供有益的经验。

专栏1 研究进程

本项研究缘起于中国社会保障学会、国际劳工组织、德国艾伯特基金会的一个基本共识：当今全球经济发展与社会保障制度处于复杂变革和挑战期。理解两者间的关系显得前所未有的重要。

这份报告的研究进程得益于多次高级别大会和研讨会的丰硕研讨和发现，以及若干轮的修订。2015年9—10月，中国社会保障学会会长先后会见了国际劳工组织社会保障高级专家、国际社会保障协会秘书长，就该项研究进行了讨论。同期，德国艾伯特基金会驻中国代表对此项研究表示鼎力支持。他们一致认为，对当今世界社会保障与经济发展关系问题进行最新专题研究具有重要性。

2016年9月，中国社会保障学会、国际劳工组织、德国艾伯特基金会在北京联合举行"全球社会保障与经济发展关系研究项目"启动会，来自中国社会保障学会、国际劳工组织、德国艾伯特基金会、国际社会保障协会，以及来自丹麦、法国、德国、日本、韩国、英国、美国等国的20多位知名专家学者参与研讨。与会者确定了该项研究的基本框架、核心观点、任务分配和时间进度安排等。2016年9—12月，七位国别报告作者分别提交了法国、德国、日本、北欧国家、韩国、英国、美国的研究报告初稿。

2017年5月，郑功成教授、舒尔茨先生、努诺·昆拉先生、李青宜女士、何文炯教授、华颖博士、鲁全副教授、仁恺先生等在北京举行研讨会，就主报告的主体内容初稿及国别报告初稿交换意见。

2017年9月，中国社会保障学会、国际劳工组织、德国艾伯特基金会在南京大学举行"全球社会保障与经济发展国际研讨会"。报告相关作者交换了意见，并进一步从与会的各国学者中听取了更广泛的意见。紧接此次会议，郑功成教授、舒尔茨先生、努诺昆拉先生、李青宜女士、何文炯教授、华颖博士、鲁全副教授、仁恺先生在南京对主报告及修订后的国别报告进行最后一次集体研讨，并对主报告的进一步修订提出意见。

2018年2—12月，三家合作机构进一步对报告进行修订。

报告最后由郑功成教授、舒尔茨先生和华颖博士定稿，以英文和中文出版。

1.2 社会保障与经济发展关系的理论假设

本节介绍了在文献中被用来解释社会保障与经济发展之间关系的主要假设。为了使论证具有一致性，首先描述了一系列的社会保障传统，这将有助于我们更好地理解社会保障与经济互动的现状，以及在当下探讨中我们所处的位置。阐明这些传统也将有助于我们更好地理解作为本报告重要组成部分的中国的情况。同时，本节还将引申一种以生产率为导向的观点，该观点旨在解释社会保障之所以存在的内在经济原因。尽管是特例论述,但无疑具有直觉上的欺骗性,因而值得置于本报告中。此外,我们还会探索社会保障的一系列"利"与"弊",这些利弊是过去数十年间全球经济(商业)周期起伏的结果,也是对社会保障与外生危机或内生危机之间相互作用所做出的回应。

> **专栏2 如何界定社会保障以及一些含义**
>
> 社会保障的定义很多,但无定论。社会存在差异且会随着时间的推移而发生变化,社会保障亦然。有时定义比较模糊,使用非特定的术语;有时是非常具体和详细的。定义可以是静态的,也可以将动态因素考虑在内。这些基准之间有许多定义。大多数专家就社会保障的一些核心要素与特征达成了共识,但在概念边界上仍存在一些悬而未决的灰色地带。
>
> 在此,我们简要地改编并思考一个由欧盟所开发的主要用于统计目的的定义(ESSPROS, 2012),国际劳工组织和其他机构如今也使用该定义。
>
> 根据该定义,社会保障包括公共机构或私营机构旨在减轻家庭与个体一系列特定风险或需求的负担而采取的所有干预措施,假定既不同时存在互惠安排,也没有个人安排(见附件1)。依照惯例,有如下风险或需求:
>
> 1. 疾病和医疗　　　　5. 家庭和子女
> 2. 残障　　　　　　　6. 失业
> 3. 老年　　　　　　　7. 住房
> 4. 遗属　　　　　　　8. 社会排斥
>
> 这个定义的起源是国际劳工组织第102号公约《社会保障(最低

标准）公约》（1952年）的术语，今天依然被作为核心参考使用。该定义列举了九个分支，这九个分支是在基于团结的筹资原则和作为个体的法定权利的基础上，通过医疗保健、疾病津贴、失业津贴、老年津贴、工伤津贴、家庭/儿童津贴、生育津贴、残障津贴和遗属津贴，在某些特定事件发生的情况下给人们提供支持。这些福利待遇必须符合最低标准（ILO，1952）。

定义中的"干预"一词表明，社会保障不仅是一项经济活动，还可能包括某些社会活动；相应地，该定义把实物福利与现金福利区分开来。

更多信息见附件1中欧洲综合社会保护统计系统（ESSPROS）对社会保障[1]的定义；读者们会意识到，这一定义在纳入私人干预方面存在明显语意问题，这意味着公共组织基于团结化筹资原则的制度与私人制度安排之间的定义界限变得越来越模糊，这很大程度上源于过去二三十年间社会风险私人化的世界趋势。

尽管上述定义是主流，但值得注意的是，联合国的国民经济核算体系（SNA）（以及欧盟的国民经济核算体系）不仅广泛涵盖了相同的需要和风险，还将教育作为一项社会需求包括在内。基于此背景，我们也将教育作为一项社会需求纳入本报告。[2] 但是，疾病期间工资的继续支付并未被作为一项社会支出纳入国民经济核算体系，而是作为了工资和薪水总额的一部分。在方法上还存在其他差异，这使得清楚理解公共论争中所使用的社会指标的统计基础十分重要。例如，特别是

1　事实上，ESSPROS使用的术语是社会保护而非社会保障。
2　从统计社会保障方法的定义来看，将教育作为一种需求（而非投资）纳入或排除出定义是有利有弊的。由于本报告聚焦于社会政策，而非统计方法或法律术语，坚持一个确切的定义并非当务之急。对社会保障一词的先验理解应足以理解本报告的内容。

> 在国际比较中，需要知道"社会支出的比例"的计算是基于 ESSPROS 型还是 SNA 式的统计数据。即便基于这两种统计方法会得出相似的数值结果，它们仍然代表着不同的内容。
>
> 主要来源：ESSPROS，2012；United Nations et al.，2009。

社会保障是国家依法实施的具有经济福利性的现金给付及服务提供等干预措施。在这些干预措施中，核心为养老金、医疗保险、失业保险、社会救助、教育福利和住房福利等项目。在本报告中，主要从经济功能的视角解释和评估社会保障这一术语及其实践。

1.2.1 社会保障传统介绍

社会保障深深植根于各种思想传统，这些思想传统对社会保障政策偏好与实践有着不同的影响，具体如下（改编自 Dixon，1999）。

1597、1601 和 1834 年欧洲济贫法[1]传统建立在济贫院的基础之上，是现代家计调查实践（不同于无条件的福利待遇）的思想渊源。

主仆传统则认为，自负盈亏者在启动可能对他人构成风险的机构时，应该对其行为的结果负民事责任（Herbert Asquith，1906；转引自 Dixon，1999）。该原则看似合理，但在企业内经常被滥用，从而使雇主（"主"）对劳动者（"仆"）的优势得以延续。

职业储备金传统，如果作为唯一的手段保留，则不能达到现代社会对社会保障的要求；但是它仍然会引起政策制定者的兴趣，尤其是作为提供额外一层次收入保障的选项。

基于互助共济、精算公平的社会保险传统，是 19 世纪至 20 世纪主要在发

---

[1] 从严格意义上来说，《济贫法》起源于英国；然而，类似的规则与实践同时在欧洲各地适用。这就是为什么我们称之为欧洲济贫法。

达国家占主导地位的、成功的社会保障形式,但近年来其对社会保障规划者的吸引力开始减退,尤其是在发展经济学方面。

马克思－列宁传统通过其正式设计所努力实现的福利国家设想,似乎与俾斯麦－贝弗里奇混合型概念存在许多交叉重叠之处。然而,相比之下,这种传统以集体权利取代个体权利、以工作纪律取代宏观财政就业政策,从而旨在使日常的社会实践直接等同于经济增长。

福利国家传统在政府充分就业导向的宏观经济和宏观财政政策的支持下,力求通过追求社会稳定和社会进步来实现资本主义的人性化,同时旨在消除人们痛苦的社会根源(Sigmund Freud;转引自 Dixon,1999)。

相比之下,市场化传统强调并关注市场的优点。这种传统信奉帕累托原则[1],认为个体是其自身福祉的最佳评判者;该传统还认为个体是理性的、有欲望的、有算计的和利己的,有着各自已知的偏好排序。

一般最低收入传统是新自由主义思想的彻底完成式,因为它提倡国家为公民提供最低限度的社会收入保障,同时将任何额外的收入保障都留给私营部门来提供。在大多数设想中,一般最低收入传统瞄准两个目标:(1)消除个体初次收入生产的必要性,从而使个体可以自由自愿地选择工作与否的同时,于日常决策中免受物质需求的制约;(2)通过用仅登记出生和死亡的最小行政单位来取代社会保障机构及机构间不可避免的互动,减少行政复杂性。

这些传统含蓄或是明确地反映了特定的主流经济学范式思想,通常辅以某些政治伦理,风险分担在其中或多或少发挥着突出作用。在成熟的现代社会福利国家里,我们通常会发现许多乃至所有这些传统都是并行不悖的,也许只是称谓有所不同。如果把经济体理解为一系列相互作用的机构,如私人家庭、企

---

[1] 帕累托原则是福利经济学中的一个术语。弱帕累托原则指出,如果 B 情形下所有个体的效用都高于 A 情形下,那么一组个体更偏好 B 的福利状况;强帕累托原则认为,如果在 B 情形下至少有一个个体有比 A 情形下更高的效用,而在 A 情形下没有人的福利状况变坏的话,那么一组个体会偏好 B 胜过 A。

业及政府机构,而经济发展是它们之间动态相互作用的结果,那么很显然,社会保障与经济之间相互依存,因为社会机构本身是经济活动参与者,并介入其他经济主体的结构和活动。从这个角度来看,创造外部条件以使各个机构能够追求最优发展道路,是经济政策的作用和艺术。如何在具体(改革)的情况下最好地设定这种条件,很大程度上取决于政策制定者对主流社会保障传统或是这些传统的混合的充分理解。缺少这种理解很容易导致预期改革成果无法实现,这在现代史上有许多例子。

1.2.2 社会保障的利与弊

标准微观经济学理论试图阐明市场(商品市场、服务市场以及劳动力市场)出清必须满足的条件(价格和成本水平)。这种做法与《费城宣言》形成鲜明对比,《费城宣言》规定:劳动力不是商品(ILO,1944)。它常常也忽略了社会保障在充分就业中的潜在作用,并隐含地(有时明确地)认为社会保障是市场出清的障碍。换言之,只要充分就业是社会的一个社会经济目标,社会保障就会被视为一项应该避免而非积极追求的事业。

纯粹的微观经济学方法不仅经常受到经济学界的批评,还受到社会学、政治学、心理学等其他社会研究专业的批评。然而,这种方法通常以其"大众化"的版本在关于社会保障利弊的公共论争中显示顽强的抵抗性,因而得以维护其重要性。历史实践中,在社会保障制度已实施的情况下,这种方法意味着制度的市场化改革。

通过反思这个分析和政策框架,并且在很大程度上遵循波普尔的科学传统(Popper,1977;Frisby,1972),现有文献包括"支持"社会保障("利")与"反对"社会保障("弊")观点的清单,如下所示(改编自Cichon等,2004)。我们在此对这些观点进行阐释,但不会详细讨论其相关性。

社会保障产生正面经济效应的例子:

● 社会保障通过减少人们生存的不安全，可以稳定内需并有助于减少过度储蓄。社会保障能促进社会安定，并为私人投资的盈利和正收益率创造环境。

● 失业保险为失业者提供了寻找合适工作的时间，从而在经济和劳动力市场结构性变化的情况下促进劳动力的调整。

● 更广泛地说，社会保障制度，包括养老金计划和社会救助，以及福利取向的制度，可以被用作支持人们接受经济改革的政策工具。

● 医疗保障和工作安全计划维持并提高了个人和集体的劳动生产率。

● 社会保障提供了一种实用的社会机制，将全球化对收入的积极效应传递给弱势人群。

● 社会保障降低了劳动力成本的均衡水平：如果社会保障缺位，进行个体储蓄的劳动者需要更高的劳动收入才能达到既定的终身收入水平。

● 社会保障向企业提供了有关国内竞争的关键变量的信息。在自治管理的情况下，制度化的社会对话有助于减少经济僵化。

社会保障产生负面经济效应的例子：

● 失业保险和社会救助津贴可作为劳动者保留工资的基准（工资水平低于该基准，则劳动者不愿意工作而更愿意领取失业津贴）。这种预期工资和福利待遇的组合增加了生产成本并阻碍某些生产活动，导致国民总收入低于其潜在水平，失业率上升，继而必须支付更多的失业津贴，因此社会保障成为导致自身想解决的问题的一个原因。

● 现收现付的养老金制度［有预先设定退休年龄和福利待遇标准，例如1952年国际劳工组织第102号公约《社会保障（最低标准）公约》］为提前退出劳动力市场的行为提供了激励。相较于没有预先设定退休年龄和福利待遇的情形，这种情况减少了劳动力的供给。这降低了经济产出从而增加了社会相对于其可用总收入的社会成本。

● 疾病津贴可以使劳动者在个人可用收入不受影响的情况下暂时离职，从而降低了劳动生产率。

- 一般来说，社会保障使个人更加依赖福利转移支付，降低了个人自主和自信生活的能力，个人无心于承担其经济失败的风险，然而个人承担其经济失败的风险是市场经济成功运转的关键。社会保障还会降低个人的储蓄意愿，然而储蓄是经济增长的必要条件。社会保障还增加生产成本从而降低国际竞争力，并对一国的国际收支平衡和货币稳定造成负面影响。

社会保障条款和待遇中还有很多这样的例子。它们通常基于片面分析，其内容取决于对个人和经济隐含或明确的、强或弱的、行为和结构的假设。上面列出的项目（包括未列出的）的关键在于它们或真或假，这取决于基本假设或实践中检验这些（片面）假设的经验材料。从理论分析的视角来看，这种情况并不如人意，因为它使社会保障以相当随意和不确定的方式嵌入到"经济学"中，并强化而非削弱了观察者们（可能还有决策者）这样一种印象：社会保障不是现代经济的组成部分，两者格格不入。[1]

反对使用这种列举正面和负面效应做法的最有力理由之一是，它仅关注有限的社会经济现实（市场），而往往忽略其他同样重要和可观察的经济现象。支持社会保障的最有力论据之一是，毕竟社会保障制度确实存在，反对社会保障的人对此别无选择，只能接受。尽管存在着纯粹的经济学上的种种困难，但社会显然已决定实施这样的社会制度。理论经济学要研究的问题之一进而应当是：为什么？

1.2.3 对社会保障的正面论证

为什么社会保障存在？这一问题可以转化为：是否有可能发现"客观"的条件，可以用于"纯粹"的经济推理，合乎逻辑地推断出社会中社会保障的存

---

[1] 在社会保障制度早已实施的情形中，从总供给和需求的宏观经济学方面，以及宏观和微观的（个人）分配问题来看，情况是不同的。

在？事实上，标准经济学理论已经形成了这样的论点，我们现在对其进行探究。在这一推论下，社会保障通过其买断/买进功能以及由此产生的对劳动生产率的积极影响而成为经济学理论的内在要素。基本上，该论点认为社会保障是一种社会工具，它买断生产过程中的非生产性劳动力（并买入高生产率的劳动力），以维持或提高由此产生的（余下）劳动力的生产力水平。[1]

该论点的核心大概可追溯至第一次世界大战前美国支持养老金的活动人士（Rodgers，1998）的讨论（即在社会养老金制度引入美国之前约30年）。它利用当代主流的边际主义的数学工具，在20世纪90年代被正式确立（Sala-i-martin，1996）。

这一论点最初仅针对养老金制度。每个人的生命中都有一个节点，从这一节点起个体（生理的）生产率下降，这一点从直观上是令人信服的。这一情况有可能会因技术进步、个体技能的退化或健康状况等的恶化影响到个体劳动生产率而提早发生。工作和经验方面的持续培训可能有助于抵消这种衰退，但存在局限性。根据一个社会（企业）的生产函数，在企业或行政部门继续雇佣生产率逐渐衰退的劳动力，从而使得年老与年轻雇员之间的生产力差距扩大，会在某一时刻给企业的总生产率带来负面影响并降低其竞争力。这一视角下，"接管"（或"买断"）生产率渐退的年老员工的制度，如社会养老保险制度，可以被诠释为一种提高生产率的制度安排；同时，因其为退休的人（被"买断"者）继续提供一定水平的收入而实现了社会目标。中国政府显然能充分理解这种情况，因为其在努力推行国企市场化改革期间就有效地利用了社会保障（见第3章）。

---

[1] 本报告作者很清楚，他们提出这一关于社会保障的论点，可能会被（错误地）批评为坚持所谓的"李嘉图式恶习（Ricardian Vice）"（Kurz，2017；Schumpeter，1954）。然而，正如李嘉图所创造的合乎逻辑的"比较优势"两百年来为促进自由和不受限制的国际贸易提供了主流经济学理由一样，买进/买断论点也可能同样被认为是为社会保障提供了理论基础。

我们认为，这个论点可以推广到几乎所有的社会保障制度，无论其是以现金还是实物提供福利待遇。例如：

儿童（现金）福利通常支持学校教育，提升未来劳动力素质，防止童工出现（童工通常会降低企业生产率）；疾病津贴使得劳动者可以在家养病，从而避免在工作场所传播疾病的可能；住院治疗是一种极端的情况，从剩余健康劳动力中买断患病劳动力（类似的还有工伤保险和护理保险）；失业保险同样适用买断理论，因为失业劳动力在分析上等同于零生产率劳动力（同一枚硬币的两面）。类似地，社会保障也可以具有经济上的买进功能，尤其是当社会项目旨在直接或间接增加（生产性）劳动力的情况下。例如，在关于为儿童提供（更多）托幼场所的当代论争中，经常使用这样的论据（以及其他论据），即此类政策为女性（母亲）提供了更多就业空间，从而有助于提高劳动力市场参与率，并促进经济增长。

另一个例子是对贫困大学生提供助学金或住房补贴，使得他们能够继续学习并提高未来劳动生产率。当然，用买断/买进论点解释社会保障的经济根源有其局限性，其他经济推论也可能（并且往往）适用，这取决于一个社会的历史和价值体系。关于社会保障的经济影响的观点不仅是理论性的，事实上，近年来，它在许多发达国家的社会政策实践中日益突出，政府开始依据经济需求，调整各自的社会保障制度。例如，通过收紧社会福利的可及性以应对人口原因导致的劳动力的减少。

中国可被视为成功应用买断功能的又一范例（见第3章）。在追求买断/买进政策时，政府容易失误，以致生产率处于次优水平：如果买断太多劳动力，剩下劳动力的生产率可能会比以前低；如果买进过多，那么同样的情况也会发生。即使并非完全不可能，也难以找到劳动力的"最佳规模"——它取决于经济未知的生产函数。换言之，没有客观正确的对策来最终应用社会保障的买断/买进功能。它的使用仅能通过社会的接受而被合法化，而这又是一个政治和社会实践的问题。

当然，经济体必须有意愿内化相关买断/买进成本，否则这种对社会保障存在的解释是无效的。必须假设通过社会保障所获得的生产率的提高明显超过相关生产成本的增加。这个假设需要经过实证检验（到目前为止还没有做过）。然而，有充分理由认为，世界范围内不同区域间和国家内部各经济体间巨大的生产力差异与（完善或不完善的）社会保障制度的可及性及其应用实践密切相关。在此基础上，这一假说似乎至少部分地证明，国际上可以观察到的生产率水平差异与社会保障制度是否具有促进生产率的能力有关。

社会保障的买断/买进功能不仅是一个学术议题。更重要的是，它提醒各国政府（和社会政策分析者）：世界范围内控制乃至减少社会支出的当代政策可能会在负面生产率效应方面面临意料之外的经济成本。的确，所有那些采用新自由主义政策（见第 2.1 节）并调整社会保障参数设计以适应其经济（商业）要求的国家，均同时造成了失业增加，或是庞大的、无生产率或低生产率的低工资部门。鉴于未来技术变革的不安全性及其对劳动力市场的潜在影响，各国政府最好积极地、以生产力为导向地利用社会保障的买断/买进功能。

社会保障既是一项人权，也是一个能够应对社会不安全的有力治理工具。

1.2.4 作为初次收入再分配工具的社会保障

在上一节中，社会保障被阐释为现代资本生产方式的必要组成部分，主要是为了现代社会这一核心构成特征的长期存在。接下来将提出另一个不同性质的观点：它将社会保障视为把收入（现金或实物）转移给没有直接参与生产过程的人群（即被买断的劳动者）的（必要）工具。从本质上说，我们认为，在某一发展阶段，基于资本的生产依赖于从直接参与生产中获得初次收入者向不直接参与生产者的资金流动，以最大化并维持用于最终消费的产品和服务的生产（以使利润最大化）。[1] 社会保障是社会组织这种资金流动的一种方便实用的方式。

> **专栏3　什么是初次收入？**
>
> "初次收入"一词是衡量一个经济体（一个社会）在某一时期（如一年）内生产的、可用于最终消费的收入的核心概念。通常，初次收入被称作国内生产总值（GDP）。GDP基本上按平衡项目计算：
>
> 总产出 − 中间消耗 = 增加值（= GDP）
>
> 其中，中间消耗是总产出的一部分，必须重新投入生产以使生产过程得以继续进行。
>
> GDP可被视为一个双重概念：它既是生产的结果，同时也是一个经济体的总（货币）收入的衡量指标。该收入与生产同时出现，并以初次劳动收入的形式分配给劳动者（劳动者的报酬）、资本所有者（利润）。这两个生产要素（劳动和资本）的分配通常被称为"初次收入分配"。这些收入可以进行再分配（通过社会保障等国家制度），可用于私人消费、政府消费、私人资本和公共资本形成的投资及出口（必须减去进口以避免重复计算）。
>
> 增加值（GDP或初次收入）是社会收入再分配的唯一来源（通常称为"二次收入"或"二次分配"）。除了GDP，社会也可以选择重新分配国家或国际积累的财富，这种财富积累不是收入流量，而是存量（源于储蓄积累）。
>
> 更多信息参见：联合国等《国民经济核算体系（2008）》（纽约，联合国，2009）.

---

[1] 为了提高可读性，在此简化了论证。众所周知，在事先制定的政策条件下，生产的最大化可以发生，而且现实通常也是如此。这包括在发达经济体中，最大化空闲时间（劳动生产率最大化使得工作时间减少）。

生产需要有效需求。有效需求的增加是生产增长的先决条件，而生产增长则会导致劳动收入与利润的增加。

从单个国家的角度来看，外部需求是这一额外需求显而易见的来源。对于各国来说，依靠外部需求可以是一个临时和过渡性的选项，但是从逻辑上来讲，由于所有国家经常账户余额总和等于零，因此并非所有国家都可以依赖外部需求。中国、德国、日本和瑞士等国家长期以来一直依赖这种外部需求，而第二次世界大战之后直至今日，主要是美国通过对外负债创造了这种需求。通过社会保障创造更多内需在理论上最简单，前提是社会转移带来的额外需求是无代价的，即它们不会影响生产成本。当前有些提议主张通过"直升机撒钱"或政府的永久赤字支出为社会福利筹资，这些提议可被视作试图在暗示社会保障的推行可以没有成本。尽管这些建议在短期内可能有助于世界经济摆脱目前的紧缩局势，但长期来看不足以为社会保障提供资金支持。

我们认为这些转移支付的资金应该来自当前生产，即它是生产过程的直接成本，因此可以减少利润或是可以改变劳动收入构成。我们会进一步解释这个观点。为了简单起见，我们假设 GDP 等于由劳动收入和资本收入（"利润"）组成的国民收入（United Nations 等，2009）。

显然，在统计分析中，当劳动收入（劳动力成本）[1]的水平（或数额）及其构成不灵活时，任何社会保障的增加都会减少利润（见专栏 3；United Nations et al.，2009）。在这种情况下，任何额外的社会支出都势必要通过利润来筹资并会减少利润，而这反过来又将引起旨在降低劳动力成本（劳动收入）的反应。

如果劳动收入的构成灵活，情况就不同了。在这种情况下，社会保障可以从劳动收入中支出，而不会对利润产生负面影响。当然，前提是劳动力成本水平（数量）保持不变。一部分劳动收入可用于支付当前的社会保障，或者对于

---

[1] 这两个词语表明对同一议题的不同视角。在会计术语中，劳动收入与劳动力成本是一致的（United Nations et al.，2009）。

养老金而言，劳动收入的支付可以推迟到劳动者退休后。[1] 许多国家的法律将基于收入的养老金视为延期工资，这适用于社会保险型养老金。

通过劳动收入为社会保障筹资，要求扣除社会保障缴费（以及其他可能需要从劳动收入中扣除的项目）后的劳动收入能够留出足够的财务空间，以使劳动者在参与生产过程期间过上体面生活。[2]

这就是为什么根据国际准则，社会保障的实施和管理应基于两方（或三方）原则，即需要雇主和雇员的参与。在现实经济中，实施社会保障可能需要在劳动和资本的收入利益之间做出妥协，因为它可能对劳动收入和利润都产生负面影响。这种妥协在增长的经济体中最容易实现，因为此时社会保障成本增加的影响甚微。就社会保障的实施而言，假定劳动力和资本平等地共享增长收益，那么国民收入的绝对水平不如其增长动态重要。

以史为鉴，可参考19世纪80年代的德国。当时其社会保障制度是在经济相对稳定的增长期推行的，而那时德国的（人均）绝对收入水平仍明显低于其主要邻国和竞争对手（Maddison，2016）。中国近年来的转型已被描述为一种经济、劳动和社会保障措施相辅相成以造福于全体人民的途径（见第3章）。

尽管上述条件通常在发达国家得到广泛满足（资本存量、产品和劳动力市场深厚而广阔），但明显的是，在非正规部门庞大但资本存量少、基于资本的生产规模小、正规劳动力市场小的国家（即发展中国家），情况却并非如此。如果正规部门太小，当试图为全民提供社会保障的时候，生产基础实际上可能会捉襟见肘。从劳动收入中的扣除额因此而需要达到过高水平，以致活跃劳动者的剩余净收入不足以支撑其体面生活。商品和服务的间接

---

[1] 这种情况下，养老金可被理解为劳动收入的延期支付。

[2] 劳动者的消费水平不仅由总劳动收入的强制扣除额决定，还由对消费品和消费服务的间接征税决定。为求简便，我们在此不详细讨论这方面的问题。

税增加会导致劳动者净收入状况恶化，因此有必要找到其他的筹资可能性（ILO，2017）。

尽管必须以一些怀疑态度看待在发展中国家迅速有效地实施全面的社会保障的可能性[1]，但社会保障有效的再分配功能已经在大多数发达国家反复得到印证，特别是欧洲和日本。在这些国家，财务规模大、管理良好的社会保障体系能够在经济危机期间有效地发挥其稳定需求的功能。2008—2010年全球金融和经济危机期间，社会保障发挥了这一功能。在欧洲，社会保障尽管还不足以完全平衡经济衰退对初次收入的影响，但为受危机影响的人群提供了重要的收入支持。宏观经济稳定效应越明显，国家的临时赤字在政治上就越能被接受，而不是通过紧缩措施减少赤字。

1.2.5　社会保障制度设计和经济表现

本章接下来转向另一个问题，即是否存在一些社会保障传统，在其对经济的影响或是与经济的互动方面，优于其他传统？从经济发展的角度来看，我们感兴趣的问题是：某些传统如何在现实中发挥作用？在探寻答案时，我们对最符合社会经济偏好的选项做出了明智的选择。

在更具体地分析最佳选择的问题时，我们将分析限于当代两类社会保障制度模式：通过缴费筹资的社会保险制度（俾斯麦模式）和通过税赋筹资的社会转移支付制度（贝弗里奇模式）。[2]

奥托·冯·俾斯麦开创的社会保险制度后来被一些分析者称之为"走了历史的好运"（Ritter，2014），尤其是因为这一制度的下列内在经济特征。

通过社会保险机制，在某些风险事件发生时，国家为劳动者提供收入替

---

[1]　如果将中国作为成功扩展社会保障的标杆国家，不应忘记，迄今为止，这一进程尚未结束，已经持续了约30年，或者说一代人的时间。

[2]　关于所用术语，请参阅第2.1节。严格地说，贝弗里奇模式是通过定额缴费来为福利国家筹资，而这可被视同为人头税或其他形式的税收。

代。在此模式下，劳动者（以及雇主和政府）依据个人收入缴纳保险费，保险待遇亦依据其（之前的）收入而定。该制度由家计调查式的社会救助制度进行补充，后者确保最低收入的水平（刚好）防止个体陷入贫困。如果要从经济上准确理解俾斯麦社会保险制度，需要意识到这一制度的筹资（收入）与福利待遇间有着天然的密切联系。这一制度特征使得劳动者有动力追求生产率最大化，从而最大化其自身工资与福利待遇。如果劳动者无法将工资提高到某个最低水平，那么所挣的福利待遇会太低，以至于无法避免贫困。这一制度需要（正规）就业，以便能够从管理上进行待遇给付。并且这一制度追求最大化就业，以期不断接近全覆盖的目标。[1]

最大化就业的要求激发了对国家引导的宏观经济促增长政策的需要，该政策使得即使工资水平处于收入分配的底端，也可获得足够高的社会保障福利。否则，如果工资太低，该制度无法使人避免贫困。经久不衰的俾斯麦模式得以在发达国家取得长久成功（这并不是说其实施总是成功的），主要有以下几方面原因：其逻辑自然，从直觉上易于理解；可以采用现收现付制或预筹基金，有多种组合方式；即使原先没有缴费积累的人，也能够得到给付（即"祖父条款"，类似中国的"老人老办法"）；技术上能够依据人口和新的经济发展情况进行参数调节；能够做到在制度内进行（某种程度的）再分配，同时保留其支持经济增长的特征。

上述最后一点尤其重要，因为只要社会经济与技术发展允许中产阶级群体的广泛存在，俾斯麦社会保险制度就将运行良好。而当中产阶级规模萎缩（或是规模一直太小，在发展中国家情况往往如此），工资收入导致福利水平不足以避免贫困时，这一制度就到达其极限，并出现社会功能失调。

---

[1] 需要特别指出的是：最大化就业一词意味着，在俾斯麦模式下，每一个体都必须参与劳动力市场工作并缴费；不遵守此规则的个体可以从该制度中获得福利待遇（该制度会照顾到这类人），但这些福利待遇仅是从制度其他参保者那里衍生出来的，即不是基于其本身的直接法定权利。

当工资水平太低，福利待遇将系统性地降到贫困线之下，需由社会救助制度化地补足。

作为社会治理工具，自治管理的俾斯麦模式促进经济发展的潜力在2008—2010年金融和经济危机中为一些欧洲国家（如奥地利、比利时和德国）所印证。这些国家积极利用社会保障为经济复苏做准备。中国在其更加漫长且复杂的转型过程中，也成功地应用了俾斯麦元素（见第3章）。

那么，贝弗里奇模式又是如何嵌套入经济发展之中的呢？贝弗里奇提出建立一种制度，在该制度下，由国家通过以下措施保障所有人免于匮乏：全体公民缴纳较低而统一的费用（人头税）；全体公民在需要之时能获得足够的现金（以及服务）；没有家计调查；如出现任何赤字，由国家填平；如果想要水平高于"免于匮乏"的保障，应当诉诸私营部门。需要注意的是，贝弗里奇模式下社会保障筹资与个人待遇享受权之间相互独立（这也是其与俾斯麦模式的核心区别），这意味着待遇水平取决于社会的定义，必须由政府历次预算来确定。由于该制度从设计上就旨在保障"免于匮乏"，因此无须社会救助家计调查。

这一制度需要充足的生产才能产生用于再分配的应税资源。但严格意义上说，从个人的角度来看，只要用于保证政府福利给付能力的税收的征缴可以不依赖于任何就业[1]，就不需要正式就业或充分就业。贝弗里奇模式的上述特征使其可以免受通过生产率与就业最大化以实现全民覆盖的长期要求的制约（俾斯麦模式有此约束），并且使个人在进行决策时可不受物质约束。换言之，这一制度模式潜在地具有高度再分配功能，对经济状况的作用仅存在于需求侧，而俾斯麦模式虽然再分配功能弱，但在供给侧和需求侧都能作用于经济。

---

[1] 贝弗里奇的政治纲领是凯恩斯主义的，包括充分就业。然而，从理论上来说，他的制度不需要个人通过就业来获得福利待遇。

通常的情况则是，一些国家的制度是结合了俾斯麦模式与贝弗里奇模式的混合型体制。例如，中国的城乡居民养老保险制度有两大组成部分：完全由政府提供的基础养老金和由个人缴费与政府补贴筹资的个人储蓄账户。这一制度具有贝弗里奇模式与俾斯麦模式的特征，以及来自新加坡和智利的个人账户元素。

2 国际视野下的社会保障和经济发展：历史经验和当代挑战

2.1 全球范围内社会保障与经济发展的历史经验

专家们的普遍共识是，现代意义上第一次社会保障立法出现在19世纪80年代的德国。在当时，这一立法以一个世纪以来不断演变的社会哲学与宗教思想为基础，是对第一次工业革命带来的社会冲击的政治回应，同时也是出于统治精英们对类似法国大革命（1789—1799年）的动乱的恐惧。

第一次世界大战前，社会保障理念与制度席卷欧洲和美国。第二次世界大战期间及战后不久，这一进程出现部分加速，于20世纪二三十年代取得些许进展，然后在美国总统罗斯福新政的社会保障立法（1935年）和英国贝弗里奇报告（1942年）之后达到高潮。第二次世界大战后，福利国家得到了前所未有的发展。在所谓的冷战时期（1945—1989年），福利国家成为国际政治的工具。

尽管确定第二次世界大战后社会保障历史趋势是可能的，但越想要确定发展的典型路径，需要描述的细节就越多。尤其是近年来，越是走向国际，就越想要区分社会保障实践的国家趋势、区域趋势和国际趋势。越是想要反思国际（联合国和国际劳工组织）公约，就越难以区分社会保障思想、设计和现实的各种当代路线。本章进行不同层次的抽象与具象化叙述。大部分内容是依据附录中的（国别）报告。在此也粗略讨论了中国的情况（见第2.1.6小节），但关于中国更详细的论述在第 3 章。因此，本章旨在全面论述，但也不可避免地有所取舍：例如，没有涉及印度或东盟地区[1]的发展。

2.1.1 遥远的过去：现代社会保障的先驱与发展动因

现代社会保障的遥远根源之一是古罗马法，它是 19 世纪出现的家长式社会保障的核心根基（Scholz，2017；Bleicken，2015；Manthe，2011）。

另一思想流派是欧洲的济贫法传统（Dixon，1999）。[2]《济贫法》（1597 年、1601 年）总结和整合了各种欧洲大陆和英国的立法。它如今被认为是欧洲中世纪之后，首部长效解决社会贫困问题的法律。与前述罗马法传统截然不同的是，英国的济贫法具有更明显的惩戒性，以期阻吓那些潜在的申请者，而非积极为其提供帮助。现在一般认为，济贫法传统的实施源于 14 世纪黑死病所导致的劳动力短缺。类似的做法在现代社会仍然存续，主要存在于英美国家的社会保障制度，但近年来在中欧和北欧也越来越多见。

尽管罗马法和西方制度化的（主要是天主教和新教的）基督信仰体系，以及"山顶布道"的强烈动机也许支持人们接受非人格化的济贫机构，但在东方情况却不大一样。[3] 相反，某些个人收入再分配的义务已在古代发展起来，富人捐赠养费给修道者和贫穷的会友，贵族和富裕家庭负担照顾寡妇和孤儿的责任（Weber，1991，1920）。中国儒家思想（孔子，公元前 551—公元前 479 年）是一个令人印象深刻的例子，在履行与社会群体需要有关的义务和承诺方面奠定了早期的思想基础（Wang，2017）。

孔子所阐述的有关理想社会的著名的大同思想，时至今日在国内外都具

---

[1] 国际劳工组织目前正在编写一份题为《亚洲老年收入安全》的报告，其中涉及东盟成员国和其他几个亚洲国家，预计于 2019 年出版。这份报告有望对本报告中的一些问题进行更深入的讨论。

[2] 参见 http://eh.net/encyclopedia/article/boyer.poor.laws.england Economic History Association（2018 年 12 月 14 日访问）。

[3] "西方""东方"在此分别用来指代西半球和东半球。"山顶布道"（又译"登山训众"）是《新约》"马太福音"中十分精彩的一段文字，集中表述了耶稣的教义和基督教的根本精神。

有影响力。它描述了这样的情况:"故人不独亲其亲,不独子其子,使老有所终,壮有所用,幼有所长,鳏寡孤独废疾者皆有所养,……力恶其不出于身也,不必为己。是故谋闭而不兴,盗窃乱贼而不作,故外户而不闭,是谓大同。"[1]

这一思想发端于约 2 500 年前,中国社会保障的实践源头甚至可以追溯至殷商时代(公元前 1600—公元前 1046 年),其救灾制度与国家起源及朝代演进相伴始终,面向士兵的优待抚恤制度始于公元前 1046 年周武王伐纣;汉文帝于公元前 179 年颁布养老令,规定国家对老年人尽赡养之义务;唐代(618—907 年)建立了完备的仓储后备制度;宋朝(960—1279 年)已有高度发达的社会救助系统及福利制度。虽然这些制度的形式与内容伴随社会经济发展与朝代变更会发生变化,但实践中一直由国家强势主导。因此,社会保障自古以来被视为中国国家治理的重要组成部分,体现出国家"父爱主义"和家国一体同构的基本特色,国家或政府在提供相应的社会保障的同时,亦规制着家庭保障,牵引着邻里互助与单位保障,国家福利制度往往与家庭保障紧密相关(郑功成,2014a)。

2.1.2　19 世纪:英国、德国和罗马教廷

1834 年,伴随着英国自由市场资本主义的发展,1597 年和 1601 年的《旧济贫法》得到修订。《新济贫法》规定,任何有劳动能力者除非进入济贫院参加劳动,否则无法接受政府的补贴或其他帮助。加之另一个原则是,济贫院收容者的状况应当比院外最贫穷的自由劳动者的状况更差,这实际上导致了饥荒。[2]地方性、周期性发生的失业,是工业化社会的新现象;其所带来的社会影响,

---

[1] 《礼记·礼运篇》。鳏寡孤独是一个汉语成语,泛指没有劳动能力而又没有亲属供养、无依无靠的人。其中,鳏指年老无妻或丧妻的男子,寡指年老无夫或丧夫的女子,孤指年幼丧父的孩子,独是年老无子女的人。

[2] 这一原则反映于当代规则中,这些规则规定,社会救助必须显著低于最低工资;社会越是允许接近贫困的工资水平(不稳定工作),这样的规定就越有问题。

《新济贫法》无法应对。如此设计的社会保障制度不仅在各个方面漠视了现代社会对人权的尊重，也从根本上违背了提高劳动生产率的最低条件。由于1834年的《新济贫法》适得其反但却存续良久，之后欧洲"更有人性的资本主义"花了近一个世纪才得以实现。

《新济贫法》是英国当时最重要的法律之一，影响并同时反映了英国直到20世纪的社会经济结构。其根本的自由放任哲学，是一种具有智力欺骗性且强有力的治理工具[1]，塑造了那些移民至美国的英国公民的态度。这就是为何19世纪80年代德国的法团主义社会保险立法模式未能在英国实现，而在美国也只得到部分实现的原因之一。

19世纪欧洲大陆讨论的核心与英国的实践方向不同，这尤其归因于罗马教廷的持续影响。罗马教廷在承载着旧罗马法的长期记忆的同时，宣扬并实践着教会慈善，同时也支撑着德国、奥地利、法国、意大利、西班牙和其他欧洲大陆国家（社会保障）的家长式倾向。

从国际视角看，在当时所有工业化国家中，德国成为首个进行现代社会保障立法的国家，有其偶然性。尽管如此，这仍然令人印象深刻：这个国家当时远非最发达的经济体，却在短短七年内实施了一套现代社会保障法律。大多数国家花了数十年才完成类似的工作（见表1）。在20世纪，这种立法设计成为其他国家争相效仿的成功蓝图。

德国本国与国际研究都对俾斯麦社会保障立法的细节进行了细致而广泛的记录，故在此不做讨论。它们充分表明，现代社会保障政策是如何偶尔地不受理想主义动机驱使的，并且政策进程一旦启动，其最终结果可能会与初始意图有何不同。这种观察并非微不足道。对德国而言，所实施的制度的设计使其人口和经济能够并且准备好以最有效的方式与之相适应。然而，德国模式的成功

---

1 社会市场经济的概念尚未获得重视。

并不能保证别的国家（通常具有不同的人口与社会经济背景）对同一制度的部分照搬会产生同样的社会和经济结果。

1891年，罗马教皇颁布了首部社会教谕[1]，以期应对劳资之间的冲突关系，尤其关注劳资双方（制度化的）合作、私有产权随附的社会责任等议题。与此同时，罗马教廷相继颁布了八份社会教谕[2]，涵盖了诸如企业管理中工人的共同决定权、劳工优先于资本、工人结社的权利，以及社会市场经济等其他议题。对上述文献的分析和结论持续影响着以天主教为主的国家的民众对社会保障的态度（虽然在实践中往往并不十分成功，令人遗憾）。[3]

表 1　　部分国家社会保障的首次立法年份与经济发展水平

	国家	工伤保险	医疗保险	养老保险	失业保险	家庭津贴	次序（依据首次社会保障立法时间）	首次对社会保障立法时的人均GDP	1883年（德国首次对社会保障立法时）人均GDP
		年份					排名	国际美元	
	1	2	3	4	5	6	7	8	9
1	澳大利亚	1902	1948	1908	1944	1941	15	3 823	4 475
2	奥地利	1887	1888	1907	1920	1948	4	2 404	2 209
3	比利时	1903	1894	1900	1920	1930	3	3 468	3 145
4	加拿大	1930	1977	1927	1940	—	23	4 847	2 090
5	丹麦	1898	1892	1891	1907	1952	2	2 555	2 299
6	芬兰	1895	1963	1937	1917	1948	17	1 492	1 230
7	法国	1898	1928	1910	1905	1932	6	2 760	2 288
8	德国	1884	1883	1889	1927	1954	1	2 143	2 143
9	希腊	1914	1922	1934	1945	1958	18	1 592	1 178
10	冰岛	1925	1936	1909	1936	1946	16	—	—
11	爱尔兰	1897	1911	1911	1911	1944	7	2 736	1 775

1　《新事通谕》（见 Leo XIII, 1891）。

2　分别颁布于1891年、1931年、1961年、1967年、1981年、1987年、1991年和2009年。

3　罗马教廷与德国政府和民间社会之间一直存在着密切的联系，财政是重要原因（德国富有的天主教教区是罗马教廷的主要捐助者）。毕竟，直到1806年（拿破仑战争结束），德意志帝国都被称作神圣罗马帝国。

续表

国家	工伤保险	医疗保险	养老保险	失业保险	家庭津贴	次序（依据首次社会保障立法时间）	首次对社会保障立法时的人均GDP	1883年（德国首次对社会保障立法时）人均GDP
			年份			排名	国际美元	
	1	2	3	4	5	6	7	8	9
12 意大利	1898	1943	1919	1919	1937	13	1 672	1 568
13 日本	1911	1927	1941	1947	1971	19	837	1 356
14 卢森堡	1902	1901	1911	1921	1947	8	—	—
15 荷兰	1901	1931	1919	1916	1939	12	3 440	3 305
16 新西兰	1908	1938	1898	1930	1926	11	3 985	3 495
17 挪威	1895	1909	1936	1906	1946	10	1 872	1 588
18 葡萄牙	1913	1935	1935	1975	1942	20	1 250	1 008
19 西班牙	1900	1942	1919	1919	1938	14	1 654	1 720
20 瑞典	1901	1891	1913	1934	1947	9	2 105	1 937
21 瑞士	1918	1911	1946	1982	1952	21	4 378	2 396
22 英国	1897	1911	1908	1911	1945	5	4 264	3 643
23 美国	1930	1965	1935	1935	1935	22	6 213	3 008
24 简单平均值	1903	1920	1918	1925	1945	—	2 949	2 249
25 变化范围	46	94	57	77	45	—	5 376	3 467
26 极大值	1930	1977	1946	1982	1971	—	6 213	4 475
27 极小值	1884	1883	1889	1905	1926	—	837	1 008

注：①第1列中所选取的是OECD国家名。
②第8和第9列引自麦迪逊（Maddison, 2003）研究中的国际与历史估算比较值。
③第25行为第26和27行之差，适用于第2至第6列，此行数据表示这些国家某项制度立法所跨越的年份。
资料来源：依据施密特（Schimidt, 2005：182）的研究整理而成，原文为德语。

2.1.3 20世纪：两次世界大战期间的社会保障

1919年，随着国际劳工组织的成立，社会保障国际化迈出重要一步（ILO，2016）。在金本位制的货币紧缩情况下，国际竞争问题需要一种国际机制，以便就社会保障立法对劳动力成本的影响进行调解，这不足为奇。

甚至在第一次世界大战之前，欧洲各国政府和美国民间社会已经实施、开展了许多以劳工为本的社会保障立法与活动（详细描述参见 Rodgers，1998）。俾斯麦模式得到了新的关注，获得了新的动力，并逐渐被应用于德国的欧洲大陆邻国。[1]

与此同时，英国的政治家和社会保护活动家认为这种由国家运营的俾斯麦社会保险模式不适合英国（Rodgers，1998）。结果这种由国家组织的社会保险（即使是采取劳资自治的形式），没有机会在英国实施。[2]

尽管英国官方对俾斯麦社会保险立法模式的态度鲜明，美国的情况则难以一言蔽之。德美之间双边往来甚多，以期探索俾斯麦模式是否可应用于美国，或是寻求其他替代方案。制度之间潜移默化地相互促进，与此同时又竞相提出最佳解决方案，这成为当时国际互动的常态之一——尽管大众对此不甚了解。简言之，美国在1935年实施社会保障制度[3]，但却未能以类似的医疗和失业保险方案来完善这一制度，这可视为制度竞争互促的结果。就像在英国一样，第一次世界大战后俾斯麦模式在美国不是特别受欢迎。（1935年）美国社会保险型的养老金的实现，主要得益于德国的工伤保险制度使其在减少（重）工业工伤事故方面取得了卓越成就（Rodgers，1988）。

除了工人（事故）补偿计划随着时间的推移逐步实施，罗斯福总统的社会保障是美国值得一提的唯一由国家运营的全国性社会保险制度。由于私人保险公司（认为其业务受到威胁）进行了大量不合常规的游说，社会医疗保险的发

1　德国的邻国对俾斯麦制度印象深刻，并不是因为立法，而是因为其系统的、集中的和现代的模式：这被视作极好的治理方式，影响且引发了欧洲内外有关社会保障的争论。

2　这一立场后来再次出现：20世纪70年代，工党政府实施了一个更彻底的（被广泛淡化的贝弗里奇模式）缴费筹资型社会保险，但这一制度在数年后被撒切尔的保守党政府（1979—1990年）所取消。

3　《美国社会保障法》（1935年8月14日）是一部规定一般福利的法案，它建立了联邦老年福利制度，并使得各州能够就老年人、盲人、被供养的和残疾的儿童、母婴福利、公共卫生以及失业补偿法的管理作出更充分的规定；建立了社会保障委员会；增加税收；以及其他目标（SSA，2016）。

展受到阻碍。[1]

1919—1939年，国际劳工组织颁布了67部公约和66项建议书。[2] 然而，在不断重演的政治竞争和国际间相互不信任的环境下，全球范围内劳动者的社会状况未有太大改善。只有少数国家的社会保障制度有所扩展或得到正式完善，其中包括德国在1927年建立了失业保险制度，法国在1928年建立了医疗保险制度。[3]

在这些年间，欧洲大陆、英国和美国之间就社会保障开展了国际咨询、立法和宪法的讨论，大多数英国参与者意识到英国的制度并不是比俾斯麦模式更有吸引力的选择。在20世纪二三十年代的英国，佃农或收入微薄的工人阶级过着十分朴素的生活，若在年老之时遭遇疾病、工伤、失业或残疾，总是有陷入贫困之虞。

当美国总统罗斯福在"新政"中加入其著名的"四大自由"时[4]，英国不得不将重大社会改革提上议事日程。受政府委托，威廉·亨利·贝弗里奇爵士（1819—1963年）于1942年提交了《社会保险与相关服务》报告（Beveridge, 1942）。该报告不仅极大地影响了英国国内的辩论与政治的概念化[5]，还激发了第二次世界大战后福利国家在全球范围内的实施。这一报告与凯恩斯主义的经济和财政政策一起，在长达25～30年的时间里，成为除苏联体制外另一种成功的制度选择；而苏联体制主要通过国家保障的充分就业，承诺使人们无匮乏之虞。

---

1 要全面了解奥巴马总统（2009—2017年）实现全民医保的困难，就必须回到第一次世界大战前后美国所开展的辩论。

2 见http：//www.ilo.org/dyn/normlex/en/f？ p=1000：12000:::NO:::（2016年11月23日访问）。

3 法国在1945年才开始实施现代社会保障制度。

4 "四大自由"即言论自由、信仰自由、免于匮乏之自由和免于恐惧之自由。

5 1942年的贝弗里奇报告对于第二次世界战后出现的西方福利国家来说，无疑是一份参考文件。其理念近来重新得到国际认可并成为发展动力。

2.1.4 20世纪：第二次世界大战后走向全球的社会保障

第二次世界大战后，社会保障在全球范围内进入繁荣期，不论是资本主义国家还是社会主义国家都纷纷建立起自己的社会保障制度。已有大量书籍和文章从不同的视角广泛描述了福利国家的发展演变及其与人口、经济的互动，并且以政治、财政经济和社会视角的分析居多。联合国，特别是国际劳工组织越加频繁地介入社会保障问题，并大规模地扩大研究、分析和宣传倡导。社会保护的概念已经成为大多数政府一般政策组合的重要组成部分，因此几无可能撤销（见图1）。但这并不意味着全球所有人口都被社会保障覆盖。尽管乍看之下让人印象深刻，但必须明白的是，图1反映的是已在本国立法中确立了某种形式的社会保障的国家所占的百分比——它并没有反映在立法中得到确认的社会保障已经在多大程度上实质性地成为了现实。该图也未区分立法覆盖所有人口的制度和（刻意或无意地）仅覆盖小部分人口的制度。

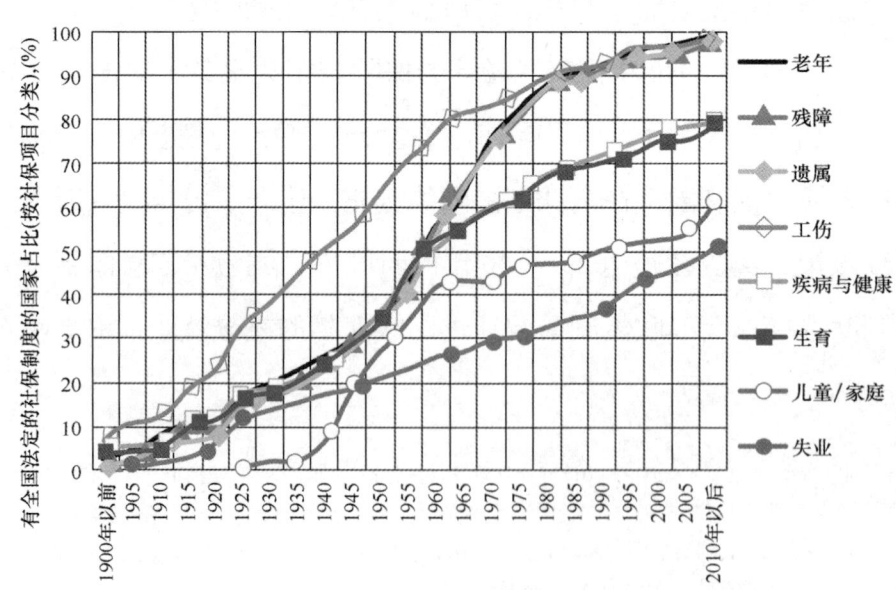

图1　1900年以前至2010年以后对社会保护项目进行全国性立法的国家占比，按政策领域分列

资料来源：ILO, 2017；基于国际劳工组织世界社会保护数据库、国际社会保障协会/美国社会保障总署（ISSA/SSA）的《全球社会保障项目》。

图 1 也未能反映社会保障在法律和 / 或实质上对人们的覆盖程度。事实上，全球有 40 亿人（即世界总人口的 55%）没有被任何社会保障福利覆盖，只有 29% 的人口能够获得全面的社会保障（ILO，2017）。

尽管这些事实并未受到严肃质疑，但全球社会保障的实施仍然不尽如人意的原因在于，社会保障不可避免地要与其他政策领域及其发展进行互动，其中有些有利于社会保障覆盖面的扩张，有些则不然。

2.1.5 第二次世界大战后西方国家社会保障的发展

在西方[1]，福利国家作为一个概念，在社会经济现实中，经历了不同的阶段：从有着强有力的政治支持和扩张阶段，到所谓巩固阶段，到过去二三十年的危机与市场化阶段。特别是欧洲福利国家最近失去了许多其早期具有解放性的推力和动力（Vaughan-Whitehead，2015a and 2015b）。现如今，福利国家常常被理解为支持经济增长的手段而不是因积极的经济发展所收获的成果（Vaughan-Whitehead，2015a）。第二次世界大战后福利国家的发展可划分为四个阶段（Hudson，2016；Judt，2010）：

- 福利国家的建立与扩张（1945 年后至 20 世纪 70 年代中期）；
- 福利国家的巩固（紧缩）（20 世纪 70 年代中期至 90 年代中期）；
- 作为投资的福利国家（20 世纪 90 年代中期以后）：从福利国家到竞争国家；
- 新的改革和未来的改革需要（2010 年代中期及以后）。

基于更详细的关于德国、英国、法国、北欧国家、美国、日本和韩国的国别报告，本小节会详细地阐述这四个阶段。对于四个欧洲案例，叙述会有所不同。这不仅是由于国别报告作者的分析视角不同，还因为欧盟从一开始[2]，便刻

---

[1] "西方"一词在此主要（但不仅仅）包括经合组织成员国。许多国家在苏联解体之前属于"东方"，现在被视为"西半球"的一部分。

[2] 见 1956 年的《罗马条约》https://eur-lex.europa.eu/legal-content/EN/TXT/?uri=CELEX：11957E/TXT（2018 年 2 月 16 日访问）。

意将社会保障政策排除在由共同规则与法规约束的主要议题之外。[1]

上述福利国家发展的四个阶段性趋势在本小节所述的所有国家中都很明显，其中，韩国和美国两国与欧洲的趋势相差较远，而日本与欧洲的差异较小。当中国开始以更加全面的社会保障来完善其社会主义市场经济之时，其他大部分作为参照的国家已经在理念上将社会保障视为一种投资，即期待福利国家为经济目的服务。然而历史告诉我们，这不是对福利国家角色和功能的唯一解释。

在全球视角下，西方目前正在寻找一个新的、范式上巩固的福利国家模式。而在反思国际典型模式及其发展的中国，被视为加入该探索的队伍。如果顺利，各国可能会发现一个新的（或者旧的）范式，它不仅可以满足人们的社会需求，而且还有助于稳定未来固有的不稳定和不平衡的全球经济发展（包括贸易关系）。

福利国家的建立与扩张（1945年后至20世纪70年代中期）

福利国家在第二次世界大战后初期的特点是：经济高速增长、失业率迅速下降、工资增长强劲，对提高所得税和社会缴费率的阻力很小；劳工权利得到改善，资本接受了社会义务；社会支出以及社会收入比率最初较低，后由于再分配性质的立法而增加。在国际上，这一政策得到了两方面的大力支持：作为固定汇率制度（"布雷顿森林体系"）中锚货币供给者的美国（DeLong，2002），以及各国领导人就凯恩斯主义宏观经济政策所达成的广泛共识（Samuelson，1983）。在福利国家扩张时期，美国的政治和凯恩斯主义宏观经济所发挥的支持作用不容小觑。与此同时，在具体实现社会保障方面，美国仍然保持适中水平。

尽管与美国的社会经济体制大为不同，但欧洲国家可以自由保留大量结构上重要的公有制企业（如法国、德国和英国）。工会在整个经济体的组织中发挥了重要作用，特别是在扩大劳工权利和改善工作条件方面：直接或间接地，工

---

[1] 应当记住的是，本报告对欧洲国家进行分组时，许多监管和行为细节方面的显著国别差异仍未被披露。

会明确承担了政治角色（和政党一起），常常对政治决策产生直接的影响。

在20世纪60年代，丹麦和瑞典大幅改变其社会结构，并且其社会支出也从相对落后的状态转变为名列前茅。日本也紧随其后（DeLong，2002）。

欧洲国家开始努力实现社会保障覆盖面最大化（从而不让任何公民掉队），但这从来不是第二次世界大战后美国社会政策的明确目标。相应地，其社会保障的改善也很有限。在直到20世纪70年代中期的一个半世纪里，在受教育的社会权利发展方面，美国一直是领先者[1]，但在收入转移和医疗保健等社会权利的发展方面滞后，仅在大萧条时期和20世纪60年代取得了飞跃，但仍落后于其他工业民主国家。这种社会发展模式可能是为何美国在19世纪和20世纪初是经济发展方面的领军者，但在第二次世界大战战后增长水平却落后的一个影响因素。

罗斯福新政是美国福利国家的转折点，但也只是昙花一现。一方面，《社会保障法》（1935年）提供基本养老金、失业和残疾保险，并以联邦最低工资（1938年）补充社会救助。这些措施让美国（在大萧条期间）在基于工作和救济的公共社会支出方面短暂地处于世界领先地位。另一方面，《社会保障法》的成就是永久性的，而工作和救济项目则可能失效。以提供全面的医疗保障来补充《社会保障法》的计划失败。政府只成功地保障了老年人（Medicare）和穷人（Medicaid）（1965年）。[2] 此外，20世纪60年代的"伟大社会"计划提供贫困救济，建立了学前教育计划，并大幅增加了对各级教育的援助。1970年，美国教育公共支出占国内生产总值的7.4%，仅次于加拿大（8.5%），在经合组织成员国中与瑞典不相上下。

因此，虽然美国的扩张性社会保障政策在第二次世界大战战后停止了，

---

[1] 在许多早期的研究中，教育并未被纳入福利国家，但是近来，尤其在欧盟转向社会投资后，教育经常被纳入福利国家的一部分。

[2] 直到2010年《患者保护与平价医疗法案》的颁布，美国才朝全民医保覆盖更迈进了一步。

但却在西欧蓬勃发展，且在 1973 年之前的 25 年间，西欧的经济增长率很高。也许有人会认为，西欧的扩张性社会政策在此期间促进了经济增长（例如，工会的工作时间与工资政策促进了劳动生产率的提高，共同决策制缓解了增长期间的动态结构变化），但学者间普遍存在的共识是，这一观点必须慎重使用，因为它很容易夸大对这一时期社会保障角色和影响的重要性的认识。

事实上，主要是投资、消费和（部分）出口驱动的经济增长，尤其是通过提高工资在初次分配中的份额，造就了日益富裕的中产阶级和出台社会政策的机会。然而人们也一致认为，社会保障政策不是阻碍或限制经济增长的原因。社会保障成本并非 1973 年经济危机的原因——这一保守的观点在第一次石油危机之后才出现。

法国的总体方案（Régime général）始于第二次世界大战战后，旨在快速覆盖全部人口。该方案起初为仅限于私营部门雇员的职业计划，目前法国的养老金和失业津贴仍然如此。家庭津贴和医疗保险现在覆盖了全部人口。

社会支出和总体经济走势基本保持一致，除了 1949—1953 年和 1961—1968 年两个时期；在这两个时期，支付的现金福利待遇增长率动态地超过了经济增速，同时（低得多的）医疗服务继续逐步增长。总之，这就是法国的社会支出比率从最初不到国民净收入的 15% 逐步上升到 1973 年的约 20% 的原因（Concialdi，2019）。

联邦德国战后紧迫的社会问题是，如何安置东部的失地和其他流离失所者中约 1 200 万名的难民（当时联邦德国总人口略高于 5 000 万人）（BMAS and BArch，2006）。最终这一问题的解决得到了失业保险、社会救助等社会项目以及临时住房配给等其他措施的支持。但这一问题的解决主要得益于 20 世纪 50 年代的蓬勃复苏和投资过程。这一过程得到了美国援助的支持：和其他欧洲国家一样，德国就业迅速增长，失业率快速下降。集体谈判制度增强了企业的组织生产力。管理层的工人共同决策制度进一步加强了劳工权利[1]，也有助于整合剩余劳动力。

直到 1960 年左右，联邦德国社会支出比率（社会支出占国内生产总值的百分比）仍然低于 20%；[2] 然后开始持续增长，1975 年达到 26.3%（BMAS and BArch，2017）——这是对第一次石油危机后经济衰退的技术回应。法定扩张主要是由数次扩大社会保险覆盖面及其他非家计调查型福利待遇所导致。联邦德国的福利制度在 20 世纪 60 年代末得到现代社会救助制度的补充，该社会救助制度旨在防止少数未就业或没有其他待遇资格的人陷入贫穷（参见对日本的进一步讨论）（Schroeder，2019）。

北欧国家的公共支出比原本较低，部分原因在于一种常见的批评观点认为，扩大社会权利会阻碍经济增长并滋生怠惰。北欧国家通过改革逐渐引入新的社会权利、覆盖更多民众，立法确定更高的福利待遇和更多的国家规定等措施，使得原本较低的公共支出比在 20 世纪 60 年代发生了巨大的变化（主要是丹麦和瑞典）。在此期间，一场变革导致了现在所说的北欧福利国家的出现，其特征有：普遍性（一个制度覆盖所有人，而不是如德国或英国的分散制度）；社会权利（基于公民身份在所有欧盟国家）；国家监管（所有欧盟国家，但存在差异）；税收筹资（除采用俾斯麦模式的国家以外的一项主要原则）；大型公共部门（不同于德国、英国等国）；本地社区策略（差异小）；高度组织化的劳动力市场（组织化程度高于德国，更大大高于英国）；关注再分配与平等（在阶层与性别方面，如同英国的公共医疗服务，而德国则更关注效率）。

这些特征是在特定的政治格局下，通过渐进式改革和 20 世纪 60 年代经济增长所创造的机会之窗而形成的。在相应的北欧政治辩论中，经济发展的目标是确

---

1 劳资合作的这一特点，实际上是由第二次世界大战战后占领联邦德国的西方盟军所引发的。它吸纳了第一次世界大战战后在英国进行过短期激烈讨论但未付诸实施的想法（Rodgers，1998）。

2 综合时间序列统计于 1960 年才开始。

保包容、社会安全、平等以及所有公民过上更好生活的机会（Petersen，2019）。

20世纪60年代，英国通过社会改革成为福利资本主义的国际典范，这些社会改革是受贝弗里奇报告的启发，并于1945—1951年实施。然而，英国错过了逐步迈向北欧模式的机会。相反，在随后数十年，英国似乎从临时的福利国家领军者退至一个更为落后的位置。这远离福利大潮的一步，主要是由于作为政治辩论永恒主题的成本争论，以及由于资金问题而产生的淡化贝弗里奇模式的妥协，而同时，凯恩斯主义的宏观经济政策没有将社会保障纳入其理论推理和财政实践中。因此，继任政府为节省社会支出而使用了成本更低廉的定向待遇给付。此外，尽管英国的社会保障制度在很大程度上是由雇主和雇员的缴费进行筹资，但却从未建立一个对所缴费用与所获待遇之间关系进行正式评估的常规程序。而与此同时，许多针对中产阶级的私营（职业）计划受控于这种技术。[1]

因此，即使支出在稳步增长[2]，英国也只能从社会保障稳定宏观经济和提高生产率的功能上获得次优收益，这很可能是导致20世纪70年代后期宏观经济稳定失败的原因之一。

第二次世界大战后，日本首先采取紧急措施援助其饱受苦难的民众，然后从零开始重新建立其制度，包括行政管理。这包括：社会救助（于1950年彻底改革并由国家负责）；20世纪50年代养老金和健康保险的全覆盖，两者均于1961年实现。两项计划均是基于社会保险原则，市町村承担国民健康保险的组织责任。在20世纪60年代，公共养老金和社会救助的现金待遇水平显著提高。与西欧类似，日本的立法旨在提高诸如智障人士等弱势群体的社会福利。日本取消了医疗待遇方面的限制；从1972年起开始支付儿童津贴；1973年，老年人可

---

[1] 精算方法由应用数学技术组成，在政治辩论中最有影响力，因为其通常被假定为自动保证了社会保障缴费者和待遇领取者之间或个人缴费与个人所领取的养老金之间的财务公平。然而，精算公平仅仅是公平的特质之一，公平是一个多维度概念，因此使用时必须谨慎（有关实践中所使用的精算方法的概述见Plamondon，2002）。

[2] 社会保障和医疗保健支出在1950年分别为国内生产总值的4.8%和3.3%，1960年为5.6%和3.1%，1970年为7.3%和3.5%，1980年为9.0%和4.4%。

免费获得医疗诊疗服务。此外,通过数部法律,日本的劳动关系也实现了现代化。

然而,同样由于战后的高经济增长率,日本社会支出比一直到20世纪70年代初期仍保持在不足5%的低水平,远低于法国、德国等国的水平。因此,日本社会保障的宏观经济供给侧和需求侧功能无法发挥其对经济的促增长和稳财政效应。然而,日本的社会保障在维护社会稳定方面发挥了良好作用,这是战后日本经济健康增长的基础(Ono,2019)。

韩国奉行"压缩式增长和公平"范式下的社会经济政策(这一政策一直持续到20世纪80年代后期),在没有重大的(再分配性的)社会保障项目情况下,通过该政策实现了显著的社会公平(主要在初次收入分配层面)。这种独特的历史经验使韩国社会深信,经济增长与制度化的社会保障之间主要为消极的相关关系,即"经济增长第一,分配第二"。总体政策取向是,所有的社会资源都应该只投资于经济增长,因为社会支出会阻碍经济发展。相应地,政府将社会支出集中在教育上(这点与美国相似)。

韩国的《工伤补偿保险法》于1964年才实施,覆盖率在当时很低。国民健康保险于1977年引入,当时的城市人口几乎占到了总人口的50%(该制度于1988年实现全覆盖)(Kim,2019)。在这一时期,韩国尚未实行公共养老金计划。

相较于其他OECD国家,韩国的社会支出比极低(处在个位数水平),这不足为奇。

在此阶段末期(1973年),石油危机来袭,其对西方各国(以及日本和韩国)民众心理影响的程度之深远甚于统计部门事后所测量的经济萧条。在财政上有足够规模的条件下,社会保障最初有效地稳定了1974年和1975年的国内总需求和个体预期。但是,大多数政府开始推迟原计划的改进,直到"另行通知"。[1]其造成的主要心理效应是人们(和政府)对"永无止境的增长"的信念被打破了,

---

[1] 在这方面法国是个例外。20世纪70年代至80年代初,其社会保障计划有了重大改进。在德意志联邦银行发挥其在欧洲货币体系中的主导作用后,法国于1983年之后开始实施成本控制政策。

并且，信奉市场理性（最小程度的国家干预）的新芝加哥学派取得了主导地位。[1] 简言之，新自由主义"反革命"隐隐逼近。

福利国家的巩固（紧缩）（20世纪70年代中期至90年代中期）

这一阶段始于布雷顿森林体系崩溃（1971年）和第一次石油危机（1973年）之后，这两起事件共同导致了全球经济的大衰退。在欧洲，德国马克成为新的锚货币，欧洲各国货币与之挂钩；并且，德国央行推行其有（恶）名的价格稳定政策[2]，对其他欧洲经济体产生了影响；凯恩斯主义共识破灭，并逐渐被货币主义新范式所取代（Friedman and Bordo，2005）；（代价高昂的）失业率上升并居高不下，工会陷入守势；社会保障的改进搁置。这些事态发展一起导致了长达一年的新滞胀现象（停滞的实际增长和通货膨胀）。在第二次石油危机（1981年）之后，许多国家的劳动收入在GDP中的占比开始下降，社会保障筹资变得更加困难。在福利方面，政府大幅削减扩张计划，并逐步开始废除早先的社会保障和劳工权利立法，日本和韩国在这方面是例外。

非常有趣的是，在这一时期（20世纪80年代中期至90年代中期），中国也削减了福利待遇以为经济结构改革做准备并提供支持（详见第3章）。

随着1976年的国际收支危机、高通货膨胀率以及失业增加，英国终于开始结束残存的贝弗里奇福利国家体制。国际货币基金组织对此提供救济，以换取社会调整项目。

1979年之后，"削减政府职能"成为激进的新自由主义的自由市场驱动改

---

1 芝加哥学派在思想上深受奥地利经济学家哈耶克的影响，米尔顿·弗里德曼是其学生和追随者。哈耶克是凯恩斯长期以来的对手。凯恩斯主义经济学是成功的福利国家的核心条件，而哈耶克的经济学则主张仅依靠市场，只允许最低限度的社会保护。当代关于一般最低收入的提议符合哈耶克主义的范式。

2 根据联邦法，保障价格稳定是德意志联邦银行（即德国中央银行）的主要任务。德国央行是否使用了正确的指标和政策来完成其任务，德国国内以及国际文献都对此进行了长期的辩论。

革方案的主调，它试图扭转在 1945—1975 年向集体主义渐进的趋势。该方案包括高调的私有化（包括大部分社会住房），一些公共服务的市场化以及推动降低税率与公共支出的总体水平。[1]

社会保障的重点是削减失业津贴以激励人们去工作。[2] 一个（处于平均收入水平的）失业者的失业津贴替代率从 1979 年的 50% 下降到 1983 年的仅 25%（Hudson，2016）。尽管在改革进程初期，不断升级的经济问题导致失业率迅速上升至第二次世界大战后前所未有的高水平，但这些削减措施还是出台了。

经济问题不断升级也是为何英国的社会支出比——尽管最初比同期的联邦德国低了约 8 个百分点——持续增长的原因之一。

欧盟的经济巨头联邦德国，通过提高缴费率和政府转移并收紧福利待遇，从财务上巩固了其社会保障制度。社会保障成本越来越被视为失业率上升的主要致因，失业率从 20 世纪 70 年代初的 0.7% 上升到 70 年代末的 9%（BMA，2016）。一些地区的社会保障覆盖面仍在扩大，但总的来说，在收紧某些福利的同时，禁止了新增项目。1989 年，德国统一前夕，社会支出比下降至 24.6%，这一比率在当时较低，是因为 GDP 增长率暂时加快（而不是由于整体待遇削减）（BMAS，2015）。

统一后的德国（1990 年以来）在 1990—1992 年短暂的经济统一繁荣时期暂时中断了社会保障的巩固进程：民主德国的社会福利待遇水平不得不大幅且快速地提高，以（部分）适应上涨的物价水平；经济回波效应导致联邦德国也略有调整提高（BMAS and BArch，2008；BMG and BArch，2004）。加上有效利用了应对民主德国大规模就业不足与失业的劳动力市场工具，以及实施新的护理保险（1994 年），这些政策在 20 世纪 90 年代将德国的总体社会支出比提高

---

[1] 如前所述，这一政策早已做好了意识形态方面的准备，主要是通过哈耶克的著作。

[2] 10 年后，德国实施了这一政策的改编版，包括住房私有化和削减失业福利。这是一个有趣的案例，也印证了一个事实：欧洲各国的社会政策不断相互激发，有时变得更好，有时变得更坏。

到比20世纪80年代（联邦德国）高出1.5个百分点。[1]

1973年，法国将社会保障作为宏观经济稳定器使用，也作为对当时德国央行紧缩货币政策的间接反应。在随后几年中，法国社会保障制度的运作能力越发受到质疑。正如在德国和美国一样，社会支出日益被视作经济增长重获动力的问题阻碍而非解决对策。20世纪80年代中期以后，社会支出比达到25%~30%的水平，这一水平在特定的基于劳动者缴费的财务体制下，被认为在经济上不可持续。在此期间，如德国一样，法国抵制了英国的市场激进主义，尽管法国并未完全忽视市场激进主义。20世纪90年代，法国开始大幅减少社会保障筹资中缴费所占比重，并代之以一般税收收入、私人家庭服务费等。[2] 换言之，支出比保持在历史水平但筹资模式有所改变，以支持商业竞争力。

在20世纪七八十年代的经济（石油价格）危机中，北欧国家比大多数其他欧洲福利国家表现更好。北欧民众对福利国家理念的高度接受及其有效的管理，促进了北欧国家抵御外部冲击和重大变化的高应变能力。通过对社会保障与经济之间，尤其是与劳动力市场间相互作用的仔细分析，使北欧国家能够更好地应对未来的挑战。事实上，在各种社会模式中，在促进将社会保障视作对人的投资的当代范式理解方面，北欧国家影响巨大。

美国实施的政策导致不平等激增。社会支出的增加主要表现为税收支出——针对社会目的的税收减免。社会税收支出与一般联邦社会支出之比从1975年的5%增加到2010年的30%（Faricy，2015）。这些税收支出绝大多数流

---

[1] 尽管德国在1990年10月实现了政治上的统一，且随后联邦德国社会保障立法迅速拓展到民主德国，但两者之前的领土在行政（和统计）上仍然保持独立，从而可以理性调整民主德国的生活水平，使其适应联邦德国。正如所预见的一样，这一转变过程在社会保障方面花了约一代人的时间，刚（成功地）完成。

[2] 在欧洲货币体系的条件下（在一个被管控的汇率体系中只容许很小的灵活度），这一政策也是对德国通过之前的巩固措施所获得的额外竞争力的滞后反应。遗憾的是，在欧盟，社会保障一直被视为成员国之间竞争的工具变量，而不是需要密切协调的政策领域。在无法进行汇率调整的欧元体系下，人们受到的影响越来越明显。

向高收入群体，因而增加了收入不平等。[1,2] 与此同时，教育支出从 1970 年的高点（GDP 的 7.4%）下降到 20 世纪 90 年代中期的低点（GDP 的 5.2%），并趋于平稳（Stephens，2019）。最低工资标准持续下降，从 20 世纪 60 年代末到 2010 年，实际最低工资大约减少了 1/3。

日本的财政政策转为紧缩，其明确意图在于避免加税。膨胀的社会支出越来越被视为不可持续。为了遏制（由 1973 年制定的免费医疗诊疗政策所导致的）医疗费用的加速上涨，引入了针对老年人的固定共同支付比率，同时，针对基于就业的健康保险计划的参保者，共付比提高了 10%。在 20 世纪 80 年代中期，财政调整旨在基于各健康保险计划所覆盖的老年人数量来平衡其费用负担。[3]

此外，为更好实现费用控制（也为了加强成员之间的公平性），在所有的公共养老金计划中实行统一的第一层次基本养老金。

为了回应社会对人口老龄化的持续关切，日本政府于 20 世纪 80 年代末启动政策，为老龄社会做准备。日本实施了一个为期数年的大型公共投资项目（"黄金计划"），以建立针对老年人的公共福利服务设施，如日托中心和养老院。该项目通过征收 3% 的消费税来筹资，于 2000 年初步完成，与此同时启动了公共长期护理保险（可能是在服务基础设施已有发展的支撑下）。日本似乎是唯一在社会（医疗和服务）政策方面如此突出地关注老龄化问题的工业化国家。

韩国继续奉行"就业第一，再分配第二"的政策，但于 1988 年实现了国民健康保险全覆盖。同年实施了一般公共养老金计划，并在 1998 年实现全覆盖。

---

1 欧盟成员国同样为了社会目标使用税收支出工具。由于估算税收减免量困难，欧盟决定不再将这些纳入 ESSPROS（见 ESSPROS）。

2 同期，作为家庭福利领域的一个工具，税收减免也在德国得到重视。相较于低应税收入或无应税收入的家庭（低应税收入或无应税收入家庭的每个孩子领取直接的固定现金津贴），更高收入的阶层反而从与儿童相关的减税中获益更多。这一政策的支持者认为该政策完全遵守了公平和再分配的收入所得税规则；反对者认为相同的政策意味着高收入家庭的儿童对国家来说比低收入家庭的儿童具有更高的绝对价值。

3 德国也引入了类似的政策。医疗控费问题对各国政府来说都是一个看起来永无止境的任务。

然而，该计划非常保守，是部分积累型的，并且由于初期仅支付少量养老金而累积了大量的储备金。此外，该基金给国家造成的财政负担微乎其微，因为它是由雇主和雇员筹资的社会保险制度。政策取向为保持相对较低的缴费率和替代率。总的来说，社会支出仍处于低水平。韩国决定采用（俾斯麦模式的）社会保险，加入了旨在利用社会保障来提高劳动生产率的国家之列。

在该阶段结束时，国际上有关社会保障的辩论，包括在欧洲和中国的，受到了 20 世纪 80 年代初智利大力推行的养老金私有化改革的巨大影响（World Bank，1994）。本报告中无法进一步详述这一改革（但已有许多著作对其进行了广泛的描述与分析，如 Gillion 等，2000），这一改革囊括了后凯恩斯主义国家观的所有元素：国家提供税收筹资的、最小程度的社会保障，通过竞争性和营利性私人机构（为负担得起的个体）提供更高水平的保障，由此将财务风险从社会团结化筹资转移给个人，并使雇主义务最小化。尽管不常见于国家论争中，但这一改革对国际辩论和社会政策发展的影响不可小觑。因为许多国家（尤其是东欧国家）的决策者深为其特点吸引。[1]

与此同时，西方福利国家——大多数正在进行调整以适应其所覆盖人口的老龄化——更加普遍地看到，它们在世界经济体系中的地位发生了巨大变化。东欧的苏联体系已然崩塌，中国已开始向国际开放。由于快速适应现代科技、大幅扩大生产，以及抓住向开放的西方消费者市场以低廉的价格进行出口的机会，中国的对外开放给其他国家带来了一定的挑战。而西方国家贸易保护主义的回应既在实践上不可行，又不符合体面的国际合作政策，同时还违背自 20 世纪 70 年代以来西方形成的市场范式。福利国家的进一步紧缩和社会保障作为对人的投资的观点的出现（见下文），可以被视作对中国开放的一种潜在临时性反应——一旦中国的平均劳动成本达到西方国家水平，这种反应就会结束。人们

---

[1] 智利的财政部长如今正和这些改革的后期影响缠斗（见第 2.1.6 小节）。

可能会笼统地认为，就像在当代中国社会保障政策背景下所做的那样（见第 3 章），社会保障与经济要求之间的矛盾在某些时期可能是无法避免的，但在总体上以及从长期来衡量，两者之间的关系是积极的和相辅相成的。

作为投资的福利国家（20 世纪 90 年代中期以后）：从福利国家到竞争国家

自苏联解体后（1989 年左右），社会保障的怀疑者和支持者都将社会保障视为一种（对人的生产力和对经济的）投资。在这一时期，北欧国家（有些矛盾地）成为了社会模式的世界典范。[1] 这种情况的发生不是因为其（持续的）高社会福利、平等或低贫困水平，而是表明社会保障与经济增长关系的逻辑发生了改变，即福利国家不再是目标，而是增强经济表现的手段。

一些研究者将这种新范式称为"竞争国家"，就像德国和英国一样，它的出现是对全球化的回应。一种新的"传统智慧"出现，认为社会政策是一种可以促进经济增长和提高国家竞争力的公共投资。的确，在（经典的）社会保障逻辑中，经济发展是社会保障扩张的前提。在此，最终目标是社会包容、消除贫穷、再分配、平等以及创造机会平等。在（新的）增长—竞争—创新逻辑中，社会保障对促进国民经济的发展而言至关重要。北欧福利国家最初是第一种社会保障模式逻辑，但在过去几十年中逐渐转变为第二种增长—竞争—创新模式。尽管制度未正式改变，其内容却发生了变化：社会风险事故的应对越来越多地从社会团结化筹资转为由个人负担；公共社会保障支出减少（甚至停止），代之以自愿或强制的个体私人安排，且对金融市场的依赖程度越来越高；社会保障的参保者变成了消费者，而非具有享受公共福利待遇权利的公民。正是在这个时候，国际社会逐渐用"社会保护"一词取代了早先的"社会保障"，前者更偏重社会安全网和解决贫困问题，而后者更侧重社会保险与中产阶级的要求。

在此期间，一个主要的（且在国际上非常成功的）意识形态推手是世界银

1　矛盾的是，其将社会保障与经济交织在一起的做法一直备受左翼政治家和社会保障专家的推崇，但却由于被认为是北欧特色而从未实现国际化突破。

行，它向那些未准备好采取智利模式的国家积极兜售（极为复杂的）瑞典养老金模式作为替代方案（World Bank，1994）。这一政策的成功得到了所谓的"华盛顿共识"的支持（Williamson，2002；Mueller，1999；见第2.1.6小节），柏林墙的倒塌和由此引发的（尤其是苏联的）政治动荡使政府忽视了反对不成熟的社会保障市场化试验的理性观点（Hagemejer and Scholz，2004）。2008—2010年的国际金融和经济危机以来，很多国家通过财政紧缩进一步收紧了社会保障政策。

因此，20世纪90年代中期（从结构上和动态上）尚存在的福利国家已经失去了其早期的大部分解放性特征（emancipating features），以至于使用"福利国家"一词来进行描述似乎已不再合理。西方国家的社会保障越来越少地在社会团结筹资的基础上为人们提供保障，而是越来越多地将风险转移给个人——因此，相当矛盾地，社会保障反而加剧了人们的不安（Judt，2010）。

本报告中有关中国的研究结果表明，在同一时期内，类似的社会保障认识在中国得以实施，但其作用方向与西方国家的趋势有所不同。相似性体现在，自20世纪80年代开始转型以来，中国就一直把社会保障作为一种治理工具，明确服务于国家现代化和经济增长进程的要求。[1] 同时，民众的心理可能也极为不同：在西方，社会改革通常强加苛刻的条件，进而被视为抹去之前的社会成就的政策；而中国的政策则有助于释放经济增长动力，并（在之后）首次为实现社会保障全民覆盖提供了空间。事实上，中国民众可能会认为，改革同时带来了前所未有的保障与经济进步。在评估这些发展时需要考虑到不同的出发点，20世纪80年代中国和西方国家之间的社会支出水平和社会保障发展水平存在极大差异，但是这种差距正在缩小。

自这个阶段开始以来，英国在1997年之后采用"第三条道路"的施政纲领，包括旨在提高人力资本、促进知识经济的供给侧社会政策（几年后，这一纲领

---

[1] 探讨当时中国和北欧学者之间是否进行了思想交流是很有趣的。

在德国引发了类似的改革，见下文）。

社会投资计划极为强调制定积极的劳动力市场政策、提供创新服务，以及求职者与私人顾问间一对一的讨论。这些新政中的一些措施包含了对那些未参与者的惩戒机制。在这些体制下，个体求职者在履行积极求职的义务方面受到监督，社会保障待遇给付的条件性日益增强，惩罚变得越发普遍。这些以及其他变化还旨在通过整合求职支持和待遇给付功能，提供个性化的一站式服务，以加大对求职者的支持。

这一通过社会保障进行惩戒的政策与"让工作有回报"的尝试结合在了一起。英国首次实施了全国最低工资，使用工作中的收入补足（in-work income top-ups）来提高低薪劳动者收入的情况大幅增加。[1] 在这方面，育儿家庭尤其受到关注，旨在消除儿童相对贫困（最终相当成功）。在此期间，英国社会支出的增速快于其他 OECD 国家，与家庭有关的支出占 GDP 的比例从 1997 年的 2.1% 上升到 2000 年的 4.0%，同时医疗卫生支出也显著增加。在 1997—2007 年，英国经济表现强劲，失业率降到约 5%，通货膨胀率自 20 世纪 60 年代以来首次在较长一段时期内保持在约 3% 的低水平。尽管不平等程度仍然较高，但是停止恶化了。

在全球金融危机之后，公众对经济和公共财政状况的担忧与日俱增，由此引发了随后（保守自由主义和保守主义）政府对社会投资模式和全球金融危机的回应。政府非但没有解决新的劳动力市场和反贫困政策的不完善及潜在不利因素，反而缩减职能、大幅削减开支、进一步收紧制度的惩罚条件。这些措施的影响仍未完全显露，此刻定论为时过早，尤其是因为对英国脱欧的后果很难判断。[2]

---

[1] 德国也引入了一个针对低收入劳动者的收入补足计划，但不如英国那么慷慨。国民最低工资实施得更晚，近来研究显示，该制度的部分功能仍然失调（Pusch，2017）。

[2] 2016 年 6 月 23 日，英国人民举行脱欧公投，近 52% 的投票者支持离开欧盟。英国政府于 2017 年 3 月 29 日启动正式脱欧程序。欧洲公约中规定了一个为期两年的脱离进程，在此期间，余下的欧盟成员国和英国必须就脱欧问题的细节进行磋商。该时期于 2019 年 3 月 28 日结束。余下所有 27 个欧盟成员国的议会都必须同意协商结果（在两年的规定期内）。

德国大刀阔斧（在 21 世纪初期）进行社会保障市场化改革。改革主要聚焦劳动力市场、养老金和医疗保险方面[1]——与英国在 1997 年及之后进行的改革遥相呼应。改革措施包括一些新的规则。在劳动力市场方面，这些新规则规定，劳动者与工资挂钩的失业保险待遇领取权停止后，只提供（微薄的）基本的（定额）援助。基本援助的领取者仍然可以享受基本医疗服务，但不再被法定养老保险所覆盖。通过合法的、高度灵活的劳动合同形式，求职者被商品化了（Pusch，2017；Amlinger，Bispinck 和 Schulten，2016）。在职业介绍所，个体求职者同其案例管理者之间的关系带有强烈的惩罚色彩（参见关于英国的讨论）；在工资协议谈判中，工会的作用被大幅削弱。

在养老金方面，新规定削弱了社会保障养老金与其经济来源（缴费工资）的关联，此举有利于职业和私人养老金。此外，德国法定退休年龄提高到 67 岁，立法规定的标准替代率降低约 1/3（BMAS 和 BArch，2016b）。[2]

在医疗保险方面，新规定明确了通过社会保险或私人保险实现全覆盖（全民强制参保）。从 2004 年开始，冗余的（财务状况不佳的）医院被关闭，余下的许多医院以效率为名而私有化。

在社会保障的以上三个领域，新规定出于成本效益的考虑而削减了行政管理。

改革的结果是催生出庞大的、工作条件不稳定的低工资行业：对于长期留在该行业的人来说，未来存在显著的老年贫困风险。

宏观经济层面，同一政策使得德国与其欧洲的主要竞争对手（如法国和意大利）相比，平均劳动力单位成本显著降低。在私人家庭部门（收入不平等日益加剧）、企业和公司部门以及政府部门出现了前所未有的三倍盈余，导致巨大

---

1 第三条道路的政策受到英国发展的启发，并且在某种程度上也是政治协调的结果（Blair，1999）。
2 两项措施都将在 2030 年前完成，目前正在推进中。

且不断增长的贸易顺差。[1]

2008—2010 年，政府、雇主和工会三方协调努力，大规模使用联邦就业机构的适当工具来对抗全球金融危机对宏观经济稳定性的破坏，德国的法团主义社会特征在此期间发挥了良好的功能。因此，2009 年德国的社会支出比增加了 2.7 个百分点[2]，充分证明了社会保障作为宏观经济收入稳定器的作用。该比率随后因经济复苏而逐渐回落。

从 1993 到 2008 年，法国保持了相对稳定的实际社会支出增长率，年增长率约为 2%——目前普遍认为这也是法国经济的长期实际增长率。因此，社会保障与国民净收入之比大体稳定。自 2008 年金融危机以来，法国经济一直停滞不前，这也解释了为何社会支出比近来上升。尽管法国没有如德国、英国那样进行全面改革，但也在逐步调整其社会保障制度以适应国民经济的需要，从而使该制度具有比 30 年前更大的异质性——社会权利日益分割，福利待遇的实际价值减少，导致早前有利于劳动者的趋势被更多的不平等和贫困所取代。因此，虽然法国并未正式加入新的国际主流话语体系，但它针对国际趋势进行了零星调整。

日本经济步入停滞期。社会政策自此被财政紧缩主导：由于年龄构成和职业背景的不同，国民健康保险的财务状况早已比其他基于就业的计划更差，而非正规就业的边缘参保者数量的激增又使情况恶化。因此，健康保险（由公共转移补贴）进行了进一步合理化，包括：

● 2006 年，共同支付比从 10% 提高到 20%，对医院和诊所的转移支付前所未有地减少了。

---

1 对于一个国家的经济而言，以下基于账目的宏观经济方程始终成立：私人家庭部门余额 + 企业部门余额 + 国家部门余额 + 相对于世界其他地方的余额 =0。因此，像德国这样有三倍盈余的国家的国民经济，一定有贸易顺差。另一个含义是投资（I）创造储蓄（S），而不是反过来，即储蓄并不是投资的先决条件（Lindner，2012）。

2 官方数字显示增加了 3.4 个百分点，但其中 0.7 个百分点是由于社会立法的变化，将私人医疗保险纳入德国 2009 年社会预算后的技术性结果。

- 基本养老金计划的财务状况与之相似,因此,来自国库的补贴在 2009 年增加。
- 为应对持续的人口老龄化,一项针对老年人的新医疗保险计划于 2008 年实施。
- 2000 年起实施的长期护理保险,在 2005 年全面改革,以更加注重预防性护理。
- 公共养老保险开始采用宏观经济指数化。

与出生率下降有关的政策仍然是日本政治议程中的主要议题。育儿现金津贴和对育儿家庭的实物支持成为社会保障政策的首要议题。在 2008 年金融危机的影响下,大众开始意识到并接受了青年人不稳定的就业状况是个问题。

加强日本社会保障制度的财务与组织基础已势在必行。税收和社会保障综合改革倡议也于 2000 年以后跃居政治议程首位。

韩国开始逐渐改变其"经济增长第一"的范式。早先的高经济增长被认为是不可持续的,取而代之的是长期适度增长的观点,以及劳动力市场灵活性的增强。全球金融危机之后,韩国实施了各种措施,这些措施增加了非正规工作的数量并加速了劳动力市场的二元化,对社会的收入和财富分配造成日益明显的不利影响。出生率的快速下降和人口老龄化现象,如今也受到公众热议。这些发展态势似乎改善了社会对社会保障的看法。

美国终于向全民医保迈进了一大步(2010 年出台了《患者保护与平价医疗法案》),如若不然,美国的社会结构不会发生任何改变。除 20 世纪 30 年代和 60 年代的短暂插曲外,利用社会保障措施,采取协调一致的行动,以提高社会的整体(经济)福祉,似乎不在美国的政治范畴之内。社会税收支出继续大规模流向高收入群体,因而加剧了收入不平等。实际最低工资持续下降,并且由于教育投入不均,收入不平等进一步加剧。基尼系数和收入在全社会排名前 1% 群体的收入份额均随着时间的推移而增加,造成这种现象的最重要原因在于劳动者的工会化程度下降，以及工会的谈判能力与政治影响相应丧失，这一发展态势正出现于全球各地。

很难判断新的竞争国家范式是否会继续形成、塑造一个新的社会保障世界秩序。那些将其经济调整为出口导向（贸易顺差）模式的国家迟早要如同中国那样去调整适应其贸易伙伴对贸易逆差所做出的反应，进而不可避免地会对社会保障产生影响。在下一小节，我们将讨论一些可能的新改革以及有充分理由可以预见的改革需要。

近年来，西方社会越来越关注社会保障在服务于商业需求方面所发挥的日益增强的作用。这是因为，社会保障能成为一种再分配工具以使人们能够有效参与分享全球化所带来的经济收益的希冀并未实现，也没有迹象表明会在将来实现。目前看来，这些发展是否能达到触发变革势头的临界状态，仍然是一个悬而未决的问题。

新的改革和未来的改革需要（2010年代中期及之后）

从某种意义上说，西方国家的社会保障政策目前正处在十字路口：社会保障政策似乎已转至本质上服务于外生商业需求的地位。规则和激励措施已经调整，致使人们只有在被证明有相应行为的情况下才能获得有效的社保覆盖，包括服从由经济命令所掌控的匿名系统的效率要求。从这一角度看，人们可能将越来越不愿意忠于已丧失早期采取有助于摆脱束缚策略的社会保障制度，这种情况直到20世纪70年代末或80年代初才逐步形成（Bosch，2015；Gauti，2015；Grimshaw，2015；Vaughan-Whitehead，2015a）。为了重获公众支持，社会政策必须改变社会保障附属品的角色并使其（再次）采取更加独立的姿态——积极寻求弥合（国家的）不平等差距，否则这种差距将因全球化而继续扩大。

这个只能在叙述中一笔带过的内容，意味着要改变关于社会保障及其受益者的学术、专业和公共论述。希冀这种情况会发生，可能是因为在过去二十年，北欧国家在共同形成、塑造当今世界的社会保障范式方面发挥了突出的作用。

首先，必须承认，北欧国家的发展迟早会产生合法性问题[1]。这种发展的一个重要组成部分是正在进行的从"经济发展为了社会保障"到"社会保障为了经济发展"的范式转变，这将给北欧国家带来什么结果还很难说。就目前而言，人们可以观察到规范性罗盘发生了改变，正偏离了集体关切，转向了更多的个人利益。作为一小群（国际比较中的）小国家的北欧国家，尽管经常被作为社会楷模，但北欧国家使其福利国家政策逆大潮流而动的选择有限。瑞典在过去20年间相当成功地影响了国际养老金改革，丹麦影响了有关劳动力市场弹性保障的讨论（Auer，2010），这些都是积极的信号。

同时，正如本节的其余部分所示，本报告涉及的所有国家都有理由和充足空间在实践中改善其社会保障制度。例如，将社会保障叙述的必要变化与现实中的切实进展相结合是很有可能的。社会政策改进的具体领域包括新的（旧的、古典的）工资问题，该问题在本报告中的五个国家中普遍存在——法国、德国、英国以及日本和韩国（在其他几个国家中不那么普遍），该问题仍很重要且嵌套于更加普遍的问题中，即纠正全球日益恶化的收入与财富分配问题；还包括一系列解决不稳定就业与失业、儿童与家庭、医疗保障、养老金、照护体系及住房等问题的必要政策。法国、德国与英国，存在着庞大的（或不断增长的）亚贫困水平工资部门，对社会福祉产生了内在的直接影响。换言之，实质性的工资增长早应实现，尤其是最低工资。[2]

更具体地说：

- 在英国和德国（也许还有北欧），必须重新审视其条件性福利体制的运行。

1　详见本报告附录之北欧报告。

2　在这方面，同属欧元区的法国和德国休戚相关（而英国可以在必要时调整其汇率）。例如，如果没有德国的配合，法国就无法解决其工资水平过低的问题。若法国如建议那样推行提高工资的政策，德国将不得不更快地提高其工资水平。如若不然，德国相较于法国的竞争力将进一步增强，法国的就业会面临更大的压力（Flassbeck，2017）。为了缓解欧元区内日益紧张的局势并为其福利待遇和工资水平的提升提供空间，德国也需要大幅提高工资水平。否则，德国的出口导向型经济模式迟早会难以为继。

各项立法中的惩戒性元素早应移除。越来越多的证据表明，近年来日益严厉的政策措施剥夺了许多公民的基本社会权利，助长了低收入和极不安全的合同签订。

- 英国和法国的住房高成本问题亟待政府采取行动去解决，同样的问题当前也出现在德国（时间上滞后一些）。20世纪90年代和21世纪头十年德国大规模的公共住房私有化使得市政当局几乎没有办法来对抗市场租金。最终，这意味着恢复促进建造更多社会住房的政策。加强对私营部门租金水平的调控可能也是一种选择。住房在日本也应成为社会政策的一个重要组成部分。尤其是鉴于家庭规模和结构的变化，住房应与社会保障相结合，旨在为各代际的经济脆弱家庭提供支持。日本的社区结构必须进行调整以适应大多数居民年龄在65岁及以上的状况。

- 如同英国一样，儿童保育在德国也是个问题。在德国，每5～6名儿童中就有1人目前生活在贫困中（Bertelsmann Stiftung，2016）。国家直接提供普遍的育儿服务似乎是个有效的解决途径。另一种选择是增加对托儿服务的国家补贴，服务的落地则交由市场。无论哪种方式，都需要采取行动解决育儿成本异常高昂的问题，日本也同样需要关注该问题。

- 英国仍然受到20世纪80年代许多前工业中心地带所实施的去工业化政策的影响。沿着贝弗里奇所设想的思路重新启动国民保险，有助于所有人清楚自己的所得与所付。在社会保障成本（及其对社会的回报）方面，所有国家都应当更加公正坦诚。

- 正如在法国一样，德国似乎早应在社会保障体系中建立一个普遍覆盖的层次。法国可以通过扩大安全网和增加最低福利待遇来实现这一目标，而德国则可以通过逐渐放弃公共养老保险的精算公平原则并代之以再分配性质的制度设计来实现这一目标（BMAS和BArch，2016a；Scholz，2009）。这两个国家都应该通过更高的税收份额来寻求社会保障筹资。否则，人们之间的收入不平等将继续增加，产生不利的经济影响（Cingano，2014）及不良的社会和政治影响（见下文北欧国家）。

● 韩国的讨论也出现同样的走向。在韩国，提出了覆盖全民的一般基本收入[1]，以回应无就业增长（jobless growth）的强劲趋势、非正规工作增多以及青年失业率的攀升。由于韩国的社会支出比仍然非常低，仅为10%，这一措施会是扩大韩国内需的最有效措施。由于涉及高昂的财政成本，目前讨论的重点是（有限的）特定人口补助金，如扩大基本养老金、引入儿童和青年津贴等与年龄相关的社会津贴。在韩国讨论的议题还包括改善国家的医疗卫生基础设施，投资经济型公共（社会）住房以刺激生育率，以及降低儿童保育和医疗保健成本，尤其是针对处于生育年龄的群体。

● 应对当前劳动力市场二元化对老年人的不利影响，日本希望在不给年轻一代带来额外负担的情况下提高公共养老金的待遇水平，这可以通过如下措施得以实现：（1）保障覆盖短时工作雇员与小微企业雇员；（2）与延长的工作年限相一致的自愿延长缴费年限；（3）充分应用宏观经济指数化以提高未来养老金领取者的福利待遇。鉴于政府的财政约束，这样的政策是否适合日本目前还有待观察。无论如何，各国都亟须扩大从事不稳定工作者的养老金覆盖，否则将损害人们对制度的忠诚度。

● 在德国，改变养老金财务可能会对医疗卫生筹资产生（积极）影响，这可能有助于解决这样一个问题：尽管强制性的健康保险覆盖全民（自2007年和2009年起），德国可能还有接近1%的人口漏保（Koschnitzke，2015）。[2]这种情况可以通过全民健康保险来解决，这一改革将使私人健康保险扮演补充性角色。

● 在美国，共和党政府向来奉行保守的政策——即本质上没有社会政策（除了税收优惠）。当今政府是否会最终废除《患者保护与平价医疗法案》（俗称"奥

---

1 德国等国也提出了类似的建议。
2 没有关于未参保人员的官方数据，估算参考的是从缴费欠款和其他间接指标中提取的信息。

巴马医改")——其尝试迄今未获成功——在本报告撰写之际还是一个悬而未决的问题。从国际社会的专业视角来看，拟定的政策犯了方向性错误，与国际建议书和公约背道而驰。

第 3 章将更详细地探讨中国的发展。

显然，本报告所涵盖的包括中国在内的所有国家，都必须寻求巩固或提升与老年人长期护理有关的政策，市政当局和地方组织应承担主要责任。应当优先加强居家医疗保健和社会服务（而不是在机构设施内）。应支持家庭参与预防措施和互助，使老年人能够尽可能长时间地保持活力。必须改善照料体弱老年人的护理人员的工作条件，并提高其工资水平。

2.1.6　1989 年之后东欧、中亚及世界其他地区社会保障的发展

世界上其他地区也进行了社会改革，尽管本报告没有或仅粗略介绍。这些改革是全球社会经济进程总体的一部分，但也有其独特性。例如，有些曾在 1990 年前后进行了公共养老金制度私有化的国家，已经开始了重新改革。自 2000 年以来：

● 一些拉美国家的改革被（包括世界银行在内）判断为失败、被撤销或是宣告违宪（厄瓜多尔和尼加拉瓜），这些拉美国家的公共养老金制度最终得以保留。阿根廷（2008 年）、玻利维亚（2010 年）、匈牙利（2010 年）、波兰（2013 年）、保加利亚（2014 年）和哈萨克斯坦（2013 年）则部分或完全重新建制。

● 更多的国家正在探索重新改革，如智利、萨尔瓦多和俄罗斯。这些逆转是否会改善参保者的物质生活水平仍有待观察，也有许多复杂的问题尚待解决。无论如何，这些反应都清楚地表明，社会在接受"去团结化"方面是有限度的。

以下简要介绍 1989 年之后东欧和中亚的发展，作为对 1989 年以后（西方）福利国家概念的范式变化取得成功的背景解释。

苏联（包括经济互助委员会成员国）的变革式发展，使社会保障处于巨大的压力之下。资本存量崩溃、恶性通货膨胀、大规模的失业与就业不足、拖欠工资、效率低下和不受信任的国家机构（包括缺乏有效的统计数据），以及其他不利的事态发展，使得继续提供社会保障（尤其是筹集所需资源）极为困难。在苏联体制下，如同计划经济时期的中国，大部分社会保障是通过企业提供的，这进一步加剧了问题。然而，不同于在中国，东欧和中亚国家因为变革而失去了本可以帮助国有企业有条不紊地、理性地向市场条件转变的治理手段。突然之间，企业及其他机构面临剧烈的市场冲击，不得不因此而暂时或永久地停止运营，或是从迅速陷入困境的国库中获得大量补贴而得以在没有收入的基础上苟延残喘。

随着企业的倒闭，社会保障制度崩溃了。尽管多数国家出现了这些急剧的变化，财政与行政管理的情形极度困难，但某些类别的福利和服务供给稳定。例如，养老金仍继续发放，医疗卫生服务维持在最低水平。值得称颂的是，社会保障机构（现独立于早前企业）的建立和区域化发展，在此条件下提供社会福利待遇给付的速度之快。这个过程伴随着国际财政支持，例如，来自世界银行以及国际和双边技术咨询的支持，尤其是通过结对项目将西方社会保障机构（主要是欧洲和美国）的技术官员与东方的技术官员联系起来。紧接这一过程的是关于最佳方案的概念性辩论，辩论发生在世界银行与国际劳工组织之间、瑞典与法国之间、支持市场经济解决方案者与支持社会市场经济解决方案者之间，等等。

金融业在促进社会保障私有化方面发挥了极大的影响。政府和民间社会在刚刚经历了国家运营的体制后，好奇且渴望从市场解决方案中获得承诺，这不足为奇。但是只有极少数人了解，在基于私有财产权的市场条件下，适当的国家行政管理（待建立）耗时且复杂，包括由此产生的法律和行政义务、企业琐事，以及它们与社会保障之间的相互联系等。同时实施新的法律制度所产生的困难可以解释为什么中国的转型更容易——中国可以集中精力进行结构变革而无须改变法律制度。1989年之后东方所进行的讨论和改革也影响了西欧的机构、大学、公民社会和游说团体，包括通过青年才俊从东方流入西方（如进入欧盟机构和世界银行）。也正是通过这些影响，西方传统的福利国家概念突然遭到了挑战。

已有研究对其中一些发展进行了详细描述和分析（Mueller，1999）。然而，更多的发展及其相应的影响（结构性的或对于个人而言的），仍有待历史学家和其他研究者去发掘。

2.2 全球社会保障与经济发展面临的新挑战

进入 21 世纪以来，伴随全球化进程的加快和互联网的发达，全球经济社会环境也发生了巨大的变化，并且还在向纵深发展，给社会保障与经济发展所处的环境带来了新的挑战，应对这些挑战构成了当今世界各国实现国家发展目标的具有战略意义的重大政策议题。

在本节，我们描述了对这个政策议程至关重要的五个方面，包括：（1）思维理念的改变；（2）全球化进程的不确定性；（3）老龄化的影响；（4）新技术革命与新业态常态化；（5）福利的刚性增长与财务可持续性之间的矛盾。

2.2.1 经济发展与社会保障关系背后的发展理念出现分歧

在社会保障制度建设中，建设制度的理念是否科学，往往是社会保障制度设计优劣的决定性因素，而制度设计的好坏又决定着技术方案有效性的高低。尽管在实践中，后者对前者会产生相应的影响，但科学理念的确立优于制度的设计，合理的制度设计优于技术方案的选择，又确实是建设社会保障体系的一条基本逻辑（郑功成，2008b）。

正如前文所述，最佳政策选择随时间推移而变化，影响着对社会保障和经济发展相互关系的理解。

从第二次世界大战结束到 20 世纪 70 年代中期，为了应对市场失灵导致的经济发展危机，凯恩斯主义盛行，多数国家的政府在发展经济的同时为提高人民生活水平而积极推行社会保障与就业政策，这是世界经济扩张的时期，也是许多国家社会保障制度日益健全的黄金时期。

然而，20世纪七八十年代，两次石油危机的爆发和随后的东欧剧变和苏联解体构成了新自由主义和货币主义同时取得成功的时代背景。1989年的"华盛顿共识"（Williamson，2002）被视为如何在实践中应用新自由主义理念的一个成熟体现。这30年，世界经济的发展与许多国家的社会保障改革与发展深受新自由主义范式的影响，其实质是主张自由的竞争、自由化、私有化和市场化，同时要求将国家的角色缩小到"守夜人"的最低限度。[1]

显然，社会保障不能不受这些事态发展的影响。新自由主义将经济增长置于社会保护之上，从而可能对各国社会政策的发展具有不容低估的负面影响。因此，东欧国家坚持采取经济"休克疗法"（Klein，2007），但并未取得预期的发展成果[2]；拉美国家作为推行"华盛顿共识"的试验地，转眼成了重灾区，近年来掀起的反新自由主义浪潮也最为激烈。许多国家的贫富两极分化现象日趋严重，整个社会的结构性危机日益显性化。当前发生在欧美地区的反全球化思潮、不断高涨的社会运动和极端主义、民粹主义等现象，表明在一个社会保障已陷入了越来越难以维持其核心功能——即在需要时提供收入保障——的世界，人们的不安全感在不断增加。维持社会安宁的难度也增加了。

过去几十年的一个核心误区是：假定收入和财富不平等问题可以通过"自动的"涓滴效应解决，即允许富人从经济增长中获取超比例的利润（在许多国家都是这样的情况），最终惠及穷人。因此，减少社会福利投资、削减社会保障不会造成伤害，而是通过这种涓滴效应来补偿。

---

[1] https://definitions.uslegal.com/n/night-watchman-state/.
[2] 像波兰、捷克等国后来取得的经济成就大部分可归因于作为欧盟成员国而受到的积极影响。

在这种发展理念的影响下，社会保障在许多国家不再被视为经济发展的重要目标，也不再被视为弥补市场缺陷和促进经济社会持续协调发展的工具。有的经济学家甚至轻易地将金融危机、债务危机乃至政治危机归咎于福利制度，掩盖了容易发生危机的资本主义制度性根源，同时也夸大了社会保障制度所谓的负面效应，导致人们无法认识到在社会经济转型过程中加强社会保障的必要性。

对社会保障与经济发展关系的曲解，会造成持续损害社会公正与经济社会协调发展的严重不良后果。当前，国际社会和各国必须以更加开放的心态，理性辨析社会保障与经济发展的积极关系。如若不然，其他紧迫的全球性问题，如贫困、气候变化、环境污染、人口增长和移民，便难有成功解决的胜算。2015年9月，联合国正式通过了17个可持续发展目标，其中包括消除贫困、消除饥饿、良好健康与福祉、优质教育、性别平等、缩小差距等问题（United Nations，2015）。要实现这些目标，就必然需要建立健全的社会保障制度并充分发挥其作用。

2.2.2 全球化进程具有不确定性

对大多数国家而言，全球化突出地表现了它的两面性特性：既是机遇，也是挑战。全球化进程通常是一个经济增长与财富积累的进程，也是使许多人的生存境况获得持续改善的进程。巴西、印度、中国和南非等发展中国家显然已经表现出这种积极影响。

尽管全球化有积极效应，但它也加剧了国际竞争与投机。最近几十年发生的一系列危机是自由贸易和资本自由流动的不可预见的交织效应的表现，再加之劳动力流动性不断增加和社会保障稳定性下降，一个国家的经济波动不可避免地殃及他国，甚至可能影响全世界。

全球化也打破了原有的劳资关系平衡，导致全球范围内的"强资本、弱劳工"格局的形成（郑功成，2002）。因为资本可以自由流动，总可以找到更廉价的（但仍有足够生产力的）劳动力。特别是对于发展中国家而言，很难不走上资本诱导型的发展道路。为了尽量减少相关的劳动力成本，必须采取福利措施使劳资关系更加平衡，工资和利润得到公平的分配。

全球化的诸多不确定性，给各国经济发展与社会保障政策带来深刻影响。面对竞争的加剧、风险的增加，是努力谋求经济与福利的同步长期发展还是以牺牲福利来取得短期繁荣，是各国必须做出的选择。只有建立在互助共济基础之上的社会保障制度，才能在全球化进程中提供稳定的安全预期，也有助于扭转当前劳工的不利地位。目前的问题是如何适应经济社会发展和新业态的出现以更好地实施社会保障。数字经济的发展确实给社会保障体系带来了新的挑战，如非标准形式就业，但信息技术的广泛应用又为应对这种挑战提供了相应的技术支撑。

2.2.3 人口老龄化快速发展对经济社会影响深远

当今世界已经迎来了人口结构大转型，全球人口老龄化进程在加快、加深，这是人类社会发展进步的巨大成果，但也给社会保障与经济发展带来了日益严峻的挑战。根据世界卫生组织定义，65岁及以上人口占总人口比达到7%时为"老龄化社会"，达到14%为"老龄社会"，达到20%为"超老龄社会"（见世界卫生组织1982年《维也纳老龄问题国际行动计划》）。2011年，德国、意大利和日本已是"超老龄社会"；瑞典、希腊、保加利亚、西班牙、法国、英国、加拿大、白俄罗斯、澳大利亚等50多个国家已是"老龄社会"；美国、俄罗斯、中国、哈萨克斯坦等多个国家属于"老龄化社会"。

老龄化程度的不断加深，对就业结构、消费结构、产业结构与整个经济的发展产生直接且巨大的影响，同时也会对社会保障制度的结构、资源配置与财政平衡等产生长远且深刻的影响。养老金支付、医疗保障支出、养老服务供给和筹资的压力会持续攀升，需要妥善应对。[1] 虽然老龄化带来的人口结构变化，构成了现在及未来社会保障与经济发展的重大挑战，但通过完善社会保障制度来应对人口老龄化已经成为国际社会的共识。[2]

面向老年人的社会保障制度在许多情况下已经开始调整，以能够发挥对经济发展的积极支持作用。在这方面，处于不同发展阶段的两个国家表现突出：

● 人口老龄化对经济发展与社会保障的影响并非一定是消极的，老龄化并不可怕。德国作为超老龄国家的代表，其经济发展依然充满着活力，社会保障也在稳健运行。这关键在于德国在 20 世纪 90 年代悄无声息的生产过程改革（Bosch，2017），并对社会保障体系特别是养老保障进行一系列重要的（主要是参数性的）适应性调整。

● 中国作为快速老龄化国家的代表，在经济发展方面取得了成功，其社会保障体系建设同样在快速发展，尤其是老年人的购买力得到了提升。尽管养老金支付压力与老年服务需求会持续上升，但劳动生产率的提高与科技进步等带来的智能化，为有效解决这些问题创造了经济与技术基础。

人口老龄化会带来一些风险，也会带来新的发展机遇，各国政府应该采取措施更加积极地应对本国老龄化进程。

国际层面，还应当设法将老龄化的成本效应置于国际竞争的争辩之外。如

---

[1] 必须承认的是，人口老龄化对平均医疗成本水平的影响相较其于养老金与养老服务成本的影响而言，在国际研究中关注较少。

[2] 正是由于人口结构变化对经济社会发展影响深远，早在 20 世纪 80 年代，联合国就开始探索如何应对人口老龄化的影响。1982 年联合国在维也纳召开第一次老龄问题世界大会，通过了包括 62 项建议在内的《老龄问题国际行动计划》。1991 年联合国大会通过了《联合国老年人原则》，确立了关于老年人地位五个方面的普遍性标准：独立、参与、照顾、自我充实和尊严。2002 年联合国在马德里召开第二次老龄问题世界大会，总结就维也纳会议后 20 年来各国在老龄问题上的行动进展，通过了《老龄化马德里政治宣言》和《老龄问题国际行动计划》，积极老龄化观念被纳入各国发展框架。此后，老龄问题不时被纳入联合国议程，2016 年在美国纽约联合国总部举行了老龄问题不限成员名额工作组第七届工作会议，集中讨论非政府组织参与老龄问题、强化促进和保护老年人人权和尊严的措施等老龄问题。

果所有国家都接受全球范围内的老龄化这一事实，同时停止对抗由之带来的成本效应，那么，老龄化就不再是经济问题了。它可能仍然对需求结构产生影响，但在社会市场经济中并不构成问题，这些经济体很容易适应。

2.2.4　新技术革命对传统产业的冲击与新业态的常态化

伴随全球化进程的是信息技术与互联网在生产方式、就业方式乃至人们的日常生活的广泛应用。人工智能的进一步发展和应用将会催化这些发展并带来变革。它们创造了新的经济增长点，也导致了社会关系特别是劳资关系发生变化，给社会保障制度及其管理带来了新的问题。

近年来发生着最新变化，人工智能与互联网催生出各种新部门和业态，电商、居家创业、智能检测等新业态蓬勃发展，新的工作方式、新的就业形态成为正在流行的新常态。它既直接影响经济发展与社会治理格局，也对现行社会保障制度提出新的挑战。随着就业灵活性、流动率的不断升高，就业场所与劳动关系呈现出许多新形态，而新的社群结构及诉求表达方式亦属新"面孔"。（郑功成，2017c）

但担忧劳动消失还为时过早，即使新技术革命背景下的工作形态会发生变化，工作的本质却不会改变；取得报酬的方式或途径可能发生变化，确保劳动者获得足够的报酬却不应改变。

在新技术革命与新业态的背景下，如何维护初次收入分配的公正性，进而不断完善社会保障制度，并确保这一制度的有效性和公正性不受冲击，亦是现阶段各国政府需要认真应对的挑战。在实践中不能指望社会保障解决初次分配中的问题，各国政府应当承担这种责任，即重视对劳动者权益的保护，不仅要提供公平的工资，还需要强化劳资关系和社会保障制度的适应性。这些需要基于稳定劳资关系、收入与财富分配格局及社会结构的深刻变化，以确保劳动者的福利权益不受损害。

2.2.5 福利刚性增长与财务可持续性的矛盾

社会福利是人的基本权利，促进福利增长是各国政府的重大责任。无论是横向的国际比较还是长期历史发展均表明，社会保障制度一旦确立，其发展速度通常超越社会经济发展。原因在于现代社会与日俱增的复杂性，以及只能通过增加公共物品和服务供给才能满足的不断增长的需求（Lindert，2010；Wagner，1876）。社会保障项目只能增加不能削减，待遇水平只能提升不能降低，这是普遍性规律（当然在实践中，个别项目可能会根据实际需要扩张或收缩，或者只是临时性项目，或者出现管理不善）。因为制度固有的向上发展的特性，社会保障制度作为国民分享国家发展成果的基本途径与制度保障，以及解决特定社会问题的重要工具，不能也不会停留在慈善类型的或是社会救助"雪中送炭"式的低水平状态，而是在运行和管理良好的情况下可以呈现出"水涨船高"现象（郑功成，2018a）。

随着人口老龄化带来的人口结构深刻变化，家庭保障功能（家庭内部的帮助和转移）也会不可避免地持续弱化。相反，养老金、医疗与养老服务等社会保障制度支出必然持续增长。这种刚性增长规律在发达国家近数十年来的发展实践中已经表现得非常充分，也开始在中国这样快速发展的发展中国家得到了体现。

以上观察必须与国家的社会支出比例（见专栏 2 对于社会保障的定义）根据经济发展周期而有增有减的情况清晰区分开来。当经济发展停滞甚至负增长时，失业率通常也会升高（这意味着出现更多的贫困家庭）；在经济繁荣时期，失业率通常下降，相应需要的公共社会支持也会减少。短期的经济周期性发展可能被已有庞大制度的财务惯性所取代，特别是具有反周期性财务稳定效果的养老和医疗保障制度。这些短期发展和长期固有惯性两者之间的复杂互动，反过来直接影响国家财政收入，也会直接影响社会保险筹资与居民的社会福利服务支付能力。这种交织且复杂的情况需要认真治理。否则，除非采取改善措施，社会保障的财务可持续性将容易受到影响。因此，开辟新的财源和进一步优化社会保障体系结构，是各国为适应未来而必须采取的政策措施。

综上，在社会保障制度定型后，福利刚性增长与财务可持续性之间确实存在着矛盾。因此，在努力促进和切实维护法定社会保障制度的公平性的同时，需要采取有效的措施以调动更多的市场资源与公共资源投向社会保障领域。

特别是在最近一轮全球金融与经济危机期间，多边国际组织就社会保障的重要性达成一定程度的协议。即使未就具体模式和支出水平达成共识，国际货币基金组织和世界银行等机构在某种程度上也就社会保障的重要性达成了一致。例如，国际货币基金组织独立评估办公室在一份报告中指出："过去十年来，国际货币基金组织加强了对社会保护的关注，因为社会保护应对了全球金融危机的后果，解决了人们对粮食和燃料价格冲击所带来影响的担忧，应对了对低收入群体和最脆弱群体的更广泛的压力。因此，国际货币基金组织已经超越了传统的'以财政为中心'的做法，认识到社会保护由于社会和政治稳定考量等更广泛的原因而具有宏观上的重要性"（IMF，2017b）。世界银行和国际劳工组织主导的"全民社会保护 全球伙伴关系"于2016年启动。这表明世界银行意识到社会保护在应对贫困和加剧的收入不平等方面的重要性（World Bank and ILO，2016）。

3 社会保障与经济发展：
　　中国的案例

短短数十年，中国从低收入国家转变为主要经济大国，取得了令人瞩目的成就。自 20 世纪 80 年代掀起从计划经济走向市场经济的经济体制改革以来，中国经济的增长速度令人印象深刻。因此并不令人惊讶的是，如今的中国是世界第二大经济体，对全球经济增长的贡献率约为 31.5%，相比之下美国约为 11.5%，欧元区为 9% 左右。[1]

中国用市场经济体制取代了早期高度集中的计划经济体制，适应了经济全球化进程。采用的策略是成功的：首先，允许地方突破既有的国家政策规定，通过实施试点，以创新的做法取代旧的做法，然后从中汲取经验教训并制定新的国家政策，最终在全国范围内全面付诸实施。然而，由于转型过程需要改变以既得利益格局和强劲的路径依赖为特征的旧制度，因此在经济体制改革和社会改革方面存在巨大的失败风险。

在中国数十年的改革和发展中，这种失败的风险显著下降。其原因是多方面的，包括政治稳定、市场广阔、生产结构向纵深发展、劳动力资源

---

[1] 所有数据部分基于作者的估算，根据是国际基金组织的 2017 年 10 月的世界经济展望数据库。参见：http://www.imf.org/external/pubs/ft/weo/2017/02/weodata/download.aspx。

丰富以及对世界开放的政策等。而其中一个核心原因是政府信赖社会保障是应对改革风险与改善民生的重要治理工具，并坚信不断发展的社会保障与经济发展之间的积极关系。简而言之，在转型过程中，政府信任并依靠对经济和劳动力市场发展与社会保障之间内在关系的妥善、积极和前瞻性处理。这种信任体现在政府有效地利用社会保障的核心功能，使得国内生产力储备井喷式发展。

这一过程同时对中国社会保障制度建设产生了积极的影响。事实上，非常明显，中国经济的快速发展为更有效和更慷慨的社会保障制度提供了物质基础，这有助于化解收入风险并不断增进人民福祉。尽管还有许多工作要做，但这一社会保障体系现在已经几乎覆盖全民。

3.1　中国社会保障制度促进经济发展的历史经验

3.1.1　中国近 40 年取得的经济发展成就

在 1978 年，中国是一个极低收入国家，处于普遍贫穷状态，国内生产总值（GDP）和人均 GDP 分别为 3 679 亿元人民币和 385 元人民币（约分别合 2 185 亿美元[1]和 229 美元）（国家统计局，2019）。此后，中国经济经历了持续高速增长：到 2017 年，国内生产总值超过 82 万亿元人民币，约合 12 万亿美元；人均 GDP 达到了 59 210 元人民币，约合 8 768 美元（国家统计局，2019）。这些数据（见图 2）表明，中国属于中等偏上收入国家行列，并正在向高收入国家迈进。但中国的发展很不平衡，东部发达地区与西部欠发达地区的差距较大。

1　本报告中的美元按照中国国家统计局公布的"历年平均汇率"折算。参见：http：//data.stats.gov.cn/easyquery.htm?cn=C01&zb=A060J&sj=2017［2018 年 10 月访问］。

图 3、图 4、图 5 和图 6 反映了中国近 40 年的经济发展进程伴随着就业结构、产业结构、城镇化率与生活水平的深刻变化。

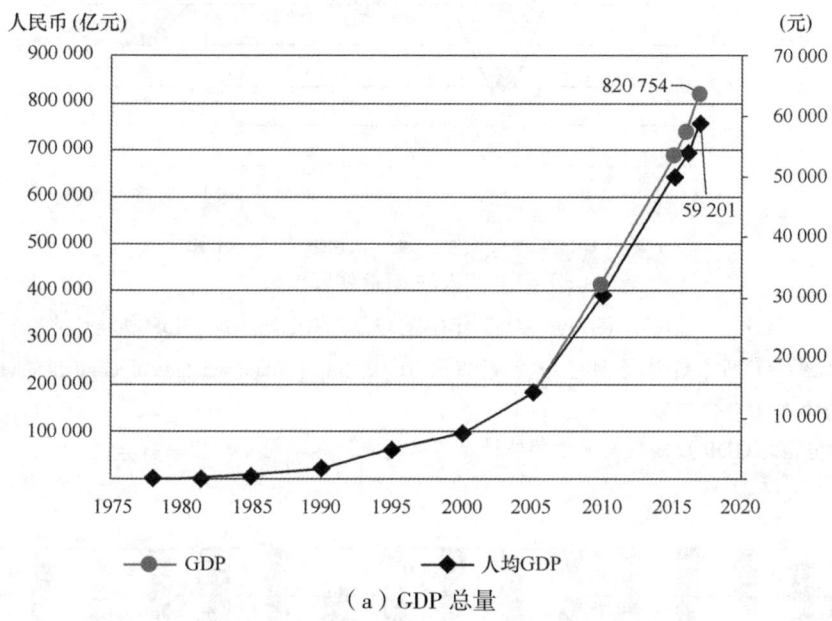

（a）GDP 总量

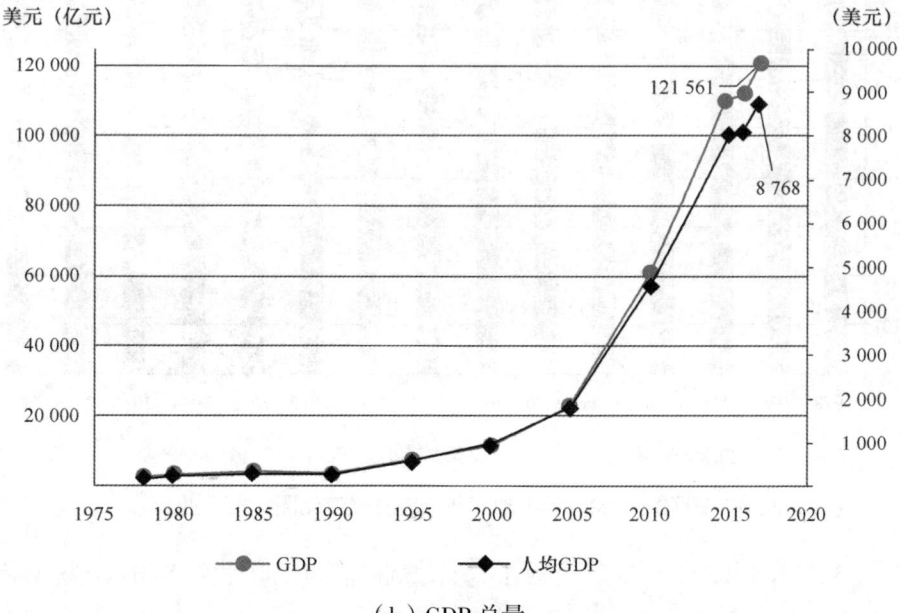

（b）GDP 总量

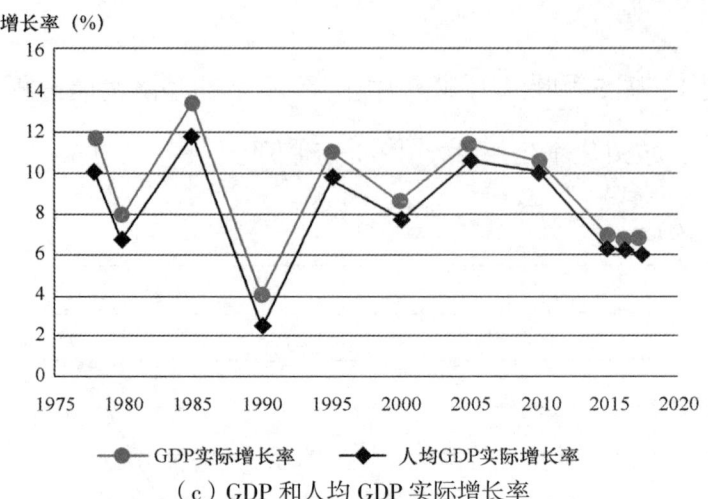

(c) GDP 和人均 GDP 实际增长率

图 2　1978—2017 年中国 GDP 总量与人均 GDP

资料来源：①国家统计局网站 国家数据。参见：http://data.stats.gov.cn/english/easyquery.htm？cn=C01（2019 年 1 月访问）。

②基于美元的 GDP 数据根据《中国统计年鉴》发布的各年份平均汇率折算。

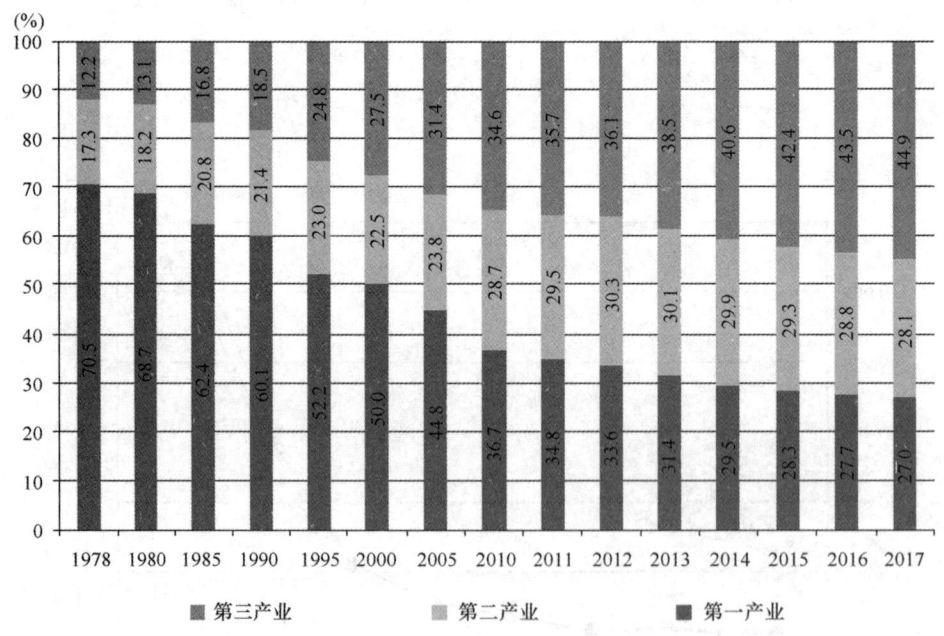

图 3　1978—2017 年中国就业结构发展变化图（按产业划分）

如图 3、图 4 所示，中国经历了整体就业结构和产业结构的典型（和快速）转型，具有现代化工业国家典型特征：第一产业的劳动者数量显著减少，同时第二产业（制造、建筑业等）和第三产业（服务业）的从业人数相应增加。第二产业产出份额的相对稳定及其就业人数，间接表明了这一产业生产率的显著提高。第二产业就业的统计稳定性掩盖了巨大的变化，现代化和市场化带来的社会保障的重点改革支撑了这些变化。

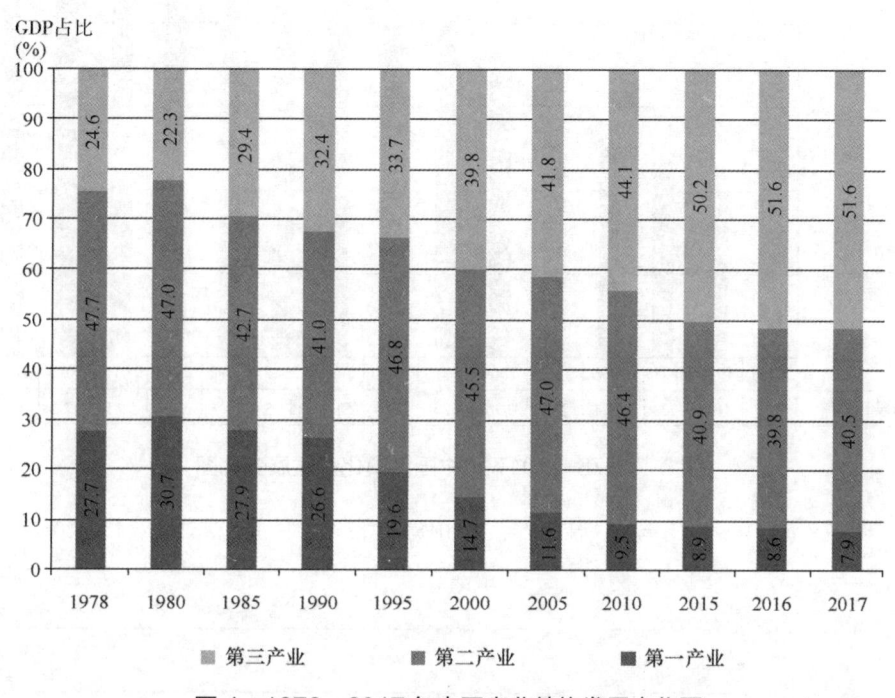

图4　1978—2017年中国产业结构发展变化图

资料来源：国家统计局.中国统计年鉴2018［M］.北京：中国统计出版社，2018.

中国的快速城镇化（见图5）给社会保障制度带来了更多的挑战。在户籍制度持续存在情况下，大量农民工依法有义务保持其在户籍地的登记，他们因此失去了事实上的医疗保障、社会救助以及其随迁子女教育的覆盖（以上只有在户籍地才能享受）。国家资源的地区配置仍然以户籍制度提供的信息为基础，由此产生的社会和管理问题目前仍存在，也是近期需要解决的问题。

同期中国减少了贫困人口6.6亿人。正如恩格尔系数下降所示，人民生计得到了显著改善（见图6）。尽管如此，绝大多数中国人口尚未达到高收入状态。全国农村贫困率虽然从2012年10.2%下降到了2018年的1.7%，但根据现行标

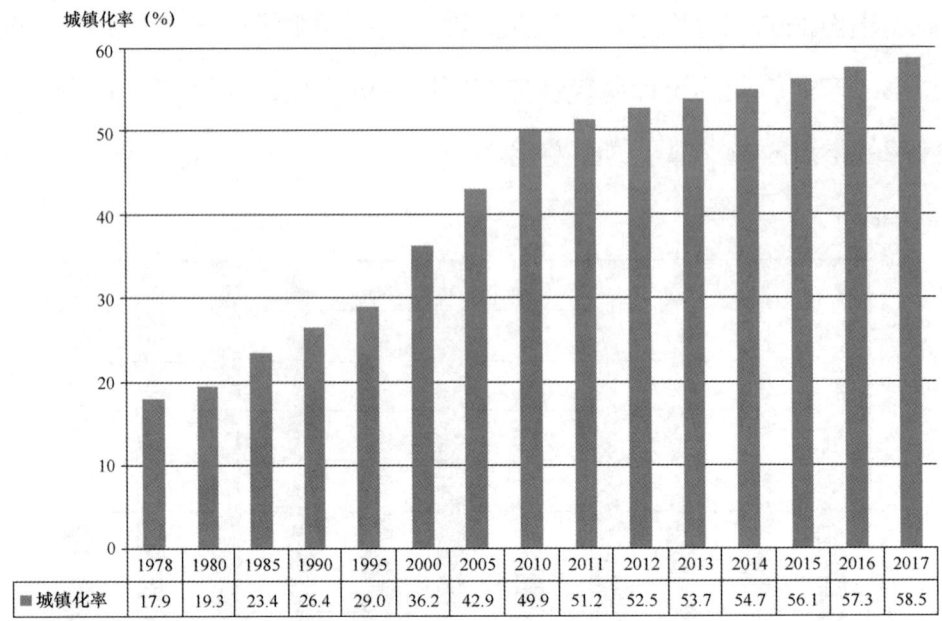

图 5　1978—2017 年中国城镇化率发展变化图

资料来源：国家统计局.中国统计年鉴2018[M].北京：中国统计出版社，2018.

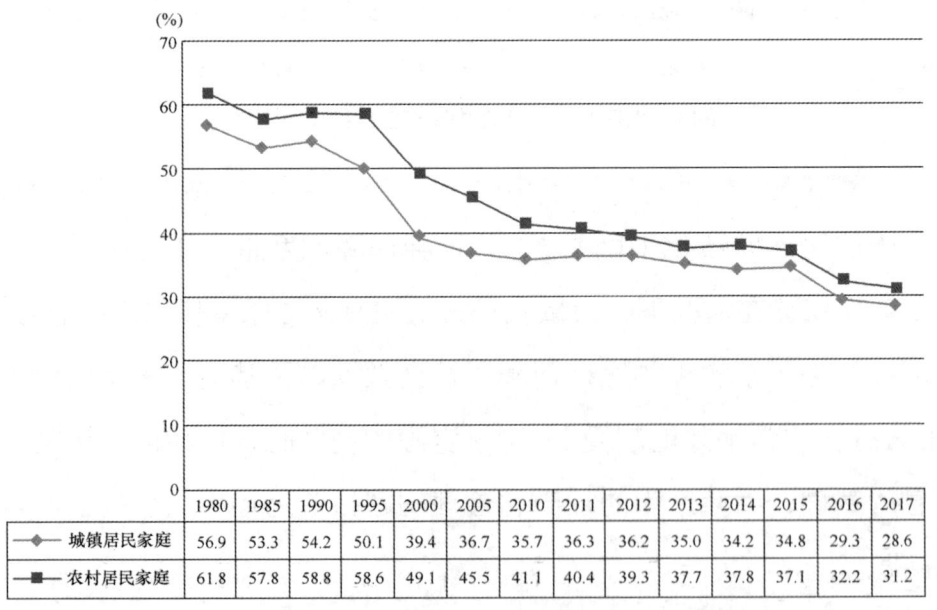

图 6　1980—2017 年中国城乡居民家庭恩格尔系数

注：恩格尔系数（Engel's Coefficient）是食品支出总额占个人消费支出总额的比重，其主要内容是指一个家庭或个人收入越少，用于购买生存性食物的支出在家庭或个人收入中所占的比重就越大。

资料来源：中华人民共和国统计局发布的历年国民经济和社会发展统计公报。

准（年人均 2 300 元人民币，2010 年不变价），截至 2018 年年底全国农村贫困人口还有 1 660 万人。[1] 中国政府的目标是在 2020 年消灭区域性整体贫困与绝对贫困现象，全面建成小康社会[2]；到 21 世纪中叶即中华人民共和国成立一百周年时，建成富强民主文明和谐美丽的社会主义现代化强国，全体人民共同富裕基本实现（习近平，2017）。

3.1.2 中国社会保障改革与发展取得的成就

在经济体制改革的触发下，中国的社会保障也在 20 世纪 80 年代中期进入全面而深刻的制度变革时期。这是为了支持经济改革进程，也是为了避免可能引发巨大社会风险的激烈变化。社会保障采取与经济改革相似的渐进改革方式，经历了从被动变革到主动变革，从自下而上到自上而下，从试点先行与逐渐推进到中央政府顶层设计与全面推进，从作为治理工具服务并服从于经济改革到独成体系的更加间接影响、维系和促进经济发展的转变过程。中国的社会保障在 30 多年的制度变革中，从基于国家—单位的制度环境转变为独立于单位的制度环境。在计划经济时代，中国曾经实行的是单位包办的社会保障制，城镇劳动者被固定在机关事业单位或国有企业，所在单位直接负责劳动者的养老、医疗、住房及其他各种福利保障，并惠及其家属，国家对城镇单位实行财政补贴；乡村人口则被固定分割在不同的基层组织，居民福利主要通过福利化的分配制度在集体成员之间实现互助，政府只负责有限的救灾济贫工作。因此，该系统高度分散和分割，因为它由各自具有独特边界的单位完全安排。中国的社会保障已经实现整体转型，即从计划经济时代的国家负责、单位包办、全面保障、板块结构、封闭运行式的社会保障制度转换成了政府主导、企业

---

[1] 国家统计局网站：http：//www.stats.gov.cn/tjsj/zxfb/201902/t20190215_1649231.html
[2] 参见《中华人民共和国国民经济和社会发展第十三个五年规划》（2016—2020）。

与个人责任分担、覆盖全民、社会化、多层次化的新型社会保障体系，实现了从国家—单位保障制到国家—社会保障制的转型（郑功成，2008a），从而可以在社会保障制度运行中使用现代管理技术，以更好地满足服务大规模人群的需要。

在2008年全球金融危机之后，中国政府加大了社会保障扩面的力度，以实现养老保险和医疗保险的全民覆盖。2009年之前，养老保险覆盖的人口不足2.5亿（包括养老金领取者），约占15岁及以上人口的23%。经过2009年、2011年、2014年和2015年的一系列改革，为城乡居民建立了养老保险制度，机关事业单位养老保险制度也与城镇职工养老保险制度并轨（参见ILO《世界社会保护报告2014—2015》）。新设立制度下的养老金包括社会养老金和个人储蓄账户养老金。医疗保险制度也采取了类似结构，职工医疗保险建立在用人单位与参保人缴费的基础之上，城乡居民医疗保险则主要依靠政府补贴，个人缴费通常只占到基金来源的1/4 ~ 1/5（关于这些制度的更多细节见下文）。

养老保险、医疗保险制度的创新政策设计以及中国政府对居民养老金与疾病医疗所承担的直接责任，是养老保险和医疗保险覆盖面迅速扩大的重要原因。

面向低收入群体的综合型社会救助制度得到全面确立，并惠及占总人口近10%的低收入家庭[1]，救助水平在不断提升。包括保障性住房建设、养老服务、残疾人保障、儿童福利等在内的其他福利制度也在改革和发展中（见专栏4）。中国建立了日益严密的社会安全网，既有效地化解了市场竞争与天灾人祸衍生出来的社会风险，也有效地促进了社会公正。

---

1 根据中国民政部《2016年社会服务发展统计公报》资料中有关最低生活保障、特困人员救助、临时救助、医疗救助、受灾人口救助受助人数，以及人力资源社会保障部有关就业救助受助人数、住房建设部有关住房救助受助人数、教育部有关教育救助受助人数综合计算后，扣除重复计算人数后获得的相对指标。

中国社会保障制度的快速发展，不仅使本国人民的福利水平与民生质量得到了大幅度提升，也对世界社会保障发展做出了重要贡献。如果不算中国，全世界社保覆盖面只有50%，算上中国达到了61%。[1] 2016年11月17日，国际社会保障协会将"社会保障杰出成就奖"授予中华人民共和国政府，以表彰中国近年来在扩大社会保障覆盖面工作中取得的卓越成就（ISSA，2016）。中国的社会保障制度目前已经成为全体人民共享国家发展成果的基本途径（郑功成，2016b）。

当然，其他因素也（一定）有助于这些发展。国际比较来看，中国的社会保障体系就财务规模而言仍然有限，因此对经济的积极财政影响只能是适度的。[2] 然而不可否认的是，多年以来，中国社会保障体系已经从被动地应对贫困的体系转化为主动地将经济发展成果重新分配给有需要的人，并惠及全体人民。

专栏4　中国社会保障制度体系框架

1. 社会救助制度

   1）最低生活保障

   2）灾害救助

   3）医疗救助

   4）教育救助

   5）特困人员救助

   6）住房救助

---

[1] 中国社保大奖的"含金量"——专访国际社会保障协会秘书长汉斯·霍斯特·康克乐伍斯基．中国政府网，2016-11-18. 参见：http://www.gov.cn/xinwen/2016-11/18/content_5134319.htm

[2] 即使完善的社会保障体系也不能指望其纠正社会的收入和财富分配不公平。要做到这一点，需要通过适当的税收政策来支持，以及有效的劳动力市场和工资协商制度。

7）就业救助

8）临时救助

2. 社会保险制度

1）养老保险

2）医疗保险

3）工伤保险

4）失业保险

5）生育保险

6）护理保险（试点中）

3. 社会福利制度

1）老年人福利

2）儿童福利

3）妇女福利

4）残疾人福利

5）教育福利

6）住房福利

4. 优抚安置制度

1）军人与军属优待

2）军人与军属抚恤

3）伤残军人安置

4）退伍军人安置

说明：①中华人民共和国国务院新闻办公室.中国的社会保障状况和政策.国务院公报，2004（32）.该政策性文件明确中国的社会保障体系由社会保险、社会福利、优抚安置、社会救助和住房保障等组成。

> ② 2010年通过的《中华人民共和国社会保险法》明确规制了养老保险、医疗保险、工伤保险、失业保险、生育保险五大险种，2017年中国政府开始在15个城市启动护理保险试点。
>
> ③ 2014年国务院颁行的行政法规《社会救助暂行办法》明确规制了最低生活保障等八项救助制度。
>
> ④ 2004年国务院颁行的《军人抚恤优待条例》明确规制了军人优待、抚恤制度，2011年国务院颁行的《退役士兵安置条例》明确了军人退役安置保障。
>
> ⑤ 中国的社会福利通常包括面向老年人、儿童、妇女与残疾人的福利津贴及相关服务，但中国理论界也将教育福利与住房福利纳入社会福利政策范畴。

中国的社会保障是由若干保障项目组成的一套制度体系，而养老保险、医疗保险、最低生活保障、教育保障、住房保障构成了这一制度体系的主要内容，并与中国经济发展存在着密切关系。以下将对主要的社会保障制度进行评估，包括讨论其发展、问题和解决方案。

社会养老保险

社会养老保险之发展

中国的社会养老保险制度始建于1951年，面向的是国有、集体企业职工，是由国家负责、企业包办的一种非缴费型养老金制度。随后亦建立了国家机关、事业单位工作人员退休金制度，并遵循了相同的原则。

20世纪80年代中期，中国一些地方开始探索超越企业的社会统筹型养老金制度。1991年国务院启动企业职工养老保险制度改革，实行国家、企业、个人三方共同负担的养老金制度，职工个人也要缴纳一定的费用，中国自此开始进入缴费型养老金时代。1995年国务院通过将社会统筹与个人账户相结合的方式来推进缴费型的财务机制，以深化养老保险改革，同时允许地方根据这一原则进行试点。1997年正式建立了面向企业职工和城镇个体劳动者的基本养老保险制度，实行社会统筹与个人账户相结合的财务模式。2009年开始，中国以财政资金为主，先后为农民和城镇非工薪居民逐步建立基本养老保险制度。参保是自愿的；为了激励参保，政府承担了为全额基础养老金提供资金并部分补贴参保者缴费的责任。2015年中国又将国家机关和事业单位工作人员纳入社会养老保险制度，非缴费型养老金制度完全被缴费型养老金制度所替代。2018年中国建立职工基本养老保险中央调剂金制度，希望借此推进这一制度走向全国统一。目前，中国已经实现基本养老保险制度政策上的全覆盖：工薪劳动者适用职工基本养老保险制度，其他社会成员适用城乡居民基本养老保险制度。

近20年来，中国社会养老保险覆盖面持续扩展，且保障待遇稳步提高。2017年全国参加养老保险的人数达到近9.155亿人，领取养老金的人数（附件2表A2第2列加第4列）达到2.662亿人。

1998—2017年，职工基本养老保险参保人数由11 203万增加到40 290万；城乡居民基本养老保险参保人数由8 025万增加到51 260万（见图7和附件2表A2）。

与此同时，基本养老保险的保障待遇都有增长（见图8和附件2中表A5）。养老金水平实现了多年连续增长。职工基本养老保险月人均基金支出从2001年的69.13美元增长到2017年的425.95美元，城乡居民基本养老保险月人均基金支出从2009年的5.96美元增长到2016年的18.77美元（国家统计局，2018）。

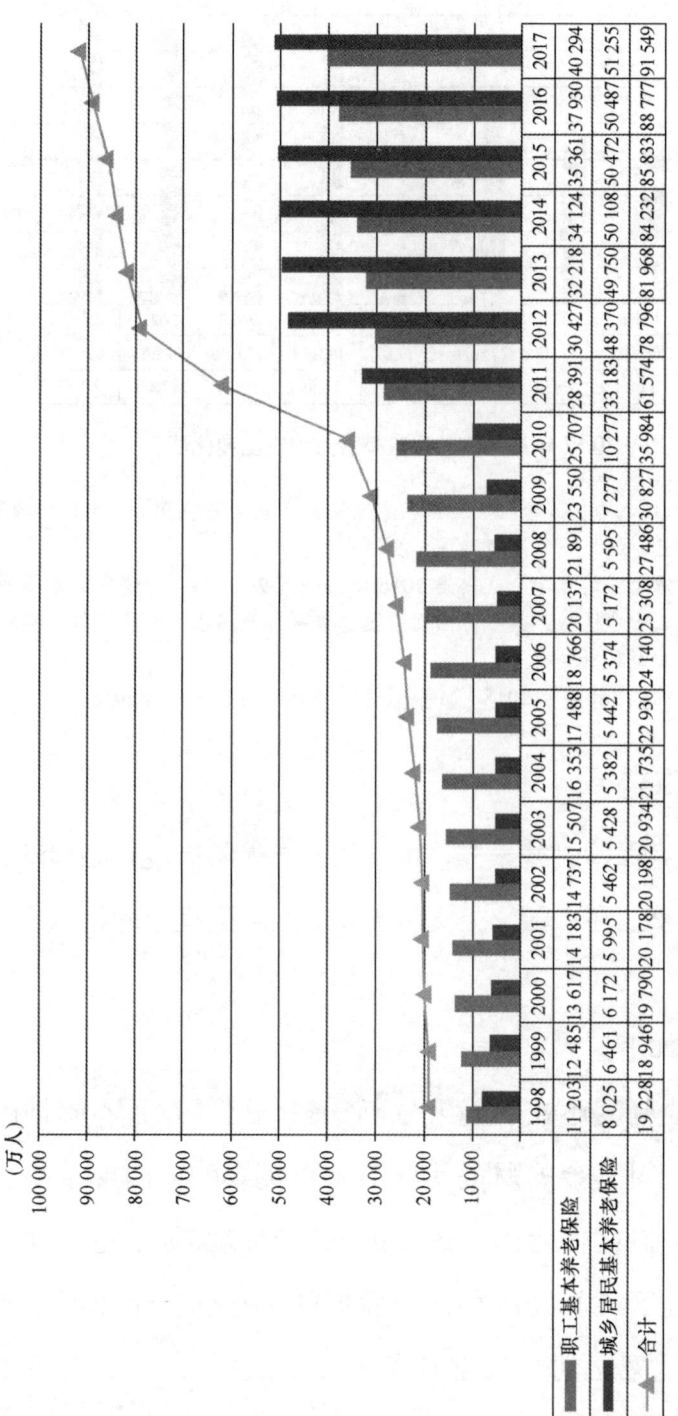

图 7 1998—2017 年基本养老保险参保人数历年变化情况

资料来源：国家统计局. 中国统计年鉴 2018 [M] . 北京：中国统计出版社，2018.

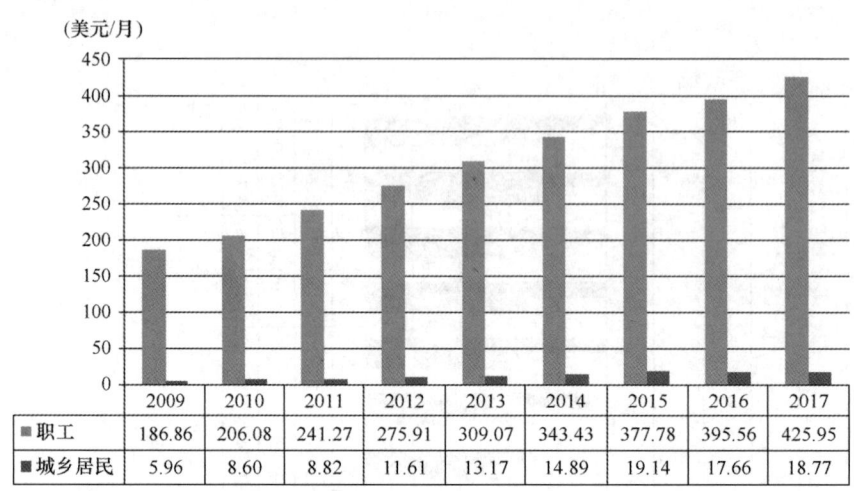

图8 2009—2017年基本养老保险基金人均支出变化情况

注：①基金人均支出用于估计人均养老金。人均养老金支出＝基金总支出/年末待遇领取人数。基金总支出最主要是养老金支出，此外还包括丧葬费、抚恤金等。

②图中城乡居民基本养老保险人均养老金支出量2016年略低于2015年，这是因为新增的养老金领取人数中，待遇水平相对较低的地区增加较多，因而全国总体平均待遇水平有所降低。实际上，各地区的待遇水平都没有降低，反而有所提高。

资料来源：国家统计局.中国统计年鉴2018［M］.北京：中国统计出版社，2018.

主要问题和解决思路

和世界上所有的养老保险制度一样，中国的养老保险制度也必须随着经济和人口的变化而不断调整。在中国，上文所描述的改革进程中的特殊历史遗留问题也要加以解决。

目前最紧迫的问题如下。

一是现行养老保险制度还处于地区分割状态，这导致了不同地区缴费和待遇给付负担不公，对基金的财务状况产生直接影响，出现了基金余缺并存的现象，使得这一制度作为国家统一的法定制度实际上沦为地方性制度安排，进而加剧了地区之间经济和社会发展的不平衡，也影响了市场经济条件下企业之间、地区之间的公平竞争（郑功成，2013）。二是不同群体之间的待遇差距较大。如机关事业单位退休人员的养老金水平普遍较高，企业退休人员的养老金水平较低,两者相差约两倍;农村老年人的养老金标准更低,目前国家规定的基础养老金最低标准仅为每人每月88元(约合13美元,按2017年平均汇率折算,下同),实际月人均养老金支出为126.72元(约合18.8美元)。[1] 人们普遍认为待遇差距过大是不公平的,如果不逐步缩小,将破坏公众对养老保险制度的认同。三是养老保险改革的转制成本尚未解决,造成的突出问题是使得在职的一代劳动者既要为自己未来的养老金储备资金,还要承担旧制度下的退休人员的养老金,形成了双重负担。1995年开始实行社会统筹与个人账户相结合的养老保险制度时,本意是维持作为公共养老金的社会统筹部分的现收现付制,对个人账户实行私人所有的完全积累制,实际上并非如此,因为低估了制度转轨的过渡期成本,迄今仍未找到妥善的解决办法。虽然筹资时由用人单位缴费形成社会统筹基金,个人缴费进入个人账户基金,但在地区分割的情形下,部分地区(如东北地区)的个人缴费因被用于支付当期的养老金而出现了个人账户空账,而另一些地区(如广东)则有大量结余。这种格局进一步增加了解决转制成本的复杂性。

为此,需要从以下几方面加以改进。

第一,需要尽快实现基本养老保险制度全国统筹。为改变地区分割导致制度扭曲的现状,中国需要加快推进全国养老保险制度统一的步伐,真正实现缴费基数计算方法、缴费率与给付办法的全国统一,以为所有劳动者提供更加公平的基本养老金保障,进而为养老保险制度的参与主体(包括企业、劳动者等)创造公平环境。中国政府在2017年决定先行建立养老保险中央调剂制度,2018年从各省、自治区、直辖市征收的职工养老保险费中统一按3%征集中央调剂金,再根据各省、自治区、直辖市退休人数按人均额计算汇总后返回各省、自治区、直辖市,以便增强区域

---

[1] 数据来自《中国统计年鉴2018》。

之间的互助共济功能，起到养老保险基金余缺调剂作用。这是走向全国统筹的过渡性办法，但还不是制度统一的全国统筹，因而需要加快改革步伐。

第二，需要缩小不同群体之间的基本养老金待遇差距。现行养老金给付办法不足以缩小不同群体之间的待遇差距，特别是财政注资型的养老金给付的差距，因此，政府应当采取一些特别措施，包括建立待遇确定和调整的协调机制。在这种机制下，可以逐步相对降低高保障人群的基本养老保险待遇，稳步提高农民等低保障人群的基本养老保险待遇，减轻他们对老年生活的后顾之忧。政府应该按照保基本的原则，兑现待遇给付，同时确保基本养老金替代率符合不低于40%的国际标准。此外，政府应确定职工养老金水平及其调整（指数化）方法，维持适度的筹资水平和年轻一代人的合理负担。鼓励中高收入群体参加职业年金和商业保险，提高补充性养老保险水平，真正形成结构合理的多层次老年收入保障体系。

第三，进一步明晰政府、企业（和其他机构）、个人在养老保险筹资中的责任。明确雇主缴费的责任及其执行至关重要，这不仅是为了养老保险制度的有序运行，而且也因为缴费是劳动力成本的一部分，是雇主在市场经济中必须接受的。雇主不应通过裁员而是应通过提高生产率的措施来应对劳动力成本。这个导向比乍一看来更重要。

中国在经历了三四十年的在很大程度上依赖（成功的）出口拉动的粗放型生产率增长后，现在将进入长期的集约型生产率增长阶段，特别是在内需导向型战略下（社会保障制度扩张是其中一个核心要素）。如下列等式所示（见专栏5），在经济范畴内，提高生产率是老龄化社会中控制养老金成本的唯一现实选择（在已使用过削减待遇、延长退休年龄等其他养老金节流措施后）。

专栏 5　养老金支出占 GDP 比重的决定因素

$$\frac{养老金}{GDP} = \frac{\overbrace{\dfrac{养老金领取人数}{退休年龄以上人口}}^{覆盖率} \times \overbrace{\dfrac{退休年龄以上人口}{15 岁以上和退休年龄以下人口}}^{人口抚养比} \times \overbrace{\dfrac{平均养老金}{平均劳动生产率}}^{待遇比率}}{\underbrace{\dfrac{就业人数}{15 岁以上和退休年龄以下人口}}_{就业率}}$$

其中,

覆盖率：养老金领取人数占退休年龄以上人口的百分比；

人口抚养比：退休年龄以上人口占 15 岁以上和退休年龄以下人口的百分比；

待遇比率：平均养老金占平均劳动生产率的百分比（平均劳动生产率定义为就业人员的人均国内生产总值）；

就业率：就业人数占 15 岁以上和退休年龄以下人口的百分比。

资料来源：改编自该欧盟委员会报告第 85 页：European Commission. 2015. *The 2015 ageing report：Economic and budgetary projections for the 28 EU Member States：2013-2060*（Luxembourg, Publications Office of the European Union）. Available at：http：//ec.europa.eu/economy_finance/publications/european_economy/2015/pdf/ee3_en.pdf[20 Feb. 2019].

由于中国养老保险的覆盖率已经达到近 100%，加之待遇给付很难削减，控制养老金成本的选择唯有降低抚养比、提高生产率和就业率。

在提高和维持生产率增长的同时创造就业，确实是社会主义市场经济中企业家的真正任务。要在企业家中平地而起实现这种商业文化并不容易，但可以通过严格落实企业的缴费义务来加以培育。与此同时，政府的职责是社会保障的组织管理和制定管理规则，使企业能够通过卸下早期社会包袱而获得自主经营权。目前，这也包括政府对历史债务[1]的承认和合理评估，以及有效解决制度转轨成本，而非通过（间接地）向当前缴费者和个人转嫁债务将问题留待以后解决。或是，政府可以承认早先启动的个人账户政策不成熟，并将相关政策退回到经典的（可能是部分积累）现收现付制。这种方式将增加养老金政策的透明性，且在财务负担方面并不会带来太大的变化。因为理论和政策实践都已经证明，无论是在现收现付制还是个人账户制下，政府都要承担兜底责任（Gillion 等，2000）。

第四，增强基本养老保险制度的可持续性。包括：通过增强这一制度的公平性、便捷性、透明度，以提高社会成员对制度的认同度和支持度；建立健全确保精算平衡的机制，增强制度设计和政策调整的科学性和依据；提高养老保险基金的投资收益率，提高制度运行效率。

第五，小步渐进地提高法定退休年龄与法定最低缴费年限。一方面，中国的法定退休年龄为男性60周岁、女性50周岁（其中女干部为55周岁）。从国际比较来看偏低，中国政府已经明确渐进性地提高退休年龄，但迄今还未出台新的政策。一个适宜的方案是，明确一个基准退休年龄目标，采取小步渐进的方式逐步推进，并针对特定人群（如重体力劳动者、教师与医生等脑力劳动者）采取弹性退休制。另一方面，中国现行的养老保险最低法定缴费年限为15年，明显偏短，有必要逐步延长，最终达到与可比国家相同的年限。这是适应人均预期寿命不断延长并有助于人们更好地按照生命周期安排工作与退休生活的必要举措。

1　这里的"历史债务"一词是指向在新制度引入之前，或者更确切地说，在新制度全面实施之前退休的劳动者支付的养老金。

社会医疗保险

社会医疗保险之发展

中国的社会医疗保险始建于20世纪50年代初。根据1951年《中华人民共和国劳动保险条例》，国家为企业职工建立了劳动保险医疗制度，随后为国家机关和事业单位工作人员建立了公费医疗制度，这两项制度实际上都是免费医疗制度。在农村，1957年开始实行农村合作医疗制度，依靠农村集体经济为农民提供一定程度的初级医疗保障。

免费医疗体制下，由企业承担在职职工与退休人员全部医疗费用。与养老保险情况一样，在20世纪80年代中期，这使得企业之间因在岗职工与退休职工健康风险结构的不同而造成负担畸轻畸重、不可持续。一些经济效益不良的企业无法报销职工与退休人员的医疗费用，企业的医疗费用负担也日益沉重。

因此，中国于20世纪90年代初期开始探索企业大病医疗费用统筹。1994年国务院选择江苏省镇江市、江西省九江市开展医疗保险改革试点，企业职工免费型医疗制度被由雇主、雇员缴费的缴费型医疗保险制度所取代。1998年正式建立城镇职工社会医疗保险制度，后来逐步扩展到几乎全体工薪劳动者。在农村，从1978年开始，因各地陆续推行家庭联产承包责任制，依托于集体经济的合作医疗制度逐步瓦解（见第3.1.4小节），农民的医疗保障由此弱化。2003年，中国开始推进农民基本医疗保险制度的试点，2007年将这一制度推广到工薪劳动者之外的城镇居民。

目前，中国已经建立了全民医疗保险制度，其中，工薪劳动者适用职工基本医疗保险（简称"职工医保"），其他社会成员适用城乡居民基本医疗保险（简称"居民医保"）。根据人力资源社会保障部发布的历年《人力资源和社会保障事业发展统计公报》以及原国家卫生计生委公布的历年《中国卫生和计划生育年鉴》，2000年参加社会医疗保险的人数（仅）为0.4亿人（不含仍然被免费医疗制度覆盖的人口），2005 年增长到 3.2 亿人，2010 年达到近 13 亿人，2017 年超过 13 亿人。这两种制度已经覆盖了中国 95% 以上的人口（城镇人口的覆盖率为 94%[1]，农村人口覆盖率达 97%[2]），基本实现了缴费型医疗保险模式下的全民医保目标（见表 2）。

表 2　　2006—2017 年中国基本医疗保险参保人数　　（单位：亿人）

年份	职工基本医疗保险		城乡居民基本医疗保险	合计
	在职参保	离退休参保		
	（1）	（2）	（3）	（4）
2006	1.16	0.42	4.10	5.68
2007	1.34	0.46	7.26	9.06
2008	1.50	0.50	9.33	11.33
2009	1.64	0.55	10.15	12.34
2010	1.78	0.59	10.31	12.68
2011	1.89	0.63	10.53	13.05
2012	1.99	0.66	10.77	13.42
2013	2.05	0.69	10.98	13.72
2014	2.10	0.73	10.51	13.34
2015	2.14	0.75	10.47	13.36
2016	2.17	0.78	7.24	10.19
2017	2.23	0.80	10.07	13.10

注：①这里的城乡居民基本医疗保险包括合并之前独立的新型农村合作医疗及城镇居民基本医疗保险，下同。2016 年以前新农合参保数据来自《中国卫生和计划生育统计年鉴》。2016 年起由于两项制度合并，参保人数统计出现较大波动。

②职工医保制度 1998 年年底建立，2000 年以后在各地陆续实施，中国公费医疗制度、劳动保险医疗制度开始逐步向基本医疗保险转型，享受公费医疗制度和劳动保险医疗保障人群逐步转移至基本医疗保险制度，但是在 2006 年以前，职工医保、公费医疗制度和劳动保险医疗制度并存。

③城乡居民基本医疗保险参保人数（第 3 列）2014 年后开始逐年减少，主要有两个原因：一是部分人员转而参加职工基本医疗保险；二是城镇居民基本医疗保险与新型农村合作医疗制度过去有重复参保的现象，两项制度整合之后，参保总数有所减少。因此，基本医疗保险参保总人数也相应减少。

资料来源：本表数据来自国家统计局公布的历年《中国统计年鉴》、人力资源社会保障部发布的历年《人力资源和社会保障事业发展统计公报》以及原国家卫生计生委发布的《中国卫生和计划生育年鉴》。

1　根据中国人力资源和社会保障部发布的《2016 年人力资源和社会保障事业发展统计公报》中的参保人数与中国国家统计局公布的同年城镇人口数计算。

2　国家卫计委：今年新农合住院费用报销比例再提高 5 百分点以上 . 新华社，2016-07-05. http：//finance.people.com.cn/n1/2016/0705/c1004-28526963.html

覆盖面扩大的同时,中国也确保了保障待遇的稳步提高(见图9)。自引入医疗保险制度以来,中低收入群体,特别是在农村地区,对于医疗服务的利用率也在持续提高。[1] 同时,自付额占医疗卫生总费用的比例从1995年的46.4%降至2014年的31.99%。[2] 这些改善部分地与职工人均基金支出从2000年时的329元人民币(39.72美元)增长到2017年的3 122元人民币(462.4美元)这一事实有关,而对于农村和城市居民而言,人均基金支出从2004年的33元人民币(3.99美元)增加到2017年的567元人民币(83.97美元)。

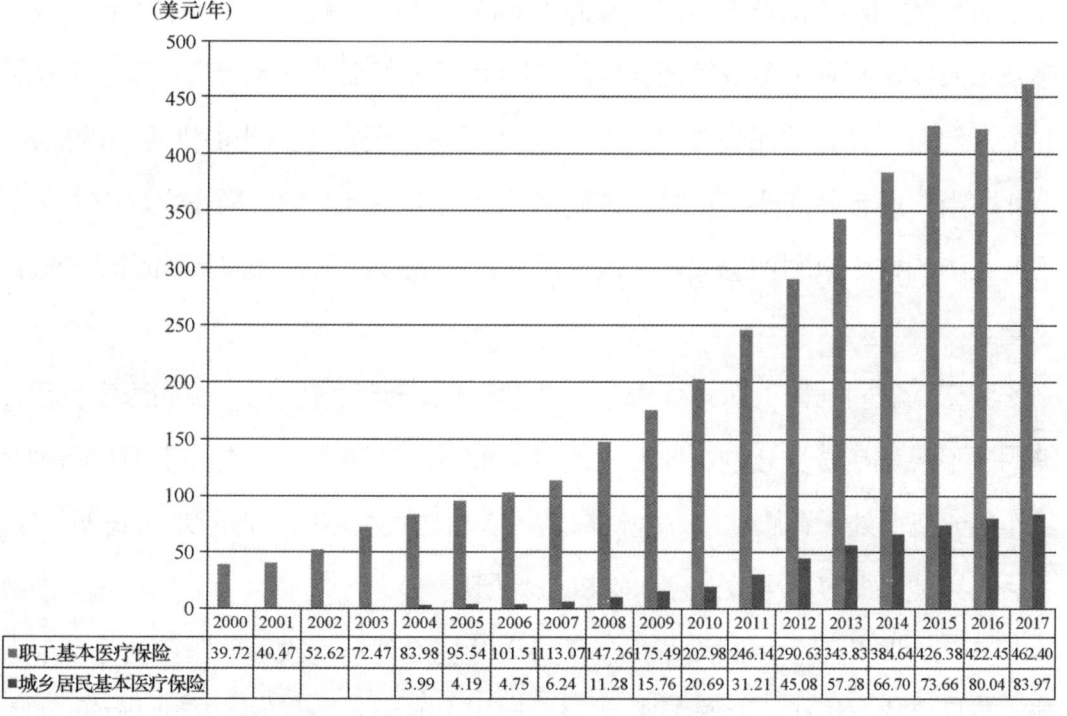

图9 2000—2017年基本医疗保险人均基金支出变化情况

资料来源:①数据来自国家统计局公布的历年《中国统计年鉴》、人力资源社会保障部发布的历年《人力资源和社会保障事业发展统计公报》以及原国家卫生计生委发布的《中国卫生和计划生育年鉴》。

②人均基金支出=基金支出/参保人数。

---

[1] 根据原国家卫生计生委历年发布的《中国卫生和计划生育年鉴》。

[2] 参见:https://data.worldbank.org/data-catalog/GDP-ranking-table(2018年10月访问)。

2018年3月，中国政府设置统一的国家医疗保障局，将原来分散在人力资源社会保障部、国家卫生和计划生育委员会[1]、民政部等部门的相应职责划入该局，这预示着中央政府将更加强有力地推进全民医保制度的建设。

当前的主要问题和解决思路

当前，中国社会医疗保险制度存在的问题主要有以下四点。

其一，职工医疗保险采取的也是与职工养老保险类似的统账结合财务机制。个人缴费占工资总额2%，全部记入个人账户；用人单位缴费占工资总额的6%，其中的30%（相当于工资总额的1.8%）记入个人账户。这种制度设计既不遵循私人保险原则也不遵循社会保险风险共担的原则。个人账户只不过是私人的个人储蓄，在花费昂贵和严重的疾病情况下，通常也不能提供足够的储备。因此，当参保者最需要支持时，该制度无法提供充足保护。换言之，有组织的互助共济的核心原则被忽视了，因此医疗保险制度的可持续发展面临着严峻的风险。

其二，农村居民的医疗保障水平依然较低，慢性病和重大疾病医疗费用保障明显不足。在城乡分割、地区分割的情形下，进城务工的农民工因户籍地与工作地分离而处于尴尬地位，他们被纳入农村居民基本医疗保险却又长期工作、生活在异地，很容易导致医疗保险权益受损。

其三，医药卫生体制改革（包括公立医院治理结构改革、医药流通体制改革、药品价格市场化改革等）滞后，衍生出过度医疗、药价虚高和腐败等问题，导致医疗保险基金存在着较为严重的浪费现象，而一些大病、慢性病却保障不足，资源使用效率有待提高。

其四，退休职工不缴纳医疗保险费的现行政策，将因人口老龄化的加速发

---

[1] 国家卫生和计划生育委员会是由原卫生部和原国家人口和计划生育委员会于2013年设立的。2018年3月，该委员会解散，其职能被纳入名为国家卫生健康委员会的新机构，旨在促进健康中国倡议，并确保为中国人民提供全面的保健服务。

展而对医疗保险制度可持续性造成越来越大的挑战。

因此，中国还需要在以下几个方面深化医疗保险制度改革。

第一，必须取消个人账户，转化为有效的基于互助共济融资技术原则的社会保险。在有效地组织时，医疗保险符合参保者的利益；如果其嵌入透明的医疗卫生系统中，则是一个具有高度再分配性质的制度安排——健康者与病人间、高收入者与低收入者间、安全工作场所劳动者与高风险工作场所劳动者间（仅举几个例子）。而在职工医疗保险中设置个人账户则严重削减了这一功能。要通过深化改革来为所需的转型做好精心准备，包括加强相关研究。

第二，加快职工医保、城乡居民医保制度的整合步伐，用统一的医疗保险制度覆盖全民，以此促进制度公平，提高运行效率。同时，在向社会保障融资方式转型的同时，将目前县级统筹提高至省级统筹（按照《社会保险法》规定）。这是缩小不同群体之间医疗保障待遇差距的唯一现实选择（就目前所观察到的情况）。还应当着力提高农村居民的基本医疗保险保障水平，这不仅能够满足日益增长的社会公平的要求，而且还会进一步提高医疗消费（对预期寿命有积极影响）和全社会的消费信心。为此，需要进一步增加政府对制度的补贴和提高个人缴费的比例。

第三，合理引导退休职工缴纳医疗保险费。应当坚持"老人老办法，新人新办法"原则，修改相关法律，规定新退休的人员应当缴纳医疗保险费；或者适当提高退休人员的养老金水平，以此换取其缴费。这种改革能够适应人口老龄化，壮大医疗保险基金，同时确保退休职工与居民医保制度覆盖下的老年人承担同样的缴费义务，享受同样的医疗保险待遇。

第四，需要加强重大疾病与慢性病医疗费用保障。在提高筹资水平的条件下，更多的资源应当用于医药费用较高的疾病治疗和医疗服务，最终为全体人民提供疾病医疗与健康保障方面的稳定预期。

第五，深入推进基本医疗保险付费机制改革。将总额控费与按人头付费、病种付费有机结合，推广按病种与疾病组付费的方式。此外，必须实施协商和协调机制，包括所有参与医疗卫生系统的利益相关者——参保人（含缴费者和患者）、医疗服务提供者（医院／医生协会）、政府、医药行业，以便对医疗服务和药品进行更合理和有效的定价，以此促进医药服务行为规范化，减少基本医疗保险及相关服务中的资源浪费，使有限的资源发挥更大的效用，并促进医药服务行业持续健康发展。在这种情况下，完善医疗保险监管体系使其拥有现代化的机构架构非常关键，该体系应该实现医疗系统各方面（包括法律、组织和统计信息及数据，所有其他利益相关者必须能够获得这些信息）的研究和知识至上，这样才能充分体现（代表）参保者的利益。

最低生活保障

最低生活保障之发展

在自 1949 年起逐步建立高度集中的计划经济体制后，社会成员均被编入某一组织（在城镇是企业与公共机构，在农村是集体经济组织），这类组织既是生产经营和公共服务等的组织者，也是社会福利和风险保障的提供者。在此基础上，国家确立了"生产自救，群众互助，并辅之以政府必要的救济"的原则，[1]奉行"救急不救穷"，以救灾和救危为主，同时对个别特别困难者实施长期救助。贫困人口主要依靠工作单位（包括农村集体经济组织）给予帮助，偶尔也能得到政府的临时性救助。只有城镇孤寡老人与儿童被政府举办的社会福利机构供养或者给予长期救济。

20 世纪 80 年代中期，继农村实行土地承包责任制改革后，城市经济体制改革逐步展开，经济结构调整和体制机制转变，国有企业产生了一批失业者，

1　该原则在 1953 年第二次全国民政会议上得以确定。

加上原先由工作单位提供的部分福利和风险保障被剥离但又没有新的替代者，这就导致了新的城市贫困群体的出现。雪上加霜的是，进入20世纪90年代中期后，越来越多的退休人员由于全国范围内的养老保险基金赤字而未能按时足额领取养老金。在社会问题日益严峻的背景下，1993年6月，上海市率先建立城市居民最低生活保障制度，不久，全国各地陆续效仿。1997年9月，国务院决定在全国普遍实施城市居民最低生活保障制度（简称"低保"）。1999年9月，国务院制定《城市居民最低生活保障暂行条例》，正式确立了全国性的面向城镇居民的最低生活保障制度。

在农村，1978年联产承包责任制推行之后，集体经济逐步弱化，农民的公共福利和风险保障也随之减弱。2001年，浙江省率先实施城乡一体化的最低生活保障制度，将全省农民纳入这一制度的保障范围。随后，许多地区纷纷建立农村低保制度，或者将城市低保制度扩展到农村。2007年，国务院决定在农村普遍实施低保制度。至此，低保制度成为保障全民基本生活的基础性制度安排。

从图10可见，中国农村贫困线近年来得到提升，而贫困发生率是持续下降的。2010年后贫困率的突然上升与新设定的农村贫困线标准有关。

30多年的农村扶贫开发（见专栏6），使贫困地区的经济和社会迅速发展，农村居民的生存和温饱问题得到基本解决，贫困人口的生活、教育、卫生状况明显好转，贫困地区的生产生活基础设施逐步改善，为经济社会长期发展奠定了基础。2010年年底，全国农村绝对贫困人口下降到2 688万人（国务院新闻办公室，2011）。1981—2012年，中国减少的贫困人口占全球减少全部贫困人口的71.82%[1]。尽管中国在消除贫困现象方面已经取得了卓越成就，但根据现行贫困线标准，2018年仍然有近1 660万农村贫困人口（国家统计局，2019）。

1　数据来自2016年12月发布的中国社会科学院和国务院扶贫办《中国扶贫开发报告2016》（扶贫蓝皮书）。

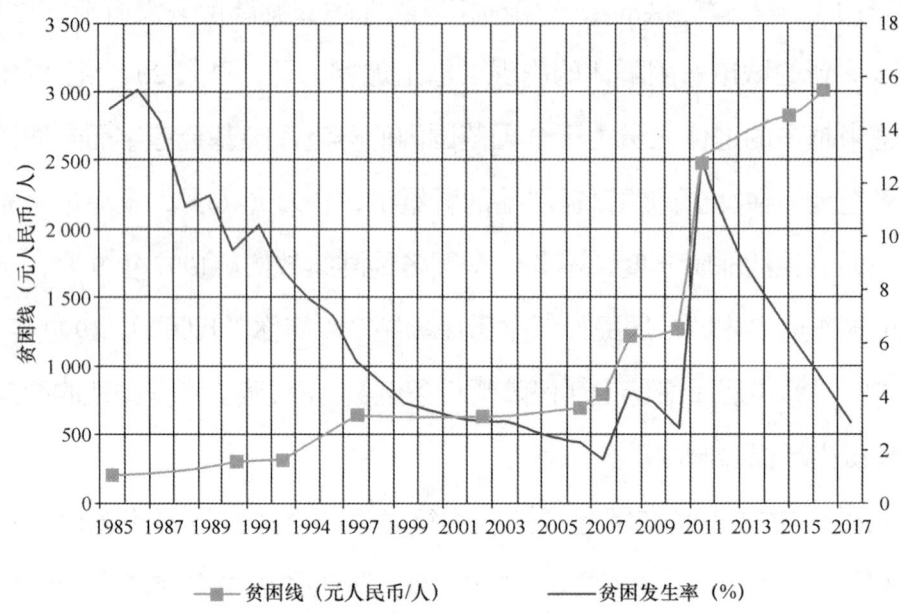

图 10　1985—2017 年农村贫困线和贫困发生率

说明：①1978 年标准，在 1978—1999 年是农村贫困标准，2000—2007 年则作为农村绝对贫困标准。
②2008 年标准，在 2000—2007 年是农村低收入标准，2008—2010 年则作为农村贫困标准。
③2010 年标准是新确定的农村扶贫标准。
资料来源：1985—1999 年农村扶贫标准、贫困人口、贫困发生率由国务院扶贫办提供。2000—2017 年的贫困人口、贫困发生率等数据来自《中国统计年鉴 2018》，贫困线标准来自国家统计局的《中国农村贫困监测报告》。

> **专栏 6　中国农村扶贫开发：加强消除贫困的措施**
>
> 　　几十年前，中国是世界上贫困人口最多的国家。1986 年，中国在农村地区开始实施针对贫困人口和贫困地区的重大扶贫开发活动。随后进行了进一步的改革，包括《国家八七扶贫攻坚计划》[1]（1994 年）、《中国农村扶贫开发纲要（2001—2010）》《中国农村扶贫开发纲要（2011—2020）》。自 2015 年以来，国家实施精准扶贫战略，旨在于 2020 年消除绝对贫困。

1　计划用 7 年时间（1994—2000 年），解决 8 000 万人贫困问题。

> 贫困地区的地方政府已将消除贫困作为其重要目标之一。通过中央财政专项投入或以地区对口支援等方式,为贫困地区分配了大量资源。中央政府还加大了消除贫困和发展毗邻贫困地区的力度。中央财政也加大了连片特困地区的扶贫开发力度,按大口径计算的中央财政和地方财政扶贫支出,2011—2014 年共计约 1.5 万亿人民币（2 410 亿美元）。[1]

2014 年,国务院颁布新的法规《社会救助暂行办法》,全面确立了包括医疗、教育、住房、就业、临时急难救助在内的综合型社会救助制度,最低生活保障作为最重要的一项制度纳入其中,并消除了城乡分割的政策痕迹。目前,最低生活保障制度是惠及人数最多、所用资金量最大、保障水平较高的社会救助项目,并成为整个社会保障体系中的核心项目。根据民政部发布的历年《民政事业发展统计公报》和《社会服务发展统计公报》,2000 年享受低保待遇的城乡居民约为 700 万人,2015 年超过 6 600 万人,2017 年超过 5 300 万人,这意味着享受最低生活保障待遇的贫困人口在经历一段时期增长后开始减少（见表 3）。

表 3　　2000—2017 年中国城乡最低生活保障基本情况

年份	城镇低保 低保人数（万人）	月平均标准（元/人）		财政支出（亿元）		农村低保 低保人数（万人）	月平均标准（元/人）		财政支出（亿元）	
		人民币	美元	人民币	美元		人民币	美元	人民币	美元
	(1)	(2)	(3)	(4)	(5)	(6)	(7)	(8)	(9)	(10)
2000	402.6	157.0	19.0	27.2	3.3	300.2				
2001	1 170.7	147.0	17.8	54.2	6.5	306.8				

---

[1] 中央财政综合扶贫投入指中央财政用于部分农村贫困地区、贫困人口能够直接受益的资金,包括专项扶贫资金投入、农业生产方面的投入、农村教育方面的投入、农村医疗方面的投入、农村社会保障方面的投入、大中型水库移民后期扶持及彩票公益金方面的投入、一般性转移支付七大类,涉及 33 项中央财政资金。地方财政扶贫投入是不完全统计。

续表

年份	城镇低保					农村低保				
	低保人数（万人）	月平均标准（元/人）		财政支出（亿元）		低保人数（万人）	月平均标准（元/人）		财政支出（亿元）	
		人民币	美元	人民币	美元		人民币	美元	人民币	美元
	(1)	(2)	(3)	(4)	(5)	(6)	(7)	(8)	(9)	(10)
2002	2 064.7	148.0	17.9	108.7	13.1	407.8				
2003	2 246.8	149.0	18.0	151.0	18.2	367.1				
2004	2 205.0	152.0	18.4	172.7	20.9	488.0				
2005	2 234.2	156.0	19.0	191.9	23.4	825.0	76.0	9.3		
2006	2 240.1	169.6	21.3	224.2	28.1	1 593.1	70.9	8.9		
2007	2 272.1	182.4	24.0	277.4	36.5	3 566.3	70.0	9.2	109.1	14.4
2008	2 334.8	205.3	29.6	393.4	56.6	4 305.5	82.3	11.9	228.7	32.9
2009	2 345.6	227.8	33.4	482.1	70.6	4 760.0	100.8	14.8	363.0	53.1
2010	2 310.5	251.2	37.1	524.7	77.5	5 214.0	117.0	17.3	445.0	65.7
2011	2 276.8	287.6	44.5	659.9	102.2	5 305.7	143.2	22.2	667.7	103.4
2012	2 143.5	330.1	52.3	674.3	106.8	5 344.5	172.3	27.3	718.0	113.7
2013	2 064.2	373.3	60.3	756.7	122.2	5 388.0	202.8	32.8	866.9	140.0
2014	1 877.0	410.5	66.8	721.7	117.5	5 207.2	231.4	37.7	870.3	141.7
2015	1 701.1	451.1	72.4	719.3	115.5	4 903.6	264.8	42.5	931.5	149.6
2016	1 479.9	494.6	74.5	687.9	103.6	4 576.5	312.0	47.0	1 014.5	152.7
2017	1 261.0	540.6	80.1	640.5	94.9	4 045.2	358.4	53.1	1 051.8	155.8

数据来源：中华人民共和国民政部2000—2017年《中国民政事业发展统计公报》和《社会服务发展统计公报》。

当前的主要问题和解决思路

中国的最低生活保障制度实施以来，为保障贫困人口的基本生活和维护社会稳定、支持经济发展做出了积极贡献，但现行制度还存在一些缺陷。

首先，保障水平偏低，并且缺乏正常增长机制，客观上影响了部分贫困人口基本收入保障权益的有效实现。

其次，低保待遇中要减去全额劳动收入，导致对有劳动能力的那部分低保对象的就业创业激励不足。

最后，管理与运行机制不完善。迄今缺乏有效的家计调查，也缺乏专业化的经办机构，实践中骗取低保待遇的现象并不罕见。同时，地方一级还存在着腐败现象，有限的低保往往达不到目标群体，偏远落后地区尤甚。这影响了包括低保制度在内的整个社会救助制度的健康发展。

因此，这一制度还需要如下改进和完善。

第一，需要加快推进最低生活保障制度城乡一体化。目前仍然存在着城乡分割的现象，造成了城乡低保对象的权益不公，应当积极推进全国统一的最低生活保障制度，确保同一地域的贫困人口在低保制度下享受到公平保障。

第二，需要改进低保标准制定和低保对象认定的财务、管理和操作办法。目前的制度是基于个人收入的家计调查型，应该考虑根据标准化的一篮子物品与服务来衡量个人或家庭的需求，并保证其适度的生活水准。

从国际经验看，基于收入的贫困计算相较于标准化的一篮子支出而言的优点在于，待遇评估和递送（以及受益人的退出机制）在管理上都更加简便。以支出为基础的一篮子计算方式的优点在于，它原则上能够更好地瞄准受益人的需求；以 CPI 为基础对保障标准进行指数化调整也比以收入为中心的方式更为合理，因之确保了待遇随着时间的推移而保持其实际价值。现实中出现的错保和漏保问题，与管理和经办机构的质量和分布状况相关。

无论如何，必须尽快而持续地推进处于基础层次的低保制度及其他救助项目走向健全，这也是完善越来越基于社会保险原则（养老和医疗）的整个社会保障制度体系的必由之路。

第三，建立健全就业创业的内生激励机制。为应对当前体制下抑制劳动力市场参与的挑战，应该制定相关规则，使得低保待遇和额外的劳动收入两者能兼而有之。一般而言，这一制度需要良好的管理，不但对待遇给付和低保对象的社会需求进行公平的管理，而且要帮助有工作能力的低保对象进入或重返劳动力市场。国际经验表明，这一制度的实施需要地方税务机关和社会救助部门间的顺畅合作。

教育福利

教育福利制度的历史演进

教育是国民立足社会的基础,也是国家发展之根本所系(郑功成,2014a)。从 1949 年开始,中国致力于全面普及初等教育、发展中等和高等教育。就教育福利制度的发展而言,大体上可以划分为三个阶段。

第一阶段:20 世纪 80 年代前,中国实施与计划经济体制相适应的全面免费教育。在城镇,有初等教育、高等教育和职业技能培训等,均属于公共福利范畴,即使是企事业单位举办的学校,也因为公有制而与国家财政紧密关联,本质上属于公共福利。在农村,以初等教育为主,由国家财政和乡村集体经济共同出资举办,也带有公共福利性质。当时的教育福利具有普遍性,但限于教育发展不足,只有极少数人能够享受高等教育。

第二阶段:在 20 世纪最后 10 多年时间,伴随着国家福利缩减,全面免费教育开始改革探索,转向多元投资的混合型教育体系。义务教育继续免费,全部由国家财政投入,中高等教育适度收费,并允许民间力量投资举办各类教育。1992 年,中国政府明确教育对国民经济发展具有先导性影响,但强调"不能过多依赖国家投资"。[1] 随后,高等教育扩招、收费和民办教育兴起,教育事业总体上得到迅速发展。高中、中等职业教育和高等教育的学校仍然以公办为主,投资以财政投入为主。在这一阶段,教育总投入大幅增加,但财政性投入比重有所下降。

第三阶段:进入 21 世纪以来,困难群体教育帮扶体系逐步完善。2001 年开始,陆续实行"两免一补"——全面免除城乡义务教育阶段学生学杂费,对农村学生和城市家庭经济困难学生免费提供教科书,对家庭经济困难寄宿生提供生活补助,实施营养改善计划。在高等教育方面,健全了奖助学金、助学贷

---

[1] 1992 年《中共中央国务院关于加快发展第三产业的决定》。

款、学费补偿贷款代偿、勤工助学、困难补助、伙食补贴、学费减免等制度，以保障困难家庭子女上大学的权益。在普通高中，采用以国家助学金为主体、学校减免学费等为补充的保障措施。对于中等职业教育，则实行以国家免学费、国家助学金为主的保障政策。同时，加强了以残疾儿童为对象的特殊教育。

政府还通过扫盲班、夜校、职业培训等途径，提高国民受教育水平和劳动技能。据联合国教科文组织的数据，全国总人口中的文盲率由1982年的39%以上下降到2010年的3%以下。[1] 1985—2016年，全国劳动力人口的平均受教育程度从6.1年上升到了10年；其中，城镇劳动力人口的平均受教育程度从7.8年上升到了11.2年，农村从5.6年上升到了8.5年。[2] 中国财政部、教育部、国家统计局发布的《2017年全国教育经费执行情况统计公报》显示，中国财政性教育经费投入由1991年的618亿元人民币（116.1亿美元）增长至2017年的3.421万亿元人民币（5 066.5亿美元），其占GDP的比重从1991年的不足3%增长至2015年的近4.3%，近几年来一直保持在4%以上。[3]

问题与改进建议

中国教育事业虽有较大发展并对经济增长起到了积极作用，但依然面临许多问题：一是人均受教育年限与发达国家相比还有较大差距，学前教育（3～6岁）和高中阶段教育福利供给仍然不足；二是教育资源配置不均衡，城乡之间、区域之间、学校之间都存在显著的差异，阻碍着资源匮乏地区劳动力素质提高，加剧了地区经济发展不平衡；三是部分地区、部分人群的义务教育未能达标，教育质量亟待提高，基础教育公平性受到质疑；四是对职业技术教育重视不够，导致高技能产业工人短缺，影响产品质量和技术进步；五是劳动力市场、收入分配和社会保障制度缺陷，导致部分大学生就业困难，使得欠发达地区和低收

---

1 参见：http://data.uis.unesco.org（2018年10月10日访问）。
2 中央财经大学《2018年中国人力资本报告》。
3 参见1992—2017年的《中国教育统计年鉴》。

入家庭教育投入动力下降。

为此，需要在以下几方面予以改进。

一方面，需要进一步扩大政府教育投入。面对城乡居民教育需求的不断增长，政府需要增加公共投入，进一步增加财政性教育支出预算。同时，深化教育体制改革，有序发展民办教育以确保其不过度且达到公立教育的质量，动员更多社会资源进入教育领域。此外，通过营造公平竞争环境，改善收入分配，提高人力资源投资回报率，增强社会成员对教育投入的积极性。

另一方面，提高免费教育年限，并加大对落后地区与贫困家庭子女的援助力度。宜将免费教育延长到12年，即将高中教育阶段纳入免费教育范畴，并确保4～6岁儿童能够普遍性地享受免费的学前教育，实现教育覆盖到所有的适龄儿童。同时，政府应加大对落后的农村地区、西部地区和边远贫困地区的财政支持力度，全面改善其办学条件，确保这些地区的教育质量。

此外，中国教育发展面临的一项重要任务是加快发展职业教育，优化教育结构。应当营造有利于职业教育发展的社会氛围，为此，可借鉴国外经验，与德国及其他有着健全职业教育体系的国家加强合作，以便更深入理解运转有效的职业教育体系的必备条件。应当提高参与职业教育的中学生比重，培养数以亿计的拥有相应技能的高素质劳动者，重点是加快培养各行业所需要的专业技术人员。

3.1.3 社会保障对中国经济发展的贡献

本小节旨在证明，中国的社会保障与经济发展保持了共同发展的正相关性。社会保障体系的日益健全和社会保障水平的持续提升，为中国的经济改革和社会转型进程创造了相对安定的社会环境（郑功成，2018a）。

社会保障待遇水平的提高直接增加了城乡居民的收入，提高了他们的购买力与消费倾向和消费能力，从而刺激了总消费。在此基础上，中国社会保障制度的变革与发展，为维护社会正义、实现超越经济领域外的国家全面发展做出了贡献。具体而言，社会保障对中国经济发展的贡献主要表现在 30 年多来如下几个方面切实的政策和改革。

一是社会保障快速发展的需求效应，培育了民生经济新增长点。社会保障制度的日益健全激发了城乡居民的消费倾向，提升了其消费能力。不断增长的养老金和社会救助等其他保障待遇，对消费产生了刺激作用。随着目前社会保障体系几乎覆盖全民、保障水平持续增长，私人家庭消费也在急剧增长，全国商品性消费继 2008 年、2012 年先后突破 10 万亿元、20 万亿元之后，2017 年社会消费品零售总额达到 36.6 万亿元（国家统计局，2018）。最终消费（包括私人家庭消费和政府消费）对中国经济增长的贡献率从 2014 年的 48.8% 增长到 2016 年的 64.6%，超过投资贡献率 22.4 个百分点。[1]

因此，消费已经成为中国经济增长的最大引擎。这在很大程度上可归因于接近全民覆盖的社会保障体系这一主要成就。

二是创设失业保险制度（1986 年）与下岗职工基本生活保障制度，为国有企业改革劳动用工制度和步入市场化提供了必要条件。在异常深刻的经济改革中，支撑中国经济大厦的国有企业处于中心位置，只有让国有企业成为真正的市场主体，才能与逐渐发展壮大的私有企业竞争。这要求通过允许用人单位和劳动者签订和终止合同（中国的术语是"双向选择"就业[2]），从而灵活化基于终生"铁饭碗"的就业安排，并将国有企业劳动者融入统一劳动力市场。中国政府意识到这种新格局很容易使工人处于不利地位。失业保险和下岗职工基本生活保障制度旨在应对失业、下岗职工可能面临的经济困难。换言之，它们都

---

[1] 消费仍是经济增长的"第一引擎"[N]．人民日报 - 海外版，2017-07-23．

[2] "双向选择"是指劳动者从过去的指令性就业向自主择业的根本性转变，用人单位从过去需要政府招工指标才能用工转向自主雇用。这种新的合同模式适应中国的市场经济改革，它增强了用人单位和雇员的自主权利，但把劳动者权益置于严峻风险之下，因此，特别需要通过健全的社会保障制度对劳动者加以保障。这类似于"弹性保障"的概念，此概念基于更容易的雇用和解雇辅以对失业人员健全的社会保障，这一概念在 20 世纪 90 年代和 21 世纪 00 年代的国际讨论中风靡一时。中国的做法在何种程度上与欧洲的实践不同，值得进一步的社会历史研究。另参见（Auer，2010）。

是服务于和促进国有企业改革的。

在这样的制度化社会保障背景下,中国经历了两次大的国有企业改革大潮。社会保护机制的建立有助于缓冲经济改革进程的影响。

第一次是20世纪80年代让国有企业从高度集权的指令性计划经济步入市场竞争环境,开始允许效益不良的国有企业走向破产,同时建立劳动合同制度,这些措施激活了国有企业与劳动力市场的活力,也为优化企业人力资源配置和提高劳动生产率创造了条件。

政府意识到,在这个过程中,摩擦与困难不可能完全避免,如破产后的失业工人就缺乏应有的制度保障。因此,1986年,国务院颁布行政法规《国营企业职工待业保险暂行规定》,建立了面向国有企业工人的失业保险制度,它标志着中国正式进入了重构与市场经济相适应的社会保险制度新时代(参见 ILO NATLEX-China)。正是由于失业保险制度的建立,国有企业改革中出现的失业工人才有了基本的生活保障和重新就业的缓冲期。

第二次是1998年启动的国有企业改革,旨在裁减国有企业中的冗员、让国有企业卸下与直接经营目的无关的负担,轻装融入市场经济。由于国有企业冗员充斥、人浮于事,以及社会负担繁重,许多国有企业效益不良,缺乏发展规划,因此,中国政府再度强力推进国有企业改革。改革同时旨在完善社会保障制度以减轻国有企业传承已久的社会负担,但若简单地采取让国有企业工人失业且不提供任何基本的临时财务支持的激进办法,不仅劳动者一时无法适应,亦有违当初用工的社会契约精神,还会产生巨大的社会震荡,这是不可接受的。

为此,中国政府在推进养老保险、社会救助及相关公共服务等发展的同时,创建了有中国特色的面向国有企业下岗职工的基本生活保障制度,即让国有企业冗员离开劳动岗位进入企业再就业服务中心,政府通过财政拨款、失业保险基金调剂、国有企业负担各占三分之一的比例筹集资金,建立下岗职工基本生活保障基金，在政策规定的期限（最长3年）内向下岗工人发放生活津贴。这一制度为1998—2003年3 000多万国有企业下岗职工提供了基本生活保障，为顺利实现国有企业裁员的目标做出了特殊的贡献，也帮助了国有企业快速融入新的市场环境，因此促进了中国经济持续高速增长（见Lee，2005）。

2016年，中国再度掀起国有企业改革高潮，这次改革以建立现代企业治理制度为目标，同时减少钢铁、煤炭等行业的过剩产能。这符合中国政府已经将治理污染和保护环境提到了优先领域、以为人民提供优良的生态环境、建设美丽中国与健康中国的现实，同时为应对全球气候变化做出努力。然而，这又涉及数以百万计国有企业职工的裁减，他们需要政府提供相应的培训，并通过足额补偿给予原有收入的应有替代。

三是实现社会保障制度从单位保障制向社会保障制转型，为市场经济改革与发展营造了相应的有利环境。这个转型非常重要。在计划经济体制下，社会保障主要是在企业层面组织起来的，社会保障的有效运行取决于履行社会保障职能的企业或机构"长生不死"，然而，这与市场经济的基本要求相矛盾，即企业必须能够因经济和财务原因而破产。从理论上讲，计划经济体制下也可以选择重组或者关闭企业，包括重组以企业为基础的社会保障，但这与社会化支持的市场解决方案相比，会有巨大的效率损失。

此外，单位保障制既将劳动者固定在不同的单位而制约着劳动者的自由流动与人力资源的优化配置，也让各个单位承担着无所不包的社会保障事务而无法真正成为市场或社会主体。

因此，中国社会保障改革的重要方向就是让社会保障走向超越单位的公共社会保障制，即在企事业单位之外建立自成体系的社会保障制度。[1] 经过

---

[1] 当然，企业与公共机构在社会保障改革后仍然是重要的参与主体，它们必须为雇员收取和缴纳社会保险费（和所得税），并在组织问题、技术等方面提供相应的专业支持。将企业和机构的经济和其他利益纳入改革后的社会保障是另一个很重要的议题。

近 30 多年的制度变革，基本实现了社会保障社会化改革任务。一方面，中国的社会保险从单位包办走向政府主导、用人单位与参保者个人缴费、专业经办机构经办，实现了社会化管理与运行。同时，这一制度几乎覆盖了全民，为各类企业成为平等竞争的市场主体创造了条件。另一方面，社会救助与社会福利亦从政府包办的狭窄格局走向汇集政府、社会及个人力量的社会化。计划经济时代的社会救助与社会福利只面向城镇中没有单位归属的孤寡老幼，改革后的社会救助与社会福利则面向全体有需要的国民（郑功成，2018b）。

四是社会养老保险制度改革和建设是促使中国经济增长的众多因素之一。由于影响路径复杂，我们很难严格地仔细区分每一因素的具体贡献，但可以从以下几个方面粗略地刻画这种积极贡献。

影响一：社会养老保险制度的转型是必要的，顺应了国有企业改革；这项制度的存在——无论在改革前还是改革后——促使政治决策层和企业管理层寻求解决方案，以维护在国有企业市场化进程中退休人员的养老金权益，这又反过来增强了大多数社会成员对改革的接受程度。

在中国，企业提供养老金的义务源于 1969 年财政部发布的《关于国营企业财务工作中几项制度的改革意见（草案）》，规定各企业承担本企业退休人员的养老金。到 20 世纪 80 年代中期，一部分国有企业大面积亏损，导致无法足额给付养老金。这一情况促使政府对养老金制度更加根本性的改革，并与预期的经济改革进程相结合。因此，80 年代中期开始国有企业改革时，中国借鉴国际上这方面的经验，开始转向以社会统筹为基础的养老金制度（而非以企业为基础）的蓝图。这保证了退休人员的养老金权益，也相对均衡了企业之间关于养老金组织和财务的负担（即所有企业同样独立于各自的养老金领取者数量），从而增强了此前负担较重的企业的经济活力，促使中国经济逐步走出了僵化的生产力低谷。

这一论点不容误解：将养老保险错误的组织结构从企业的义务中抽离出来，并帮助企业随后在市场条件下成功行事——这绝不是废除社会养老保险。相反，有充足的理由认为，基于财政上更广泛的社会团结筹资的养老金持续给付，促进了养老金领取者以及他们子孙后代对改革的支持。

影响二：养老保险的社会统筹[1]促进了劳动力的自由流动。1991年对企业职工养老金制度进行的改革，将该制度转变为由国家、企业、个人共同筹资的制度。影响二是第一个影响的直接必然结果：在市场经济体制下，企业在竞争环境中经营，必须能够吸引到所需数量和质量的劳动力。这反过来要求劳动力可以自由流动。在这样的条件下，保障每个劳动者的养老金需要一个独立并高于企业（和其他机构）的体系，该系统承担所有必要的管理杂务。通过这样的方式，可以使企业的交易成本和整个社会的交易成本最小化（Coase，1937）。

影响三：统一的城乡居民基本养老保险制度的建立，进一步加强了改革的接受度，也提振了消费能力和信心。2009年，中国确立了农村老年人与城镇非工薪居民的（统一的）基本养老金权益。考虑到各种国际讨论，这项几乎实现全民养老金覆盖的改革，是一种符合劳动力市场发展的现代方法，是"不让任何一个人掉队"的社会政策的体现，完全符合中国的共享发展理念和国际劳工组织《第202号建议书 关于国家社会保护底线的建议书》。这一制度以财政投入为主要资金来源，辅之以参保人的个人缴费，虽然待遇给付水平不高，但是显著地直接增加了所有农村老年人与此前缺乏社会养老保险的城镇非工薪老年人的福利，进而直接提升了这一群体当期的消费能力和对于未来的消费信心。

影响四：退休职工养老金持续增长[2]，既提升了养老金领取者的消费信心，

---

[1] 中国的社会统筹均是相对于计划经济时代的单位统筹而言的，既包括财务统筹，更体现在组织与管理上。
[2] 中国过去15年职工养老金持续增长，是特定时期基于老一代退休职工养老金水平偏低而采取的补偿性措施，它与社会平均工资和CPI并无直接关联性。今后会建立指数化的调整机制。

也提振了家庭消费。2005—2015 年，按照中央政府的大致规定，养老金给付标准年均增长 10%；2016 年增长 6.5%，2017 年增长 5.5%。在此，本报告使用基金人均支出（年度基金支出总额／年底养老金领取者人数）估算养老金的增长（见图 11）。养老金的大幅增长直接提高了退休人群的消费能力与消费信心，包括其家庭成员，因为家庭成员可以把更多的收入用于自己的消费，而不是为自己父母的养老进行储蓄。

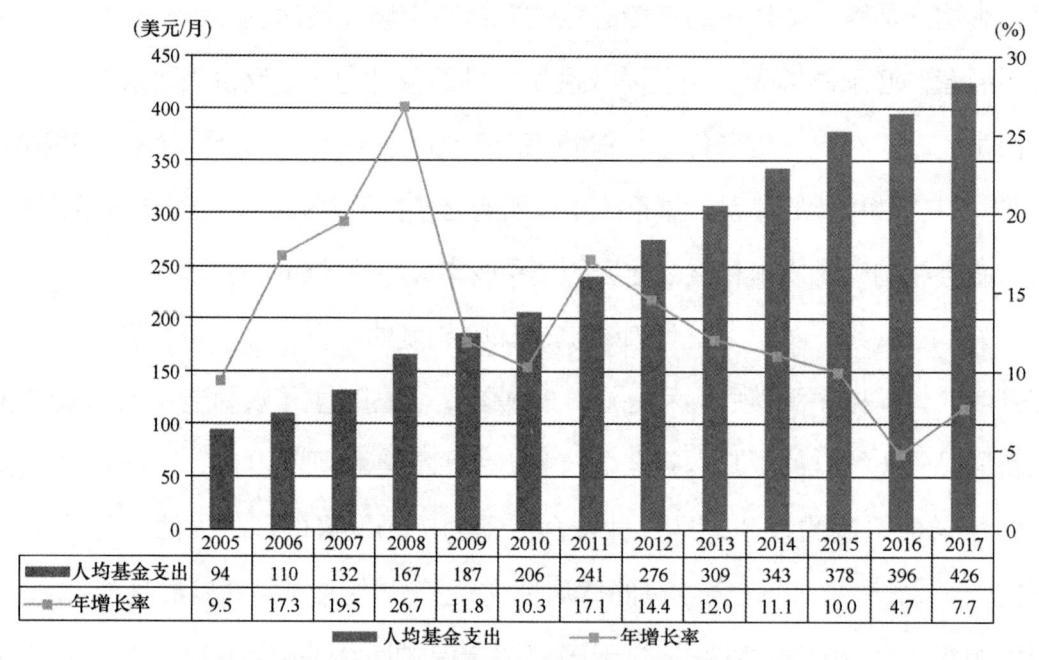

图 11　2005—2017 年职工基本养老保险人均基金支出增长情况

数据来源：所有数据来自《中国统计年鉴 2018》。

影响五：部分积累的基本养老保险（基金结余）支持了经济发展。中国现行基本养老保险制度采用部分积累制筹资模式，因而有一定规模的基金结余，并且主要集中于各地的财政专户或相应的银行。虽然投资回报率不高，但这些资金（见图 12 和附件二中表 A3）都通过各种渠道进入经济领域，促进了经济的增长。

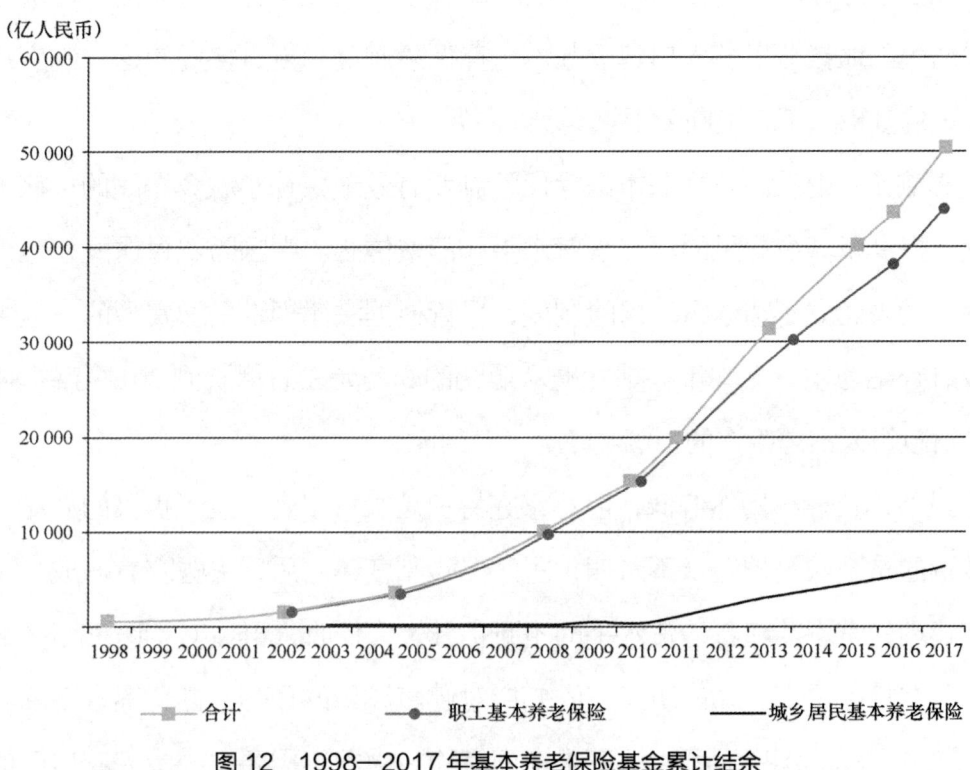

图 12　1998—2017 年基本养老保险基金累计结余

数据来源：所有数据来自《中国统计年鉴 2018》。

五是与养老保险制度类似，社会医疗保险制度改革和建设对中国经济发展具有积极影响，主要表现在以下几个方面。

影响一：社会医疗保险制度更公平地保障了全体社会成员的疾病医疗，也均衡了不同企业的组织与财务负担，顺应了国有企业改革和市场经济体制的建立。改革前，免费医疗制度只能保障城镇劳动者及其家属，劳动者不能自由流动，农村人口被完全排除在制度之外，而每个企业则要各自承担本单位职工及其退休人员的医疗费用。成立较早的企业往往因退休人员多而不堪重负，直接影响了职工的医疗保障权益，这些权益随着独立于企业的医疗保险制度的引入重新获得了保障。

在企业层面，医疗保险产生了与养老保险（详见上文）类似的效益增强效应，社会医疗保险还使得用人单位之间的医疗费用负担也相对均衡。特别是为农村居民与城镇非工薪人口建立基本医疗保险制度，更直接促使这一制度在覆盖全民的基础上不断走向公平。

影响二：财政注资型基本医疗保险制度有效地减轻了城乡居民的疾病后顾之忧，提高了城乡居民的医疗消费水平和消费信心。中国为农村居民和城镇非工薪劳动者建立了基本医疗保险制度，尽管根据法律规定是缴费型的，但主要以政府补贴为主，人均年补贴标准从最初的 3 美元左右增长到 2017 年约 84 美元，财政投入占总筹资的 70% 左右。

虽然筹资标准仍然偏低，但对家庭特别是农村家庭产生了积极的效应。相当数量的贫困农民曾经从不看病，医疗保险制度建立后，去医院看病成为个人健康管理的常态。随着筹资水平的不断提升，中低收入群体对于医疗服务的利用率也在持续提高。如前所述，人们应对健康风险的预防性储蓄需求下降。诚然，城乡居民的疾病后顾之忧还未全面解除，中国还需要进一步完善自己的医疗保险制度。

影响三：社会医疗保险促进了医药产业规模与收入的发展。全民医疗保险制度的建立对医疗服务提供者的收入和生产发展，以及医药产业有着积极的影响。事实上，对医疗保险（以及其他医疗服务融资体系）而言，个人缴费通常是获得使用医疗服务权利的基础，而家庭（以及企业和纳税人）的缴费往往流向医疗服务提供者和健康产业（技术和制药）。随着对全民医疗保险制度补贴的不断增加（如前所述）和同步增长的人均医疗卫生支出，中国医疗服务提供者和制药业所获取的资源也随之增加。

目前，医疗服务机构的业务收入中 50% 以上来自于基本医疗保险基金的支付。根据国家卫生健康委公布的《中国卫生健康统计年鉴 2018》，2017 年年底，全国共有 31 056 家医院，床位数超过 610 万张（约每 230 人一张床位，即每千人床位数约 4 张），分别比 2012 年增长逾 34% 和 47%（国家卫生健康委，2018）。

根据原国家卫生计生委的数据，2015 年，全国规模以上制药企业数量达到 7 116 家，规模总产值接近 2.7 万亿人民币（4 298.8 亿美元），规模总资产接近 2.5 万亿人民币（3 940.9 亿美元），行业销售收入近 2.6 万亿人民币（4 100.1 亿美元），行业利润总额约 2 627 亿人民币（421.8 亿美元），这些指标分别比 2011 年增加 25.41%、75.84%、89.34%、75.85% 和 75.82%。

六是最低生活保障制度的建立（城镇居民 1999 年建立，农村居民 2007 年建立），标志着中国的社会救助制度从基于人道转向人权，从补救性救济转向制度性救助，不仅有效地保障了贫困人口的基本生活，有助于维护社会稳定，也促进了经济转型和发展。

一方面，低保制度顺应城乡经济体制转型，有效地保障了贫困人口的基本生活。这使得国有企业可以不再承担原来肩负的救助本单位贫困人口的责任，成为真正的市场主体（见上文养老保险、医疗保险部分的讨论）。同时，建立城镇最低生活保障制度后，也有效地解决了城镇新贫困人口的基本生活问题，使得城市经济体制改革得以持续。再看农村，低保制度的建立对因疾病、天灾人祸和竞争失利等因素造成的贫困人口提供了基本生活保障，这是中国农村经过深刻社会经济变革后依然保持稳定发展的重要原因。

另一方面，最低生活保障制度稳定并促进了贫困人口的消费。贫困人口获得低保待遇后，一般直接用于购买生活资料，满足有效需求。此外，低保资金源于税收，特别是来自高收入群体所缴纳的税收，将这部分税收支付给低收入家庭具有很强的收入再分配效应。

七是其他的社会改革也直接推动着国民经济持续高速增长。在社会保障领域，在失业保险、养老保险、医疗保险和社会救助之外，还有一些其他改革也改善了经济增长的环境。在此，我们聚焦以下三个方面。

首先，公共教育事业大发展，源源不断地为中国经济增长提供着高素质的劳动力。在国民经济持续高速增长的背景下，据中国教育部、国家统计局、财政部关于2017年全国教育经费执行情况统计公告[1]，财政性教育经费投入从1991年的约116亿美元增长至2017年的5 066亿美元，其占GDP的比重从1991年不足3%增长至2012年的4%，近几年来一直保持在4%以上。

这使得教育事业获得持续发展，包括全民九年制义务教育，高等教育、职业教育均得到了特别重视和发展。中国在保持财政投入适度增长的同时，通过调动民间资源发展教育事业，增加了全社会的教育投入，使高等教育进入了大众化时代。职业技术教育的发展，不仅增加了青少年的受教育机会，而且提高了全社会人力资本水平，增加了高素质劳动力供给，支撑着中国劳动生产率的持续提高。1996—2015年，中国劳动生产率年平均增速为8.6%，高于同期世界平均水平。[2] 虽然劳动生产率的提高并不能仅仅归因于教育的发展，还得益于总体投资和生产过程的改进，但教育的发展仍然是提高劳动生产率的关键先决条件。

目前，中国劳动年龄人口平均受教育年限已经超过10年，高于世界平均水平，新增劳动力平均受教育年限达到13年左右，接近中等发达国家平均水平[3]，处于发展中国家前列。高等教育毛入学率[4]由1978年的2.7%提升到了2017年的45.7%[5]，超过中高收入国家平均水平，中国已经进入了高等教育大众化时代。[6] 这将有益于支撑中国经济持续发展，并使人口红利由数量型向质量型转变，它预示着中国经济未来发展将拥有更多高素质的劳动者。

教育的提供也是一项经济活动。作为国民经济的重要组成部分，教育事业的发展直接贡献于经济增长。根据统计，1978—2017年，中国普通高等学校由

1　参见：http：//www.moe.gov.cn/srcsite/A05/s3040/201810/t20181012_351301.html.

2，3　数据来自国家统计局国际统计信息中心发布的《世界经济统计公告》，http：//finance.sina.com.cn/stock/usstock/c/2016-09-19/doc-ifxvyqvy6701963.shtml.

4　高等教育毛入学率指高等教育在学人数与适龄人口之比。适龄人口是指18～22岁年龄段的人口数。

5　数据来自教育部《2017年全国教育事业发展统计公报》。

6　中共教育部党组. 发展具有中国特色世界水平的现代教育［J］. 求是，2017（16）.

598 所增加到 2 631 所；特殊教育学校由 292 所增加到 2 107 所；学前教育机构由 163 952 所增加到 255 000 所[1]。普通中小学和中等职业教育机构因计划生育政策带来的人口变化和体制改革等因素有所减少。接受教育的人口大幅度增加，由 1985 年的 2.3 亿增长到 2015 年的 3.4 亿人；相应地，教育法人单位从业人数由 1985 年的 1 261 万人增加到 2015 年的 1 915.3 万人。按 GDP 分行业计算，2016 年教育行业增加值接近 2.7 万亿人民币（3 960 亿美元），占当年 GDP 的 3.6%。[2] 这只是教育对于国家经济产出的直接贡献。为了在 20 世纪末的亚洲金融危机期间刺激经济增长，中国大幅度扩大了高等教育的入学率，以之作为增加消费和内需的一项关键举措。

其次，城镇居民住房自有化改革极大地激活了房地产业的发展，不仅使人民的居住条件持续得到大幅度改善，同时也成为了国民经济增长的重要支柱性产业。在计划经济时代，中国城镇居民住宅均为所在单位或政府提供的公共房屋，人均住房面积不足 10 平方米。20 世纪 90 年代中国掀起大规模的住房体制改革，改革的核心内容是在原来由国家或单位提供公共房屋的城镇居民住房福利基础上推行住宅自有化，由此而催生规模日益巨大的房地产业，并迅速成为中国经济增长的支柱性产业。在房地产业市场化条件下，居民居住条件也迅速得到改善。中国社会科学院的调研表明，2015 年受访家庭居民住房自有率为 95.4%，其中城镇居民家庭住房自有率为 91.2%，19.7% 的家庭拥有两套以上的住房（李培林等，2015）。政府只对低收入困难群体提供有限的公共房屋。

因此，住房改革去福利化是中国房地产业快速成长并成为国民经济支柱性产业的根本推手。不过，住房改革去福利化也助长了房地产行业的泡沫，对低收入家庭不利。因此，自 2009 年起，中国政府开始推进大规模的保障性

---

[1] 教育部《2017 年全国教育事业发展统计公报》。
[2] 国家统计局《中国统计年鉴 2018》。

住房建设，以此确保低收入家庭住有所居，这应当是中国住房改革在经历了从国家福利到住宅私有化后，步入针对低收入家庭的适度福利化发展阶段（见专栏7）。

> **专栏7　中国的住房保障改革与发展——从去福利化到重归社会保障体系**
>
> 住房保障是中国社会保障体系的重要组成，主要包括如下两项：
>
> 1. 保障性住房制度。它由政府出资，目标群体是低收入困难家庭。有两种情形：一是政府兴建公共房屋，直接分配给没有住宅或者住宅条件不足以满足起码居住条件的低收入困难家庭，该项政策适用于城镇居民；二是政府出资帮助改造处于危险状态的住宅，该项政策同时适用于城乡居民。
>
> 2. 住房公积金制度。它只适用于城镇在职职工，由用人单位与职工个人按照工资额的5%～12%等额缴纳住房公积金并存入职工个人账户，专门用于职工住房消费支出。在实践中，通常只有机关事业单位与国有企业参加。此外，机关事业单位还对无住房职工或住房面积未达到规定标准的职工发放现金补贴。
>
> 在20世纪80年代前，中国在城镇建立的是与计划经济体制相适应的公共住房制度，采取实物配给制；农村居民则可以按照政府制定的规则，经过批准后自主建房。由政府大包大揽的城镇住房制度造成了低效率和住房分配不公等现象，产生了租不养房、不能维持住房简单再生产、居民住房条件和质量改善缓慢等一系列问题。
>
> 20世纪90年代，中国对城镇住房制度进行改革。调动市场主体参与住宅建设，后来发展到追求住房商品化、自有化，房地产业很快

成为国民经济发展的支柱性产业,城镇居民的住房条件因此得到显著改善,人均住宅建筑面积从1978年的6.7平方米增加到2016年的33平方米。同时,2003年以来,房地产投资一直呈上升趋势,占全社会固定资产投资规模仅次于制造业。2016年全国房地产增加值占GDP的比重是6.5%,还带动了包括钢铁、煤炭等上游行业和用气、用电等下游产业的大发展。2017年房地产业和建筑业就业人口超过3 080万,占当年城镇就业总人数的17.5%(国家统计局,2018),仅低于制造业。因此,中国住房改革后,房地产业对国民经济总体就业的拉动作用非常显著。

中国推进住房商品化改革也带来了一些消极后果,这就是出现了房地产市场"过热"和"泡沫"现象。一些中低收入群体则无法承受房价快速上涨,住房成为一个社会问题。为此,1995年开始实施"安居工程",旨在解决城镇中低收入家庭的住房问题。1999年开始实施廉租房制度。2009年明确了政府为低收入困难家庭提供保障性住房的福利政策,并对煤炭采空区、林场、农垦中的棚户区进行大规模改造,对农村地区有安全隐患的危房进行改造。根据2011年制定的《国民经济与社会发展第十二个五年规划纲要》,国家明确的方针是加快构建以政府为主提供基本保障、以市场为主满足多层次需求的住房供应体系。

根据国家统计局的数据,2011—2017年,中国各级政府财政累计用于保障性住房的支出超过36 250亿元(近5 370亿美元,按2017年年平均汇率折算),从2010年的1 755亿元(259亿美元)增长到2017年的6 552亿元(近970亿美元),年均增长约为32%以上。

> 住房保障制度作为中国社会保障体系的有机组成部分，需要稳定发展。当前需要解决的主要问题是进城务工的农民工群体的住房问题，同时出台相关政策鼓励住房租赁业发展，并制定保障性住房退出机制和完善住房公积金制度。

最后，社会福利服务向社会资本开放创造了新就业并改善了民生。近几年来，基于养老、健康、儿童、教育等民生方面的支出持续增长，中国政府在努力增加公共投入和提供基本公共服务的同时，实行对社会资本开放的政策，促使私人资本投向这些服务领域的投资规模持续扩张。因此，福利领域正在吸引越来越多的劳动力就业，并成为民生经济新增长点。例如，中国民政部《2017社会服务发展统计公报》显示，截至2017年年底，全国注册登记的提供住宿的各类社会服务机构3.2万个，其中注册登记为事业单位的机构1.8万个，注册登记为民办非企业单位的机构1.3万个，再加上企业投资的营利性养老机构，社会或企业投资建设的养老机构占注册养老机构总数40%以上。这些依靠社会力量兴建的社会服务机构，既满足了一部分人群护理服务的需求，亦增加了社会就业。这种现象在健康服务领域同样存在。因此，向社会资本开放社会福利领域，壮大了社会保障体系的物质基础，也更好地满足了有需要者的需求。

八是社会保障制度在中国遭遇经济发展危机时发挥了关键性的促进作用。

最能够全面、综合地反映社会保障制度促进中国经济发展的是1998年和2009年两个时节点。这两个重要时节点的共同背景是在不利的国际金融危机背景下，中国的经济发展也遇到了危机，而政府采取了包括扩张投资、刺激消费等多种措施，社会保障制度发挥了特别重要的作用。它不仅有效地保护了人民免受经济危机的影响，而且直接提振了人民的消费信心与消费能力，从而有助于中国能够率先走出国际经济危机阴影并很快恢复国民经济持续增长。

1997年东南亚爆发金融危机,构成了不利的外部环境。在国内,由于一段时期内偏重经济增长而忽略了保障民生,社会保障制度改革亦偏重控制政府支出而未能够顾及劳动者的合法权益,一度出现数以百万计的退休人员不能按时足额领取养老金、许多职工不能报销医疗费用等现象,造成了城市新贫困人口剧增、社会不安全感急剧上升,并直接衍生了居民消费率下降、企业库存剧增、国有企业亏损面急剧扩大等问题。国民经济有可能陷入危机。

1998年,中国政府意识到消费不旺是由于社会保障欠缺所致,便将社会保障改革与制度建设摆到政府工作的头等重要位置上,强力落实"两个确保、三条保障线"[1],同时建立面向低收入困难群体的最低生活保障制度,推进医疗保险改革与住房体制改革,还建立了应对未来人口老龄化高峰的社会保障战略储备基金[2]等。虽然财务规模仍然有限,但通过全面落实这些重大的社会保障制度,不仅解决了城乡居民的现实困难,也重振了人们对社会保障制度的信心,提振了居民消费,有效地化解了当时的社会风险,创造了较为安定的社会环境。社会保障制度的健全是随后得以全面推进各项重大改革并实现国民经济再次持续高速增长的关键原因(郑功成,2017c)。

---

[1] "两个确保,三条保障线"是1998年中国政府采取的综合社会保障措施。其中,"两个确保"包括:一是确保国有企业下岗职工的基本生活,在国有企业普遍建立下岗职工再就业服务中心,由再就业服务中心为下岗职工发放基本生活费,并为他们缴纳社会保险费,所需资金由政府财政、国有企业和失业保险基金三方共同筹集,同时,组织下岗职工参加职业指导和再就业培训,引导和帮助他们实现再就业;二是确保离退休人员的基本生活,保证按时足额发放基本养老金。"三条保障线"包括:一是国有企业下岗职工在再就业服务中心最长可领取3年的基本生活费;二是下岗职工失去工作2年期满仍未实现再就业的,可继续领取失业保险金,领取时间最长为两年;三是享受失业保险金期满仍未就业的,可申请领取最低生活保障金。

[2] 社会保障战略储备金,全称为全国社会保障基金,是中国政府于2000年建立并用以应对2030年后老龄化高峰期养老金支付需要的战略储备基金,它来源于国家财政拨款、国有资产划拨等,同时接受地方政府委托管理一部分积累的养老保险基金。该基金原由人力资源社会保障部、财政部共同管理,2018年改由财政部单独管理,由全国社会保障基金理事会依法负责投资运营,其投资收益继续充实基金。截至2018年,该基金资产总额为29 632万元,约合4 300亿美元,相当于同年GDP的3.3%。

2008 年全球经济危机，中国经济也深受其害，外贸锐减，进出口额下降，许多企业破产，失业工人增加。当时正在制定中的《社会保险法》也受到了来自工商界的阻力，到 2010 年 10 月才得以顺利通过。在全球范围内，大多数国家在很短的时间内迅速从一揽子刺激计划转向紧缩措施，其效果并不理想。相比之下，中国维持了经济增长刺激措施，并进一步健全了社会保障体系。这场危机使得中国的发展模式从不可持续的出口导向型转向内需驱动型，但如果不能有效地解除城乡居民在养老、医疗、住房、教育等方面的后顾之忧，内需就不可能调动起来。没有国内消费增长助力，中国经济面临步入低谷无法自拔的风险。因此，在 2009 年，中国政府逆可能出现的经济发展低潮而动，强力推进各项社会保障制度建设，具体包括：

● 开始为农民建立养老保险制度并很快实现了养老保险制度覆盖全体适龄人口的目标。

● 启动三年医改计划并很快实现医保接近覆盖全民的目标。

● 同年还掀起大规模的保障性住房建设。

此外，再加上在四川汶川大地震后的救灾与灾后重建、扩大高等学校招生规模等方面加大投入力度，城乡居民的社会保障水平普遍得到大幅度提升。这些重大举措迅速安定了人心，减轻了人民的后顾之忧，也增加了城乡居民的收入，促使居民消费增长并逐渐成了拉动国民经济增长的第一大引擎，经济实力显著增强。中国成功的关键在于对危机的迅速反应、果断决策以及对既定政策坚定的执行力（郑功成，2017c）。

总之，回顾中国以往几十年的发展，如果没有在 1998 年、2009 年两个关键时节点上强力推进社会保障制度建设，不可能有 1998 年、2009 年后的快速发展新局面。它证明的是，不重视社会保障，经济发展也不会一帆风顺，发生危机更难以自拔。因此，发展社会保障和维护与促进经济发展不仅不相互矛盾，在结构良好的情况下还可以相得益彰地发展（郑功成，2017c）。

从更广泛的视角来看，中国通过使用社会保障作为政策工具应对两次经济危机，这呼应了经济危机通常伴随着社会保障的发展（包括社会保障制度结构的调整与优化）之国际与历史经验。中国情况的特别之处在于，这些反应迅速而强劲，而西方国家政府在危机引发的社会保障制度健全方面通常采取更加试探性和不情愿的态度。欧盟在 2008—2010 年金融和经济危机之后的紧缩取向就是一个例子。

3.1.4 中国处理经济发展与社会保障关系的经验

中国的经济发展成就为世界所公认，已经成为当今世界经济增长的主要引擎；中国的社会保障改革与发展也取得了巨大成就，引起国际社会的广泛关注。这两项成就不是偶然地重叠在一起，而是有着非常紧密的内在关联性，也证实了过去其他发达经济体同样观察到的趋势。中国的经验主要包括以下五个方面，可作为未来国家政策发展方向的指导方针（郑功成，2018a）。

指导方针一：坚持经济增长与社会保障之间相辅相成的关系

本节提出的关于社会保障措施与经济发展之间相互作用的确凿证据，应该足以证明，要避免任何政治或经济行为使这种关系处于风险之中或受到质疑。追求经济增长的首要目的，是快速摆脱贫困状态、维持已有的生活水准并通过尽可能公平的分配持续不断地改善人民生活。特别是进入 21 世纪后，中国采取这种模式并且通过社会保障与国民经济共同发展注入了新的动力，中国正在收获这种政策的成功。例如，财政收入大幅增长，据中国财政部公布的《2009 年全国财政收入决算表》和《2017 年全国财政收支情况》数据，仅个人所得税收入就从 2009 年的 578 亿美元，增长到 2017 年的

1 772 亿美元。

不断增长的财政收入无疑成了政府支持和共同为社会保障筹资的主要资金来源。财政收入增长的进程也是政府持续加大对社会保障及公共卫生与公共教育投入的进程，这使得社会保障体系日益健全，人民福利也一直以较快的速度持续增长（见 3.1.3 节）。

中国的发展实践证明了一个基本观点：经济发展是保障与改善民生的基础和前提，健全的社会保障是维持和提高经济生产力的目的和基础。只有将两者有机关联，实现良性循环，国民经济才能在科学发展之路上行稳致远，实现可持续而均衡的发展。若忽视这个道理，有可能错失中国经济的长期积极发展（见指导方针二）。

指导方针二：必须将社会保障作为保障与改善民生的基本制度安排，这需要坚持福利水平与经济发展水平相适应，防止因社会保障滞后或超前而损害经济增长

中国政府在遵循指导方针一、注重强调保障与改善民生的进程中，将社会保障制度摆到了极为重要的地位，公共投入的增长速度快于财政收入的增长速度。该政策必须坚持下去，直至中国的社会支出比例达到国际上可比国家的水准（这些国家的水平也可能发生变化，而且有差异），这样才能与中国不断增长的经济实力相匹配。表 4、表 5 为本指导方针提供了统计证据。

表 4 所揭示的是从 2007 年到 2017 年，中国一般公共预算收入增长了 2.4 倍，而社会保障与就业支出、医疗卫生与计划生育支出、教育支出增长三项加总的增速略快，为 2007 年的 3.6 倍。总支出占 GDP 之比重也从近 7.1% 增长到约 8.4%。如果再加上各项社会保险基金，这种物质基础更加雄厚。

表4 2007—2017年中国公共预算支出表

年份	一般公共预算收入		社会保障与就业支出		医疗卫生与计划生育支出		教育支出		支出合计		GDP占比(%)	支出总增长率(%)
	亿人民币	亿美元	亿人民币	亿美元	亿人民币	亿美元	亿人民币	亿美元	亿人民币	亿美元		
2007	51 321.78	6 749.31	8 514.24	1 119.71	3 554.91	467.51	7 122.32	936.65	19 191.47	2 523.87	7.09	
2008	61 330.35	8 830.74	9 795.92	1 410.48	4 178.76	601.68	9 010.21	1 297.35	22 984.89	3 309.51	7.15	19.77
2009	68 518.30	10 030.49	9 164.21	1 341.56	4 951.10	724.80	10 437.54	1 527.97	24 552.85	3 594.33	7.05	6.82
2010	83 101.51	12 275.87	9 130.60	1 348.78	5 333.37	787.85	12 550.02	1 853.91	27 013.99	3 990.54	6.57	10.02
2011	103 874.43	16 082.62	11 109.40	1 720.04	6 429.51	995.47	16 497.33	2 554.24	34 036.24	5 269.75	7.02	25.99
2012	117 253.52	18 574.82	12 585.52	1 993.75	7 425.11	1 176.26	21 242.10	3 365.09	41 252.73	6 535.09	7.65	21.20
2013	129 209.64	20 863.15	14 490.54	2 339.75	8 279.90	1 336.93	22 001.76	3 552.57	44 772.20	7 229.25	7.58	8.53
2014	140 370.03	22 851.15	15 968.85	2 599.60	10 176.80	1 656.70	23 041.71	3 751.01	49 187.36	8 007.32	7.63	9.86
2015	152 269.23	24 447.57	19 018.69	3 053.54	11 953.18	1 919.14	26 271.88	4 218.08	57 243.75	9 190.76	8.34	16.38
2016	159 604.97	24 028.57	21 591.45	3 250.60	13 158.77	1 981.06	28 072.78	4 226.36	62 823.00	9 458.02	8.49	9.75
2017	172 592.77	25 562.48	24 611.68	3 645.20	14 450.63	2 140.26	30 153.18	4 465.95	69 215.49	10 251.41	8.43	10.29

资料来源：中华人民共和国国家统计局. 中国统计年鉴 2018 [M]. 北京：中国统计出版社，2018.

表 5 反映的是近 40 年中国卫生费用支出发展情况，卫生总费用占 GDP 之比从 3% 增长到 6.3%。这一增长很大程度上归因于社会医疗保险支出。医疗费用的增长弹性长期处于 2 左右的水平，鉴于此前中国的支出水平非常低，这是社会卫生政策的积极发展。然而，正如国际研究所表明的那样，医疗卫生费用支出存在饱和点，一旦超过饱和点，额外的支出将不再能够改善人们的健康状况而只能服务于医疗服务提供者的利益与健康产业的利润追求。总体而论，中国社会保障水平在持续提高，但社会保障总支出占 GDP 比重约为 13% 左右，较之 OECD 国家平均水平偏低。中国政府意识到社会保障水平还需要进一步提升，并一直在做这方面的努力。

表 5　　1978—2017 年中国卫生费用支出结构表

年份	卫生总费用								卫生总费用占 GDP%
	合计		政府卫生支出		社会卫生支出		个人卫生支出		
	亿人民币	亿美元	亿人民币	亿美元	亿人民币	亿美元	亿人民币	亿美元	
1978	110.21	65.46	35.44	21.05	52.52	31.20	22.52	13.38	3.00
1980	143.23	95.59	51.91	34.64	60.97	40.69	30.35	20.25	3.15
1985	279.00	95.00	107.65	36.66	91.96	31.31	79.39	27.03	3.09
1990	747.39	156.25	187.28	39.15	293.1	61.28	267.01	55.82	4.00
1995	2 155.13	258.07	387.34	46.38	767.81	91.94	999.98	119.74	3.54
2000	4 586.63	554.05	709.52	85.71	1 171.94	141.57	2 705.17	326.77	4.62
2005	8 659.91	1 057.16	1 552.53	189.52	2 586.41	315.74	4 520.98	551.90	4.68
2010	19 980.39	2 951.53	5 732.49	846.81	7 196.61	1 063.09	7 051.29	1 041.63	4.98
2015	40 974.64	6 578.68	12 475.28	2 002.97	16 506.71	2 650.23	11 992.65	1 925.48	6.05
2016	46 344.90	6 977.24	13 910.30	2 094.20	19 096.70	2 875.01	13 337.90	2 008.02	6.20
2017	52 598.28	7 790.26	15 205.87	2 252.12	22 258.81	3 296.72	15 133.60	2 241.42	6.30

资料来源：国家统计局. 中国统计年鉴 2018 [M]. 北京：中国统计出版社，2018.

指导方针三：坚持共建与共享相结合，建立以权利义务相结合的社会保险为主体的社会保障体系

社会有多种选择来创造并维持经济发展与改善民生之间的良性循环，共同点是形成人人参与建设的社会和制度氛围。中国社会普遍崇尚劳动，因此，中国是世界典型的以工作和劳动生产力为导向的社会之一，其实现良性循环的方式是将社会保障转变为政府、企业、个人多方共同参与和负责的制度体系，该体系的核心是基于风险分担、互助共济的社会保险原则（也包括精算公平的元素）（Scholz，2015；Dixon，1999）。

中国确立的是以基于劳动者的社会保险为主体的制度体系。其中养老保险、医疗保险是最重要的保障项目。社会保障的这种设计特点一般是基于这样的理念，即用人单位与个人都须依法缴纳保险费，于后才能享受相应的养老保险与医疗保险待遇。这种权利与义务相结合的制度安排，实质上是追求共建共享社会保障制度，应当是一条理性的改革与发展之路。需要强调的是，政府补贴对社会保障制度覆盖面的快速扩大起到了很重要的作用，包括城乡居民养老保险、医疗保险制度的建立与发展，以及低保对象与重度残疾人参加养老保险与医疗保险，均与政府补贴有直接关系。

指导方针四：高度重视消除贫困，通过作为基础的社会保险制度，以及有效的社会救助和基本福利服务，保障人们的基本生活

处于贫困和脆弱经济状况的人群往往只能找到不稳定的低工资或无工资的工作和就业安排，因此指导方针三所概述的（缴费型）制度往往不足以帮助他们摆脱困境，严重残障者往往也面临类似的情况：必须向包括这些人群在内的需要帮助的人提供社会保障。这可以通过各种方式来完成，例如：经过家计状况调查，直接向他们提供津贴或服务；在适当和管理适用的情况下，还可以通过提供政府支持的养老保险和医疗保险专项缴费，使得穷人积累权益，同时各项社会保险获得相应的收入。这表明，政治策略可以确保高覆盖面水平从而创造社会保障文化。社会保险、社会救助、扶贫项目的互补设计和携手共进，在国际上已经证明是非常有效的（如在法国、德国、北欧国家等），也适用于现代中国，且应该在中国得到更多的运用。

指导方针五：在明确的增长导向政策中，采取渐进改革策略，是中国成功处理社会保障改革的复杂问题的关键。未来的改革需要坚持这种方式，它也可以被视作其他国家改革政策模板

中国过去30多年的社会保障改革在社会、经济和政治上都是一项有风险的事业。社会上的风险在于，新的系统要实施，而旧的系统必须继续运行。经济上的风险在于，社会保障改革是计划经济成功向社会主义市场经济过渡的先决条件，但社会保障改革以前还没有经过检验（没有全面的模板）。在政治上，经济和社会保障改革影响了整个社会，鉴于人们的心态普遍存在着惯性，必须让人确信预期政策的优势。

为什么中国化解了改革过程中的风险？大体有三个原因。

（1）明确的增长导向，着眼于培育和不断壮大中产阶级。社会和政治稳定得到保持，因为社会保障改革建立在明确的经济增长导向上，这一导向贯穿始终。社会广泛接受这些改革措施的原因是绝大多数劳动者和退休者的收入不断增长，人民生活水平普遍提高。

例如，20世纪80年代初期农村推行家庭联产承包责任制[1]时，农民的集体福利被削减，但土地承包后延期获得的收益大大超过了福利即期减少的份额，从而并未引起农民的持续抗议。类似方式在城镇继续演进，从免费医疗到参保缴费的社会医疗保险，从不用缴费且高替代率的退休金到缴费型且替代率逐渐降低的社会养老保险。从某种意义上说，中国非常明智地在走向富裕之前就实施了改革——一旦富裕起来，类似的社会改革（降低替代率等）就很难实现了，发达国家（欧洲）就是例子。

劳动者与其他居民的初次分配收入不断增加，同时出现了较为广泛的中

---

1 农民将国家的土地承包，将相当数量的农产品上缴给国家后，超出配额的部分则由农民自由处理，可在自由市场出售。

产阶级。这个群体对社会救助和反贫困服务的依赖程度较低，同时又有能力为自己的老年和医疗健康储蓄。这能够为政府反贫困政策所需资金提供财政空间。

（2）渐进改革的策略。与经济改革相适应，原有的社会保障制度也必须通过改革加以重塑，其长期目标是在社会主义市场经济条件下，构建与其良性互动的全面社会保障体系。然而，在新制度尚未全面建立并运行时，原有社会保障制度必须继续发挥作用。

为了实现这一转变，必须同时解决诸多问题，因此众多主体、个人和机构不得不卷入了这一改革中。他们必须具备必要的知识，这对于大量借鉴国际经验的主体而言是个问题。为了能够应对错误的发展、失误或失败，同时也吸取成功的经验，政府采取了谨慎的做法，使得在必要情况下可以快速调整行动方向，不会导致风险过度积累。先决要求和条件有着谨慎界定，做出决策的方式使得改革后的社会保障能够逐渐发挥预期的作用，同时旧的社会保障结构相应被替代。中国社会保障改革仍未完成，还需要继续改革以最终实现全面而深刻的制度变革。

（3）自下而上的方法。自下而上的改革策略也使得所有人的态度是积极的。具体而言，选择个别地区进行试点，进行预定的改革，然后总结经验，形成国家层级的改革方案，最后自上而下地进行推广。这种改革方式不仅为改革者提供了更多参考，还为公众逐渐了解并适应新的制度安排提供了过渡期。

综上所述，回顾性地看，渐进改革策略与以长期初次收入增长替代短期福利损失的策略相结合，作为推进社会保障制度变革并不断发展的中国方案，确实是优选方案。与此同时，中国社会普遍认识到这一政策的合理性，它是在灵活市场经济条件下促进经济发展、保持稳定的经济增长率和完善社会保障制度的必须。

3.2 主要社会经济挑战和政策建议

3.2.1 中国面临的主要挑战

中国正在快速步入现代化，经济和社会发展显著改善，但经济发展在持续几十年的高速增长后，已经进入了中高速增长的新常态。在经济全球化的背景下，和其他区域和国家一样，中国的发展也面临着多种挑战。

1. 经济发展面临着结构调整、产业升级、增长方式转换的压力

社会保障是这一发展的一部分，并且还需要进一步发展，直至中国成为有着完善社会保障制度和具有中国特色的福利国家。

中国经济发展面临挑战。正如2016年9月习近平主席在杭州召开的B20峰会（G20峰会配套活动）上指出的："我们清醒认识到，中国经济发展不少领域大而不强、大而不优，长期以来主要依靠资源、资本、劳动力等要素投入支撑经济增长和规模扩张的方式已不可持续，中国发展正面临着动力转换、方式转变、结构调整的繁重任务"（习近平，2016）。

中国经济从粗放型到集约化生产率增长的必然转变，对于社会保障的制度设计和管理都具有重要的影响。正如本报告所示，社会保障制度的设计可以对经济增长起到支持作用。中国社会保障制度的进一步发展，需要尊重社会保险与社会救助之间独立而又互补的功能。

各个社会保障机构的管理和服务必须实现现代化，特别是在信息技术解决方案方面，从而能够处理大量的社会保障业务以及促进机构间的交流和协调。还需要增加这些机构中训练有素的工作人员的数量，以服务于机构所覆盖的参保者。

此外，如何让社会保障适应新常态，推动社会经济和社会保障的协调发展，保持和强化社会保障制度设计中促进增长的元素，以维持集约化而非粗放型的较高速度的经济增长，是一大挑战，但同时也是可实现的。中国经济其他领域的现代化已经证明了这一点。

2. 地区之间、城乡之间发展不平衡和社会不平等现象加剧

一方面，从东部沿海到西部内陆呈现经济和社会发展方面的重大不平衡现象。沿海地区接近高收入国家水平，北京、上海和天津等城市的人均 GDP 超过 15 000 美元，西部欠发达地区仍处于中等收入偏下水平，个别贫困地区（在国际比较中）甚至处于低收入水平。[1]

不仅如此，在城乡之间也因长期的户籍制度壁垒及公共资源配置失衡等原因而存在着较大差距，2017 年全国城镇居民可支配收入是农村居民的 2.7 倍。

另一方面，中国在努力使所有人的生存境况得到普遍改善的同时，不同群体之间的收入差距也在扩大，基尼系数[2]长期居于 0.4 以上的高位。2008 年全国居民收入基尼系数高达 0.491，2009 年以来虽连年下降，但 2015 年仍达 0.462，2017 年又回升到了 0.467。[3]

同时，目前的社会保障统筹层次低，社会保险制度安排仍然处于地区分割状态，多数社会保障项目在职工与居民之间也存在制度分割，这在一定程度上拉大了经济的失衡。在亿万富豪人数快速增加的同时，还有大规模的贫困人口等待着国家与社会的援助。据中国政府公布的数据，截至 2018 年年底，农村贫困人口还有近 1 660 万人，他们处于需要政府援助的绝对贫困状态。

地区及城乡之间发展失衡与社会不平等现象加剧，既影响国民经济的持续健康发展，也影响社会公正，并可能破坏社会稳定。在这些方面，中国与全球其他地区和国家面临着类似的问题。在现代化进程中，中国将必须在国内认真应对这些问题，同时也要在国际上（如，联合国和 20 国集团峰会）与其他国家

1　甘肃、贵州、云南等省 2017 年的人均 GDP 只有约 5 000 美元。参见国家统计局. 中国统计年鉴 2018[M]. 北京：中国统计出版社，2018.

2　基尼系数是根据劳伦茨曲线所定义的判断收入分配不均等程度的指标。基尼系数是比例数值，在 0 和 1 之间，0.4 是国际公认的贫富差距偏大的警戒线。

3　数据来源为国家统计局。

齐心协力。

3. 少子高龄化现象日益显性化与传统保障机制持续弱化

伴随社会发展进步所带来的生育率下降与人均预期寿命持续延长，加上以往几十年推行独生子女政策，中国少子高龄化现象日益显性化。在这方面，中国显然面临着与许多发达国家一样的挑战。根据原国家卫计委发布的《中国家庭发展报告（2015年）》，中国家庭已经从大家庭型转向小型化，核心家庭占六成以上，家庭户平均规模仅为3.02人，二三人家庭成为家庭类型主体，单人家庭、空巢家庭[1]不断涌现。[2] 大约1.5亿个家庭为独生子女家庭，80岁以上的高龄老年人年均递增100万以上。在儿童照料和养老等方面，家庭照料模式正在面临着日益严峻的挑战，对社会服务需求较大。与此同时，传统的邻里互助因人口的高流动性而被适用于"陌生人社会"[3]的隐性或显性规则所替代，传统的功能强大的单位保障制因市场经济改革被瓦解。家庭保障、邻里互助、单位保障等传统保障机制的快速弱化，使城乡居民对社会化保障及服务的需求急剧上升，亟待国家和社会来填补。

4. 社会保障制度还未完全成熟，面向老年人、儿童、残疾人的基本公共服务供给不足

中国社会保障改革采取的是试点先行、渐次推进的策略，虽然取得了积极的成就，但渐进改革也必然因路径依赖而存在着历史局限性，现行社会保障制度的一些缺陷仍然需要加以解决。

---

1 空巢家庭，是指家庭中因子女外出工作或学习导致的老人独居现象。
2 2015家庭发展报告：空巢老人占老年人总数一半. 人民网, 2015-05-13. http://politics.people.com.cn/n/2015/0513/c70731-26995290.html
3 陌生人社会，是相对中国传统的熟人社会而言的。在过去，由于人口缺少流动性，世代居住的处所和工作单位都非常稳定，邻里之间也非常熟悉，从而被称之为是熟人社会。30多年来，伴随工业化、城镇化的快速发展，人口流动性也不断升高，即使居住在同一社区，邻里之间往往并不相识，农民工更是很难融入城镇社区。这种现象增加了人们的不信任感和社会运行的成本。

例如，法定养老保险还停留在地区分割统筹状态，全国统一的法定目标尚未实现；缴费满15年可领取全额养老金的规制陷入僵化，影响制度的可持续发展；医疗保险还分为职工与居民两大群体，退休人员不需缴纳医疗保险费的法律规制亟待改进；中央政府与地方政府的社会保障责任还未能够明确划分；社会保障管理体制需要深化改革才能最终定型。同时，在家庭保障功能持续弱化的条件下，数以亿计的老年人口、儿童以及8 000多万残疾人，均迫切需要相应的社会福利与社会化服务，但目前国家与社会还无法全面满足这些群体的诉求，既影响了民生保障与民生质量，也不利于民生经济发展。因此，要真正促进中国社会保障制度理性地走向成熟、定型，还需要更加科学的顶层设计和全面促进相关服务的发展，这方面的任务非常繁重。

同时，当社会保障体系走向成熟定型时，费用也会持续上升（包括人口结构因素所导致的），一些国家采取了看似容易的解决方案，即将风险从国家转移到个人（以个人账户和/或私有化的形式，包括养老金制度），但这些国家的改革实践并不完全成功。例如，在1981—2011年，有36个国家把公共养老金由给付确定型现收现付制（NDB）部分或全部转换为缴费确定型积累制（FDC），一些实施部分积累制的国家还同时把未积累的部分从NDB制度转换为点数制和记账制（NDC）。但最近的情况表明，36个国家中有21个撤回了这项改革，其中有9个国家全部撤回（Wang，Williamson和Cansoy，2016）。因此，中国在促使本国的社会保障体系走向成熟定型时，更加需要政治智慧。

5. 中国正面临着大规模人口流动、快速工业化与城市化、社会结构转型，以及各种新业态的出现等变化

这些变化既对经济发展产生直接影响，也对社会保障及其发展提出了新的挑战（郑功成，2018a）。

特别是以互联网、人工智能为代表的科技进步与新经济，对人们的工作方式与生活方式产生了直接影响，进而影响着经济社会结构变化，也给传统的社会保障经办方式带来前所未有的挑战。只有实质上现代化的社会保障管理机构才能够在维护参保者利益的同时，长期适应这种变化。中国政府在确定社会保障的指导方针时，宜继续推行旨在平衡市场化解决方案（作为公共计划的补充，适用于少数高收入者）和社会保障核心原则（针对中等收入和低收入群体）的政策。这些核心原则不仅是本报告明确和隐含的依据，也是国际劳工组织和其他国际组织公约与建议书的基础。

3.2.2 对中国政府的政策建议

如前所述，中国在近几十年总体上实现了社会保障与经济发展的良性互动，但当前遇到的多种挑战表明两者之间的关系还需要进一步理顺，才能更好地实现共同发展。特别是必须更多的在集约化而非粗放型经济增长的视角下，看待社会保障对增长的促进作用。本报告对中国政府的建议如下。

1. 切实解决好内生动力[1]不足问题，以使国民经济继续保持中高速增长

中国经济发展面临着出口增速拐点已经来临、低劳动成本优势逐渐减弱、供需结构性矛盾突出、地区与行业走势在分化、资源环境压力日益增大等现实问题，再依靠传统的粗放型增长模式难以为继，必须转向高质量发展。

必须继续保持中高速增长，并持续壮大支撑社会保障制度的物质基础（财务空间）。切实解决好经济增长内生动力不足问题成了最大挑战，因此，中国经济需要走向形态更高级、分工更优化、结构更合理、质量更提升的新发展阶段。这意味着要把经济增长动力更多放在创新驱动和扩大内需特别是消费需求上。为此，应当同时充分发挥好政府在公共领域中的决定性作用和市场在资源配置中的决定性作用，在有针对性地解决城乡居民实际困难和尽快扩大中等收入群体的条件下，让经济发展成果通过社会保障制度更多、更好、更公正地惠及民

---

[1] 内生动力是指源自国家、组织内部或个人自身的动力。经济发展的内生动力即是指来自本国的社会消费与科技创新等。

生。这必须辅之以促进生产力发展和工资增长的政策。

同时，将为全体人民提供稳定安全的社会保障预期摆到国家发展的重要位置上（郑功成，2016c）。这是持续释放居民消费潜力、进一步激活经济增长内生动力、促使国民经济继续保持中高速增长的必要举措，也是真正跨越所谓"中等收入陷阱"的必要举措，还是稳步走向共同富裕的必由之路（郑功成，2016d）。

2. 尊重社会保障与国家治理关系的历史逻辑，强化中央政府统筹责任，真正构建有序组合的多层次社会保障体系（郑功成，2017c）

面对新的挑战，需要将社会保障体系作为一个内容完整、结构优化的整体纳入国家治理体系，让其切实担当起促进社会公正、实现共享发展的历史使命，为全体人民享受世代福祉提供基本途径与制度保障。

为此，特别需要对社会保障制度结构与功能异化保持警惕，防止动摇社会保障制度互助共济、稳定安全预期的根本。加强政府的责任显然有助于实现这一目标。

中国需要采取正式制度与非正式制度有机结合，普惠性制度与特惠性制度双层构架，政府与市场、社会、家庭与个人等多支力量相融合，真正构建有序组合并且具有适度弹性的多层次化社会保障体系。在这一过程中，坚持政府主导并确保中央政府统筹规划的权威具有必要性、重要性。应该进一步强化政府对社会保障的财政责任，在地区分割的情形下特别需要强化中央政府的统筹责任，从而建设积极和健全的社会保障体系，并与时俱进地优化制度体系结构。在地区发展失衡的条件下，可以允许一定时期内存在差距，但任何时候都不能动摇统一制度的目标和扭曲通向目标的路径（郑功成，2016e）。应当尽可能地通过社会保障制度的统一来促使公共资源在全国范围内得到更为公正的配置，让社会保障成为缩小地区差距、实现地区之间公正与协同发展的重要手段。

中央政府宜担负起做好社会保障体系顶层设计、推动社保立法、合理配置资源、维护制度统一的重大责任。同时，重塑高效率的社会保障运行机制，包括健全治理优良的经办机构，充分利用大数据等信息技术[1]，提升制度运行的预测、预警与监控能力。在坚持结构与运行稳定的同时也要保持一定的灵活性，以适应新业态、人口流动性等发展势头。还要赋予社会保障制度自我调节与不断修正的能力。

3. 坚持以共享为社会保障制度的基石，实行多元主体共建共治

随着社会保障改革的进行，中国已经确立了共享发展的新理念，它是对以往单纯强调鼓励部分人先富起来的矫正，更是健全社会保障制度的理论基石。在社会保障改革中，如果动摇共享之根基和互助共济之根本，必定导致制度异化。若要实现这一制度可持续发展，须在政府主导下，充分调动各方积极性，让各方主体参与共建共治。在实践中，社会保障只有在强制性的情况下才能起到很好的作用，自愿性的制度只有辅助的补充功能。实践也证明，由于各种原因，政府不宜垄断社会保障的管理，而是应该将相关职能留给利益相关者。

一方面，社会保障肩负收入再分配职能，必须由政府主导，但当前完全由行政系统包揽制度立法、行政监管、具体业务经办的局面不利于这一制度的健康发展（郑功成，2004b），其改革方向应当是"让立法机关、行政机关、司法机关与经办机构各司其职、各负其责"（郑功成，2016a）。同时，还应当让代表不同群体利益的工会、雇主组织、残联等参与制度设计、监督制度运行。只有这样，才能确保各方主体有效地参与共建共治，这是维护社会保障制度健康持续发展的重要条件，也非常符合国际社会普遍认同的由三方利益相关者参与社会保障政策制定与管理的原则。另一方面，慈善与互助是自愿性共享机制，同

---

[1] 有必要将数据保护等问题考虑在内，以保护社会保障数据系统中包含的个人信息。

样需要大力发展。中国有家庭保障、邻里互助等优良传统,劳动者的职业福利曾十分发达,但现在这些传统日益式微,并不利于动员更多社会保障资源和提供社会保障服务(郑功成,2011)。因此,社会保障政策还需要与家庭政策、机构福利等有机协同,同时促进互助、慈善及志愿服务不断发展,这将有利于不断壮大整个社会保障体系的物质基础,为更好地满足人民不断增长的福利诉求创造条件。

4. 促进并维护就业与社会保障良性互动

社会保障与就业实质上是共享与共建的关系,两者之间的良性互动在很大程度上决定着社会保障与经济发展的良性互动。因此,在处理两者关系时,需要在提供合理激励和确保人人有充足保障之间找到均衡点。在政策设计中,应当同时考虑到就业与社会保障相互关联与相互促进的问题。为此,中国宜坚持与就业关联的以社会保险为主体的社会保障制度发展取向,将健全社会保障制度作为提升就业质量的重要指标,让全体劳动者依法获得相应的社会保险。

同时,进一步完善非收入关联型的社会救助以及财政补贴的保障项目(如居民养老金等)并确保适度的待遇给付,继续帮助符合条件的低收入人口与残障人士参与社会保险,以确保没有人被排斥在社会保障制度之外。为全民提供由税收筹资、水平适度的定额养老金,与就业和社会保障相关联的原则并不冲突。

还需要尽快建立护理保险制度,尽可能推进企业年金等与职业相关的福利,以为劳动者提供更加全面的保障。同时,逐步提高劳动报酬占 GDP 之比重,为此,政府应当鼓励工资协商谈判。此外,社会保障制度也要有利于促进就业,包括:坚持保障水平适度,不构成影响就业的负担;促进劳动者就业创业,发挥积极的政策效应;强化失业保险预防失业和提升劳动者就业能力的作用,让社会救助具有激励就业的功能,使之变成积极的制度安排;全面发展社会保障体系，释放大量有质量的就业岗位，特别是面向老年人、儿童、残障人士、妇女的各项福利和社会服务，以及健康保障、慈善事业，都是值得开拓并具有巨大空间的新兴就业领域（郑功成，2017d）。

5. 重视发展教育福利与社会福利服务

宜以全面覆盖当地常住人口为目标，向以农民工为主体的流动人口中的适龄儿童提供作为公共服务的义务教育；适时将义务教育年限从现行的9年制延长到12年制。同时，增加对职业教育的公共投入，以增强职业教育的福利性。

中央政府宜加强对义务教育与职业教育的支持力度，以全面实现人口红利从数量型向质量型转化。在社会福利服务方面，特别需要加强儿童福利事业和老年人福利事业，宜将托儿所、幼儿园纳入儿童福利范畴并提供相应的预算保障，将退休人员人力资源再开发纳入养老服务体系。中国还应扩充残疾人福利中的教育内容以更好发挥残疾人的才能和劳动贡献。残疾人应被平等地视为具有生产力的劳动力，并应平等地参与面向未来工作的技能培训。这些福利项目的扩展将使中国未来发展的人力资源更加丰富并具有质量。

6. 重视社会保障法制建设，让社会保障制度尽快运行在法治轨道上（郑功成，2018a）

成熟的社会保障制度必定运行在法治轨道上。然而，基于中国渐进改革的历史路径，现行社会保障制度还缺乏必要且充分的法律规制与保障，其后果不仅会损害这一制度应有的稳定性、权威性与公信力，也容易导致对社会保障与经济发展关系的认识产生波动。

因此，有必要加快制定综合性的《社会保障法》和《社会福利法》《社会救助法》等基本法律，以及《儿童福利法》《老年人福利法》《残疾人福利法》等专门法律，尽快修订完善《社会保险法》《军人保险法》等法律。在这一过程中，政府应该致力于将所有法律法规集合成一套系统的卷章（不仅包括纸质的，酌情也应提供电子版），这样使相关信息对全体国民更加透明。有了健全的法律保障，公众便会有稳定安全的社会保障预期，人民对社会保障制度的信心也必定提升，这对于激发人们参加社会保障的积极性，进而维护这一制度的健康持续发展将大有裨益。

中国需要加快对照国际劳工组织第 102 号公约（《社会保障最低标准公约》）审查自身制度，以批准这一公约。在中国进一步努力实现现代化和发展其社会保障制度的同时，确保社会保障制度在法治轨道上运行是一项重大任务。

4 总结

4.1 全球经济发展与社会保障关系的基本历史经验和理论共识

本报告回顾了一个多世纪以来全球社会保障与经济发展关系的历史演进，总结了两者间关系的理论阐述与一般规律，重点介绍了中国 40 多年来经济发展与社会保障关系的演进，并辅之以欧洲国家、美国、日本和韩国等发达国家的社会保障与经济发展之历史经验。在回顾这些基本历史经验与由此产生的理论共识的基础上，本报告达成了以下核心共识。

第一，社会保障制度是促进社会公正、弥补市场失灵、实现共享发展的不可替代的制度安排。

历史证明，社会保障制度的产生，既是为了解决当时遭遇的现实社会问题或者解除经济发展遭遇的困境，亦有着深远的人文主义思想渊源和人们对社会公正的固有追求。在过去一个半世纪的时间里，社会保障越发证明了它在促进社会正义和有效应对经济危机有害影响方面发挥的建设性作用。19 世纪末在德国引入的俾斯麦社会保障体系极大地缓和了劳资关系，提高了劳动生产率，支持了国家的国际竞争力，从而促进了德国的国民经济发展和持久繁荣。在 20 世纪，俾斯麦社会保障的基本原则演变成了全球鼓舞人心的成功故事。作为罗斯福新政的重要组成部分，美国 1935 年制定的《社会保障法》是 20 世纪最严重经济危机的宝贵良药。它通过纠正自由放任经济体制的内在缺陷，在大萧条时期挽救了资本主义。英国1942年的贝弗里奇报告对第二次世界大战后福利国家在英国和全球的发展产生了重大影响，加强了社会团结，促进了经济复苏。

第二，经济增长和社会保障不仅是任何发展模式的两个关键组成部分，也应该被视为现代发展中同一枚硬币的两面。

在现代经济中，以市场原则为基础的经济发展为社会保障创造着物质基础，而社会保障为动荡不定的经济体注入了稳定性。从理论出发，经济发展和社会保障通常是互相交织的社会制度。可以说，社会保障制度的发展和存在有内在的经济原因（见 1.2 节以及 Coase, 1937），显然两者之间存在着紧密的联系。在不接受其经济前提条件和基础的情况下，社会保障就会面临着缺乏可持续性的问题；反之亦然，没有社会保障，经济发展将变得不稳定，并且面临崩溃的高风险，价值从而也会大打折扣。

历史表明，在市场经济中，社会保障的成本通常与短期商业（利润）利益相冲突。获取利润是市场经济所固有的，因此这种冲突不可避免。经济发展和社会保障发展的相互依存并不意味着两种制度和平共存。恰恰相反，为了释放社会保障带来的提高生产力的效应，不同国家或区域的各利益相关方在不同的历史时期都必须承受经济利益和社会利益之间或多或少的激烈冲突，同时实施了冲突解决机制，以避免社会经济僵局。这种机制也是必要的，以避免社会保障沦为短视、固有商业利益的附属品。制定相应的规则以平衡利益、造福各方过去是（现在仍然是）治国理政和整个社会的艺术。

第三，在现代社会，社会保障往往是一个全面综合的制度体系，包括各种待遇给付、不同的项目和筹资来源。发达国家的社保支出规模占 GDP 的 25% 左右，而通常社保收入的 1/3 或以上来自于政府（纳税者），其余的可能来自雇主和雇员的强制缴费以及其他来源，如自愿缴费或投资回报。

社会保障的核心功能包括：基于有组织的社会团结这一有国际共识的原则

进行风险分担，促进社会正义和社会凝聚力，保障基本收入安全和提供基本公共服务。疾病、工伤事故、残障、失业、贫困、长寿等个人风险，不仅是每个公民所关心的问题，而且在个人生命周期中实际上被暴露在其前。

在这些风险成为现实的情况下，提供应对这些风险的制度和服务不仅是人们的合理诉求，也是政府的重大使命。市场机制和非政府组织在必要时作为社会保障的补充，通常得到支持并纳入政府主导的框架。这包括旨在扩大社会保障物质基础和避免制度运行失灵的市场监管。

国际上，大多数发达国家将其 GDP 的 25% 左右（有时甚至更多）用于社会保障。这一比例的估计数基于是否涵盖教育的成本而有所不同。中国目前的社会支出占 GDP 的 13%，是发达国家支出水平的一半左右。

第四，社会保障总体上有利于长期经济增长和国民福利水平提升，但不同制度设计具有不同的经济效应。

当社会保障很好地适应国家的社会和经济结构时，会产生非常积极的直接和间接生产力效应。除德国、美国、英国等大国的发展经历可资借鉴外，还可以发现，北欧国家的高福利水平不是繁荣的阻碍，而是提升了人力资本积累和创新能力，也实现了社会保障与经济增长的良性互动。日本、韩国在 20 世纪下半叶的经济腾飞与社会保障制度的建立是同步进行的，以生产力为导向的福利政策有力地支持了其经济增长。

同时，不同的社会保障项目对经济发展的影响是不同的，这取决于制度设计是更多的公平取向还是效率取向（见 1.2.5 小节）。

例如，对于低收入国家而言，社会救助制度可以显著地提高低收入群体的收入水平和提振消费需求，从而对经济产生直接影响。对高收入国家而言，社会救助的需求侧效应则是有限的。经典的社会保险制度免除了人们的后顾之忧，从而提高了国民的边际消费倾向，进而有利于经济增长。社会福利服务有助于拉动相关第三产业的发展，从而有利于经济增长方式的转变和产业结构的升级。

免费教育直接提高了人们的整体文明水平,同时可以支持人口红利从数量型到质量型的转变。

以上所提到例子可能与经济发展有不同的互动,这取决于它们的设计是更偏向俾斯麦模式还是贝弗里奇模式。

第五,从全球范围来看,社会保障在不同地区的发展是不平衡的,最近显现出了不稳定的倾向。而中国 40 多年的发展实践,证实了经济发展与社会保障可以实现良性互动与共同发展。

欧洲国家因工业化而最早建立现代社会保障制度。制度的设计伴随着该地区社会经济的发展而不断发展,尽管其在发展中也会出现一些波折,但欧洲国家的社会保障水平确实仍是全球最高的。欧洲的经验对世界其他地区社会保障制度的设计仍然具有启发性。日本(韩国稍逊一筹)几十年来一直在建立现代的全面社会保障制度。美国的社会保障因其社会结构与奉行个人主义的文化而独树一帜,其水平不如欧洲,但亦有相对健全的社会保障制度,还有自愿性的慈善机制。拉丁美洲地区的社会保障水平总体上居于中等状态。非洲(南非例外)与南亚地区,因发展落后而还停留在主要依靠社会救助与临时的反贫困项目、税收支撑的有限福利或是覆盖面很窄的社会保险这一阶段。

中国 40 多年的发展值得注意,因为其经济体制改革触发并影响了中国社会保障改革。在从计划经济向市场经济转变的进程中,社会保障也经历了全面而深刻的制度变革,变革的结果是社会保障覆盖面迅速从覆盖少数人扩展到覆盖全民。社会保障水平尽管仍然相对较低,但伴随快速增长的经济也在持续地提高。这种变革既为中国经济改革和持续增长创造了稳定的社会环境和发展条件,更为全体人民分享国家发展成果提供了制度保障。

中国的发展道路及发展成就,再次证明了社会保障与经济发展可以相得益彰地共同发展——正如"先发国家"的发展。

第六，经济全球化给各国社会保障与经济发展带来了各种新挑战。

经济全球化与区域竞争、老龄化、人口流动与社会结构变迁，科技进步与信息化以及由此带来的新业态、非标准就业形式与生活方式的改变，均构成了各国经济发展与社会保障的新挑战。

4.2 结论和对各国的政策建议

在市场经济中，劳动力不断面临着被视为商品的危险。劳动力不是也不应该是商品，特别是因为劳动力价格（即工资）同时也是人们（家庭）对经济产生需求的手段。历史表明，从长远来看，正是社会保障与劳工标准的结合，防止了劳动力成为商品。在这种情况下，市场经济已经转变为社会市场经济。

在市场经济中，关心市场活动的短期收益者与关心公平的社会保障者之间固有冲突的强度在不同时期、不同区域和不同国家都有很大差异。

从长远来看，历史证明，按照符合市场的要求"优化"社会保障既不必要也不可取。在合理的范围内且避免超出制度承受能力的情况下，必须接受两个政策领域之间的内在冲突并找到平衡。这种平衡在社会市场经济和社会主义市场经济中都是至关重要的。

在世界范围内，过去三四十年是一个经济利益较之社会公平和社会保障而言占据优势地位的时期。在西方，这一事态发展导致大多数经合组织国家（迄今发达）的福利体制明显紧缩；在社会保障未发展或欠发达的其他地区，社会保障的发展明显落后于经济发展，并且（通常）达不到西方所实现的社会保障水平。

这些国家的共同发展实践表明，社会保障在经济衰退时期发挥了积极的经济需求和供给侧效应，从而促进而非阻碍经济的快速复苏。此外，很多国家利用危机后的复苏来加强各自的社会保障制度，这不仅是为了下一阶段的经济衰退未雨绸缪，而且旨在促进社会公正并维系社会经济的健康可持续发展。社会保障事实上构成了国家治理的制度基石。

必须全面理解不同社会保障项目与经济发展的相互作用，以便能够优化社会保障与一般经济要求之间相互冲突而又支持的关系。

在此背景下，中国走上了一条非常有趣和特别的社会保障发展道路。在最初社会保障待遇给付水平（包括医疗低水平供给）相当低（目前仍然偏低），并且不受国际劳工组织任何社会保障和劳动规范约束的情况下，中国决定在20世纪70年代末将其计划经济转变为竞争性（社会主义）市场经济。中国社会主义市场经济的核心特征可能意味着企业完全暴露于市场竞争，但部分企业的所有权仍然掌握在国家或公共机构手中。[1] 因此，公共企业和私人企业在平等的基础上竞争。

从这一点出发，并考虑到市场愿景，中国政府利用社会保障作为核心手段，以支持（对人们）产生影响的经济结构调整过程。其目的是在财务上缓冲该过程的影响，同时也利用社会保障调整劳动力结构并重新配置劳动力，以满足新经济环境的要求：建立新的失业保险为临时失业人员提供短期收入支持；养老金制度被用于提前退休；采取了专门的反贫困措施，以避免失业劳动力暂时陷入困境。多年来，主要是城市劳动力和市民享有这些措施。近10多年来，农村人口被纳入社会保障政策。

换言之，在西方和中国，过去40多年的统治范式主要由经济思维所占据。与西方不同，中国的社会保障制度仍处于起步阶段，因而具有优势：中国公众没有期望"过高的"社会保障福利待遇；也没有复杂的立法或司法系统（如西方那样专注于保护个人权利和应得权益）阻碍政府在适当时候做出必要的决定。这种初始"简单"的社会保障体系，可以在需要时进行实质性的调整，这显然有助于实现预期目标，但也不应该低估巨大困难。从国际视角来看，中国政府

---

[1] 这不同于"社会"市场经济，其所有权主要是私有的，国家所有权保持在最低限度。

利用转型过程将中国的社会保障体系向着国际劳工组织第 102 号公约所述的一套经典的制度和功能设计塑造。这将使中国最终能够批准第 102 号公约和其他相关公约，如 1967 年的《残疾、老年和遗属津贴公约》（第 128 号）。

西方国家无法对社会保障进行这种"工具性的"使用。原因在于：西方国家的社会保障是在复杂的立法和相互依存的制度安排中实施的；社会保障还是社会力量较量的结果，在一些国家，这些社会力量至今仍然活跃。一个明显的例外可能是德国，其"2010 年议程"改革也将社会保障"工具化"为实现经济目标的手段。在中国，过去 40 多年中社会保障的积极影响主要来自其对劳动力结构调整的支持，其次是通过宏观经济需求效应产生；在西方，社会保障对经济的积极影响主要是通过其（成本引起的）劳动生产率效应，以及通过其在国民收入中所占的高份额支出（宏观经济需求效应有助于在危机时期稳定西方经济体）而产生的。

尽管中国目前正在深化包括社会保障在内的改革，新制度的定型还需要通过进一步的顶层设计才能走向完善，但已经取得的巨大进展，对世界各国特别是发展中国家在妥善处理社会保障以实现经济发展这一方面具有重要的启迪作用。

本报告建议各国采取以下政策，以同时促进社会保障和经济的发展。

（1）研究表明，各国政府必须同等重视经济发展和社会保障发展，实现两者同步发展应被国际公认为善治的理性目标。为此，必须加强劳工权利以及人们对其个人福利待遇权利的意识。此外，必须智慧地利用社会保障对提高生产率和增加分配公平的隐性和显性影响，以支撑国内需求。

（2）发达国家应该继续追求高水平的社会保障政策。人口老龄化和国际竞争不应成为进一步紧缩社会政策的"借口"。相反，社会应准备好继续为所有无法获得初次收入的人过上体面生活而提供资金。这可能意味着，至少在暂时的人口老龄化时期，支出将高于最近的水平。可能需要探索新的社会保障筹资形式。国家（政府）应继续保留对社会保障的主要责任；由政府保证足够的能维持个人体面生活的最低福利水平。只应将补充层次（即所谓的第二或第三层）分配给私营部门或作为个人的责任。

（3）鉴于中国作为一个经济体的重要国际角色及其在塑造国际社会保障讨论和态度方面日益重要的作用，中国应该继续走实施制度化社会保障的扩张性道路，加强促进个人应享权利的政策。养老金已经近乎全覆盖，其他社会政策领域也必须取得类似成功，包括免费教育、家庭福利、医疗保健、消除贫困、工作场所保护和工伤事故保险等。此外，中国应提高社会支出相对水平，以赶上其他现代经济体的支出水平。

（4）发展中国家或是正在发展社会保障作为其经济发展一部分的国家，应认真研究中国的情况。虽然中国案例是特殊且通常不是完全适用的，但它包含了旨在同时促进经济和社会保障发展的政策所要汲取的经验教训。国际劳工组织的公约可以帮助制定国家社会政策目标，中国过去40多年的发展为实现这些目标所需的具体政策提供了灵感。

（5）国际社会没有必要放弃社会保障价值观，也没有必要减少或废除社会保障公约。恰恰相反，国际社会应坚持社会公正、"人类命运共同体"和可持续包容性发展的价值观；这些价值观应该相应地指导社会保障和经济发展的实践。为了避免社会保障不恰当地成为国际竞争的工具，请国际社会继续努力以支持社会保障和劳工权利领域的共同规则和公约。再国有化和保护主义的新趋势，使得劳动力转变为"商品"，这种状况必须停止并得以扭转，这包括从社会保障立法中撤销惩罚性的元素。

（6）需要采取国际协调的稳步举措，寻求社会政策领域的新均衡。为了在这一过程中保持稳定，理性的做法是坚持社会保障的基本原则并保证充分发挥其有效的功能，同时在适当的经济增长下谋求进一步发展。

（7）在政府主导的社会支出水平较高或将要提高的情况下，社会保障的运作机制必须适应信息技术和智能化的变化。在政府财政（包括社会保障）必须迅速应对不受控制、制造危机的全球金融市场对社会和经济造成的无法预见的不利影响时，这一点尤其必要。展望工业 4.0、劳动力市场 4.0，以及现代化工业特别是制造业部门的可能发展，社会保障必须做好相应调整的准备，包括采取旨在维持和稳定其财务基础的创新方法。

总之，让所有公民以更好和更公平的方式从国家发展成果中受益，应该是这一适应进程中的一个关键目标。这将有助于促进经济平稳发展。因此，发达经济体在调整其社会保障体系时，应优先考虑维持和促进社会正义，包括保持或设定适当的待遇水平标准。欠发达经济体则需要聚焦于解决当前的贫困问题，同时加强社会保障的制度化建设（在这方面，国际劳工组织的第 202 号建议书可作为直接参考）。

附件 1

社会保障的定义

以下文本摘自欧洲综合社会保护统计系统 ESSPROS（2012），为了更便于阅读，做了微小的编辑改动。为了确保本报告的语言连贯性，我们将 ESSPROS 中所使用的"社会保护（social protection）"一词替换为了"社会保障（social security）"。这两个术语在国际劳工组织的出版物中可互换使用，在英语国家同样如此。但是，美国所使用的"福利（welfare）"一词与英国所使用的"社会保障（social security）/社会保护（social protection）"之间存在一些冲突。

社会保障的常规定义

15. 关于社会保障的范畴没有普遍接受的定义，也没有适合所有目的的定义（包括汇编统计数据）。因此，有必要对社会保障的范畴做出常规定义，并尽可能在国际层面上满足社会政策分析和数据收集的需要。本节首先提出了一个一般性定义，与 ESSPROS 的核心制度及其模块有关，下文各段进一步解释和具体说明了该定义。

16. 社会保障包括公共机构或私人机构旨在减轻家庭和个人一系列既定风险或需求的负担的所有干预措施。前提是既没有同时存在的互惠安排，也不存在个体的安排。

按照惯例，可能导致社会保障出现的风险或需求如下：

（1）疾病/医疗；

（2）残疾；

（3）老年；

（4）遗属；

（5）家庭/儿童；

（6）失业；

（7）住房；

(8)其他社会排斥。

17. 定义中的"干预"一词应从最广义的角度理解,以涵盖对待遇给付和相关管理成本的筹资,以及实际提供的福利待遇。

18. 在社会保障框架内所提供的福利可以多种形式,但在核心制度中,它们仅限于:

(1)给被保护者的现金支付;

(2)对被保护者支出的补偿;

(3)直接提供给被保护者的实物或服务。

19. 干预必须是来自公共机构或私营机构的,排除了所有私人家庭或个体间以礼物、亲属帮助等形式进行的直接资源转移,即使其目的是保护接受者免受第16段中所列风险或需要的影响。

出于实际原因,诸如慈善募捐、圣诞节募捐等小规模的、非正式的和偶然的援助,自然灾害发生时的临时人道主义援助和紧急救助也不包括在该定义中。

19A. 一般来说,最常参与干预的主体有:

社会保障基金;中央、州和地方政府机构;自治和自我管理的养老保险基金;保险公司(在丹麦,运营劳动力市场养老金的养老保险基金可以将这些养老金的管理委托给保险公司);互助会;直接向现任和前任雇员提供福利的公共雇主或私人雇主;私人福利与救助机构[例如,红十字会、葡萄牙的宗教基金会(Casa Misericordia),以及(罗马天主教的)慈善组织(Caritas)]。

20. 第16段所列的风险或需求清单有两个目的。一方面,将社会保障的范畴限定在欧洲语境中所认为的最相关的领域。另一方面,在各成员国的机构、规则和社会传统大相径庭的情况下,它是编制可比统计数据的工具。这些风险和需求界定了提供资源与福利的主要目的,无关乎其背后的法制或体制结构。在这种情况下,习惯使用社会保障功能这一术语。

21. 功能是根据其最终目的而定的,而不是根据社会保障的分支或立法条文而定。例如,不能简单地将由养老基金所发放的福利待遇完全归于老年保障功能,因为其中某些福利也许是为了缓解受益者因养家者死亡而产生的需求(这就属于遗属保障功能),或因丧失参加经济和社会活动的身体能力而产生的需求(这就要被划分为残障保障功能)。ESSPROS仅将功能细分适用于社会保障福利待遇,而不适用于收入。实际上,一种单一的收入类型可以被用来为数个不同的功能提供资金。

23. 社会保障的常规定义规定，干预措施不涉及同时的互惠安排。这应当被视为将任何接受者被要求提供某种等价物以作为交换的干预措施排除在社会保障范围之外。例如，提供给家庭的有息贷款就不是社会保障，因为借款者承诺还本付息。类似地，医疗保障及其他供给的费用的自付部分也不被归为社会保障。这并不排除社会保障福利可能以受益者采取某些行动（如参加职业培训项目）为条件，只要这种行为不具有工薪工作或出售服务的性质。

24. 干预不应包括同时存在的互惠安排，这一原则对于区分由雇主直接提供给员工的社会保障和构成总工资和薪水的资金流两者尤为重要。

24A. 雇主为雇员福利而进行的任何可合理视为工作补偿的支出不被视为社会福利。例如：生活费津贴、地方津贴和外派津贴，通勤补贴，雇主在储蓄计划下向雇员支付的款项，给在职雇员提供的免费住房或住房津贴，员工子女托儿所，公休假和年假的假期工资，为员工及其家人提供体育、娱乐和度假设施。

25. 然而，当雇主所提供的互惠安排不是同时进行时，则该支出归类为社会保障。例如，由雇主支付的退休和遗属养老金、给退休员工的免费住房等都是社会福利（即使该项福利权源于员工之前曾为雇主服务）。同理，当员工因生病、生育、残疾、裁员等而无法工作时，继续支付的工资和薪水也被归类为由雇主提供的社会保障。

26. 此外，根据国民账户的定义，社会保障不包括雇主为了自己以及员工的利益的支出，因为这对雇主的生产过程是必需的。

26A. 例子包括：员工在履行职责过程中的津贴或差旅费报销、工作性质要求的体检、工作场所提供的无法用于员工家庭的食宿（如客舱和宿舍）。

27. 因此，在实践中，雇主直接向雇员提供的社会保障仅限于：

（1）在员工因疾病、意外或生育等而无法工作期间所继续支付的正常或减少的工资和薪水；

（2）支付给雇员所供养的子女及其他家庭成员的法定专项津贴；

（3）与工作性质无关的医疗保健。

28. 社会保障不包括个人或家庭完全出于个人利益而主动投保的所有保险。例如，向私人人寿保险持有者所支付的整笔款项或年金不被视为社会保障。

29. 这一规则并不意味着所有个体政策都被排除在社会保障之外。当雇主以保险的形式提供社会保障时，有时允许或甚至要求以个体参保者名义参保。

30. 这一规则也并不意味着所有的集体合同都必须归类为社会保障。仅出于获得折扣的目的而集体投保的保险政策（如医疗旅游团体险政策）就不属于社会保障。

31. 如果一项保险政策是基于社会团结的，无论其是否由被保险人主动投保，则将其纳入ESSPROS的范畴。如果一项政策的缴费与受保者个体所面临的风险不成比例，那么该保险政策就是基于社会团结。

31A. 通常基于社会团结原则的保险类型有：专门面向同一职业或行业人群的制度；互助会提供的保险；以政府为基础的自愿保险，向某些类别的家庭（如小商贩或其他低收入群体）开放（有时被称为选择加入）。

32. 值得注意的是，社会团结是保险计划被归类为社会保障计划的充分条件，但不是必要条件。具体来说，

（1）根据法律或条例，某些群体有义务参加指定的保险计划；

（2）如员工及其供养家属根据集体工资协议都被保险，则即使该保险不是基于社会团结原则，亦被包含在ESSPROS的范畴中。

32A. 难以划定边界的是所谓的外包，即法律允许人们退出由社会保障管理的一般性计划，而通过其他渠道获得保障。法律规定强制性覆盖（尽管没有具体的计划）或一项保险政策取代政府计划的事实并不是将其归类为社会保障的充分理由。在这些例子中，社会团结的标准可以作为有用的指导。如果替代选择是一个公司计划、职业计划、工会制定的计划或其他互助计划，可被视为基于社会团结原则。因而这些情况可被划入ESSPROS的范畴。当一个人从一种社会保障基金或公司计划中退出，与商业保险公司签订个人保单时，这种情况需单独分析，因为社会团结原则可能仍然适用。英国的个人养老金计划就是一个例子。

附件 2

附　表

表 A1　　1978—2017 年中国 GDP 总量与人均 GDP

年份	GDP（亿元）						人均 GDP（元）（按年中人口数计）				
	人民币	名义增长率（以人民币计）(%)	美元	名义增长率（以美元币计）(%)	购买力平价	名义增长率（以购买力平价计）(%)	实际增长率(%)	人民币	名义增长率（以人民币计）(%)	美元	购买力平价	实际增长率(%)
1978	3 679	13.2	2 185				11.7	385	11.9	229		10.2
1980	4 588	11.9	3 062	16.1			7.8	468	10.6	312		6.5
1985	9 099	25.0	3 098	−0.9			13.4	866	23.4	295		11.9
1990	18 873	9.9	3 946	−13.5	11 199		3.9	1 663	8.3	348	987	2.4
1995	61 340	26.1	7 345	30.2	22 524	13.3	11.0	5 091	24.7	610	1 869	9.8
2000	100 280	10.7	12 113	10.7	37 037	11.0	8.5	7 942	9.9	959	2 933	7.6
2005	187 319	15.7	22 867	16.9	66 393	15.0	11.4	14 368	15.1	1 754	5 093	10.7
2010	412 119	18.2	60 879	19.3	124 574	11.9	10.6	30 808	17.7	4 551	9 313	10.1
2015	685 993	7.0	110 140	5.5	197 263	8.0	6.9	50 028	6.4	8 032	14 386	6.4
2016	740 061	7.9	111 416	1.2	213 100	8.0	6.7	53 680	7.3	8 082	15 457	6.2
2017	820 754	10.9	121 561	9.1	231 214	8.5	6.8	59 201	10.3	8 768	16 677	6.2

注：世界银行的 PPP 转换因子参见以下网址：https：//data.worldbank.org/indicator/PA.NUS.PPP？contextual=default&end=2017&locations=CN&start=1990&view=chart.

数据来源：国家统计局，参见：http：//data.stats.gov.cn/english/easyquery.htm？cn=C01［Jan. 2019］.

表 A2　　1978—2017 年中国基本养老保险参保人数历年变化情况　　（单位：万人）

年份	职工基本养老保险		城乡居民基本养老保险		合计
	在职参保人数	离退休人数	60 岁以下参保人数	60 岁以上领取人数	参保人数
	（1）	（2）	（3）	（4）	（5）
1998	8 475.8	2 727.3	7 965.2	59.8	19 228.1
1999	9 501.8	2 983.6	6 371.0	89.8	18 946.2

续表

年份	职工基本养老保险		城乡居民基本养老保险		合计
	在职参保人数	离退休人数	60岁以下参保人数	60岁以上领取人数	参保人数
	（1）	（2）	（3）	（4）	（5）
2000	10 447.5	3 169.9	6 074.5	97.8	19 789.7
2001	10 801.9	3 380.6	5 887.0	108.1	20 177.6
2002	11 128.8	3 607.8	5 338.4	123.4	20 198.4
2003	11 646.5	3 860.2	5 230.1	197.6	20 934.4
2004	12 250.3	4 102.6	5 176.9	205.5	21 735.3
2005	13 120.4	4 367.5	5 140.2	301.7	22 929.8
2006	14 130.9	4 635.4	5 018.6	355.1	24 140.0
2007	15 183.2	4 953.7	4 779.9	391.6	25 308.4
2008	16 587.5	5 303.6	5 083.0	512.0	27 486.1
2009	17 743.0	5 806.9	5 942.1	1 335.2	30 827.2
2010	19 402.3	6 305.0	7 414.2	2 862.6	35 984.1
2011	21 565.0	6 826.2	24 025.7	9 156.8	61 573.7
2012	22 981.1	7 445.7	34 987.3	13 382.2	78 796.3
2013	24 177.0	8 041.0	35 982.1	13 768.0	81 968.1
2014	25 531.0	8 593.4	35 794.5	14 313.0	84 231.9
2015	26 219.0	9 142.0	35 672.0	14 800.0	85 833.0
2016	27 826.3	10 103.4	35 576.8	15 270.3	88 776.8
2017	29 268.0	11 026.0	35 657.0	15 598.0	91 549.0

注：①表中"城乡居民基本养老保险"（第3列和第4列）之居民是指所有农村居民和城镇中非工薪适龄（16~59岁）人口，在2010年及以前仅指"农村社会养老保险"，从2011—2013年为"农村社会养老保险"和"城镇居民基本养老保险"合并数据，2014年开始为制度整合后的"城乡居民基本养老保险"。

②在20世纪80年代末，中国部分地区曾经试行过农民自愿参加、个人缴费的储蓄型养老保险办法，但因缺乏财政支持而未能够得到发展，并出现了基金流失、待遇严重偏低甚至无法兑现待遇等问题，因此，中国政府于1998年明令停止这种做法，已经参保的农民作为遗留问题处理。2009年，中国政府正式推进财政注资型农民养老保险，并在2011年推广到城镇非工薪适龄人口，2012年年底实现了制度全覆盖。

数据来源：人力资源社会保障部发布的历年《人力资源和社会保障事业发展统计公报》，国家统计局公布的历年《中国劳动统计年鉴》，郑功成著述的《中国社会保障30年》。

表A3　　　　　　　1998—2017年中国基本养老保险基金累计结余

年份	职工基本养老保险		城乡居民基本养老保险		合计	
	亿人民币	亿美元	亿人民币	亿美元	亿人民币	亿美元
	（1）	（2）	（3）	（4）	（5）	（6）
1998	587.8	71.00			587.8	71.00
1999	733.5	88.61			733.5	88.61

续表

年份	职工基本养老保险		城乡居民基本养老保险		合计	
	亿人民币	亿美元	亿人民币	亿美元	亿人民币	亿美元
	（1）	（2）	（3）	（4）	（5）	（6）
2000	947.1	114.41			947.1	114.41
2001	1 054.1	127.35			1 054.1	127.35
2002	1 608.0	194.27			1 608.0	194.27
2003	2 206.5	266.58	259.3	31.33	2 465.8	297.91
2004	2 975.0	359.44	285.0	34.43	3 260.0	393.87
2005	4 041.0	493.30	310.0	37.84	4 351.0	531.15
2006	5 488.9	688.54	354.0	44.41	5 842.9	732.95
2007	7 391.4	972.04	412.0	54.18	7 803.4	1 026.22
2008	9 931.0	1 429.93	499.0	71.85	10 430.0	1 501.78
2009	12 526.1	1 833.71	681.0	99.69	13 207.1	1 933.41
2010	15 365.3	2 269.78	422.5	62.41	15 787.8	2 332.20
2011	19 496.6	3 018.61	1 231.2	190.62	20 727.8	3 209.23
2012	23 941.3	3 792.68	2 302.2	364.70	26 243.5	4 157.39
2013	28 269.0	4 564.52	3 006.0	485.37	31 275.0	5 049.89
2014	31 800.0	5 176.79	3 845.0	625.94	35 645.0	5 802.73
2015	35 345.0	5 674.81	4 592.0	737.27	39 937.0	6 412.08
2016	38 580.0	5 808.23	5 385.0	810.71	43 965.0	6 618.94
2017	43 885.0	6 499.75	6 318.0	935.75	50 203.0	7 435.50

注：表中"城乡居民基本养老保险"（第3列和第4列）在2010年及以前仅指"农村社会养老保险"，从2011—2013年为"农村社会养老保险"和"城镇居民基本养老保险"合并数据，2014年开始为制度整合后的"城乡居民基本养老保险"。

数据来源：人力资源社会保障部发布的历年《人力资源和社会保障事业发展统计公报》，国家统计局公布的历年《中国劳动统计年鉴》。

表 A4　　　　1978—2017 年中国基本养老保险参保人数　　　　（单位：万人）

年份	参保人数合计	职工基本养老保险			城乡居民基本养老保险
		合计	在职参保人数	离退休人数	
1978				314.0	
1980				816.0	
1985				1 637.0	
1986				1 805.0	
1987				1 968.0	
1988				2120	
1989	5 710.3	5 710.3	4 816.9	893.4	
1990	6 166.0	6 166.0	5 200.7	965.3	

续表

年份	参保人数合计	职工基本养老保险			城乡居民基本养老保险
		合计	在职参保人数	离退休人数	
1991	6 740.3	6 740.3	5 653.7	1 086.6	
1992	9 456.2	9 456.2	7 774.7	1 681.5	
1993	9 847.6	9 847.6	8 008.2	1 839.4	
1994	10 573.5	10 573.5	8 494.1	2 079.4	
1995	10 979.0	10 979.0	8 737.8	2 241.2	
1996	11 116.7	11 116.7	8 758.4	2 358.3	
1997	11 203.9	11 203.9	8 670.9	2 533.0	
1998	11 203.1	11 203.1	8 475.8	2 727.3	
1999	12 485.4	12 485.4	9 501.8	2 983.6	
2000	13 617.4	13 617.4	10 447.5	3 169.9	
2001	14 182.5	14 182.5	10 801.9	3 380.5	
2002	14 736.6	14 736.6	11 128.8	3 607.8	
2003	15 506.7	15 506.7	11 646.6	3 860.2	
2004	16 352.9	16 352.9	12 250.3	4 102.6	
2005	17 487.9	17 487.9	13 120.4	4 367.5	
2006	18 766.3	18 766.3	14 130.9	4 636.4	
2007	20 136.9	20 136.9	15 183.2	4 953.7	
2008	21 891.1	21 891.1	16 587.5	5 303.5	
2009	23 549.9	23 549.9	17 743.0	5 806.9	
2010	35 984.1	25 707.3	19 402.3	6 305.0	10 276.8
2011	61 573.3	28 391.3	21 565.0	6 826.2	33 182.0
2012	78 796.3	30 426.8	22 981.1	7 445.7	48 369.6
2013	81 968.4	32 218.4	24 177.3	8 041.0	49 750.1
2014	84 231.9	34 124.4	25 531.0	8 593.4	50 107.5
2015	85 833.4	35 361.2	26 219.2	9 141.9	50 472.2
2016	88 776.3	37 929.7	27 826.3	10 103.4	50 847.1
2017	91 549.0	40 294.0	29 268.0	11 026.0	51 255.0

数据来源：国家统计局.2018中国统计年鉴[M].北京：中国统计出版社，2018.

表 A5　　2001—2017 年中国基本养老保险基金人均支出变化情况

年份	职工基本养老保险		城乡居民基本养老保险	
	人民币/月	美元/月	人民币/月	美元/月
	（1）	（2）	（3）	（4）
2001	572.21	69.13		
2002	656.66	79.34		
2003	673.99	81.43		
2004	711.36	85.95		
2005	770.90	94.11		
2006	880.31	110.43		
2007	1 003.44	131.96		
2008	1 161.10	167.18		
2009	1 276.41	186.86	40.70	5.96
2010	1 395.04	206.08	58.21	8.60
2011	1 558.32	241.27	56.98	8.82
2012	1 741.70	275.91	73.30	11.61
2013	1 914.15	309.07	81.59	13.17
2014	2 109.63	343.43	91.47	14.89
2015	2 352.97	377.78	119.20	19.14
2016	2 627.44	395.56	117.33	17.66
2017	2 875.93	425.95	126.73	18.77

注：①基金人均支出 = 基金支出/年末待遇领取人数，基金人均支出用于估计人均养老金。
②美元对人民币汇率来自《中国统计年鉴 2018》公布的历年平均汇率。
③表中城乡居民基本养老保险人均养老金支出量（第 3 列和第 4 列）2016 年略低于 2015 年，这是因为新增的养老金领取人数中，待遇水平相对较低的地区增加较多，因而全国总体平均待遇水平有所降低。实际上，各地区的待遇水平都没有降低，反而有所提高。
数据来源：人力资源社会保障部发布的历年《人力资源和社会保障事业发展统计公报》，国家统计局公布的历年《中国劳动统计年鉴》。

表 A6　1985—2017 年中国农村贫困线、贫困人口和贫困发生率

年份	1978 年标准 贫困标准（元/人）	1978 年标准 贫困标准（美元/人）	1978 年标准 贫困人口（万人）	1978 年标准 贫困发生率（%）	2008 年标准 贫困标准（元/人）	2008 年标准 贫困标准（美元/人）	2008 年标准 贫困人口（万人）	2008 年标准 贫困发生率（%）	2010 年标准 贫困标准（元/人）	2010 年标准 贫困标准（美元/人）	2010 年标准 贫困人口（万人）	2010 年标准 贫困发生率（%）
1985	206	70.1	12 500	14.8								
1986	213	61.7	13 100	15.5								
1987	227	61.0	12 200	14.3								
1988	236	63.4	9 600	11.1								
1989	259	68.8	10 200	11.6								
1990	300	62.7	8 500	9.4								
1991	304	57.1	9 400	10.4								
1992	317	57.5	8 000	8.8								
1993	—	—	—	—								
1994	440	51.1	7 000	7.7								
1995	530	63.5	6 540	7.1								
1994	—	—	—	—								
1997	640	77.2	4 962	5.4								
1998	635	76.7	4 210	4.6								
1999	625	75.5	3 412	3.7								
2000					625	75.5	3 209	3.5				
2001					630	76.1	2 927	3.2				
2002					627	75.8	2 820	3				

续表

年份	1978年标准			2008年标准			2010年标准		
	贫困标准（元/人）	贫困标准（美元/人）	贫困人口（万人）	贫困发生率（%）	贫困标准（元/人）	贫困标准（美元/人）	贫困人口（万人）	贫困发生率（%）	贫困标准（元/人）	贫困标准（美元/人）	贫困人口（万人）	贫困发生率（%）
2003					637	77.0	2 900	3.1				
2004					668	80.7	2 610	2.8				
2005					683	83.4	2 365	2.5				
2006					693	86.9	2 148	2.3				
2007					785	103.2	1 479	1.6				
2008					1 196	172.2	4 007	4.2				
2009					1 196	175.1	3 597	3.8				
2010					1 274	188.2	2 688	2.8	2 300	339.7	16 567	17.2
2011									2 536	392.6	12 238	12.7
2012									2 625	415.8	9 899	10.2
2013									2 736	441.8	8 249	8.5
2014									2 800	455.8	7 017	7.2
2015									2 855	458.4	5 575	5.7
2016									3 000	451.7	4 335	4.5
2017											3 046	3.1

注：中国农村贫困线标准远低于国际上普遍接受的联合国开发计划署的标准，还有较大的提升空间。

数据来源：1985—1999年农村扶贫标准、贫困人口、贫困发生率等数据由国务院扶贫办提供，2000—2017年的贫困人口、贫困发生率等数据来自《中国统计年鉴2018》；贫困线标准来自国家统计局的《中国农村贫困监测报告》。

参考文献

Amlinger, M. ; Bispinck, R; Schulten, S. 2016. The German minimum wage: Experiences and perspectives after one year. in *WSI Report*, No. 28e.

Auer, P. What's in a name? The rise (and fall?) of flexicurity. in *Journal of Industrial Relations*, 2 July 2010. Available at: http://journals. sagepub. com/doi/pdf/10. 1177/0022185610365646 [17 June 2018].

Bertelsmann Stiftung. 2016. Kinderarmut in Deutschland waechst weiter mit Folgen fuers ganze Leben. (Nuernberg, Germany, Bundesagentur fuer Arbeit). [*Child poverty continues growing in Germany with lifetime implications* (Nuernberg, Germany, Federal Employment Agency). Available at: https://www. bertelsmann-stiftung. de/de/themen/aktuelle-meldungen/2016/september/kinderarmut-in-deutschland-waechst-weiter-mit-folgen-fuers-ganze-leben/ [18 July 2017].

Beveridge, W. H. 1942. *Social insurance and allied services*: *Report*. (London, HMSO).

Blair, T. ;Schroeder, G. 1999. *Europe*: *The third way* (*Die neue Mitte*). London and Berlin, Labour Party and Sozialdemokratische Partei Deutschlands, Available at: https://web. archive. org/web/19990819090124/http://www. labour. org. uk/views/items/00000053. html [8 Feb. 2017].

Bleicken, J. 2015. The army of Augustus. in *Augustus*: *The biography*. New York, Penguin, [Original published in German: Jochen Bleicken: *Augustus*: *Eine Biographie* (Berlin, Alexander Fest Verlag, 1998; paperback-edition consulted: Hamburg, Germany, Rowohlt, 2010].

Bonss, W. 1982. *Die Einuebung des Tatsachenblicks*: *zur Struktur und Veraenderung empirischer Sozialforschung*. Frankfurt am Main, Suhrkamp,

[*Exercising our views on subject-matters: about structure and transformation of empirical sociological research*].

Bosch, G. 2015. The German welfare state: From an inclusive to an exclusive Bismarck model:in D. Vaughan-Whitehead (ed.): *The European social model in crisis*: *Is Europe losing its soul*？ (Geneva, Cheltenham, UK and Northampton, MA, ILO and Edward Elgar Publishing).

—. 2017. Exportorientiertes Wachstumsmodell: Die Agenda 2010 sollte Probleme loesen, die es nicht gab. [*Germany's export-oriented growth model*: *The Agenda 2010 was supposed to solve problems which did not exist*], 15 Aug. Available at: https://makroskop. eu/2017/08/die-agenda-2010-sollte-probleme-loesen-die-es-nicht-gab/ [16 Aug. 2017].

Bundesagentur fuer Arbeit (BMA). 2016. Arbeitslosigkeit im Zeitverlauf - Monats-/Jahreszahlen (ab 1950). Nuernberg: Bundesagentur für Arbeit. [*Federal Employment Agency*: *Unemploymnet – long-term time series* (*as of 1950*)].

Bundesarchiv: Denkschrift. Undated. *Ueber die Hoehe der finanziellen Belastung, welche durch die Alters- und Invalidenversicherung der Arbeiter voraussichtlich hervorgerufen werden wird* (Berlin). [Federal Archives: Memorandum. Undated. *On the level of financial burden resulting from the implementation of the workers' old-age and invalidity insurance* Berlin. [Delivered prior to Bismarck's pension legislation in order to fix benefit levels and contribution rates.]

Bundesministerium fuer Arbeit und Soziales (BMAS). 2015. Sozialbudget 2014. http://www. bmas. de/SharedDocs/Downloads/DE/PDF-Publikationen/a230-14-sozialbudget-2014. pdf?__blob=publicationFile&v=2, accessed September 23, 2015.

—. 2016a. *Entwicklung der privaten Altersvorsorge 2001 bis 2016*. (Berlin, Bundeministerium fuer Arbeit und Soziales). Available at: http://www. bmas. de/DE/Themen/Rente/Zusaetzliche-Altersvorsorge/statistik-zusaetzliche-altersvorsorge. html [23 Nov. 2016]. [*Development of the number of private pension contracts 2001 to 2016* (Berlin, Federal Ministry of Labour and Social Affairs]

—. 2016b. *Gesamtkonzept zur Alterssicherung* , Berlin. [*Comprehensive old-age security concept*].

Available at: http://www. bmas. de/SharedDocs/Downloads/DE/Thema-Rente/

gesamtkonzept-alterssicherung-detail. pdf?__blob=publicationFile&v=6 [11 Dec. 2016].

—. 2017. *Sozialbericht. Teil B: Sozialbudget* [*Social report. Part B: Social budget*] (Berlin). Available at: http://www. bmas. de/SharedDocs/Downloads/DE/PDF-Publikationen/a-101-17-sozialbericht-2017. pdf?__blob=publicationFile&v=2 [12 Jan 2018].

Bundesministerium für Arbeit und Soziales und Bundesarchiv (BMAS and BArch). 2006. *Geschichte der Sozialpolitik in Deutschland seit 1945. Band 9: Deutsche Demokratische Republik 1961–1971. Politische Stabilisierung und wirtschaftliche Mobilisierung.* Nomos: Baden-Baden. [Federal Ministry of Labour and Social Affairs and Federal Archives. 2006. *History of social policy in Germany since 1945, Vol 9: German Democratic Republic 1961–1971: Political stabilisation and economic mobilisation*].

—. 2008. *Geschichte der Sozialpolitik in Deutschland seit 1945. Band 10: Deutsche Demokratische Republik 1971–1989. Bewegung in der Sozialpolitik, Erstarrung und Niedergang.* Nomos: Baden-Baden. [Federal Ministry of Labour and Social Affairs, and Federal Archives. 2008. *History of social policy in Germany since 1945, Vol.10: German Democratic Republic 1971–1989: Social reforms, rigidity, and decline*].

Bundesministerium fuer Gesundheit und Bundesarchiv (BMG and BArch). 2004. *Geschichte der Sozialpolitik in Deutschland seit 1945. Band 8: Deutsche Demokratische Republik 1949–1961. Im Zeichen des Aufbaus des Sozialismus.* Nomos: Baden-Baden. [*Federal Ministry of Health and Social Security, and Federal Archives. 2004. History of social policy in Germany since 1945, Vol. 8: German Democratic Republic 1949–1961: Under construction of socialism*].

Central Committee of the Communist Party (CCCP). 2015. *13th Five-Year Plan for Economic and Social Development of the People's Republic of China (2016–2020)*, Translated by Compilation and Translation Bureau (Beijing). Available at: http://en.ndrc. gov. cn/newsrelease/201612/P020161207645765233498. pdf [Dec. 2016].

Central Committee of the Communist Party; State Council. 1992. *Decision on accelerating the development of the tertiary industry* (Beijing) [in Chinese]. 中共中央和国务院. 中共中央国务院关于加快发展第三产业的决定. 1992.

China Centre for Human Capital and Labour Market Research. 2018. *China *human capital report 2018* (Beijing, Central University of Finance and Economics Press) [in Chinese]. Available at: http://humancapital. cufe. edu. cn/info/1020/2454. htm. 中央财经大学中国人力资本与劳动研究中心. 中国人力资本报告 2018[M]. 北京：中央财经大学出版社, 2018.

Chinese Academy of Social Sciences (CASS); State Council Poverty Alleviation Office (SCPAO). 2016. *China Poverty Alleviation and Development Report 2016*, Poverty Reduction Blue Book (Beijing) [in Chinese]. 中国社会科学院和国务院扶贫办. 中国扶贫开发报告 2016, 扶贫蓝皮书. 2016(12).

Cichon, M.; Scholz, W.; van de Meerendonk, A.; Hagemejer, K.; Bertranou, F.; Plamondon, P. 2004. *Financing social protection* Geneva, International Labour Office and International Social Security Association.

Cingano, F. 2014. *Trends in income inequality and its impact on economic growth*, OECD Social, Employment and Migration Working Papers, No. 163. Paris, OECD Publishing. Available at: http://dx. doi. org/10. 1787/5jxrjncwxv6j-en [1 Feb. 2017].

Coase, R. H. 1937. "The nature of the firm", in *Economica*, Vol. 4, No. 16. Available at: https://www. colorado. edu/ibs/es/alston/econ4504/readings/The % 20Nature% 20of% the% 20Firm% 20by% 20Coase. pdf [11 Nov. 2014].

Concialdi, P. 2019. *Economic development and social security in France: The mid-1980s turning point*. Background paper to the Chinese version of this report. Beijing, CAOSS.

Confucius. Undated. The conveyance of rites, in Dai, S. (ed.): *The Book of Rites*. Beijing, Confucian Classics. Available at: https://ctext. org/liji/li-yun [19 Feb. 2019].

DeLong, B. J. 2002. *Macroeconomics*, Revised edition. New York, McGraw-Hill.

Dixon, J. E. 1999. *Social security in global perspective*. Westport, CT, Praeger.

European Commission. 2015. *The 2015 ageing report: Economic and budgetary projections for the 28 EU Member States, 2013–2060*. Luxembourg, Publications Office of the European Union. Available at: http://ec. europa. eu/economy_finance/

publications/european_economy/2015/pdf/ee3_en. pdf [20 Feb. 2019].

European System of Accounts. 2010. *European System of Accounts*. Luxembourg, Office for Official Publications of the European Communities.

European System of Integrated Social Protection Statistics (ESSPROS). 2012. *European System of Integrated Social Protection Statistics Manual*. Luxembourg, Office for Official Publications of the European Communities.

European Union; International Labour Office. Undated. *A Review of Global Fiscal Stimulus. International Institute for Labour Studies* (IILS). Available at: http://www. ilo. org/wcmsp5/groups/public/---dgreports/---inst/documents/publication/wcms_194175. pdf [18 Aug. 2018].

Faricy, C. G. 2015. *Welfare for the wealthy*: *Parties, social spending and inequality in the United States*. Cambridge, Cambridge University Press, p p. 140.

Flassbeck, H. 2017. Europaeische Arbeitskosten: Unter deutschem Einfluss auf deflationaerem Pfad. Teile 1 - 3. https://makroskop. eu/2017/04/europaeische-arbeitskosten-unter-deutschem-einfluss-auf-deflationaerem-pfad-1/ [15 Apr. 2017]. [*European labour costs*: *Deflationary tendencies under German impact*.]

Friedman, M. ; Bordo, M. D. 2005. *The optimum quantity of money*. London and New York, Transaction Publishers.

Frisby, D. 1972. The Popper-Adorno Controversy: The methodological dispute in German Sociology. in *Philosophy of the Social Sciences*, Vol. 2, pp. 105–119.

Gauti, J. 2015. Frances social model: Between resilience and erosion, in D. Vaughan-Whitehead (ed.): *The European social model in crisis*: *Is Europe losing its soul*? Geneva, Cheltenham, UK and Northampton, MA, ILO and Edward Elgar Publishing, pp. 121–174.

Gillion, C. ; Turner, J. ; Bailey, C. ; Latulippe, D. (eds.) 2000. *Social security pensions*: *Development and reform*. Geneva, International Labour Office.

Gleeson-White, J. 2012. *Double entry. How the merchants of Venice shaped the modern world and how their invention could make or break the planet* . London, Allen Jane. [Book consulted in its German edition: *Die doppelte Buchfuehrung und die Entstehung des modernen Kapitalismus* (Soll & Haben)].

Gray, J. 2007. Naomi Klein's critique of neo-liberalism, The Shock Doctrine, is both timely and devastating. in *The Guardian*, 15 Sep. Available at: https://www.theguardian.com/books/2007/sep/15/politics [11 Nov. 2017].

Grimshaw, D. 2015. Britains social model: Rapid descent from liberal collectivism to a market society. in D. Vaughan-Whitehead (ed.): *The European social model in crisis*: *Is Europe losing its soul*? Geneva, Cheltenham, UK and Northampton, MA, ILO and Edward Elgar Publishing, pp. 553–613.

Hagemejer, K. ; Scholz, W. 2004. Nachhaltig, sicher und angemessen？ Die Reformstrategie der Weltbank und die Rentenreformen in Polen, Ungarn, Tschechien und anderen osteuropaeischen Laendern. Eine Neubetrachtung (Soziale Sicherheit in Europa). in *Deutsche Rentenversicherung*, Vol. 11/12 [*Sustainable, safe and adequate？Revisiting the pension reforms in Poland, Hungary, Czech Republic and other countries of the region and the World Bank pension agenda*].

Hudson, J. 2016. *From welfare state to competition state? The evolving relationship between social security and the economy in the United Kingdom* York, UK, University of York.

International Labour Organization (ILO). 1944. Declaration concerning the aims and purposes of the International Labour Organization. Declaration of Philadelphia, 26th General Conference of the International Labour Organization, Philadelphia, 10 May. Available at: http://www.ilo.org/wcmsp5/groups/public/---asia/---ro-bangkok/---ilo-islamabad/documents/policy/wcms_142941.pdf [5 Oct. 2014].

—. 1952. Social Security (Minimum Standards) Convention, 1952 (No. 102. Geneva. Available at: http://www.ilo.org/dyn/normlex/en/f?p=NORMLEXPUB:12100:0::NO::P12100_INSTRUMENT_ID:312247 [10 Dec. 2016].

—. 2012. Social Protection Floors Recommendation, 2012 (No. 202. NORMLEX Information System on International Labour Standards (Geneva). Available at: http://www.ilo.org/dyn/normlex/en/f? p=NORMLEXPUB:12100:0::NO::P12100_ILO_CODE:R202 [29 Nov. 2017].

—. 2014. *Building economic recovery, inclusive development and social justice*: *World social protection report 2014/15* . Geneva.

—. 2016. ILO constitution: 1919. Geneva. Available at: https://www.ilo.org/public/libdoc/ilo/1920/20B09_18_engl.pdf.

—. 2017. *World social protection report 2017–19*: *Universal social protection to achieve the Sustainable Development Goals*. Geneva.

International Labour Organization (ILO) NATLEX-China. Undated. China: Regulations on unemployment insurance for staff and workers of state-owned enterprises. Promulgated by the State Council by Decree No. 110, 4 Dec. 1993. unofficial translation. Available at: http://www.ilo.org/dyn/natlex/docs/WEBTEXT/49694/65117/E93CHN01.htm [19 Jan. 2019].

International Monetary Fund (IMF). 2017a. *World economic outlook*: *Update*, July. Washington, DC.

—. 2017b. *The IMF and social protection*: *2017 evaluation report*. Washington, DC, Independent Evaluation Office, IMF. Available at: http://www.ieo-imf.org/ieo/files/complctcdevaluations/SP%20-%202017EvalReport.pdf [19 Jan. 2019].

International Social Security Association (ISSA). 2016. Government of China receives international social security award. Press release, 17 Nov. Available at: https://www.issa.int/en/-/government-of-china-receives-international-social-security-award [Oct. 2018].

International Social Security Association (ISSA), Social Security Administration (SSA). Various years. *Social security programs throughout the world*. Geneva and Washington, D.C.

Judt, T. 2010. *Ill fares the land*. New York, NY, Penguin.

Kim, Y. 2019. *Limits of economic growth without welfare*: *The experience of the Republic of Korea*. Background paper to the Chinese version of this report. Beijing, CAOSS.

Klein, N. 2007. *The shock doctrine*: *The rise of disaster capitalism*. New York, Metropolitan Books/Henry Holt.

Konfuzius. 2017. Gespraeche (Lun-yu). Stuttgart, Reclams Universal Bibliothek. Aus dem Chinesischen von Ralf Moritz. [*The analects*, translated from

Chinese by Ralf Moritz].

Koschnitzke, L. 2015. *Krankenversicherung: Die Schutzlosen. Trotz gesetzlicher Pflicht leben hunderttausende Menschen in Deutschland ohne Krankenversicherung. Die aktuelle Fluechtlingskrise verschaerft das Problem* [*Health insurance: The non-protected. Despite legal obligation hundreds of thousands of people live without health insurance in Germany. The current refugees crisis intensifies the problem*] (Hamburg, Germany, ZEIT). Available at: http://www. zeit. de/wirtschaft/2015-10/krank-ohne-versicherung-selbstaendigkeit-abstieg [19 Jan. 2019].

Lee, C. K. 2005. *Livelihood struggles and market reform: (un)making Chinese labour after state socialism* (Geneva, United Nations Research Institute for Social Development). Available at: https://www. econstor. eu/bitstream/10419/148803/1/862974275. pdf [19 Jan. 2019].

Leo XIII .1891."Rerum Novarum: Encyclical of Pope Leo XIII on capital and labour", in *Libreria Editrice Vaticana*. Available at: http://w2. vatican. va/content/leo-xiii/en/encyclicals/documents/hf_l-xiii_enc_15051891_rerum-novarum. html [8 Dec. 2016].

Li, P. ; Cheng, G. ; Zhang, Y. 2015. *Social Blue Book: Analysis and projection of China's social situation in 2016*.Beijing, Social Sciences Academic Press [in Chinese]. 李培林，陈光金，张翼．社会蓝皮书：2016年中国社会形势分析与预测[M]．北京：社会科学文献出版社，2015.

Li, S. ; Jingyong, Z. 2003. "Can education provide sufficient human capital for a moderately prosperous society?", in *Xinhua News Agency*, 12 Mar. [in Chinese]. 李术峰，张景勇．教育，能否为全面小康提供足够人力资本[N]？新华社，2003-03-12.

Lindert, P. H. 2010. *Growing public: Social spending and economic growth since the 18th century* (Los Angeles, CA, University of California).

Lindner, F. 2012. *Saving does not finance Investment: Accounting as an indispensable guide to economic theory*, Working Paper 100. Duesseldorf, Germany, Macroeconomic Policy Institute. Available at: https://www. boeckler. de/pdf/p_imk_wp_100_2012. pdf [19 Jan. 2019].

Lister, R. 2013. Benefit cuts: How the language of welfare poisoned our social security. in *The Guardian*, 1 Apr. Available at: https://www. theguardian. com/commentisfree/2013/apr/01/language-welfare-social-security [27 Dec. 2017].

Maddison, A. 2003. *Historical statistics*: *The Maddison Project* (Groningen, Netherlands, University of Groningen). Available at: http://www. ggdc. net/maddison/oriindex. htm [11 Nov. 2016].

—. 2016. *The Maddison Project* (Groningen, Netherlands, University of Groningen). Available at: http://www. ggdc. net/maddison/maddison-project/home. htm [10 Nov. 2016].

Manthe, U. 2011. *Geschichte des Roemischen Rechts*, 4. Auflage [*History of Roman Law*]. Munich, C. H. Beck. [Chinese translation available].

Ministry of Civil Affairs (MCA). Various years (2010–18). *Statistical bulletin on social services development 2009–17*. Beijing. 中华人民共和国民政部. 2009—2017 年《社会服务发展统计公报》.

—. Various years (2000–09). *Statistical bulletin on civil affairs development* (Beijing). 中华人民共和国民政部. 2000—2009 年《中国民政事业发展统计公报》.

Ministry of Education (MOE). 2017. "Leading CPC group of the Ministry of Education: Develop modern world level education with Chinese characteristics", in *Qiushi Journal*, Vol. 16 [in Chinese]. 中共教育部党组. 发展具有中国特色世界水平的现代教育［J］. 求是, 2017(16).

—. Various years. *Statistical yearbook on education*. Beijing. 教育部历年《中国教育统计年鉴》. 北京：人民教育出版社.

—. 2018. *Statistical bulletin on the development of education 2017*. Beijing. 教育部. 2017 年全国教育事业发展统计.

Ministry of Finance (MOF, Ministry of Education (MOE), National Bureau of Statistics (NBS). 2018. *Statistical bulletin on the implementation of educational funds in China 2017*. Beijing. Available at: http://www. moe. gov. cn/srcsite/A05/s3040/201810/t20181012_351301. html [Nov. 2018] 中国财政部，教育部，国家统计局. 2017 年全国教育经费执行情况统计公报. 参见：http://www. moe. gov. cn/srcsite/A05/s3040/201810/t20181012_351301. html.

Ministry of Human Resources and Social Security (MHRSS). Various years.

Statistical bulletin on human resources and social security development (Beijing). 中国人力资源和社会保障部. 历年《人力资源和社会保障事业发展统计公报》.

Mueller, K. 1999. *The political economy of pension reform in Central-Eastern Europe*. Northampton, MA, Edward Elgar Publishing.

National Bureau of Statistics (NBS). 2016. *An International comparison report of labour productivity* . Beijing.

—. 2019. National data. Available at: http://data. stats. gov. cn/english/easyquery. htm?cn=C01 [Jan. 2019].

—. Various years. *Statistical yearbook*. Beijing. 历年《中国统计年鉴》.

—. Various years. *Statistical bulletin on national economic and social development* (Beijing). 历年《国民经济和社会发展统计公报》.

—. Various years. *Labour statistical yearbook* (Beijing). 历年《中国劳动统计年鉴》.

National Health Commission (NHC). 2018. *China statistical yearbook of health*, Beijing. 中国卫生健康委. 中国卫生健康统计年鉴 2018.

National Health and Family Planning Commission (NHFPC). 2016. *China family development report 2015* (Beijing). 国家卫生计生委. 中国家庭发展报告 (2015 年).

—. Various years. *China Statistical Yearbook of Health and Family Planning*, Beijing. 中国国家卫生计生委. 历年中国卫生和计划生育统计年鉴.

National Poverty Alleviation Office (NPAO). 2017. Leading Party Group of Poverty Alleviation Office of the State Council of CPC: Five years of poverty alleviation and endeavours. in *People's Daily*, 17 Oct. [in Chinese]. 中共国务院扶贫办党组. 脱贫攻坚砥砺奋进的五年［N］. 人民日报, 2017-10-17.

Ono, T. 2019. *Historical development and current issues for social security in Japan*. Background paper to the Chinese version of this report. Beijing, CAOSS.

Ortiz, I. ; Cummins, M. ; Karunanethy, K. 2017. *Fiscal space for social protection and the SDGs: Options to expand social investments in 187 countries*,

Extension of Social Security Working Paper No. 48. Geneva and New York, International Labour Office, UNICEF and UNWOMEN. Available at: http://www. social-protection. org/gimi/gess/RessourcePDF. action?ressource. ressourceId=51537 [19 Jan. 2019].

Pal, K.; Behrendt, C.; Lger, F.; Cichon, M.; Hagemejer, K. 2005. *Can low-income countries afford basic social protection*? *First results of a modelling exercise*: *Issues in social protection*, Discussion Paper 13. Geneva, International Labour Office.

Payandeh, M. 2012. The united nations, military intervention, and regime change in Libya. in *Virginia Journal of International Law*, Vol. 52, No. 2. Available at: https://ssrn. com/abstract=1930993 [19 Jan. 2019].

People's Daily. 2016. Chinese government received ISSA Award for Outstanding Achievements in Social Security. 19 Nov. [in Chinese]. 中国政府获国际社会保障杰出成就奖［N］. 人民日报, 2016-11-19.

—. 2017. Whose jobs will be replaced by artificial intelligence? 21 Apr. [in Chinese]. 人工智能, 会"砸"谁的饭碗［N］? 人民日报, 2017-04-21.

Petersen, K. 2019. *Growth for welfare or welfare for growth*? *The changing relationship between economic development and social security in the Nordic countries*. Background paper to the Chinese version of this report. Beijing, CAOSS.

Plamondon, P.; Drouin, A.; Binet, G.; Cichon, M.; McGillivray, W. R.; Bdard, M.; Perez-Montas, H. 2002. *Actuarial practice in social security*. Geneva, International Labour Office and International Social Security Association.

Popper, K. 1977. *The logic of scientific discovery*. Fourteenth edition. London, Routledge. [First published in German: Logik der Forschung (Wien, Springer, 1934)].

Pusch, T.; Seifert, H., 2017. Mindestlohngesetz: Fuer viele Minijobber weiterhin nur Miniloehne. Policy brief No. 9. Duesseldorf, Wirtschafts- und Sozialwissenschaftliches Institut, Hans-Boeckler-Stiftung. [*Germany's minimum wage law*: *Many mini-jobbers still only earn mini-wages*]. Available at: http://www. boeckler. de/14_107083. htm [19 Jan. 2019].

Ritter, G. A. 2014. The creation of the German pension insurance and its major characteristics, revision of a lecture at Thanks, Otto! 125 Years of Pensions and New Global Perspectives conference, Berlin, 28–29 Oct. (Handout) Avalable at: https://helpage. app. box. com/s/4zxpaajj9gv2g9c785tl/file/24147825195 [19 Jan. 2019].

Rodgers, D. T. 1998. *Atlantic crossings*: *Social politics in a progressive age.* Cambridge, MA and London, Harvard University Press and Belknap Press.

Sala-i-Martin, X. 1996. *A positive theory of social security*. Journal of Economic Growth, 1:277-304. Boston, June.

Samuelson, P. A. 1983. *Foundations of economic analysis*, Enlarged edition . Cambridge, MA, Harvard Economic Studies.

Schmidt, M. G. 2005. Sozialpolitik in Deutschland. Historische Entwicklung und internationaler Vergleich. Dritte Auflage. Wiesbaden, Germany, Verlag fuer Sozialwissenschaften [*Social policy in Germany*: *Historical evolvement and international comparison. Third edition*].

Scholz, W. 1992. Methodische, statistische und prognostische Aspekte der Rentendynamisierung in Ostdeutschland [*Methodological, statistical and prognostic aspects of the pension adjustments in East-Germany*]. in Verband Deutscher Rentenversicherungstraeger (ed.): *Deutsche Rentenversicherung*. Frankfurt am Main, Deutsche Rentenversicherung. pp. 550–569.

—. 2009. *The social budget of Germany*: *Keeping the welfare state in perspective.* Duesseldorf, Germany, Hans Boeckler Stiftung.

—. 2015. Financing social security out of contributions: About origins, present discussions and prospects of a success story. in *International Social Security Review*, Vol. 68, No. 4.

—. 2017. Global social security in political and economic contexts: Historical experiences and current trends. in *China International Social Security Review*, Vol. 1, No. 1, pp. 135–152.

—. Cichon, M. ; Hagemejer, K. 2000. *Social budgeting*. Geneva, ILO and ISSA.

Schroeder, W. 2019. *Historical experience of the interaction between economic* development and social security. Current core problems in reaction national and global developments. Search of solutions for the future. Background paper to the Chinese version of this report Beijing, CAOSS.

Social Security Administration (SSA). 2016. Preamble to *the* Social Security Act of 1935. SSA (US), Historical links. Available at: https://www. ssa. gov/history/35act. html#PREAMBLE [23 Nov. 2016].

State Council Information Office (SCIO). 2011. *China's rural poverty alleviation and development*, White Paper (Beijing) [in Chinese]. 中华人民共和国国务院新闻办公室．中国农村扶贫开发的新进展白皮书．2011-11-16.

State Council Poverty Alleviation Office (SCPAO). 2017. Leading CPC Group of Poverty Alleviation Office of the State Council: Five years of poverty alleviation and endeavour. in *People's Daily*, 17 Oct. [in Chinese]. 中共国务院扶贫办党组．脱贫攻坚砥砺奋进的五年［N］．人民日报, 2017-10-17.

Stephens, J. D. 2019. *The welfare state and economic development*: *The United States in comparative perspective*. Background paper to the Chinese version of this report. Beijing, CAOSS.

Supreme Court. 2002. *Compulsory Education Law of the People's Republic of China* (Beijing, Supreme People's Court of the People's Republic of China. Available at: http://en. chinacourt. org/public/detail. php? id=135 [Oct. 2018].

United Nations General Assembly. 2015. Transforming our world: The 2030 Agenda for Sustainable Development. Resolution adopted by the General Assembly on 25 Sep. (A/RES/70/1). Available at: http://www. un. org/ga/search/view_doc. asp?symbol=A/RES/70/1&Lang=E [19 Jan. 2019].

United Nations (UN); Statistical Office of the European Union (EUROSTAT); International Monetary Fund (IMF); World Bank; Organisation for Economic Co-operation and Development (OECD). 2009. *System of National Accounts 2008*, Luxembourg, New York, Paris, Washington, United Nations. Available at: http://unstats. un. org/unsd/nationalaccount/sna2008. asp [13 Dec. 2018].

United States Congress. 1776. *Declaration of Independence. The unanimous Declaration of the thirteen United States of America*. Philadelphia, PA, US Government. Available at: https://upload. wikimedia. org/wikipedia/commons/8/8f/

United_States_Declaration_of_Independence. jpg [Oct. 2018].

Vaughan-Whitehead, D. (ed.). 2015a. *The European social model in crisis. Is Europe losing its soul*? Geneva and Cheltenham, UK and Northampton, MA, ILO and Edward Elgar Publishing.

—. 2015b. The European social model in times of crisis: An overview. in D. Vaughan-Whitehead (ed.): *The European social model in crisis*: *Is Europe losing its soul*? Geneva, Cheltenham, UK and Northampton, MA, ILO and Edward Elgar Publishing. pp. 1 and 65.

Wagner, A. 1876. Grundlegung der Politischen Oekonomie. Teil I: Grundlagen der Volkswirtschaft. Leipzig, C. F. Winter. [*Political economy. Volume I*: *basic economics*.]. Available at: https://archive. org/details/grundlegungderp00wagngoog/page/n9 [19 Jan. 2019].

Wang, W. 2017. Thoughts on social security within the framework of the ideal of great harmony. in *Chinese Social Security Review*, Vol. 1, No. 1, pp. 114–124 [in Chinese, with abstract in English].

Wang, X. ; Williamson, J. B. ; Cansoy, M. 2016. Developing countries and systemic pension reforms: Reflections on some emerging problems. in *International Social Security Review*, Vol. 69, No. 2.

Weber, M. 1905. *The Protestant ethic and the spirit of capitalism* New York, Penguin Books, 2002.

—. 1991. *Die Wirtschaftsethik der Weltreligionen. Konfuzianismus und Taoismus. Schriften 1915–1920*. Tuebingen, MWS I/19 [*The religion of China*: *Confucianism and Taoism. Writings 1915–1920*].

Williamson, J. 2002. "What Washington means by policy reform", in J. Williamson (ed.): *Latin American adjustment*: *How much has happened*?. Washington, DC, Institute for International Economics.

World Bank. 1994. *Averting the old-age crisis*: *policies to protect the old and promote growth*. New York, Oxford University Press.

—. 2017. *Health expenditure*: *China*. Washington, DC. Available at: https://data. worldbank. org/indicator/SH. XPD. PCAP?locations=CN [Oct. 2018].

World Bank; International Labour Office (ILO). 2016. World Bank and ILO announce new push for universal social protection. Press release. Available at: http://www. worldbank. org/en/news/press-release/2016/09/21/world-bank-ilo-announce-new-push-for-universal-social-protection; http://www. ilo. org/global/topics/social-security/WCMS_378991/lang--en/index. htm [10 Oct. 2018].

World Health Organization (WHO). 1982. *The Vienna International Plan of Action on Ageing* (Geneva).

Xi, J. 2016. A new starting point for China's Development: A New Blueprint for Global Growth. Opening remarks, B20 Summit, Hangzhou, 3 Sep. G20 Information Centre. Available at: http://www. g20. utoronto. ca/2016/160903-xi. html [10 Oct. 2018].

—. 2017. Secure a decisive victory in building a moderately prosperous society in all respects and strive for the great success of socialism with Chinese characteristics for a new era: Xi Jinping's report to the 19th CPC National Congress. in *People's Daily*, 28 Oct. [in Chinese]. 习近平：决胜全面建成小康社会 夺取新时代中国特色社会主义伟大胜利——在中国共产党第十九次全国代表大会上的报告［N］．人民日报, 2017-10-28.

Zheng, G. 2002. *Globalization of labour and social security*. Beijing, China Labour and Social Security Publishing House [together with Zheng Yushuo, in Chinese]. 郑功成，郑宇硕．全球化下的劳工与社会保障［M］．北京：中国劳动社会保障出版社, 2002.

—. 2004a. From welfare education to mixed plural-education system China's educational benefits and human capital investment. in *Research on Education Tsinghua University*, Vol. 25, No. 5 [in Chinese]. 郑功成，从福利教育走向混合型的多元教育体系——中国的教育福利与人力资本投资，清华大学教育研究，第 25 卷第 5 期, 2004 年 10 月．

—. 2004b. From centralized government administration to self-governance by stakeholders: The future model of administration of social insurance in Chin. in *Journal of Renmin University of China*, Vol. 5 [in Chinese]. 郑功成，从政府集权管理到多元自治管理——中国社会保险组织管理模式的未来发展［J］．中国人民大学学报，2004（5）．

—. 2008a. *China's social security: A review of 30 years of progress* Beijing,

People's Publishing House [in Chinese]. 郑功成 . 中国社会保障 30 年［M］. 北京：人民出版社 , 2008.

——. 2008b. *China's social security reform and development strategy*: *Ideas, goals and action plan* (Beijing, People's Publishing House [in Chinese]. 郑功成 . 中国社会保障改革与发展战略 —— 理念、目标与行动方案［M］. 北京：人民出版社 , 2008.

——. 2011. The historical view and global vision of the development of contemporary social security. in *Economics Information*, No. 12 [in Chinese]. 郑功成 , 当代社会保障发展的历史观与全球视野［J］. 经济学动态 , 2011(12).

——. 2013. Top-level design to deepen the reform of the pension system in China. in *Teaching and Research*, Vol. 12 [in Chinese]. 郑功成 . 深化中国养老保险制度改革顶层设计［J］. 教学与研究 , 2013(12).

——. 2014. The historical logic of the evolution of China's social security. in *Journal of Renmin University of China*, Vol. 1 [in Chinese]. 郑功成 . 中国社会保障演进的历史逻辑［J］. 中国人民大学学报 , 2014(1).

——. 2016a. *China's social security development report 2016*. Beijing, People's Publishing House [in Chinese]. 郑功成 . 中国社会保障发展报告·2016［M］. 北京：人民出版社 , 2016.

——. 2016b. *Main report on the development of China's social security*: *A review of the 12th Five-Year Plan and outlook on the 13th Five-Year Plan*. Beijing, People's Publishing House [in Chinese]. 郑功成 , 中国社会保障发展总报告 ——"十二五"回顾与"十三五"展望［M］. 郑功成 . 中国社会保障发展报告·2016. 北京：人民出版社 , 2016.

——. 2016c. Properly handle the relationship between economic development and the improvement of people's livelihood. in *People's Daily*, 1 Nov. [in Chinese]. 郑功成 . 正确处理经济发展与改善民生的关系［N］. 人民日报 , 2016-11-01.

——. 2016d. The key points and paths of expanding middle income groups. in *Guangmin Daily*, 29 June [in Chinese]. 郑功成 . 扩大中等收入群体的要点与路径［N］. 光明日报 , 2016-06-29.

——. 2016e. A Chinese social security issue elicited by the story of a German farmer. in *Global Times*, 13 Sep. [in Chinese]. 郑功成 . 一个德国老农引出的中国社

保命题[N].环球时报,2016-9-13.

—. 2017a. A proper view on the relationship between social security and economic growth. in *Guangmin Daily*, 25 Mar. [in Chinese]. 郑功成. 正确看待社会保障与经济发展的关系[N].光明日报,2017-3-25.

—. 2017b. Great times call for great wisdom. in *Popular Tribune*, Vol. 1 [in Chinese]. 郑功成. 大时代需要大智慧[J].群言,2017(1).

—. 2017c. Social security and public governance: Historical logic and future options. in *Chinese Social Security Review*, Vol. 1, No. 1 [in Chinese; abstract in English]. 郑功成. 社会保障与国家治理的历史逻辑及未来选择[J].社会保障评论,2017(1).

—. 2017d. Make social security and employment mutually strengthening pillars to people's livelihood. in *Wenhui*, 16 Mar. [in Chinese]. 郑功成. 让社保与就业成为相互促进的民生支柱[N].文汇报,2017-3-16.

—. 2018a. China's Social Security and Economic Development: Retrospect and Prospect. in *Journal of Renmin University of China*, Vol. 1 [in Chinese]. 郑功成. 中国社会保障改革与经济发展:回顾与展望[J].中国人民大学学报,2018(1).

—. 2018b. Forty Years of Social Security in China (1978-2018): Institutional Transformation, Path Selection and Chinese Experience. in *Teaching and Research*, Vol. 11 [in Chinese]. 郑功成. 中国社会保障40年变迁(1978—2018)——制度转型、路径选择、中国经验[J].教学与研究,2018(11).

附录：国别报告

德国经济发展与社会保障体系建设：
历史经验与未来方案

［德］沃尔夫冈·施罗德　塞缪尔·格里夫 [1]

随着时间的推移，德国福利国家出现了一个社会保险制度和经济发展的复杂网络。这个网络适应着不断变化发展的条件，但是从未放弃依赖个人有偿就业的基本资金筹集模式。德国福利体制被认为是社会保障制度的先驱。19世纪末，德国就已建立了工伤、医疗和养老保险。除了社会保险之外，该体系还涵盖由联邦、州、市或者福利机构支持的社会权利和基础设施。德国福利国家由于其众多不同的元素，被称之为福利多元主义。以有偿就业为基础的社会保险制度的资金筹集，给德国企业带来财政压力，这可能会直接影响它们在经济全球化中的竞争力。

在德国福利多元体系里，通过各种各样的行动者、机构和工具为广泛的社会阶层实施社会融合和保障。一方面，德国福利国家的基本结构显示出非凡的连续性；另一方面，这个体系历经了频繁的修订和调整过程。自20世纪80年代以来，关于福利国家在财政和实质内容方面调整的争论从未停止。这导致了几乎所有社会保障领域发生类似变化，包括不同服务提供者之间更多的竞争以及更大程度地激活被保障的个体。

一、历史经验

1883—1889年，与其最强大的国际竞争对手相比，德国处于不发达的状态。然而，正

1　［作者简介］沃尔夫冈·施罗德（Wolfgang Schroeder），德国卡塞尔大学（University of Kassel）社会科学学院教授。主要研究方向：政治学。塞缪尔·格里夫（Samuel Greef）博士，德国卡塞尔大学（University of Kassel）社会科学学院博士。主要研究方向：福利政治学。

　　［译者简介］胡文秀，中国人民大学中国社会保障研究中心博士生，中国社会保障学会秘书处学术助理。

　　［翻译审校］华颖，中国社会科学院人口与劳动经济研究所助理研究员。

是在这些年，德国建立了半政府性质的社团组织，这些组织在工伤、医疗和养老方面提供保障。表1显示了德国是社会保障的先行者，像美国这样经济上更为发达的国家，是在后来才开始建立现代福利国家的。

表 1　　　　　　　　　　　　　社会保障制度建立年份及经济表现

国家	工伤保险	医疗保险	养老保险	失业保险	家庭支持	根据社会政策制定时间的排名	该国第一部社会法制定年份时的经济发展	德国第一部社会法制定年份时的经济发展（1883）
							人均国内生产总值（国际美元）	
比利时	1903	1894	1900	1920	1930	3	3 468	3 145
德国	1884	1883	1889	1927	1954	1	2 143	2 143
荷兰	1901	1931	1919	1916	1939	9	3 440	3 305
法国	1898	1928	1910	1905	1932	6	2 760	2 288
奥地利	1887	1888	1907	1920	1948	4	2 404	2 209
丹麦	1898	1892	1891	1907	1952	2	2 555	2 299
挪威	1895	1909	1936	1906	1946	8	1 872	1 588
瑞典	1901	1891	1913	1934	1947	7	2 105	1 937
英国	1897	1911	1908	1911	1945	5	4 264	3 643
美国	1930	1965	1935	1935	1935	12	6 213	3 008
加拿大*	1930	1977	1927	1940	1945*	13	4 847	2 090
日本	1911	1927	1941	1947	1971	11	837	1 356
意大利	1898	1943	1919	1919	1937	10	1 672	1 568
均值	1903	1918	1915	1922	1945	7	2 968	2 252

*注：家庭支持项下的家庭津贴是加拿大第一个全民项目。

资料来源：Manfred Gustav Schmidt. *Sozialpolitik in Deutschland : Historische Entwicklung und internationaler Vergleich*.VS Verlag für Sozialwissenschaften, 2005.

自19世纪80年代通过俾斯麦的社会法建立社会保障制度以来，出现了5种塑造德国社会保障模式结构的因素：（1）对生活水平的关注；（2）根据社会保险框架内标准的雇佣关系，基于有偿就业缴费的资金筹集；（3）以公共社会保险机构为主导的多元结构，公共社会保险机构是由雇主和工会代表组成的自治机构；（4）后续护理和现金转移支付优先于预防；（5）以有一位男性养家者的"正常家庭"作为典型情况。因为这些结构因素基本上在20世纪所有的历史动荡中幸存下来，所以艾斯平—安德森在他的类型学中将德国、法国和奥地利一起归为"保守的"福利国家。[1]根据艾斯平—安德森几十年来"保守"的文章，保守福利国家特点是改革的意愿和能力低，他将其描述为"冷冻的福利国家景观"。[2]然而，尽管存在这些结构和路径依赖的限制，从20世纪90年代开始，德国福利国家为了应对部分功能的失调亦进行了广泛的改动。

2014年[3]，社会保险制度支出约占所有社会支出的2/3。[4]由于大部分人口都从这些支出中受益，因而社会保障是福利国家最重要的组成部分。社会保障的收支随着政治决策、经济状况、劳动力市场及社会面临的挑战而发生变化。因此，社会支出比率及其随着时间的推移可以作为这些变化的指标。基于这个前提，我们可以看到自1945年以来，德国福利国家发展的五个阶段。

（重新）建立阶段（1945—1960年）。这一阶段是战争余波期和战后时期，采用了魏玛共和国时期（1919—1933年）和俾斯麦19世纪的福利国家来重建社会保障制度。虽然以强大的结构连续性为基础，但福利国家的重建是由于经济的快速崛起，连带着高增长率和低失业率所促成的。独立于政府和企业的自由集体谈判，是为（独立自主的）产业关系而设立的法定框架（*Tarifautonomie*, 1949）。这一阶段奠定的其他基础包括在公司管理中引入了劳工共同决定的制度（*Mitbestimmung*, 1951）、雇员参与和投诉的权利（*Betriebsverfassungsrechte*, 1952），以及1957年养老金改革。这些年社会支出比率低于20%。[5]

扩张阶段（1961—1975年）。这一阶段的特征是社会保障的不断扩张，直到社会支出比率达到26.3%。例如，旨在预防贫困的联邦社会救助法（*Bundessozialhilfegesetz*, 1961）引入了新的现代社会保障权利要求。最重要的是，社会福利的权利得到了扩展。

巩固阶段（1976—1989年）。第一次石油价格危机（1973年）终结了充分就业。在20世纪70年代初期，失业率为0.7%。但是在这一阶段末，失业率上升到了9%。因为这个发展变化，社会保险制度（由于与工资高度相关的筹资模式）收入下降而支出上涨（如失业

---

[1] Gøsta Esping-Andersen. *The Three Worlds of Welfare Capitalism*, Princeton. Princeton: Princeton University Press, 1990.

[2] Gøsta Esping-Andersen. *Welfare States in Transition: National Adaptations in Global Economies*.London: Sage, 1996.

[3] 2014年的社会预算支出为8 500亿欧元，其中5 100亿欧元拨给了社会保障体系。

[4] 社会支出比率表示为社会福利支出占GDP的百分比。

[5] Bundesministerium für Arbeit und Soziales (BMAS). *Sozialbudget* 2014.http://www.bmas.de/SharedDocs/Downloads/DE/PDF-Publikationen/a230-14-sozialbudget-2014. pdf?__blob=publicationFile&v=2. Berlin. Federal Ministry of Labour and Social Affairs, 2015.

福利）。随后的巩固阶段，福利在特定领域依然在延伸（如妇女养老金），但总体而言，"一些社会福利严重减少，一些福利被取消"。[1] 到这个巩固阶段结束时，社会支出比率已经降到了 24.6%。[2] 这个下降的部分原因是经济状况的改善和 GDP 的增长。

德国统一和引入新福利阶段（1990—2002 年）。这一阶段的特征是德国的统一和随后西德制度向东德的扩展。与此同时，被国家保险制度覆盖的工作在减少。尽管如此，强制的长期照护保险（*Pflegeversicherung*，1995）作为第五个险种加入社会保险体系中。然而，建立新保险的法律也引入了服务提供者之间的竞争和更多的财务约束。伴随着 2001 年的养老金改革（称为"李斯特"年金，以当时的劳工部长命名），引入了一项新的国家补贴的积累型养老金计划作为第三层次，亦即第一层次强制的现收现付制和第二层次企业养老金的补充。[3] 在这一阶段，社会支出比率从 25% 上升到 29.5%。

重建和巩固阶段（2003 年以来）。2004 年的劳动力市场改革——被称为"2010 议程"，通常被认为是德国福利国家的历史转折点——是非常具有争议的。一方面，它给劳动力市场带来了更多的灵活性，使失业率大幅下降；另一方面，就业的上涨是以增加不稳定的就业关系和扩大低工资部门为代价的（见图 2）。在社会保障的发展方面，这个改革促成了在新的社会保障法典（SGB Ⅱ）中的（联邦）失业救助（Arbeitslosenhilfe，SGB Ⅲ）和针对就业人员（*Sozialhilfe*，BSHG）的（基于市级的）社会救助的合并。这项举措使得此前严格分离的劳工政策和针对穷人的政策得到了整合和重新定义。

在金融和银行业危机的背景下（2008—2010 年），社会政策被认为是稳定经济的因素，像短期工作这样的工具被（重新）发现并且作为经济政策手段而被积极地运用[4]。在刺激需求的同时，就业保障型的劳动力市场政策能够搭建通往下一阶段经济增长的桥梁。这主要归功于社会伙伴（工会和雇主协会）和德国社团主义传统的复兴。[5]

养老金制度方面，法定退休年龄已由立法增加到 67 岁（从 2029 年起全面实施）。2008 年，

1　Manfred Gustav Schmidt.*Sozialpolitik in Deutschland: Historische Entwicklung und internationaler Vergleich*,Wiesbaden.VS Verlag für Sozialwissenschaften, 2005.

2　Bundesministerium für Arbeit und Soziales（BMAS）. *Sozialbudget 2014*. http://www.bmas.de/SharedDocs/Downloads/DE/PDF-Publikationen/a230-14-sozialbudget-2014.pdf?__blob=publicationFile&v=2.Berlin.Federal Ministry of Labour and Social Affairs, 2015.

3　Manfred Gustav Schmidt.*Der deutsche Sozialstaat: Geschichte und Gegenwart*, Munich, C.H. Beck,2012.

4　Wolfgang Schroeder.*Vorbeugende Sozialpolitik weiter entwickeln*, Weiterdenken Diskussionspapiere des Landesbüros NRW.Bonn.Friedrich-Ebert-Stiftung, 2014（1）.

5　Wolfgang Schroeder.*Eigene Stärke braucht Kooperationspartner*.Mitbestimmung, 2013（4）.

社会支出比率稳定在27%左右。从2009年开始,"李斯特"个人账户(积累型)养老金制度已被纳入社会支出比率计算当中;不过,社会支出比率大致保持在29%左右。[1] 我们在表2中总结了这些发展变化。我们可以看到,自20世纪70年代中期开始,经过多年的扩张,社会支出比率从2000年开始一直保持稳定。

表2　　　　　　　社会支出比率、社会保障缴费及人均国民总收入

年份	社会支出比率（占GDP百分比）	雇员社会保障缴费率（占总工资百分比）					人均国民总收入（欧元）
		所有缴费	法定养老保险制度	医疗保险	失业保险	强制长期照护保险	
1960	18.3	12.2	7	4.2	1		2 792
1970	20.2	13.25	8.5	4.1	0.65		5 945
1980	25.7	16.2	9	5.7	1.5		12 808
1990	24.1	17.8	9.35	6.3	2.15		20 658
2000	28.8	20.5	9.65	6.75	3.25	0.85	25 983
2010	29.8	20.23	9.95	7.9	1.4	0.975	32 137
2016	29.4	19.33	9.35	7.3	1.5	1.175	37 130*

*注：按2015年数据计算的估算。

资料来源：Manfred Gustav Schmidt, *Sozialpolitik in Deutschland*: *Historische Entwicklung und internationaler Vergleich*, Wiesbaden, VS Verlag für Sozialwissenschaften, 2005; Sozialpolitik-aktuell, *Sozialleistungsquote 1960–2015*, http://www. sozialpolitik-aktuell. de/tl_files/sozialpolitik-aktuell/_Politikfelder/Finanzierung/Datensammlung/PDF-Dateien/abbII1a. pdf, Duisburg, Institut Arbeit und Qualifikation der Universität Duisburg-Essen, 2016.

二、社会保障制度当前存在的主要问题

近年来,围绕一些主要问题和挑战存在争论,而这些问题和挑战需要德国福利国家做出新的结构性回应。

（一）人口变化和社会老龄化

自20世纪80年代以来,人口变化一直是激烈讨论的主题,这是因为德国是全球出生率最低的国家之一。总和生育率从1960年的2.4%下降到2015年的1.5%,低于替代水平。

---

[1] Bundesministerium für Arbeit und Soziales（BMAS）. *Sozialbudget 2014*.Berlin.Federal Ministry of Labour and Social Affairs, 2015.

只有在过去几年，生育率才略微上升（如从 2006 年的 1.33% 上升到 2015 年 1.5%）。[1] 与此同时，越来越多的老年人和越来越少的年轻人共存，因此老年抚养比（养老金领取者和劳动人口之间的比率）正在上升。表 3 清楚地显示这一发展趋势，包括按年龄划分的人口分组、中位数年龄及老年抚养比的变化，到 2060 年的预测趋势表明社会老龄化是一个持续进程。

表 3　德国人口发展情况（1950—2060 年）

		1950	1960	1970	1980	1990	2000	2010	2020	2030	2040	2050	2060
年龄分组（百分比）	65+	10	12	14	16	15	17	21	23	28	31	32	33
	20~64	60	60	56	58	63	62	61	60	55	53	52	51
	<20	30	28	30	27	22	21	18	18	17	17	16	16
中位数年龄		34.9	34.2	33.8	36.2	37.1	39.6	44.1	46.3	47.6	49.8	50.9	50.5
老年抚养比		16	19	25	27	24	27	34	38	50	58	60	65

注：从 2020 年开始，预测值基于以下情景：出生率为每位妇女生育 1.4 个孩子；在 2060 年出生的儿童预期寿命为男孩 84.8 岁、女孩 88.8 岁；从 2021 年起，每年的净移民数为 10 万人。

资料来源：Statistisches Bundesamt（2016）.

如果再考虑到出生时的预期寿命，我们就会发现，不仅老年人比例在增长，而且预期寿命在过去几十年也一直在提高，将来也会是这个趋势。这些发展变化对养老金筹资、医疗卫生体系和劳动力市场产生重大的影响。移民在中期内并不能够扭转这个变化趋势。此外，社会的老龄化以及医疗技术的进步显然会给福利国家的筹资带来新的挑战。

（二）劳动社会的结构变革

劳动世界的结构变革呈现几个紧密交织的维度。一方面，伴随着向以服务业为基础的社会转型，就业正由制造业转向服务业；另一方面，这会导致总增加值的变化（见图 1）。

1　Eurostat. *Total fertility rate*.1960–2013.http://ec.europa.eu/eurostat/statistics-explained/images/6/62/Total_fertility_rate % 2C_1960 % E2 % 80 % 932013_ % 28live_births_per_woman % 29_YB15-de.png.Luxembourg, 2014; Statistisches Bundesamt, *13. Koordinierte Bevölkerungsvorausberechnung für Deutschland*, https://www.destatis.de/bevoelkerungspyramide/.Wiesbaden, Federal Statistical Office, 2016.

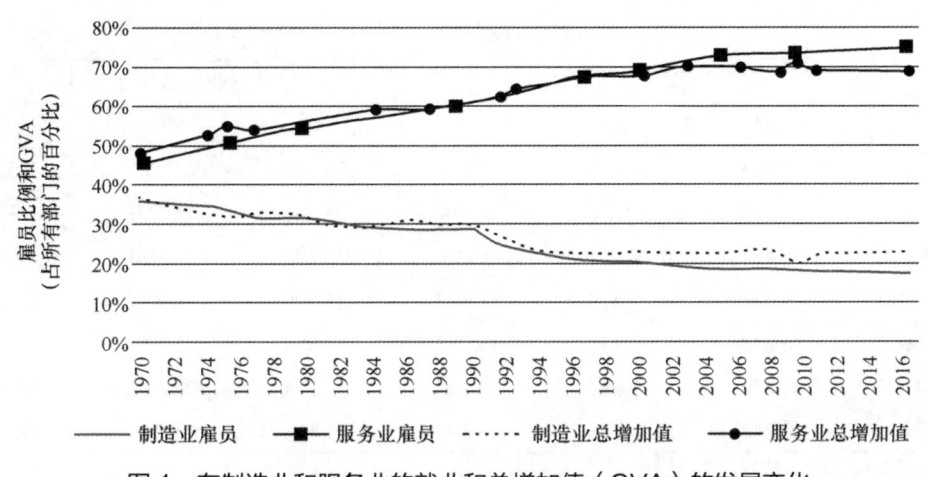

图1 在制造业和服务业的就业和总增加值(GVA)的发展变化

资料来源:Statistisches Bundesamt(2016、2017).

这个描述的变化导致了所谓的非典型就业的增长和低工资部门的增长(见图2)。

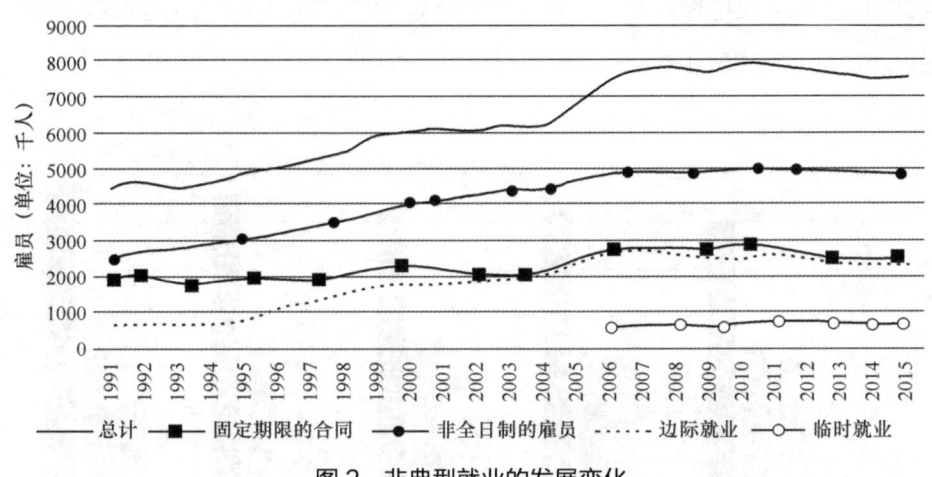

图2 非典型就业的发展变化

资料来源:Statistisches Bundesamt(2016).

此外,在1960—2015年女性就业人数增长了一倍多(见表4)。这表明劳动力潜力和为社会保险制度缴费的人数有所增加,但也意味着在经济动荡时期对福利国家会有更高的要求。

由于女性就业人数的增加,福利国家需要更加完善的基础设施,这意味着需要更多的儿童保育中心、更多的全日制学校等。总的来说,近年来,劳动力市场变得更为灵活多样、受限制更少,但也不那么安全且更加不平等。

表 4　　就业和就业人数的发展情况（1960—2015 年）

年份	有偿就业（千人）			就业人数（千人）		
	总计	男性	女性	总计	男性	女性
1960	25 203	15 710	9 494	25 344	15 773	9 573
1970	25 320	5 066	9 254	25 480	16 150	9 329
1980	26 428	16 516	9 913	27 194	16 896	10 299
1990	29 033	17 410	11 623	31 000	18 350	12 650
2000	36 232	20 439	15 793	39 950	22 433	17 517
2010	38 270	20 637	17 633	41 214	22 333	18 882
2015	39 242	20 845	18 398	41 183	21 964	19 219

资料来源：Statistisches Bundesamt（2016）.

（三）不平等

按照收入分配和不平等程度的国际标准，长期以来，德国被视为平等主义的国家。但是，自 20 世纪 90 年代中期以来，不平等现象开始增加。基尼系数是社会不平等的一个指标。图 3 用基尼系数比较了根据艾斯平—安德森的划分，分别代表着不同福利国家和社会保障类型的三个国家。[1]

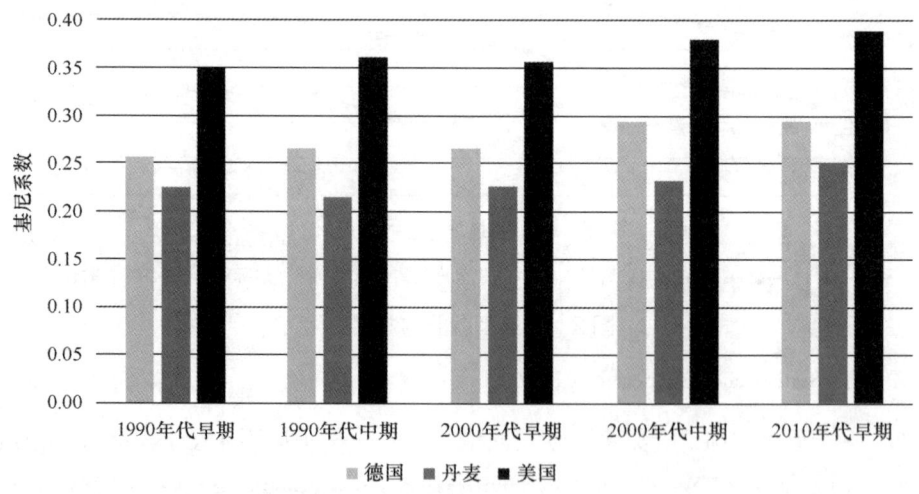

图 3　基尼系数的发展情况

资料来源：Sachverständigenrat zur Beurteilung der gesamtwirtschaftlichen Entwicklung. *Mehr vertrauen in Marktprozesse: Jahresgutachten 2014/15*。http://www. sachverstaendigenrat-wirtschaft. de/fileadmin/dateiablage/gutachten/jg201415/JG14_ges. pdf, Wie sbaden, German Council of Economic Experts, 2015.

1　Gøsta Esping-Andersen.*The Three Worlds of Welfare Capitalism*.Princeton.Princeton University Press, 1990.

北欧福利模式（如丹麦）展现了比自由主义模式（如美国）更低的基尼系数。德国代表着保守型福利体制，处在中间位置，然而在过去的几十年里德国出现了日益加剧的不平等。造成这种现象的原因是单身家庭和单亲家庭的增加，以及工会力量的减弱和集体谈判覆盖面的下降。这些发展变化导致了收入差距越来越大，且高收入者收入不断上涨。与此同时，低工资服务部门的强力扩张导致了收入贫困的加剧。2008年，OECD指出，德国有19%的家庭没有任何的就业收入，这个比例在所有OECD国家中最高。自20世纪90年代以来，贫困风险率一直在15.7%左右。

从财富分配来看，我们可以看到在最高收入10%的家庭中实质性的财富积累（见表5）。近年来，这个趋势更加明显。相反，收入处于下半部分的家庭的净财富实际上已经缩减了。

表5　　　　　　　根据 EVS 和 SOEP 的财富分配情况

	占全部净财富百分比（%）						
	根据 EVS（收入和消费的抽样调查）				根据 SOEP（德国社会经济调查）		
年份	1998	2003	2008	2013	2002	2007	2012
最高10%的家庭	45.1	49.4	52.9	51.9	55.7	56.7	53.4
低于50%的家庭	2.9	2.6	1.2	1.0	1.4	1.5	1.5

资料来源：Bundesministerium für Arbeit und Soziales（BMAS）. Armuts-*und Reichtumsbericht:Verm-ögensverteilung.*
http://www.armuts-und-reichtumsbericht.de/DE/Indikatoren/Gesellschaft/Vermoegensverteilung/vermoegensverteilung.html.Berlin.Federal Ministry of Labour and Social Affairs, 2016.

长期以来，德国有一个相对平等的工资模式，但是在过去几十年里，我们观察到对应不同资格等级的工资差距日益扩大。具有高级或者中等资格等级的雇员从上涨的工资中获益最多（见图4），而没有资格等级的雇员则面临重大的损失。

年轻人受到工资下降的严重影响。对于学者来说尤其如此。在2002—2010年间，30岁的全职受雇佣的学者面临着13个百分点的收入损失（见图4）；而在同一时期，40岁的学者收入上升了1个百分点。

总体而言，低工资部门的不断扩张和实际工资水平的下降对社会保障支出和收入方面都构成压力，因而对福利国家产生直接的影响。一方面，社会保障主要取决于依赖收入水平的缴费。另一方面，低工资部门给许多劳动者和未来领取养老金人员带来新的贫困风险，因而需要更多的社会支出。例如，其中一个后果就是老年贫困的风险越来越高。

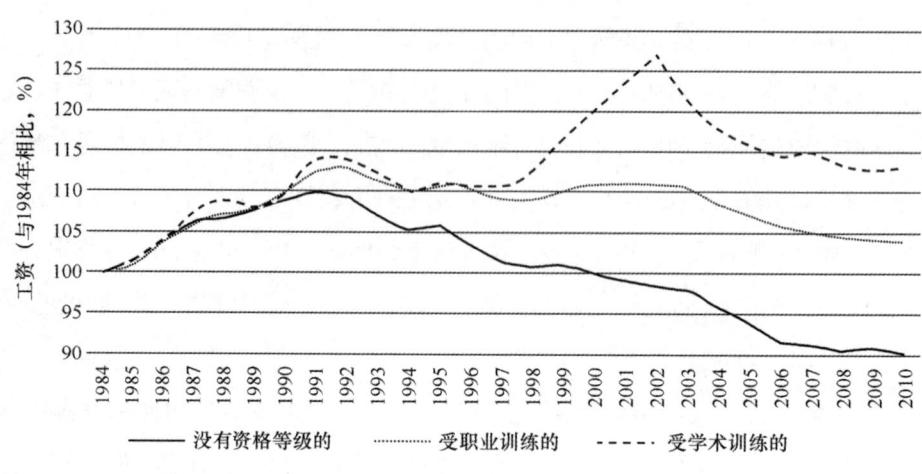

图 4　根据资格等级的工资发展情况

注：从 1984—2010 年，根据资格等级的实际每日总薪酬指数；以 1984 年 =100 计算，30 岁的男性全职雇员。约阿希姆·穆勒（Joachim Möller）基于对数工资函数的计量经济学假设进行计算。描述性变量为常量、6 个虚拟变量，即资格等级、年龄、年龄的平方及所有交互项；数据库：S-IAB。

资料来源：Ulrich Walwei. *Geringqualifizierte: Beschäftigungssituation und Möglichkeiten der Aufwärtsmobilität. lecture,* 21 September 2014; Joachim Möller. Die Entwicklung der Lohnunterschiede nach Qualifikation und anderen Merkmalen. Paper Presented at the Forum Lohnentwicklung GIB NRW, 25 April, Düsseldorf.http://www.landderfairenarbeit. nrw. de/files/mais/content/Galerien/Forum% 20Lohnentwicklung/Duesseldorf_VortragMoeller.pd，2013.

（四）激活和减少开支

很长一段时间，德国曾被认为"欧元区病人"。[1] 之后，德国成为了欧洲的先驱。"从欧元区病人到经济巨星"。[2] 正如"德国劳动力市场奇迹"[3] 所指出的那样，劳动力市场的发展在这一变化中起了非常显著的作用。在很大程度上，这是哈茨改革的一个效果：2003—2005 年的劳动力市场改革决定性地促进了劳动力市场的改善。按照定义，衡量失业率下降就是一个很好的例子（见图 5）。即使是在 2009 年以后的经济危机期间，失业率也仅仅是在短期内上升，且上升幅度不大。

在劳动力市场改革过程中，重新融入有偿就业的工具（如公共就业计划和长期培训）以及与激活劳动力市场政策相关的支付也受到严密的审查（见图 6）。在国际比较中，关

---

[1] *The Economist.* The Sick Man of The Euro.http://www.economist.com/node/209559, 1999, 3 June.

[2] Christian Dustmann, et al. "From Sick Man of Europe to Economic Superstar: Germany's resurgent economy." *Journal of Economic Perspectives,* 2014, 28（1）.

[3] Ulrich Walwei.*Curing the Sick Man: The German Labour Market on the Way to Good Health?* IAB Report, http://doku.iab.de/aktuell/2014/aktueller_bericht_1402.pdf, 2014, 15 April.

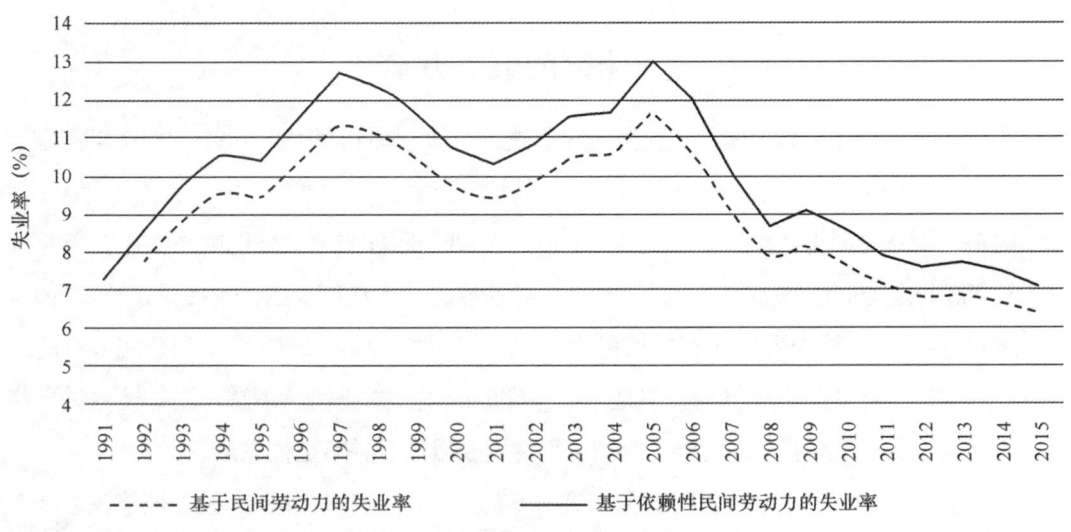

图 5　失业率的发展情况

资料来源：Bundesagentur für Arbeit.Arbeitslosigkeit im Zeitverlauf：Monats-/Jahreszahlen（ab 1950）.Nuremberg，Federal Employment Agency，2016.

于激活劳动力市场政策的支出，德国或多或少处在较低水平。整体而言，哈茨改革的目标——从消极被动的劳动力市场政策转向积极的劳动力市场政策——并没有实现。激活劳动力政策支出的减少，与低技能岗位向高技能岗位的流动性下降有关。

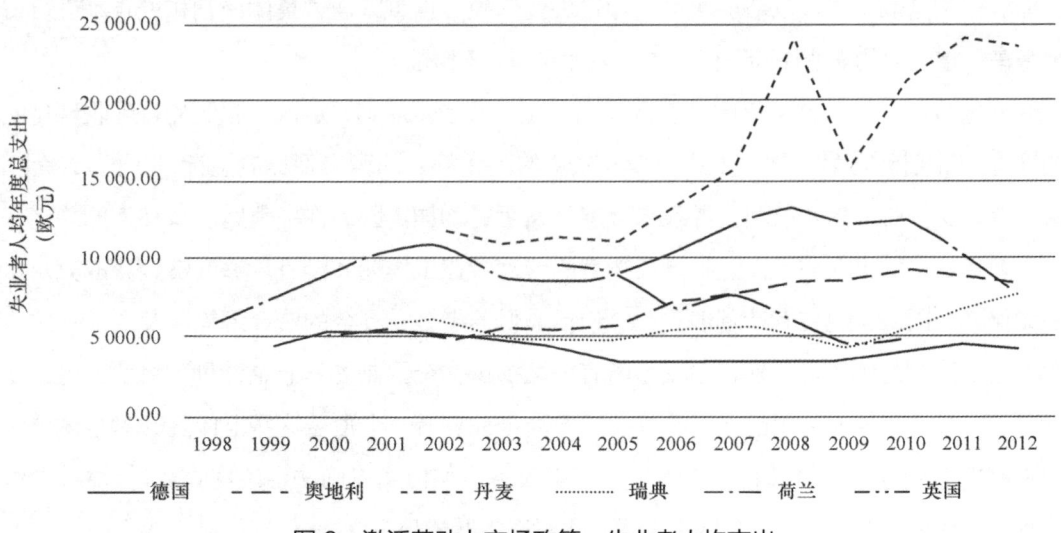

图 6　激活劳动力市场政策：失业者人均支出

资料来源：Wolfgang Schroeder, Sascha Kristin Futh, Bastian Jantz. *Wandel durch Annäherung? Reformaktivitäten europäischer Wohlfahrtsstaaten im Vergleich*. Berlin. Friedrich-Ebert-Stiftung, 2015.

三、未来的解决方案

为了应对人口变化、个体化以及全球化的挑战，德国福利国家在 1995—2007 年实施了许多影响深远的改革。在这些改革之后，德国的福利国家状况如何？

财务。财务方面得到整固。这是因为国民在养老、医疗方面更多的财务支出，以及国家在养老和失业方面削减福利。此外，社会保险制度在更大程度上由税收提供资金。并且，自从 2005 年开始，德国经济一直保持稳步增长——除了 2008—2010 年受到金融危机的影响——这创造了更多的工作机会。但是，已经完成的整固措施仍然不够。还需要更进一步的改革，因为从长期来看，最重要的改革项目在资金筹集上并不是很充足。

医疗。多年来，一个全民医疗保险计划（*Bürgeroder Volksversicherung*）被建议为现有的法定和私人医疗保险双重体系的替代方案。全体国民和各种收入水平的公民都应该强制参加统一的法定医疗保险计划，而私人医疗保险将只是作为一个补充。这意味着法定医疗保险收入将会更高，初级卫生保健的服务水平将更高。另外的优点包括能更容易和更高质量地获得保险福利以及更高的效率，从而节约费用。

劳动力市场。目前，失业保险并没有包括足够的预防元素。可以引入获得进一步培训和发展的权利，在失业保险内形成一个附加层次。这意味着在资格培训阶段可以不用工作且能够得到全额工资。该新层次可以通过失业保险，也可以通过集体谈判和税收来进行资金筹集。重组后的失业保险可以在失业发生前进行预防。

养老金。2001—2004 年的养老金改革把焦点放在了从第一层次（强制的、现收现付制的养老金计划）向第三层次（基于个人账户的国家补贴的积累型养老金计划）的转移上。人们有理由担心，这个改革会导致未来老年贫困的增加。因为许多家庭没有私人的养老保障。尤其是，低收入的无技能和低技能型的劳动者在工作期间没有足够的资金获取充足水平的保障。因此，现在有计划建立一个包括最低养老金、混合的资金筹集以及更加关注企业养老金计划的体系。此外，建议为所有公民提供一个强制的养老金计划。目前，有许多针对公务员（*Beamte*）和自雇者的单独的养老金计划。一个覆盖这些群体且针对全体公民的强制性养老金计划将具有一些优势。如果公务员和自雇者向法定的现收现付计划缴费，将有助于在短期内止住养老金水平下降和缴费率上升的势头。[1]

---

[1] 然而，长期来看，这些额外的缴费者也要求（高的）养老金（公务员通常有着特别高的预期寿命），因而不能解决由人口因素导致的养老金筹资问题。只要德国力求为所有的公民提供体面的生活，那么在未来就不得不向老年一代分配更多的资源。在这方面，德国与世界上大多数国家处境相同。

预防性的社会政策。这个概念包含了以尽早、集中的和以服务为导向的方式向人们投入时间和精力。[1] 它旨在赋予个人自主实现社会参与的权利。为此必须建立新的福利机构、工具、途径和获取支持。在个人的一生中应该尽可能早地赋权,从而打破早期童年阶段根深蒂固不平等的起始局面。通过这种方式,可以使个人尽可能平等地获取机会。预防性的社会政策从有助于提高现有机构运行效率的质变开始。为了有效地以目标为导向的工作,这需要高质量的社会服务。

福利国家对不同经济状况的调整是处于不断变化的状态。过去,方向发生了变化,但范式并没有改变。未来的改革必须要以符合社会和经济条件的方式进行,要考虑到社会凝聚力、社会保护、社会参与和个人发展。到目前为止,在很长一段时间里,德国企业的竞争力没有受到福利国家重建和稳定的社会支出比率的影响。然而,因为未来更进一步的调整措施可能面临不一样的情况,所以今后采取措施必须要考虑到福利国家和经济的网络关系。

1　Wolfgang Schroeder. "Arbeitsgesellschaft und vorsorgender Sozialstaat." in *Arbeit ist keine Ware*, Freiburg. Herder Verlag,2009:181–197.

英国社会保障与经济关系的演变：
从福利国家到竞争国家？

[英] 约翰·哈德森[1]

一、历史经验

（一）从福利领头羊到福利落后者

艾斯平－安德森（1990，1999）[2]在其对资本主义国家福利制度有划时代意义的比较研究中，将英国描述为他所划分的自由主义福利体制的国家。在该体制下，劳动力的去商品化程度微弱（即社会权利相对适度），试图通过社会干预再分配的意图最小化（因为经过家计调查的干预措施以最贫困群体为目标），而且经济宽裕的人群有选择由私营部门提供服务和保险的强烈动机（因为福利国家的首要目标是充当安全网）。

除英国的全民健康服务体系之外，这是对当今英国社会保障[3]体系主体的合理特征描述。尽管总体而言，英国的福利供给比美国的更为宽泛，但仍然明显低于主要的西欧和北欧邻国。事实上，如图1所示，过去几十年来，英国公共和强制性私人支出的总体水平（根据经合组织的社会支出数据库提取的数据）保持在经合组织国家的平均水平，即通常情况下占GDP之比约比美国高四到五个百分点，但比丹麦，法国和德国低六到七个百分点。

尽管英国的社会干预规模相对适中，但是其在第二次世界大战后福利国家的全面发展往往被视为英国的历史关键时刻。事实上，2011年"英国社会态度调查"报告指出，51%

---

1 [作者简介] 约翰·哈德森（John Hudson），英国约克大学教授（University of York, United Kingdom）。主要研究方向：福利国家。

[译者简介] 华颖，中国社会科学院人口与劳动经济研究所助理研究员。

2 Esping-Andersen, G. The Three Worlds of Welfare Capitalism. Cambridge: Polity Press, 1990.

Esping-Andersen, G. The Social Foundations of Post-Industrial Economies. Oxford: Oxford University Press, 1999.

3 在英国，"社会保障"一词通常只用来指收入维持计划，主要是现金转移支付；医疗保健在本文中也有所提及，但本文中"社会保障"一词是指收入维持计划，特别是在用于分析支出数据时。

的受访者认为"创建福利国家是英国最值得骄傲的成就之一",而对这一说法持异议者仅占15%(Clery et al,2013)。[1]这或许反映了这样的事实:在第二次世界大战暗无天日之中,英国政府提出在战争结束后社会权利将得到根本性的延伸,因此社会政策在为国家提供未来积极愿景方面发挥了至关重要的作用。事实上,正是在战争期间,英国才开始使用"福利国家"这一说法。1941年,约克大主教威廉·坦普尔(William Temple)用"福利国家"来对比希特勒在德国所追求的"战争国家"。[2]

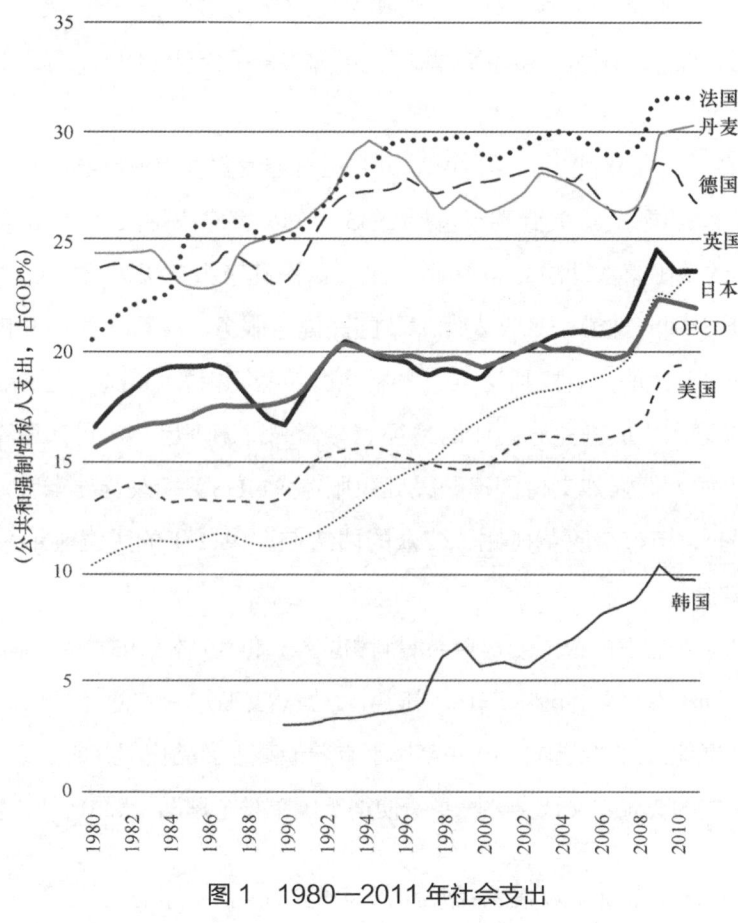

图1　1980—2011年社会支出

数据来源:OECD SOCX Database

1　Clery, E., Lee, L and Kunz, S., Public Attitudes to Poverty and Welfare, (1983–2011): Analysis using British Social Attitudes data. London: National Centre for Social Research, 2013.

2　Lunt, N., From welfare state to social development: winning the war of words in New Zealand. Social Policy and Society.2008, 7(4): 405–418; Timmins, N.The Five Giants: a *Biography of the Welfare State*. London: Fontana Press, 1995.

首次提出"福利国家"的时机并非偶然：1942年出版的著名的《贝弗里奇报告：社会保险和相关服务》勾勒了一个激进和受欢迎的计划，以解决贝弗里奇认为的五大主要社会弊病："贫困（收入不足）""懒惰"（失业）、"肮脏"（住房条件差）、"无知"（教育不足或质量低）和"疾病"。贝弗里奇报告为解决这些社会弊病提供了一个全面的愿景，并且在社会保障方面，描绘了一个"抵制收入能力中断和被破坏的社会保险计划"[1]，该计划基于统一缴费的缴费原则，在相关风险事件发生时，缴费者获得定额的待遇给付作为回报。贝弗里奇主张这一点，部分原因是他通过对当时制度的反思得出这样的结论："英国人所渴望的是以缴费获取待遇，而非从国家获得免费津贴"，还因为"民众对任何形式家计调查的普遍反对"[2]。

正是在1945—1951年战后工党政府受贝弗里奇启发实施大量社会改革后，很多人认为英国成为了"福利国家"。关键改革包括1945年的《家庭津贴法》、1946年的《国家保险法》、1948年的《国家救助法》和1946年的《国民健康服务法》。这些改革大大增加了国家对社会事务干预的规模——收入保障、国民健康服务、教育、住房和就业服务都在扩展——同时强调公民的社会权利[3]。与这些社会改革密切相关的是对凯恩斯主义经济管理策略的支持，以之作为促进充分就业的途径。尽管民意调查显示，贝弗里奇的建议中有一些更受支持 [如人们强烈支持创建国民健康服务（NHS）和改善养老金，而对寡妇津贴的支持却较弱]，但整个改革抓住了公众的情绪点。1942年的民调显示88％的受访者赞成该计划的实施[4]。

尽管受贝弗里奇启发的模式无疑存在漏洞和弱点，但1945—1951年实施的社会改革使英国成为彼时福利资本主义的国际典范。事实上，虽然艾斯平－安德森[5]把英国归为自由主义的福利体制，但他认为"英国在1950年属于有着最高去商品化程度的国家行列：战后引入的贝弗里奇模式的普遍主义社会公民身份使得英国享誉全球"。然而，从比较视角看，英

1　Beveridge, W. H. B. Social *insurance and allied services*. HMSO: London, 1942.

2　Beveridge, W. H. B. Social *insurance and allied services*. HMSO: London, 1942.

3　Dwyer, P.,Understanding Social Citizenship: Issues for Policy and Practice.（Second ed.）（Understanding welfare: Social Issues, policy and practice series）. Bristol: The Policy Press, 2010；

Hudson, J. and Lowe, S. *Understanding the Policy* Process. Bristol: The Policy Press, 2009.

4　Hudson, J., Lunt, N., Hamilton, C., Mackinder, S., Meers, J.and Swift, C.Exploring Public Attitudes to Welfare over the Longue Durée: Re-examination of Survey Evidence from Beveridge.Beatlemania, Blair and Beyond. Social Policy & Administration,2016（50）: 691–711.

5　Esping-Andersen, G. *The Three Worlds of Welfare Capitalism*. Cambridge: Polity Press, 1990.

国似乎从 20 世纪 50 年代初暂时的福利国家领头羊角色转换到随后几十年中落后的地位。这是为何又是如何发生的呢？

（二）战后福利共识的淡化

虽然人们普遍认为"战后福利共识"推动了英国福利国家在 20 世纪五六十年代和 70 年代大部分时期的稳定增长，但这种共识的深度存疑。毫无疑问，当时大体上积极的政治气氛促使福利国家总体规模稳步增长。如图 2 所示，在这几十年里，社会保障和国民健康支出扩张了（虽然国民健康服务领域的支出起步蹒跚）。这两个领域的支出占 GDP 之比分别为 1950 年的 4.8% 和 3.3%，1960 年的 5.6% 和 3.1%，1970 年的 7.3% 和 3.5%，1980 年的 9.0% 和 4.4%。

图 2　1948—2013 年公共支出的发展

数据来源：Institute for Fiscal Studies and Office of Health Economics

然而，即使支出稳步增长，关于成本的争议仍然是政治辩论的焦点，筹资问题经常产生的妥协结果冲淡了贝弗里奇模式。最著名的例子是，1951 年引入的对一些牙科和光学服务的收费，导致了曾担任卫生部长并被广泛认为是 NHS 建筑师的奈·贝文（Nye Bevan）辞职。当时看并不明显，但回顾起来显而易见的是，尽管贝弗里奇的愿景是建立以保险为基础的社会保障制度，即缴费型的保险而非家计调查型的待遇给付占主导地位，但历届政府都发觉使用成本更低的定向福利给付（targeted benefits）的诱惑难以抵抗。如图 3 所示，基于缴费的待遇给付占社会保障待遇给付支出之比在 20 世纪 60 年代中期达到 72% 的峰值，20 世纪 80 年代迅速下降；与此同时，自 1982 年以来，基于家计调查的福利已经占到社会保障支出总额的 1/4 ~ 1/3。

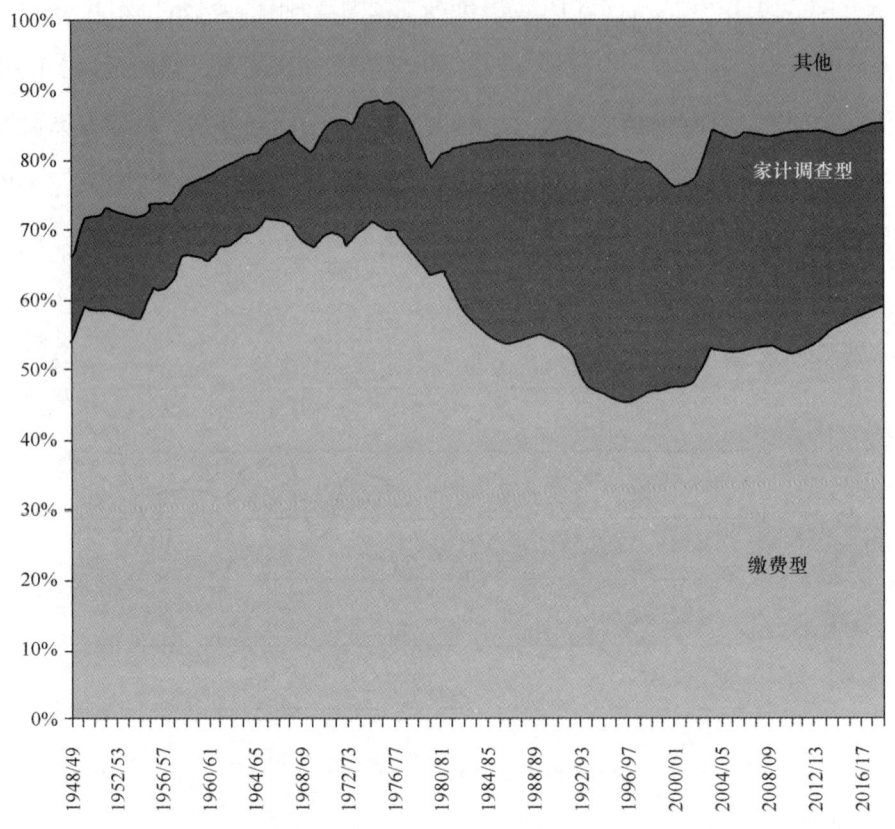

图 3　按财务机制划分的社会保障待遇给付份额

数据来源：HM Treasury

第二次世界大战后的数十年，贝弗里奇设想的保险原则未得以完全制度化的原因有很多。首先，尽快实现社会改善的压力使得 1945—1951 年的战后政府在国民保险基金（National Insurance Fund）尚未成熟之前就开始支付养老金，这意味着该制度一直运行在现收现付而不是精算的基础之上。其他相关原因包括：待遇给付设定在贝弗里奇所建议的充足水平以下，导致通过额外的经家计调查的收入以补充最贫穷人群收入的压力增大。更为关键的是，一旦确定了相对较低的福利水平，再将其提高到适当水平的政治和财政成本是具有挑战性的，尤其是因为花费更少的定向补充福利总是可作为替代性的备选项。到 20 世纪 50 年代中期，政府接受了一项独立评估的结论，即将养老金提高到贝弗里奇设想的水平将会给公共财政造成过重成本。这反过来又为更多地通过基于家计调查的收入补贴或基于特定意外事件的待遇给付，来解决最贫困者的收入不安全问题奠定了基础。[1]

这导致的结果之一就是英国的社会保险原则比其他欧洲国家弱。尽管雇员、雇主和个体经营者的国民保险缴费（National Insurance Contributions，NICs）除了一部分纳入国民健康服务（NHS）之外，均被纳入国民保险基金且只能被政府用于缴费型的福利支出，然而国民保险缴费与政府用于缴费型的福利支出之间并无真正的精算关系。因此，许多专家认同米尔利斯（Mirrlees）等[2]的观点：英国的"国民保险不是真正的社会保险计划，只是一项收入税。且现行制度使得政治家们大玩国民保险缴费的把戏，但又不承认这些缴费本质上是劳动收入征税的一部分"。这个制度运作缺乏透明度，很可能使得政府更容易削弱破坏保险原则，而非出现另外一种情况，即国民保险基金本身的财务可行性从来就不是真正的政治辩论议题。

在个人层面保险原则也是微弱的。虽然每个公民的缴费记录作为获得一些主要福利的条件从而是重要的，但贝弗里奇模式中的统一给付额意味着个人缴费与福利给付之间的关联微弱。举例来说，求职者津贴（失业津贴的主体）既有基于缴费的，也有基于家计调查的变体，但两者的基本给付率没有差别。从长远来看，这很可能使英国的制度容易受到削减，因为低福利水平意味着较之福利待遇收入是相关型的情况，对经济状况较好的公民吸引力较弱。[3]

然而，非缴费给付的增长，一定程度上也是应对贝弗里奇模式某些缺陷而施策之结果。也许其中最值得注意的是，缴费型模式对女性固有的歧视，它是基于男性养家模式设计的，即"围绕着有能力在工作中建立长期的、不间断的缴费记录的典型全职（男性）劳动者而建立"。[4]对养老金权利的影响尤为深刻，女性由于照护活动和/或在劳动力市场中处于更为边缘的地位，其缴费记录中断的倾向高，只有少数人有资格

1　Social Security Committee.Fifth report: The Contributory Principle, 7 June 2000 HC 56-I 1999-2000, 2000.

2　Mirrlees, J., Adam, S., Besley, T., Blundell, R., Bond, S., Chote, R., Gammie, M., Johnson, P., Myles, G. and Poterba, J.*Tax by Design*. Oxford: Oxford University Press, 2011.

3　Hudson, J, Hwang, G-J & Kuhner, S.Between Ideas, Institutions and Interests: Analysing Third Way Welfare Reform Programmes in Germany and the United Kingdom.*Journal of Social Policy*, 2008，37（2）：207-230.

4　Colwill, J.Beveridge, women and the welfare state, *Critical Social Policy*, 1994（14）：53-78.

领取全额养老金。[1] 20 世纪 60 年代贫困的"再发现"以及竞选中出现的新"贫困游说团体"也为采取新的干预措施制造了压力，挑战了福利国家已经消除贫困和需求的这一臆想[2]。

围绕这些问题的政治因素逐渐削弱了保险原则，最终由 20 世纪 70 年代发生的数次短期经济危机终结了福利国家共识。20 世纪 60 年代，相对滞后的经济增长开始成为关注焦点，1973 年石油危机、上涨的通货膨胀压力、攀升的失业率以及日趋紧张的劳资关系之综合效应，最终酿成了重大经济危机。在 20 世纪 70 年代中期，英国出现了严重的通货膨胀问题，1975 年零售物价指数（RPI）达到了 24% 的高峰，更关键是，这同时伴随着失业率的迅速攀升（图 4）。此段"滞胀"时期削弱了对已构成战后福利共识核心的凯恩斯主义经济框架的信心，引发了精英经济政策界的深入争论。[3]

但是，1976 年推动一个新范式的势头加速了，当时国际收支问题导致英国向国际货币基金组织（IMF）寻求紧急支持，给予的支持部分基于废除战后共识的某些要素。随着公共支出的减少、通货膨胀率的上升，政府、企业主和工会之间的关系趋紧，特别是在 1978—1979 年发生的劳资冲突（所谓"情绪不满的冬天"）即是紧张关系的明显升级。在一些人看来，这是整个战后贝弗里奇－凯恩斯模式遭遇系统性危机的证据，其中包括保守党党首玛格丽特·撒切尔（Margaret Thatcher），她在 1979 年当选首相常被视作是战后福利共识明确的结点。[4]

（三）撒切尔的政府职能缩减

撒切尔社会和经济改革议程的核心是承诺"缩减政府职能"。她发起了一场激进的、由自由市场驱动的"新自由主义"改革，旨在扭转之前一个世纪尤其是 1945—1975 年逐渐走向集体主义的方向。改革包括高调的私有化举措（含一些主要的国有产业和大部分社会住房存量）、一些公共服务的市场化，以及推动降低税率和公共支出的整体水平[5]。

---

1 Thane, P.The 'scandal' of women's pensions in Britain: how did it come about? *History and Policy*, March 2006.

2 Walker, A., Gordon, D., Levitas, R., Phillmore, P., Phillipson, C., Salomon, M. and Yeates, N.（Eds）.*The Peter Townsend Reader*. Bristol: The Policy Press, 2010.

3 Pemberton, HR & Oliver, MJ.Learning and change in 20th-century British economic policy' Governance.2014, 17（3）: 415－441, 2014.

4 Hudson, J., and Lowe, S. *Understanding the Policy Process*. Bristol: The Policy Press, 2009.

5 Kavanagh, Dennis. Thatcherism and British politics: the end of consensus? Oxford Oxford University Press,1990.

附录：国别报告　187

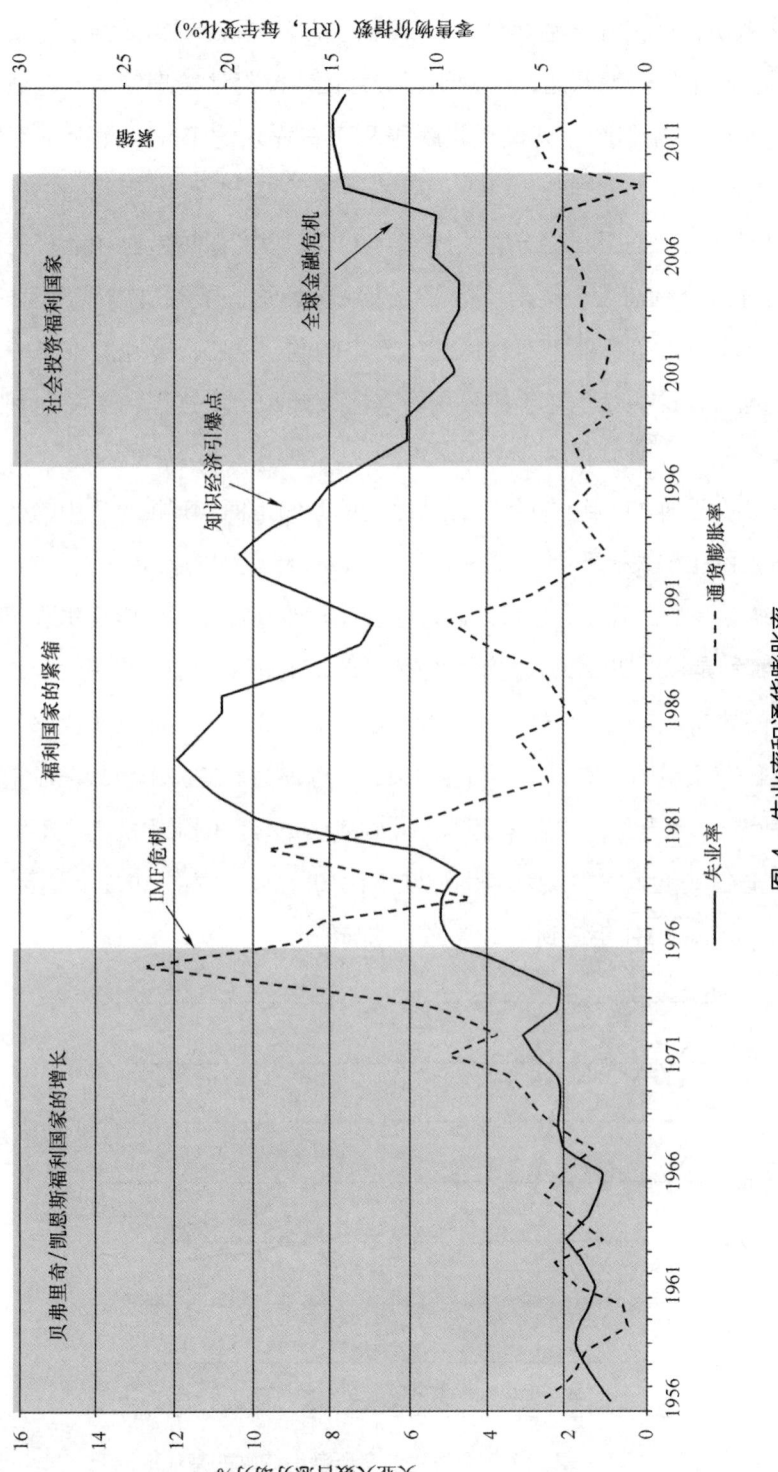

图 4　失业率和通货膨胀率

数据来源：OECD

看似可以这么说，此前几十年集体主义策略的某些方面造成了英国经济表现欠佳。例如，从20世纪60年代后期开始，一种明显的社团主义经济管理策略已经被试用，政府希望利用收入和价格控制作为管理通货膨胀和工资需求的工具。然而，不断加剧的劳资冲突一再破坏这些过程，同时工资上涨可能导致了20世纪70年代的物价上涨。将失败的私营公司国有化也是历届政府的关键部署工具，政府保护就业和经济关键部门的愿望促使其收购一部分制造业。但是，批评人士认为，这些干预措施尽管保护了就业，但几乎没有解决汽车制造等行业相对较低的生产率问题，这些行业越发难与（联邦）德国和日本的对手竞争，这些竞争对手的公司看来在设计和生产过程中更好地利用了最新技术。

然而，无论导致英国20世纪70年代经济困境的原因是何，其相对适中的社会保障或健康支出似乎不太可能是关键致因。如图1所示，1980年英国的社会支出占GDP之比几乎低于（联邦）德国8个百分点。尽管如此，社会保障改革却成了由撒切尔改革驱动的计划的主要部分，特别是针对失业工人的福利成为了改革的靶子。图5使用比较福利权益数据库（CWED）的数据，展现了个体失业者的津贴相对于先前平均收入替代率的下滑，从1979年撒切尔上任首相伊始时的50%下降到1983年的25%。这些削减却是在撒切尔夫人任下早期的经济问题不断升级、失业率迅速上升到战后史无前例水平的情况下发生的。如图4所示，失业率在20世纪50年代中期到70年代初为2%左右，1979年达到了约5%，到1982年超过了10%，1984年达到了12%左右的峰值。

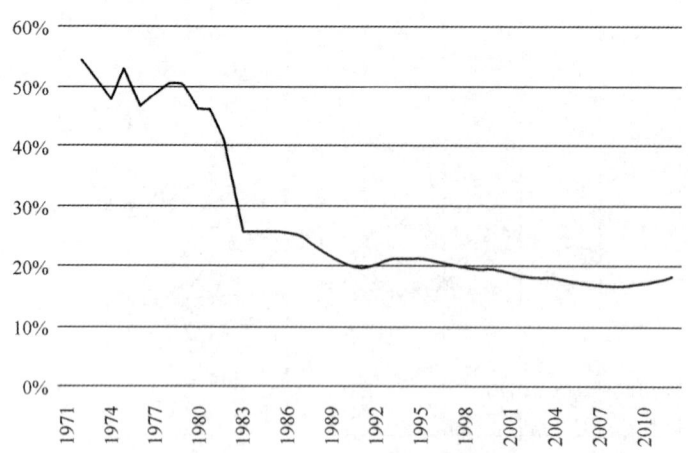

图5　1971—2011年个体失业者所获得津贴的替代率

数据来源：Comparative Welfare Entitlements Dataset (CWED)

与此同时，撒切尔在任期间引入了大幅减税（见表 1），所得税的基本税率和较高税率，以及公司税的标准税率大幅下降。总的来说，这些政策变化标志着社会和经济政策的重点明显转移，撒切尔在其任期头几年经济问题加剧时拒绝改变这一进程同样也是标志。[1] 撒切尔以其"绝不妥协"而闻名，作为政治家，她坚定地一心贯彻自认为对增加英国的经济财富有必要的激进方案。如图 4 所示，她执政的 11 年（1979—1990 年），以及随后她的保守党同僚约翰·梅杰（John Major）担任首相的几年中（1990—1997 年），英国的失业率居高不下。事实上，从撒切尔任首相的 1979 年起，这个数字从来没有回降到当时 4.7％的水平。尽管通货膨胀率确实急剧下降，但在 1990 年前后飙升，随后几年再次下降。鉴于撒切尔最初捍卫货币主义的经济学而不是凯恩斯主义的策略，20 世纪 90 年代早期显而易见的是，撒切尔和梅杰政府均将稳定价格优先于保护就业。事实上，1991 年，财政大臣（财政部长）诺曼·拉蒙特（Norman Lamont）承认了这一点，他向议会宣布"失业率上升和经济衰退是我们为拉低通货膨胀而不得不付出的代价，这个代价非常值得。"见 1991 年 5 月 16 日下议院辩论。

表 1　　　　　　　　　　　　　税率的变化

	收入税		公司税（标准税率）
	基本税率	较高税率	
1975/1976	35％	40％~75％，83％	52％
1980/1981	30％	40％~60％	52％
1985/1986	30％	40％~60％	40％
1990/1991	25％	40％	34％

数据来源：Institute for Fiscal Studies

这样一种说法在战后福利共识时代不可想象。这一状态正如有学者[2]所描述的，英国从"福利国家"转变为不再重视社会权利的"竞争国家"，提高全球市场经济竞争力成为政府的首要任务，这使得经济目标居于优先地位。该进程是否提升了英国的经济竞争力是有争议的。若做一全面评估，会非常明显看出不同部门和地区间有得有失。图 6 详细展示了英国经济整体增长水平，并辅以经合组织国家的估计增长值用于

---

[1] Kavanagh, Dennis. *Thatcherism and British politics: the end of consensus*? Oxford:Oxford University Press, 1990.

[2] Evans M, Cerny P., Globalisation and social policy[J]. Developments in British social policy, 2003（2）：19-40.

比较。在 1979—1997 年保守党政府执政期间,和 1971 年以来的大部分时期一样,英国的经济增长率非常紧密地贴合了经合组织的总体趋势,但有几点明显的差异。第一个是 20 世纪 80 年代初由于嵌入新的经济策略,英国经济衰退更为严重。随后,在 20 世纪 80 年代中期起的几年中,英国经济增长相对强劲,其经济表现领先于主要邻邦,以致有人赞颂英国的经济"奇迹"。然而这个时期是短暂的,90 年代初增速放缓至接近于零,1991 年出现经济萎缩,而英国大部分邻国(以及经合组织作为整体)继续保持稳定增长。

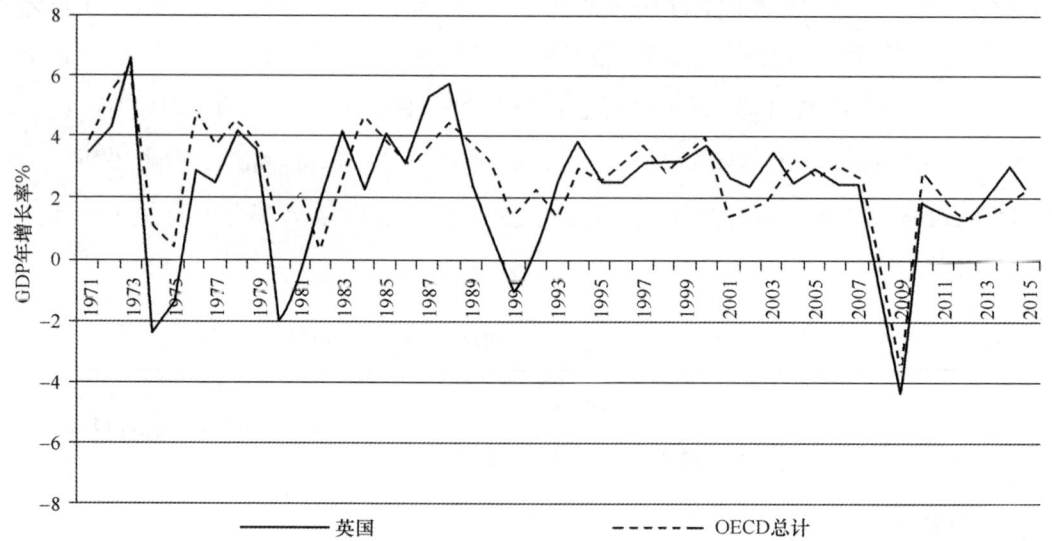

图 6　经济年增长率

数据来源:OECD

这样的经济成绩在增长和通货膨胀的表现上喜忧参半,而在失业率方面表现无疑不佳。高企的失业率、跟跄的增长及下降的收入和公司税率对其他领域都有重大影响。如图 2 所示,虽然削减了待遇的慷慨程度,但社会保障总体支出水平继续上升,这尤其是因为失业率的居高不下。这些变化反过来又大大削弱了 20 世纪 80 年代后期税收和福利制度的再分配效应,导致 1984—1990 年的不平等以国际标准来看异常高的速度增长(见图 7),并且大体上延续至今。[1]

---

[1] Atkinson, A. B. *Inequality: what can be done*? London: Harvard University Press, 2015.

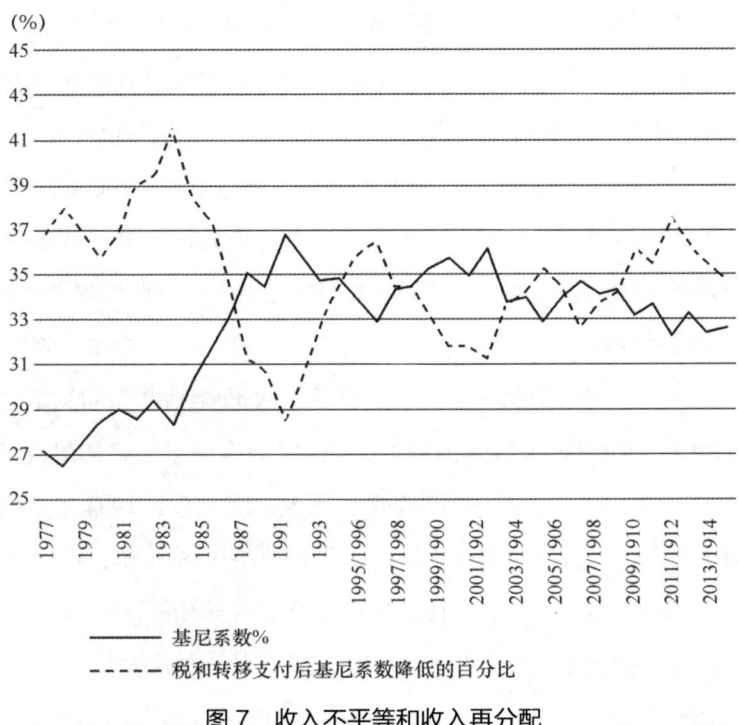

图 7 收入不平等和收入再分配

数据来源：Office for National Statistics

除了这些明显的变化之外，同期还有详细的体制结构改革，这主要是 1986 年《社会保障法》的结果。囿于篇幅在此无法进行详细讨论，有学者[1]认为，关键的目标（对工作代际的福利）是简化制度和改善工作激励。在制度简化方面，收入支持取代了补充福利。补充福利涉及各种特定具体情况的待遇给付，而收入支持的组合方式较少，包括申领者有特定需求时可能获得更少的附加和/或酌情支付的待遇。在工作激励方面，1986 年的法案旨在通过家庭补贴（Family Credit）体系扩大和延伸工作相关的福利，确保有子女的低收入家庭的有偿工作。约翰·梅杰延续了这些改革，加强了积极寻找工作以领取失业津贴的要求，其标志是 1996 年以求职者津贴取代失业津贴，对这项福利的新命名本身即表明了政府的意图。[2]

虽然在此我们的核心关注点是撒切尔改革的经济和分配效应，但必须强调的是，撒切尔的方案在瓦解战后福利共识方面是有争议的。尽管表面看，其政治上是成功的——撒切

---

[1] Bennett, F. and Millar, J.Social Security: reforms and challenges' in Millar, J. (Ed) Understanding Social Security (2nd Edition). Bristol: The Policy Press, 2009.

[2] Wright, S.Welfare to Work' in Millar, J. (Ed) *Understanding Social Security* (2nd Edition). Bristol: The Policy Press, 2009.

尔率领其政党在三次大选中取得了决定性的胜利，并且她是英国一百年以来任期最长的首相，但英国政体的制度性构成夸大了公众对撒切尔支持的程度。尽管她在1979年、1983年和1987年大选中获得了下议院的多数席位，但其政党从未在这些选举中占有超过44%的公众投票。[1] 此外，公众态度调查显示，处于撒切尔社会政策议程核心的对社会保障供给的削减鲜有公众支持。现实情况恰好相反，公众态度的历史分析表明，对这些改革的对抗性反应，促成了公众在20世纪80年代对扩张而非紧缩社会保障待遇的强烈支持[2]。许多工会也积极反对撒切尔改革议程，撒切尔1979年当选后，由于劳资纠纷减少的工作日数急剧上升：仅1979年9月一个月内就达1 170万天，是第二次世界大战后的峰值。撒切尔上任的第一年，12个月累积工作日损失数是自从1931年12月有记录以来的最高值，约为3 220万。[3] 1984—1985年发生的煤矿工人分裂性争端，很大程度上造成1984年大约2 710万天的工作日损失。为了表明这些数值的相对水平，来看21世纪的头十年，平均每年损失的工作日仅为69.2万。简言之，20世纪80年代是英国社会、政治和经济动荡的十年。无论对经济的影响如何，撒切尔的改革在随后的几十年中给英国的社会和政治生活蒙上了阴影。正如帕金斯[4]在撒切尔夫人的讣告中所言，撒切尔是"20世纪下半叶英国政治最具统治力和最分裂的力量……她对经济、社会和英国全球地位的认识继续塑造着英国政治"。

（四）布莱尔与社会投资福利国家的兴起

尽管工党最初反对撒切尔的政策转变，并在1983年大选竞选活动中提出宣言主张加强国家干预，但在尼尔·金诺克（Neil Kinnock，1983—1992年）的领导下，他们开始转向接受这种新范式的部分要素。1994年托尼·布莱尔当选党首加速了这一进程，1997年他成为英国首相时，推行"第三条道路"的计划，以寻求贝弗里奇和撒切尔策略的调和。[5]

---

1 Audickas, L., Hawkins, O. and Cracknell, R., *UK Election Statistics*: 1918–2017. House of Commons Library Briefing Paper CBO7529,2017.

2 Hudson, J., Lunt, N., Hamilton, C., Mackinder, S., Meers, J., and Swift, C.Exploring Public Attitudes to Welfare over the Longue Durée: Re-examination of Survey Evidence from Beveridge, Beatlemania, Blair and Beyond. Social Policy & Administration, 2016（50）：691-711.

3 Office for National Statistics. *UK labour market statistical bulletin: August* 2017. London: ONS, 2017.

4 Perkins, A. Margaret Thatcher obituary. *The Guardian*, 8 April 2013.

5 Lister, R. Work for those who can, security for those who cannot, A Third Way in social security reform or fractured citizenship, in R. Edwards and Glover（eds）, *Risk & Citizenship: Key issues in welfare*, London: Routledge, 2001.

Powell, M., 'New Labour and social justice', in M. Powell（ed）Evaluating New Labour's Welfare Reform, Bristol: Policy Press, 2002.

就协调社会和经济政策目标而言，这种新策略的关键并不是重返凯恩斯主义的需求管理方法，而是转向供给侧的策略，其重点在于提高人力资本，而非控制货币供应和通货膨胀。布莱尔"第三条道路"的设计师之一安东尼·吉登斯（Anthony Giddens）阐述了这样的愿景："宏观经济政策的目标是保持低通货膨胀率，限制政府借贷，采取积极的供给侧措施来促进增长和高就业"。[1] 同样，在社会政策方面，他主张"尽可能投资于人力资本……是福利改革的主旨，也是政府应对知识经济而必须采取的行动……"。当被问及政府的三大优先事项时，布莱尔附和了吉登斯的表述，他的回答"教育、教育和教育"广为人知。在与时任德国总理施罗德的一份长篇联合声明中，他们阐述了共同的"第三条道路"愿景，认为"当务之急在于人力和社会资本投资"。[2]

这一社会投资议程对社会保障政策有重大影响。积极劳动力市场政策的发展得到高度重视，包括一系列新政：提供创新的服务和求职者与个人顾问间一对一的讨论。针对不同群体推出了五项不同的新政策：青年新政、25岁以上人群新政、50岁以上人群新政、单亲父母新政、残障人群新政。这些新政中的一些项目是强制性的，如若被视作不参加则面临处罚（如对于25岁以下青少年失业达六个月者）；对一些群体的自愿性条款在接下来历次改革中也将逐步转变为强制性的。

在这些制度安排下，个体求职者应该接受积极寻找工作的义务，社会保障待遇给付的条件性稳步增强，处罚也变得越发普遍。[3] 重要的机构改革标志着重点的转变，包括新建名为"就业中心+"的公共就业服务机构。[4] 它是由隶属于不同政府部门的两个大型行政机构进行重大改组而形成的：即教育和就业部的就业服务机构、社会保障部的福利局。这只是广泛的工作重组的一部分，其他还包括社会保障部更名为工作和养老金部。这些变化标志着基调的改变，布莱尔经常引用的目标是"为能工作者提供工作，为不能者提供保障"。[5] 同时，这些变化也体现了通过将求职支持和待遇给付功能相结合来改善对求职者的支持，

---

1 Giddens A. *The Third Way and its Critics*. Cambridge: Polity Press, 2000.

2 Blair, T. and Schroeder, G. Europe: The Third Way/Die Neue Mitte. London: Labour Party, 1999.

3 Dwyer, P. Creeping Conditionality in the UK: From Welfare Rights to Conditional Entitlements? *Canadian Journal of Sociology*, 2004, 29（2）256–287.

4 Stafford, B. and Kellard, K., 'Reforming the public sector: personalised activation services in the UK' in R van Berkel and B Valkenburg（Eds）*Making it Personal: Individualising activation services in the EU*. Bristol: The Policy Press, 2007.

5 Blair, T. Foreword in Department for Social Security, *New Ambition for Our Country: A new contract for welfare*, London: Stationary Office, 1998.

以提供更加"用户友好化"和个性化的一站式服务的意图。

以上与"让工作有收益"的尝试相结合。英国首次引入了全国最低工资,在职收入补足的使用显著增加(主要通过税收抵免的形式)以提高低收入人群的收入,特别是聚焦于有子女家庭的税收抵免。这主要是因为布莱尔政府做出了减少并最终消除儿童相对贫困的激进承诺。图8凸显了在托尼·布莱尔(1997—2007年)和戈登·布朗(2007—2010年)领导下的工党政府对支出的大幅度重塑,税收抵免支出占全部社会保障和税收抵免支出的份额由1996/1997年度的6%上升至2009/2010年度的15%。

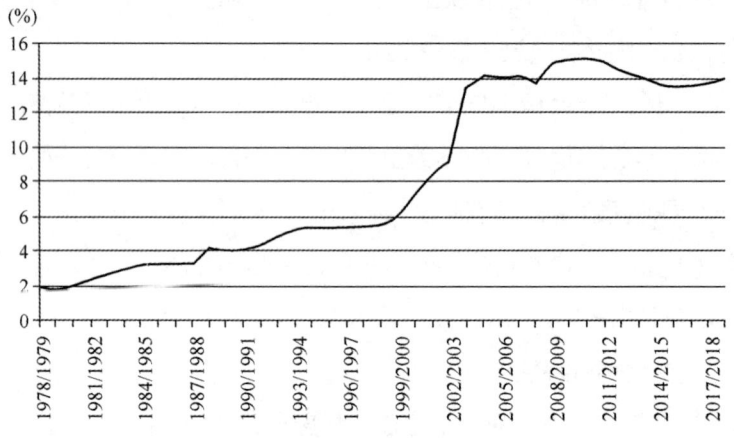

图8 税收抵免支出占全部社会保障和税收抵免支出的份额

数据来源:HM Treasury

布莱尔/布朗议程包括投资方面真正的内容真正的投资维度;那些年社会支出上升的速度与比经合组织更快(见图1),特别是NHS支出明显增加(见图2),而经合组织划分为家庭政策的支出(主要是对有子女家庭的现金转移支付)从1997年占GDP的2.1%上升到2010年的4.0%。布莱尔时期(1997—2007年)的经济表现强劲,英国的增长超越了许多邻国,以经合组织标准衡量依然强劲(见图6)。失业率下降至自20世纪70年代以来未曾见的5%的低值,大大低于欧元区的水平;同时通胀率自20世纪60年代以来首次较长时期保持在3%左右(见图4)。不平等没有实质性的减少,但是不平等的增长至少止住了(见图7),以儿童为重点的干预的确也显著减少了儿童相对贫困(定义为生活在低于中位等值收入60%的家庭)。据经合组织的报告,儿童贫困率从1995年的30%下降到2007年的23%,2010年在戈登·布朗任下进一步下降到19.4%,这是一个与国际趋势背道而驰的显著成就。

尽管英国取得了令人瞩目的成就,但在推行的社会投资策略上仍然存在着薄弱环节。布莱尔时期长期的经济增长掩盖了许多（尽管不是全部的）不足。然而在布朗于2007年出任首相后不久，全球金融危机爆发。由于英国经济的核心是庞大的银行业，英国受到了极大冲击，经济事实上因之而深度萎缩（见图6）。布朗在曾经担任英国财政大臣的十年间，凭借其谨慎的公共财政管理策略赢得了良好的声誉，英国在经合组织中的公共债务水平最低。然而，布朗的三年首相生涯中，全球金融危机却使其大部分工作功亏一篑：英国一些主要银行需要数十亿英镑的紧急援助，税收收入由于经济迅速萎缩而下降，公共财政出现严重赤字，这些使得政府债务总额占GDP之比从2007年的47%跃升至2011年的91%（见图9）。

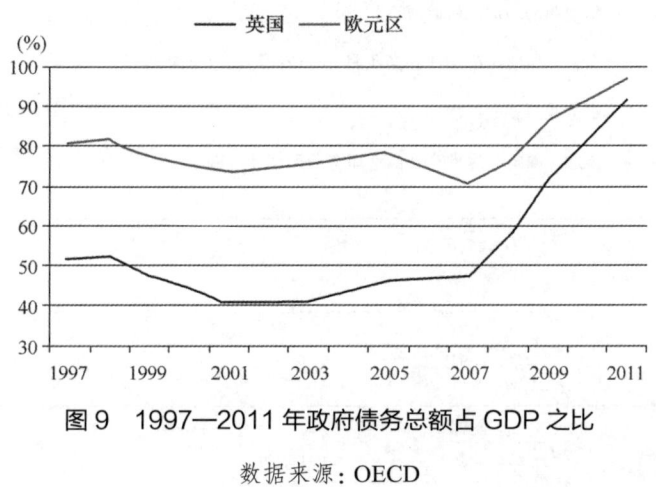

图9　1997—2011年政府债务总额占GDP之比

数据来源：OECD

公众对于经济和公共财政状况日益加重的担忧是工党在2010年大选中失势的关键。戴维·卡梅伦（David Cameron）接替布朗担任首相，在2010—2015年执掌保守党—自民党联合政府。2015年开始，保守党单独组建多数党政府，但卡梅伦在脱欧公投后辞职，特蕾莎·梅（Theresa May）2016年7月继任成为首相。特蕾莎·梅在2017年6月召集新一届大选，希望保守党以此获得更多议会席位以推行脱欧的愿景，但是选民给出了一个不明朗的结果，使其成为下议院最大党党首，但保守党未能取得议会多数席位。目前的政策环境很大程度上反映了卡梅伦政府对布莱尔—布朗投资模式和全球金融危机的反应，以及特蕾莎·梅正在努力应对的英国脱欧危机。现在是该调整方向的时候了。

二、当代发展

图4和图6的数据表明，自21世纪70年代以来，屡次深度衰退已经影响了英国经济，但在这些数字背后是经济从工业模式转向后工业模式的痛苦转型。在撒切尔任下，国家从

关键的经济部门迅速撤退，加速了去工业化的进程。在一些地区，如造船、煤矿和钢铁等曾在 20 世纪 70 年代基本上属于国有且曾作为当地劳动力市场和经济基石的主要行业，遭遇急速收缩，在许多情况下甚至行业已消亡。[1]

如图 10 所示，在国家层面，就业岗位逐渐从制造业转移至金融、保险、房地产和商业服务行业。1997 年布莱尔担任首相时，后者的增加值份额已经多出 5 个百分点，就业份额高出 2 个百分点；至布莱尔 2007 年卸任，两者在增加值和就业份额上的差距已经分别扩大至 25 个百分点和 11 个百分点。

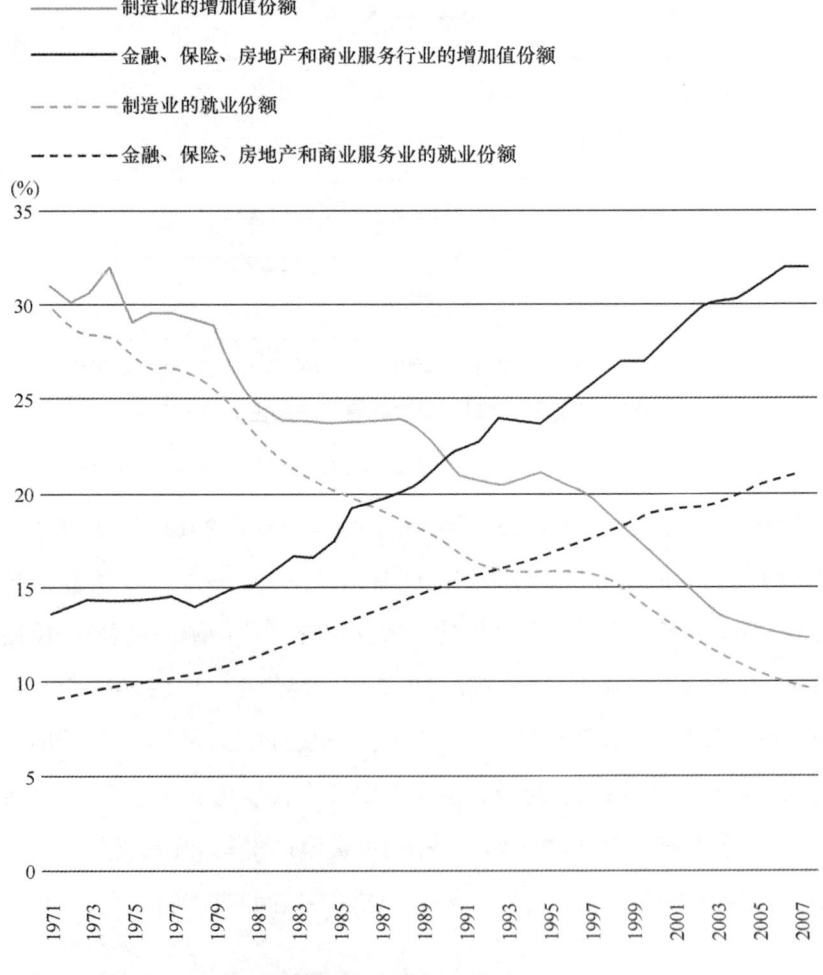

图 10　后工业经济的崛起

数据来源：OECD STAN Database

1　Hudson, J.and Lowe, S., *Understanding the Policy* Process. Bristol: The Policy Press, 2009.

随着在此期间伦敦牢固地成为引领全球的金融中心,这种发展策略似乎有不少值得称道之处。然而,英国由于其庞大的金融服务部门而在全球金融危机受到相对沉重的打击;此外,新经济也带来了其他重大的社会挑战。至关重要的是,此前几十年社会政策和经济政策趋势的相互强化往往是带来这些当代挑战的根源。

劳动力市场日益两极分化是许多后工业经济体中普遍存在的现象,但却给英国带来了特殊的挑战,因为如学者[1]所描述的"糟糕而可爱的工作"之间的差距日增。这一进程也存在空间分布,一些曾经是工业中心的地区提供了相对而言少的"可爱的"工作。布莱尔-布朗政府承认日益灵活和积极的劳动力市场政策可能会扩大低工资部门数量,增加的税收抵免待遇给付试图解决这个问题。但有人认为,这种做法成为了向低工资雇主提供实质补贴;有学者[2]已经把它标榜为"企业福利"的一方面。此外,尽管在职福利有所增加,许多就业家庭的收入仍然很低,几乎 2/3 的贫困儿童生活在就业家庭中[3]。

很明显,英国的社会保障体系需要特别着力解决主要与劳动力市场两极分化相关联的深层次不平等现象。联合国儿童基金会[4]最近的一份聚焦于有子女家庭不平等状况的报告提供了相关佐证。它计算了处于收入分布底部(第 10 个百分位)和中位数之间的儿童的相对收入差距。结果显示,2013 年,欧洲国家中只有保加利亚在收入转移前比英国有更大的差距。然而,英国非常注重对有子女家庭的收入进行补贴,这使得英国在收入转移之后的差距居于最小之行列。这凸显了尽管英国的新经济在创造相对较高就业水平方面取得了成功,但为了支持这种低工资就业的增长,来自社会保障的大量工资补贴必不可少。

住房市场为我们提供了经济和社会政策变化相互增强的又一佐证。撒切尔的旗舰政策之一就是所谓的"购买权",即允许地方政府社会住房的租户以低于市场的价格购买房屋。这一政策,加之对新建社会住房建设的资金支持有限,导致社会租赁部门规模大幅缩小。在英格兰,1981 年社会住房的住户占家庭总数的 32%,到 1991 年这一比例下降至 23%,

---

[1] Goos, M and Manning, A. Lousy and Lovely Jobs: the Rising Polarization of Work in Britain. *The Review of Economics and Statistics*, 2007(89). 118-133, 2007.

[2] Farnsworth, K. *The British Corporate Welfare State: Public policies for private companies*. Sheffield: Sheffield Political Economy Research Institute, 2015.

[3] Belfield, C., Cribb, J., Hood, A. and Joyce, R. *Living Standards, Poverty and Inequality in the UK*: 2015. London: Institute for Fiscal Studies, 2015.

[4] Unicef, *Fairness for Children: A league table of inequality in child well-being in rich countries*(Innocenti Report Card 13). Unicef Innocenti Research Centre: Florence, 2016.

而在 2007 年全球金融危机初期仅为 18％。[1] 住房金融化除了推动金融服务业的发展、增加住房成本并使英国经济容易受到房地产泡沫的影响之外，还给社会保障体系带来了新负担，尤其是对针对私人租房者无法支付住房成本的住房救助给付（住房补贴）的需求不断增长。随着全球金融危机后抵押贷款融资越发困难，私人租赁部门已成为特别的压力来源。英国相对自由的住房市场意味着私人租房者通常将其收入的 40％ 用于房租，而欧洲的平均值为 28％。越发严峻的可负担性问题部分导致 2008 年以来私人租赁部门的住房补贴申领人数上升了 42％。根据英国住房联合会的统计[2]，每年约 93 亿英镑的住房补贴流向私人房东，现在占社会保障预算的 14％。

需要补充的是，住房成本上涨加之高额的儿童照护成本，大大降低了许多有年幼子女的就业家庭的实际可支配收入。英国男性和女性的劳动力市场参与率都高于欧洲和 OECD 的平均水平，自 2005 年以来女性劳动力市场参与率高于 70％。根据 OECD 家庭数据库，在英国，全职收入为平均工资 150％ 的双薪家庭的儿童照护净成本高于其他经合组织国家（2012 年）。这反映了英国主要采取市场化的方式提供儿童照护，同时，历届政府的主要做法是寄希望于通过现金转移和税收抵免来缓解市场对家庭收入造成的压力。

然而，尽管英国 21 世纪头十年面临与日俱增的压力，2010 年以来的做法并没有填补 1997 年以后出现的社会投资模式的空白。缩减国家职能作为第二次世界大战以来最大单笔削减支出的激进紧缩计划的一部分，再次被提上议程。此外，还削减了许多服务，特别是地方一级的福利待遇大幅度削减，包括设定家庭可以获得的资金支持总额的封顶线等。

待遇提供的基调和方式也发生了重大变化。处罚体系似乎变得严厉许多，待遇给付的约束条件增强。如图 11 所示，2010 年求职者津贴（Job Seekers Allowance）申领者中移交接受处罚的人数急剧增加。一些研究者明确地将惩罚倾向的增强与慈善组织运营的食品银行的快速增长联系起来。[3] 据估计，2011/2012 年度至 2013/2014 年度，食品银行提供的食品包裹数量每年增加 600％ 以上。[4]

---

[1] Department for Communities and Local Government [DCLG], *Housing in England 2006/07*, DCLG: London, 2008.

[2] Bachelor, L.UK tenants pay more rent than any country in Europe: British renters pay a higher proportion of their wages as well as higher rents, according to the National Housing Federation. *The Guardian, Wednesday* 24 June, 2015.

[3] Loopstra, R., Fledder, J., Reeves, Aaron. and Stuckler, D. *The impact of benefit sanctioning on food insecurity: a dynamic cross-area study of food bank usage in the UK*. University of Oxford Sociology Working Papers, Paper Number 2016–03.

[4] Lambie-Mumford, H., Snell, C. and Hunt, T. *Heat or Eat?* SPERI British Political Economy Brief No. 19, 2016.

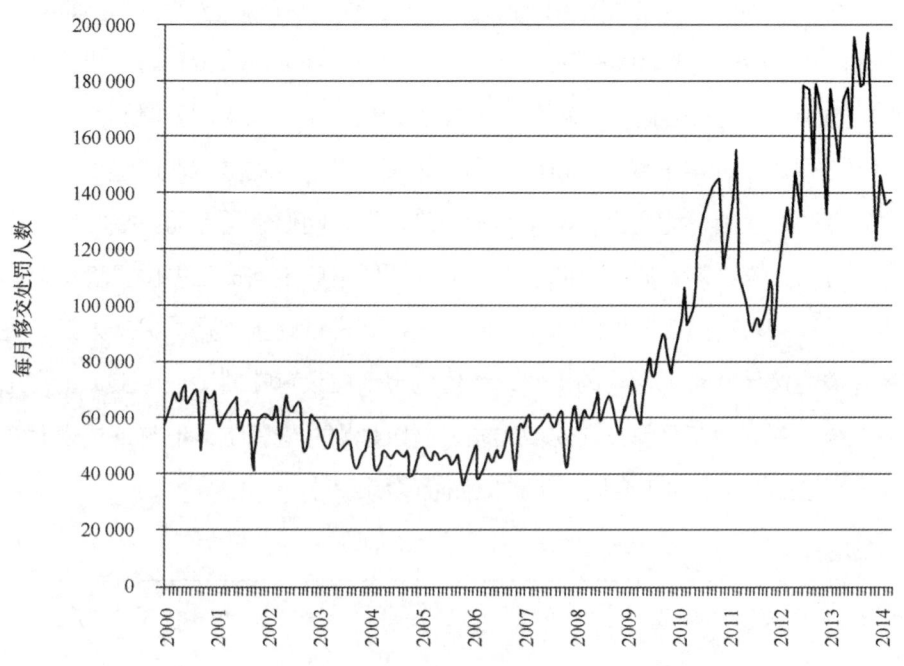

图 11 求职者津贴移交处罚人数

数据来源：DWP stat-xplore

随着最近的、也许是自贝弗里奇以来最重要的社会保障改革，即统一福利（Universal Credit）的全面实施，条件性（conditionality）制度将进入全新领域。作为 2012 年《福利改革法案》的核心，统一福利以全新的一套递送机制为前提，并将成为工作年龄人群非保险型福利给付的核心内容。它取代六项现有的基于家计调查的福利和税收抵免（儿童税收抵免、住房福利、收入支持、基于收入的求职者津贴、与收入相关的就业和支持津贴、工作税收抵免），将以上全部归并为单项基于家计调查的收入补充体系。该体系针对所有失业或低收入的处于工作年龄的成年人。至关重要的是，统一福利将作为一种动态调整的收入补充来运作，旨在根据申领者工作收入的变化来逐渐调整收入支持的额度，以确保"工作是有收益的"。由于这一制度涵盖了就业和失业两种情况，因此许多申领者在两种状态间切换时无须提出新的待遇要求。随着申领者有偿工作收入的变化，其从统一福利制度中获得的支持金额将随之升降。但这也意味着条件制度将首次延伸到就业的情况中[1]，并且可能出现一些就业者和自雇佣者因面临受到处罚的威胁而不得不谋求新工作或额外工作的情况。

---

[1] Simmons, D.Escalating Conditionality'，Child Poverty Action Group Bulletin Issue 225.December 2011, http://www.cpag.org.uk/content/escalating-conditionality, 2011.

有人对统一福利如何与某些类型的雇佣关系相互作用有所顾虑，尤其是高度临时性的、不为员工提供任何每周工作时间保证的"零时工合同(zero hours contracts)"。据估计，近3%的英国劳动力受雇于此种合同，相较之下，21世纪初头十年的大部分时间里，这一比例约为0.5%（见图12）。近年来越加严苛的惩罚规则可能助长了这类就业的增长，而且统一福利对零时工合同的使用可能产生的影响尚不明确，但方向似乎是有助于临时性工作的进一步发展。一方面，统一福利的推行似乎有可能削弱低薪雇主向员工提供更稳定合同的积极性，因为统一福利将在员工工作时间减少时介入对其进行财务支持。另一方面，统一福利的领取者将被迫接受零时工合同的工作，给付的灵活应该意味着（理论上）工作总是能改善处境的；统一福利制度目前正在逐步实施，所以规则并未固定，但有证据表明，已经有申领者因为拒绝接受"零时工合同"下的雇佣而受到惩罚。

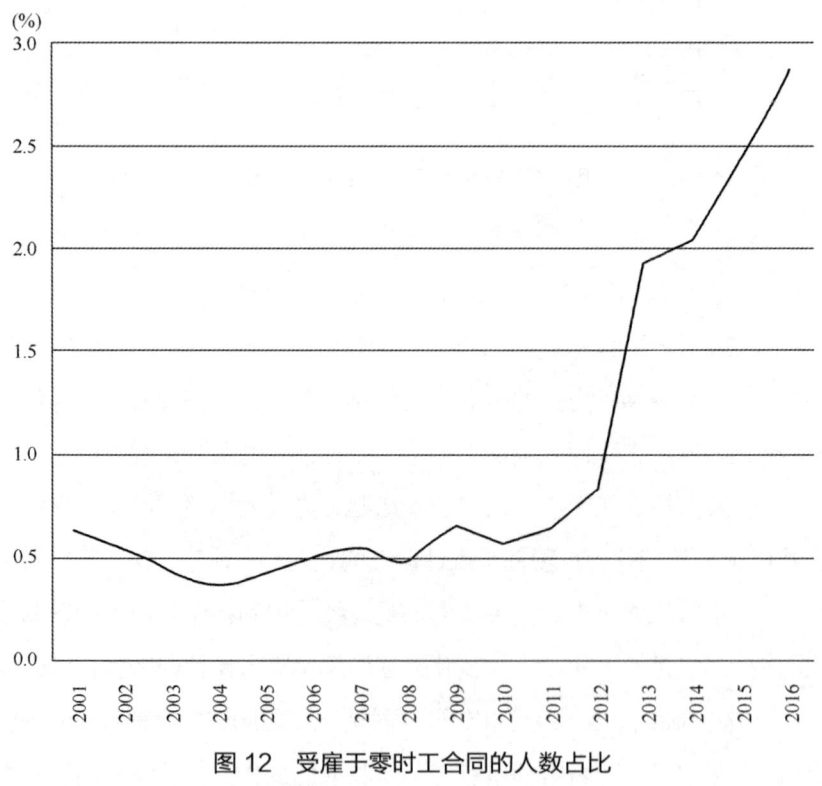

图12　受雇于零时工合同的人数占比

数据来源：Office for National statistics

三、未来解决方案

英国目前正处于经济和政治具有不确定性的重要历史性时期。政治体制日益破裂和棘手：历经英国分裂的公投（苏格兰独立，选民以微弱差距否决），退出欧盟的公投（所谓"脱欧"，选民以微弱差距表决通过）。加之全球金融危机和深度紧缩方案的影响，使得人们对当前和未来的不确定性非常担忧。社会和经济不平等可能在脱欧公投中扮演了重要但非决定性的作用，尤其是在英格兰，那些在20世纪80年代以来受到经济和社会政策变化不利影响的社区对脱欧表示了更强烈的支持。正如有学者[1]所言，许多投票支持离开欧盟的人群极有可能受到20世纪80年代以来各届政府所倡导的经济和社会转变的不利影响。

对英国社会保障和经济的审视是不全面的，很少提及国民健康服务和养老金，仅是注意到这些方面的总体筹资压力。这反映了关于社会保障原则和经济影响方面的重大政治辩论都集中在对劳动年龄人群的支持上。尽管有围绕国家投入资金不足、国家养老金的覆盖范围和充足性、国民健康服务的市场化，以及私人养老金计划缺陷的争论，但国民健康服务和养老金一直得到强有力的公众支持。[2]即使在经济困境期福利国家被"指指点点"时，国民健康服务和养老金也很少成为被攻击的靶子。事实上，自2010年以来，国家养老金和国民健康服务已经明确地从紧缩方案中被豁免，然而这是公共支出的两个最大项目。这凸显了推动当前社会保障政策走向的是政治而非经济上的必要性。

这种情况在英国由来已久。当然，社会支持的总成本和这些支出给经济带来的机会成本在不同时期反复地引起担忧。关于"福利"的争论主要是由道德上的考量所驱动。通常分为以下两个阵营：（1）主张强大的社会权利造成向"不值得帮助的穷人"提供财务支持从而削弱工作激励的风险；（2）强调贫困和弱势的结构性原因，强调社会正义优先于工作激励。这种分歧至少可以追溯到1905年皇家济贫法和困难救济委员会时期。彼时围绕如何实现1834年济贫法现代化的问题经过了四年的讨论，提出了分别反映以上两个思想学派的两份报告。[3]

从历史比较视角来看，英国的社会保障改革方案引入了越来越多的惩罚性干预措施，即常常提供吝惜的支持以促进人们尽快去工作。这样的策略以"劣等待遇（less eligibility）"的理念（即领取福利者的境遇必须劣于获得最低工作报酬的工人）嵌入了1834年的济贫法

---

[1] Ellison, N.The whys and wherefores of Brexit'. in J Hudson, C Needham & E Heins（eds）, *Social Policy Review*. Bristol: The Policy Press, 2017（29）.

[2] Hudson, J., Lunt, N., Hamilton, C., Mackinder, S., Meers, J., and Swift, C.Exploring Public Attitudes to Welfare over the Longue Durée: Re-examination of Survey Evidence from Beveridge, Beatlemania, Blair and Beyond. Social Policy & Administration,2016（50）691–711.

[3] Jones K. *The Making of Social Policy in Britain: from the Poor Law to New Labour*. Athlone, London, 2000.

中。正是济贫法极端的惩戒性质造成了贝弗里奇所强调的对家计调查方式的敌意。然而，正如上文所述，最终没有足够的政治意愿来实现贝弗里奇所设想的另一种主要基于缴费的制度。

正如哈罗普（Harrop）[1]所言，英国面向工作年龄人群的社会保障体系已经演化为由缴费型的、家计调查型的、普遍福利和私人补充性保障组成的"大杂烩"。改革的选项包括试图追求其中一条"纯粹的"路线，但在英国更有望成功的方式是强化以上每种类型保障，同时继续融合四者。但是，如哈罗普所指出的，也是贝弗里奇（1942）[2]在其著名报告中所强调的那样，任何社会保障改革都需要一套更广泛的支持手段的配合，同时国家要在社会保障现金福利制度永远无法解决的一些根本性问题上发挥更加积极的作用。

一是低工资问题。如上文所示，英国的社会保障制度助长了低工资和灵活的就业市场，在职贫困成为日益严重的社会问题。解决这个问题需要提高最低工资。重要的是，在这方面政府最近采取了一些措施，例如，引入新的"最低生活工资（Living Wage）"，尽管仍低于使所有在岗职工家庭摆脱贫困的水平，但这仍将大大提高最低工资水平。

二是需要反思获得待遇的条件制度之运作情况。越来越多的证据表明，越发严苛的做法一方面使得许多公民有迫切需要的时候被剥夺了基本社会权利，另一方面又助长了低薪和极度没有保障的零工时合同的兴起。

三是需要采取紧急措施解决英国住房的高成本问题。这终究需要推动建造更多的住房，特别是更多的社会住房。加强对私人部门租金水平的监管也是一个选择。

四是儿童照护问题。直接由国家提供全民儿童照护将是最简便和最有效的方式，但鉴于现有服务提供者的抵制，这将会面临政治挑战。另一选择是国家对儿童照护提供更多的补贴，并将服务供给交由市场。无论哪种方式，都需要对异常高的儿童照护成本采取行动。

五是国家需要持续干预，以刺激某些地区的就业增长并创造就业机会。尽管已经过去了三四十年，但20世纪80年代的去工业化仍然影响着许多前工业中心地区的经济。这些地区通常也是最强烈支持英国脱欧的，这反映了他们有被政策制定者忽视的感觉。仅凭社会保障一己之力，无论其具有多么积极的劳动力市场政策元素，都不能使工业衰退的地区获得重生。

1　Harrop, A. For Us All. *Redesigning Social Security for the 2020s*, 2016.

2　Beveridge, W. H. B. *Social insurance and allied services*. HMSO: London, 1942.

最后，若能对个人的投入和回报更加坦诚，那么社会保障的未来可能更具可持续性。20世纪80年代以来，英国的个人所得税税率相对较低，政府借款往往填补了空白，而国民保险是与实际支出脱钩的"神秘收费"。需要提高收入税，这不仅应针对收入前1%人群，而且应将目标群体面向收入前20%或前30%的人群。但很少有政治家热衷于这件事，这或许因为很少有公民明白得到了多少回报。按照贝弗里奇的设想重启国家保险，可以帮助全民意识到他们从（应该）被要求向其缴费的制度中受益几何。

法国的经济发展与社会保障：
以20世纪80年代中期为转折点

［法］皮埃尔·龚夏尔第[1]

和许多富裕的发达国家一样，在法国，社会保障制度是劳动者与公民日常生活的一部分。有一个指标可反映这一事实：当前，社会支出大约占国民净收入的1/3。

尽管此前有过一个仅覆盖部分人口、对法国的经济结构影响有限的零散残缺的项目体系，但法国社会保障制度更加系统性和可量化的显著发展却主要始于第二次世界大战以后。一直到20世纪70年代，社会保障支出的增加无疑对法国的经济发展起到了积极的推动作用。这一时期的经济增长率达到了前所未有的（高）水平，社会支出的增加与经济的蓬勃发展几乎并行不悖。社会保障的发展与规范的雇佣合同的建立一起构成了劳资之间社会妥协的一部分，这种社会妥协成功缓解了市场力量对收入平等和人民福祉的内生性不利影响。在法国，社会保障的发展还极大地促进了工业劳动场所的人性化和劳动力市场总体状况的改善。在一个整合的框架内，劳动者的去商品化及其与社会保障制度日益紧密的联系是这一时期的关键特征。

第一次石油价格危机及其对经济主体的直接与间接影响，"扰乱了"这种妥协。劳动收入占国民净收入的比重在1973—1982年大幅度地增加，但却在这之后以更大的幅度下降，并于20世纪80年代末达到了前所未有的低水平。尽管20世纪70年代的这种增长在很大程度上是对惊人的经济增长的一个技术性反应，但它随后的下降却主要是因为相对于资本而言，劳动者的地位开始逐渐式微。

这种情形至今依旧。与此同时，政府开始放松对金融领域的管制，进而催生一种经济体制。在这种体制中，金融机构的主导地位是理解法国社会经济发展的一个关键特点。个

---

[1] ［作者简介］皮埃尔·龚夏尔第（Pierre Concialdi），法国经济与社会研究中心（Institute de Recherches Économiques et Sociales）研究员。主要研究方向：福利国家。

［译者简介］杨无意，中国人民大学中国社会保障研究中心博士生，中国社会保障学会秘书处学术助理。

［翻译审校］华颖，中国社会科学院人口与劳动经济研究所助理研究员。

人责任、社会权利碎片化及社会保障市场化是这个时期的一些重要特征,而缓慢的经济增长同样也是这个时期的特征。

本文对这些发展进行了更加详细的分析。第一部分描述了法国社会保障制度的历史经验。该部分对社会保障支出的宏观经济趋势及其对人口覆盖率和社会福利待遇给付水平的相关影响进行了一个总体概述,重点关注养老金计划、医疗保障体系和失业计划。第二部分则涉及法国社会保障制度目前面临的主要挑战。这些挑战包括人口老龄化、社会保障筹资的相关问题以及失业与未适当就业的发展情况。第三部分探讨了成功应对这些挑战的一些可选项,即通过改进社会保障制度使之适应被金融机构利益主导的全球化世界经济的新特征。

一、历史经验

同许多其他国家一样,19世纪的工业革命对法国社会的发展产生了深远的影响。在人类历史进程中生产率第一次稳定且快速地提高。在此背景之下,分配问题迅速升至社会政治议程前列。社会保障权利及其相关待遇的确立,同增加工资报酬和减少工作时间的斗争一道,成为对生产力进步成果再分配的又一重要工具。

除经济的剧变之外,还发生了其他结构性变化。随着日益壮大的工人阶级的出现——这个阶级脱离了传统的和以农村社区为主的支持形式(通过家庭、行业协会或宗教)——对和现代工业发展相关的职业风险保障的需要也在日益增加,而在现代工业发展的初期,工伤事故保护并未得到很大重视。

19世纪末与20世纪初相交之际,社会救助制度开始发展,但仅惠及一小部分人口。尽管在20世纪的头几十年里有过一些建立强制性社会保障制度的尝试,但却只有在第二次世界大战之后,随着1945年社会保障计划的实施,现有的法国社会保障制度才开始发展起来。1945年制定了总体方案(General Scheme/Régime Général),旨在迅速覆盖整个人口。然而,从早前的计划中受益的雇员(矿工、公务员、铁路工人、正规部门中的其他雇员)却不愿因参加一项单独的、统一的计划而失去其既得利益。自雇佣劳动者也拒绝与工薪阶层同列,并担心一个综合(普遍的)制度的潜在成本。因此,总体方案开始仅针对私营部门雇员而发展,法国的社会保障制度是以职业为基础组织起来的。养老金和失业津贴至今仍是这样的情况,而家庭津贴和医疗保险现在则普遍覆盖且惠及全民。

本文重点关注总体方案,这一方案是当前的主要制度,将近3/4的法国社会保障总支出由其产生和分配。

（一）社会保障的宏观动态

2015年，货币型与实物型的社会保障（SP）待遇在国民净收入（NNI）[1]中的占比略微超过1/3，大约为1950年占比水平的3倍（见图1）。

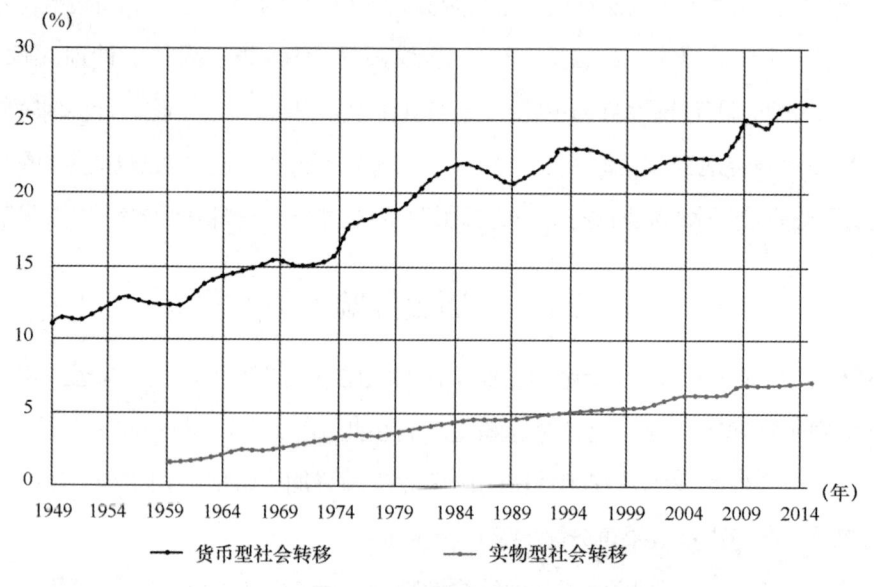

图1　社会保护转移占国民净收入的百分比

资料来源：作者根据法国国家统计和经济研究所（INSEE）公布的国民经济核算等数据整理计算所得。

然而，社会保障的扩张并不是线性的。此外，在分析时，将国民收入动态的特定时期和社会保障支出动态均考虑在内，有助于更好地理解占比的变化。这种方法使我们能够区分过去三个不同时期（见图2）。

● 1940—1973年：在此期间，经济增长率相当高而平稳。除两个时期（1949—1953和1961—1968年）外，社会支出增长率与这一趋势相一致。这些短暂的社会保障支出"过度增长"时期，基本解释了这一时期社会支出占比的长期增加。

● 1973—1993年：经济增长放缓，并且经济变得更具周期性。在向新增长体制转变期间，社会福利待遇的增长率逐渐接近经济增长率。1973年之后，社保转移与国民净收入比值的增加集中在经济衰退期。换言之，这些（占比）增加是（经济）增长乏力的结果。

---

[1] 国民净收入（NNI）被定义为国内生产总值（GDP）加上来自国外的工资、薪水及财产所得的净收入，减去因损耗与报废而导致的固定资本资产（住宅、建筑、机器、运输设备和实体基础设施）折旧。参见：OECD. *Net National Income*. https://data.oecd.org/natincome/net-national-income.htm. Paris：Organisation for Economic Co-operation and Development, 2016.

● 1993—2015年：1993—2008年全球金融危机，社会支出的年增长率相当稳定，平均为2%左右，目前该数值被认为是经济的长期可持续实际增长率。因此，社保转移与国民净收入比值趋于稳定，而变化主要反映了经济的波动。自2008年以来，经济一直停滞不前，这解释了自那时起社保转移与国民净收入比值的增加。

一直到第一次石油价格危机之前，社会保障的发展始终与经济增长同步。政策制定者的共识是，社会保障是对生产力增长成果进行再分配以确保均衡和公平共享的经济发展的一种方式。社会保障还是一个反（经济）周期的工具，是政府为避免严重的经济危机而推行的凯恩斯主义干预政策的一部分。

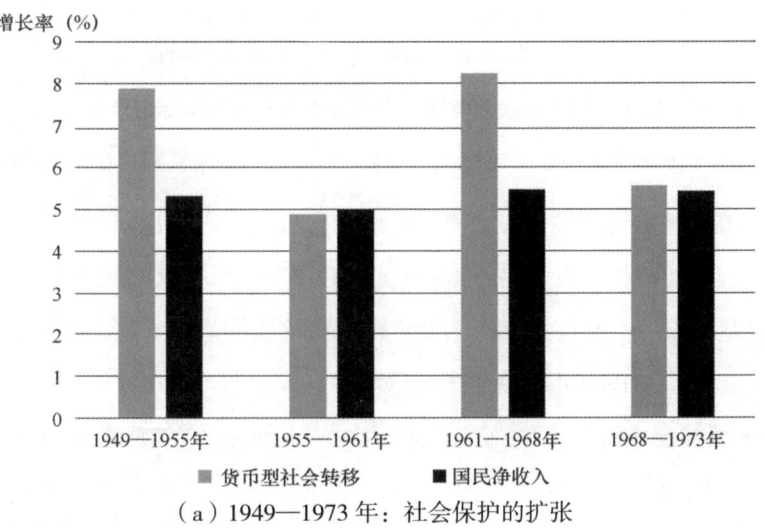

（a）1949—1973年：社会保护的扩张

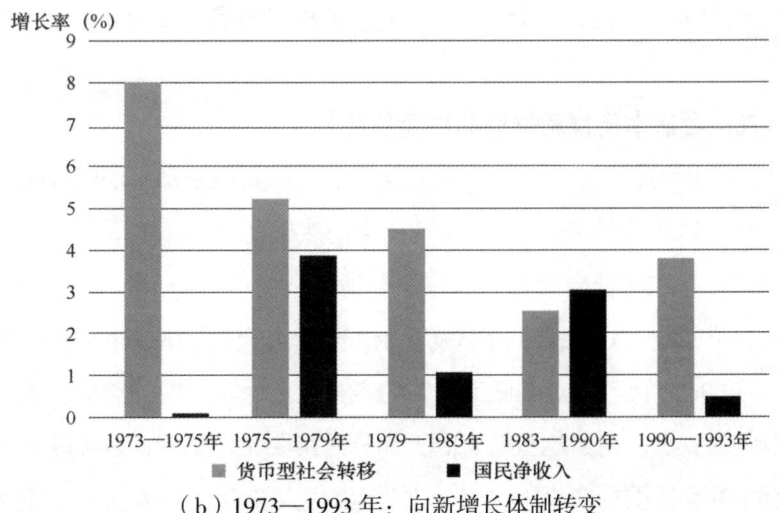

（b）1973—1993年：向新增长体制转变

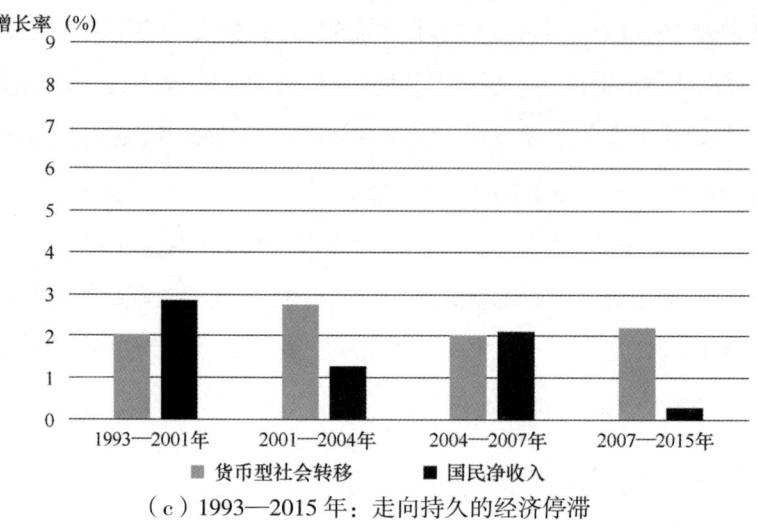

（c）1993—2015年：走向持久的经济停滞

图2 货币型社会转移与国民净收入的平均实际增长率

资料来源：作者根据法国国家统计和经济研究所（INSEE）的国民经济核算等数据整理计算所得。

第一次石油价格危机之后，失业率升高，大部分社会需求也随之升高。这导致社会支出的急剧增加。与此同时，工资仍滞留在过去的生产率增长趋势上。这两个因素——失业增加和工资协定的惯性——同第二次石油价格危机的压缩效应一起，减少了初次收入中的利润占比，这个比重在1982年下降到一个低水平。

1982年之后社会党政府所实施的政策旨在恢复利润。工资限制与社会支出控制导致了20世纪80年代劳动收入占比的急剧下降。与此同时，一个新的范式出现：失业的致因并不在于国内和国际的需求不足，而是源于"过高的"劳动成本。供给侧政策开始在随后几十年里占据主导地位，荼毒至今。这对社会保障筹资、设计及社会保障制度的目标均产生影响。

（二）筹资、覆盖率及福利待遇的主要趋势

由劳资双方共担的、与收入相关联的社会缴费，一直以来都是法国社会保障筹资的主要来源。2015年，这些缴费在全部收入中的比重仍然超过60%（见图3）。

然而，随着取代这些社会缴费一部分的一种新型税收（Contribution Social Généralisée，CSG）的出现，该比重在20世纪90年代初开始下降，这一进程在20世纪90年代后期加速。同时，在20世纪90年代实行对"低工资"的雇主社会保障缴费的豁免，这一举措旨在降低劳动成本以促进就业。由于这些豁免的一部分是由税收资助的，这项政策还导致了社会保障资源总量中社会缴费的减少。这一变化背后的主要驱动力是雇主社会缴费的减少。自

20世纪70年代中期以来,所有社会缴费在社会保障筹资当中的占比下降了15个百分点,雇主社会缴费的占比也下降了。

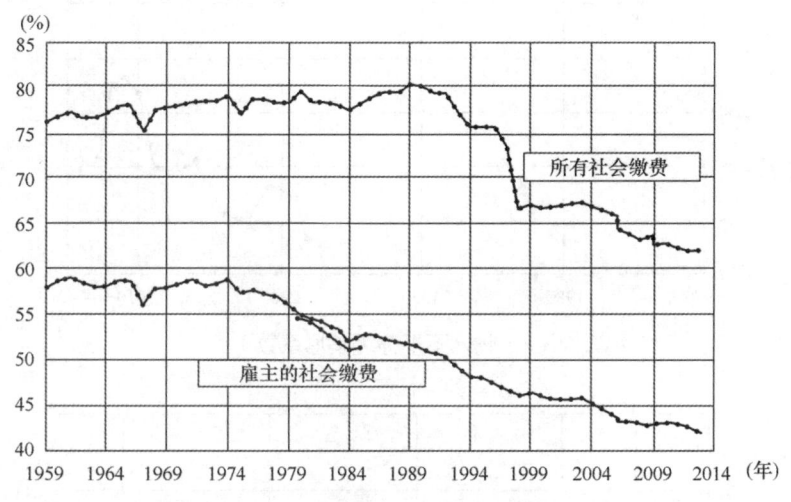

图3　社会缴费在社会保护筹资中的比重

资料来源:作者根据法国国家统计和经济研究所(INSEE)的国民经济核算等数据整理计算所得。

社会保障筹资的变化通常反映了社会保障目标的变化。如前所述,这些变化可概括为从团结和再分配向责任和个体化的转变。例如,直到20世纪80年代,一些最低收入项目是由针对私营(企业)职工的总体方案资助的。[1] 1979—1984年,还存在一个针对临时及长期失业劳动者的单项失业计划。该计划由社会缴费和政府补贴共同筹资,前者负担2/3,后者负担1/3。当时,总体方案的目标仍然是将全体人口整合到一个共同的框架内。

20世纪80年代及之后发生的变化逐渐改变了这种逻辑。最低收入计划开始完全由财政资助,并根据失业时长将失业计划一分为二。在养老金计划中,所谓的"非缴费型"福利不再由社会缴费提供资金(1993年),并且在20世纪90年代推出了针对低工资劳动者的在职福利。随着社会权利的日益分割,以及实际待遇价值从总体上来看降低,当前社会保障制度比30年前的异质性大得多。

尽管难以描绘出这些定性变化和总体不平等及贫困指标之间的统计相关性,但毫无疑问,它们逆转了此前不平等和贫困减少的趋势(见图4)。

1　针对成年残障人士(1976—1983年)和单亲家长(1976—1999年)。

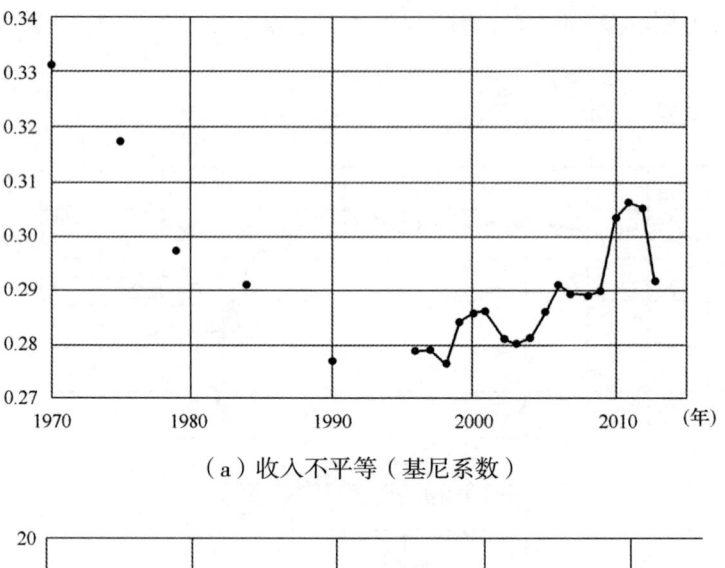

(a) 收入不平等（基尼系数）

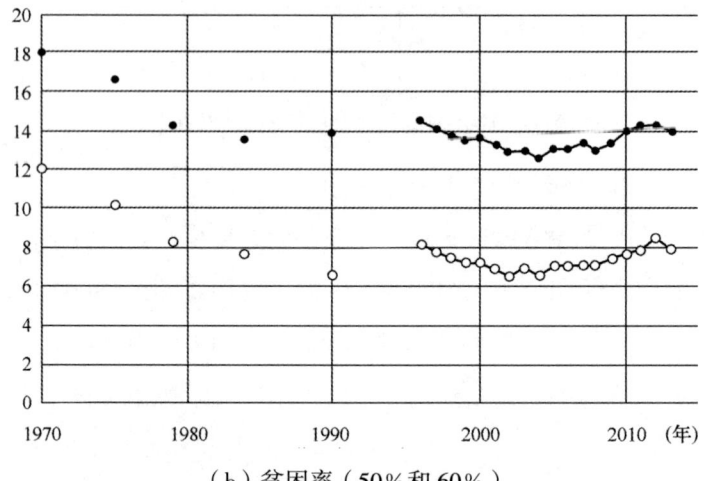

(b) 贫困率（50%和60%）

图4　1970—2010年的不平等和贫困

资料来源：作者根据法国国家统计和经济研究所（INSEE）数据整理计算所得。

（三）社会保障与经济：政策和范式

可以通过考虑两个主要议题来对社会保障与经济之间的关系进行分析。第一个议题是关于社会保障对劳动力和资本市场运行的潜在(理论的)影响或实际(经验的)影响。问题是，社会保障是否会（或不会）改善这些市场的运行，并因此对整个经济产生积极或消极的影响？第二个议题涉及社会保障对人口经济福祉的影响，这最终是任何经济活动的目标。这个议题又引出了两个问题：社会保障的再分配效应是否显著地减少了不平等及其相关社会成本？社会保障是不是满足社会需求的有效途径，而这些需求是否本可以通过市场机制（更好地）被满足?

在此部分，笔者会针对主要的社会保障项目来探讨这些问题，并在可能的情况下，就法国的经验提供一些证据。讨论的重点是养老金、医疗服务、失业与社会救助制度。

1. 养老金

直至 20 世纪 70 年代，对退休计划的主要关注点是这些计划的覆盖面和福利待遇的充足性。1962 年发布的一份报告[1]就养老金的低水平发出了警告，20 世纪 70 年代两本有影响力的书[2,3]也指出了法国社会尤其是老年人群的高贫困率。20 世纪七八十年代初所实施的养老金改革试图通过以下措施来解决这个问题：扩大养老金计划（1972 年）的覆盖面，提高待遇水平和老年人最低收入保障水平（20 世纪 70 年代和 80 年代初），以及将法定退休年龄降至 60 岁（1983 年）等。结果，老年人口贫困率从 1970 年的 32% 急剧下降到 1984 年的 8%。毫无疑问，在当时，养老金政策极大地提升了老年人的经济安全，并增强了他们在财务上和实践中的自主权。

1983 年降低法定退休年龄的举措遭到了批评，理由是它会强制性地把老年劳动者挤出劳动力市场。但经验证据表明，情况并非如此。老年人劳动力市场参与率降低的趋势早在 20 世纪 70 年代中期便开始了。[4] 事实上，在 20 世纪七八十年代，养老金政策还是解决大规模失业的政府政策的一部分。20 世纪 70 年代和 80 年代初，在两次石油价格危机的背景下，这场大规模失业在法国出现。提前退休计划在 20 世纪 70 年代初开始发展，并且养老金政策被视为缓解失业状况的一个途径。这些政策为老年劳动者提供了必要的经济支持（通过失业津贴和亲属的一些支持）。

因此，在 20 世纪 80 年代中期，养老金计划在全国范围内相当成功地达到了其目标，即为老年人提供充足的收入，让他们能过上体面的生活。与此同时，公职人员和各级政府——无论是由社会党还是保守党执政——均开始对（由）日益增长的老年人口（造成的）所谓的经济负担表示担忧。换言之，公共养老金不再被视作为老年人提供经济支持的一个问题解决方案，而被当作了一个问题。这引发了一系列旨在削减老年福利待遇的"改革"。结果，这些改革目前的实际趋势是降低了养老金制度的相对慷慨度。未来若不进行制衡的

1　Pierre Laroque.*Rapport de la Commission d'étude des Problèmes de la Vieillesse*.Paris: L'Harmattan, 1962.

2　René Lenoir. *Les Exclus*.Paris：Seuil, 1974.

3　Lionel Stoleru.*Vaincre la Pauvreté dans les Pays Riches, Collection Champs*. Paris: Flammarion, 1977.

4　Didier Blanchet, Jean-Alain Monfort. *L'âge et la Durée de Retraite Depuis 50 Ans*, Insee première, Paris: *French National Institute of Statistics and Economic Studies*, 1996（448）.

改革，老年人的相对处境将会进一步显著恶化，并退回到 20 世纪 70 年代中期的水平（见图 5）。

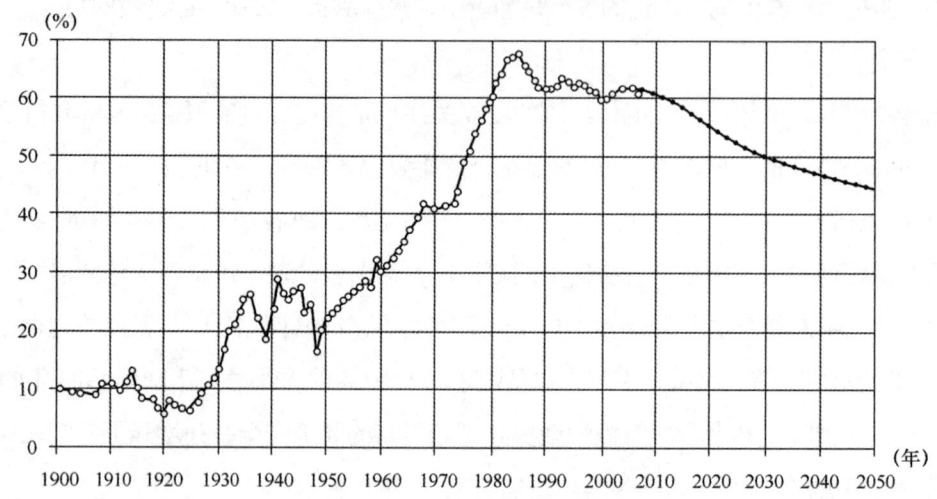

图 5　养老金制度的"慷慨度"（平均养老金／人均 GDP）：一个宏观评估

注："平均养老金"＝公共养老金支出总额／60 岁及以上人口数。此公式将养老金计划对老年人的（收入）替代率的差异和覆盖率的差异均考虑在内。

资料来源：Anne Reimat, "Histoire Quantitative de la Prise en Charge de la Vieillesse en France, XIXe-XXe Siècles : Les Régimes de Retraites," Economies et Sociétés, 2001, No.28; COR, *Evolutions et Perspectives des Retraites en France*: Rapport Annuel du Conseil D'Orientation des Retraites, Paris, Pensions Advisory Council, 2017.

另一项改革大大降低了退休者通过有偿劳动来补充其养老金的可能性。由于目前养老金待遇可能（至少部分地）被视作仅补贴未获得充足养老金者和需要额外收入的退休者的有偿就业，这可能改变了社会转移的理念。这一改革还可能加剧了就业市场上劳动者之间的竞争，进而给工资造成下行的压力。

除对劳动力参与率的经济影响外，养老金计划还可能影响资本市场的运转。这取决于所使用的待遇给付方式。经济学理论认为，如果养老金计划的筹资方式是现收现付制，即用当期的社会缴费来支付当期的养老金，则可能会降低私人家庭的储蓄率，并因此减少投资，最终降低经济增长率。这一观点被用于法国的辩论中以向公众兜售基金积累制的养老金方案。然而，到目前为止，法国并不存在大规模的基金制计划，尽管这些储蓄计划的比重正随着时间的推移而增加。[1] 当前，法国绝大多数的养老金（计划）仍然采用现收现付的

1　DREES.*Les Retraités et Les Retraites*.Paris: Direction de la Recherche, des études, de l'évaluation et des statistiques, 2015.

筹资方式。无论是基本养老金还是在私营企业职工的养老金收入中占比很大（约40%）的补充养老金均是如此。尽管存在这种"非典型的"养老金筹资方式，但法国的家庭储蓄率是欧盟中最高的之一。[1]因此，在法国案例中不存在挤出效应。[2]

2008年的金融危机也凸显了通过社会缴费来为养老金筹资的一些积极作用。在危机期间及之后，基金积累制养老金计划损失了近20%的价值，并且相对于所作出的给付承诺而言，许多养老基金的资金目前仍非常不足。根据最近的一项研究，美国和英国的大部分养老金计划资金不足，总赤字率为18%。[3]这对养老金领取者来说是一个真正的威胁，并且可以说，真正的养老金定时炸弹并非人口方面的，而是财务方面的。在法国的制度体系下，养老金领取者没有受到金融危机的毁灭性影响。但这并不意味着法国的养老金筹资没有问题，因为经济衰退影响就业，并减少了社会缴费的征收额。但是，应对这种情形所需的调整可以由政府监督，并且最脆弱的老年人遭受的损失少于普通的养老金领取者。这凸显了现收现付制养老金计划相较于基金制而言更大的灵活性。

其他研究也指出，对养老金领取者的公共转移不仅提高了他们的经济自主权和经济安全，而且还为传统形态的家庭内部团结提供了新的支持。换言之，在公共转移与家庭内部的私人转移之间并不存在挤出效应。相反，这些研究最可靠的结论是，在公共转移与私人转移之间存在着某种形式的互补，以至于老年人生活水平的提高也会惠及他们最年幼的亲属，而且可能缓解了失业率上升对最年轻世代的剧烈影响。

2. 医疗服务

法国的医疗服务由医院（公立的和私立的都有）与私人执业者（医生及其他医疗专家和医疗辅助人员）提供。目前这些服务在卫生总费用中的比重略超过70%（见表1）。一直到20世纪80年代初，医疗费用上涨背后的主要驱动力是医院支出增加。自那时以后，床位数大幅度减少：公共部门撤除了近1/4的床位，私营部门则撤除了将近1/5。结果是，医

1　Lucy apRoberts, Pierre Concialdi.Pension Reform and Personal Provision of Retirement Income in France. in Jim Stewart, Gerard Hughes（eds.）, *Personal Provision of Retirement Income: Meeting the Needs of Older People?*Cheltenham: Edward Elgar, 2009.

2　德国等其他国家同样如此。事实上，这个问题所涉甚广，无法在本报告中进行讨论。例如，与广为接受的（错误的）认知基本相反，银行并不需要任何储蓄来为投资提供资金，而诸如"投资基金"等其他金融中介则需要。

3　Citigroup.*The Coming Pensions Crisis: Recommendations for Keeping the Global Pensions System Afloat.*New York: Citi Global Perspectives & Solutions, 2016.

院支出份额从1980年的54%下降到2010年的46.4%。同一时期，医疗卫生支出的增长率较前一时期（1950—1980年）也明显下降（见表2）。

表1　卫生支出结构（占总支出的百分比）　（%）

年份	医院	私人执业者	药品	其他
1955	36.6	29.6	29.1	4.7
1980	54.0	24.9	17.8	3.3
2010	46.4	25.1	19.7	8.8

资料来源：作者根据法国研究、科研、评估和统计局（DREES），以及国家卫生总费用核算等数据整理计算所得。

表2　医疗卫生支出年均增长率　（%）

年份	医院	私人执业者	药品
名义支出			
1950—1980	16.3	15.0	14.1
1980—2010	5.8	6.4	6.7
数量			
1950—1980	7.8	6.6	10.8
1980—2010	2.2	3.9	6.3
价格			
1950—1980	7.9	7.9	2.9
1980—2010	3.5	2.4	0.4

资料来源：作者根据法国研究、科研、评估和统计局（DREES），以及国家卫生总费用核算等数据整理计算所得。

自20世纪70年代中期以来，为遏制医疗费用的上涨并平衡医疗保险基金账户，各种方案被付诸实施。首批方案试图通过提高来自患者的筹资（通过社会缴费）和患者的医疗支出来实现这些目标。自20世纪90年代以来，也实行其他改革措施以收紧对公共医疗卫生支出的控制。这些改革措施进一步增加了患者的自费支付[1]，并在公共医疗卫

1　自费支付可能包括直接支付（对不在保险报销范围内的药品和服务的付费）、共同支付（参保患者需要承担一部分治疗费用和药品费用），以及对优待的非正式支付。

生系统中推行了结构性变革,在医院中尤为如此(Tarification à L'activité,T2A)。大约从2005年起,公立医院和私立医院中所有医疗、外科及产科服务都是按服务付费。与许多其他欧洲国家一样,这一改革旨在将内部市场或准市场引入医疗服务的供给中。这为多种形式的外包做好了准备,包括长期外包合同,通常被称为公私合作模式(PPPs)。[1]

所有这些变化一方面影响患者的医疗服务费用,另一方面也影响了这些服务的质量。

就医疗服务的财务成本来看,法国的医疗保险制度是一个双层构架。第一层通过各种强制计划提供基本的保险项目,第二层由"互助"(非营利)保险公司或纯私有的(营利)保险公司提供的补充保险项目构成。

被强制医疗保险计划覆盖的人口比重从1960年的76%左右上升到1980年的99.2%。据估计,现在有99.9%的人口被覆盖。公共医疗卫生支出在总支出中的比重增加(见表3)的确部分地反映了这种覆盖率的提高。从那时起,绝大部分人口得到了覆盖,且这个比例是(衡量)强制医疗保险计划"慷慨度"的一个良好指标。

由表3可知,过去30年公共医疗卫生支出的占比有所下降,且对于非医院支出(私人执业者)来说,这种下降相当显著。平均来看,这种下降被低估了。自21世纪初以来,长期疾病计划开始实施,使越来越多的参保者能够从医疗卫生支出的全额报销中受益。[2]因此,平均比重没有反映出大多数未能从该计划中受益者的情况,并且对这些人来说,公共支出占比更低。例如,在总体方案中,药品的平均报销比例从1995年的70.6%提高到2011年的77.7%。然而,这一上升主要是由长期疾病计划受益者比重的增加所驱动的。对于没有从这一专项计划中受益的普通劳动者来说,报销率则低得多,从2000年的60%降至2011年的57%。

表3	各类公共医疗卫生支出在总支出中的百分比		(%)
年份	1950	1980	2010
医院	54.6	88.2	90.9
私人执业者	52.9	76.7	63.0
运输	100.0	96.0	91.8

---

[1] 公私合作模式可以采取多种形式,例如,医院建筑和技术设备的筹资及租赁、维修服务的提供,以及公立医院的民营化管理。

[2] 对于某些疾病,长期疾病计划允许对由社会保障(疾病保险)部分支付的医疗服务费用进行全额报销。

续表

年份	1950	1980	2010
药品及药物治疗	47.2	65.6	65.8
其他医疗支出	14.6	21.9	42.1
合计	51.0	79.9	75.7

资料来源：作者根据法国研究、科研、评估和统计局（DREES），以及国家卫生总费用核算等数据整理计算所得。

由于医疗服务费用的攀升，越来越多的人在获得医疗服务方面受到了限制，尤其在未参加任何补充保障项目的情况下。这促使一个特殊的家计调查式计划，"全民医疗保险"（CMU，简称全民医保）在 2000 年建立。该计划给最贫困人口提供基本保险项目（基本全民医保）和免费的补充保险项目（补充全民医保）。由于全民医保所规定的参保者最高收入（上限）非常低，因此在 2005 年推出了另一项福利待遇，对不符合全民医保参保条件但收入又未超过全民医保收入上限 135% 的人员，可以购买补充医疗保险进行补贴。最终，在 2013 年一项集体协议得以签署，以向所有雇员普及这些补充医疗保险计划，并且法律规定从 2016 年 1 月 1 日起所有企业都必须强制执行。

总之，当前法国的医疗保险制度由两个强制层次构成。第一层次是公办的；第二层次，即补充层，则由私营保险公司提供。

在这个全局性的、复杂的系统中，存在着各种各样的有关医疗保障制度与经济发展相互关联的问题。在此，笔者主要关注以下三个方面。

医疗服务的公共覆盖与可及性。医疗服务费用的增加的确会对其可及性产生明显的影响，并因此而影响人口的健康状况。定期调查显示，由于经济原因，越来越多的人决定不寻求治疗。[1] 这种现象在非稳定就业劳动者中更加明显。[2] 这种就诊延迟往往会反映在健康状况的衰退和病症的恶化中，而这最终会让社会付出更加昂贵的代价。资源与门诊服务的匮乏还会导致最贫困的家庭到医院的急诊部门进行治疗。而如果他们在门诊进行治疗的话，费用原本会便宜很多。最终，所有这些因素都对人口健康和

---

[1] Nicolas Célant, et al.*Enquête sur la Santé et la Protection Sociale 2012*, Les rapports de l'IRDES.Paris：Institut de recherche et documentation en économie de la santé, 2014（556）.

[2] Catherine Chauveaud, et al. *Le "Non-recours" Aux Soins des Actifs Précaires*.Document de Travail de l'ODENORE, Grenoble: Observatory on Non-take-up of Social Rights and Public Services, 2010（2）.

医疗费用产生了不利影响。还有一个日益严重的问题则与医疗服务可及性中的区域不平等有关。[1]

医疗服务和保险的提供。强制性补充私人健康保险的推行的确使保险成本明显增加。私人自愿健康保险的管理成本比强制性的公共计划高出 5 倍以上。

就医疗服务提供而言，引入 T2A 似乎并未达到其目标。一些研究者指出，医院之间竞争的加剧已经对医疗服务质量产生了不利的影响。其他研究则表明，这项政策极大地损害了该行业从业者的工作条件，尤其是护士和大部分资历低的医院职工。[2]而这又反过来影响了所提供的服务的质量和这些员工的健康状况。

失业、工作条件与健康。在过去的 20 年中，许多企业经历了工作场所的重构。诸如岗位轮换、管理层级精简、自我指导的工作团队和即时全面质量管理等新的工作方法被采用。一些研究调查了这些做法对工伤和心理压力的影响。结果表明，对劳动者而言，这些做法与更高的工伤风险及更多的心理不适相关，因此意味着它们可能会对工作条件造成不利影响。[3]结果便是，这可能会导致旷工并影响员工的工作满意度，而这又可能反过来给劳动生产率造成消极影响。

必须提及失业与工作不安全对健康的影响。许多国家的流行病学研究表明，失业对人们的健康状况有不利影响。例如，长期失业与更高的自杀率有关。[4]更普遍地来看，失业与死亡风险的增加有关，尤其是对那些处于职业生涯早期或中期的人来说。[5]工作不安全和失业还构成了抑郁症状加剧的重大风险。[6]这在法国有据可查。据估计，与 2007 年年末的失

1　Laure Com-Ruelle, et al.*Recours Aux Soins Ambulatoires et Distances Parcourues par les Patients: Des Différences Importantes Selon L'accessibilité Territoriale Aux Soins*, IRDES.Questions D'économie de la Santé, Paris：Institut de recherche et documentation en économie de la santé, 2016（219）．

2　Samia Benallah, Jean-Paul Domin.Réforme de L'hôpital: Quels Enjeux en Termes de Travail et de Santé des Personnels? *Revue de l'IRES*, 2016（91–92）．

3　Philippe Askenazy, et al. New Organizational Practices and Working Conditions: Evidence from France in the 1990s. *Recherches économiques de Louvain,* 2002, 68（1）．

4　Allison Milner, et al.Long-term Unemployment and Suicide: A Systematic Review and Meta-analysis.*Plos One,* 2013, 8（1）．

5　David J. Roelfs, et al. Losing Life and Livelihood: A Systematic Review and Meta-analysis of Unemployment and All-cause Mortality.*Social Science & Medicine*,2011, 72（6）．

6　Tae Jun Kim, Olaf von dem Knesebeck.Perceived Job Insecurity, Unemployment and Depressive Symptoms: A Systematic Review and Meta-analysis of Prospective Observational Studies.*International Archives of Occupational and Environmental Health*, 2016, 89（4）．

业状况相比，失业率的上升可能是造成2008—2010年自杀事件增加近600起的原因。[1]然而，如果将所伴随的更大的死亡风险考虑在内，则失业对健康的影响大得多。按照目前的失业率，估计每年有14 000例死亡与失业有关。[2]因此，失业成为一个重大公共卫生问题。

（四）失业与社会救助制度

社会救助制度包括各种各样的给付项目，大多在地方一级运作。在这一小节中，重点介绍各种类型的最低收入保障计划。

第一道安全网的保障对象为老年人。战前养老金制度的崩溃促使一项针对老年劳动者的家计调查式福利项目在20世纪40年代诞生。1956年，这道安全网被加以改革完善；在20世纪70年代至80年代初，其待遇水平进行了大幅调整。从20世纪50年代至60年代，老年人最低收入保障制度发挥了重要的作用：20世纪50年代末，有3/4的退休者获得了最低收入保障（而现在则不到8%）。1957年还建立了一个针对低于法定退休年龄的残障人士的专项计划。

20世纪70年代，在法国，那些被遗漏在高速经济增长之外，并暂时或永久地被排斥在劳动力市场外或是在劳动力市场上处于不利地位的人得到了越来越多的关注。这导致了以特定类型的人口为保障对象的其他最低收入保障项目的建立。这些特定类型的人口包括：残障人士（AAH，1975年）、单身父母（API，1976年）[3]和寡妇（及鳏夫）（AV，1981年）。

随着失业率的上升，1982—1984年，社会党政府对失业制度的规定进行了更改，以减少失业津贴方面的公共支出。因此，一个由国家财政资助的专项最低收入保障项目（ASS）被制定出台，为那些参加了失业保险制度但待遇领取资格已用尽的失业者提供救助。然而，由于大部分失业者未获得任何失业津贴[4]，大规模失业引发了人们对未获得任何支持的退休年龄以下的成年失业者的"新贫困"问题的担忧。因此，1988年，一项取得了广泛政治共识的针对所有25岁以上成年人的一般最低收入保障计划（RMI）被制定出台。最后，随着就业团结收入（Revenu de Solidarité Active RSA）取代了RMI，以及针对单身父母的最低收入保障项目（API）与RSA的合并，一项重大的变革于2009年发生了。

目前，约有410万人获得各类最低收入保障中的一项，并且有将近11%的人口（包括伴侣和子女）靠着这些最低保障待遇来维持生计。对这些安全网的公共支出合计达GDP的

---

1 Moussa Laanani, et al. Association Entre Taux de Chômage et Suicide, Par Sexe et Classe D'âge, en France Métropolitaine, 2000–2010.*Bulletin Épidémiologique,* 2015（1–2）.

2 Pierre Meneton, et al. Le Chômage: Un Problème de Santé Publique Majeur. *Revue de l'IRES,* 2017（91–92）.

3 该计划主要针对的是有3岁以下子女的单身父母。

4 目前，约一半的失业者没有获得任何失业津贴。

1.1%。RSA的受助者在这些待遇领取者中占46%，第二大群体（25%）则为残障人士。

创建于20世纪80年代的最低收入保障计划（ASS和RMI）的待遇水平比其他现存的最低收入保障计划低得多。这解释了为何自20世纪80年代中期以来平均最低保障收入有所下降（见图6）。

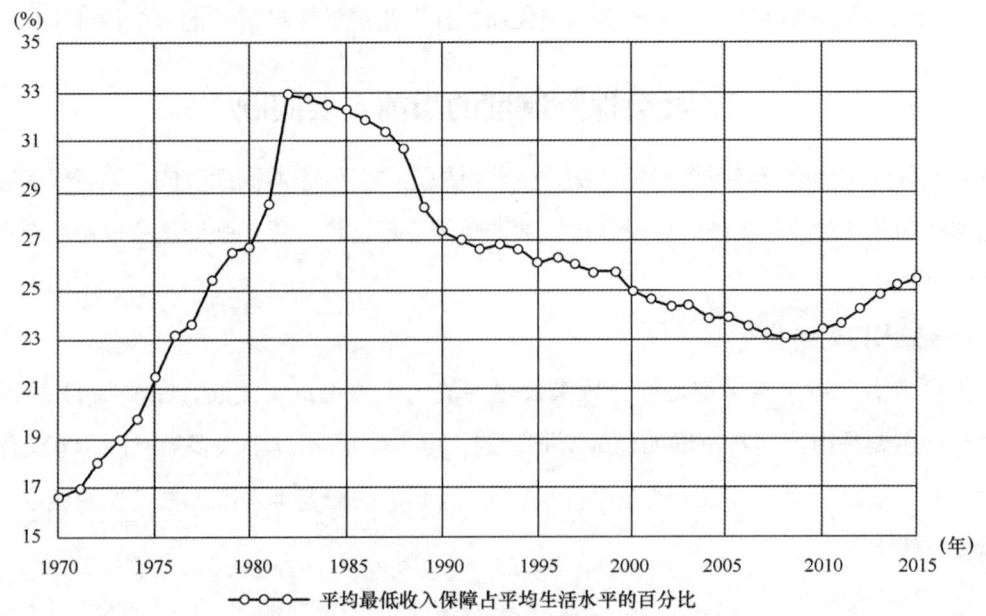

图6 与平均生活水平相比的最低收入保障

资料来源：作者根据法国研究、科研、评估和统计局（DREES），以及法国国家统计和经济研究所（INSEE）的数据整理计算所得。

20世纪90年代末，大量官方报告就RMI的潜在反向激励作用发出了警告。这促使了2009年RSA的诞生。RSA取代了RMI，并意在增强就业激励。然而，到目前为止，几乎没有任何研究能够支持有关这种反向激励效应的假设。根据对基本福利待遇领取者的一项调查，有72%的人在积极地寻找工作。[1] 而在那28%的未求职者中，40%的人提到了健康问题，仅0.5%的人表示"从经济利益的角度来看，工作反而是不划算的"。这些结果与此前对RMI的领取者的一项调查结果一致，该调查对这些待遇领取者在过去18个月的活动轨迹进行了研究。[2] 主要研究结果如下：一方面，接受救助的失业者在求

---

[1] Belleville-Pla, A. Les Trajectoires Professionnelles des Bénéficiaires de Minima Sociaux. *Études et Résultats*, 2004（320）.

[2] Danièle Guillemot, et al. Trappe à Chômage ou Trappe à Pauvreté: Quel est le Sort des Allocataires du RMI? *Revue économique*, 2002, 53（6）.

职方面非常积极，很少拒绝工作，更不用说出于经济原因（拒绝工作）。他们更可能面临劳动力需求不足。另一方面，在接受了工作的受助者中，约 1/3 的人并不获得经济上的收益。但是，对他们中的大部分人来说，就业增进了福利。对 RMI 的领取者而言，更多是掉入贫困陷阱的风险，而非掉入失业陷阱的风险。事实上，他们往往从事的是"劣质工作"并始终被困在次要部门，流动到由"优质工作"组成的主要部门的可能性非常低。[1]

二、社会保障制度的当前主要问题

社会保障正面临着各种各样的挑战，这些挑战是许多国家共同面临的。笔者仅简要地提出这些问题并对业已实施的应对这些挑战的政策进行讨论，重点强调这些政策所存在的某些局限或缺陷。

（一）人口老龄化

人口老龄化数十年来都是社会政策议题中的一个关键词。然而，在法国的情形下，这种趋势主要是由预期寿命增加趋势所驱动的（见表4）。不同于大多数欧洲国家，法国的生育率一直以来都相当高（处在更替水平）。因此，法国老年人口比重增加的速度将慢于欧盟整体。

表 4　关键的人口统计学指标

	生育率（%）		65岁时的预期寿命（男性，岁）		65岁及以上人口的比重（%）	
	2013 年	2060 年	2013 年	2060 年	2013 年	2060 年
法国	2.02	1.98	18.9	23.0	17.8	24.8
欧盟 28 国	1.60	1.76	17.6	22.4	18.4	28.4

资料来源：EU. *The 2015 Ageing Report: Economic and Budgetary Projections for the 28 EU Member States* (2013–2060), European Economy.Brussels: European Commission, 2015.

人口老龄化被认为对养老金支出和医疗卫生支出均有影响。

1. 老龄化与养老金

所有欧盟国家业已实施的养老保险制度变革已经导致——并将继续导致——养老金的大幅度削减。将欧盟国家作为一个整体来看，覆盖率和待遇水平的下降将"填补"未来 50

---

[1] 此外，在对再就业困难进行解释时，其他问题（健康、交通、育儿、资质欠缺等）在许多情况下比经济激励更加重要。

年里人口老龄化所造成的新增公共支出的80%左右（见表5）。[1] 少数几个国家的覆盖率和待遇水平的下降将超过人口老龄化带来的压力（超出幅度为20%左右），法国是其中之一。

表5　　　　　　　　2013—2060年公共养老金支出和变化的主要致因

	公共养老金（GDP的%）		主要致因（2013—2060年）			
	2013年	2060年	抚养比	覆盖率	待遇水平	其他
法国	14.9	12.1	6.7	-3.2	-4.7	-1.6
欧盟	11.3	11.1	7.2	-2.6	-3	-1.8

资料来源：EU. *The 2015 Ageing Report: Economic and Budgetary Projections for the 28 EU Member States*（*2013–2060*）, European Economy. Brussels: European Commission, 2015（3）.

从经济学的角度来看，养老金削减的必要性遭到了质疑。遵循舒尔茨所提出的观点，一些研究者认为，未来的人口变化应该不会导致劳动年龄人口经济负担的增加。[2] 原因就在于，在任何时候，劳动人口都必须从经济上供养年老与年幼的人口。此外，失业者和非经济活动人口也必须由劳动人口来供养。因此，经常被用来为削减公共养老金支出辩护的老年抚养比，并不是一个评估未来人口变化结果的恰当经济指标。如表6所示，在未来50年里，经济抚养比几乎不会增大，并且，即使把年轻人和老年人的总体成本差异考虑在内，这一结果仍然成立。[3]

表6　　　　　　　　法国和欧盟28国的抚养比

	2013—2060年的变化（%）		
	老年	人口	经济
法国	53.5	27.3	3.1
欧盟28国	80.0	48.9	6.5

各抚养比的定义：老年抚养比：65岁以上人口与15~64岁人口比值；人口抚养比：65岁及以上人口与15岁以下人口之和，与15~64岁人口的比值；经济抚养比：非劳动人口与劳动人口的比值。

资料来源：EU. *The 2015 Ageing Report*：*Economic and Budgetary Projections for the 28 EU Member States*（*2013–2060*）, European Economy. Brussels: European Commission, 2015（3）.

1　EU.*The 2015 Ageing Report: Economic and Budgetary Projections for the 28 EU Member States*（*2013–2060*）, European Economy.Brussels: European Commission, 2015（3）.

2　James H. Schulz.The Economics of Aging, Dover：Auburn House, 1988; Pierre Concialdi.*Demography, Employment and the Future of Social Security Financing*, Financing social protection in Europe.Helsinki：Ministry of Social Affairs and Health, 1999.

3　Pierre Concialdi.Demography, the Cost of Pensions and the Move to Pension Funds.*Review of Political Economy*, 2006, 18（3）.

这些表格阐明了一个事实，即主要问题不是一个有关劳动者向"非劳动者"的转移水平的经济问题；它主要涉及的是这些转移的组织以及支持经济依赖人口所需要的公共转移与私人转移的相应比重。对养老金领取者的转移通常采取强制缴费的形式，而绝大多数对年轻人的转移则是以私人现金和实物支出的形式在家庭内部进行。这在经济资源分配方式上存在本质差异，且引起了一个政治问题。

如果考虑替代方案的后果，这种选择的政治维度也是相当清楚的。事实上，我们不太可能看到，目前正在进行的转变会减少依赖人口的供养成本，尤其是养老金的成本。正如国际货币基金组织及世界银行公布的许多研究所记载的那样[1]，向私有化养老金转变并不一定会降低养老金的总成本。相反，这意味着转制成本、增加的行政成本和更多的财政补贴，这会导致劳动者养老金成本的全盘增长。因此，几乎没有任何经济上的理由支持从公立养老金制度转变为私有化的养老金制度。而这也的确是过去20年法国及其他所有欧盟成员国所做的选择，对老年贫困会产生巨大的和可能意想不到的后果。

2. 老龄化和医疗支出

正如多项研究所载且和一些传统观念相反的是，人口老龄化不会对医疗支出产生重要影响。如果通过将人口统计预测应用到按年龄分组的医疗卫生支出观察情况中来简单地模拟未来的医疗卫生支出，就会有这种情况。但是这个方法没有考虑到，按年龄组观察到的医疗卫生支出情况随着时间的推移而快速变化。法国的情况也证实了这一点。研究表明，老龄化只解释了医疗卫生支出增长的很小一部分，主要的驱动因素是实践中的变化，最重要的是所谓的技术变革。[2,3] 欧盟委员会的预测也得出同样的结论。[4]

（二）社会保障筹资

伴随着持续的经济危机和大规模失业，社会保障筹资议题一直都是个关键问题，特别

---

[1] Peter Orszag, Joseph Eugene Stiglitz.Rethinking Pension Reform: Ten Myths about Social Security Systems, in Robert Holzmann; Joseph Eugene Stiglitz（eds.）. *New Ideas about Old Age Security: Toward Sustainable Pension Systems in the 21st Century,* Washington, D.C., World Bank, 2001.

[2] Michel Grignon.*Les Conséquences du Vieillissement de la Population sur les Dépenses de Santé,* IRDES, Questions D'économie de la santé. Paris：Institut de recherche et documentation en économie de la santé, 2003（66）.

[3] Brigitte Dormont, et al.Health Expenditure Growth: Reassessing the Threat of Ageing.*Health Economics,* 2006, 15（9）.

[4] EU.*The 2015 Ageing Report: Economic and Budgetary Projections for the 28 EU Member States*（2013–2060），European Economy.Brussels: European Commission, 2015（3）.

是在法国的情形中，社会支出的资金来源中有很大一部分仍来源于社会缴费。由社会缴费向税收的转变以及雇主社会缴费豁免的推行，都旨在促进就业并减少失业。当前一个越来越普遍的共识是，这些政策并没有成功地减少失业。多项研究表明，这些政策反而增加了贫困，并导致越来越多的劳动者困于没有出路的工作，因而使被困在低工资陷阱中的劳动者对社会保障的需求增加。这可能是过去 20 年里所实施政策的另一个"意料之外"的效应。

从宏观层面来看，2008 年的金融危机助推了关于社会保障筹资的讨论。和所有欧洲国家一样，在法国，公共赤字增加，政府会强调削减社会开支是减少公共债务的必要条件。然而，这些观点可能会在以下两个方面受到挑战。

一方面，在大多数欧洲国家，公共债务不是来源于社会保障管理部门的任何债务（见表 7）。尽管在大多数国家社会保障待遇的确是公共支出的最大一部分，但几乎所有国家的社会保障行政管理机构在公共债务总额中的比重都是零或是非常低。在这种背景下，削减社会保障待遇对减少公共债务几乎没有任何影响。

表 7　部分欧洲国家 2015 年社会保障行政管理机构在公共债务和公共支出中的比重　（%）

	占公共债务之比	占公共支出之比
爱沙尼亚	0.0	13.6
塞浦路斯	0.0	21.6
拉脱维亚	0.0	24.7
克罗地亚	0.0	40.8
葡萄牙	0.0	26.5
斯洛伐克	0.0	31.6
斯洛文尼亚	0.0	38.2
意大利	0.0	39.9
保加利亚	0.0	36.2
卢森堡	0.0	42.1
捷克	0.0	13.1
希腊	0.0	33.3
德国	0.1	43.3

续表

	占公共债务之比	占公共支出之比
丹麦	0.1	4.6
匈牙利	0.2	30.0
奥地利	0.6	33.6
罗马尼亚	1.3	31.0
西班牙	1.6	33.9
比利时	1.9	35.0
瑞典	2.0	12.8
芬兰	2.4	35.5
波兰	4.9	40.1
荷兰	8.2	38.3
法国	10.9	46.6
立陶宛	23.6	34.8
欧盟	2.5	31.6
欧元区	3.2	40.1

资料来源：欧盟统计局（Eurostat）。

另一方面，从经济学的角度来看，人们可以批评"削减社会支出会对经济增长产生积极影响"这一假设。事实上，这一假设支持的政策得到了国际货币基金组织及其他国际组织的提倡，并对一些国家的人口健康产生了巨大的影响，比如希腊。[1] 然而，数年前，国际货币基金组织的首席经济学家承认，财政整顿对经济增长的影响与低于预期的增长率相关，因为"财政乘数明显高于预测者所默认假设的"。[2]

另一个补充性的并且可能更加有趣的解释是，不同类型的公共支出存在着显著的异质性：财政乘数从国防（支出）的 −9.8 到卫生（支出）的 +4.3 不等（见图 7）。[3] 用作者的话来说："国内经济对政府支出的吸收程度的不同似乎可以解释这些差异。国防与显著扩大的贸易逆差有关，而卫生和教育则对贸易逆差没有影响。"

1　Noelle Burgi. Le Démantèlement Méthodique et Tragique des Institutions Grecques de Santé Publique. *Revue de l'IRES,* 2017（91–92）.

2　Olivier Blanchard, Daniel Leigh. *Growth Forecast Errors and Fiscal Multipliers,* IMF Working Paper. Washington, D.C: International Monetary Fund, 2013.

3　Aaron Reeves, et al. Does Investment in the Health Sector Promote or Inhibit Economic Growth? *Globalization and Health,* 2013, 9（43）.

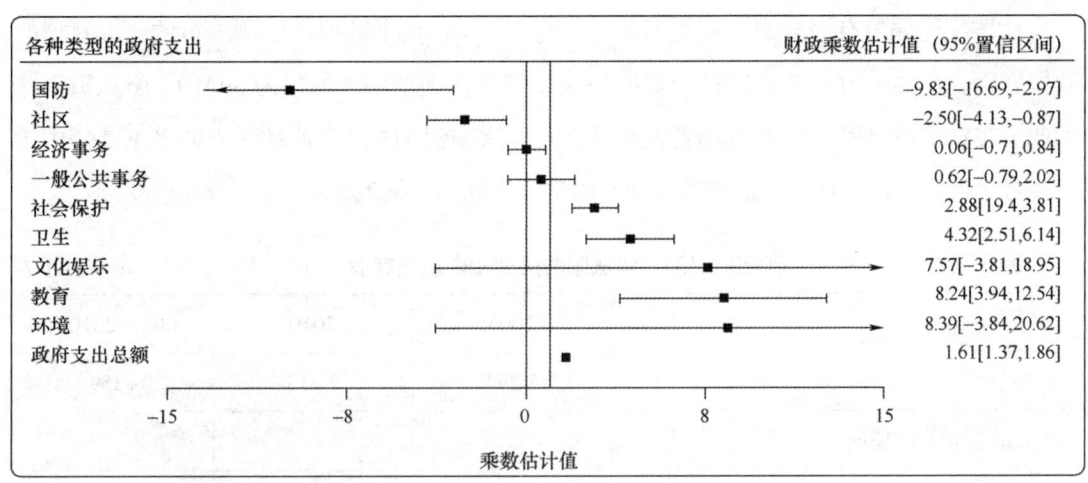

图 7 各类政府支出的财政乘数

资料来源：Aaron Reeves, et al. Does Investment in the Health Sector Promote or Inhibit Economic Growth? *Globalization and Health*, 2013, 9（43）.

（三）失业、就业不足、低工资及其他形式的未适当就业[1]

对所有的社会保障制度来说，失业都是个显而易见的巨大挑战，因为它在侵蚀制度资源的同时使人们对社会保障的需求增加。然而，单独一个数字并不能全面反映劳动者所面临的各种就业问题。非典型就业（短期合同、临时工作、有补贴的短期工作）在 20 世纪八九十年代的大部分时间里急剧增加。在 1982—1997 年间，新增工作岗位中有九成是非典型的工作。

就业不足，以及更笼统地说，各种形式的未适当就业也急剧增加。按照国际劳工组织的定义，可以区分"定量"就业不足（或"非自愿的非全日制"劳动者，即愿意工作更多的劳动者）和"定性"就业不足（指那些不得不从事低于他们的技能或经验水平的工作的劳动者）。

过去 30 年，定量就业不足急剧增加。自 20 世纪 90 年代早期以来的有关就业不足的数据可通过欧盟统计局历年的劳动力调查（Labour Force Surveys）获得。尽管有一些方法和概念上的变化[2]，但可以估计的是，自 20 世纪 90 年代初以来，就业不足者的数量翻了一番以上，增加了 100 万人。换言之，非但失业没有减少，就业不足也大量增加。

  1　译者注：在多数情形下，"underemployment"和"inadequate employment"都被作为可互换的同义词。然而，作者在文中对这两个概念的使用却暗示二者之间或许存在一些差别。结合原文语境，译者将此处及下文中的"underemployment"和"inadequate employment"分别译作"不充分就业"与"未适当就业"。

  2　就业不足定义的最新变化发生在 2009 年，由此导致了约 25 万人从统计数据中"消失"。

法国统计局没有报告定性就业不足。然而，一个法国非政府组织所进行的研究获得的数据表明，2003—2010 年，这种形式的失业非常迅速地增加（增幅为 30%）。所从事工作远低于其技能或经验水平的劳动者人数从 240 万增加到 315 万。这种现象似乎主要集中于年轻劳动者群体，并且这也是未适当就业的主要推动力（见表 8）。

表 8　　2003—2010 年法国的失业和未适当就业　　　　　　　单位：千人

年份	2003	2010	2003—2010 年
A. 失业	2 294	2 653	+359
B. 未适当就业的情况			
1. 低工资就业	3 732	3 785	+54
2. 非典型工作	2 546	2 744	+198
3. 不充分就业	3 773	4 743	+970
4. "恶劣的"工作条件	1 735	1 932	+196
5. 想另谋工作的劳动者	2 375	2 620	+245
C. 未适当就业的情况（无重复计算）	9 165	10 075	+910
失业率（%）	8.5	9.4	+0.9
未适当就业率（%）	33.9	35.5	+1.6

资料来源：ACDC, Les Autres Chiffres du Chômage, http://acdc2007.free.fr/（Paris）.

过去 20 年来法国实施的旨在抗击失业的政策显然没有到达其目标。更普遍的是，大部分已实施的就业政策对劳动力市场产生了不利影响。随着低工资工作的增加，劳动者被困在这种工作岗位的风险也明显增加[1]——至少在短期内。与此同时，失业与低工资工作之间的转换也变得越加频繁。[2] 而且似乎不存在任何明显的跳板效应（Springboard Effect），把这些从事劣质工作的劳动者引到某种正规的工作岗位上。[3]

1　Pierre Concialdi, Sophie Ponthieux.Low Pay and Poor Workers: A Comparative Study of France and the USA. *Transfer,* 2000, 6（4）.

2　Pierre Concialdi.Employment at All Costs? Limits and Shortfalls of French Employment Policies.in Marc Humbert, Yoshimichi Sato（eds.）, *Social Exclusion: Perspectives from France and Japan,* Melbourne：Trans Pacific Press, 2012.

3　Pauline Givord, Lionel Wilner.*Les Contrats Temporaires: Trappe ou Marchepied vers L'emploi Stable?*INSEE, Documents de Travail, Paris: French National Institute of Statistics and Economic Studies, 2009（4）.

三、如何成功应对当前的挑战

过去30年里，对法国社会保障制度所做的改变已逐渐地——但无疑也实质性地——改变了制度的基本理念。无论是社会党还是保守党（执政），政府推行的成本控制政策，同样削减了社会保障制度的覆盖面和待遇水平。为"调整"社会保障制度以使其适应全球化的新制约和所谓的数字化时代而年复一年作出的政策决断导致了结构性的变化。

这一结果是不是政策制定者有意为之，仍将会在长时间内难以得出定论。

不管答案是什么，事实上这些政策并没有达到他们所提倡的目标。因此，人们就再次改革的必要性达成了某种程度的共识。然而，社会参与者、政策制定者和研究者对这些改革内容的理解和认知差异甚大。一般来说，研究者们形成了两种相互对立的主要观点，两者争论不休。[1,2]

所谓的传统观点强调在市场条件下社会保障对经济正常运行的潜在不利影响。然而，很难在经济学文献中找到这个观点的有力经验支持。研究者们强调，当代经济学主流理论并未提供一个良好的框架来分析这个问题，并因此对社会保障制度的实际积极影响视而不见。

抛开并超越任何经济学的辩论，还需要在更广泛的框架内设计社会保障，包括通过监管来驯服市场的措施。按照波兰尼（Polanyi）的观点，社会保障首先是一种旨在保护劳动者免受市场力量影响的社会反应，在此基础上，则可以认为，在放松对劳动力市场和金融市场管制的同时，不仅没有加强社会保障，反而通过愈发糟糕的安全网的恢复性政策去削弱它，这无异于抱薪救火。[3] 困难在于，力争进一步放松市场管制的呼声很难为历史（实证）经验所反驳。正如弗雷德·布洛克（Fred Block）所说："由于社会总是从市场自我调节的全面实验中抽身而退，其理论家们总是可以声称，任何失败都不是由于政策设计，而是由

---

[1] Anthony Barnes Atkinson.The Economics of the Welfare State: An Incomplete Debate.in *The Welfare State in Europe: Challenges and Reforms,* European Economy, Luxembourg: Official Publications of the European Communities, 1997（4）.

[2] Assar Lindbeck.Welfare State Dynamics.in *The Welfare State in Europe: Challenges and Reforms,* European Economy, Cheltenham, Edward Elgar, 1997（4）.

[3] Karl Polanyi.*The Great Transformation: The Political and Economic Origins of Our Time*.Foreword by Joseph Eugene Stiglitz，introduction by Fred Block, Boston: Beacon Press, 2001.

于实施中缺乏政治意愿。因此，市场自我调节的信条无法被历史经验抹杀"[1]。

必须通过考虑社会保障的目标（即其社会可持续性）来分析社会保障制度所面临的挑战和应对这些问题所需要的可能解决方案，从而给人们提供充足的覆盖和福利待遇。

上文表明，社会保障制度呈加速下行的趋势。如果不进行改革，未来几十年，尽管整个社会会变得前所未有的富裕，但社会保障制度提供的福利待遇将会更差。不平等和贫困将会增加。为了解决这个问题，我们可以借鉴托尼·阿特金森（Tony Atkinson）的提议，他的这本著作是基于几十年的经验和研究。[2]

第一个提议涉及经济运行。在此，笔者仅简要介绍与劳动力市场运行直接相关的提议。由于对大多数人来说，工资是唯一的收入来源，因此给劳动者提供公平和充足的工资以使他们无须依赖社会救助待遇来维持生计就显得非常关键。第一个提议与失业问题有关，即政府应当确定预防与减少失业的明确目标，并相应向有意愿者按最低工资标准提供公共就业保障。考虑到当前法国大规模的失业，人们也可以质疑延长决定退休年龄的趋势。延长法定退休年龄将增加劳动力供给。

第二个重要的提议是，应该有一个全国性的薪酬政策，涵盖按生存工资设定的法定最低工资等事项。在法国的情形下，这种生存工资意味着将目前的最低工资增加40%左右。最低工资并非通常所定义的社会保障体系的正式组成部分，但它是所有社会政策的基础，因为它决定了所有低收入工作者的生活条件。

还有一条行动路线则是扭转社会权利的分割趋势，实现社会保障制度某种类型的全覆盖。就短期而言，第一步是要提高现有的安全网和福利待遇的最低标准。在法国，这显然已成为当务之急。根据法国国家贫困及社会排斥观察所（ONPES）近期的一项研究，约40%的人口未获得过上体面生活所需的充足资源。[3]

当然，这些变化需要增加社会支出。阿特金森的书中对这个问题进行了讨论，并且他指出这些改革从财务上来看是可持续的，故在此笔者不会就这一定量问题展开详细的论述。另一个问题则涉及社会保障制度的筹资渠道。这是一个因国家而异的具体问题。在法国的

1　Fred Block.Introduction, in Karl Polanyi.*The Great Transformation: The Political and Economic Origins of Our Time*.Beacon Press, 2001.

2　Anthony Barnes Atkinson. *Inequality: What Can be Done?*Cambridge：Harvard University Press, 2015.

3　ONPES.*Reference Budgets: Assessing the Needs to be Met for an Effective Participation in Society. 2014–2015 Report*. Paris: French National Observatory on Poverty and Social Exclusion, 2015.

情形下，争论焦点仍然是社会缴费和税收之间的区别。然而，正如有研究表明的那样，每个国家的税收制度都取决于不同的政治体制，而这些体制均发端于特定的历史。[1] 因此，对于如何在中国的情境下解决这个问题，如果没有基于该国社会政策文献的完善健全的评估，基本不可能得出任何确切的结论。

---

1 Sven Steinmo. *Taxation and Democracy: Swedish, British and American Approaches to Financing the Modern State*. New Haven: Yale University Press, 1993.

北欧国家经济发展和社会保障之间的动态关系——为福利而增长还是为增长而福利？

[丹麦]克劳斯·彼得森[1]

北欧模式是享誉世界的社会模式。自20世纪20年代以来，北欧模式就在社会保障、善治与先进性方面为其他国家所效仿。[2]北欧模式因平衡了经济发展和社会保障而备受赞誉。例如，北欧国家在社会保障、幸福与信任指数、财富水平、平等、性别平等和减贫等方面的国际排名几乎总在前十。对此可以理解为，北欧地区的经验表明了社会保障与经济发展完美共存的可能性。用北欧理事会（北欧国家间合作的主要论坛）的话来说：

"福利国家对于经济有益。北欧国家采取了相对类似的制度化发展模式。在所有北欧国家中，国家和公共部门主要通过投资于基础设施、教育、科研和社会福利的方式在经济领域扮演了重要角色。尽管北欧国家的税收水平很高，当论及经济发展时福利国家仍被视为其优势之一。福利国家不仅造福了全体人口，而且对经济起到了正面影响。公共部门和福利服务帮助北欧国家培养了高技能劳动力，维持了较高的就业水平。再加上稳定的公民社会、强大的民主传统和有效的监管体系，促成了广泛的社会资本的出现，这是北欧经济的主要支柱之一。"[3]

然而，本文的目的不在于对北欧模式再一次进行赞誉或验证北欧理事会上述论点的正确性[4]。本文旨在提供一个历史性描述，揭示北欧模式发展背后的潜在政治逻辑或规范性理念，以及它们近来发生的变化。在模式长期稳定和对国际压力、经济危机成功适应的表象

---

1 [作者简介]克劳斯·彼得森（Klaus Petersen），南丹麦大学福利国家研究中心主任（Head of Centre for Welfare State Research, University of Southern Denmark, Odense）。

[译者简介]陶冶，中国人民大学中国社会保障研究中心博士，中国社会保障学会秘书处学术助理。

[翻译审校]华颖，中国社会科学院人口与劳动经济研究所助理研究员。

2 Hilson, M. *The Nordic model: Scandinavia since 1945*. London: Reaktion Books, 2008.

3 Nordic Council. *Business and the economy*, 2016.http://www.norden.org/en/fakta-om-norden-1/business-and-the-economy [24 October 2017].

4 Barth, E.; Moene, K.O.; Willumsen, F.The Scandinavian model: An interpretation. in *Journal of Public Economics*, 2014：60-72.

背后，也正在发生一些变化。事实上，我们观察到两种"北欧模式"，这两种模式有时共存、有时彼此独立。一方面，北欧拥有因高水平的社会保障、再分配和经济现代化而为福利国家比较研究所称颂的"经典"社会保障模式；另一方面，我们看到，在一个以全球竞争为特征的世界中，北欧模式被描绘成一个成功且具有竞争力的模式。例如，《福布斯》杂志将北欧国家列入最适合营商的国家[1]；2013年年初《经济学人》杂志的头版上写道：下一个超级模式：为什么世界应该看一看北欧国家。当人们仔细阅读就会发现，《经济学人》杂志所谈论的并不是福利国家，而是经济意义上的福利。讨论的焦点是创新能力、竞争力和改革能力。

因此，有两种北欧模式——社会保障模式和增长/竞争/创新模式。两者有着不同却互相关联的逻辑。在社会保障模式逻辑下，经济增长和发展是社会保障扩张的前提条件，其最终目标是社会融合、抗击贫困、再分配与平等，以及创造机会平等。这些是北欧福利国家的经典目标。在增长/竞争/创新模式逻辑下，社会保障被视为促进国民经济增长的方式，其最终目标是经济增长、创新和国际竞争力。北欧福利国家模式起初是这两种模式中的第一种，但在过去几十年中逐渐转变为第二种模式。这在社会和政治方面都产生了影响。

接下来，本文将概述北欧福利国家社会保障与经济增长之间的历史关系，并讨论最近几十年的发展如何给这种关系带来根本性变化。

一、经典北欧福利国家的经济发展和社会保障

丹麦、挪威和瑞典在推行基本社会保障改革方面都是先驱国家[2]。和其他欧洲国家一样，在这些国家发生的第一波社会改革主要是由对工业化和市场经济影响的担忧所推动的。包括社会民主主义劳工运动参与者、农民、社会自由主义者、慈善组织、保守派和社会政策专家在内的一群迥然相异的行动者均提出了这些担忧。其结果是在1900年左右推出了一系列社会改革措施，其中包括养老金、医疗保险、工伤保险以及稍后推出的失业保险（以及各种儿童福利改革）。

这是基于完全不同的原则的一套混合改革，在北欧国家之间和内部都有差异[3]。但事后

---

1 Forbes. *Best countries for business*, 2016. http://www.forbes.com/best-countries-for-business/list/［24 October 2017］.

2 Christiansen, N.F. et al.（eds）. *The Nordic welfare state: A historical re-appraisal*. Copenhagen: Museum Tusculanum Press, 2006.

3 Kuhnle, S. et al.（eds）. *The Nordic model of welfare*（in Chinese）. Shanghai: Fudan University Press, 2010.

看来，我们可以看到后来成为北欧模式重要原则的几条规律：
- 改革具有普遍性（覆盖全体人口的综合项目）
- 重点是税收筹资（随着时间的推移越来越多）
- 国家组织了改革并担任最后出资人

从今天的视角来看，这些初始步骤在待遇和社会权利方面都相当温和。社会权利（公民对国家的权利主张权）的想法在20世纪30年代才获得了强有力的立足点。

此外，早期的北欧福利国家在政治上受到争议。自北欧福利国家历史的第一天起，关于经济增长和社会保障的争论就从未停止。与其他欧洲国家一样，一个多世纪以来，对北欧社会改革和高税收的批评者认为，扩大的社会权利将阻碍经济增长、滋生怠惰，并有损个人和家庭自给自足的道德义务。这种批评——"走向地狱的道路铺满了善意""社会改革威胁经济发展"——在许多情况下阻碍了社会民主党和社会自由派的改革议程，认为国家的作用（只应）是为所有公民创造平等的机会和提供基本的社会保障（而不是全面综合的福利国家）。但逐渐地，社会改革带来了覆盖更多人的新社会权利、更高的福利和更多的国家调控。

这种发生在几十年间的发展，是观念、政治、外部和经济因素之间复杂的相互作用的结果。

为福利国家改革打开大门的关键之一是预防性社会政策的理念，这是从20世纪二三十年代逐渐发展起来的。预防性社会政策的关键论点是它是合理的（科学的），从长远来看可以节省资金。通过这种方式，社会政策被视为对社会及其未来的投资。但与此同时，对早期干预的更多关注也为更强的国家干预打开了大门——尤其是在家庭政策方面。

推动社会改革议程的其他重要关键是两次世界大战和20世纪30年代深刻的经济危机的综合影响。这些外部事件显然是国家调控和税收增长的推动力，并表明了国家在这些危机时刻作为"最后出资人"的重要性。

然而，如果就1945年以前社会支出占GNP的比重而言，福利国家的角色是十分有限的。20世纪30年代到50年代之间的时期显示了发展的方向，但北欧福利国家的大变革只发生在20世纪六七十年代。

二、增长极限或北欧福利国家的危机

在20世纪40年代中后期，按照欧洲标准，北欧国家的公共支出（占GDP的百分比）相对较低。但这种情况在 20 世纪 60 年代发生了巨大改变。正如我们从图 1 中看到的那样，从 20 世纪 60 年代开始，丹麦和瑞典从支出较少的国家发展到支出较多的国家之列。

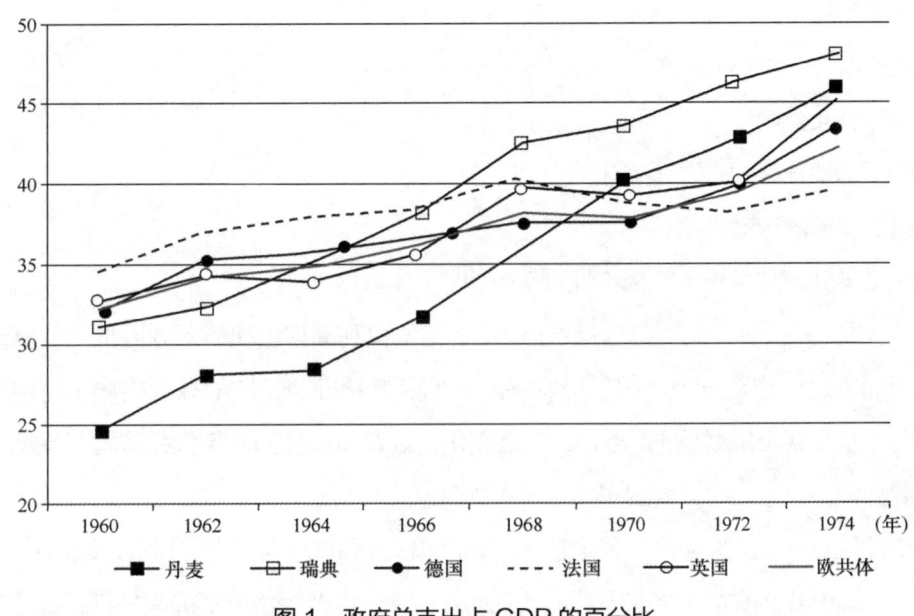

图 1　政府总支出占 GDP 的百分比

数据来源：Organisation for Economic Co-operation and Development（OECD）. *OECD Economic Outlook*, 1982（32）: 161.

这是北欧社会的一次引人注目和迅速的变化——它发生在经济增长率非常高的时期（见图 1、表 1）。公共支出占 GDP 的比例加倍，而且这是发生在 GDP 显著增长和失业实际上不存在的时期。笔者认为谈论北欧福利在 20 世纪 60 年代的重大变革是合理的。

表 1　　　　　　　　　　　北欧国家年均增长率　　　　　　　　　　　（%）

	1870—1913 年	1913—1950 年	1950—1973 年	1973—2001 年
丹麦	2.66	2.55	3.81	2.06
瑞典	2.17	2.74	3.73	1.83
挪威	2.12	2.93	4.06	3.30
芬兰	2.74	2.69	4.94	2.57

来源：Hilson, *M. The Nordic model: Scandinavia since* 1945. London: Reaktion Books, 2008.

这种变化的结果是我们现在称之为北欧福利国家的出现,北欧福利国家的特点:

- 普遍性(人人享有同一制度)
- 社会权利(基于公民身份)
- 国家调控
- 税收筹资(主导原则)
- 大型公共部门
- 基于本地社区的方式(变化的空间小)
- 组织严密的劳动力市场
- 注重再分配和平等(阶级、性别)

在本文的框架内,无法勾画导致这种特定类型福利国家出现的不同因素间的复杂相互作用。简而言之,这是一个世纪以来发展起来的制度特征、特定的政治格局(特别是社会民主党的力量及其形成联盟的能力)、增量变化,以及20世纪60年代经济增长创造的机会窗口的混合体。

在20世纪60年代的北欧政治辩论中,我们可以找到一个强有力的想法,即建立一个"良性循环",[1] 其中社会改革、国家干预、谈判而非冲突,以及经济发展齐头并进,以走向更光明的未来。经济增长(经济现代化和工业化)是这一战略的重要组成部分,我们也发现了一些教育改革的例子,将扩大职业培训和区域发展倡议作为核心要素。但这些目标均与福利有关:经济发展旨在确保实现社会融合、平等和使所有公民过上更好生活的社会保障目标。

其中一个例子就是将女性纳入劳动力市场。[2] 在20世纪40年代,北欧只有大约25%~30%的女性参与劳动力市场活动。从20世纪60年代开始,这种情况开始发生重大变化,并且在20世纪80年代,女性的劳动力市场参与率达到60%以上,并从那时起逐步接近男性就业率水平。女性经济状况的这种巨大变化至少在两个方面与福利国家有关。一方面,福利国家的发展为女性创造了就业机会,特别是在护理和教育部门。另一方面,福利国家(或者说它背后的政治力量)系统地制定了政策推动或拉动女性进入劳动力市场。这尤其包括大幅度扩大儿童的公共日托服务和改革育儿假制度。其背后的政治逻辑是,社

---

1 Kettunen, P. Reinterpreting the historicity of the Nordic model. in *Nordic Journal of Working Life Studies*, 2012, 2(4): 21-43.

2 Åmark, K. Women's labour force participation in the Nordic countries during the twentieth century. in N. F. Christiansen et al. (eds), 2006: 299-334.

会投资（如优质日托）对儿童有利，并使女性能够更好地掌控自己的生活和职业，而劳动力规模的扩大有利于经济发展。

三、福利国家的新逻辑

从北欧福利国家的黄金时代（1950—1980 年）走向今天，我们发现在指导社会保障与经济发展关系的范式上发生了一场无声的重大变革或变化。[1] 从表面上看，状况可能看起来非常相似：北欧基本的福利国家制度依然存在，北欧福利国家仍然具有较高水平的社会权利、福利和再分配水平，以及全面的社会保障体系。北欧福利国家在 20 世纪 70 年代、90 年代乃至 21 世纪的经济危机中生存下来。北欧社会已经能够适应全球化和国际金融市场的新世界。北欧福利国家——至少比其他大多数欧洲福利国家——为未来的人口变化做了更充足准备。

然而，如果我们仔细观察，也可以看到变化。北欧模式作为世界模式中的超级模式的重新出现[2]与高社会福利、平等或低贫困率本身并无太大关系。最重要的是，这表明社会保障与经济增长关系的逻辑已经发生了变化。我们仍然可以看到相同的制度，但它们现在正在遵循一种新的逻辑。福利国家不再是目标，而是增强经济表现的手段。这听起来像是一种非黑即白的情形，实际上当然更为复杂：在丹麦和瑞典失业者的境遇仍然比在世界其他地方更好，但与此同时，肯定也与 20 世纪六七十年代的情形不同。

通向这种新范式——一些研究人员称之为"竞争国家"[3]（与旧的"福利国家"形成对比）——的道路在北欧国家非常相似。这是全球化、移民和老龄化社会等结构性变化给福利国家带来挑战的结果，但它首先是一种认知上的变化：一种不同的框架，一种理解福利国家意义的新方式。这是由对福利国家的批评所驱动的。新自由主义和左翼对普惠型福利国家批评的综合影响使得古典福利国家毫无抵御之力。一种新的"普遍观点"出现，平等、社会融合、社会保障和机会均等等古典美德让步于这样一种观点，即认为社会政策是一种应加强经济增长和国家在世界市场中竞争力的公共投资。

在丹麦，2013 年财政部部长宣称竞争国家是新的福利国家。[4] 在瑞典，中右翼政府在 2012

1，3　Pedersen, O. K. *Konkurrencestaten* [Competition states]. Copenhagen: Hans Reitzels Forlag, 2011.

2　*The Economist*. The Nordic countries: The next supermodel. special report, *Northern lights*, 2013（2）.

4　Petersen, J. H. *Pligt og ret. Ret og pligt: Refleksioner over den socialdemokratiske idéarv* [Duty and right. Right and duty: Reflections on the Social Democratic idea]. Odense: University of Southern Denmark Press, 2014.

年瑞士达沃斯经济论坛上发布了一本关于"北欧之路"的小册子,认为北欧的经验表明了社会福利与经济发展之间的积极相互作用。[1] 该报告认为,成功的"北欧资本主义"可以作为世界的典范。

这并不是说范式是错误的。在北欧国家建立社会保障与经济发展之间的积极关系有很好的理由。然而,这种范式的变化似乎也会对社会保障产生影响。它给福利国家留下了裂缝,使得处理全球化、老龄化社会、个体化等结构变化的社会后果变得更加困难。

下文将以丹麦为例,简要说明一些可能预示着北欧福利国家价值体系变化的趋势。

边缘化(和污名化)。在过去的几十年里,我们目睹了对"非生产性公民"污名化的加深。这一群体非常多样化,涵盖残障人士、精神疾病确诊患者、长期失业劳动者、移民,甚至"与市场不太相关"专业(如戏剧科学或消亡语言专业)的大学生。政治家和媒体谈论这些群体的方式已经发生了重大转变,不是将他们视作弱小脆弱、需要帮助的群体,而是更倾向于强调他们的个人责任和其对社会的责任。[2] 政府报告、公开辩论和一系列旨在使劳动力市场以外的人的生活更不具吸引力的新的工作福利政策已经提出了上述论点。这包括对工作能力的严格审查(甚至有病人在被审查时被迫将病床带到工作场所的例子)、限制提供长期待遇的项目,或者由于工作记录不佳而削减福利。我们肯定会找到"大棒加胡萝卜"的例子,但平衡已经改变,更倾向于使用严格的大棒政策。

二元化。有些群体(通常是最弱势的群体)面临更严厉的福利国家政策,而富裕群体(庞大的中产阶级及以上的成员)往往有更好的选择。这可能是"二元化"公共政策[3]的结果,也是对私人替代方案日益重视的结果。福利政策中二元化的最明显例子是移民政策。在这方面,北欧国家现在都有着双轨制:一个非常严苛的系统试图让难民和非技术移民离开这些国家,另一个非常友好的系统(低税率、快速通道等)试图吸引高技术移民。私人替代方案的增长在创造一个更加分化的福利国家中起着重要作用。由于新自由主义对"消费者自由选择"的要求和预算限制,市场条件下的福利生产显著增长。结果,通常通过教育券或有吸引力的税收减免激励,使越来越多的家长选择私立学校而非公立学校;针对某些群

---

[1] Kettunen, P.et al.The Nordic model and the rise and fall of Nordic cooperation.in J.Strang(ed.):*Nordic cooperation:A European region in transition*(London,Routledge),2016:69-92.

[2] Petersen, J. H. *Pligt og ret. Ret og pligt: Refleksioner over den socialdemokratiske idéarv* [Duty and right. Right and duty: Reflections on the Social Democratic idea]. Odense: University of Southern Denmark Press, 2014.

[3] Emmenegger, P.et al.(eds).The age of dualization:*The changing face of inequality in de-industrialized societies*, International Policy Exchange Series.Oxford:Oxford University Press.

体的私人健康保险提供更快速、更优质的治疗；私人（集体或个人）养老金计划将分割未来养老金待遇领取者群体。其结果是，北欧福利国家的一个关键特征，即"普遍主义"或一种模式覆盖全体公民的状况正逐渐发生变化。我们不再享有相同的普遍政策——我们甚至可能不在同一个社会保障体系中。

不平等。如果我们遵循国际排名（通常以基尼系数衡量），北欧国家在世界上最平等的国家之列。但过去十年来收入不平等一直在增加。年轻人和移民等人群的贫困率一直在显著增长。如果我们看看健康等其他指标，也会发现社会群体之间的差异越来越大。例如，在哥本哈根的两个邻近地区，平均预期寿命有六七年的差距。这也反映了空间不平等日益增长的重要性。在一些地区（主要是大城市周围），经济发展且社会福利标准相对较高，而农村地区情况看起来更为不乐观（社会问题集中、失业、低税基等）。

合法性问题。从长远来看，这里探讨的问题可能会导致合法性问题。如果通过选择私人医疗保险、私立学校和私人养老金来退出普遍福利计划，公民是否会继续支持普遍福利计划并支付高额税收？我们可能正在走向一个更少关注集体而更多受个人利益驱动的社会。我们可能面临代际冲突：下一代可能是并不比父母生活更好的第一代。这种新的国际竞争范式的成本和收益都不是平等分布的，我们开始看到抗议派别包括富裕阶层（主张税收减免）和那些感受到威胁的人（往往期待新的右翼民粹主义政党）。并且从整体上看，人们对政客越来越不信任。

四、北欧福利国家将去往何处？

北欧案例并不是反对经济增长重要性的论据。如果没有非常有利的宏观经济历史环境，北欧福利国家会大不相同。北欧福利国家成功的部分原因正是通过受调控的市场经济培育了增长与福利的关系，这是为了社会保障的经济发展。当然，有必要对福利国家制度进行持续的改革和调整。福利国家应该是动态的，并且总是随着历史（社会和经济）环境的变化而变化。但是，这些政策变化不能脱离规范性目标或理念。这正是推动北欧福利国家发展的原因："更美好的明天"的梦想和对这个"更美好的明天"的理解，包括诸如包容性、人人享有社会保障、平等机会和平等化等规范理想。这就是代际之间的交易（社会契约）：我们现在投资，希望为我们的孩子创造一个美好的未来。当然，结果远非完美。北欧社会保障体系一直存在着裂痕和错误，需要加以修复和纠正。但是，最近几十年来，出现了比以前更多、更深的裂缝，规范性指南也发生了变化。这一发展的一个重要部分是范式从"为了社会保障而发展经济"向"为了经济发展而建设社会保障"的转变。

这是好事还是坏事取决于政治态度。市场解决方案的坚定信奉者可能将此视为实现旧梦。但对于那些相信包容、平等和社会稳定等目标，以及相信国家（甚至社会）的作用是为最脆弱的人群提供社会保障的人们来说，未来看起来更具威胁性。

参考文献

① Albrekt Larsen, C.; Goul Andersen, J.How new economic ideas changed the Danish welfare state: The case of neoliberal ideas and highly organized Social Democratic interests. in *Governance*, 2009, 22（2）: 239–261.

② Andersen, T.M.; Bergman, M.; Hougaard Jensen, S. E.（eds）. *Reform capacity and macroeconomic performance in the Nordic countries*. Oxford: Oxford University Press, 2014.

③ Petersen, J.H.; Petersen, K.; Christiansen, N.F.（eds）. *Dansk Velfærdshistorie* [Danish welfare story], Vols.1–6, Odense: Odense University Press.

比较视野中的美国：福利国家与经济发展

[美] 约翰·史蒂芬斯[1]

一、术语界定：福利国家与发展

在对福利国家进行界定时，笔者遵循马歇尔（T.H.Marshall）有关社会公民权的经典文献，并把范围拓宽。Marshall 论述道：

"我所指的（公民权的）社会要素，是从少许的经济福利与保障权到充分分享社会传统和按照社会普遍标准过文明人生活的权利的整个范围。"[2]

可见，Marshall 所指的不仅仅是获得公共转移与公共服务。他意图将这一概念扩展到积极参与社会的权利。这是他对公共教育进行广泛探讨的原因。而由于公共教育先于被广泛认为是首部现代社会立法的 1883 年德国俾斯麦《疾病保险法》的诞生，它通常不被视作现代福利国家的一部分。公民社会权利的主要特征在于其使得对公共转移、货物和服务的主张成为必需，而"所主张的公共转移、货物和服务与主张者的市场价值并不相称"。[3] 这是他最常被引用的断言的基础，即"在 20 世纪，公民身份和资产阶级制度一直处于对抗状态"。[4]

在界定发展方面，笔者遵循阿马蒂亚·森（Amartya Sen）的人类能力方法。Sen 在 20 世纪 90 年代的研究把人类的繁荣、增强人的能力作为发展的目标，但又不止于此。他把幸福从被动的消费品转变为行动的更多可能性。Sen 认为，"幸福"不仅包括增加满足感或减少痛苦，还包括人类做自己想做的事、"过自己所珍视的那种生活"的能力。[5] 尽管在其他条

---

[1] [作者简介] 约翰·史蒂芬斯（John D. Stephens），北卡罗来纳大学教授（University of North Carolina at Chapel Hill）。主要研究方向：福利国家，政治科学。

[译者简介] 杨无意，中国人民大学中国社会保障研究中心博士生，中国社会保障学会秘书处学术助理。

[翻译审校] 华颖，中国社会科学院人口与劳动经济研究所助理研究员。

2，3 Marshall, T.H. *Citizenship and social class*. in T.H. Marshall and Tom Bottomore. *Citizenship and Social Class*, London: Pluto Press, 1950：1–51.

[4] 在许多早期的研究中，教育未被作为福利国家的一部分，但近来，特别是在欧盟转向社会投资之后，它更经常被包括在内。

[5] Sen, Amartya. *Development as Freedom*. New York: Knopf, 1999.

件不变的情况下，人均国民生产总值的增加将增强人类的平均能力，但分配的结果也会影响到人类能力的发展。

二、内生增长理论与福利国家：定量实证证据

20 世纪 80 年代以来，内生增长理论逐渐取代新古典增长模型，成为长期经济增长的主导理论。[1] 这对于我们的探讨意义重大，因为内生增长理论假设福利国家的结果，尤其是人力资本存量，是经济增长的重要决定因素。此外，该理论认为，收入不平等应该会拉低经济增长，而这推而广之应当意味着再分配的社会政策将会对经济增长产生积极的影响。

大多数经济增长的实证研究都是以成年人口的平均受教育年限来衡量人力资本存量。近来，哈努谢克和沃斯曼（Hanushek and Woessmann）的研究表明，用这种方法测量人力资本存量实际上大大低估了人力资本存量对经济增长的影响。[2] 他们将人力资本操作化为对中学生进行的可比标准化测试的认知技能得分。在一个还包含了人均国民生产总值初始水平的等式中，将平均受教育年限代之以认知技能得分后，他们发现，被解释的经济增长变化从 25% 上升到 73%。当两个技能变量都在等式中时，平均受教育年限是不显著的。[3] 笔者与合著者在对 Hanushek 和 Woessmann 的数据进行再分析时，将对物质资本的投资加入分析中后发现，技能变量的系数比物质资本投资的系数大 50%。[4]

是什么导致了劳动力中的高人类技能水平？如何解释在内生增长理论的实证检验中发现的收入平等与经济增长之间的联系？这两个问题的答案是密切相关的。为了阐明这两个问题，我们可以借助经合组织根据 2008—2013 年国际成人能力评估项目（Programme for the International Assessment of Adult Competencies，PIAAC）进行的成人技能调查（Survey of

---

1　对于内生增长理论在上一代经济理论建设过程中的演进，见：Lucas（1988）；Barro（1991）；Romer（1986, 1990, 1994）；Persson and Tabellini（1994）；Perotti（1996）；Aghion and Howitt（1998）；Glaeser et al.（2004）and Helpman（2004）。

2　Hanushek, Eric A. and Woessmann, Ludger.The Role of Cognitive Skills in Economic Development. *Journal of Economic Literature*, 2008.

3　Hanushek, Eric A. and Woessmann, Ludger.Do Better Schools Lead to More Growth? Cognitive Skills, Economic Outcomes, and Causation. *Journal of Economic Growth*, 2012.

4　Evans, Peter; Evelyne Huber and John D. Stephens. The Political Foundations of State Effectiveness. in Miguel Centeno, Atul Kohli, Deborah Yashar and Dinsha Mistree（eds.）*State Building in the Developing World*. Cambridge: Cambridge University Press, 2017：380–408.

Adult Skills，SAS）所收集的数据。[1] 国际成人能力评估项目及其20世纪90年代中期的前身——国际成人识字研究（International Adult Literacy Study），将调查研究与测试相结合。在这两项研究中，对参与国成年人口随机样本进行三个领域（识字、数学和文件处理）的一般技能标准化测试。结果数据是迄今为止对经合组织国家成年人口人力资本存量最好和最具可比性的数据。出于分析需要，笔者将三个测试得分的平均值作为因变量（见表1）。

可以这么认为，对促进人力资本发展项目的支出是平均技能水平的一个很强的决定因素。对这类支出的一个合理衡量标准是儿童早教和照护支出，初等、中等和高等教育支出以及积极劳动力市场政策支出的相加指数。以上全部以国民生产总值的百分比表示。的确，这种人力资本支出测量与平均成人技能水平测量高度相关（$r=0.70$）。

伊芙琳·胡贝尔（Evelyne Huber）和笔者曾提出，技能水平，尤其是底端技能水平的一个主要致因是父母一代的贫困与不平等程度。[2] 事实上，父母一代的（见下文）及平均成人技能调查得分的不平等程度很高（$r=-0.79$）。贫困与社会排斥削弱了学生利用为其所提供的教育机会的能力。贫困家庭幼童在接受正规教育时的劣势是有据可查的。许多研究"发现在社会弱势家庭出生的儿童，其健康、教育和总体福利情况往往更差"。[3] 研究者发现，社会情感因素，比如对学术与学校的喜爱、教师支持、同辈价值观以及心理健康，导致了贫困学生的成就差距。[4] 对学习的不充分支持与拒绝顺从期望和自律的同侪压力，社会化过程往往持续阻碍教育成功。家庭因素被认为是预测成就和犯罪的最有力因素，紧随其后的是"好朋友"的影响。[5] 当然，学校和邻里的构成同样重要。[6]

这些微观层面的关系也体现在宏观层面的贫穷和不平等水平、认知技能水平和分布之间的关系上。学校制度的性质可以减少或强化阶级不平等对教育不平等的影响。社会不平

1　OECD.*OECD Skills Outlook 2013: First Results from the Survey of Adult Skills*. Paris: OECD, 2013.

2　Huber, Evelyne and John D. Stephens, *Development and Crisis of the Welfare State: Parties and Policies in Global Markets*. Chicago: University of Chicago Press, 2001.

3　Fergusson, David. M; L. John Horwood and Joseph M. Boden.The transmission of social inequality: Examination of the linkages between family socioeconomic status in childhood and educational achievement in young adulthood. *Research in Social Stratification and Mobility*, 2008. 26.

4　Becker, Bronwyn E. and Suniya S. Luthar.Social-Emotional Factors Affecting Achievement Outcomes Among Disadvantaged Students: Closing the Achievement Gap. *Educational Psychologist*, 2002, 37（4）.

5　Duncan, Greg J.; Johanne Boisjoly and Kathleen Mullan Harris.Sibling, Peer, Neighbor, and Schoolmate Correlations as Indicators of the Importance of Context for Adolescent Development. *Demography*, 2001, 38（3）.

6　Van Ewijk, Reyn and Peter Sleegers.The effect of peer socioeconomic status on student achievement: A meta-analysis. *Educational Research Review*, 2010, 5.

等程度、社会现代化水平和学校制度都解释了教育成就不平等的跨国差异。[1] 当学校制度是按成绩分班时,社会选择偏向于特权群体,会维持或加剧阶级不平等。同样的观点也适用于强烈依赖私立学校的制度。

表 1 中位成人技能的决定因素
(国际成人能力评估项目 PIAAC/ 成人技能调查 SAS 2008—2013 年)

平均人力资本支出 1980—2010 年	4.508	**	1.806	
基尼系数 劳动年龄			-1.392	***
常数	239.031	***	293.506	***
R^2	0.45	**	0.61	***
观测值	15		15	

注 ** 表示 0.01 的水平下显著,*** 表示 0.001 的水平下显著。

表 1 中的分析表明,父母一代的不平等事实上是后代中位技能水平的一个很强的决定因素。我们对中位成人技能调查得分和 1980—2010 年的平均人力资本支出进行了回归,接着对来自卢森堡收入研究(Luxembourg Income Study,LIS)第一轮或第二轮(早至 20 世纪 80 年代中期)的人力资本支出和税收及转移支付后不平等数据进行了回归。在衡量不平等和成人技能的时间点上存在着 25 ~ 30 年的差异,这一差异大致相当于一代人。可以看出,人力资本支出模型解释了平均成人技能调查得分 45% 的变化,而对父母一代人力资本支出和可支配收入不平等的回归解释了成人技能调查得分 66% 的变化。因此,即便是把共同解释的变化完全归因于人力资本投资(一个不可靠的观点),父母一代的不平等仍然解释了平均成人技能的显著变化。正如笔者与合著者之前的研究所表明的,福利国家再分配是可支配收入不平等的一个强有力的决定因素,而福利国家的规模则是福利国家再分配的最重要决定因素。[2,3,4] 因此,笔者认为,福利国家转移支付项目通过减少不平等进而提高劳动者后代的技能水平,从而有助于促进长期增长。

---

1 Mark, Gary N. Cross-National Differences and Accounting for Social Class Inequalities in Education. *International Sociology*, 2005, 20(4).

2 Bradley, David;Evelyne Huber;Stephanie Moller;Francois Nielsen and John D. Stephens. Distribution and Redistribution in Post-Industrial Democracies. *World Politics*, 2003, 55(2).

3 Huber, Evelyne and John D. Stephens. Income Inequality and Redistribution in Post-Industrial Democracies: Demographic, Economic, and Political Determinants. *Socio-Economic Review*, 2014, 12(2).

4 在笔者的分析中,对福利国家规模(社会支出占 GDP 的百分比)的测量并未包括教育支出。

三、长期历史视野下美国福利国家的发展

传统观点认为美国福利国家的发展始于20世纪30年代经济大萧条和罗斯福新政,并且只对早期进行分析,解释福利国家在此前为何没有发展。[1,2,3] 然而,当把教育纳入其中后,显然必须追溯到19世纪初,甚至是18世纪末美国的初创期。美国的头一百年是初等公共教育的扩张期,一度接近全民覆盖、强制和免费,至少在北部和西部地区如此。[4] 新国家是个农业国,因而土地所有权结构是形塑其余社会结构的最重要特征。大地产、奴隶制的南部和全国其他地区之间有明显的分隔,后者以家庭农场主为主导。在某些州(而非联邦政府)的支持下,地方社区资助初等教育。中产阶级家庭农场主足够壮大,可以通过地方税来支持学校。

美国这些地区社会结构的相同方面,导致了基于男性普选权的民主的发展。[5] 此外,在对美洲经济发展的研究中,恩格曼和索科洛夫(Engerman and Sokoloff)认为,同以大地产、奴隶制或其他类型的奴役制、受限的教育与较低的识字率、受限的选举权以及高度的不平等为特点的美国南部和拉丁美洲大部分地区相比,美国北部和西部(以及加拿大)社会结构与制度的特点,即家庭农场的主导、高教育水平、广泛的选举权和因之实现的经济平等,正是这些地区经济快速发展的原因。[6]

这些相同的体制和社会结构特征导致了19世纪末20世纪初中等教育的扩张,到20世纪中叶基本实现了中等教育的全民覆盖。Goldin 和 Katz 指出,这种"第二次伟大的教育变革将扩大欧洲和美国青年受教育程度的差距……一个直到20世纪后半叶才会再次开始缩小的差距"。[7] 紧随这种中等教育扩张的是二战后高等教育的激增。

---

1 Amenta, Edwin. *Bold Relief: Institutional Politics and the Origins of Modern American Social Policy*. Princeton: Princeton University Press, 1998.

2 Skocpol, Theda. *Protecting Mothers and Soldiers*. Cambridge: Harvard University Press, 1992.

3 替 Skocpol(1992)说句公道话,她的确对参加美国内战的联邦老兵的养老金发展进行了广泛的分析。然而,正如她明确指出的,这个养老金计划并不是之后美国养老金发展的奠基石。

4 Goldin, Claudia and Laurence F. Katz. *The Race between Education and Technology*. Cambridge: Harvard University Press, 2008.

5 Rueschemeyer, Dietrich; Evelyne Huber Stephens and John D. Stephens. *Capitalist Development and Democracy*. Chicago: University of Chicago Press, 1992.

6 Engerman, Stanley L. and Kenneth L. Sokoloff, *Economic Development in the Americas since 1500*. Cambridge: Cambridge University Press, 2012.

7 Goldin, Claudia and Laurence F. Katz. *The Race between Education and Technology*. Cambridge: Harvard University Press, 2008.

与此相反，在其他社会政策领域，美国落后于欧洲。[1] 导致这一现象的最重要原因在于美国在劳工组织方面落后于大多数欧洲国家。[2,3] 产业工人阶级的行列被一波波移民充斥，这些移民分隔了工人阶级，而包括钢铁产业、汽车产业、电力产业等在内的制造业核心直到大萧条前都保持着无组织状态。

当然，大萧条和罗斯福政府（1933年）是美国福利国家的转折点，但很少有人认识到它是多么大的一个转折，但同时又是多么短暂。它不只是1935年通过的《社会保障法》。《社会保障法》提供基本的养老金、失业和残疾保险，以及由工资税加上所得税筹资的社会救助。1938年设立联邦最低工资。有研究指出，"在经济大萧条期间，美国在公共社会支出方面成为世界领先者，这是基于工作与救济，而非社会保险。"[4] 社会保障法案的条款是永久性的成就，而工作与救济计划则会失效。此外，以全面医疗保健服务来补充社会保障的计划，也是民主党多年来的选举承诺，却并未成功。约翰逊（Johnson）政府在1965年敲定了仅覆盖老年人（老年医疗保健制度，Medicare）和穷人（医疗救助制度，Medicaid）的项目。[5] 直到2010年时任总统奥巴马（Obama）的《患者保护和平价医疗法案》（PatientProtee—tion and Affordable—Care Act）实施个体强制参保，美国才迈向了全民医保。

除了针对老人和穷人的医疗保障外，约翰逊总统的"伟大社会"计划（Great Society）还提供贫困救济，建立了学前教育项目"领先计划"（Head Start），并大幅增加了对各级教育的援助。老年医疗保健制度由工薪税筹资，其他项目则由一般性税收，主要是累进所得税筹资。最低工资增加并在1968年达到历史最高水平。公共教育支出在这一时期达到顶峰：1970年，美国的公共教育支出占国民生产总值的7.4%，在经合组织国家中仅次于加拿大（8.5%），与瑞典不相上下。[6]

图1展示了一名普通美国产业工人的失业保险和养老金替代率。残障保险为劳动者

---

[1] Hicks, Alexander. *Social Democracy and Welfare Capitalism: A Century of Income Security Politics*. Ithaca: Cornell University Press, 1999.

[2] Stephens, John D. *The Transition from Capitalism to Socialism*, London: Macmillan, 1979.

[3] Hicks, Alexander. *Social Democracy and Welfare Capitalism: A Century of Income Security Politics*. Ithaca: Cornell University Press, 1999.

[4] Amenta, Edwin. *Bold Relief : Institutional Politics and the Origins of Modern American Social Policy*. Princeton: Princeton University Press, 1998.

[5] Maioni, Antonia. *Parting at a Crossroads: The Emergence of Health Insurance in the United States and Canada*. Princeton: Princeton University Press, 1998.

[6] David Brady, Evelyne Huber and John D. Stephens, Comparative Welfare States Data Set. University of North Carolina and WZB Berlin Social Science Center, 2014.

提供 67% 的替代率。美国是唯一没有政府病假工资和儿童津贴项目的后工业民主国家。由共和党（控制的）国会和民主党总统克林顿（Clinton）于 1996 年立法通过的社会救助计划远不如其前身慷慨。对贫困家庭的支持更为重要的是负所得税。所得税抵免（Earned Income Tax Credit，EITC）于 1975 年实施，1986 年首次大幅扩张，其后在四部法律中继续得到扩张，最近一次是在 2009 年，即奥巴马执政首年。所得税抵免抵消社会保障和医疗保险工薪税，如果劳动者的收入足够低，所得税抵免可以给其带来实际的现金补助。

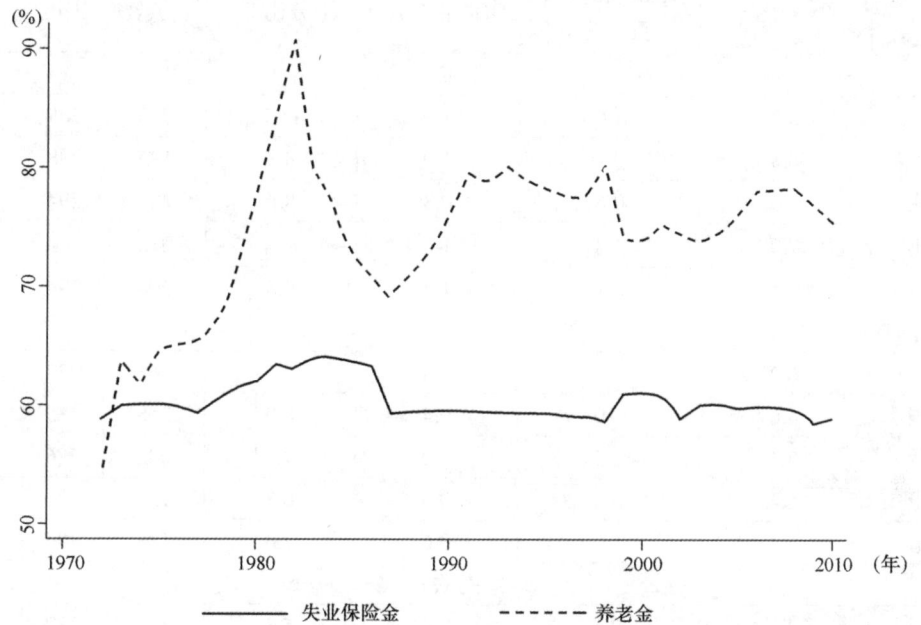

图 1　普通生产工人的失业保险和养老保险替代率（1970—2010 年）

资料来源：LyLew Scruggs, Detlef Jahn, kati kuitto. Comparative Wecfare Entit lemenets Dataset. http://cwedz.org/.

图 1 所示的养老金替代率在 20 世纪 70 年代末期与 80 年代初期的增长，是由法定福利待遇上涨、生活成本指数化、高通货膨胀以及实际工资的缓慢增长共同造成的。立法者原本并未打算将福利待遇提高到那样一个高水平（90% 的替代率），而且从长远来看制度难以负担。因此在 20 世纪 80 年代中期，民主党（控制的）国会和共和党总统里根（Reagan）同意削减福利待遇和提高社会保障工薪税。[1]

---

[1] Béland. Daniel, *Social Security: History and Politics from the New Deal to the Privatization Debate*. Lawrence: University Press of Kansas, 2005: 138–62.

图 1 显示，养老保险制度和失业保险制度的福利待遇在 20 世纪 80 年代中期之后保持平稳，残障保险同样如此。除此之外，"伟大社会"之后美国福利国家的发展确实有悖常理。教育支出从 1970 年的高水平降低到 90 年代中期 5.2% 的低水平，并在这一水平上趋于平稳。如表 2 所示，在其他人力资本支出类别上，美国同样是低水平的。

表 2 成年人口的人力资本支出和技能存量

	公共教育支出（占 GDP 百分比）	积极劳动力市场政策支出（占 GDP 百分比）	日托支出（占 GDP 百分比）	总计（占 GDP 百分比）	经合组织国家识字测试		
					第 5 百分位	中位	第 95 百分位
北欧							
丹麦	8.2	1.6	1.9	11.7	213	289	353
芬兰	6.3	0.9	1.0	8.2	195	288	363
挪威	7.0	0.6	0.8	8.4	207	294	363
瑞典	7.0	1.3	1.6	9.9	216	304	386
均值	7.1	1.1	1.3	9.5	208	294	366
西欧							
比利时	6.2	1.1	0.8	8.1	163	277	359
德国	4.6	1.0	0.4	6.0	208	285	359
荷兰	5.4	1.3	1.0	7.7	202	286	355
瑞士	5.4	0.6	0.3	6.3	150	271	349
均值	5.4	1.0	0.6	7.0	181	280	356
南欧							
意大利	4.6	0.6	0.6	5.8	114	237	325
葡萄牙	5.3	0.6	0.4	6.3	96	229	334
均值	5.0	0.6	0.5	6.1	105	233	329
英语系国家							
澳大利亚	4.8	0.3	0.4	5.5	146	274	359
加拿大	5.1	0.3	0.2	5.6	145	280	372
爱尔兰	4.8	0.7	0.1	5.6	151	263	353
新西兰	6.4	0.4	0.7	7.5	158	272	361
英国	5.2	0.3	0.9	6.4	145	267	360
美国	5.2	0.1	0.3	5.6	133	272	371
均值	5.3	0.4	0.4	6.0	146	271	363

资料来源：David, Brady, Evelyne Huber, John D. stephens. Comparative Welfave States Data set. University of Morth Carolina and WZB Berlin Social Sciece Center, 2014.

有研究表明，社会支出的增加主要是以"税收支出"的形式出现，如对私人养老金计划或私人医疗保险缴费等社会目的的税收减免。[1,2] 社会税收支出占普通联邦社会支出的比例从 1975 年的 5％上升到 2010 年的 30％。[3] 这些社会税收支出绝大部分流向了高收入群体，因而加剧了收入不平等。从 20 世纪 60 年代末到 2010 年，实际最低工资下降了约 1/3。Faricy 的时间序列数据分析显示，社会税收支出的增加发生于共和党控制国会期间，而最低工资的增加主要发生于民主党执政期间。

结果便是不平等急剧上升，如图 2 所示。鉴于国民收入中流向高收入群体的份额增加，自 1979 年以来中位收入家庭几乎未从经济增长中获益也就不足为奇了。[4] 在表 2 中，我们看到美国人力资本投资下降的结果。最后三列中的数值是经合组织在 20 世纪 90 年代中期所进行的国际成人识字率测试的得分，所使用的方法与前述成人技能调查（SAS）的一样。底端技能基础尤其糟糕，这反映了一个事实：即无论是用收入最高的 1％人群所占财富份额来衡量还是用基尼系数来衡量，在经合组织国家中，美国的不平等程度都是最高的。

胡贝尔和史蒂芬斯（Huber and Stephens）的研究显示，美国与其他英语系国家基尼系数上升的一个原因是这些国家教育支出的减少。[5] 数据支持 Goldin 和 Katz 的观点，即由于美国与其他英语系的民主国家以及美国都没有对教育进行投资，技能偏向型的技术变革导致了教育工资溢价的上升，进而导致收入不平等的加剧。[6] 然而，后工业国家基尼系数的上升与收入最高的 1％人群所占财富份额的增加，最重要的原因均是工会力量式微。[7,8]

1　Faricy, Christopher G. *Welfare for the Wealthy: Parties, Social Spending, and Inequality in the United States*. Cambridge: Cambridge University Press, 2015：140.

2　Hacker, Jacob S. *The Divided Welfare State: The Battle Over Public and Private Social Benefits in the United States. Cambridge*: Cambridge University Press, 2002.

3　Faricy, Christopher G. *Welfare for the Wealthy: Parties, Social Spending, and Inequality in the United States*. Cambridge: Cambridge University Press, 2015.

4　Nolan, Brian; Max Roser; Stefan Thewissen. Stagnating median incomes despite economic growth: Explaining the divergence in 27 OECD countries. http://voxeu.org/article/economic-growth-stagnating-median-incomes-new-analysis.

5　Huber, Evelyne and John D. Stephens.Income Inequality and Redistribution in Post-Industrial Democracies: Demographic, Economic, and Political Determinants.*Socio-Economic Review*,2014, 12（2）.

6　Goldin, Claudia and Laurence F. Katz. *The Race between Education and Technology*. Cambridge: Harvard University Press, 2008.

7　Huber, Evelyne and John D. Stephens.Income Inequality and Redistribution in Post-Industrial Democracies: Demographic, Economic, and Political Determinants.*Socio-Economic Review*,2014, 12（2）.

8　Huber, Evelyne;Jingjing Huo and John D. Stephens.Power, Policy, and Top Income Shares. *Socio-Economic Review*, 2017,0（0）.

表 3 中来自卢森堡收入研究和经合组织的数据显示了相对于其他后工业民主国家而言，美国福利国家在减少贫困和不平等方面的表现。再分配措施是针对户主为 17～66 岁的家庭，按（市场收入基尼系数 – 可支配收入基尼系数）／市场收入基尼系数进行计算。老年贫困率则是低于中位家庭收入水平 50％ 的老年人所占百分比。应当牢记的是，从世界范围来看，福利国家，尤其是北欧与欧洲大陆国家，在减少不平等和贫困方面的表现最佳，但美国在这两项上毫无疑问是垫底的。

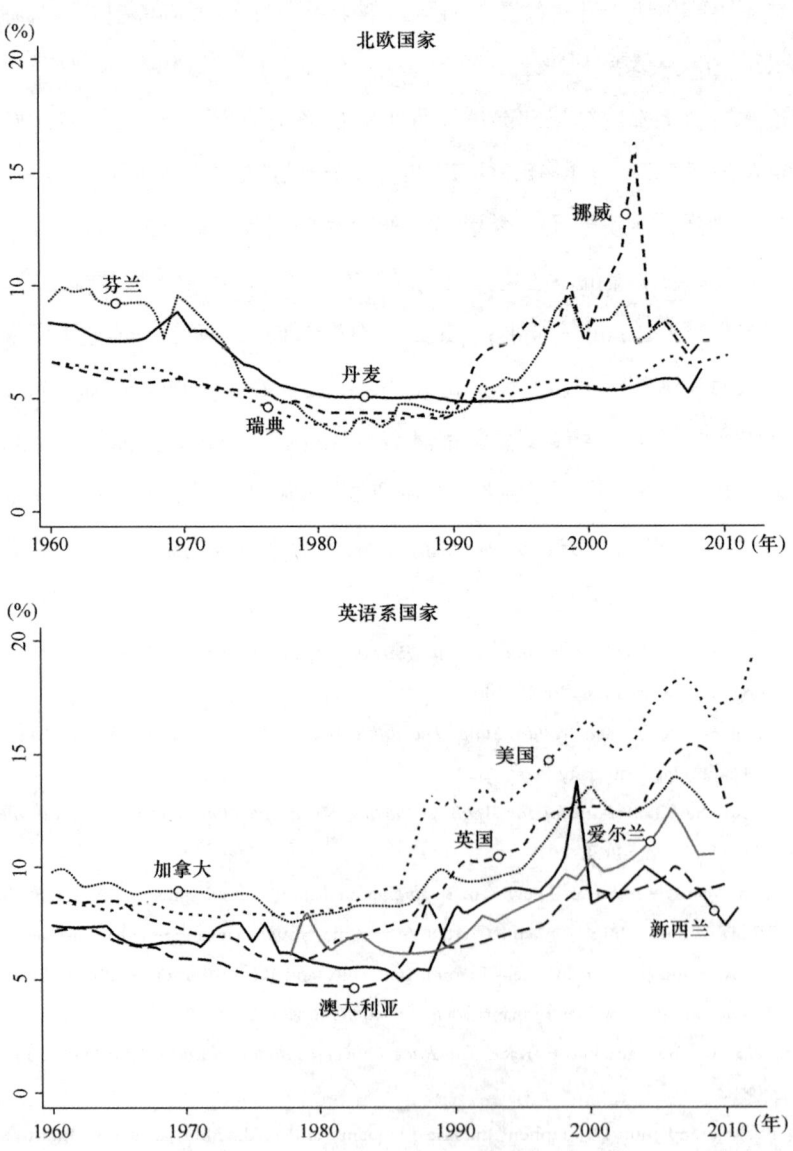

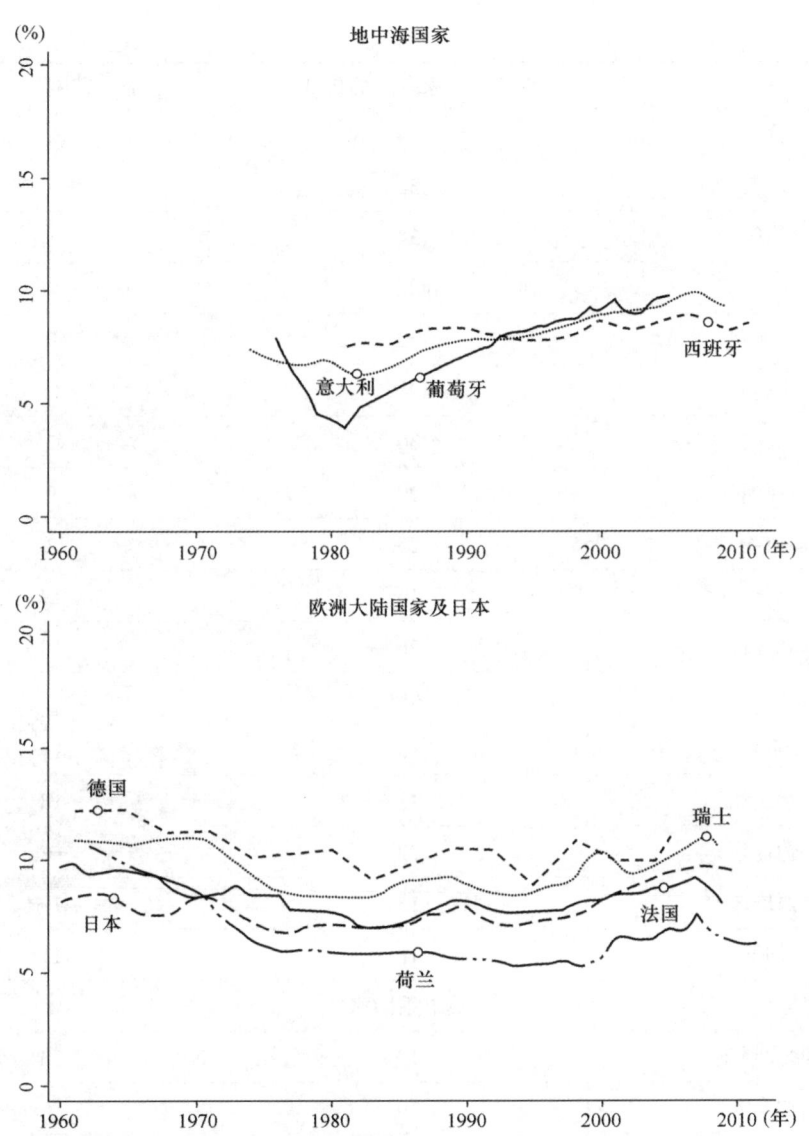

图 2　按生产体制与国家划分的收入前 1% 的人所占财富份额（1960—2010 年）

资料来源：Huber, Evelyne; Jingjing Huo and John D. Stephens.Power, Policy, and Top Income Shares.Socio-Economic Review, 2017.

表 3　　　　　　　　　劳动年龄家庭间的再分配与老年贫困年

	劳动年龄家庭间的再分配	老年贫困率（%）
北欧		
丹麦	36	8
芬兰	33	10

续表

	劳动年龄家庭间的再分配	老年贫困率（%）
挪威	34	8
瑞典	32	7
均值	34	8
西欧		
奥地利	32	9
比利时	21	15
法国	30	7
德国	29	9
荷兰	25	2
瑞士	16	17
均值	26	10
南欧		
希腊	15	14
意大利	18	18
葡萄牙	23	…
西班牙	15	19
均值	18	17
英语系国家		
澳大利亚	19	23
加拿大	19	7
爱尔兰	25	24
新西兰	21	…
英国	18	17
美国	13	23
均值	19	19

注：…代表数据不可得。

资料来源：David, Brady, Evelyne Huber, John D. stephens. Comparative Welfave States Data set. University of Morth Carolina and WZB Berlin Sciece Center, 2014.

鉴于评估内生增长理论的实证研究结果，美国的长期（1960—2010年）经济增长慢于经合组织的平均水平（后者 2.5%，前者 2.1%）也就不足为奇了。[1] 因此，美国陷入了一个低社会投资、不平等加剧、低增长和人力资本贫乏的恶性循环。

奥巴马执政的头两年（2009—2010 年），是国会参众两院均由民主党人控制的时期。这两年见证了自约翰逊的"伟大社会"计划以来的首次重大社会政策创新，即《患者保护和平价医疗法案》的通过。该法案通过扩大医疗救助和要求未被雇主所提供计划覆盖的个体购买医疗保险（"个体强制参保"），扩大了覆盖面，并给低收入家庭提供补贴以帮助其购买保险。该法案使得 90% 以上的美国人被医疗保险覆盖。共和党在 2010 年的选举中获得了对众议院的控制权，从那时起至 2016 年年末，共和党人进行了 50 多次投票试图废止该法案，但（撤销该法案的）议案却从未被参议院所采纳。即便参议院通过了，也会被奥巴马所否决。当 2016 年的大选使共和党控制了参众两院和白宫后，《患者保护和平价医疗法案》有可能会被废除，但共和党无力废除该法可能意味着法案将比大多数观察家所以为的更具有韧性。

四、结 论

在过去两个世纪里，与欧洲相比，美国经历了令人眼花缭乱的社会经济转变。在 19 世纪中期，除南部地区以外，整个国家高度民主、教化良好，在高人力资本水平的基础上有平等的收入分配，因而教育工资溢价低、财产分配平等。这些特点促成了美国从建国到大萧条前的高水平经济增长。然而，美国却是福利国家中的落后者，仅实施了一战前四个社会计划中的一个，希克斯（Hicks）在他对这一时期的研究中考察了这些社会项目。[2] 笔者曾将此归因于弱劳工运动，Hicks 的分析支持这一观点。[3,4]

在 20 世纪的头 75 年里，美国继续保持着教育上的领先地位。在经济大萧条期间，劳工运动与其他社会运动高涨，罗斯福政府利用这一新契机通过了《社会保障法案》，订立了最低工资，甚至还在社会支出方面一度将美国推至发达国家前列。然而，美国仍然未能通

---

1 David Brady, Evelyne Huber and John D. Stephens. Comparative Welfare States Data Set. University of North Carolina and WZB Berlin Social Science Center, 2014.

2 Hicks, Alexander. *Social Democracy and Welfare Capitalism: A Century of Income Security Politics*. Ithaca: Cornell University Press, 1999.

3 Stephens, John D. *The Transition from Capitalism to Socialism*, London: Macmillan, 1979.

4 Hicks, Alexander. *Social Democracy and Welfare Capitalism: A Century of Income Security Politics*, Ithaca: Cornell University Press, 1999.

过国民健康保险,尽管这在民主党的议程中占有重要地位。

约翰逊的"伟大社会"计划将社会议程向前推进,通过了医疗保险和医疗救助相关法案,增加了各级教育投资,制定了反贫困计划,并将实际最低工资提高到了美国的历史最高水平。美国在教育方面保持了其领先地位。[1] 在此之后,社会政策各领域的主流趋势都是消极的,教育支出持续下降,其他领域的公共社会政策日渐式微,直到奥巴马执政时期。而在共和党掌权时期,不平等的社会税收支出增加。到 20 世纪 90 年代中期,美国的中位技能水平低于多数经合组织国家,底端技能则更差。因此,美国的不平等激增,同时经济增长缓慢。

---

1 尽管因为没有成人技能调查型测试得分数据而无法肯定,但美国不太可能是中位人力技能水平方面的领先者,也几乎可以确定美国在技能分布底端表现糟糕。因为由于办学经费依赖于地方财产税,多数成年非裔美国人上的是实施种族隔离的学校,多数穷人上的是教学质量很差的学校。

日本社会保障的历史发展与当前问题

[日] 小野太一[1]

一、历史发展

（一）第二次世界大战后

日本社会保障制度[2]的起源可追溯至19世纪明治维新后。1874年，首部《济贫法》出台；1922年，《健康保险法》颁布，其主要目的在于确保工厂工人和矿工的健康；1938年制定的《国民健康保险法》为农民等生活在农村地区的人提供了必要的医疗服务；《工人养老保险法》于1942年实施，这项立法的一个动机便是在战时为工业投资积累资本。

这些社会保障法律框架在第二次世界大战后依然存在，但随后出现的恶性通货膨胀等破坏因素和经济混乱，几乎摧毁了社保制度的现实物质基础。基于日本《宪法》第25条（自1947年5月生效），第二次世界大战后社会保障制度的重建简直需要从零开始，其中规定：每个人都应享有维持健康、文化生活之最低标准的权利。在生活的各方各面，国家都应努力促进并推广社会福利、安全以及公共卫生。

迫于当时的紧急情况，工作重点首先投向了健康和福利政策，以确保并改善营养供给、重建卫生设施、预防传染性疾病等。此外，工作重点还包括促进日本劳动关系现代化的主要立法，如《劳动基准法》《工会法》《劳动关系调整法》（1947年）。《公共救助法》（1946年）规定，在紧急情况下通过家计调查为经济困难者提供现金和实物支持。这一立法在1950年经历了彻底改革，引入了处理行政投诉以及表达现代人权的条款，反映了《宪法》第25条的理念（对国家责任的要求）。《儿童福利法》和《身体残障者福利法》分别于1947年和

---

1 [作者简介]小野太一，日本政策研究大学院大学教授[Taichi Ono, Professor, National Graduate Institute for Policy Studies (GRIPS), Tokyo]。主要研究方向：社会政策，福利国家。

[译者简介]黄莎，中国人民大学中国社会保障研究中心博士生，中国社会保障学会秘书处学术助理。

[翻译审校]华颖，中国社会科学院人口与劳动经济研究所助理研究员。

2 在本文中，作者所使用的"社会保障"一词指各种健康和福利措施，如公共卫生、社会救助、社会福利、医疗保险、公共养老金，以及失业保险、工伤保险、积极的劳动力市场政策等劳工政策。

1949 年颁布，前者主要致力于照顾孤儿，后者旨在照顾受伤士兵等战争伤员，这些人在非军事化时期不允许享受特殊待遇。

1950 年，政府社会保障咨询委员会呼吁制定全面的社会保障制度。该委员会指出，社会保险应成为社会保障制度的核心，因为个人缴费的筹资方式将会激发公民的自我责任感。通过以社会保险为社会保障制度的核心的方式保持了战前医疗筹资制度基本架构的完整，通过 1948 年的国民健康保险改革，市町村（作为最基础的地方自治体）已经可以自行决定启动强制性的全民覆盖，以保障那些未被其他制度如基于就业的医疗保险所覆盖的国民。该制度于 1958 年再次进行改革，相关法律要求所有市町村承担提供国民健康保险的责任，国民健康保险最终于 1961 年实现全覆盖。与此同时，国家养老金开始实施（1961 年），实现了公共养老保险的全覆盖。上述两个制度都表明了日本社会保障制度在战后时期快速现代化的特点。

20 世纪 60 年代，在经济繁荣和人口构成较为年轻的背景下，公共养老金和社会救助的现金福利水平得到了显著提高。旨在提高老年人、智力或精神障碍者等不同弱势群体的社会福利的立法在日本国会得以通过。医保所覆盖的治疗范围限制得以取消。1972 年开始实行儿童津贴制度，这是大多数西欧国家已经启动的制度，日本终得以将最后一项欠缺的儿童福利加入社会保障制度中。在这一不断完善的时期，终极成就是在 1973 年引入了老年人免费医疗诊疗政策。

1973 年秋，第一次"石油危机"对日本经济造成了冲击。与其他许多国家一样，由于发行政府债券以弥补赤字，日本的财政平衡在 20 世纪 70 年代恶化。

20 世纪 80 年代初，这一政策变得越来越难以持续，在"不加税实现财政重建"的口号下，日本财政政策转向了紧缩政策。社会保障支出增加，尤其是因免费医疗诊疗政策造成的医保费用加速增长，导致对社会保障支出增长的担忧开始高居政策议程。为抑制支出增长，日本政府采取了一系列措施，其中一个重要的举措是无论是门诊还是住院，对老年人重新引入了医疗保险共付的固定金额[1]，对以就业为前提的医保制度的受保人引入 10% 的共付比例而非固定的支付金额，药品花费也包括在内。[2] 为均衡各种不同医保制度所负担的覆盖老年人的费用成本，20 世纪 80 年代中期实施了财政调整机制。通过在覆盖不同群体的

---

[1] 门诊病人一个月 400 日元，住院病人一天 300 日元。

[2] 被以就业为前提的保险制度覆盖的（参保者的）被供养人当时必须支付 20%（住院）或 30%（门诊）的费用。被国民健康保险覆盖的被供养人，门诊服务和住院服务均需支付 30% 的共付费用。

所有7个（当时的）制度中引入统一的第一层次（基本养老金），公共养老金也引入了成本调整机制。这一举措不仅旨在稳定养老金制度，而且也提高了被保险群体之间的公平性。[1]

由于人口持续老龄化，对社会保障未来的担忧仍是20世纪80年代后期的核心政治问题。针对这些担忧，政府未雨绸缪，启动了系列政策，应对老龄化社会。一项规模巨大的多年公共投资项目（黄金计划）启动，如通过日托中心或养老院为老年人提供福利服务。其目的在于解释为何额外征收3%的消费税，以获得公众认同。该投资项目于2000年4月初步完成，此时公共长期护理保险制度在20世纪90年代服务基础设施发展的支撑下得以启动。

（二）21世纪

为刺激内需，日本实施了持续低利率和过度借贷，结果20世纪80年代后期出现经济泡沫，该泡沫在1990年崩溃。然而尽管增速较慢，日本经济仍保持了持续增长直到1997财年。1997财年日本（名义）GDP达到历史最高点。[2]自此，日本经济进入漫长的停滞期，原因在于经济泡沫导致了家庭、企业和金融机构的资产负债表调整，以非制造业和中小型企业为主的生产率增长乏力，20世纪90年代和21世纪初期人口下降（劳动力投入减少）及资本贡献减少。[3]

全球化浪潮也对日本形成了冲击。税收减少以及公共财政为促进经济复苏而实施的反复刺激使得国家财政状况恶化。健康保险的缴费收入获得政府预算转移支付，实现了合理化。健康保险的共付比一律[4]由20%上调至30%[5]，且由公共健康保险制度按统一的费用表（通常每两年修订一次）向医院和诊所支付的待遇额在2006年以前所未有的幅度削减。

---

1 在这项改革中，为所有公民引入了第一层次的基本养老金，包括以就业为前提的制度。雇员养老保险等以就业为前提的制度实行了改革，提供与收入相关的第二层次养老金。国家养老金的参保者只获得第一层次的基本养老金，以就业为前提的制度的参保人员因改革而获得第一层次和第二层次的养老金。公共养老金制度的平等性和连贯性得以同时实现。由于基本养老金的资金来源于国家补贴和人均共担的（当时的）七项养老制度的缴费（因此调整了不同制度间年龄结构的失衡），财务稳定性也得以确保。

2 直到最近。根据内阁府2017年9月发布的"GDP季度测算：2017年4—6月（第二次初步测算）"，2016财年的名义GDP比1997财年的多了4.8万亿日元。

3 见2015年度日本经济和公共财政年度报告（东京，内阁府）。

4 老年人（75岁以上或到2014年3月底已年满70岁的人为10%，70~74岁的为20%，收入超过一定份额的为30%）及儿童（6岁以下即义务教育前为20%）例外。

5 由公共健康保险覆盖的医疗服务的实际共付比例通常低于30%：20世纪70年代中期建立了一项高额医疗服务费用补贴制度，该制度根据受保人的收入水平，对超过上限的共同支付额进行部分报销。

同时，面对人口老龄化的加剧，为促进社会保障制度的稳定性和合理性，对如下制度作出了重大的结构性变革：

- 健康保险（通过引入一项以老年人为对象的新制度）
- 长期护理保险（通过鼓励预防及非机构护理）
- 公共养老金［引入一种称为"宏观经济指数化"的自动平衡机制，其中使用价格指数或工资指数对养老金进行定期调整，同时考虑人口结构变化（对活跃人口和非活跃老年人口）的隐性成本（负担）效应］。[1]

鉴于 2008 年年末全球金融危机的影响以及之后严重的经济衰退，公众开始以更加严肃的态度接受了中青年的不稳定就业状况。尽管这点很重要，但与之形成反差的是，经济停滞下就业危机——伴随着产业结构变化和非正规就业扩散——早已以"秘密"方式进入日本劳动力市场。

应对与出生率下降相关的问题的政策依然突出，并被明确列入日本的政治议程。同时，对育儿家庭——即在经济停滞中挣扎的年轻工作一代——的育儿现金津贴和实物支持攀升至社会保障政策议程的首位。

由于不同的人口构成，基于市町村的国民健康保险制度的财务状况本就比其他以就业为前提的制度更加糟糕，又因无法获得正规就业的边缘参保者人数的激增，其财务状况进一步恶化。

基本养老金的财务状况面临着类似的困境；2009 年，在税收没有增加的情况下，国家财政对其补贴已经增加。虽然仍需简化社会保障制度的繁文缛节，但加强日本社会保障体系财政基础的政策已成为必然。消费税被视为满足当前需求的理想来源，这是因为消费税是在包括养老金领取者在内的各代中平等分担的。因此，在 21 世纪头十年的后期，一项所谓的"社会保障和税收综合改革"倡议跃居政治议程之首。

二、社会保障制度面临的主要问题

（一）当前问题

显而易见，与人口相关的三个问题——人口老龄化、出生率下降以及前两者（加上几乎没有跨境净移民）所导致的人口减少——是日本当前社会经济转型的主要原因，更不用说社会保障政策了。

---

[1] 然而，由于例外条款，宏观经济指数化直到 2015 年才得以实施。

截至 2016 年 4 月 1 日，日本女性总人口中有超过 30% 的人年龄在 65 岁以上（男女都算，则 65 岁以上的老年人占总人口的 27.3%）。日本经济活跃年龄总人口（女性和男性）的比例约为 60%，是经合组织中这一比例第二低的国家。[1] 这些统计数据表明，日本是世界上人口"最老"的国家。相关变化体现在家庭构成上，单人家庭、仅含一对夫妇的家庭和老年家庭的数量正在上升，而核心家庭以及三代同堂家庭的数量正在下降。从 2010—2015 年各年龄组情况可以看出[2]，随着女性的劳动参与率不断提高，对老人和儿童照护的社会服务需求随之增加。

不断变化的经济结构也对社会保障政策产生了显著影响。经济仍旧停滞不前。根据"目标"情景，即便是在"经济振兴"的乐观情况下，政府预测的实际增长率仅为 2% 左右。[3] 失业率虽然低于国际"常态"，且近年来呈下降趋势，但长期内失业率已明显上升。[4] 此外，非正规就业人口比例从 1985 年的 16.4% 增加到 2015 年的 37.5%。[5] 其中一些人不享有以就业为前提的社会保障，无论是健康保险还是公共养老金，两者通常需要的缴费更低，但提供的待遇更高。[6]

自 1961 年实现健康保险和公共养老金全覆盖以来，社会保障支出在半个多世纪中持续增长，无论是其绝对数额还是 GDP 占比都是如此（见图 1）。[7] 与 1951 财年相比，2014 年社会保障福利的名义量的增速远超过名义 GDP 的增速（社会福利增至原有的 714 倍，GDP

---

[1] 仅高于以色列，但非就业一代的构成则完全不同（OECD 2013 年数据）。

[2] 相关资料来自厚生劳动省的《劳动经济白皮书 2016》。

[3] 根据日本政府 2017 年 1 月所作的中长期经济和财政预测分析，在经济复苏情景下，预计 2022 年财年实际增长率为 2.4%。

[4] 以简单的算术平均数计算，总人口的失业率在 1981—1995 年为 2.5%，而 1996—2010 年，这一数字跃升至 4.5%（根据 2015 年，日本统计局的劳动力调查）。

[5] 非正规就业包括非全日制工、临时工、派遣工、合同工。然而，应该注意到，自 2013 年起，年轻劳动者（15～54 岁）中出现了从非正规就业向正规就业的净转移。

[6] 许多非正规劳动者如果在较小的公司工作且每周劳动时间少于一定的小时数，就不能享受以就业为前提的社会保障。如果其年薪低于标准额（由法规规定），这些非正规劳动者可以以"受供养的家属"身份，享有其家庭成员（通常是配偶）以就业为前提的社会保障。在其他情况下，这些非正规劳动者自然加入国家养老金和国民健康保险，在大多数情况下，公共养老金月缴费额更高，但提供较少的待遇（仅为第一层次）；健康保险月缴费额更高，但提供的待遇是一样的，特殊情况下还提供一些现金给付。

[7] 从历史来看，短期内出现过不同于社会保障支出的 GDP 占比增长的例外情况，最近一次例外情况发生在 2013 财年和 2014 财年。社会保障支出 GDP 占比之所以下降，原因在于经济实现了强劲增长，并取消了养老金待遇的例外条款，因而出现了不同于最初公式的情况。

增至89倍）。然而，当前的公共社会支出（GDP占比）仅比经合组织平均水平（21.0%）高出2.1个百分点（23.1%）；尽管日本人口老化，但仅就老年支出而言，日本与许多欧洲国家相差无几甚至更低。[1]

因此，关注的焦点不应局限于支出的绝对规模——尽管必须要进行持续审查以提高效率——但更应关注确保是否有税收或缴费等适当的资金来源支撑此类支出。财政状况的恶化凸显了迅速解决这一问题的紧迫性，以避免失去市场和未来子孙后代对日本的信心，后代可能会将社会保障误认为是20世纪错误决策而不公平地遗留下来的强加于其肩上的沉重负担。

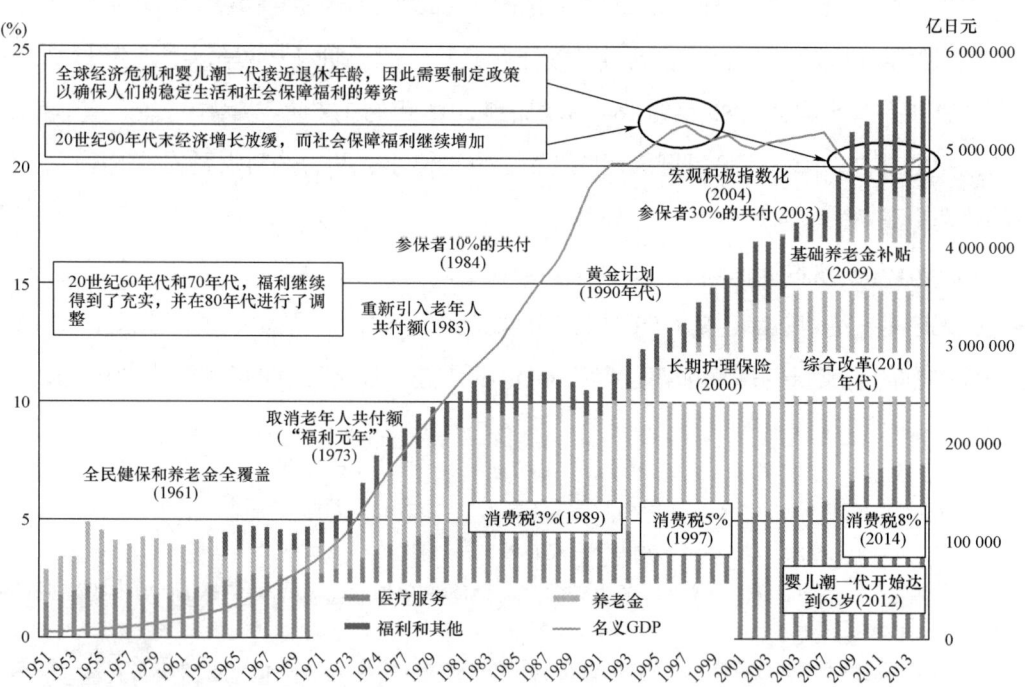

图1　社会保障福利的GDP占比和名义GDP（1951—2014年）（单位：亿日元）

（二）政治背景

20世纪下半叶至今，日本社会保障制度取得了进展，但却有两个相互矛盾的口号：一个是以社会可持续性为中心，即"增加待遇"；另一个则是以财务可持续性为中心，即"待遇与负担之间实现平衡"。在此期间，政府主要由自民党（LDP）或以自民党为中心的政党联盟领导，策略性地在两个口号之间摇摆，以使社会保障制度适应社会经济变革。21世纪

---

[1] 数据来自2016年OECD的社会支出数据库。

头十年的后期,"社会保障和税收综合改革"倡议是在自民党领导的政府下进行的,尽管当时首相经常变动。这一倡议在日本民主党(DPJ)领导的联盟内阁时期得以延续,民主党在2009年下议院选举中击败自民党及其盟友,其政治支持主要来自工会。虽然民主党与自民党在公共养老金和儿童照料制度改革的优先次序和设计方面存在着一些差异,但在强化社会保障制度以减轻公众的焦虑以及增加(不可避免的)税收的必要性上却达成了广泛共识。因此,2011年6月达成了一项所谓的三方协议,将消费税率从5%逐步提高到10%,以将增税用于加强社会保障制度。这是在民主党在2010年的上议院选举中失利,败给自民党及其少数派盟友,政治权力遭到削弱后达成的。

这种政治协议之所以成为可能,只是因为日本整个公民社会存在着以下共识:社会保障在现代社会中有着无可争议的价值,社会保障不应受制于政党政治,在经济增长放缓、"超老龄化"和人口减少的背景下为实现制度可持续发展对社会保障制度进行改革具有必要性。专栏1中摘录的政府报告措辞体现了这种共识。

专栏1 将令人确信的社会保障制度传给后代

改善社会保障制度极大地促进了"长寿"。医疗保险和长期护理保险都扩大了保障范围;人人都可以得到适当的医疗和护理服务,人们的寿命因此已经延长。通过养老保险提供的收入保障使人们能够安享长寿。

我们不能忘记,由于社会保障制度,我们已经实现了人类长久以来追求的长寿社会梦想。长寿社会印证了社会保障制度的成功,也正是这种成功促使我们走向老龄化社会,现在又出现了社会保障制度可持续性的问题。我们必须将这个极好的社保制度交到子孙后代手中,这也就是我们需要进行这项改革的原因。

资料来源:摘录自日本全国社会保障改革理事会最终报告的前言(2013年8月)。

(三)社会保障的贡献及待改善的领域

专栏2中列出了综合改革的内容。其中,多项措施自2014年4月以来已经实施,同时消费税率也提高到了8%。此处引用的综合改革议程中列出的政策以及政府报告中的自我评估,揭示了日本社会保障制度所作的贡献以及需要改进的领域。在日本第二次世界大战后的历史中,社会保障制度保障和稳定了人民的生活,使人们能应对一生中的各种风险事件——年老、残疾、疾病、伤亡,尤其是贫困,并同时改善了公共卫生和营养。这些政策大有裨益,包括促进长寿、健康、公共安全、通过共同的归属感来凝聚社会团结,以及即便是在近期的经济停滞期间也能通过维持稳定的消费流或创造与护理有关的工作岗位来支持经济发展等,因而受到人们的广泛欢迎。因此,改革医疗保障、长期护理和公共养老金主要是为了在人口结构变化和经济增长乏力背景下改善可持续性、促进代际平等。另外,正如之前所提到的,对于当前一代的劳动者,他们过去往往被视为受到终身雇佣惯例的保护,因此社会脆弱性比老年人要小,但对当前一代劳动者的政策相比之下已经滞后。因此,通过综合改革,拓展了福利和服务的内容和覆盖,增加了对儿童和家庭政策的公共投资,改善了对非正规就业人员的社会保障覆盖。

> **专栏2 "社会保障和税收综合改革"的主要内容**
>
> a. 儿童和家庭政策
> - 解决幼儿园和托儿所等候名单的问题。
> - 投资一系列儿童保育服务,如为患病的儿童提供托儿所、为哺乳母亲提供设施,以满足工作父母的需求。
> - 促进工作场所的变化,使其更加适合家长,包括改善育儿假、缩短工作时间、提供性别中立的工作环境。
>
> b. 医疗和长期护理服务
> - 增强医院功能和床位可及性,使其合理化,改善医院提供者间的合作,以优化每个地区的服务提供。
> - 加强预防措施。
> - 以更低的成本,改善居家护理,提高生活质量。
> - 建立综合社区护理体系。
> - 全面改革国民健康保险,实现财务的可持续性。
> - 区分医疗保健和长期护理福利的优先次序(增加高收入老年人的共同支付等)。
>
> c. 养老金
> - 将政府雇员的公共养老金统一并入雇员养老保险制度中。
> - 通过消费税确保基本养老金(占待遇给付的一半)补贴有稳定的财务来源。
> - 引入"宏观经济指数化"*,以抑制当前老年人口待遇的增长,确保现收现

付制度下当前工作一代的未来待遇水平，固定最高缴费率保持不变。
- 将雇员养老保险的覆盖范围扩大到每周工作时间较短的劳动者。
- 缩短最短缴费期（从25年减少至10年）。
- 为低收入的基本养老金领取者提供补充型现金津贴（延后的）。

d. 财政可持续性
- 提高消费税税率（2014年4月从5%提高到8%。原本计划从2015年10月起提高到10%，但推迟到2019年10月执行）。

* 于2004年通过，但由于例外条款，直到2015年才执行。

三、未来解决方案

尽管由于担心消费税对经济增长产生负面影响，进一步将消费税税率提升至10%之举措已经推迟两次（2014年11月和2016年6月），但综合改革议程中提出的充实、稳定和优化社会保障制度的大多数措施都已制定。同时，改革之初的高昂势头，在持续了约十年后，也逐渐消失。除了注意确保待遇和负担之间的均衡，笔者还考虑了在后综合改革时期的当下需要解决的四个关键问题。

首要任务。后综合改革时期的首要任务应该是稳步实施改革所制定的或将要制定的政策。对于医疗保障而言，供给侧（医疗服务提供者）改革已明显落后。日本的许多医院由于历史原因是非营利性的私营实体，医院应该适应其经营所在地由"超级老龄化"带来的不断变化的需求。在许多地区，医院所配备的急症护理病床数超过预期需求，而康复服务和老年居家护理服务的床位数却很少；此外，在一些地方可以看到医院病床总量过剩。各地需要对各医院所提供的服务构成进行合作性的决策。

关于老年人的长期护理，在各地组织综合社区护理体系是重中之重。市町村作为政治决策的最小独立单位，也是公共长期护理保险制度的承保人，应主动行动。市町村一个方便是加强为身体和心理脆弱的老年人（包括那些患有老年失智症者）提供居家医疗保健和居家社会服务的联合服务，老年人在家中的生活质量会优于在医院或养老院。综合社区护理的另一个方便是鼓励采取预防措施和家务互助，以帮助老年人保持活跃和健康。还应推广各种措施，为需要照顾体弱老年人的家庭提供支持。

对于儿童照料和支持育儿家庭，应采取全面的措施，包括为单亲家庭提供现金津贴和咨询（实物）服务，提供更多各种儿童照管服务来鼓励妇女的劳动参与、促进婚姻和谐，并为母婴建立本地综合支援诊所（芬兰母婴照护制度的日本版）。以上必须持续推进。此外，幼儿园教师以及体弱老年人的照护者的工作条件和工资得到了改善。这些举措得到了"全民动态参与"倡议的积极倡导，这项倡议是现任内阁的一项旗舰性的国内政策，该政策将消除妇女劳动参与障碍视为经济振兴的关键。

对于公共养老金而言，提高养老金待遇水平而不给年轻一代带来额外负担的措施已列入讨论议程，包括：

● 进一步将雇员养老保险的覆盖范围扩大到短时工，或扩大到在非强制参保的工作场所工作的雇员，如一些微型企业。

● 与工作年限和寿命的延长相一致，自愿延长缴费年限。

● "充分"应用宏观经济指数化，提高未来养老金领取者的待遇。[1]

然而，这些只是 2016 年 12 月国会通过的改革法案中的部分内容。进一步鼓励老年人的劳动参与，包括延迟退休年龄，是另一个应对的重要领域。这不仅是为了充实公共养老金福利待遇，而且也是为了促进身心积极和健康的生活方式。

第二个问题与包括医药物在内的医学科学进步有关。医学科学的进步有利于人类，但同时也因人类寿命延长而对社会保障筹资构成了挑战，不仅对医疗保障，而且对养老金和长期护理都是如此。为了确保社会保障筹资的可持续性，同时使所有人能平等地获得、共享科学进步的裨益，需要更加积极地优化现行制度。居家护理不仅可以改善患者的生活质量，还可以减少不必要且昂贵的住院治疗。制度优化的另一个例子（迄今仍是实验性的）是将成本效益分析引入到统一费用表下的医疗器械和药品定价中，这一举措从 2016 财年开始试行。

第三个问题涉及促进社会保障与其他相关领域的政策组合，例如，住房或本地社区振兴等问题。在日本，尽管住房救助是在公共救助制度下予以发放的，穷人或其他社会弱势群体（需支付）的公共住房租金是被折减过的，最近的立法也将贫困租户的租房补贴纳入穷人服务和支持体系（该体系在公共救助基础上提供"二级社会安全网"），然而住房往往被视为超出社会保障的政策范围。考虑到不断变化的家庭结构（见本文第二部分），应该加

---

[1] 目前，即使根据最初的宏观经济指数化公式应减少名义金额，现行规则中仍存在维持名义金额的例外条款。根据宏观经济指数化的规定，雇主和雇员的缴费率上限是固定的。由于制度是基于没有缓冲储备基金的现收现付制，因此，对当前养老金领取者的超额给付必须通过减少未来领取者的待遇水平来抵消。

大力度采取住房和社会保障相互协调的综合方法，为各代经济脆弱的家庭提供支持。另一个具有潜在生产力的社会政策领域便是社区发展。20世纪70年代，婴儿潮一代聚集生活的农村地区和一些城郊社区，现已"空巢"，其大多数居民年龄超过65岁。在这些地区引入上述的综合社区护理体系，就等同于社区发展的任务。在那里，老年人被鼓励作为志愿者或有偿劳动者，与志愿组织或社会企业家一道，参加各种社区活动。这种社会参与可能也有助于预防老年脆弱。在一些城市，已经有一些进步活动人士和杰出的社区领袖采取了这些举措，这种积极的社区发展有望在全国范围内扩展。

第四个问题是要解决综合改革中未纳入的情况。其中一类问题包括与贫困和不平等有关的议题，特别是贫困家庭儿童，或因孤儿身份、虐待或遗弃而处于不利地位儿童的福利和教育问题。"全民动态参与"倡议下的各项政策，包括上述儿童照料和对育儿家庭的支持，可以解决这些问题。这一倡议应该继续下去。此外，扩大雇员养老保险覆盖范围的政策（见专栏2）侧重于低收入者、中青年劳动者，以及在非正规、不稳定的就业条件下的劳动者。进一步扩展覆盖范围是可取的。针对穷人的服务与支援体系有望得到有效实施。促进对人力资本开发的投资是另一项重要的政策，应加强职业教育和培训，使中青年都能获得必要的技能，以在向服务导向型数字经济的转型中生存下来。若不公正诚实地处理不平等和贫困问题，将会破坏社会团结感，并可能造成人群之间的裂痕。

对资本主义社会中社会保障价值的共识，一直是社会保障制度全面改革的推动力，使社会保障制度在实现升级和现代化的同时获得必要的资金，即便是在20世纪90年代末以来经济停滞的条件下，这包括2000年公共长期护理保险的引入以及21世纪头十年的综合改革。在公众中培养社会保障基本原则——正如社会保障咨询委员会1995年的建议中所称的"独立意识（自我责任感）和社会团结（互助）"十分重要。那些旨在推进社会保障以服务于其所负责群体的人应始终牢记这一点。

韩国的经验：没有福利制度的经济增长局限

[韩]金渊明[1]

韩国是一个进入工业化较晚的国家，从20世纪60年代才开始其工业化进程，而在同一时期大多数西方国家已经成为工业化经济体。虽然在20世纪60年代早期，韩国仍然是一个典型的农业社会，但在接下来的30年里，韩国迅速进入了工业化阶段。由于从20世纪60年代到90年代中期的高经济增长率，韩国得以从最不发达的国家之列一跃为最发达的国家之一，进而摆脱了几个世纪的绝对贫困。换句话说，与日本和中国台湾地区一道，韩国成为第二次世界大战后取得成功经济发展的"东亚奇迹"。

世界银行的一份报告显示，直到20世纪80年代后期东亚的经济增长实现了收入分配的公平，而非加速收入的不平等。[2]特别是韩国在很短的时间内实现了"压缩增长"和公平。有趣的是，这种相对公平的增长模式主要是在初次劳动收入分配上实现的，即没有适当的（再分配性的）社会保障计划。这种独特的韩国历史经验使其社会坚信经济增长与社会福利之间的负向关系，这种关系被称为"经济增长第一，分配第二"。这使得韩国的人们普遍认为所有社会资源都应仅投资于经济增长，因为社会支出本身会阻碍经济增长。

韩国的高经济增长持续了几十年，但在1997年亚洲经济危机之后经济增速大幅下降。与此同时，低出生率和人口老龄化在21世纪趋势更加明显。此外，1997年之后，当劳动力市场变得更加灵活时，以不良工作条件为特征的非正规就业者人数迅速增加，并促使劳动力市场更加明显地二元化。这些基本的社会经济变化意味着韩国在经济和社会方面都面临着可持续性危机。

---

1 [作者简介]金渊明，韩国中央大学社会政策系教授（Yeon-Myung Kim, Professor of Social Policy, Chung-Ang University, Republic of Korea）。主要研究方向：社会保障，福利国家。

[译者简介]陶冶，中国人民大学中国社会保障研究中心博士，中国社会保障学会秘书处学术助理。

[翻译审校]华颖，中国社会科学院人口与劳动经济研究所助理研究员。

2 World Bank.*The East Asian miracle: Economic growth and public policy*.New Oxford: Oxford University Press.

在这种情况下，最近的讨论对经济与福利之间负面关系的范式表示质疑，认为经济增速下降、低出生率和劳动力市场的二元化正是现有"没有分配的经济增长战略"的结果。因此，为了解决当前和未来的社会经济挑战，韩国社会必须增加劳动收入所占份额，并积极扩大社会福利。

在本文中，作者将介绍这种新兴范式的经济和社会背景，讨论有关当前挑战的政策理念和建议。韩国如今的政坛上也在就这些政策理念和建议进行辩论。

一、经济奇迹时期经济与社会福利之间的关系

日本、中国大陆和中国台湾地区、韩国等后发工业化国家和地区以在短时间内实现高收入水平而闻名，这种现象被称为"压缩发展"或"压缩增长"。西方社会用了一个多世纪的时间才达到同样的收入水平。[1] 1960 年工业化进程开始时，韩国是一个典型的农业国家，城市人口在总人口中的比例仅为 28%。但是，如图 1（左轴）所示，仅仅 30 年后，即 1990 年，城市人口比例增加到 74%，几乎与经合组织的总体平均比例（73%）相同。

这表明韩国在短短 30 年内就成功地发展为一个完全工业化的经济体。快速的工业化伴随着经济的高速增长。从 1960—1990 年，韩国的 GDP 年均增长率接近 9%，普通民众的实际收入也在增加[2]，所有人都从增长中受益。1960 年人均国内生产总值仅为 79 美元，1990 年增加到 7 521 美元，2015 年增加到 27 982 美元。经济高增长为那些从农村迁移到城市地区的人口创造了就业机会。

韩国的经济增长主要来自出口导向的经济部门。韩国政府积极支持出口，同时利用第二次世界大战后逐步建立的自由贸易范式。1960 年，进出口额与国民总收入的比率（作为一个衡量经济开放程度的指标）仅为 15.4%，但在 1990 年增加到 53.6%，2014 年增加到 98.6%。因此，正是成功融入世界经济使韩国得以实现其快速增长。

"东亚奇迹"因其伴随经济发展的广泛公平的收入分配而得到认可，韩国是"最典型的"案例。根据上述世界银行的报告，在对 1965—1989 年 40 个国家的经济增长与收入不平等关系的分析中，韩国的人均 GDP 增长率最高，且 1997 年经济危机前的收入不平等程度最低。

1　Whittaker, D. et al. *Compressed development in East Asia*. ITEC Working Paper 2007: 7-29（Kyoto, Doshisha University, Institute for Technology, Enterprise and Competitiveness）.

2　韩国的社会经济指标来源于韩国银行经济统计系统，http://ecos.bok.or.kr/。

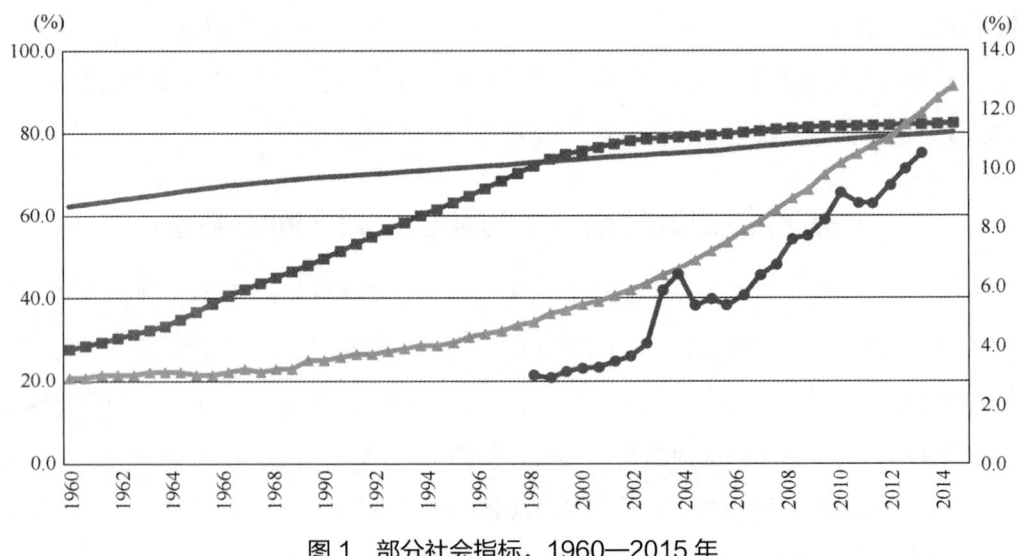

图1　部分社会指标，1960—2015年

来源：经合组织国家相关社会指标是2016年12月20日从世界银行获取；韩国相关社会指标是2016年12月20日从韩国统计局韩国统计信息服务指标中获取。

高额的教育投入在保证韩国压缩增长期的公平发展方面发挥了重要作用。1970年，一般性政府支出中的教育支出占比为22%，与经济发展支出占比相当。直到20世纪80年代后期，这部分占比始终保持在20%左右，代表着对人力资本的高投资。

然而，韩国对社会保障项目的投入占比相对较小。1970年社会发展支出仅占政府总支出的13%左右。[1] 从这个意义上说，韩国在压缩发展时期的社会政策具有"生产主义"特征，这意味着社会政策从属于经济增长。[2]

在"压缩增长"时期，韩国创造了大量的工作岗位，工资发挥了工资收入者的社会保障的作用。与此同时，强大的家庭关系维持了家庭内部的私人收入转移支付，为那些面临失业或老龄化等社会风险的人扮演了隐性的社会保障体系。如图1（右轴）所示，1960年65岁以上人口的比例仅为2.9%，而到1990年则增加到5%；供养老年人口的费用主要由家庭承担。

---

[1] 社会发展支出包括住房、医疗和社会保障开支。

[2] Holliday, I. Productivist welfare capitalism: Social policy in East Asia. in *Political Studies*, 2000, 48（4）: 706–723.

因此，在没有社会保障这样强有力的再分配制度的情况下，"压缩增长"同时实现了经济增长和公平的收入分配。它使得社会上遵循这样一种思维范式，即社会福利的扩张可能导致有限的社会资源流入非生产性部门，从而阻碍经济增长。这种对经济增长与收入分配之间联系的负面认识后来成为一个主要的政治口号（所谓的"经济增长第一，分配第二"范式）。这种主导了韩国社会几十年的模式，在经济快速增长期结束后即自1997年以来，首次面临挑战，主要是在两位自由进步派总统金大中和卢武铉的任期内。

当然，在压缩的经济发展时期，社会保障在制度化方面取得了一些进展，但覆盖率和福利水平均极为有限，且国家干预和财政承诺最小化。韩国首个社会保险制度法律——《工业事故赔偿保险法》——于1964年实施，但覆盖范围非常狭窄。1977年国民健康保险建立，当时城市人口已接近总数的50%，在1988年该制度实现全覆盖。此后普遍性的公共养老金制度建立，当时城市人口的规模已达到70%，该制度在1998年也实现了全覆盖。值得注意的是，1988年的国民养老金制度是部分积累制而非现收现付制的，因为养老金待遇领取者的数量很少，从而能够积累庞大的养老金储备。此外，该基金对国家的财政负担微乎其微，因为它是作为社会保险制度运作的，雇主和雇员都应该对其进行缴费。

这些举措的滞后和社会保障制度的不成熟，以及通过保险筹资都导致了韩国社会支出的低水平。如图1（右轴）所示，韩国的社会支出在1990年仅占GDP的3%左右，当2010年老年人口占总人口的比例超过10%后才逐步达到10%。考虑到经合组织成员国在20世纪60年代初期、美国在1970年的社会支出几乎占国内生产总值的10%，[1]可以说明韩国的社会支出水平之低。

随着1997年亚洲金融危机爆发，"经济增长第一，分配第二"的范式开始面临重大转折。首先，持续的高速经济增长终于结束，韩国经济进入长期低增长阶段。在1997年亚洲金融危机之后实行的劳动力市场灵活性措施增加了非正规工作（主要是临时工、非全日制工和派遣工）的数量，加速了劳动力市场的二元化。此外，很明显，出生率的迅速下降和人口老龄化将导致潜在增长率下降，以及供养老年人口的巨大成本。许多工业化国家普遍见证了这些发展趋势。在韩国，它们的速度和程度被认为更快和更为严重。

1　OECD.Social spending is falling in some countries, but in many others it remains at historically high levels.in *Social Expenditure Update*, Nov., Paris：Directorate for Employment, Labour and Social Affairs, 2014.

因此，这些变化被认为是对韩国社会可持续性和包容性增长的威胁，并导致对经济增长与社会福利之间关系之负面态度的质疑。在下一节中，将研究这些新观点的经济背景和社会背景。

二、社会经济挑战和可持续增长的危机

（一）劳动力市场的变化：二元化与劳动和资本收入的不平等

1997年亚洲金融危机给韩国劳动力市场带来了重大变化。特别是，从那时起，非正规劳动者的数量迅速增加，因为许多公司开始使用他们来取代正规劳动者。根据韩国统计信息服务处（KOSIS）的数据[1]，2001年对非正规劳动者数量的首次官方记录显示，他们占工资和工薪收入者总数的26.8%（364万人），2016年达到32.0%（616万人）。工会认为这个数字被低估了：根据工会估计，2001年非正规劳动者的比例为55.7%（737万人），2016年为43.6%（839万人）。[2]非正规劳动者在工作条件方面遭受严重歧视，从而大大降低了生产成本，这是韩国劳动力市场几乎平分为二（二元化）的一个因素。根据政府数据，非正规劳动者的平均工资目前仅为正规劳动者的53.4%。90/10收入不平等比率[3]从1990年的3.86增加到2014年的4.79，表明领薪劳动者之间的收入差距有所增加。正规劳动者和非正规劳动者之间社会保险覆盖率的差距同样巨大：正规劳动者的国民养老金覆盖率为82.0%，而非正规劳动者的覆盖率仅为36.9%；在就业保险方面，非正规劳动者的覆盖率只是正规劳动者的一半（分别为42.5%和82.4%）。[4]

收入指标中的这种不平等模式也可以在资本和劳动力之间的（初次）收入分配中观察到。根据经合组织的数据，假设自营职业者的劳动收入与工资收入者的劳动收入相同，劳动收入份额从1990年的83%下降到2012年的72%。[5]在根据雇员和自雇人员构成变化进行调整后，劳动收入份额仍然从1996年的79.8%下降到2012年的68.1%。[6]20世纪90年

---

[1] 所有数据来源于韩国统计信息服务处（KOSIS），http://kosis.kr/[2018-02-01]。

[2] Kim, Y.S. *The number and working conditions of non-regular workers*. KLSI Issue Paper No.4，Seoul：Korea Labor & Society Institute，2016.

[3] 指收入最高的10%人群与收入最低的10%人群的收入之比。

[4] Statistics Korea. *Supplementary results of the economically active population survey by employment type* Daejeon，2016.

[5] *Unit labour costs—annual indicators：Labour income share ratios*. http://stats.oecd.org. Paris. Directorate for Employment, Labour and Social Affairs，2016.

[6] Lee, B.H. *Labor income share in Korea：Measuring issues and trends*，e-Labor News No.159（Issue Paper），2015.https://www.kli.re.kr/downloadBbsFile.do?atchmnflNo=11033（Sejong, Korea Labor Institute）.

代以后，资本与劳动力之间的初次收入分配维持了一种有利于资本的结构。

因此，自20世纪90年代以来，社会不平等现象变得更加严重，"带着公平的经济增长"的范式成了谜。人们越来越认识到经济增长的重点是大公司及其正规劳动者（的利益）；结果，对未实现公平分配的批评变得更加普遍。与此同时，低工资、非正规劳动者的数量增加，加上劳动收入份额下降，导致人们担心私人家庭消费将下降，从而阻碍潜在的经济增长。这种情况引发了对"经济增长第一，分配第二"范式的批评，并揭示了加强劳动力市场规制和扩大社会福利以改善一般收入分配的必要性。

（二）人口变化：生育率降低和人口老龄化

韩国是经历了最消极的人口转变的国家之一。出生率在1980年为2.8，在2001年降至1.29，并在过去15年中保持在1.3以下，显示出"超低出生率"现象（KOSIS）。每年出生的孩子数量从1980年的86万减少到2015年的44万——在35年内减少了近一半。相反，出生时的平均预期寿命从1970年的62岁增加到2015年的82岁，即增加了20岁（KOSIS）。根据韩国统计局[1]的人口预测，到2060年，65岁以上人口的比例将达到总人口的41.0%，比28个欧盟国家的预测平均值28.4%高出12.6个百分点。[2] 特别是，生产性人口占比将从2015年的73.4%下降到2060年的49.6%。

人们一致认为，人口构成的这些变化将威胁韩国社会的可持续性，并且相关挑战需要突破性的解决方案。但是，在确定解决方案方面存在实质的冲突。所谓主流[3]的支持经济增长的观点认为，必须控制社会福利的扩张，以抑制与人口老龄化相关的福利成本的扩大。持相反立场者认为，即使国家的财政可持续性处于危险之中，也应该采用扩张性财政政策，社会福利应该随着税收的增加而扩大。具体而言，这一立场提出了大规模的财政投资，以提振低出生率和增加老年人口的社会支出，从而防止（否则不可避免）韩国经济的生产潜力下降。

（三）进入低经济增长的漫长时期

在1997年经济危机之后，1998—2014年韩国经济的年增长率降至4%。根据战略与财政部（2016年）的长期经济展望，21世纪20年代韩国的潜在经济增长将进一步下降至2%，2030年后将降为1%——这主要是基于假设的持续低出生率，以及进一步的人口老龄化。

1　Statistics Konea. *Population projection*：2015-2060 .in Korean press release Daejeon，2016.

2　European Commission.*The 2015 Ageing Report：Economic and budgetary projections for the 28 EU Member States*（2013-2060）.European Economy series.Brussels：Directorate-General for Economic and Financial Affairs，2015.

3　在本文中，"主流"一词表示那些推动了"经济增长第一，分配第二"主流意识形态的群体。更具体地说，这些群体由特别是来自财政部门的保守政党、政府官员和官僚、大公司的首席执行官和保守的大众媒体组成。

毫无疑问，韩国经济已进入长期低增长阶段。这就使得关于社会福利支出与经济产生的总收入之间关系的争论更加重要。低预期的经济增长意味着靠增长创造的财政空间有限。正因为如此，主流讨论者开始以悲观预测为借口，提出抑制社会福利的扩张，而理解经济与福利之间积极关系的支持福利的团体则强烈要求确保增加福利资源。

为了讨论韩国经济增长与社会福利之间的关系，重要的是了解韩国高度开放的经济的核心。20世纪60年代以后，韩国的经济高增长率是以大公司为主导的出口导向型经济政策的结果。数十年的出口导向型经济增长将韩国的开放经济推向全球顶级水平。经济的开放程度可以通过出口和进口之和与GDP的关系来衡量。事实上，2014年韩国这一比例为95.9%，是所有经合组织国家中最高的，甚至是日本（38.5%）的两倍多。[1]这种经济开放引发了扩大社会福利的矛盾方面。主流观点认为，对于像韩国这样的出口导向型国家来说，公司的国际竞争力很重要，这是由出口商品和服务的价格共同决定的。价格尤其受到社会保险额外筹资的进一步财政负担的负面影响，劳动力成本的增加降低了国家的国际竞争力。因此，该派观点认为，在开放经济中，高水平的社会支出是经济增长的障碍。反对者认为，决定竞争力程度的不是劳动力成本，而是单位劳动力成本，即与公司生产率相关的劳动力成本，而经济的开放性是生产力的永久触发因素。此外，由于开放经济体直接受到世界经济起伏的影响，完善的社会福利制度对稳定国内经济、实现产业结构的顺利调整和减少社会混乱至关重要。

（四）主流观点对可持续性危机的回应

本节探讨了主流观点为应对韩国"可持续发展危机"而提出的政策策略，并探讨了这些策略如何看待经济与社会福利之间的关系。

主流观点对可持续性危机的回应可以在2016年战略与财政部发布的《2060年长期财政展望》（以下简称LFO 2060。有人认为，财政部门在实现东亚国家的经济奇迹方面发挥了重要作用[3]。在此背景下，LFO 2060可被视为重要的报告，它显示解决可持续性危机的主流政策取向。事实上，在报告发布时，战略和财政部提交了一项法案，以加强金融监管，并制定旨在抑制福利计划扩张的实际政策）中找到。在长期低经济增长的情况下，LFO 2060

1　*OECD Factbook* 2015–2016：*Economic, environmental and social statistics*，2016.

2　Ministry of Strategy and Finance.*Long-term fiscal outlook* 2060.Sejong，2016.

3　Johnson，C.The developmental State：Odyssey of a concept.in M.Woo-Cumings（ed.），*The developmental State*.Ithaca，NY：Cornell University Press，1999.

清楚地显示了主流观点的政策方向，以及其对如何调整经济与福利之间关系的理解。LFO 2060 预测，由于人口减少，韩国的潜在经济增长率将大幅下降，这将导致难以通过提高税收以支付老年人的高福利支出。因此，基于无政策变化假设（图 2 中的情景 2），由于养老金和医疗保障成本增加，社会支出在 2060 年的 GDP 中占比将达 22.8%。当把福利（支出）加到政府的其他一般支出中，社会支出占比将在 2060 年达到 28%，与经合组织成员国目前的社会支出水平相当。在这种情况下，国家（主要是国内）债务将从 2015 年的 GDP 的 40.1% 增加到 2060 年的 62.4%。如果作为对策，把由政府自行决定的支出每年减少 10%，国家债务将保持在目前的水平（2060 年为 38.1%，见图 2 中的情景 1）。如果引入新的昂贵的福利计划，到 2060 年债务将达到 GDP 的 88.8%（见图 2 中的情景 3）。显然，战略和财政部更喜欢并积极推行情景 1，将国家债务维持在当前水平。因此，LFO 2060 的关键信息是，为了维持韩国的财政稳健[1]，国家的支出不应再增加，主要目标应该是抑制因预期人口因素所引致的福利支出的增加。

战略和财政部将未来的福利支出视作阻碍财政可持续性的最具威胁性的因素。因此，LFO 2060 提出了抑制新的福利计划并约束养老金、医疗保障及长期护理计划支出的政策，以克服与经济低增长相关的问题。这清楚地表明，主流群体仍然坚持现有的范式，将社会福利视为阻碍经济增长的主要因素。

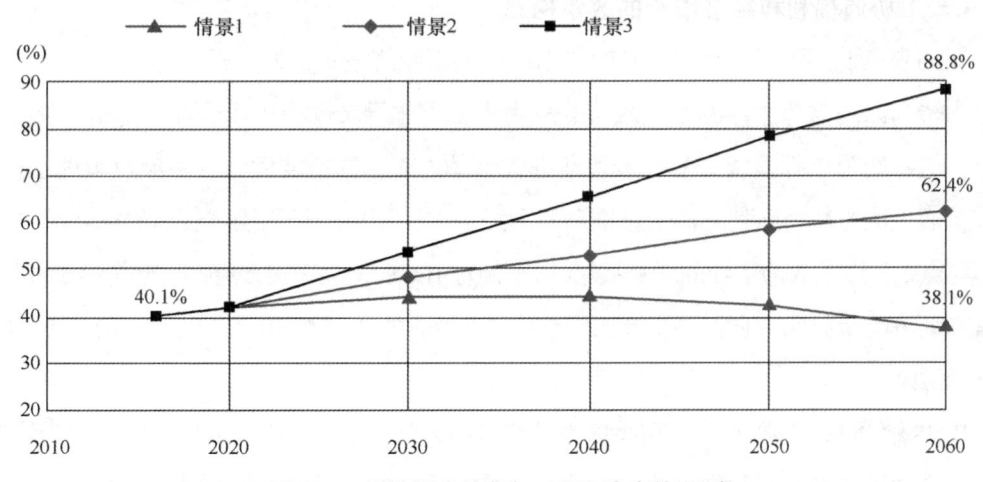

图 2　一般性政府债务与 GDP 比率的预测

来源：作者对战略和财政部数据（2016）的重新整理

---

[1] 对于这些主流群体而言，财政稳健性非常重要。在财政稳健的基础上，韩国政府能够积极采用扩张性财政政策，这使韩国能够迅速摆脱两次经济危机（1997 年亚洲金融危机和 2008 年全球金融危机）。

三、对可持续经济增长的政策理念与建议

1997年12月，当韩国社会的可持续性危机变得更加明显时，一个相对进步的党派击败了历史悠久的保守派并两次获得政权（金大中政府，1998—2002年；卢武铉政府，2003—2007年）。两位总统优先考虑分配政策和扩大社会福利。特别是，两任政府还试图在政治上重建经济增长与社会福利之间的关系。金大中总统的政府专注于"生产性福利"的讨论，强调社会福利的生产性方面。因此，通过扩大社会保险覆盖面以及促进受益人享有公共援助这一个体"权利"，向普遍性迈出了实质性的一步[1]。同样，卢武铉总统的政府采用了"社会投资"范式，创造了一种新的政策话语，被称为"经济与福利之间的良性循环"，推动了儿童保育以及老年人社会照顾服务实现巨大进步。然而，因为保守党在2008年重新获得了政治权力，这些政治努力未能取代现有"经济增长第一，分配第二"的主要范式。新保守派政府回到了以大公司为主导的外向型经济战略，而分配政策失去了优先地位。然而，在社会危机加深的情况下，倡导扩大社会福利和分配政策作为确保韩国社会可持续性之主要工具的主张也越来越响亮。在这一背景下提出的一些政策建议将在下文阐释，这些政策建议现已为新任总统文在寅的政府所采纳。政府目前正在制定一项倡导扩大社会福利和分配政策的详细方案。

（一）协调福利和经济增长的政策构想

新的观点批评了"没有福利制度的出口导向型经济增长"的范式，并开始将重点从出口导向转向以内需为主导的增长政策、从由大公司主导转向由中小企业主导的经济增长。此外，这些新观点都强调分配政策和渐进式劳动力改革的重要性。与主流政策理念相反，这种新模式认为社会福利的扩大是推动韩国经济逆转预期的长期经济衰退的重要因素。在新的观点中，以收入为主导的增长战略（以下简称ILGS）是文在寅政府（从2017年5月开始）的官方经济政策导向，它强调了开放经济中社会保障的必要性和社会投资视角。下文将就此进行讨论。

ILGS解释说，韩国社会的可持续性危机是由大公司主导的出口战略所固有的局限性导致的，这种战略导致劳动收入减少，进而使得内需减少和家庭消费下降。在韩国，以三星和LG等大公司为首的出口部门占最终总需求的比例从1990年的22.5%增加到2014年的

---

[1] Kim, Y.M.Beyond East Asian welfare productivism in South Korea.in *Policy and Politics*, 2008, 36（1）: 109-125.

36.2%，而同期私人国内消费的比例从41.0%降至33.6%。[1] 然而，出口部门中大公司的利润并未在国内再投资，而是保留在公司中。此外，随着大公司的生产基地转移到国外，其创造国内就业的能力急剧下降。

ILGS对韩国社会的诊断是，劳动收入份额减少和低工资的非正规劳动者比例增加，导致收入不平等加剧，最终导致家庭消费和国内需求减少。因此，从这个角度来看，国内私人家庭收入的提高是促进经济增长的关键。因此，ILGS非常重视改善劳动力市场的初次收入分配；引入最低收入保障，包括提高最低工资；改善非正规劳动者的工作条件；工资增长与生产力提高相匹配。[2] 在同一背景下，强调通过社会保障项目加强二次收入分配（本文稍后将对此进行解释）。通过这种方式，收入导向型增长理论认为，社会福利的扩张可以通过促进国内消费（国内消费由于韩国经济结构而严重不足）来促进经济增长。

因此，社会福利是一种宏观经济稳定器。通过改善社会福利可以实现对这一功能的改进。如上所述，作为最开放的经合组织经济体，韩国直接受到全球经济波动的影响。然而，由于社会支出水平较低（2014年占国内生产总值的10%），其社会保障制度在世界经济衰退时稳定国内经济方面具有根本性的局限。此外，社会保险的特点是规定了待遇与缴费之间的强相关性，这使得社会保障的收入维持功能对于那些被遗留在劳动力市场之外的人和年轻的毕业生（young school leavers）来说尤其薄弱。另外，由于失业保险金水平很低，就业培训项目不足，很难迅速回应对开放经济非常重要的产业结构调整。因此，为了维护韩国开放经济的稳定，扩大社会福利至关重要。

虽然ILGS强调了需求方面，但社会投资观点侧重于劳动力供给方面，即劳动力的质量和数量。这种观点主张通过投资于人力资本来发展个人就业能力，是欧盟社会政策的一个重要范例。[3] 在韩国，社会投资视角在扩大儿童保育服务和积极的劳动力市场政策方面做出了巨大贡献。据分析，韩国的低生育率实际上是由儿童保育费用高造成的，因而对儿童保育服务进行了大量投资。因此，家庭政策支出仅占2000年国内生产总值的0.1%，而到2014年迅速增加到1.2%。与此同时，对低收入失业者和青年劳动者的积极劳动力市场政策

---

[1] Bank of Korea. *The Korean economy based on the 2014 input-output statistics*. Seoul, 2016.

[2] 在此背景下，文在寅政府在2018年将法定最低工资提高了16.4%，现在的重点是将公共部门非标准劳动者的地位转为长期就业的政策，并解决私营部门中标准和非标准工作两者之间不平等的工作条件。

[3] Leoni, T. Social investment: A guiding principle for welfare state adjustment after the crisis?. in *Empirica*, 2016, 43（4）：831–858.

得以加强，并且在同一时期相关支出从占国内生产总值的 0.2% 上升到 0.5%。[1] 但是，关于这些政策的产出存在一些争议。例如，尽管儿童保育服务有了广泛的改善，但低出生率和青年失业率没有变化。

（二）福利扩张的政策建议

过去，韩国社会福利扩张的合理性在于追赶西方福利国家、保护社会权利和分摊社会风险。然而，促进私人家庭消费、确保稳定就业和降低私人福利成本构成了最近扩大社会福利的主要理由。

由于韩国经济无就业增长、非正规工作的增加以及青年失业率的上升趋势，基本收入的构想突然引起重视。基本收入支持者认为，此类计划是扩大韩国国内需求的最有效方法。然而，由于建立普遍性基本收入制度耗资巨大，讨论的重点放在了扩大老年人现有的现金津贴，并根据人口分类建立新的普遍社会津贴之上。文在寅政府承诺在 2022 年前将基本养老金水平从每月 20 万增加到 30 万韩元；从 2018 年起，0~5 岁的儿童将普遍享受儿童保育津贴。此外，那些被排除在就业保险之外的年轻人将获得临时"青年求职津贴"。

正在讨论的一项提议是将部分国民养老金储备投资于保障公共福利基础设施。2015 年，国民养老基金相当于国内生产总值的约 34%，其中绝大多数储备投资于股票和债券等金融产品。这项提议实际上是由现任执政党提出的，该执政党是 2016 年 4 月大选时的反对党。他们认为至少有 25% 的新增的养老金储备（价值 10 万亿韩元）每年应该用于建造公共出租房屋，尤其是提供给年轻人的公租房，以及扩大公共医疗保健和福利设施。该政策提案的主要目标之一是通过降低年轻育龄人口的住房、儿童保育和医疗保健成本来提高出生率，并促进早婚。[2] 在这届新政府的领导下，这项被称为"国民养老基金社会投资"的政策也正在取得成果。

该提议也可以作为减少由营利性医疗和社会服务提供者（目前在韩国占主导地位）所带来的私人福利成本的措施。例如，公立医院病床的数量仅占总数的 10%，公立托儿服务提供者仅占所有服务提供者的 6.5%，只有约 2.6% 的长期护理机构是公共机构。医疗和社会护理部门通过私人第三方支付系统运营，因此，私人提供者的市场支配地位意味着结构性问题，因为它过度使用公共财政。如果将国民养老金储备的一部分用于确保公共提供者，则可以将其用作医疗和社会护理服务的费用调控器。文在寅政府宣布了一项大规模增加公

---

[1] *Social Expenditure Database.* http://www.oecd.org/social/expenditure.htm .Paris:Directorate for Employment, Labour and Social Affairs，2016.

[2] 韩国女性的平均初婚年龄曾是 24.8 岁，男性曾是 27.8 岁，但是到 2014 年则分别变为了 30.0 岁和 32.6 岁。

共儿童和老年人护理的政策，计划于 2018 年实施。

另一项政策建议将社会福利的扩张与创造优质就业机会联系起来。在目前无就业增长突出的韩国社会中，过去几年在社会照护领域创造了许多就业机会，例如托儿所教师、护理和社会工作者。[1] 然而，社会照护领域的企业很多只是提供极端恶劣劳动条件工作的小企业，并且其中许多是非正规就业。考虑到社会护理服务部门的这些结构性弱点，政策提案建议，需要通过在每个地方政府区域建立社会服务团体来创造高质量的工作。它还建议由当地政府直接运营养老院和护理设施，当地政府也应直接雇用幼儿园教师和护理人员。因此，这项政策建议的关键是在社会服务和医疗保健部门创造高质量的公共就业。文在寅政府已宣布在公共部门创造 81 万个新工作岗位，占韩国总就业人数的 3%，其中约 34 万个将在公共福利设施内和通过扩大公共医疗卫生服务创造。

四、结　论

围绕社会福利与经济增长之间正向关系的讨论之所以在韩国不流行，是因为韩国的经济史表明了在工业化时期经济的快速增长与公平的共存。此外，自 20 世纪 90 年代以来主导世界的新自由主义意识形态支持了经济增长与公平之间负相关关系的历史意识形态，这在韩国社会中更为根深蒂固。在这里，自 20 世纪 90 年代中期以来的负面根本变化甚至激发了对旧的主导范式的重新评估。然而，越来越多的人主张，为了支持经济增长的可持续性，更公平地分配财富是必不可少的。即使是传统上曾强调经济增长的世界银行，也开始关注极端经济不平等对经济增长的负面影响。[2] 这种新趋势令人鼓舞，因为它最终可能有助于改变主导范式。就韩国而言，重新建立经济与社会福利之间关系的新观点不仅仅是学术建议。2017 年 5 月上台的文在寅政府正在积极推动收入导向型增长政策，以实现经济增长与福利扩张之间的正向关系。大多数欧洲福利国家是在经济发展的黄金时期发展起来的。韩国在去工业化和全球化时期开始发展成为一个福利国家，这一时期提供了一个完全不同的环境。如上所述，文在寅政府的举措可能尤其会对新兴产业产生一些影响。

1　2011—2015 年这些服务部门创造了约 28 万个工作岗位。

2　Dabla-Norris, E.et al. Causes and *consequences of income inequality*: *A global perspective*. IMF Staff Discussion Note 15/13 . Washington, DC: International Monetary Fund, 2015.

This report offers a comprehensive overview and interpretation of the interplays of economic and social policy developments at the global level and in historical perspective. While showing an abundance of literature (and views) regarding social policy in the Western hemisphere, it fills the research gap in understanding the way China has supported its past decades of impressive economic development through proactive expansion and use of social security and its related institutions. The authors conclude that the positive trade and growth effects of globalization – triggered by the opening up of China that began in 1978 – provided a window of opportunity for the Chinese social security system. China' state-led expansionary social security policy had positive impacts on the country's economic development and, therefore, at the least, deserves the world's social policy makers' attention.In contrast, the West simultaneously consolidated its social security systems, including through state-retrenchment and privatization and, later, in a context of intensified austerity, thus contributing to economic stagnation, unemployment and growing poverty. Again, social policy makers are invited to re-consider mainstream social policy approaches. The authors hope to be able to prove that positive interaction between and joint progress of social security and economic development can be achieved, which is not only the historical experience proven by the Western hemisphere, but also consolidated by China's story in recent decades.

ILO Regional Office for Asia and the Pacific
United Nations Building, 11th Floor
Rajdamnern Nok Avenue
Bangkok 10200, Thailand
Tel.: +66 2288 1234, Fax.: +66 2288 3062
Email: BANGKOK@ilo.org
www.ilo.org/asia

—. 2016b. *Main report on the development of China's social security: A review of the 12th Five-Year Plan and outlook on the 13th Five-Year Plan*. Beijing, People's Publishing House [in Chinese].

—. 2016c. Properly handle the relationship between economic development and the improvement of people's livelihood. in *People's Daily*, 1 Nov. [in Chinese].

—. 2016d. The key points and paths of expanding middle income groups. in *Guangmin Daily*, 29 June [in Chinese].

—. 2016e. A Chinese social security issue elicited by the story of a German farmer. in *Global Times,* 13 Sep. [in Chinese]

—. 2017a. A proper view on the relationship between social security and economic growth.in *Guangmin Daily*, 25 Mar. [in Chinese]

—. 2017b. Great times call for great wisdom. in *Popular Tribune*, Vol. 1 [in Chinese]

—. 2017c. Social security and public governance: Historical logic and future options. in *Chinese Social Security Review*, Vol. 1, No. 1 [in Chinese; abstract in English].

—. 2017d. Make social security and employment mutually strengthening pillars to people's livelihood. in *Wenhui*, 16 Mar. [in Chinese].

—. 2018a. China's Social Security and Economic Development: Retrospect and Prospect. in *Journal of Renmin University of China*, Vol. 1 [in Chinese].

—. 2018b. Forty Years of Social Security in China (1978-2018): Institutional Transformation, Path Selection and Chinese Experience. in*Teaching and Research,* Vol. 11 [in Chinese].

Xi, J. 2016. A new starting point for China's Development: A New Blueprint for Global Growth. Opening remarks, B20 Summit, Hangzhou, 3 Sep. G20 Information Centre. Available at: http://www.g20.utoronto.ca/2016/160903-xi.html [10 Oct. 2018].

—. 2017. Secure a decisive victory in building a moderately prosperous society in all respects and strive for the great success of socialism with Chinese characteristics for a new era: Xi Jinping's report to the 19th CPC National Congress. in *People's Daily,* 28 Oct.[in Chinese].

Zheng, G. 2002.*Globalization of labour and social security.* Beijing, China Labour and Social Security Publishing House, 2002. [together with Zheng Yushuo, in Chinese].

—. 2004a. From welfare education to mixed plural-education system China's educational benefits and human capital investment. in *Research on Education Tsinghua University*, Vol. 25, No. 5 [in Chinese].

—. 2004b. From centralized government administration to self-governance by stakeholders: The future model of administration of social insurance in Chin. in *Journal of Renmin University of China*, Vol. 5 [in Chinese].

—. 2008a. *China's social security: A review of 30 years of progress.*Beijing, People's Publishing House. [in Chinese].

—. 2008b. *China's social security reform and development strategy: Ideas, goals and action plan* Beijing, People's Publishing House. [in Chinese].

—. 2011. The historical view and global vision of the development of contemporary social security, in *Economics Information*, No. 12 [in Chinese].

—. 2013. Top-level design to deepen the reform of the pension system in China. in *Teaching and Research,* Vol. 12 [in Chinese].

—. 2014. The historical logic of the evolution of China's social security. in *Journal of Renmin University of China,* Vol. 1 [in Chinese].

—. 2016a. *China's social security development report 2016.* Beijing, People's Publishing House. [in Chinese].

Available at: https://archive.org/details/grundlegungderp00wagngoog/page/n9 [19 Jan. 2019]

Wang, W. 2017. Thoughts on social security within the framework of the ideal of great harmony. in *Chinese Social Security Review*, Vol. 1, No. 1, pp. 114-124 [in Chinese, with abstract in English].

Wang, X.; Williamson, J.B.; Cansoy, M. 2016. Developing countries and systemic pension reforms: Reflections on some emerging problems. in *International Social Security Review*, Vol. 69, No. 2.

Weber, M. 1905. *The Protestant ethic and the spirit of capitalism.* New York, Penguin Books, 2002..

—. 1991. *Die Wirtschaftsethik der Weltreligionen. Konfuzianismus und Taoismus. Schriften 1915-1920.* Tuebingen, MWS I/19. [*The religion of China: Confucianism and Taoism. Writings 1915-1920*].

Williamson, J. 2002. "What Washington means by policy reform", in J. Williamson (ed.): *Latin American adjustment: How much has happened?*.Washington, DC, Institute for International Economics.

World Bank. 1994. *Averting the old-age crisis: policies to protect the old and promote growth.* New York, Oxford University Press.

—. 2017. *Health expenditure: China.* Washington, DC. Available at: https://data.worldbank.org/indicator/SH.XPD.PCAP?locations=CN[Oct.2018].

World Bank; International Labour Office (ILO). 2016. World Bank and ILO announce new push for universal social protection. Press release. Available at: http://www.worldbank.org/en/news/press-release/2016/09/21/world-bank-ilo-announce-new-push-for-universal-social-protection; http://www.ilo.org/global/topics/social-security/WCMS_378991/lang--en/index.htm [10 Oct. 2018].

World Health Organization (WHO). 1982. *The Vienna International Plan of Action on Ageing* (Geneva).

in *People's Daily*, 17 Oct. [in Chinese].

Stephens, J. D. 2019. *The welfare state and economic development: The United States in comparative perspective*. Background paper to the Chinese version of this report. Beijing, CAOSS.

Supreme Court. 2002. *Compulsory Education Law of the People's Republic of China*. Beijing, Supreme People's Court of the People's Republic of China. Available at: http://en.chinacourt.org/public/detail.php?id=135[Oct. 2018].

United Nations General Assembly. 2015. Transforming our world: The 2030 Agenda for Sustainable Development. Resolution adopted by the General Assembly on 25 Sep. (A/RES/70/1). Available at: http://www.un.org/ga/search/view_doc.asp?symbol=A/RES/70/1&Lang=E[19 Jan. 2019].

United Nations (UN); Statistical Office of the European Union (EUROSTAT); International Monetary Fund (IMF); World Bank; Organisation for Economic Co-operation and Development (OECD). 2009. *System of National Accounts 2008*. Luxembourg, New York, Paris, Washington, United Nations. Available at: http://unstats.un.org/unsd/nationalaccount/sna2008.asp [13 Dec. 2018].

United States Congress. 1776. *Declaration of Independence. The unanimous Declaration of the thirteen United States of America*. Philadelphia, PA, US Government. Available at: https://upload.wikimedia.org/wikipedia/commons/8/8f/United_States_Declaration_of_Independence.jpg. [Oct. 2018].

Vaughan-Whitehead, D. (ed.). 2015a. *The European social model in crisis. Is Europe losing its soul?* Geneva and Cheltenham, UK and Northampton, MA, ILO and Edward Elgar Publishing.

—. 2015b. The European social model in times of crisis: An overview. in D. Vaughan-Whitehead (ed.): *The European social model in crisis: Is Europe losing its soul?* Geneva, Cheltenham, UK and Northampton, MA, ILO and Edward Elgar Publishing. pp. 1 and 65.

Wagner, A. 1876. Grundlegung der Politischen Oekonomie. Teil I: Grundlagen der Volkswirtschaft. Leipzig, C. F. Winter. [*Political economy. Volume I: basic economics.*].

und internationaler Vergleich. Dritte Auflage. Wiesbaden, Germany, Verlag fuer Sozialwissenschaften. [*Social policy in Germany: Historical evolvement and international comparison. Third edition*].

Scholz, W. 1992. Methodische, statistische und prognostische Aspekte der Rentendynamisierung in Ostdeutschland. [*Methodological, statistical and prognostic aspects of the pension adjustments in East-Germany*]. in Verband Deutscher Rentenversicherungstraeger (ed.): *Deutsche Rentenversicherung*. Frankfurt am Main, Deutsche Rentenversicherung.pp. 550-569.

—. 2009. *The social budget of Germany: Keeping the welfare state in perspective* (Duesseldorf, Germany, Hans Boeckler Stiftung).

—. 2015. Financing social security out of contributions: About origins, present discussions and prospects of a success story. in *International Social Security Review*, Vol. 68, No. 4.

—. 2017. Global social security in political and economic contexts: Historical experiences and current trends. in *China International Social Security Review*, Vol. 1, No. 1, pp. 135-152.

—. Cichon, M.; Hagemejer, K. 2000. *Social budgeting*. Geneva, ILO and ISSA.

Schroeder, W. 2019. *Historical experience of the interaction between economic development and social security. Current core problems in reaction national and global developments. Search of solutions for the future.*Background paper to the Chinese version of this report. Beijing, CAOSS.

Social Security Administration (SSA). 2016. Preamble to *the* Social Security Act of 1935., SSA (US), Historical links. Available at: https://www.ssa.gov/history/35act.html#PREAMBLE [23 Nov. 2016].

State Council Information Office (SCIO). 2011. *China's rural poverty alleviation and development*, White Paper (Beijing) [in Chinese].

State Council Poverty Alleviation Office (SCPAO). 2017. Leading CPC Group of Poverty Alleviation Office of the State Council: Five years of poverty alleviation and endeavour.

People's Daily. 2016.Chinese government received ISSA Award for Outstanding Achievements in Social Security, 19 Nov.[in Chinese].

—. 2017. Whose jobs will be replaced by artificial intelligence? 21 Apr. [in Chinese].

Petersen, K. 2019. *Growth for welfare or welfare for growth? The changing relationship between economic development and social security in the Nordic countries*. Background paper to the Chinese version of this report. Beijing, CAOSS.

Plamondon, P.; Drouin, A.; Binet, G.; Cichon, M.; McGillivray, W.R.; Bdard, M.; Perez-Montas, H. 2002. *Actuarial practice in social security.* Geneva, International Labour Office and International Social Security Association.

Popper, K. 1977. *The logic of scientific discovery.* Fourteenth edition. London, Routledge. [First published in German: Logik der Forschung (Wien, Springer, 1934)].

Pusch, T.; Seifert, H., 2017. Mindestlohngesetz: Fuer viele Minijobber weiterhin nur Miniloehne. Policy brief No. 9. Duesseldorf, Wirtschafts- und Sozialwissenschaftliches Institut, Hans-Boeckler-Stiftung. [*Germany's minimum wage law: Many mini-jobbers still only earn mini-wages*] Available at: http://www.boeckler.de/14_107083.htm [19 Jan. 2019].

Ritter, G.A. 2014. The creation of the German pension insurance and its major characteristics, revision of a lecture at Thanks, Otto! 125 Years of Pensions and New Global Perspectives conference, Berlin, 28-29 Oct. (Handout) Avalable at: https://helpage.app.box.com/s/4zxpaajj9gv2g9c785tl/file/24147825195 [19 Jan. 2019]

Rodgers, D.T. 1998. *Atlantic crossings: Social politics in a progressive age*. Cambridge, MA and London, Harvard University Press and Belknap Press.

Sala-i-Martin, X. 1996. *A positive theory of social security*. Journal of Economic Growth, 1:277-304. Boston, June.

Samuelson, P.A. 1983. *Foundations of economic analysis,* Enlarged edition. Cambridge, MA, Harvard Economic Studies.

Schmidt, M.G. 2005. Sozialpolitik in Deutschland. Historische Entwicklung *productivity*.Beijing.

—. 2019. National data. Available at: http://data.stats.gov.cn/english/easyquery.htm?cn=C01 [Jan. 2019]

—.Various years. *Statistical yearbook,* Beijing.

—.Various years. *Statistical bulletin on national economic and social development,* Beijing.

—.Various years. *Labour statistical yearbook,* Beijing.

National Health Commission (NHC). 2018. *China statistical yearbook of health,* Beijing.

National Health and Family Planning Commission (NHFPC). 2016. *China family development report 2016,* Beijing.

—.Various years. *China Statistical Yearbook of Health and Family Planning,* Beijing.

Ono, T. 2019. *Historical development and current issues for social security in Japan.* Background paper to the Chinese version of this report. Beijing, CAOSS.

Ortiz, I.; Cummins, M.; Karunanethy, K. 2017. *Fiscal space for social protection and the SDGs: Options to expand social investments in 187 countries,* Extension of Social Security Working Paper No. 48. Geneva and New York, International Labour Office, UNICEF and UNWOMEN. Available at: http://www.social-protection.org/gimi/gess/RessourcePDF.action?ressource.ressourceId=51537 [19 Jan. 2019].

Pal, K.; Behrendt, C.; Lger, F.; Cichon, M.; Hagemejer, K. 2005. *Can low-income countries afford basic social protection? First results of a modelling exercise: Issues in social protection*, Discussion Paper 13.Geneva, International Labour Office.

Payandeh, M. 2012. The united nations, military intervention, and regime change in Libya.in *Virginia Journal of International Law*, Vol. 52, No. 2. Available at: https://ssrn.com/abstract=1930993[19 Jan. 2019].

apr/01/language-welfare-social-security [27 Dec. 2017].

Maddison, A. 2003. *Historical statistics: The Maddison Project* (Groningen, Netherlands, University of Groningen). Available at: http://www.ggdc.net/maddison/oriindex.htm[11 Nov. 2016].

—. 2016. *The Maddison Project* (Groningen, Netherlands, University of Groningen). Available at: http://www.ggdc.net/maddison/maddison-project/home.htm[10 Nov. 2016].

Manthe, U. 2011. *Geschichte des Roemischen Rechts*, 4. Auflage [*History of Roman Law*]. Munich, C.H. Beck.[Chinese translation available].

Ministry of Civil Affairs (MCA). Various years (2010–18). *Statistical bulletin on social services development 2009-17*. Beijing.

—. Various years (2000-09). *Statistical bulletin on civil affairs development* (Beijing).

Ministry of Education (MOE). 2017. Leading CPC group of the Ministry of Education: Develop modern world level education with Chinese characteristics, in *Qiushi Journal*, Vol. 16 [in Chinese].

—.Various years. *Statistical yearbook on education,* Beijing.

—. 2018. *Statistical bulletin on the development of education 2017. Beijing.*

Ministry of Finance (MOF)，Ministry of Education (MOE)，National Bureau of Statistics (NBS). 2018. *Statistical bulletin on the implementation of educational funds in China 2017*.Beijing. Available at: http://www.moe.gov.cn/srcsite/A05/s3040/201810/t20181012_351301.html [Nov. 2018]

Ministry of Human Resources and Social Security(MHRSS). Various years. *Statistical bulletin on human resources and social security development*. Beijing.

Mueller, K. 1999. *The political economy of pension reform in Central-Eastern Europe*. Northampton, MA, Edward Elgar Publishing.

National Bureau of Statistics (NBS). 2016. *An International comparison report oflabour*

Chinesischen von Ralf Moritz. [*The analects,* translated from Chinese by Ralf Moritz].

Koschnitzke, L. 2015. *Krankenversicherung: Die Schutzlosen. Trotz gesetzlicher Pflicht leben hunderttausende Menschen in Deutschland ohne Krankenversicherung. Die aktuelle Fluechtlingskrise verschaerft das Problem* [*Health insurance: The non-protected. Despite legal obligation hundreds of thousands of people live without health insurance in Germany. The current refugees crisis intensifies the problem*] (Hamburg, Germany, ZEIT). Available at: http://www.zeit.de/wirtschaft/2015-10/krank-ohne-versicherung-selbstaendigkeit-abstieg[19 Jan. 2019].

Lee, C.K. 2005. *Livelihood struggles and market reform: (un)making Chinese labour after state socialism* (Geneva, United Nations Research Institute for Social Development). Available at: https://www.econstor.eu/bitstream/10419/148803/1/862974275.pdf[19 Jan. 2019].

Leo XIII. 1891. "Rerum Novarum: Encyclical of Pope Leo XIII on capital and labour", in *Libreria Editrice Vaticana*. Available at: http://w2.vatican.va/content/leo-xiii/en/encyclicals/documents/hf_l-xiii_enc_15051891_rerum-novarum.html[8 Dec. 2016].

Li, P.; Cheng, G.; Zhang, Y. 2015. *Social Blue Book: Analysis and projection of China's social situation in 2016* (Beijing, Social Sciences Academic Press [in Chinese].

Li, S.; Jingyong, Z. 2003. "Can education provide sufficient human capital for a moderately prosperous society?", in *Xinhua News Agency*, 12 Mar.[in Chinese].

Lindert, P. H. 2010. *Growing public: Social spending and economic growth since the 18th century* (Los Angeles, CA, University of California).

Lindner, F. 2012. *Saving does not finance Investment: Accounting as an indispensable guide to economic theory*, Working Paper 100. Duesseldorf, Germany, Macroeconomic Policy Institute. Available at: https://www.boeckler.de/pdf/p_imk_wp_100_2012.pdf[19 Jan. 2019].

Lister, R. 2013. Benefit cuts: How the language of welfare poisoned our social security. in *The Guardian*, 1 Apr. Available at: https://www.theguardian.com/commentisfree/2013/

—. 2016. *ILO constitution: 1919*. Geneva. Available at: https://www.ilo.org/public/libdoc/ilo/1920/20B09_18_engl.pdf

—. 2017. *World social protection report 2017-19: Universal social protection to achieve the Sustainable Development Goals*. Geneva.

International Labour Organization (ILO) NATLEX-China. Undated. China: Regulations on unemployment insurance for staff and workers of state-owned enterprises. Promulgated by the State Council by Decree No. 110, 4 Dec. 1993. unofficial translation. Available at: http://www.ilo.org/dyn/natlex/docs/WEBTEXT/49694/65117/E93CHN01.htm[19 Jan. 2019].

International Monetary Fund (IMF). 2017a. *World economic outlook: Update,* July. Washington, DC.

—. 2017b. *The IMF and social protection: 2017 evaluation report*. Washington, DC, Independent Evaluation Office, IMF. Available at: http://www.ieo-imf.org/ieo/files/completedevaluations/SP%20-%202017EvalReport.pdf[19 Jan. 2019].

International Social Security Association (ISSA). 2016. Government of China receives international social security award. Press release, 17 Nov. Available at: https://www.issa.int/en/-/government-of-china-receives-international-social-security-award [Oct. 2018].

International Social Security Association (ISSA)，Social Security Administration(SSA). Various years. *Social security programs throughout the world*.Geneva and Washington, D.C.

Judt, T. 2010. *Ill fares the land*. New York, NY, Penguin.

Kim, Y. 2019. *Limits of economic growth without welfare: The experience of the Republic of Korea*. Background paper to the Chinese version of this report. Beijing, CAOSS.

Klein, N. 2007. *The shock doctrine: The rise of disaster capitalism*. New York, Metropolitan Books/Henry Holt.

Konfuzius. 2017. Gespraeche. Lun-yu. Stuttgart, Reclams Universal Bibliothek. Aus dem timely and devastating", in *The Guardian*, 15 Sep. Available at: https://www.theguardian.com/books/2007/sep/15/politics[11 Nov. 2017].

Grimshaw, D. 2015. Britains social model: Rapid descent from liberal collectivism to a market society. in D. Vaughan-Whitehead (ed.): *The European social model in crisis: Is Europe losing its soul?* Geneva, Cheltenham, UK and Northampton, MA, ILO and Edward Elgar Publishing, pp. 553-613.

Hagemejer, K.; Scholz, W. 2004. Nachhaltig, sicher und angemessen? Die Reformstrategie der Weltbank und die Rentenreformen in Polen, Ungarn, Tschechien und anderen osteuropaeischen Laendern. Eine Neubetrachtung (Soziale Sicherheit in Europa). in *Deutsche Rentenversicherung,* Vol. 11/12 [*Sustainable, safe and adequate? Revisiting the pension reforms in Poland, Hungary, Czech Republic and other countries of the region and the World Bank pension agenda*].

Hudson, J. 2016. *From welfare state to competition state? The evolving relationship between social security and the economy in the United Kingdom.* York, UK, University of York.

International Labour Organization (ILO). 1944. Declaration concerning the aims and purposes of the International Labour Organization. Declaration of Philadelphia, 26th General Conference of the International Labour Organization, Philadelphia, 10 May. Available at: http://www.ilo.org/wcmsp5/groups/public/---asia/---ro-bangkok/---ilo-islamabad/documents/policy/wcms_142941.pdf [5 Oct. 2014].

—. 1952. Social Security (Minimum Standards) Convention, 1952 (No. 102). Geneva. Available at: http://www.ilo.org/dyn/normlex/en/f?p=NORMLEXPUB:12100:0::NO::P12100_INSTRUMENT_ID:312247 [10 Dec. 2016].

—. 2012. Social Protection Floors Recommendation, 2012 (No. 202). NORMLEX Information System on International Labour Standards (Geneva). Available at: http://www.ilo.org/dyn/normlex/en/f?p=NORMLEXPUB:12100:0::NO::P12100_ILO_CODE:R202 [29 Nov. 2017].

—. 2014. *Building economic recovery, inclusive development and social justice: World social protection report 2014/15.* Geneva.

European System of Integrated Social Protection Statistics (ESSPROS). 2012. *European System of Integrated Social Protection Statistics Manual*. Luxembourg, Office for Official Publications of the European Communities.

European Union; International Labour Office. Undated. *A Review of Global Fiscal Stimulus*. *International Institute for Labour Studies* (IILS). Available at: http://www.ilo.org/wcmsp5/groups/public/---dgreports/---inst/documents/publication/wcms_194175.pdf[18 Aug. 2018].

Faricy, C. G. 2015. *Welfare for the wealthy: Parties, social spending and inequality in the United States*. Cambridge, Cambridge University Press. pp. 140.

Flassbeck, H. 2017. Europaeische Arbeitskosten: Unter deutschem Einfluss auf deflationaerem Pfad. Teile 1-3. https://makroskop.eu/2017/04/europaeische-arbeitskosten-unter-deutschem-einfluss-auf-deflationaerem-pfad-1/[15 Apr. 2017]. [*European labour costs: Deflationary tendencies under German impact.*]

Friedman, M.; Bordo, M.D. 2005. *The optimum quantity of money*. London and New York, Transaction Publishers.

Frisby, D. 1972. The Popper-Adorno Controversy: The methodological dispute in German Sociology. in *Philosophy of the Social Sciences*, Vol. 2, pp. 105-119.

Gauti, J. 2015. Frances social model: Between resilience and erosion. in D. Vaughan-Whitehead (ed.): *The European social model in crisis: Is Europe losing its soul?* Geneva, Cheltenham, UK and Northampton, MA, ILO and Edward Elgar Publishing, pp. 121-174.

Gillion, C.; Turner, J.; Bailey, C.; Latulippe, D. (eds.) 2000. *Social security pensions: Development and reform*. Geneva, International Labour Office.

Gleeson-White, J. 2012. *Double entry. How the merchants of Venice shaped the modern world and how their invention could make or break the planet*. London, Allen Jane. [Book consulted in its German edition: *Die doppelte Buchfuehrung und die Entstehung des modernen Kapitalismus* (Soll & Haben)].

Gray, J. 2007. "Naomi Klein's critique of neo-liberalism, The Shock Doctrine, is both *capital report 2018* (Beijing, Central University of Finance and Economics Press) [in Chinese]. Available at:http://humancapital.cufe.edu.cn/info/1020/2454.htm.

Chinese Academy of Social Sciences (CASS); State Council Poverty Alleviation Office (SCPAO). 2016.*China Poverty Alleviation and Development Report 2016*, Poverty Reduction Blue Book (Beijing) [in Chinese].

Cichon, M.; Scholz, W.; van de Meerendonk, A.; Hagemejer, K.; Bertranou, F.; Plamondon, P. 2004. *Financing social protection.* Geneva, International Labour Office and International Social Security Association.

Cingano, F. 2014. *Trends in income inequality and its impact on economic growth,* OECD Social, Employment and Migration Working Papers, No. 163. Paris, OECD Publishing. Available at: http://dx.doi.org/10.1787/5jxrjncwxv6j-en [1 Feb. 2017].

Coase, R.H. 1937. "The nature of the firm", in *Economica,* Vol. 4, No. 16. Available at: https://www.colorado.edu/ibs/es/alston/econ4504/readings/The%20Nature%20of%the%20Firm%20by%20Coase.pdf[11 Nov. 2014].

Concialdi, P. 2019. *Economic development and social security in France: The mid-1980s turning point.* Background paper to the Chinese version of this report. Beijing, CAOSS.

Confucius. Undated. The conveyance of rites, in Dai, S. (ed.): *The Book of Rites*. Beijing, Confucian Classics. Available at: https://ctext.org/liji/li-yun [19 Feb. 2019].

DeLong, B.J. 2002. *Macroeconomics,* Revised edition. New York, McGraw-Hill.

Dixon, J. E. 1999. *Social security in global perspective.* Westport, CT, Praeger.

European Commission. 2015. *The 2015 ageing report: Economic and budgetary projections for the 28 EU Member States, 2013-2060* (Luxembourg, Publications Office of the European Union. Available at: http://ec.europa.eu/economy_finance/publications/european_economy/2015/pdf/ee3_en.pdf[20 Feb. 2019].

European System of Accounts. 2010. *European System of Accounts*. Luxembourg, Office for Official Publications of the European Communities.

gesamtkonzept-alterssicherung-detail.pdf?__blob=publicationFile&v=6 [11 Dec. 2016].

—. 2017. *Sozialbericht. Teil B: Sozialbudget* [*Social report. Part B: Social budget*] (Berlin). Available at: http://www.bmas.de/SharedDocs/Downloads/DE/PDF-Publikationen/a-101-17-sozialbericht-2017.pdf?__blob=publicationFile&v=2[12 Jan 2018].

Bundesministerium für Arbeit und Soziales und Bundesarchiv (BMAS and BArch). 2006. *Geschichte der Sozialpolitik in Deutschland seit 1945. Band 9: Deutsche Demokratische Republik 1961-1971. Politische Stabilisierung und wirtschaftliche Mobilisierung*.Nomos: Baden-Baden. [Federal Ministry of Labour and Social Affairs and Federal Archives. 2006. *History of social policy in Germany since 1945, Vol 9: German Democratic Republic 1961-1971: Political stabilisation and economic mobilisation.*].

—. 2008. *Geschichte der Sozialpolitik in Deutschland seit 1945. Band 10: Deutsche Demokratische Republik 1971-1989. Bewegung in der Sozialpolitik, Erstarrung und Niedergang.* Nomos: Baden-Baden. [Federal Ministry of Labour and Social Affairs, and Federal Archives. 2008. *History of social policy in Germany since 1945, Vol. 10: German Democratic Republic 1971-1989: Social reforms, rigidity, and decline*].

Bundesministerium fuer Gesundheit und Bundesarchiv (BMG and BArch). 2004. *Geschichte der Sozialpolitik in Deutschland seit 1945. Band 8: Deutsche Demokratische Republik 1949-1961. Im Zeichen des Aufbaus des Sozialismus.* Nomos: Baden-Baden. [*Federal Ministry of Health and Social Security, and Federal Archives.* 2004. *History of social policy in Germany since 1945, Vol. 8: German Democratic Republic 1949-1961: Under construction of socialism*]

Central Committee of the Communist Party (CCCP). 2015. *13th Five-Year Plan for Economic and Social Development of the People's Republic of China (2016-2020),* Translated by Compilation and Translation Bureau (Beijing). Available at: http://en.ndrc.gov.cn/newsrelease/201612/P020161207645765233498.pdf [Dec. 2016].

Central Committee of the Communist Party; State Council. 1992. *Decision on accelerating the development of the tertiary industry* (Beijing) [in Chinese].

China Centre for Human Capital and Labour Market Research. 2018. *China human subject-matters: about structure and transformation of empirical sociological research*].

Bosch, G. 2015. The German welfare state: From an inclusive to an exclusive Bismarck model. in D. Vaughan-Whitehead (ed.): *The European social model in crisis: Is Europe losing its soul?* (Geneva, Cheltenham, UK and Northampton, MA, ILO and Edward Elgar Publishing).

—. 2017. Exportorientiertes Wachstumsmodell: Die Agenda 2010 sollte Probleme loesen, die es nicht gab, [*Germany's export-oriented growth model: The Agenda 2010 was supposed to solve problems which did not exist*], 15 Aug. Available at: https://makroskop.eu/2017/08/die-agenda-2010-sollte-probleme-loesen-die-es-nicht-gab/[16 Aug. 2017].

Bundesagentur fuer Arbeit (BMA). 2016. Arbeitslosigkeit im Zeitverlauf - Monats-/Jahreszahlen (ab 1950). Nuernberg: Bundesagentur für Arbeit. [*Federal Employment Agency: Unemploymnet - long-term time series (as of 1950)*].

Bundesarchiv: Denkschrift. Undated. *Ueber die Hoehe der finanziellen Belastung, welche durch die Alters- und Invalidenversicherung der Arbeiter voraussichtlich hervorgerufen werden wird* (Berlin). [Federal Archives: Memorandum. Undated. *On the level of financial burden resulting from the implementation of the workers' old-age and invalidity insurance.* Berlin. [Delivered prior to Bismarck's pension legislation in order to fix benefit levels and contribution rates.]

Bundesministerium fuer Arbeit und Soziales (BMAS). 2015. Sozialbudget 2014. http://www.bmas.de/SharedDocs/Downloads/DE/PDF-Publikationen/a230-14-sozialbudget-2014.pdf?__blob=publicationFile&v=2, accessed September 23, 2015.

—. 2016a. *Entwicklung der privaten Altersvorsorge 2001 bis 2016*. (Berlin, Bundeministerium fuer Arbeit und Soziales). Available at: http://www.bmas.de/DE/Themen/Rente/Zusaetzliche-Altersvorsorge/statistik-zusaetzliche-altersvorsorge.html [23 Nov. 2016]. [*Development of the number of private pension contracts 2001 to 2016* (Berlin, Federal Ministry of Labour and Social Affairs]

—. 2016b. *Gesamtkonzept zur Alterssicherung*, Berlin. [*Comprehensive old-age security concept*].Available at: http://www.bmas.de/SharedDocs/Downloads/DE/Thema-Rente/

References

Amlinger, M.; Bispinck, R; Schulten, S. 2016. The German minimum wage:Experiences and perspectives after one year. in *WSI Report,* No. 28e.

Auer, P. 2010. What's in a name? The rise (and fall?) of flexicurity. in *Journal of Industrial Relations*, 2 July. Available at: http://journals.sagepub.com/doi/pdf/10.1177/0022185610365646 [17 June 2018].

Bertelsmann Stiftung. 2016. Kinderarmut in Deutschland waechst weiter mit Folgen fuers ganze Leben. (Nuernberg, Germany, Bundesagentur fuer Arbeit). [*Child poverty continues growing in Germany with lifetime implications* (Nuernberg, Germany, Federal Employment Agency). Available at: https://www.bertelsmann-stiftung.de/de/themen/aktuelle-meldungen/2016/september/kinderarmut-in-deutschland-waechst-weiter-mit-folgen-fuers-ganze-leben/[18 July 2017].

Beveridge, W.H. 1942. *Social insurance and allied services: Report* (London, HMSO).

Blair, T.; Schroeder, G. 1999. *Europe: The third way (Die neue Mitte)*.London and Berlin, Labour Party and Sozialdemokratische Partei Deutschlands, Available at: https://web.archive.org/web/19990819090124/http://www.labour.org.uk/views/items/00000053.html [8 Feb. 2017].

Bleicken, J. 2015. The army of Augustus.in *Augustus: The biography*. New York, Penguin, [Original published in German: Jochen Bleicken: *Augustus: Eine Biographie* (Berlin, Alexander Fest Verlag, 1998; paperback-edition consulted: Hamburg, Germany, Rowohlt, 2010].

Bonss, W. 1982. *Die Einuebung des Tatsachenblicks: zur Struktur und Veraenderung empirischer Sozialforschung*. Frankfurt am Main, Suhrkamp,[*Exercising our views on*

Table A6 Poverty line and impoverished population and poverty headcount ratio in China's rural areas, 1985-2017

	Standard in 1978				Standard in 2008				Standard in 2010			
Year	Poverty line (CNY per person)	Poverty line ($ per person)	Impoverished population (10,000 persons)	Poverty headcount ratio (%)	Poverty line (CNY per person)	Poverty line ($ per person)	Impoverished population (10,000 persons)	Poverty headcount ratio (%)	Poverty line (CNY per person)	Poverty line ($ per person)	Impoverished population (10,000 persons)	Poverty headcount ratio (%)
1985	206	70.1	12,500	14.8								
1986	213	61.7	13,100	15.5								
1987	227	61.0	12,200	14.3								
1988	236	63.4	9,600	11.1								
1989	259	68.8	10,200	11.6								
1990	300	62.7	8,500	9.4								
1991	304	57.1	9,400	10.4								
1992	317	57.5	8,000	8.8								
1993	–	–	–	–								
1994	440	51.1	7,000	7.7								
1995	530	63.5	6,540	7.1								
1994	–	–	–	–								
1997	640	77.2	4,962	5.4								
1998	635	76.7	4,210	4.6								
1999	625	75.5	3,412	3.7								
2000					625	75.5	3,209	3.5				
2001					630	76.1	2,927	3.2				
2002					627	75.8	2,820	3				
2003					637	77.0	2,900	3.1				
2004					668	80.7	2,610	2.8				
2005					683	83.4	2,365	2.5				
2006					693	86.9	2,148	2.3				
2007					785	103.2	1,479	1.6				
2008					1,196	172.2	4,007	4.2				
2009					1,196	175.1	3,597	3.8				
2010					1,274	188.2	2,688	2.8	2,300	339.7	16,567	17.2
2011									2,536	392.6	12,238	12.7
2012									2,625	415.8	9,899	10.2
2013									2,736	441.8	8,249	8.5
2014									2,800	455.8	7,017	7.2
2015									2,855	458.4	5,575	5.7
2016									3,000	451.7	4,335	4.5
2017											3,046	3.1

Note: The Chinese poverty standard is significantly less ambitious than the internationally accepted United Nations (UNDP) one, leaving much room for improvement.

Table A5 Average per capita fund expenditure under the basic old-age pension scheme in China, 2001-2017 (CNY and $)

Year	Pension scheme for employees		Pension scheme for urban and rural residents	
	CNY per month	$ per month	CNY per month	$ per month
	(1)	(2)	(3)	(4)
2001	572.21	69.13		
2002	656.66	79.34		
2003	673.99	81.43		
2004	711.36	85.95		
2005	770.90	94.11		
2006	880.31	110.43		
2007	1,003.44	131.96		
2008	1,161.10	167.18		
2009	1,276.41	186.86	40.70	5.96
2010	1,395.04	206.08	58.21	8.60
2011	1,558.32	241.27	56.98	8.82
2012	1,741.70	275.91	73.30	11.61
2013	1,914.15	309.07	81.59	13.17
2014	2,109.63	343.43	91.47	14.89
2015	2,352.97	377.78	119.20	19.14
2016	2,627.44	395.56	117.33	17.66
2017	2,875.93	425.95	126.73	18.77

Note:(i) Per capita fund expenditure = total annual fund expenditure / end-of-the-year number of pensioners. The per capita fund expenditure is used to estimate the per capita pension.
(ii) CNY–$ conversion on basis of the yearly average exchange rates compiled in *China Statistical Yearbook 2018* (NBS, 2018).
(iii) Per capita pension provided under the residents' scheme (columns 3 & 4) declined slightly in 2016. The reason is that a majority of the newly added pension recipients came from regions with a relatively small pension benefit, thus reducing the national average. Overall, per capita pension for all regions rose rather than declined.
Source: MHRSS, various years (*Statistical Bulletin on the Development of Human Resources and Social Security*); NBS, various years (*China Labour Statistical Yearbook*).

Table A4 Number of basic old-age insurance participants in China, 1978-2017 (10,000 persons)

Year	Total number of participants	The basic old-age insurance for urban employee			The basic old-age insurance for urban and rural residents
		Total	Employees	Retirees	
1978				314.0	
1980				816.0	
1985				1,637.0	
1986				1,805.0	
1987				1,968.0	
1988				2120	
1989	5,710.3	5,710.3	4,816.9	893.4	
1990	6,166.0	6,166.0	5,200.7	965.3	
1991	6,740.3	6,740.3	5,653.7	1,086.6	
1992	9,456.2	9,456.2	7,774.7	1,681.5	
1993	9,847.6	9,847.6	8 008.2	1,839.4	
1994	10,573.5	10,573.5	8,494.1	2,079.4	
1995	10,979.0	10,979.0	8,737.8	2,241.2	
1996	11,116.7	11,116.7	8,758.4	2,358.3	
1997	11,203.9	11,203.9	8,670.9	2,533.0	
1998	11,203.1	11,203.1	8,475.8	2,727.3	
1999	12,485.4	12,485.4	9,501.8	2,983.6	
2000	13,617.4	13,617.4	10,447.5	3,169.9	
2001	14,182.5	14,182.5	10,801.9	3,380.5	
2002	14,736.6	14,736.6	11,128.8	3,607.8	
2003	15,506.7	15,506.7	11,646.6	3,860.2	
2004	16,352.9	16,352.9	12,250.3	4,102.6	
2005	17,487.9	17,487.9	13,120.4	4,367.5	
2006	18,766.3	18,766.3	14,130.9	4,636.4	
2007	20,136.9	20,136.9	15,183.2	4,953.7	
2008	21,891.1	21,891.1	16,587.5	5,303.5	
2009	23,549.9	23,549.9	17,743.0	5,806.9	
2010	35,984.1	25,707.3	19,402.3	6,305.0	10,276.8
2011	61,573.3	28,391.3	21,565.0	6,826.2	33,182.0
2012	78,796.3	30,426.8	22,981.1	7,445.7	48,369.6
2013	81,968.4	32,218.4	24,177.3	8,041.0	49,750.1
2014	84,231.9	34,124.4	25,531.0	8,593.4	50,107.5
2015	85,833.4	35,361.2	26,219.2	9,141.9	50,472.2
2016	88,776.8	37,929.7	27,826.3	10,103.4	50,847.1
2017	91,549.0	40,294.0	29,268.0	11,026.0	51,255.0

Source: NBS, 2018 (*China Statistical Yearbook 2018*).

Table A3 Accumulated balances of the basic old-age pension system fund in China, 1998-2017 (100 million CNY and $)

Year	Pension scheme for employees		Pension scheme for urban and rural residents		Total	
	Hundred million CNY	Hundred million $	Hundred million CNY	Hundred million $	Hundred million CNY	Hundred million $
	(1)	(2)	(3)	(4)	(5)	(6)
1998	587.8	71.00			587.8	71.00
1999	733.5	88.61			733.5	88.61
2000	947.1	114.41			947.1	114.41
2001	1,054.1	127.35			1,054.1	127.35
2002	1,608.0	194.27			1,608.0	194.27
2003	2,206.5	266.58	259.3	31.33	2,465.8	297.91
2004	2,975.0	359.44	285.0	34.43	3,260.0	393.87
2005	4,041.0	493.30	310.0	37.84	4,351.0	531.15
2006	5,488.9	688.54	354.0	44.41	5,842.9	732.95
2007	7,391.4	972.04	412.0	54.18	7,803.4	1,026.22
2008	9,931.0	1,429.93	499.0	71.85	10,430.0	1,501.78
2009	12,526.1	1,833.71	681.0	99.69	13,207.1	1,933.41
2010	15,365.3	2,269.78	422.5	62.41	15,787.8	2,332.20
2011	19,496.6	3,018.61	1,231.2	190.62	20,727.8	3,209.23
2012	23,941.3	3,792.68	2,302.2	364.70	26,243.5	4,157.39
2013	28,269.0	4,564.52	3,006.0	485.37	31,275.0	5,049.89
2014	31,800.0	5,176.79	3,845.0	625.94	35,645.0	5,802.73
2015	35,345.0	5,674.81	4,592.0	737.27	39,937.0	6,412.08
2016	38,580.0	5,808.23	5,385.0	810.71	43,965.0	6,618.94
2017	43,885.0	6,499.75	6,318.0	935.75	50,203.0	7,435.50

Note: Columns 3 & 4, until 2010 includes only "rural residents"; from 2011 and 2013, include both rural residents and urban residents covered by two schemes, respectively. Since 2014, the pension scheme for rural residents and the pension scheme for urban residents were merged, i.e. as of this date the numbers include one integrated scheme.

Source: MHRSS, various years (*Statistical Bulletin on the Development of Human Resources and Social Security*); NBS, various years (*China Labour Statistical Yearbook*).

Table A2 Number of participants and pensioners of the basic old-age pension system in China, 1978-2017 (10,000 persons)

Year	Pension scheme for employees		Pension scheme for urban and rural residents		Total
	Employees	Retirees	Participants younger than 60	Pensioners aged 60 or older	No. of participants
	(1)	(2)	(3)	(4)	(5)
1998	8,475.8	2,727.3	7,965.2	59.8	19,228.1
1999	9,501.8	2,983.6	6,371.0	89.8	18,946.2
2000	10,447.5	3,169.9	6,074.5	97.8	19,789.7
2001	10,801.9	3,380.6	5,887.0	108.1	20,177.6
2002	11,128.8	3,607.8	5,338.4	123.4	20,198.4
2003	11,646.5	3,860.2	5,230.1	197.6	20,934.4
2004	12,250.3	4,102.6	5,176.9	205.5	21,735.3
2005	13,120.4	4,367.5	5,140.2	301.7	22,929.8
2006	14,130.9	4,635.4	5,018.6	355.1	24,140.0
2007	15,183.2	4,953.7	4,779.9	391.6	25,308.4
2008	16,587.5	5,303.6	5,083.0	512.0	27,486.1
2009	17,743.0	5,806.9	5,942.1	1,335.2	30,827.2
2010	19,402.3	6,305.0	7,414.2	2,862.6	35,984.1
2011	21,565.0	6,826.2	24,025.7	9,156.8	61,573.7
2012	22,981.1	7,445.7	34,987.3	13,382.2	78,796.3
2013	24,177.0	8,041.0	35,982.1	13,768.0	81,968.1
2014	25,531.0	8,593.4	35,794.5	14,313.0	84,231.9
2015	26,219.0	9,142.0	35,672.0	14,800.0	85,833.0
2016	27,826.3	10,103.4	35,576.8	15,270.3	88,776.8
2017	29,268.0	11,026.0	35,657.0	15,598.0	91,549.0

Note: (i) (columns 3 & 4) Urban and rural residents refer to non-salaried urban and rural population in the 16-59 age group. Until 2010, merely include only "rural residents"; from 2011 and 2013, include both rural residents and urban residents covered by two schemes, respectively. Since 2014, the pension scheme for rural residents and the pension scheme for urban residents were merged, i.e. as of this date the numbers include one integrated scheme.

(ii) In the late 1980s, some rural areas piloted voluntary old-age pension scheme characterized by individual contribution and saving account. It proved to be unsustainable due to the lack of government financial support. Problems including the loss of funds, extremely low or unpaid pensions emerged. In view of this, the Chinese government suspended this practice in 1998; and those insured by then were considered as legacy issues. Later in 2009, the Government launched the government-partial-funded pension system for rural residents, which further extended to non-salaried urban population in the 16–59 age group in 2011 and achieved full basic pension coverage in 2012.

Source: MHRSS, various years (*Statistical Bulletin on the Development of Human Resources and Social Security*); NBS, various years (*China Labour Statistical Yearbook*); Zheng, 2008.

Annex 2. Additional tables

Table A1 China's total GDP and GDP per capita, 1978-2017

Year	Total GDP (hundred million)							Per capita GDP (mid-year population)				
	CNY	Nominal growth rate (based on CNY, %)	$	Nominal growth rate (based on $,%)	Purchasing power parity (PPP)	Nominal growth rate (based on PPP,%)	Real growth rate(%)	CNY	Nominal growth rate (based on CNY %)	$	Purchasing power parity (PPP)	Real growth rate(%)
1978	3,679	13.2	2,185				11.7	385	11.9	229		10.2
1980	4,588	11.9	3,062	16.1			7.8	468	10.6	312		6.5
1985	9,099	25.0	3,098	−0.9			13.4	866	23.4	295		11.9
1990	18,873	9.9	3,946	−13.5	11,199		3.9	1,663	8.3	348	987	2.4
1995	61,340	26.1	7,345	30.2	22,524	13.3	11.0	5,091	24.7	610	1,869	9.8
2000	100,280	10.7	12,113	10.7	37,037	11.0	8.5	7,942	9.9	959	2,933	7.6
2005	187,319	15.7	22,867	16.9	66,393	15.0	11.4	14,368	15.1	1,754	5,093	10.7
2010	412,119	18.2	60,879	19.3	124,574	11.9	10.6	30,808	17.7	4,551	9,313	10.1
2015	685,993	7.0	110,140	5.5	197,263	8.0	6.9	50,028	6.4	8,032	14,386	6.4
2016	740,061	7.9	111,416	1.2	213,100	8.0	6.7	53,680	7.3	8,082	15,457	6.2
2017	820,754	10.9	121,561	9.1	231,214	8.5	6.8	59,201	10.3	8,768	16,677	6.2

Note: The World Bank PPP conversion factors are available at: https://data.worldbank.org/indicator/PA.NUS.PPP?contextual=default&end=2017&locations=CN&start=1990&view=chart.
Source: NBS. 2019. National data. Available at: http://data.stats.gov.cn/english/easyquery.htm?cn=C01 [Jan. 2019]

is a company scheme, a professional scheme, a scheme established by a trade union or another kind of mutual benefit scheme, cover is presumed to be based on the principle of social solidarity. These cases, therefore, fall within the scope of the ESSPROS. When a person contracting out of a social security fund or a company scheme takes out an individual policy with a commercial insurance company the case should be examined individually, as the principle of social solidarity may still apply. The Appropriate Personal Pension Schemes in the United Kingdom are an example.

29. This rule should not be interpreted as meaning that all individual policies are excluded from social security. When social security is provided by the employer in the form of insurance, it is sometimes allowed, or even required, that the policies be taken out in the names of the individual participants.

30. Nor does this rule imply that all collective contracts must be classified as social security. Insurance policies that are taken out collectively with the sole purpose of obtaining a discount, as for example, a joint sickness policy covering a group of people travelling together, are not classified as social security.

31. An insurance policy is included in the scope of the ESSPROS if it is based on social solidarity, whether or not it is taken out on the initiative of the person insured. An insurance policy is based on the principle of social solidarity if, as a matter of policy, the contributions charged are not proportional to the individual exposure to risk of the people protected.

31A. Types of insurance that are often based on the principle of social solidarity are: schemes which are established specifically for persons belonging to the same profession or trade; insurance offered by mutual benefit societies; government-based voluntary schemes open to certain categories of households, such as small businessmen or other low-income groups (This is sometimes referred to as opting in).

32. It is noted that social solidarity is a sufficient, but not necessary, condition for an insurance scheme to be classified as a scheme of social security. Specifically,
>   (i) where by law or by regulation certain groups of the population are obliged to participate in a designated insurance scheme.
>   (ii) where employees and their dependants are insured as a consequence of collective wage agreements, the insurance is included in the scope of the ESSPROS even if it is not based on the principle of social solidarity.

32A. Difficult borderline cases arise from the so-called contracting out, where the law allows people to leave the general scheme managed by the social security fund and acquire security through other channels. The simple fact that coverage is compulsory by law (although no particular scheme is specified) or that an insurance policy replaces a government scheme, is not sufficient reason to classify it as social security. In these instances, the criterion of social solidarity can be a useful guide. If the alternative chosen of living allowances, local allowances and expatriation allowances, allowances for transport to and from work, payments made by employers to their employees under saving schemes, free housing or housing allowances to active employees, crèches for the children of employees, holiday pay for official and annual holidays, sports, recreation and holiday facilities for employees and their families.

25. However, where the reciprocal arrangement from the employee is not simultaneous, the expenditure is classified as social security. For example, retirement and survivors' pensions paid by an employer, free housing to retired employees and so on are social benefits (even if the right to the benefit arises from the previous period of service with the employer, that is, work during active life being the reciprocal arrangement). Following the same reasoning, the continued payment of wages and salaries while an employee is unable to work during sickness, maternity, disability, redundancy and so on is classified as social security provided by the employer.

26. Furthermore, in line with national accounts definitions, social security does not include expenditure by employers which is to their own benefit as well as to that of their employees because it is necessary for the employers' production process.

26A. Examples are allowances for or reimbursement of travelling expenses incurred by the employees in the course of their duties, medical examinations required by the nature of the work and accommodation provided at the workplace that cannot be used by the employees' households, such as cabins and dormitories.

27. In practice, therefore, social security provided directly by employers to their employees is limited to:
   (i) the continued payment of normal, or reduced, wages and salaries during periods of absence from work as a result of sickness, accident, maternity etc.
   (ii) the payment of statutory special allowances for dependent children and other family members.
   (iii) health care which is not related to the nature of the work.

28. Social security excludes all insurance policies taken out on the private initiative of individuals or households solely in their own interest. For instance, the payment of a capital sum or an annuity to the holder of a private life insurance policy is not considered to be social security.

20. The list of risks or needs given in paragraph 16 has two purposes. On the one hand it restricts the scope of social security to the areas which are felt to be most relevant in the European context. On the other hand, it is a tool for producing comparable statistics where the institutions, regulations and social traditions of the Member States diverge widely. The various risks and needs define the primary purposes for which resources and benefits are provided, irrespective of legislative or institutional structures behind them. In this context, it is customary to use the term functions of social security.

21. Functions are defined in terms of their end-purpose, not in terms of given branches of social security or pieces of legislation.For instance, the benefits granted by a pension fund cannot simply be classified in their entirety under the Old age function, as some benefits may have the purpose to relieve the beneficiary from needs related to the death of a breadwinner (which belong to the Survivors function) or to the loss of the physical ability to engage in economic and social activities (which are to be classified under the Disability function). The ESSPROS applies the functional breakdown exclusively to social security benefits, and not to receipts. It is recognized, in fact, that a single type of receipts can be used to finance benefits under several different functions.

23. The conventional definition of social security stipulates that the intervention does not involve a simultaneous reciprocal arrangement. This should be conceived as excluding from the scope of social security any intervention where the recipient is obliged to provide simultaneously something of equivalent value in exchange. For instance, interest-bearing loans granted to households are not social security because the borrower commits himself to paying interest and to refund the capital sum. Likewise, the portion of the full cost of health care and other provisions that beneficiaries are required to meet personally falls outside the field of social security. This does not preclude that social security benefits may be conditional on some action to be undertaken by the beneficiary (such as taking part in a vocational training programme), provided that this action does not have the character of salaried work or sale of services.

24. The principle that the intervention should not involve a simultaneous reciprocal arrangement is particularly important for distinguishing social security provided directly by employers to employees from the flows which make up gross wages and salaries.

24A. Any expenditure by employers for the employees' benefit that can reasonably be regarded as compensation for work is not considered a social benefit. Examples are:cost

(iii) Old age
(iv) Survivors
(v) Family/children/
(vi) Unemployment
(vii) Housing
(viii) Social exclusion not elsewhere classified.

17. The word intervention in the definition should be understood in its broadest sense to cover the financing of benefits and related administration costs, as well as the actual provision of benefits.

18. Benefits granted within the framework of social security can take many forms; however, in the Core system, they are limited to:
   (i) cash payments to protected people
   (ii) reimbursements of expenditure made by protected people
   (iii) goods and services directly provided to protected people.

19. The condition that the intervention must come from public or private bodies excludes from the definition of social security all direct transfers of resources between private households or individuals in the form of gifts, help to relatives and so on, even if their purpose is to protect the recipient from the risks or needs listed in paragraph 16.

For practical reasons, small-scale, informal and incidental types of support such as whip-rounds, Christmas collections, ad-hoc humanitarian aid and emergency relief in the event of natural disasters, which do not require regular management and accounting, are also excluded from the definition.

19A. Generally, the bodies most frequently intervening are:
social security funds; central, state and local government agencies; autonomous and self-administered pension funds; insurance companies(in Denmark the pension funds running labour market pensions can delegate the administration of these pensions to insurance companies; mutual benefit societies); public employers or private employers providing benefits to their current and former employees directly; private welfare and assistance institutions: for instance, the Red Cross, the Portuguese religious foundation Casa Misericordia and the (Roman Catholic) charitable organization Caritas.

Annex 1. Definition of social security

The following text is an excerpt from ESSPROS (2012), with a few marginal editorial changes for better readability. For purposes of consistent language in this report we have replaced the term social protection, which is the term used in ESSPROS, with social security. Both terms have been used in ILO publications interchangeably; this is also widely the case in the English-speaking world where some conflict exists between the American term "welfare" and the British terms "social security" and "social protection".

The conventional definition of social security

15. There is no universally accepted definition of the scope of social security, nor does there exist one that suits all purposes (including the compilation of statistics). It is therefore necessary to formulate a conventional definition of the scope of social security which meets as well as possible the needs of social policy analysis and data collection on an international level. This chapter begins with a general definition, relevant to both the Core system of the ESSPROS and its modules that is further explained and specified for use in the Core system in the following paragraphs.

16. Social security encompasses all interventions from public or private bodies intended to relieve households and individuals of the burden of a defined set of risks or needs, provided that there is neither a simultaneous reciprocal nor an individual arrangement involved.

> The list of risks or needs that may give rise to social security is, by convention, as follows:
> (i) Sickness/Health care/
> (ii) Disability

increased, the operation mechanisms of social security must be adapted to changes in information technologies and intelligence. This is especially necessary in times when government finance (including social security) must swiftly counter the unforeseeable detrimental effects on societies and economies of uncontrolled crisis-producing global financial markets. Looking ahead to the likelihood of Industry 4.0, Labour Market 4.0 and modernized industrial, especially manufacturing sectors, social security must be prepared to adapt accordingly, including through innovative methods aiming to maintain and stabilize its financial basis.

Letting all citizens benefit in a better and equitable manner from the fruits of national development should be a crucial goal of this adaptation process. This will contribute to stimulating smooth economic development. Therefore, when developed economies adjust their social security systems, priority should be given to maintaining and promoting social justice, including by maintaining or setting adequate standards for benefit levels. Less developed economies need to focus on addressing the immediate poverty issues while stepping up social security system institutionalization (ILO Recommendation No. 202 can be of direct reference in this regard).

Given its important international role as an economy and its growing role in shaping international social security discussions and attitudes, China should continue its expansionary path of implementing institutionalized social security, and policies of fostering individual entitlements should be intensified. With nearly 100 per cent pension coverage, similar success must be achieved in other social policy fields: free education, family benefits, health care, poverty eradication, workplace protection and work accident insurance, among others. Furthermore, China should increase its relative social spending levels to catch up with the spending levels of other modern economies.

Developing countries or countries in the middle of developing social security as part of their economic development should carefully study the case of China. Although specific and usually not 100 per cent applicable, it contains lessons to be learned for policies aiming to simultaneously foster economic and social security development. While ILO Conventions can help formulate national social policy goals, China's past four decades of development offers inspiration for the policies required to achieve those goals.

There is no need for the international community to give up social security values or to reduce or abolish social security conventions. Rather, the contrary is true. The international community should adhere to the values of social justice, a shared future for all humankind and sustainable inclusive development. These values should guide the practice of social security and economic development accordingly. To avoid social security unduly becoming an instrument of international competition, the world community is invited to renew its efforts in substantiating common rules and conventions in the field of social security and labour rights. New trends of re-nationalization and protectionism that have allowed labour to be transformed into a "commodity" must come to a halt and be reverted; this includes withdrawing punitive elements from social security legislation.

There is need to take internationally coordinated steady steps to seek new equilibria of ruptured policy fields. To introduce stability to this search, it is rational to uphold the fundamental principles of social security and to guarantee their effective functionality while pursuing further development under appropriate economic growth.

When and where government-led social spending levels are high or are to be

institutional arrangementsand had been the result of social forces, which are still lively today in some countries. One notable exception is possibly Germany, with its Agenda 2010 reforms, in which social security was also "instrumentalized" as a means to achieve economic goals. While the positive effects of social security over the past 40 years in China came mainly from its support to the restructuring of the labour force and, to a lesser degree, by way of its macroeconomic demand effects, in the West, social security exerted its positive effects on the economy mainly through its (cost-induced) labour productivity effects and by way of its large share of spending in national incomes (the macroeconomic demand effects helped stabilize the Western economies in periods of crises).

Although China is currently in the midst of deepening its reforms, including social security, because the system requires further overarching designs to move towards maturity, the tremendous progress that has been achieved can serve as an important example for countries around the globe, particularly for developing countries in terms of achieving economic development through the proper handling of social security.

This report recommends the following policies for countries to foster both social security and economic development:

The research findings suggest that governments must equally emphasize economic as well as social security development and that achieving synchronized development of both should be internationally accepted as a rational goal of good governance. To this end, labour rights must be strengthened together with people's consciousness of their individual welfare entitlements. Furthermore, the implicit and explicit impacts of social security on enhancing productivity as well as on distributional fairness must be intelligently used to support domestic demand.

Developed countries should continue pursuing policies of high-level social security. Population ageing and international competition should not be used as "excuses" for further retrenchment of social policy. Rather, societies should prepare to continue financing a decent living for all persons who have no access to primary income. This may imply, at least for the transitory population-ageing period, higher than recently achieved spending levels. New forms of social security financing might need to be explored. The State (government) should retain the main responsibility for social security; it is governments that guarantee sufficient minimum benefit levels that allow for individuals' decent living. Only additional (so-called second or third layers) should be allocated to the private sector or individual and personal responsibility.

provisions) and not bound by any of the ILO social security and labour norms, China decided at the end of the 1970s to transform its planned economy into a competitive (socialist) market economy. The core characterization of its "socialist" market economy may have meant that enterprises were fully exposed to market competition, but ownership of some enterprises remained in the hands of the State or public institutions.[1] Thus, both public enterprises and private enterprises were competing on equal footing.

From that starting point and with the market vision in mind, the Government used social security as the core means to bolster the implications (for people) of the economic restructuring process. The intent was to financially buffer the impact of that process but also to use social security to restructure and reallocate the labour force to the requirements of the new economic setting: A new unemployment insurance was set up to provide short-term income support for persons temporarily unemployed; the pension system was used for early retirement; and specific anti-poverty measures were employed to avoid temporary hardship of labour that had lost employment. For many years, urban-based workers and other citizens mainly took advantage of these measures; the rural population was included in social security policies a decade ago.

In other words, in the West as well as in China, the ruling paradigm of the past four decades was dominated by economic thought. Unlike the West, China had an advantage due to its social security system still in a nascent status, and the Chinese general public did not expect "too much" from social security benefits. Nor was there complex legislation or judicial systems (focused on protecting individual rights and entitlements, as was the case in the West) hindering the Government from taking necessary decisions in due time. This situation of an initially "simple" social security system that allowed for tangible adjustments as and when required clearly helped achieve the intended goals, although the enormous difficulties should not be underestimated. From an international perspective, the Government used the transformation process to shape the social security system towards the classical institutional and functional design, as described in ILO Convention No. 102, which will allow China to eventually ratify it and other relevant Conventions, such as the Invalidity, Old-Age and Survivors' Benefits Convention, 1967 (No. 128).

Such instrumental use of social security was not available to Western countries, where social security had been implemented in complex legislation and interdependent

---

[1] This differs from "social" market economies, where ownership is predominantly private, with state ownership being kept to a minimum.

History has shown that, in the long run, it is social security in combination with labour standards that prevents labour from being a commodity. Where this is the case, market economies have turned into social market economies.

The intensity of the inherent conflict in market economies between persons who are mainly interested in the short-term gains of their market activities and persons interested in equitable social security has varied significantly over the past, and by region and country.

Over the very long term, history proves that it is neither necessary nor advisable to "optimize" social security, such that it complies with the requirements of the market. Within reasonable boundaries and avoiding system overstretch, any intrinsic conflict between the two policy fields must be endured and a balance found. This balance is vital in social as well as in socialist market economies.

Over the past three to four decades, economic interests worldwide gained dominance over social equity and social security. In the West, this development resulted in a pronounced retrenchment of the (hitherto well-developed) welfare state in most the OECD (if not all) countries. In other regions, where social security was undeveloped or underdeveloped, the evolvement of any social security clearly lagged behind economic development and did not (usually) reach the social security levels achieved in the West.

Common experience of these countries demonstrates that during economic downturns, social security fosters rather than impedes rapid recovery through positive economic demand- and supply-side roles. Also, many countries used post-crisis recoveries for strengthening their social security system not only to be prepared for the next phase of downturn but also to promote social justice and maintain sound and sustainable socioeconomic development. Social security, de facto, has become an institutional cornerstone of state governance.

It is imperative to comprehensively understand the interaction of different social security programmes with economic developments to optimize the mix of conflicting and supportive relations between social security and economic requirements at large.

In this context, China took a very interesting and specific social security development path. With initially quite low-and still low-social benefit levels (including low health sound social protection system. Generally, social security in the Latin American region is at medium levels, while Africa (except for South Africa) and Southern Asia, being less developed, are still substantially relying on social assistance, ad hoc anti-poverty projects, limited benefits financed through taxation and/or social insurance coverage on a narrow basis.

China's development over the past four decades is noteworthy because its social security overhaul was triggered by and was influenced by the economic system reform. While shifting from the planned to a market economy, social security underwent comprehensive and profound system change, the result of which was rapid expansion of social security coverage, from initially covering only a few to the whole population. Along with rapid economic growth, benefit levels-although still relatively low-have been constantly improving. The overhaul has not only created a stable social environment and supportive conditions for China's economic reform and sustained growth but also provided an institutional guarantee ensuring that all people's livelihoods can benefit from the fruits of national development.

China's development pattern and achievements thus confirms again, as had been done by its predecessors in development, that social security and economic development complement and facilitate each other.

Sixth, economic globalization has confronted social security and economic development of all countries with old and new challenges.

Economic globalization, regional competition, population ageing, migration, social structure changes, progress in science and information technology followed by emerging new industries, non-standard forms of employment and lifestyle changes present new challenges to economic development and social security around the globe.

4.2 Conclusions and policy recommendations for countries

In market economies, labour is continuously in danger of being treated as a commodity-which it is not, and should not be, not the least because the price for labour (wage) is at the same time the means by which people (households) exert demand on the economy.

Korea in the second half of the twentieth century was synchronized with the establishment of their respective social security system, with productivity-oriented welfare policy strongly supporting economic growth.

At the same time, different social security schemes exert dissimilar impacts on economic development, depending on whether they are more efficiency or more equity oriented by design (see section 1.2.5).

For example, in countries with generally low-income levels, social assistance programmes can substantially increase the income of lower-income groups, strengthen consumer demand and thus have direct impact on the economy. Naturally, in higher-income countries, the demand effects of social assistance are limited. Here, often classical social insurance counters people's insecurities, thus increasing their marginal consumption propensity and thereby contributing to economic growth. Social welfare services help to drive the development of tertiary industries, thereby facilitating adjustment of economic growth patterns and helping to upgrade industry structures. Free education directly improves people's overall civil standingwhile it can support the transformation of the demographic dividend from quantity to quality.

All these examples might interact differently with economic developments, depending on whether they are more of a Bismarckian or a Beveridgean design.

Fifth, the international development of social security is imbalanced among regions, recently showing tendencies of instability. The past four decades of China's practice confirms that positive interaction and joint progress of economic development and social security can be achieved.

Owing to their industrialization, European countries were the first to establish modern social security. Chosen system designs have progressed in conjunction with the region's socioeconomic development. Despite some twists and turns in the process, European countries still have the highest social security levels in the world. Also, Europe's experience still serves as inspiration for social security design to the rest of the world. Japan (less so the Republic of Korea) has been building a modern comprehensive social security system for decades. Owing to the country's societal fabric and individualistic culture, social security of the United States stands out as a unique type. Its welfare level is not as high as Europe's, yet along with (voluntary) charity, it also has a relatively

Third, in modern societies, social security is generally a comprehensive system comprising various benefits and different schemes and funding sources. Its total spending in developed countries takes shares of around 25 per cent of GDP, while often one third or more of social security revenue is provided by the government (taxpayer), whereas the rest may come from mandated employer and employee contributions and other sources, like voluntary contributions or investment returns.

The core functions of social security include risk-sharing based on internationally agreed principles of organized social solidarity, promotion of social justice and social cohesion, guarantees of basic income security and provision of basic public services. Given the individual risks of sickness, work accident, disability, unemployment, poverty, longevity and others, these are concerns of which every citizen is not only interested in but effectively exposed to throughout their life cycle.

Availability of institutions and services addressing these risks in case they materialize is not only a justified appeal of people but also a major government mission. Market mechanisms and NGOs, where necessary as institutions for complementing social security, are usually supported and integrated into government-led frameworks. This includes market regulations aiming to expand social security's material basis and to avoid system failure.

Internationally, most advanced countries spend around one quarter (sometimes more) of their GDP on social security. Estimates vary also because of different ways of including or excluding the costs of education systems. China, with a social expenditure ratio of 13 per cent of GDP, is around halfway to reaching advanced countries' spending levels.

Fourth, social security is generally supportive to long-term economic growth and improvement of national welfare, yet different scheme designs have different economic effects.

When well adapted to a country's societal and economic fabric, social security exerts very positive direct and indirect productivity effects. In addition to the experiences of countries like Germany, the United States and the United Kingdom, the Nordic countries demonstrate that high welfare levels are no hindrance to prosperity but can enhance human capital accumulation and innovation and achieve positive interaction between social security and economic growth. The economic take-off in Japan and the Republic of an important part of US President Roosevelt's New Deal, the Social Security Act of 1935 in the United States was a valuable antidote to the most serious economic crisis of the twentieth century. It saved capitalism from collapsing during the Great Depression by way of rectifying inherent defects of laissez-faire economics. Britain's 1942 Beveridge report significantly influenced the development of the post-World War II welfare state, nationally and internationally, which strengthened social solidarity and accelerated economic recovery.

Second, economic growth and social security are not only two key components of any development model but should be seen as two sides of the same coin in modern development.

In modern economies, economic development on the basis of market principles created the material basis for social security, while social security, in return, introduced stabilization into economies that would otherwise have been volatile and erratic.

Theoretical considerations suggest that economic development and social security are generally intertwined societal systems. It can be argued that there are intrinsic economic reasons for the development and existence of social security institutions (see section 1.2 and Coase, 1937), and, obviously, there are tight links between the two. Without accepting its economic preconditions and foundations, social security faces a lack of sustainability. And, vice versa, without social security, economic development will become volatile and run a high risk of collapsing, thus greatly compromising its value.

History teaches that in market economies, the costs of social security are usually in conflict with short-term business (profit) interests. Achieving profits is inherent to market economies; hence, this conflict is unavoidable. The mutual dependency of economic and social security development does not imply that both systems co-exist in peace. To the contrary, to unleash the productivity-enhancing effects of social security, more or less intense conflicts between economic and social interests had to be withstood at various times in history and in different countries or regions by all stakeholders alike, while conflict-resolution mechanisms were implemented to avoid socioeconomic stalemate. Such mechanisms were also necessary to avoid social security becoming dependent on immediate and immanent business interest. It was (and still is) the art of state leadership and of societies at large to set respective rules for the balancing of interests to the advantage of all.

4. Summary

4.1 Basic historical experience and theoretical consensus on the relationship between global economic development and social security

Through a global perspective, this report reviews the evolution of the relationship between social security and economic development over the past century. In the preceding chapters, the report reviews theoretical explanations and universal rules of the interrelations of both; it also focuses on China's experiences over the past four decades and compares with an assessment of historical experiences of social security and economic development in selected developed countries (in Europe as well as the United States, Japan and the Republic of Korea). Based on the review of these core historical experiences and the resulting theoretical consensus, the report reaches the following core consensus.

First, social security is indispensable in promoting social justice, compensating for market failures and contributing to shared and equitable development.

History shows that the emergence of social security systems was not only the result of solving political problems or eliminating economic predicaments but that they have their origins in humanistic thought as well as in peoples' intrinsic pursuit of social justice. Over the past one and a half centuries, social security increasingly proved its constructive role in promoting social justice and in countering the detrimental implications of economiccrises. The Bismarckian social security system, introduced in Germany at the end of the nineteenth century, greatly improved industrial relations as well as labour productivity and supported the country's international competitiveness, thereby promoting its national economic development and lasting prosperity. In the course of the twentieth century, its basic principles evolved into a globally inspiring success story. As

delay(Zheng, 2018a).

A mature social security system is bound to run under the rule of law. Nevertheless, owing to the historical approach of progressive reform, the existing social security system lacks the necessary and adequate legal regulations and guarantees. This has undermined the stability, authority and credibility of the system and further resulted in fluctuations in the perception of the relationship between social security and economic development.

Given this reality, China needs to step up the legislation on general laws, including a social security law, a social welfare law and a social assistance law, as well as specific laws, such as a child welfare law, an older persons welfare law and a disabled persons welfare law, and revise and improve existing laws, such as the Social Insurance Law and the Soldiers Insurance Law.The Government should put all legislation into one systematically elaborated volume containing all laws and by-laws (in hard copy as well as electronically, as appropriate) to make the related information transparently accessible to Chinese citizens. A well-established legal guarantee would give the public a stable and secure expectation of social security and thus is bound to boost people's confidence in the social security system. This is of great significance in stimulating people's enthusiasm for participating in social security and to safeguard the healthy and sustainable development of the system.

China needs to step up the process of reviewing its system in relation to ratification of the Social Security (Minimum Standards) Convention, 1952 (No. 102). As China further pursues its endeavour to modernize itself and develop its social security system, ensuring that it is in line with the rule of law constitutes a major task.

and the Government should encourage collective wage bargaining. The social security system should be conducive to promoting employment: keeping an appropriate benefit level without weighing too heavily on the jobs; encouraging workers to seek jobs or start new businesses and bringing into play the positive policy effects; adding the role of preventing unemployment as well as strengthening workers' competency into the unemployment insurance; turning social assistance into a proactive system that encourages employment; and developing the social security system in all respects to generate a large quantity of jobs of high quality. In particular, a variety of welfare services for older persons, persons with disabilities, children and women, as well as health care and charitable causes, are emerging sectors of employment worth exploiting because they have tremendous space to grow (Zheng, 2017d).

Fifth, attach enhanced importance to educational benefits and social welfare services.

Compulsory education should be made accessible as a public service to all permanent urban residents, with and without local urban household registration, including the children of the migrating population. Also, compulsory education should be extended from the current nine years to 12 years. And public input to vocational education should be increased to enhance its welfare nature.

The central Government should intensify its efforts to support compulsory education and vocational education so as to shift the demographic dividend from quantity-oriented to quality-oriented in all respects. In terms of social welfare services, China needs to improve services for children and older persons in particular; services for children should be extended to cover nurseries and kindergartens with sufficient budget, and for older persons it should incorporate the human resource re-development of retirees. China should also enrich the educational elements in the welfare for persons with disabilities to make better use of their talents and labour contributions. People with disabilities should be equally regarded as productive members of the labour force as non-disabled persons and should be equally included in skills training for jobs of the future. All these expansions in social welfare would improve China's future human resources in both quantity and quality.

Sisth, attach great importance to the legislation on social security, and make the social security system run under the rule of law framework without further

fledged work unit welfare provision are fading, resulting in untapped potential of social resources in providing social welfare services (Zheng, 2011). To rectify the situation, social security policies, family policies and institutional welfare need to be coordinated to create synergy.

China should promote mutual help, charity and volunteer services, which will consolidate the material foundation of the overall social security system and create conditions in which individual people's needs can be better met.

Fourth, Maintain a positive interaction between employment and social security.

The relationship between social security and employment is, in essence, the relationship between sharing and collaboration. To a large extent, the benign interaction between these two determines the positive interplay between social security and economic development. China needs to strike a balance between providing proper incentives and ensuring that everyone has sufficient protection while dealing with the relationship between employment and social security. In policy design, both the correlation and the mutual promotion between employment and social security should be taken into account. It is thus better for China to adhere to constructing a social security system that centres on employment-related social insurance, takes the improvement of the social security system as a crucial indicator in terms of uplifting the quality of employment and makes sure that all workers have legitimate access to social insurance schemes.

To ensure that no one is excluded from the social security system, non-earning related schemes, such as social assistance and tax-subsidized schemes (rural and urban resident pensions, for example), need further improvement; moderate benefits should be guaranteed. Proper subsidies should be provided to the eligible low-income population and people with disabilities to help them pay their social insurance contribution. A modest but decent flat pension for all, paid out of taxation, would not conflict with the principle of an employment-social security nexus.

In addition, long-term care insurance must be put in place without further delay, and enterprise pension and other occupation-related benefits should be expanded to provide an all-around guarantee for workers.

The share of labour remuneration in relation to overall GDP should gradually increase, system structure and operation must be maintained but, at the same time, kept flexible as appropriate so that it can easily adapt to non-standard forms of employment, population mobility and other possible developments. The social security system should also be endowed with capabilities of self-recalibration and constant improvement.

Third, continue to take social sharing as a cornerstone of social security and implement the principle of stakeholder collaboration and co-governance in practice.

With its social security reforms, China has instituted a new development philosophy of shared growth. It is not only a rectification to the previous skewed notion that some people are encouraged to become wealthy ahead of others but also a theoretical cornerstone to the improvement of the social security system. If the principle of solidarity sharing and mutual help is not implemented and maintained when reforming social security, the latter will deviate from its norm. Also, sustained development can only be achieved when the Government takes the lead, while stakeholders must be encouraged to participate in collaboration and co-governance. In practice, social security only functions well when it is mandatory; voluntary settings can only have auxiliary top-up functions. It has proven good practice, for various reasons however, for a government not to monopolize the management and the administration of social security but to leave these functions to the stakeholders.

Social security bears the role of income redistribution and must be led by the Government. Yet, the current pattern, characterized by monopolized power of the administrative branch (government) over legislation, administrative oversight and implementation undermines the long-term development of social security (Zheng, 2004b). The reform goal should be to "let the legislative, administrative and judicial departments and the operational agencies shoulder their respective obligations and fulfil their own duties" (Zheng, 2016a). Meanwhile, the trade unions, employers' organizations and the Federation of Disabled Persons representing the interests of different groups should be included in the designing and overseeing of the system. Only in this way can China ensure that all parties are participating in collaboration and co-governance. This is a critical condition for the healthy and sustained development of the system and would clearly be in line with internationally agreed principles of tripartite stakeholder involvement in social security policy formulation and administration. Also, more efforts are needed to cultivate charity and mutual help, which are the voluntary mechanisms for sharing benefits. However, the tradition of family-based protection and neighbourhood watch as well as the once full-field into the system of public governance to let it co-shoulder the historical mission of promoting social justice and sharing the fruits of development. The social security system should aim to systematically contribute to the well-being of all people for generations to come.

To achieve this end, China needs to be highly wary of the departure from the normal structure and functions of its social security system and refrain from shaking the social security system's foundation, hinging upon mutual help and stable anticipation. Reinforcing the responsibility of the Government can clearly contribute to this end.

China needs to combine the formal and informal systems, establishing a two-tier system that will universally cover the population while maintaining schemes targeted at certain societal groups. The concerted efforts of the Government, the market, society, families and individuals need to come together in a well-organized and multilayered social security system to give it the proper flexibility and resilience it needs to cope with crises. In the process, governments must take the lead and the central Government should have the authority to plan in a coordinated way. The fiscal responsibility of governments should be reinforced, and the role of overarching coordination of the central Government should be strengthened to rectify the regionally segmented system and thus institutionalize a positive and sound social security system that keeps pace with the changing times. Given the reality of the existing imbalances, gaps are unavoidable for certain periods of time. Nevertheless, this should be no excuse for not unifying the system at the national level or achieving the goal with the wrong steps (Zheng, 2016e). China should spare no effort to achieve a more equitable allocation of public resources nationwide by integrating its social security system, turning it into an important tool to bridge the regional gaps and to promote fair and coordinated development.

The central Government could take on major responsibilities for formulating the national design of social security, pushing forward relevant legislation and distributing resources rationally while maintaining an integrated system. It is necessary to reshape and modernize the operating mechanisms of social security to ensure its high efficiency by developing well-governed operating agencies and taking full advantage of information technologies and big data.[1] On this basis, social security administration will enhance its capacity of forecasting and early warning as well as monitoring. Equally, a stable

---

[1] It would be important to take issues, such as data protection into account, to secure and protect private individual information contained in their social security data systems.

export growth, diminishing competitive edge of (low) labour costs, sharpening structural contradictions between supply and demand, diverging regional and industrial trends and increased pressure on resources and the environment. This requires a switch to high-quality growth.

It is imperative to maintain economic growth at a medium to high speed and to continue consolidating and widening the material basis that bolsters the social security system (fiscal space). Addressing the problem of the inadequate endogenous dynamic in economic growth has become the biggest challenge. Thus, it is incumbent upon China's economy to head for a more advanced stage of development, which is characterized by a more sophisticated division of labour, a better structure and improved quality of the economy. This means more emphasis on innovation-driven growth and the expansion of domestic demand, especially consumer demand. China should give more attention (than hitherto) to the decisive role of the Government in those policy areas that are considered public domain while leaving the crucial role of resource allocation (as much as possible and advisable) to the market. Under the conditions of (i) addressing the difficulties of urban and rural residents in a well-directed manner and (ii) expanding the middle-income groups without further delay, China should let people's livelihood benefit more from the fruits of economic development livelihoods through the social security system in a better and fairer way. This can only be successful if complemented by a pro-productivity and pro-wage growth policy.

Providing all people with a stable and secure expectation for social security should be prioritized as a national development strategy (Zheng, 2016c). This is not only a necessary measure to keep unleashing the consumption potential, further activate the domestic impetus of economic growth and maintain the national economic growth at a medium to high speed, but it is an indispensable move to stride over the so-called middle-income trap and is the only way to common prosperity (Zheng, 2016d).

Second, give full consideration to the historical logic of the relationship between social security and public governance, strengthen the responsibility of the central Government for coordination and build a well-organized and multilayered social security system (Zheng, 2017c).

In the face of the new challenges, China should take social security as a holistic system with integrated schemes and optimized structure and incorporate it as one core policy

Fifth, China is experiencing charges of large-scale internal migration, rapid industrialization and urbanization, social structure transformation and the emergence of new business forms. All these developments have direct influence on economic growth while presenting challenges to social security and its further improvement (Zheng, 2018a).

In particular, the advancements in science and technology, such as the Internet and artificial intelligence as well as the new economy, have exerted direct impact on people's work and life, resulting in economic and social structure changes. They are also bringing about unprecedented challenges to the traditional operation mode of social security. Only a substantially modernized social security administration will be able to adapt to the resulting changes in the long term while protecting the interests of a scheme's members. The Government, which steers the guidelines of China's social security system, is well advised to continue pursuing policies aiming to balance marketization solutions (applicable as a complement to the public scheme for the few top income earners) with the core social security principles (for the middle- and low-income groups) that form the explicit and implicit basis of this report and the foundation of ILO and other organizations' Conventions and Recommendations.

3.2.2 Policy recommendations for the Government of China

As described in previous sections, China has achieved a positive interaction between social security and economic development over the past decades. Yet, the multiple challenges faced by China indicate that the relationship between these two needs to be further clarified so as to achieve common development. In particular, social security's growth-enhancing role must increasingly be seen under the perspective of intensive rather than extensive economic growth. This report thus makes the following recommendations for the Chinese Government.

First, address the problem of insufficient endogenous impetus[1] of the national economy to keep it growing at moderately high speed.

China's economic development cannot be sustained on the basis of its past extensive growth experience because it is confronted with many challenges, including reduced

---

[1] Endogenous impetus refers to the internal forces that originate from the State, organizations and individuals. The internal forces driving economic growth come from domestic consumption and technical innovation.

individuals have access to a full pension after contributing only for 15 years turns out to be rigid and undermining of the sustainable development of the system.

Beneficiaries of the health insurance have been divided into two groups: employees and residents. The regulation that retirees do not have to contribute needs to be rectified.

The division of responsibilities between the central and local governments has not been clarified yet. And the social security administration system can only be optimized and fully formed by deepening the reform.

With the weakening role of the family in providing security, hundreds of millions of older persons and children as well as more than 80 million persons with disabilities are in urgent need of social welfare services. Currently, however, neither the State nor society are capable of satisfying their needs in all respects, which has not only undermined the security and quality of people's livelihoods but also impeded the economic development related to people's livelihoods.

Therefore, further reforms call for more well-informed top-level design and overall development of relevant services to move towards a mature and solid social security system. This is, without doubt, an onerous task for China.

When a social security system starts to mature and costs start going up, including due to the demographic transition, some countries follow an apparently easy solution of transferring the risk from the State to individuals, in the form of individual accounts(and/or privatization, including with pensions). However, the reforms in these countries have turned out to be not entirely successful. In the global pension reform between 1981 and 2011, for example, 36 countries introduced a full or partial move from non-financial defined benefit to financial defined contribution (Wang, Williamson and Cansoy, 2016); if partial, the unfunded part was often changed from non-financial defined benefit to a point scheme or to a non-financial defined contribution scheme. Of those 36 countries that had introduced systemic reforms (full or partial), 21 countries had reversed the reform by 2016, including nine countries that completely reversed the systemic reform and nine that partially reversed the reform(Wang, Williamson and Cansoy, 2016). This teaches that political wisdom is needed when China pursues to builda mature and fully formed social security system.

the National Health and Family Planning Commission, the size of Chinese families has shrunk, with the nuclear families now accounting for more than 60 per cent of all households. And the average household size is smaller than 3.02 persons, with the family of two or three members the dominant type, but one-person households and so-called empty-nest families are emerging (NHFPC, 2016).[1] Around 150 million families are one-child families, and the number of persons aged 80 or older rises by more than one million annually. In terms of childcare and older-person care, the traditional pattern of family care has encountered mounting challenges, thus calling for social services. Due to the high mobility of the population, the traditional neighbourhood watch has been replaced by (implicit or explicit) rules applying to a "stranger society",[2] and the traditional work unit-based welfare provisions that were once omnipotent collapsed with the market economy reform. The erosion of traditional financial and in-kind security mechanisms based on the family, the neighbourhood and the work units has led to soaring demand from urban and rural residents for social security and services, which requires immediate action by the State and society.

Fourth, the social security system is not full-fledged yet, and the supply of basic public services for older persons, children and people with disabilities are inadequate.

In reforming its social security, China adopted a progressive strategy that first entailed trials (pilots), which have thus far achieved positive results. Yet inevitably, there are historical constraints and path dependencies, leaving deficiencies in the existing social security system that still need to be addressed.

For instance, the statutory pension system remains fragmented and, being operated at the regional level, the goal of national pooling has not yet been achieved. The stipulation that

---

[1] Empty-nest families are families in which elderly adults have no supporting child around, who, thus, live alone or with a spouse.
[2] "Stranger society" is a term relating to the traditional Chinese "acquaintance society". In the past, due to the low level of population mobility, people lived and worked in the same community for generations and were closely bonded with neighbours, termed "acquaintance society". In recent three decades, along with the rapid industrialization and urbanization, the mobility of the population has been rising. People living in the same community nowadays likely see their neighbours as strangers. It is even more difficult for migrating workers to integrate into urban communities. This adds to distrust among people and to the costs of maintaining a functioning society.

Furthermore, while China is striving to improve all people's living conditions, the income gap among different groups is widening, with the Gini coefficient[1] chronically above 0.4. According to the National Bureau of Statistics, China's Gini coefficient stood at 0.462 in 2015, down from a peak of 0.491 in 2008, but edged up to 0.465 in 2016, 0.467 in 2017 (NBS, 2018).

The current social security system is also contributing to additional economic imbalances in that it remains segmented. This segmentation is largely attributable to the absence of larger geographical pooling and the continued existence of the two separate schemes for residents and employees. While the group of billionaires is growing rapidly, a large number of impoverished people are desperate for public assistance. The Government announced that nearly 16.6 million rural residents lived in poverty as of the end of 2018. These households live in absolute poverty and are in need of government assistance.

The imbalances among regions and between urban and rural areas as well as the increasing social inequality not only affect the sustainable and sound development of the national economy but also undermine social justice and potentially social stability. In these respects, China has similar problems as other regions and countries around the globe. In the course of modernization, China will have to address these problems seriously at home but also in concert with the other nations at the international level (for example, with the United Nations and the Group of Twenty summits).

Third, the ageing of China's population, coupled with the low fertility rate, has become increasingly evident while traditional security mechanisms are increasingly fading.

With a declining fertility rate and a higher average life expectancy credited to social development and progress as well as the implementation of the one-child policy over the past years, the issue of population ageing and low fertility rate is outstanding. In respect of these challenges, China has clearly joined many developed countries. According to

---

[1] A measure of inequality in income distribution, it expresses the size of the area between a theoretical perfect equality Lorenz curve and the real concave Lorenz curve of a country or another entity to the size of the area under the equality line. The value is between 0 and 1. A value of more than 0.4 is alarming because it points at an excessive rich-poor income gap.

China's necessary switch from extensive to intensive productivity growth has important implications for the social security design and administration. As shown in this report, the design of a social security system can be supportive to economic growth. For the further development of the system, China needs to respect a separate but complementary functioning of social insurance and social assistance.

To allow the handling of large numbers of social security cases as well as to promote interinstitutional exchange and coordination, the administration of respective social security institutions and services must be modernized, particularly in terms of information technology solutions. It is also important to increase the number of well-trained staff persons devoted to serving the members covered by their institutions.

In addition, it is a major challenge to adapt social security to the new normal-to propel coordinated development between the economy and social security of the society and to maintain and deepen the growth-enhancing design of social security as one means to maintaining intensive rather than extensive economic growth at a relatively high speed. It is doable, however, as the examples of modernization in other sectors of China's economy prove.

Second, development imbalances prevail among regions and between urban and rural areas and thus worsen social inequality.

Significant imbalances in terms of economic and social development exist between the country's eastern coast and the western inland. The coastal region converges with the level of high-income countries; cities such as Beijing, Shanghai and Tianjin are blessed with GDP per capita of more than $15,000. In contrast, the landlocked western regions are relatively underdeveloped, with a middle-lower-income level and some impoverished regions are (in international comparison) even at the lowest income levels.[1]

There is also a huge urban-rural gap, which, inter alia, results from the long-lasting effects of the barriers of the household registration (*hukou*) system and an uneven allocation of public resources. In 2017, the disposable income of urban residents was 2.7 times that of rural residents.

---

[1] For example, the provinces of Gansu, Guizhou and Yunnan had a GDP per capita of around $5,000 in 2017 (NBS, 2018).

knowledge of and adapt to the new situation.

In summing up, as a plan to propel the reform and development of social security, the step-by-step approach combined with a strategy of replacing short-term welfare losses with long-term primary income growth has, retrospectively, turned out to be optimal. Chinese society has widely understood the rationale of this policy as necessary to promote economic development, maintain a solid economic growth rate and enhance social security in a flexible market economy.

3.2 Major socioeconomic challenges and policy recommendations

3.2.1 Challenges confronting China

China's modernization is continuing at unprecedented speed, with significant improvements in its economic and social developments. Yet, after the rapid growth over the past decades, the economy has embarked on a new normal of medium-to-high growth. Against the background of economic globalization, China is, like other regions and countries, confronted with multiple challenges.

First, economic development faces the pressures imposed by structural adjustment, industrial upgrading and transformation of the growth model.

Social security is part of this development and needs to be further developed until China broadly joins the ranks of other countries with complete social security systems and, with its own specific characteristic, becomes a welfare state.

China's economic development is facing challenges. At the Business 20 summit (on the sidelines of the Group of Twenty summit) in Hangzhou Province in September 2016, President Xi Jinping pointed out: "We are keenly aware that many sectors of China's economy are not strong or competitive enough, despite their big sizes. Over the years, they have depended on input of resources, capital and labour force to achieve growth and expand scale. But this model is no longer sustainable. China now faces the challenging task of changing its growth drivers and growth model and adjusting its economic structure" (Xi, 2016).

urban areas: The earlier free medical care was replaced with health insurance that collects contributions, and the pension system-once having a high replacement rate and requiring no contributions-was turned into a contributory system at reduced replacement rates. In a sense, China was wise enough to implement the reforms before it became rich. Once becoming rich, similar social reforms (with cuts in replacement rates and the like) would most probably be as difficult to achieve as in the developed (European) world.

Growing primary incomes of the workforce and other residents accompanied the emergence of a relatively broad middle class that was less dependent on social assistance and anti-poverty services but able to save for their own old age and health needs. This fostered the Government's fiscal space required for financing anti-poverty policies.

(ii) The step-by-step approach: The social security system had to be reformed in conformity with the economic reform. The long-term goal was clearly defined: to build a comprehensive social security system that interacts well with a socialist market economy. The functionality of the existing social security structures and institutions must nonetheless be maintained as long as the new system (or elements thereof) was not fully established nor functioning.

To manage this transition, many issues had to be addressed at the same time and, accordingly, many, actors, persons and institutions had to be (and were) involved. And they had to be equipped with the necessary knowledge, which was a problem for the actors who draw heavily on international experience. To ably react to false developments, mistakes or failures but also to take up positive developments, the Government took a careful approach that allowed it to change direction fast, if needed, without letting risks unduly materialize. Prerequisites and conditions were carefully defined, and decisions were made in a way that enabled the reformed social security to gradually assume its intended roles and old social security structures be given up accordingly. As far as it is still incomplete, China's social security reform continues working on completing the institutional overhaul.

(iii) The bottom-up approach: A dominantly positive attitude of all people was supported by adopting a bottom-up approach. This meant choosing selected local areas as pilot zones, carrying out intended reforms, drawing lessons that well informed a national reform plan and eventually implementing it top-down. This approach provided not only additional knowledge to reformers but also a buffer period for the public to gain in-hand progress of social insurance and social assistance and poverty-relief programmes have proven very effective internationally (in France, Germany and the Nordic countries, for instance) and is also appropriate for modern China, where its use should be heavily expanded.

FIFTH GUIDELINE: The strategic step-by-step reform approach within a clearpolicy of growth orientation has proven essential for China to successfully master the complex issues of social security reform. This approach should be maintained for future reform needs. It can also be taken as a template for reform policy in other countries.

China's social security transformation over the past three decades has been a risky undertaking-socially, economically and politically. Socially because a new system was to be implemented while the old system had to continue functioning. Economically due to the transition from a planned economy to a socialist market economy, but with social security reform as a prerequisite for success, which had not been tested before (there was no comprehensive template). Politically because the economic and social security reforms affected the whole society, which, given the usual societal inertia of prevailing attitudes, had to be convinced of the advantages of the intended policy.

There are basically three reasons why the risks in the reform process did not materialize:

(i) The clear growth orientation with focus on the creation of a prosperous middle class: Social and political stability was and is maintained because the social security reforms were nested into a clear economic growth orientation, initiated during the reform process and maintained ever since. The reason for broad societal acceptance of these measures is that the incomes of the vast majority of workers and retirees continued to grow, and people's living standards generally increased.

For example, in the early 1980s, when the contract responsibility system[1] was introduced in rural areas, the welfare of farmers was curtailed. Yet, the (immediate) welfare losses were exceeded by a wide margin by the (lagged) income gains from the land contracts; thus, any sustained resistance to the reform was avoided. Similar patterns evolved in

---

[1] Also known as the household responsibility system. The Government gave farmers a quota of goods to produce, and they received compensation for meeting the quota. If they went beyond the quota, farmers were allowed to sell the excess in the free market at unregulated prices.

is to create a social and institutional environment that allows and expects everyone to contribute. China is a society in which the virtues of work are highly valued. It is one of the world's leading work and labour productivity-oriented societies, achieving the virtuous cycle by converting social security into a multi-stakeholder system in which the Government, enterprises and individuals are jointly responsible and where the core of the system is based on social insurance principles of risk sharing and mutual help (and including elements of actuarial fairness) (Scholz, 2015; Dixon, 1999).

Labour-based social insurance became a cornerstone of China's socioeconomic system with the pension and health insurance as the most system-relevant schemes. Such design features of social security are generally based on the conviction that access to benefits is provided only after both the individual and employer have paid their contributions. Such a system, linking entitlements with obligations is essentially a social security system of collaboration and sharing and constitutes a rational path of reform and development. Government subsidization has had an important role in rapidly extending social security coverage. Government subsidies directly contribute to the establishment and development of the urban and rural residents' pension and health insurance schemes as well as pension and health insurance coverage for subsistence allowance recipients and persons with severe disabilities.

FOURTH GUIDELINE: Attach great importance to eradicating poverty by complementing the social insurance-based system with effective social assistance and other basic welfare provisions, thus guaranteeing people a basic livelihood.

Because people in poverty and vulnerable economic conditions often find themselves in unstable and low-paid or non-remunerated work and employment arrangements, the (contributory) system, as sketched under the third guideline, is often insufficient to help them climb out of their situation. People with severe disabilities are typically in a similar situation. These and other persons in need of help must be given access to social security. This can be done in various ways, such as by directly providing a means-tested subsistence allowance in cash or in kind and, where appropriate and administratively applicable, through the provision of earmarked government-sponsored contributions to old-age insurance and health insurance through which persons who are poor can accumulate entitlements. At the same time, the respective schemes would receive corresponding revenue. It shows that the political scheme can ensure a high level of coverage and thus create a social security culture. The complementary design and hand-

Table 5 shows China's spending on health care over the past four decades. Expenditure as a share of GDP rose from 3 per cent to 6.3 per cent. This increase was largely due to the expenditure on health insurance. The growth elasticity of health was equal to around 2 over the long run. Given that China comes from very low spending levels, this development is highly welcome under social health policy perspectives. International research suggests, however, there are saturation levels beyond which additional health spending will not improve the health status of the population but only serves the income interests of health providers and the profit interests of the health industry. Generally speaking, the spending levels of China's social security have constantly improved, yet the total spending on social security as a share of GDP (at 13 per cent) remains lower than the average for the OECD countries. Acknowledging that spending levels on social security need to be further increased, the Government has been intensifying its efforts.

Table 5   Structure of health care expenditure in China, 1978-2017

(100 million CNY and $)

Year	Total cost of health care								As a share of GDP (%)
	Total		Government spending on health care		Social spending on health care		Individual's spending on health care		
	CNY	$	CNY	$	CNY	$	CNY	$	
1978	110.21	65.46	35.44	21.05	52.52	31.20	22.52	13.38	3.00
1980	143.23	95.59	51.91	34.64	60.97	40.69	30.35	20.25	3.15
1985	279.00	95.00	107.65	36.66	91.96	31.31	79.39	27.03	3.09
1990	747.39	156.25	187.28	39.15	293.1	61.28	267.01	55.82	4.00
1995	2,155.13	258.07	387.34	46.38	767.81	91.94	999.98	119.74	3.54
2000	4,586.63	554.05	709.52	85.71	1,171.94	141.57	2,705.17	326.77	4.62
2005	8,659.91	1,057.16	1,552.53	189.52	2,586.41	315.74	4,520.98	551.90	4.68
2010	19,980.39	2,951.53	5,732.49	846.81	7,196.61	1,063.09	7,051.29	1,041.63	4.98
2015	40,974.64	6,578.68	12,475.28	2,002.97	16,506.71	2,650.23	11,992.65	1,925.48	6.05
2016	46,344.90	6,977.24	13,910.30	2,094.20	19,096.70	2,875.01	13,337.90	2,008.02	6.20
2017	52,598.28	7,790.26	15,205.87	2,252.12	22,258.81	3,296.72	15,133.60	2,241.42	6.30

Source: NBS, 2018 (*China Statistical Yearbook 2018*).

THIRD GUIDELINE: Follow the principle of joint contribution and shared benefits and build a social security system based mainly on social insurance principles that link individual and institutional rights with individual and institutional obligations.

Societies have various options to create and maintain the virtuous cycle between economic development and improvement of people's livelihoods. A common denominator

Table 4 Public budget expenditure in China, 2007-2017　　　　　　　　　　　　(100 million CNY and $)

Year	Revenue in the general public budget		Expenditure on social security and employment		Expenditure on public health and family planning		Expenditure on education		Aggregate expenditure		Share in GDP (%)	Overall growth rate (%)
	CNY	$	CNY	$	CNY	$	CNY	$	CNY	$		
2007	51,321.78	6,749.31	8,514.24	1,119.71	3,554.91	467.51	7,122.32	936.65	19,191.47	2,523.87	7.09	
2008	61,330.35	8,830.74	9,795.92	1,410.48	4,178.76	601.68	9,010.21	1,297.35	22,984.89	3,309.51	7.15	19.77
2009	68,518.30	10,030.49	9,164.21	1,341.56	4,951.10	724.80	10,437.54	1,527.97	24,552.85	3,594.33	7.05	6.82
2010	83,101.51	12,275.87	9,130.60	1,348.78	5,333.37	787.85	12,550.02	1,853.91	27,013.99	3,990.54	6.57	10.02
2011	103,874.43	16,082.62	11,109.40	1,720.04	6,429.51	995.47	16,497.33	2,554.24	34,036.24	5,269.75	7.02	25.99
2012	117,253.52	18,574.82	12,585.52	1,993.75	7,425.11	1,176.26	21,242.10	3,365.09	41,252.73	6,535.09	7.65	21.20
2013	129,209.64	20,863.15	14,490.54	2,339.75	8,279.90	1,336.93	22,001.76	3,552.57	44,772.20	7,229.25	7.58	8.53
2014	140,370.03	22,851.15	15,968.85	2,599.60	10,176.80	1,656.70	23,041.71	3,751.01	49,187.36	8,007.32	7.63	9.86
2015	152,269.23	24,447.57	19,018.69	3,053.54	11,953.18	1,919.14	26,271.88	4,218.08	57,243.75	9,190.76	8.34	16.38
2016	159,604.97	24,028.57	21,591.45	3,250.60	13,158.77	1,981.06	28,072.78	4,226.36	62,823.00	9,458.02	8.49	9.75
2017	172,592.77	25,562.48	24,611.68	3,645.20	14,450.63	2,140.26	30,153.18	4,465.95	69,215.49	10,251.41	8.43	10.29

Source: NBS, 2018 (*China Statistical Yearbook 2018*).

The growing fiscal revenue has undoubtedly become the main source of funding for the Government to support and co-fund social security. Fiscal space has grown substantially and offered the Government opportunity to sustainably increase the inputs to social security, public health care and public education, thus making the social security system increasingly sound and enhancing people's welfare at a relativelyrapid and continuous speed (see section 3.1.3).

China's practice has consolidated the view that economic development is the foundation as well as the prerequisite for guaranteeing and improving people's livelihoods and that sound social security is the purpose as well as the basis for maintaining and increasing economic productivity. Only by interlinking the two and thus creating a virtuous cycle can the national economy progress steadily and achieve sustainable and balanced development. Ignoring these insights risks losing long-term positive developments of China's economy (see the next second guideline).

SECOND GUIDELINE: Social security must assume its role as a fundamental system to guarantee and improve people's livelihoods. This requires that benefit levels keep pace with economic capacities, such that social security neither under-demands nor overstretches the economy's possibilities to maintain sufficient economic growth.

In observing the first guideline while focusing on guaranteeing and improving people's livelihoods, the Government prioritized social security, channelling public inputs into the system faster than the general revenue grew. This policy must be maintained until China's social expenditure ratio has reached, in line with growing economic capacities, the levels of its international peers (which, equally, might be changing or varying). Tables 4 and 5provide statistical evidence for this guideline.

Table 4 reveals that, from 2007 to 2017, revenue in the general public budget **grew 3.4 times** while aggregate expenditure on social security and employment, on health care and family planning and on education increased slightly faster (3.6 times). The share of the aggregate expenditure in GDP climbed from nearly 7.1 per cent to 8.4 per cent. If the social insurance were included in the time series, the material foundation of social security would prove even more solid.

From a broader perspective, the Chinese reacted to the two periods of financial and economic crises by using social security as a policy tool. This echoes the international and historical experiences in which economic crises were often accompanied by the development of social security, including fostering and improving its structures. The Chinese case is special in that these reactions came quickly and were robust, whereas governments in the West have often taken a more tentative and reluctant approach to crisis-induced social security improvements. The austerity-orientation of the European Union in the aftermath of the 2008-2010 financial and economic crises is an example.

3.1.4 China's experience of the relationship between economic development and social security as guidelines for the future

As a major engine of the world economy, China's economic performance is widely recognized. The remarkable results the country has achieved through its social security reforms and development also have attracted attention from the international community. These two achievements do not coexist by chance-they are intrinsically and mutually linked, confirming the trend that was also observed in other developed economies in the past. China's experiences include the following five aspects that can also be considered guidelines for future national policy orientation(Zheng, 2018a).

FIRST GUIDELINE: The mutually reinforcing interrelationships between social security and economic growth must be maintained.

The solid evidence presented in this chapter regarding the interaction between social security measures and economic progress should be enough to justify avoiding any political or economic action that puts this interrelation at risk or questions it. The predominant purpose of economic growth is to swiftly eradicate poverty, maintain achieved living standard levels and, as much as possible, continue to improve them through equitable distribution. China adopted this paradigm at the start of the twenty-first century and gave it fresh momentum by developing social security and the national economy under a common growth approach. China is now harvesting the success of this policy. For example, fiscal revenue has increased significantly. Revenue from individual income tax alone has increased, from $57.8 billion in 2009 to $177.2 billion in 2017 (MOF, 2010 and 2018).

plummeted, the volume of imports and exports decreased, numerous enterprises went bankrupt and large numbers of workers became unemployed. The Social Insurance Law under deliberation at that time encountered resistance from businesses, not passing until October 2010. Globally, most countries quickly moved from their stimulus packages to austerity measures with undesirable effects. In contrast, China maintained stimulus measures for economic growth and further developed its social security system. It was this crisis that changed China's growth orientation from unsustainable export-led to domestic demand-led, in which pensions, health care, housing and education would have prominent roles in easing people's concerns. In the absence of higher domestic consumption, China's economy was in danger of becoming stuck in a trough with difficulty to get back on a previous track in the short term. Therefore, in 2009, the Government countered the sluggish economic growth by resolutely pushing forward the institutionalization of the country's social security system. Measures adopted included:

- the setting up of a pension scheme for rural residents, intending to attain the goal of covering all residents of qualifying age instantly;
- commencing a three-year reform plan for the social health insurance to achieve near universal health coverage within a short period; and
- embarking on large-scale construction of government-subsidized housing (see section 3.1.2).

In addition, after the Wenchuan earthquake in 2008 in south-western China's Sichuan Province, the Government began increasing inputs to disaster relief, post-disaster reconstruction and college enrolment expansion. As a result, the overall welfare level of urban and rural residents was considerably uplifted. These measures not only reassured people by reducing their anxieties and increasing and stabilizing their cash and in-kind incomes, they also increased personal consumption, helping to turn it into the biggest driver of national economic growth. China's economic strength rebounded. Central to the success were swift reactions to the crises, decisive policy-making and strong resolution to implement planned policy (Zheng, 2017c).

In concluding, a closer look at China's development over the past few decades indicates that without the robust steps of institutionalization of social security in 1998 and 2009, the former rapid growth could easily have come to a halt. If no importance had been attached to social security, it would be unlikely for the economy to develop smoothly, let alone bounce back amid the financial crises. Social security and the economy are thus not necessarily antagonists but, if well organized, can mutually strengthen each other (Zheng, 2017c).

absence of social security, the Government placed social security reform and institutionalization at the top of its agenda, emphasizing the implementation of "two guarantees, three security lines".[1] The subsistence allowance scheme covering residents living in financial difficulties and the health insurance reform were rolled out, the housing system was boosted and the Social Security Strategic Reserve Fund[2] was established to prepare for the population ageing in the future. The implementation of these major social security schemes, although still modest in financial size, helped to resolve the short-term predicaments of urban and rural residents, enhanced people's longer-term confidence in the social security system and thus supported recovery of domestic private consumption. In this way, they helped to reduce social risks and provided social stability for economic development. The improvements on social security were one of the critical reasons why all major subsequent reforms could be pushed ahead and why the national economy re-attained rapid growth (Zheng, 2017c).

In 2008, China's economy fell victim to the global financial crises: foreign trade

---

[1] The term "two guarantees, three security lines" refers to the comprehensive social security measures adopted by the Government in 1998. The "two guarantees" refers to (i) guaranteeing the basic livelihood of workers laid off from state-owned enterprises and (ii) guaranteeing timely and full pension payments to the enterprises' retirees. The state-owned enterprises were obliged to set up re-employment centres responsible for delivering the basic living allowances to the laid-off workers and to pay on their behalf social insurance contributions, which were co-financed by the Government. The "three security lines" refers to (i) the basic living guarantee allowance for laid-off workers from state-owned enterprises, which was delivered by re-employment centres for a maximum of three years. If the workers remain unemployed after three years, they are entitled to (ii) an unemployment insurance benefit for a maximum of two years. If the laid-off workers remain unemployed after two years of protection under the unemployment insurance, they can claim (iii) the minimum living allowance for urban residents.

[2] The Social Security Strategic Reserve Fund was set up by the Government in 2000 to prepare for the pension payment after 2030, when population ageing is expected to reach its peak. It is mainly financed through government funding and state assets, though it is also entrusted by some local governments to run their pension funds. The fund, which was jointly administered by the Ministry of Human Resources and Social Security and the Ministry of Finance, started to be solely administered by the Ministry of Finance in 2018. The National Council for Social Security Fund operates the fund. As of 2018, the fund accumulated approximately $430 billion in assets, representing 3.3 per cent of GDP in the same year.

Development 2017, by the end of 2017, 32,000 social service institutions providing accommodations registered with civil affairs authorities, among which 18,000 were registered as public institutions and 13,000 were private non-profit organizations. As well, there was an increasing number of for-profit social service institutions invested by enterprises. Thus, 40 per cent of all social service institutions were invested by enterprises or the non-government sector.Such non-government social service facilities not only meet the nursing needs of people but also create more jobs. The same applies to the field of health services. Therefore, opening social welfare services provision to social capital not only consolidates the material basis for bolstering the social security system but also better satisfies people's needs.

Eighth, the social security system hasa critical and supportive role in tackling the latest economic crises.

Telling empirical demonstrations of the positive impact of China's social security system on boosting its economic growth emerged in 1998 and 2009 during the two major international financial crises, which did not leave China unaffected. The Government adopted a variety of measures, including investment expansion and consumption stimulation. Amid the crisis, the social security system had a prominent role: It not only protected people from crisis impacts but also directly boosted people's confidence and capacity to consume, thus helping the national economy to overcome both crises relatively swiftly and re-embark on the path of growth.

The Asian financial crisis that began in 1997 created an unfavourable international environment for China's then still export-led growth policy. Domestically, priorities had been oriented towards economic growth with only little focus on people's livelihoods. Reforms of social security were dominated by the Government's cost-containment policies, which resulted in workers' legitimate entitlements and interests being infringed through millions of full or partial pension payment defaults while workers' medical costs were not reimbursed. In addition, the number of urban residents in poverty soared, which fed a growing sense of insecurity in the society and resulted in declining resident consumption, mounting enterprise inventories and deteriorating economic and financial conditions in the state-owned enterprises. The national economy risked becoming stuck in crisis.

In 1998, having realized that slagging consumption was also a result of the price-bubble effects on the property markets, began to emerge. Middle- and low-income groups could not afford the surging housing prices, thus housing turned into a social problem. To rectify this, the Government embarked in 1995 on the National Housing Project with the goal of addressing the housing problem of urban middle- and low-income families. This was followed by the Low-Rent Housing System in 1999. In 2009, it was made explicit that low-income households living in difficulty were to be provided with government-subsidized housing; meanwhile, the renovation of areas with closed coal mines, forest farms and shantytowns was conducted on a large scale, and dilapidated houses with potential safety hazards in rural areas were reconstructed. This work is still ongoing. According to China's Twelfth Five-Year Plan for Economic and Social Development, 2011-2015, the building of a housing-supply system was to be done more quickly, with basic housing support provided by the Government and multiple levels of demand to be met primarily by the market.

From 2011 to 2017, the total expenditure of government at all levels on subsidized housing was more than CNY3,625 billion (nearly $537 billion, based on yearly average exchange rate of 2017). Government spending on subsidized housing rose at a rate of 32 per cent, from CNY175.5 billion ($25.9 billion) in 2010 to CNY655.2 billion (nearly $97 billion) in 2017 (NBS, various years).

As an integral part of China's social security system, the housing benefits scheme needs to develop steadily. The following measures are essential at the current stage: (i) properly address the housing problem of rural-to-urban migrant workers; (ii) adopt policies to promote the rental housing industry; (iii) formulate exit rules for government-subsidized housing; and (iv) improve the housing provident fund scheme.

Finally, social welfare services opened up to private social capital, which triggered new employment and improved people's well-being. In recent years, spending on pensions, health care, children's upbringing, education and other aspects of people's livelihoods showed sustained increases. The Government is now striving to divert more resources to public investment, provide more basic public services and adopt a policy of opening up towards social capital, which has already led to a constant expansion of private capital invested in the services industry. As a result, the welfare sector is engaging increasing numbers of workers and generating new areas for economic growth related directly to people's livelihoods.According to the *Statistical Bulletin on Social Service* residents. (ii) The Government finances the renovation of homes in run-down urban areas and dilapidated rural houses.

2. Housing provident fund scheme applicable only to urban workers. The employer and employee contribute an equal amount, ranging from 5 per cent to 12 per cent of the gross wage, to the housing provident fund, which is deposited in the employee's individual account and used exclusively for housing-related expenditure. In practice, however, it is usually government departments, public institutions and state-owned enterprises that participate in this scheme. Additionally, government departments and public institutions hand out cash allowances to their employees who own no home or whose living space falls short of the prescribed level.

Before the 1980s in urban areas, China had a public housing system based on allocation, in line with the planned economy. Back then, rural residents were allowed to build their own house in accordance with government regulations after getting approval. However, the government-monopolized urban housing system also created drawbacks, such as low efficiency and unfair housing allocations, and gave rise to an array of problems, including lack of resources for maintenance, failure to sustain re-investment in housing and sluggish improvement of housing conditions and quality.

In the 1990s, China began reforming its urban housing system. Market resources were mobilized into the field of home building. Later, housing commodification and home ownership became explicit goals. As a result, the real estate industry soon became a pillar industry for economic growth, and the housing conditions of urban residents have improved significantly. The per capita living space rose from 6.7 square metres in 1978 to 33 square metres in 2016. Since 2003, real estate investment has been on the rise, becoming the second-largest social fixed-asset investment, after the manufacturing sector. In 2016, the real estate value added accounted for 6.5 per cent of GDP, giving a boost to the downstream (steel and coal, for example) and upstream (gas and electricity, for example) industries. In 2017, more than 30.8 million people were employed in the real estate and construction industries, taking up 17.5 per cent of the total urban employment (NBS, 2018), second only to manufacturing. Following China's housing reform, the real estate industry had a prominent stimulating effect on overall employment and the economy.

In advancing housing commodification, negative consequences, such as overheating and

Then, a new policy of housing ownership replaced the earlier distributive urban housing system, invigorated the real estate industry, improved people's living conditions and constituted an important pillar of economic growth. Under the planned economy, all urban residential dwellings consisted of public housing provided by the work units or the government, with less than 10 square metres per capita living space. In the 1990s, this system underwent extensive overhaul. The focus was to introduce housing ownership based on the previous public housing benefits provided by the work units or the Government in urban areas, resulting in the establishment and fast expansion of a real estate industry that instantly became a core pillar of China's dynamic growth. With the marketization of the housing industry, residents' living conditions were greatly improved. A sample poll by the China Association of Social Security suggests that in 2015, the home ownership rate was 95.4 per cent, with 91.2 per cent of urban households owning at least one housing property and 19.7 per cent owning more than two (Li,Cheng andZhang, 2015).Only the households in poverty or with low income are entitled to restricted public housing that the Government continues to provide.

This de-welfare reform in the housing system lies at the root of the rapid growth of China's real estate industry and its role as a core pillar of its economy. However, it also fuels the real estate bubble and disadvantages low-income families. In 2009, the Government began developing large-scale government-subsidized housing to ensure that low-income families have at least a rudimentary place to live. Following an institutional shift from a welfare-oriented housing allocation system to a market-oriented one focused on housing privatization, China is now heading towards a moderate return to a welfare-oriented housing policy targeting low-income families(see box 7).

Box 7
Reform and development of China's housing benefits:
Returning from de-welfare to social security

As an important component of China's social security system, housing benefits include the following two schemes.

1. Government-subsidized housing. Financed with government funds, it targets low-income households living in difficulties. There are two situations: (i) The Government constructs subsidized housing units and allocates them to low-income households with no housing or housing below subsistence level. This policy is also applicable to urban underpin the sustained growth of China's labour productivity. From 1996 to 2015, the average annual growth rate of the country's labour productivity was 8.6 per cent, higher than the global average level (NBS, 2016).Although the increase of productivity rates cannot be attributable to improved education alone but also to the overall investment and production process, improved education is a critical prerequisite for improving productivity.

At present, the average length of schooling of China's working-age population exceeds ten years, longer than that of the world average. The average length of education of persons entering the labour force is around 13 years, which is close to the average level of moderately developed countries and high for developed countries (NBS, 2016). The gross enrolment ratio in higher education[1] increased from 2.7 per cent in 1978 to 45.7 per cent in 2017 (MOE, 2018), exceeding the average level of high- and middle-income countries and showing that China is in an era of popularized higher education (MOE,2017). This is conducive to bolstering sustainable development of China's economy and turning the demographic dividend from a quantity-oriented type into a quality-oriented one, and indicating that additional productivity effects exerted by a larger number of high-quality workers might be expected in the future.

Providing education is an economic activity. As an important part of the national economy, the development of education directly contributes to economic growth. According to government statistics, the number of colleges and universities in China rose from 598 in 1978 to 2,631 in 2017; the number of special schools rose from 292 to 2,107, and the number of preschool institutions grew from 163,952 to 255,000 in the same period (MOE, 2018). The number of primary and secondary schools and secondary vocational education institutions declined due to demographic changes following the family planning policy and institutional reforms. The number of people receiving education surged to 340 million in 2015, from 230 million in 1985. The number of people engaged in educational legal entities increased from 12.6 million in 1985 to nearly 19.2 million in 2015. In 2016, the added value of the education industry was nearly CNY2.7 trillion ($396 billion), accounting for 3.6 per cent of GDP (NBS, 2018). This is, however, only the direct contribution of education to national output. To drive economic growth during the Asian financial crisis at the end of the twentieth century, China expanded enrolment in higher education as a critical move to expand consumption and domestic demand.

---

[1] The ratio of young people aged 18-22 years acquiring higher education.

urban subsistence allowance scheme addresses problems regarding the basic livelihood of newly emerged poor persons, enabling the reform of the urban economic system to proceed.

As for rural areas, the subsistence allowance scheme provides a basic living guarantee for persons impoverished due to illness, natural and human-made disasters and competition failures. This explains why rural China has maintained steady development despite its profound social and economic changes.

On the other hand, the subsistence allowance scheme stabilizes and increases the consumption of poor persons. After receiving the allowance, the beneficiary would normally spend it on living necessities. That the subsistence allowance scheme is financed through tax revenues largely collected from high-income groups and paid to low-income households endows the system with a strong income redistribution effect.

Seventh, other social reforms also directly promoted the sustained and rapid growth of China's economy.
There have been other reforms in the sphere of social security beyond unemployment insurance, pensions, health care and social assistance that improved the conditions for economic growth. We focus on three aspects.

First of all, significantly improved public education keeps generating high-quality labour. Bolstered by the sustained and rapid economic growth, fiscal expenditure on education increased from around $11.6 billion in 1991 to $506.6 billion in 2017[1]. Its share in GDP rose from less than 3 per cent in 1991 to 4 per cent in 2012 and has maintained this level ever since (NBS, various years).

Consequently, China's education system has embarked on continuous improvement, including nine-year compulsory education for all, which gives special prominence to higher education and an intensified focus on vocational education. While maintaining a moderate growth of public financial input, China mobilized resources also in the private sector to develop education and to increase overall educational investment, ushering in popularized higher education. The development of vocational education has not only brought more opportunities for children to receive education but also raised the human capital level of the society and increased the supply of high-quality labour, which will

---

[1] See:http://www.moe.gov.cn/srcsite/A05/s3040/201810/t20181012_351301.html.

providers and on the pharmaceutical industry. Indeed, as is normal for health insurance (including other financing systems), individual contribution payment is the basis for acquiring the entitlement to make use of the health system. The contributions collected from private households (and enterprises and the taxpayer) are usually channelled to health providers and health industries (technology and pharmaceutical). With growing subsidization (previously described) of the universal system and the parallel rise of per capita health spending, the collected resources of the medical service providers and pharmaceutical industries grew consequently.

Currently, more than 50 per cent of the revenue of medical service providers is covered by the health insurance fund. At the end of 2017, 31,056 hospitals with more than 6.1 million beds were registered across the country (representing, on average, around 230 persons per one bed, or around four beds per 1,000 population). These numbers imply an increase of the number of hospitals by slightly more than 34 per cent and beds by 47 per cent from 2012 (NHC, 2018).

In 2015, there were 7,116 large pharmaceutical enterprises (an increase of 25.4 per cent from 2011), with a total production value hitting nearly CNY2.7 trillion ($429.88 billion) (an increase of 75.8 per cent from 2011), their total assets reaching nearly CNY2.5 trillion ($394.09 billion) (an increase of 89.3 per cent from 2011), the industry's revenue out of sales culminating at nearly CNY2.6 trillion ($410.01 billion) (an increase of 75.9 per cent from 2011) and the total profit being CNY262.7 billion ($42.18 billion) (an increase of 75.8 per cent from 2011) (NHFPC, various years).

Sixth, the establishment of the subsistence allowance scheme (1999 for urban and 2007 for rural residents) shifted the social assistance system from humanitarian aid to protecting human rights and from residual relief to institutionalized assistance. It has not only guaranteed the basic livelihood of the impoverished parts of the population and helped to maintain social stability but also facilitated economic transformation and development.

On the one hand, the subsistence allowance scheme adapts to the transformation of the urban and rural economies because it guarantees the basic livelihood of persons who are poor. This allowed the state-owned enterprises to take on their intended role as market participants (see previous discussion on pensions and health) because they no longer had to provide help to their impoverished employees. The establishment of the and workers were not supposed to move freely across different enterprises. The rural population was completely excluded from the system. Because enterprises bore all medical costs of their employees and retirees, those established in the early days had more retirees and thus were overwhelmed by such heavy burden, and workers' right to free access to health services were often, de-facto, infringed. With the introduction of health insurance independent of single enterprises, this right was re-established.

On the side of the enterprises, similar business-enhancing effects took place, as in the case of pension schemes (as previously explained): Social health insurance fairly balanced employers' health-related labour costs. In particular, the establishment of health insurance for rural residents and urban non-salaried residents resulted in an increasingly fairer system on the basis of universal coverage.

SECOND IMPACT: The fiscally funded health insurance has effectively alleviated urban and rural residents' worries and concerns regarding the costs of illness and uplifted their consumption level and consumption confidence. Although of contributory nature by law, the health insurance scheme for rural and urban non-salaried residents is mainly funded by the Government. The annual subsidy per capita increased from initially $3 to $84 in 2017, reflecting an overall fiscal share in revenue of around 70 per cent.

Although total revenue remains low, positive effects on private households have been generated, especially in rural areas. Prior to the implementation of the health insurance, large numbers of impoverished rural residents never saw a doctor. Since the introduction of the health insurance, it has become normal in rural areas to see doctors as a way of individual health management. As the revenue collected increases, the utilization rate of medical services by middle- and low-income groups will continue to rise. As already indicated, the need to make precautionary individual savings addressing health risks has decreased. Admittedly, people's worries and concerns about the cost of illness have not been fully eliminated; thus, China still needs to further improve its health insurance system.

THIRD IMPACT: the health insurance boosted the number and revenue of medical and pharmaceutical industries. The introduction of (universal) health insurance had positive impacts on the development of income and production of medical service

FIFTH IMPACT: **The partially funded basic pension system (fund balances) bolsters economic development.** As China adopts the partially funded basic pension, there is a considerable amount of accumulated funds, of which most are in the special fiscal accounts or banks across the country. Although the rate of return on investment has been modest, these funds (see figure 12 and table A3 in Annex 2) enter the economic sector through various channels and contribute to boosting economic growth.

Figure 12   Accumulated balances of the basic old-age pension system fund, 1998-2017

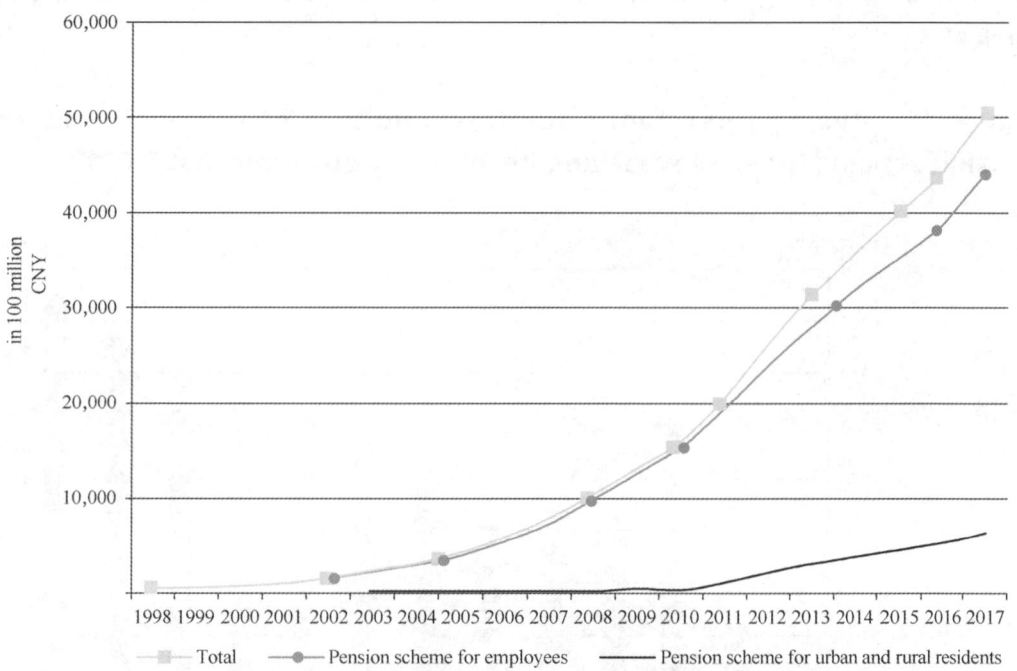

Source: NBS, 2018 (*China Statistical Yearbook* 2018).

Fifth, similar to the pension insurance scheme, the reform and institutionalization of the health insurance system have exerted positive influence on China's economic development. Such positive effects manifest themselves mainly in the following aspects.

FIRST IMPACT: **China's health insurance system has guaranteed more equitable medical care for all citizens, neutralized the respective organizational and cost burden for enterprises and conformed to the reform of the state-owned enterprises and the establishment of the market economy.** Prior to its reform, free medical care was only accessible to urban workers and their family members,

FOURTH IMPACT: **The continuous growth of retirees' pensions[1] has fostered pensioners' consumer confidence and further enhanced private households' consumption.** Pension payments increased at the growth rate broadly stipulated by the central Government, on average, by 10 per cent from 2005 to 2015, standing at 6.5 per cent in 2016 and 5.5 per cent in 2017. Here, the per capita fund expenditure (total annual fund expenditure divided by end-of-the-year number of pensioners) is used to estimate the growth of pensions (see figure 11). The substantially increased pensions directly enhanced the consumption capacity and confidence of pensioners, including that of their family members, who could spend more of their income on own-consumption purposes (rather than reserving parts of their income for their older parents).

Figure 11 Average per capita fund expenditure of the basic old-age pension scheme for employees and its annual growth rate, 2005-2017

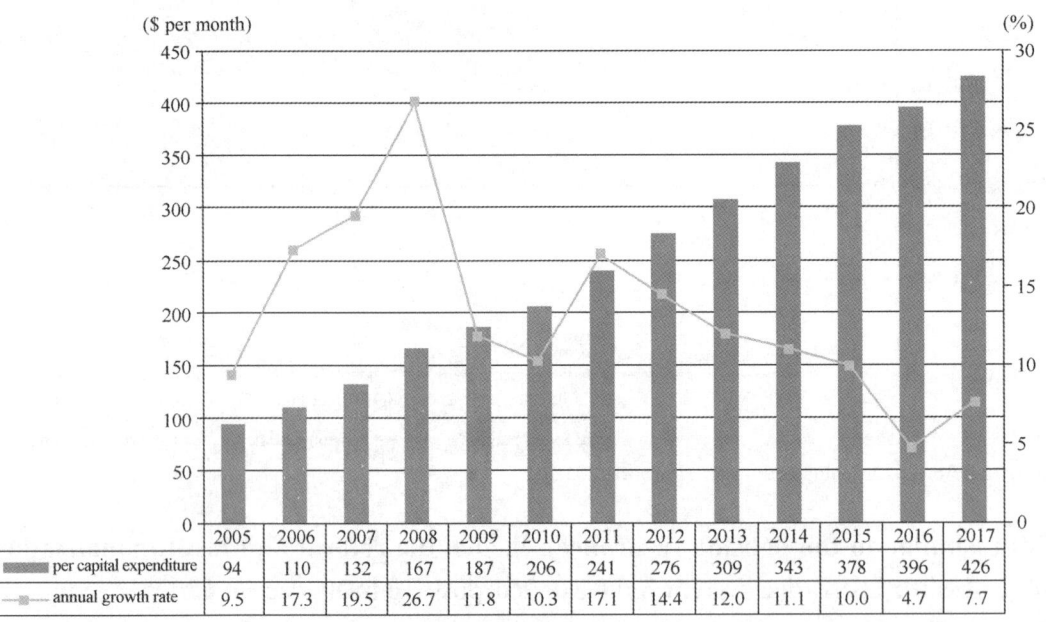

	2005	2006	2007	2008	2009	2010	2011	2012	2013	2014	2015	2016	2017
per capital expenditure	94	110	132	167	187	206	241	276	309	343	378	396	426
annual growth rate	9.5	17.3	19.5	26.7	11.8	10.3	17.1	14.4	12.0	11.1	10.0	4.7	7.7

Source: NBS, 2018 (China Statistical Yearbook 2018).

---

[1] The continuous growth of pension for retirees in China for the past 15 years is a compensatory measure for a given period of time to the earlier generation of retirees receiving a relatively low level of pension. It has no direct correlation with the average social wage and the Consumer Price Index. China plans to introduce mechanism for indexation of pensions in payment.

The argument here must not be misunderstood: It is the false organizational set-up of the pension system that was removed from enterprises' obligations and helped them later to act successfully under market conditions-it was by no means the abolishment of social pensions. To the contrary, it can be argued that the continued payment of pensions, from financially broader-based solidarity financing, fostered not only pensioners' support of the reforms but also that of their children and grandchildren.

SECOND IMPACT: Social pooling[1] of the pension system facilitated the free flow of labour. A reform of the pension system for enterprise workers in 1991 turned the system into one jointly funded by the State, enterprises and individuals. The second effect is a direct corollary to the first impact: A market economy with enterprises pursuing their operations in a competitive environment must be able to attract the number and quality of labour needed for their endeavours. This, in turn, requires that labour is free to move. Under such conditions, guaranteeing pensions in old age to each individual worker requires a system that is independent of and overarching the enterprises (and other institutions) and that takes on all necessary administrative chores. This way, not only will enterprises' transaction costs be minimized but also those of the society at large (Coase, 1937).

THIRD IMPACT: The establishment of a common basic pension system for urban and rural residents further enhanced reform acceptance, consumption capacity and confidence. In 2009, China acknowledged the (common) basic rights of rural older persons and non-salaried urban residents alike. Considering the respective international debate, this reform, which achieved almost universal pension coverage, reflected a modern approach consistent with labour market developments. It was an expression of a social policy of "leaving no one behind" and fully in line with China's principle of achieving shared growth and with ILO Social Protection Floors Recommendation, 2012 (No. 202). Despite its moderate payments, the system, funded mainly through fiscal inputs and supplemented by individual contributions from insured people, has directly improved the welfare of urban and rural seniors who were previously not covered by any pension scheme. And it has thus instantly strengthened the current consumption capacity of this population group and enhanced their consumption confidence for the future.

---

[1] China's social pooling, which includes pooling in terms of finance, organization and management, is a comparative term to the pooling by work units during the planned economy.

professional agencies, nearly covers the entire population, thus creating widely equal conditions for institutions and enterprises operating in the market. At the same time, social assistance and social welfare services have been transformed from government-exclusively-arranged to socialized schemes with responsibilities shared by the Government, society and individuals. Only older persons and children who had no work unit or people to depend on were entitled to social assistance and social welfare services in the era of the planned economy; after the reform, social assistance and social welfare services became universally accessible, depending on need (Zheng, 2018b).

Fourth, the reform and institutionalization of the public pension is one of the numerous contributors to China's economic growth. Owing to complicated channels of influence, we can hardly tell the share of each contributing factor, yet it can be roughly demonstrated through the following aspects.

FIRST IMPACT: **The transformation of the public pension system was necessary and in conformity with the reform of state-owned enterprises; the very existence of the system, before and after its reform, forced political and enterprise-level management to seek solutions that maintained pensioners' rights during the process of state-owned enterprise marketization, which, in turn, bolstered acceptance of the reforms by a large stratum of society.**

In China, enterprises' obligation to provide pensions stemmed from the Opinions on the Reform of State-Owned Enterprises Financial Systems (Draft) issued by the Ministry of Finance, which came into effect in 1969 and stipulated that enterprises were duty bound to provide pensions to their retirees. During the mid-1980s, a number of state-owned enterprises were suffering extensive deficits, which was causing millions of full or partial pension payment defaults. This eased the Government's decision to reform the pension system more fundamentally, in conjunction with the economic reform process. Thus, when the reform of the state-owned enterprises kicked off, China turned to the blueprint of a social pooling-based pension system (as opposed to an enterprise-based system), for which international experience was available and which guaranteed pensioners their entitlements. This neutralized the pension-specific organizational and financial burden among enterprises (made all enterprises equally independent of their respective number of pensioners), thereby strengthening the economic vitality, especially of the hitherto disadvantaged enterprises and supporting China's economy to get out of its rigid productivity trough.

In 2016, China initiated another round of reforming state-owned enterprises. This time, the goal is to establish modern corporate governance structures as well as to reduce overcapacities in the steel, coal and other industries. This is in line with the Government's priority of pollution control and environmental protection so as to provide people with good environment, build a beautiful and healthy China and tackle global climate change. These envisaged steps, however, possibly comprise millions of job cuts in the state-owned enterprises, which calls for proper training and retraining of unemployed workers as well as due replacement of earlier remuneration through adequate compensation.

Third, the shift from work unit-based welfare provisions to a social security system has created a beneficial room for the reform and development of the market economy. This shift was important. When social security is largely organized at the enterprise level, as was the case under the planned economy, its effective functioning depends on the existence of the enterprise or the institution carrying out the social security function. This, however, contradicts the fundamental requirement in market economies that enterprises must be able to go bankrupt due to economic and financial reasons. In theory, re-organizing enterprises (including their closure) can also be achieved under the conditions of a planned economy (including re-organization of enterprise-based social security) but, in comparison to socially bolstered market solutions, only at the expense of enormous efficiency losses.

Moreover, the institutional setting based on work units (*danwei*) not only limits worker flexibility within the different work units but also impedes the inter-institutional free flow of the labour force and thus negatively affects the possibilities of human resource optimization in the production process. It burdens the work units with onerous tasks of welfare provision, reducing their capacities to adapt to and compete in markets or society.

It was, therefore, a crucial move of China's social security reform to make social security organizationally independent of enterprises and public institutions (employers).[1] After 30 years of effort, this target has largely been attained. Indeed, the reformed social security system, government-led, funded by employers and employees, and widely operated by

---

[1] Of course, enterprises and public institutions continue to be important stakeholders under the reformed social security system: they must collect and transfer contributions (and income tax) from their employees as well as provide expertise, where appropriate, in terms of organizational issues, technology and the like. The incorporation into reformed social security of enterprises' and institutions' economic and other interests is, however, a different topic (although important).

The Government was aware that frictions and hardship could not be fully avoided in this process, for example, the livelihoods of the unemployed workers would be left unprotected. Therefore, as a measure to bolster such detrimental social developments, the State Council issued a decree in 1986 entitled, Interim Provisions on Unemployment Insurance for the State-Owned Enterprises Workers. It aimed to establish a national unemployment insurance system. In terms of social institution design, the decree marked the beginning of a new era of social insurance compatible with market economy requirements (ILO NATLEX-China, undated). Thanks to the unemployment insurance, basic livelihoods of the unemployed workers of state-owned enterprises were guaranteed, at modest levels, for some time. A buffer period was granted to the workers for re-entering the labour market.

Starting in 1998, the second round of reform aimed at reducing the number of redundant workers, unloading all such burdens from state-owned enterprises that were not related to their immediate business purposes so that they could be more easily engaged in market competition. It was triggered by the experience that many state-owned enterprises turned out to be overly burdened with redundant (but still paid) workers, often at large scale, and weighty social obligations, resulting in enterprises' poor performance in terms of production, profitability and vision for further development. At the same time, the reform also aimed to further improve the social security system to alleviate the long-term social obligations of the state-owned enterprises. The theoretical market-radical option to release workers without at least temporary financial support was unacceptable. If this approach had been adopted, the unemployed workers would have had dire difficulties in adapting to the changes, the spirit of social contract would have been tarnished and the society would have suffered turbulences.

Thus, in addition to the pension scheme, social assistance and public services, the Government set up a basic livelihood guarantee scheme with salient Chinese features, specifically targeted at supporting the laid-off workers of state-owned enterprises. The laid-off workers were to register at re-employment service centres to receive (for a maximum period of three years) a living allowance provided by the basic livelihood guarantee fund, which was co-financed by the Government, the unemployment insurance fund as well as the state-owned enterprises, each of them contributing one third to the fund. From 1998 to 2003, the basic livelihood guarantee scheme not only covered a basic livelihood for more than 30 million laid-off workers but also facilitated, as intended, the effective downsizing of the overall workforce of the state-owned enterprises and helped them to integrate fast into the new market conditions, thereby promoting sustained and rapid economic growth (Lee, 2005).

Second, the establishment of the unemployment insurance (1986) and the basic livelihood guarantee scheme for laid-off workers paved the way for the reform of the labour contracting system and the marketization of the state-owned enterprises. Main addressees of China's far-reaching economic reform were, and still are, the state-owned enterprises, which are at the core of the economy. Only by letting these enterprises become participants in the market in a real sense were they enabled to compete with the thriving private enterprises. This required the flexibility of employment arrangements that were based on labour contracts with permanent tenure by allowing both employers and employees to conclude and terminate contracts (called "two-way selection"[1]) and thus the incorporation of state-owned enterprise workers in the general labour market. The Government was, however, aware that this new pattern could easily put workers in a disadvantageous position. Unemployment insurance and the basic livelihood guarantee scheme for laid-off workers were intended to bolster possible economic hardship of unemployed andlaid-off workers-both schemes took a serving position to facilitate the reform of the state-owned enterprises.

It is against this institutional social security background that China carried out two rounds of reforms in the state-owned enterprises. The establishment of social protection mechanisms contributed to buffering the effects of the economic reform process.

The first round took place in the 1980s, during which the state-owned enterprises were moved from their operations within the highly centralized planned economy to competitive market conditions. Those state-owned enterprises that did not perform were allowed to go bankrupt, with the new labour contracting system accommodating this policy. These measures helped to invigorate the state-owned enterprises and the labour market and paved the way for optimizing human resource allocation and improving labour productivity.

---

[1] The term "two-way selection" stipulates the autonomy of workers and employers in both job choice and hiring, which is a radical shift from the directed employment and quota hiring system of the past. This new contractual pattern accommodates China's market-oriented economic reforms. While it put labour rights at severe risk, the reform move called for workers' protection through a sound social security system. This is akin to the flexicurity concept based on easier hiring and firing coupled with sound social protection for the unemployed that had been in vogue in the international debates of the 1990s and 2000s. To what extent China's practice differs from, for example, the European realization is open to further socio-historical research(See also Auer, 2010).

3.1.3 The contribution of social security to China's economic growth

This section demonstrates that China's social security system achieved and maintained positive relationships and joint developments with the country's economic development. China's increasingly full-fledged social security system, with its rising benefits, has contributed to creating stability for the economic reform and societal transformation process (Zheng, 2018a).

Increasing levels of social security benefits have directly boosted the incomes of urban and rural residents and have enhanced their purchasing power and their propensity and capacity to consume, thereby stimulating aggregate consumption. On this basis, the reform and development of China's social security system has contributed to upholding social justice and attaining comprehensive national development beyond a narrower economic meaning. In detail, the contributions of social security towards this process manifested themselves in the following aspects of tangible policy and reform over the past three decades.

First, the demand effects of the rapid progress in social security created additional overall growth. The constantly improving (towards being fully developed) social security system has stimulated urban and rural residents' propensity and capacity to consume. The growing pensions and other benefits, such as social assistance, are stimulating consumption. Because the present social security system nearly covers the entire population and benefits continue to grow, private household consumption shows enormous spikes: National commodity consumption surpassed CNY10 trillion in 2008 and CNY20 trillion in 2012, and the total retail sales of consumer goods exceeded CNY36.6 trillion in 2017(NBS, 2018). The contribution of final consumption (private household consumption plus state consumption) to the country's economic growth grew from 48.8 per cent in 2014 to 64.6 per cent in 2016, which exceeds the contribution of investment by 22.4 percentage points.[1]

Consumption has thus evolved into the major driver of China's economic growth, which to a large extent can be attributed to the primary achievement of a social security system of close to universal coverage.

---

[1] See *People's Daily*: "Consumption remains the 'primary engine' of economic growth", 22 July 2017, Overseas edition (in Chinese).

Fifth, defects in the labour markets, income distribution and social security system have led to some college graduates having difficulty finding jobs and has discouraged undeveloped areas and low-income families from investing in education.

Therefore, improvements are required in the following aspects:

First, increase government inputs to education. Faced with the growing demand of urban and rural residents for education, the Government needs to increase its input and further raise its budget for expenditure on education. It should deepen the reform of the education system, develop private education in a regulated and orderly manner to control its excesses and ensure the system follows the standards of public education to encourage more social resources flow into the education sector. In addition, by creating a level playing field, China can improve the income distribution, raise the return on investment in human resources and inspire citizens to invest personally in education.

Second, extend the length of free education and intensify efforts to help children in underdeveloped areas and impoverished families. It would be wise to prolong free education to 12 years. To realize the goal that the education system covers all children of school age, incorporate the senior high school education into free education and ensure that children aged 4-6 years have universal access to free preschool education. As well, governments should intensify financial support for underdeveloped rural areas and western regions and remote and poverty-stricken areas, improve education infrastructure and schooling conditions and ensure education quality.

Third, step up the development of vocational education and optimize the structure of the education system. China needs to create a social atmosphere conducive to the development of vocational education. It can draw on lessons from international experience and strengthen international cooperation with countries with well-established systems of vocational training (Germany, for example) for a deeper understanding of the requisites for a functional system of vocational education. It is imperative to increase the proportion of secondary-school students receiving vocational education and cultivate hundreds of millions of high-quality workers equipped with skills. Current policy priorities should accelerate the cultivation of professional and technical personnel who are needed across all sectors of the economy.

The Government has significantly enhanced the education levels and working skills of nationals through various means, including literacy classes, night school and vocational training. According to data from the United Nations Educational, Science and Cultural Organization, the illiteracy rate nationwide dropped from 39 per cent in 1982 to 3 per cent in 2010.[1] The average length of schooling of the workforce nationwide grew from 6.1 years in 1985 to 10 years in 2016, while that of rural workers rose from 5.6 years to 8.5 years and urban workers increased from 7.8 years to 11.2 years.(China Centre for Human Capital and Labour Market Research, 2018). China's fiscal expenditure on education increased from CNY61.8 billion ($11.61 billion) in 1991 to CNY3.421 trillion ($506.65 billion) in 2017 (MOF, MOE and NBS, 2018); its share in GDP rose from less than 3 per cent in 1991 to nearly 4.3 per cent in 2015 and to more than 4 per cent in recent years (MOE, 1992 through 2017).

Problems and recommendations

Although China's education system has developed greatly and has a positive role in economic growth, it is still confronted with many problems:

First, there is still a big gap between China and developed countries in terms of per capita average length of schooling and the supply of the education benefits to pre-primary education for children aged 3 to 6 years. Upper secondary education remains inadequate.

Second, the allocation of resources on education is uneven. There are distinct gaps between urban and rural areas, among regions and among schools, hindering the improvement of labour quality in resource-scarce regions and aggravating the imbalance of economic development among regions.

Third, compulsory education in some areas fails to meet the standard. The quality of education needs to be improved, and the fairness of the elementary education is under question.

Fourth, too little importance is attached to vocational education. This has resulted in a shortage of high-skilled industrial workers and is hampering product quality and technological progress.

---

[1] See http://data.uis.unesco.org (accessed 10 Oct. 2018).

education was predominant, funded by the central and local governments and the rural collective economy with the feature of public benefits. Despite its universal character, the education system was underdeveloped and only a few people had access to higher education.

II. During the last decade of the twentieth century, as state welfare was curtailed, free education for all was reformed. The education system became financially hybrid-funded by multiple parties. While compulsory education would continue to be free of charge, completely funded by the central and local governments, moderate fees were charged for higher and secondary education. The non-government sector was allowed to invest in and run various types of education institutions. In 1992, the Government made clear that education has a leading role for national economic growth but underlined the importance of not relying excessively on state investment. As a result, higher education enrolment and the number of tuition-charged and privately run schools surged, and the education system generally experienced rapid development. In the area of senior high school education, secondary vocational education and higher education, public schools were still predominant, with the bulk of inputs coming from the central and local governments. During this period, the total educational investment increased substantially, yet the share of fiscal expenditure on education declined.

III. Since the beginning of the twenty-first century, the supporting system for disadvantaged groups has improved progressively. In 2001, the policy of two exemptions and one subsidy was introduced. Students from urban and rural areas are exempted from tuition and other fees during the period of compulsory education, free textbooks are provided to rural and urban students with financial difficulties, a living allowance is offered to boarding students from impoverished families and a nutrition improvement programme is available. In terms of higher education, scholarships, student loans, tuition and loan compensation, subsidies for persons in financial difficulties, meal allowances and tuition waivers have been enhanced to ensure that students with financial difficulties can access a university education. In high schools, protection measures centring on a national grant have been adopted, with tuition waivers as a supplementary measure. As for secondary vocational education, policies centring on tuition waivers and national grants have been put in place. And special education for children with disabilities has been strengthened.

is that benefit assessment and delivery (as well as the exit rules for beneficiaries) are administratively easier to handle than a system based on a standard expenditure basket. However, the advantage of an expenditure-based basket is that, by principle, it can be better targeted to the beneficiary's needs; the indexation of benefits on the basis of the Consumer Price Index is more logical than in an income-focused system because it ensures that benefits maintain their real value over time. Variance of exclusionary and inclusionary targeting errors correlates highly with the quality and density of administration.

In any case, urgent and consistent progress must be made to complete China's overall social security system, which is increasingly based on social insurance principles (pensions and health care), with a sound basic layer comprising the subsistence allowance and other social assistance schemes.

Third, establish system-immanent incentive mechanisms for employment and entrepreneurship. To address the challenge of disincentives to labour market participation under the current system, rules should be established to allow for the combination of benefits and additional labour income. Generally, such a system requires a good administration that not only manages benefits and beneficiaries' social needs in a fair way but also helps beneficiaries with working capacities to (re-)enter the labour market. International experience shows that implementation of such a system requires smooth cooperation between local tax offices and social assistance offices.

Education benefits

Evolution of education benefits

Education is the foundation for people to establish themselves in society and is also the cornerstone of a nation's development (Zheng, 2004a). Since 1949, China has endeavoured to popularize primary education and develop secondary and higher education. Generally, the evolution of education benefits in China can be divided into three stages:

I. In the pre-1980s, education was free for all and compatible with the planned economy. In the urban area, there was primary education, higher education and skills training for workers, all falling within the category of public benefits. Due to public ownership, schools organized by enterprises and public institutions were closely tied to state finance, essentially within the realm of public benefits. In the rural areas, elementary

Problems and solutions

Since its implementation, the subsistence allowance scheme has contributed to guaranteeing a basic livelihood of persons who are poor, maintaining social stability and supporting economic development. Yet, defects remain in the current system.

First, the low level of protection and the absence of a standardized indexation mechanism have eroded the fundamental rights to basic income security of some impoverished beneficiaries of the scheme.

Second, the incentive for beneficiaries with work capacities to seek jobs or to start a new business is inadequate because benefits from the subsistence allowance scheme are deducted by the full amount of the beneficiary's earned income.

Third, the mechanism for managing and running the system needs to be reformed. Effective means tests and specialized agencies are not well established, often resulting in benefit frauds. Moreover, corruption at the local level is a major issue, and quite often the already-limited allowances cannot reach the target groups, particularly in remote areas. These defects harm the sound development of the *dibao* system as well as the social assistance system as a whole.

Hence, the system needs the following improvements:

First, further advance the urban-rural integration of the subsistence allowance scheme. The urban-rural division still exists and has led to an unfair division of rights and entitlements between the rural and urban beneficiaries. A nationally unified scheme should be established to ensure that fair support to persons who are poor can be guaranteed within the same region and according to the same rules.

Second, improve the financial, administrative and methodological means for setting the minimum living standard for the allowance and for targeting qualifying beneficiaries. The current system is means tested, based on a person's income. A change should be considered towards measuring a person's or household's needs on the basis of a standardized basket of goods and services that would be judged as guaranteeing a modest standard of living.

International experience shows that the advantage of income-based poverty measurement assistance programmes (see table 3). It has become a core scheme within the whole social security system. According to the *Statistical Bulletin on Civil Affairs Development* and the *Statistical Bulletin on Social Service Development* issued by the Ministry of Civil Affairs (various years), the number of urban and rural residents receiving the subsistence allowance was around 7 million in 2000, increasing to more than 66 million and then more than 53 million in 2015 and 2017, respectively. The decline in 2017 indicates that, after experiencing growth for a certain period, the number of impoverished individuals who received the benefit is decreasing due to the decrease in poverty incidence.

Table 3   Subsistence allowance scheme, 2000-2017

Year	Urban					Rural				
	Number of beneficiaries (10,000 persons)	Average monthly standard (per person)		Financial expenditure (hundred million)		Number of beneficiaries (10,000 persons)	Average monthly standard (per person)		Fiscal expenditure (hundred million)	
		CNY	$	CNY	$		CNY	$	CNY	$
	(1)	(2)	(3)	(4)	(5)	(6)	(7)	(8)	(9)	(10)
2000	402.6	157.0	19.0	27.2	3.3	300.2				
2001	1,170.7	147.0	17.8	54.2	6.5	306.8				
2002	2,064.7	148.0	17.9	108.7	13.1	407.8				
2003	2,246.8	149.0	18.0	151.0	18.2	367.1				
2004	2,205.0	152.0	18.4	172.7	20.9	488.0				
2005	2,234.2	156.0	19.0	191.9	23.4	825.0	76.0	9.3		
2006	2,240.1	169.6	21.3	224.2	28.1	1,593.1	70.9	8.9		
2007	2,272.1	182.4	24.0	277.4	36.5	3,566.3	70.0	9.2	109.1	14.4
2008	2,334.8	205.3	29.6	393.4	56.6	4,305.5	82.3	11.9	228.7	32.9
2009	2,345.6	227.8	33.4	482.1	70.6	4,760.0	100.8	14.8	363.0	53.1
2010	2,310.5	251.2	37.1	524.7	77.5	5,214.0	117.0	17.3	445.0	65.7
2011	2,276.8	287.6	44.5	659.9	102.2	5,305.7	143.2	22.2	667.7	103.4
2012	2,143.5	330.1	52.3	674.3	106.8	5,344.5	172.3	27.3	718.0	113.7
2013	2,064.2	373.3	60.3	756.7	122.2	5,388.0	202.8	32.8	866.9	140.0
2014	1,877.0	410.5	66.8	721.7	117.5	5,207.2	231.4	37.7	870.3	141.7
2015	1,701.1	451.1	72.4	719.3	115.5	4,903.6	264.8	42.5	931.5	149.6
2016	1,479.9	494.6	74.5	687.9	103.6	4,576.5	312.0	47.0	1,014.5	152.7
2017	1,261.0	540.6	80.1	640.5	94.9	4,045.2	358.4	53.1	1,051.8	155.8

Source: MCA, 2000 to 2017 (*Statistical Bulletin on Civil Affairs Development* and *Statistical Bulletin on Social Service Development*).

> **Box 6**
> **Poverty alleviation and development in rural China:**
> **Stronger measures to eliminate poverty**
>
> As the country with the largest impoverished population in the world a few decades ago, China initiated in 1986 a significant poverty alleviation and development campaign in rural areas, targeting impoverished individuals and regions with a high prevalence of poverty. Further reforms followed, including the 8-7 National Plan for Poverty Reduction (1994),[1] the National Programme for Rural Poverty Alleviation (2001-2010) and the National Programme for Rural Poverty Alleviation (2011-2020). Since 2015, the State has implemented the strategy of targeted poverty alleviation to eliminate absolute poverty by 2020.
>
> Local governments in poor regions have made poverty elimination one of their important goals. A large quantity of resources has been allocated to poverty-stricken areas through, for example, the central Government's special investment or regional counterpart support. The central Government has also intensified efforts to eradicate poverty and develop contiguous areas of extreme poverty. Calculated on the basis of a wider statistical scope, from 2011 to 2014, expenditures of the central and local governments on poverty alleviation amounted to nearly CNY1.5 trillion ($241 billion).[2]

In 2014, the State Council issued the Interim Regulations on Social Assistance,which established a comprehensive social assistance system encompassingmedical, education, housing, employment and temporary assistance. The subsistence allowance, as the bedrock, was incorporated and the policy vestiges of urban-rural division were eradicated. Currently, the subsistence allowance scheme has the largest number of beneficiaries, the largest amount of expenditure and a high level of benefit payments among the social

---

[1] Aimed at lifting 80 million people out of poverty within seven years(1994-2000).
[2] The central Government's funding for coordinated poverty alleviation refers to funding that is diverted to some poor rural areas to directly benefit people in poverty. It involves 33 funds and includes seven categories: the special fund for poverty alleviation, the fund for agricultural production, the fund for education in rural areas, the fund for rural health care, the fund for rural social security, the fund for providing continuing aid to residents relocated to make way for the construction of large and medium-sized reservoirs and the fund from lottery, as well as general transfers. Data concerning local government funding for poverty alleviation are incomplete.

Figure 10   Poverty line and poverty headcount ratio in rural areas, 1998-2017

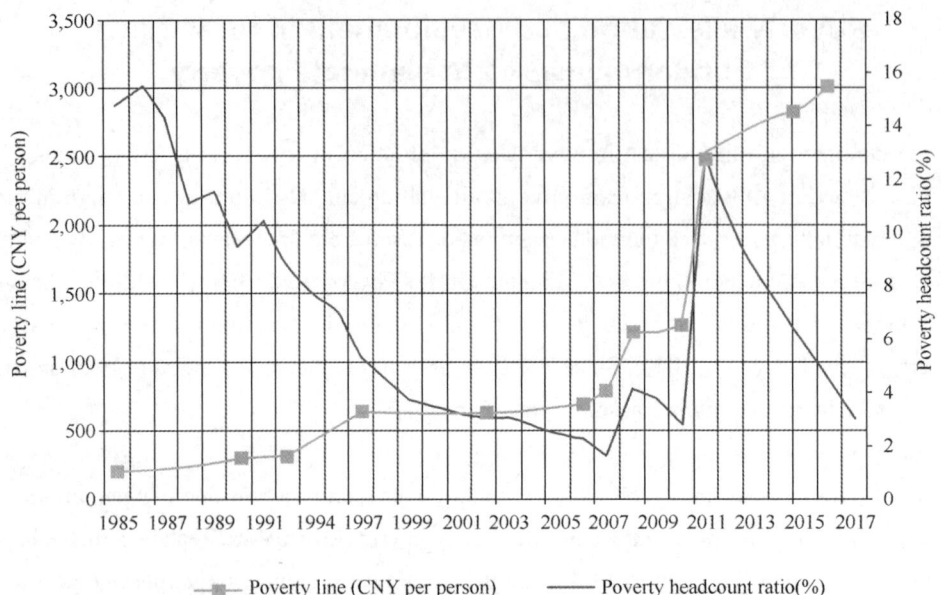

Note: (i) The standard in 1978 is the standard of rural poverty from 1978 to 1999 and is regarded as the standard of absolute poverty in rural areas from 2000 to 2007.
(ii) The standard in 2008 is the standard of low income in rural areas from 2000 to 2007, and is regarded as the standard of poverty in rural areas from 2008 to 2010.
(iii) The standard in 2010 is a newly set standard of poverty alleviation in rural areas.
(iv) Data from 1985 to1999 are provided by Poverty Alleviation Office of the State Council.
(v) Data from 2000 to 2017 are from NBS, 2018 (*China Statistical Yearbook 2018* and *Poverty Monitoring in Rural China*).

More than 30 years of constant poverty alleviation and development in rural areas (see box 6) has brought about rapid economic and social progress in poor areas. It has guaranteed the basic livelihood of rural residents, ameliorated their living conditions, improved education and sanitation for poor individuals, improved the production and living infrastructure in poverty-stricken areas and thus laid foundations for long-term socioeconomic development. At the end of 2010, the rural population living in absolute poverty decreased to nearly 26.9 million (SCIO, 2011). From 1981 to 2012, the number of people who were lifted out of poverty in China accounted for 71.8 per cent of the world's total (CASS and SCPAO, 2016). Despite China's remarkable achievements in eradicating poverty, nearly 16.6 million rural people still lived on income below the current poverty line in 2018 (NBS, 2019).

interim assistance from the central and local governments. Only the widowed seniors and orphaned children in rural areas were supported or given long-term relief by government-run social welfare facilities.

In the mid-1980s and following the introduction of reform to the household contract responsibility system in rural areas, the reform of the economic system in the urban areas was rolled out. The adjustment of the economic structure and the transformation of institutions and mechanisms gave rise to unemployment in the state-owned enterprises. The detachment from work units of welfare and social protection measures resulted in a new group of impoverished persons in urban areas. This was compounded by an increasing number of retirees who failed to receive their full pension on time due to nationwide deficits in pension funds beginning in the mid-1990s. Against the backdrop of mounting social problems, the Shanghai government took the lead in establishing a subsistence allowance scheme for urban residents in June 1993. The whole country soon followed suit. In September 1997, the State Council activated a subsistence allowance scheme for urban residents across the country. In September 1999, the State Council formulated the Provisional Regulations on the Subsistence Allowances for Urban Residents, formally establishing a national scheme for urban residents.

In rural areas and after the implementation of the household contract responsibility system in 1978, the collective economy gradually began to weaken, and the public welfare and hedge against the contingencies of life of rural residents shrank. The Zhejiang provincial government took the lead in implementing the Urban-and-Rural-Integrated Subsistence Allowance system and expanded it to cover all rural residents across the province in 2001. Subsequently, many regions set up a subsistence allowance scheme for rural residents or extended the one for urban residents to rural areas.

In 2007, the State Council decided to fully implement the subsistence allowance scheme in the rural areas. The subsistence allowance scheme has become the fundamental institution in guaranteeing the basic livelihood of citizens across the country.

As shown in figure 10, the poverty line in rural China was raised over recent decades, yet the poverty headcount ratio has been declining. The hike of the poverty headcount ratio after 2010 is linked to the newly set poverty line standard in rural areas.

should be put into the treatment of costly diseases and related health services to cover the respective costs (for rural and urban residents alike), and provide all with stable expectations about health care services.

Fifth, push forward the reform of the provider payment mechanism of health insurance by introducing mixed forms of payment (global budgeting, capitation payment plus case-based payment). It is advisable to develop case-based payment and payment by diagnosis-related groups. Also, consultation and coordination mechanisms must be implemented, including all stakeholders to the health system [the insured members, contributors and patients, health service providers (hospitals and medical associations), government and medical industry]. This aims at more rational and effective pricing of the medical services and the pharmaceuticals to be paid by health insurance to promote the standardization of medical care and reduce the resource waste in health insurance and relevant services, enabling the limited resources to have a greater role and facilitating sustainable development of the medical services industry. In this context, it is important to further develop the health insurance administration into a modern agency structure that achieves research and knowledge supremacy in all health system respects (including legal, organizational and statistical data, to which all other stakeholders must have access), such that health insurance members' interests are adequately represented within the health system.

Subsistence allowance

Evolution of the subsistence allowance

Under the highly centralized planned economy system built up after 1949, all citizens were registered with a certain organization (enterprises and public institutions in urban areas and collective economic organizations in rural areas), which was not only the organizer of production and public services but also the provider of social welfare and protection against risk. Based on that system, the State upheld the principle of "self-rescue through production, mutual help among civilians, while supplemented by necessary aid of the government"[1] and the principle of help the starving people but not the poor. Guided by these principles, the State assumed disaster relief and emergency response as its major responsibilities while also providing long-term aid for individuals living in extreme difficulties. People living in poverty mainly relied on assistance from their work unit (including collective economic organizations in rural areas) and occasionally received

---

[1] This principle was established at the Second National Conference on Civil Affairs in 1953.

First, close the individual health accounts and transform them into effective social insurance, based on the technical principles of mutual-help financing. When effectively organized in the interests of their members and if nested into a transparent overall health system, health insurance is a societal institution with a high level of redistribution-from the healthy to the sick, the high-income earners to the lower-income earners, those working at safe workplaces to those at health-risk exposed workplaces (to name a few). Individual health accounts for workers severely undermines this function. The required transformation is to be carefully prepared by deepening the reform, including research.

Second, speed up the integration of the schemes for employees and residents until the whole population is covered with a unified health insurance system. This will promote fairness of the system as well as improve its operational efficiency. The transformation to social security financing must be paralleled by widening the regional organization from the currently mainly county-based pooling at the provincial level (as stipulated by the Social Insurance Law). This is the only realistic option to reduce the considerable gaps in protection levels between health insurance members in different counties (as currently observed). Also, efforts should be undertaken to raise the protection level provided by the health insurance for rural residents. This would not only fulfil the requirement of increasing social fairness but also further elevate medical consumption (with positive implications for life expectancy) and the consumption confidence of the society more generally. The Government's subsidization of the system as well as the portion of individual contributions should be further increased.

Third, guide retired workers to pay their contributions to health insurance. The principle of "old rules apply to older persons and new rules to the newcomers" (similar to a grandfather clause) should be adhered to. The relevant laws should be amended to provide that newly retired people should contribute to health insurance. A feasible option is to raise the pension for the retirees, as appropriate, in exchange for their contribution payments. Such reform helps to adapt to population ageing, enrich health insurance revenue and ensure equal obligations for contributions as well as equal health insurance benefits among retired workers and other older persons covered by the scheme for residents.

Fourth, extend protection coverage of the health insurance to serious and chronic diseases (an imperative). On condition of increasing revenue collected, more resources

Problems and solutions

The major problems in China's health insurance are fourfold:

First, the health insurance for employees adopts a financial model of combining social pooling with individual accounts similar to the pension scheme for employees. Employees contribute 2 per cent of their gross wage payments to individual accounts; and 30 per cent of the employer's contribution (employer's contribution is equal to 6 per cent of gross payroll) is allocated to the individual account (equivalent to an implicit contribution rate of 1.8 per cent). The design of individual accounts follows neither private insurance principles nor social security principles of risk pooling. Individual accounts are nothing but private individual savings, which, in the case of costly or severe diseases, normally lack sufficient reserves. Consequently, the system fails to sufficiently protect the insured members when its support is mostly needed. In other words, core principles of organized mutual help are disregarded, and thus the sustainable development of the health insurance system is put at severe risk.

Second, the protection level of the health insurance for rural residents remains low. Health insurance for chronic and other costly diseases is evidently inadequate. With the urban-rural divided and the regional segmented system, rural-to-urban migrant workers are in a dilemma because their place of household registration differs from their place of work. They are theoretically covered by the rural residents' scheme, yet their health insurance rights are easily jeopardized because they do not have access to health insurance where they actually live and work.

Third, the reform of the pharmaceutical and health care system (governance structure of public hospitals, pharmaceutical distribution system and market-oriented pricing of pharmaceuticals) is lagging, giving rise to problems of excessive medical treatment, overinflated pharmaceutical prices and corruption. Consequently, health insurance funds are severely wasted, whereas coverage for severe and chronic diseases is insufficient. The efficiency of resource utilization needs to be improved.

Fourth, the current policy requiring no health insurance contribution from retired workers, coupled by the accelerated population ageing, is presenting mounting challenges to the sustainability of the health insurance system.

Therefore, China needs to deepen social health insurance reform in the following respects:

(see figure 9). Since the introduction of the health insurance, the utilization rate of medical services by middle- and low-income groups, particularly in rural areas, has continued to rise.[1] Meanwhile, the out-of-pocket expenditure as a share of national health expenditure has decreased, from 46.4 per cent in 1995 to 31.99 per cent in 2014.[2] These improvements are partially related to the fact that the per capita fund expenditure for employees increased from CNY329 ($39.72) in 2000 at the onset to CNY3122 ($462.4) in 2017, while for rural and urban residents it increased from CNY33 ($3.99) in 2004 to CNY 567 ($83.97)in 2017.

In March 2018, the Government set up the National Healthcare Security Administration. The health protection duties that used to be dispersedly carried out by the Ministry of Human Resources and Social Security, the National Health and Family Planning Commission[3] and the Ministry of Civil Affairs were transferred to this new administration, indicating that the central Government will promote universal health protection in a stronger way.

Figure 9 Per capita fund expenditure of the health insurance and its changes, 2000-2017

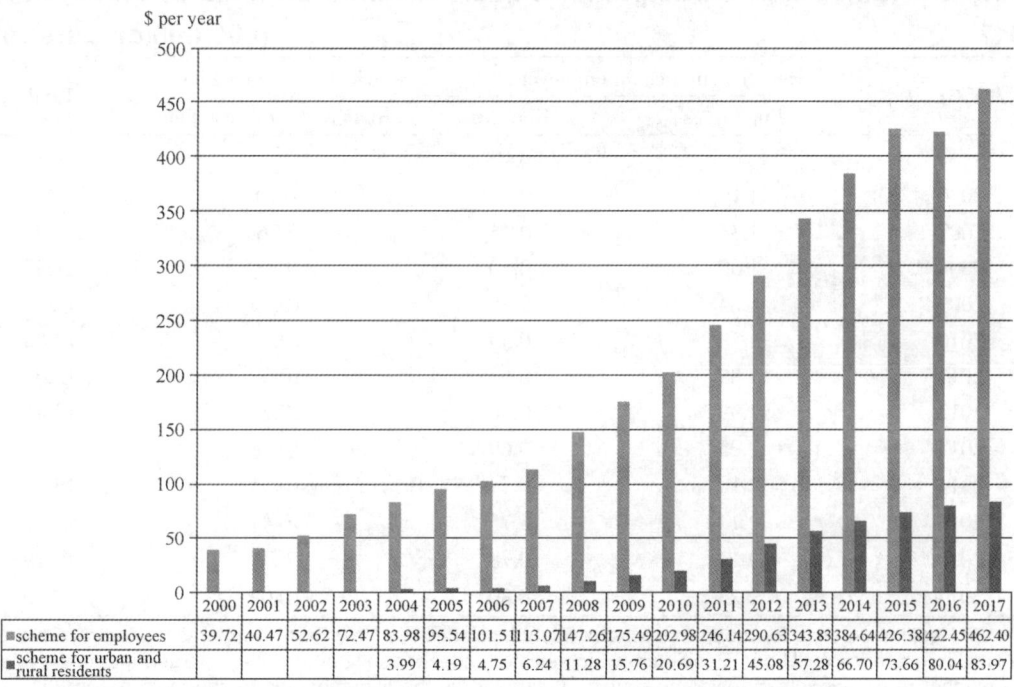

Note: Per capita fund expenditure = total annual fund expenditure / end-of-the-year number of participants.
Source: NBS, various years; MHRSS, various years; NHFPC, various years; MOH, various years.

---

[1] See NHFPC, various years (*China Statistical Yearbook of Health and Family Planning*).
[2] See https://data.worldbank.org/indicator/SH.XPD.OOPC.CH.ZS (accessed 10 Oct. 2018).
[3] The National Health and Family Planning Commission was created from the former Ministry of Health and National Population and Family Planning Commission in 2013. In March 2018, this ministry was dissolved and its functions were integrated into the new agency called the National Health Commission, aiming to promote the Healthy China Initiative and ensure the delivery of comprehensive health services for the Chinese people.

In 2003, China began to pilot the health insurance for rural residents. In 2007, the system was extended to cover urban residents who were non-salaried workers.

As of now, China has established a universal health insurance system that consists of a scheme for employees and a scheme for urban and rural residents and other non-salaried citizens. In 2000, the number of people enrolled in health insurance was (only) 40 million (excluding those who remained in the free health care system). This number climbed to 320 million in 2005, nearly 1.3 billion in 2010 and more than 1.3 billion in 2017 (MHRSS,various years;NHFPC, various years). More than 95 per cent of China's population (94 per cent for the urban population and 97 per cent for the rural population) is covered by one of the health insurance schemes, almost achieving the intended goal of near universal health coverage under the contributory insurance system (see table 2).

Table 2   Numbers of participants in basic health insurance in China, 2006-2017   (100 million persons)

Year	Health insurance for employees		Health insurance for urban and rural residents	Total
	Employees	Retirees		
	(1)	(2)	(3)	(4)
2006	1.16	0.42	4.10	5.68
2007	1.34	0.46	7.26	9.06
2008	1.50	0.50	9.33	11.33
2009	1.64	0.55	10.15	12.34
2010	1.78	0.59	10.31	12.68
2011	1.89	0.63	10.53	13.05
2012	1.99	0.66	10.77	13.42
2013	2.05	0.69	10.98	13.72
2014	2.10	0.73	10.51	13.34
2015	2.14	0.75	10.47	13.36
2016	2.17	0.78	7.24	10.19
2017	2.23	0.80	10.07	13.10

Note: (i) Health insurance for urban and rural residents includes the New Rural Cooperative Medical Care and the Health Insurance for Urban Residents, which existed independently before they merged into one system. The number of participants in residents scheme fluctuated as the two schemes began to merge in 2016.The same applies to relevant tables in subsequent sections of the report.
(ii) The health insurance for employees was established at the end of 1998 and has been carried out across the country since 2000. China's free medical care and labour insurance system are beginning to transform into the health insurance system, covering participants of the former two systems; before 2006, the three systems coexisted.
(iii) The gradual decline of participants in the scheme for urban and rural residents (column 3) since 2014 is because some participants left the residents' scheme for the employees' scheme, and the other reason is that before the integration of rural and urban schemes, some people were simultaneously insured by both schemes. As the two schemes began to merge, the number of the residents' scheme members declined slightly and so did the total number of people covered by basic health insurance (column 4).
Source: NBS,various years; MHRSS, various years; and NHFPC, various years.

In addition to greater coverage, China also ensured that benefit levels would increase steadily intellectuals, flexible retirement approaches should apply. Moreover, being only 15 years, the statutory minimal length of years of contribution payment to become eligible for a pension is overly low. It needs to be extended gradually until it reaches levels of the international peers. This is considered a necessary step to adapt to the constant increasing of average life expectancy and to help people better arrange work and retirement over their life cycle.

Social health insurance

Evolution of social health insurance

The health insurance was established in the early 1950s. Under the Regulations on Labour Insurance of the People's Republic of China in 1951, the State established the labour insurance and health care system for workers in enterprises and subsequently set up the public health care system for employees in government departments and public institutions. These two systems were free of charge. In rural areas, the rural cooperative medical care system was implemented in 1957, counting on the rural collective economy to provide modest primary health care for rural residents.

Under the free health care system, the enterprises bore all the medical costs of their workers and retirees. As with pensions, this led, by the mid-1980s, to unsustainable inequalities in the respective burdens on enterprises, which, inter alia, depended on the health risk structure of their employed labour force as well as their retirees. Enterprises performing poorly in economic terms failed to reimburse the medical expenses of their workers and retirees, and the health cost burden on enterprises was generally mounting.

Experiments with pooling health costs began in the early 1990s, with the pooling of the costs of serious (expensive) diseases.

In 1994, the State Council chose Zhenjiang (in Jiangsu Province) and Jiujiang (in Jiangxi Province) as pilot zones to test reform options for the health insurance. The free medical care for enterprise workers was replaced by the health insurance system (requiring contribution payments by employees and employers).

In 1998, the health insurance system for urban employees was formally established and subsequently expanded to nearly cover all the urban employees.

In rural areas beginning in 1978, the cooperative medical care system, which depended on the collective economy, gradually fell apart due to the implementation of the contract-responsibility system (see section 3.1.4), thereby weakening the medical care of rural residents.

Because China's coverage ratio has reached nearly 100 per cent and benefits cannot be reduced, the only options for pension cost control are reducing the dependency ratio and increasing productivity together with the employment ratio.

Creating employment while improving and maintaining productivity growth is, indeed, the genuine task of entrepreneurs in socialist market economies. Where it does not yet exist, achieving this business culture among entrepreneurs is not easy but can nevertheless be fostered by strict enforcement of enterprises' contribution payment obligations. At the same time, the Government's role is to organize administration and administrative rules of social security, such that enterprises can be empowered to develop their businesses that they had been given by removing their earlier social obligations. At this moment, this also includes the Government recognizing and properly assessing the historical debt[1] of the pension system and resolving the issue of the system-transition costs rather than shifting the solution into the future by (indirectly) loading the debt upon current contributors and individuals. Alternatively, the Government could admit that the earlier embarkment on individual accounts policies was premature and revert respective policies to the classical (possibly partially funded) pay-as-you-go methods. This will enhance the transparency of pension policies but will not change much in terms of financial burden because it has been proven theoretically as well as in political practice that the Government will always be the guarantor of last resort, be this under pay-as-you-go or individual accounts (among others) (Gillion et al., 2000).

Fourth, improve the sustainability of the pension system. Measures include improving the fairness, convenience and transparency of the system to elevate people's recognition of and support for the system; setting up and improving mechanisms to ensure actuarial balance and making the system design and policy adjustment more scientific or evidence based; and increasing the rate of return on pension fund investments as well as improving the operational efficiency of the pension system.

Fifth, increase the statutory retirement age and minimal length of contribution in a gradual approach. The statutory retirement ages at 60 for men and 50 for women (55 for female officials) are low in international comparison. The Government has decided to increase the retirement age in a gradual way, yet no policy has been introduced. A feasible option is to first set a retirement age as a benchmark, and then approach it step by step. For special groups of people, such as manual labourers with heavy workloads, teachers, doctors and other

---

[1] The term "historical debt" here refers to the pension payments to workers who retired before the inception of the new system or, rather, before it was fully operational.

downsize but, rather, counter labour costs through measures that enhance productivity. This orientation is of much more importance than it looks at first glance.

After 30 years of extensive productivity growth pulled very much by (successful) export orientation, China will now enter a likely long phase of intensive productivity growth, especially under the envisaged domestic-oriented demand strategy [in which social (security) system expansion is one core element]. As the following equation shows (see box 5), productivity growth is, in economic categories, the only realistic option to keep pension costs under control in an ageing society (after benefit reductions through entitlement cuts or retirement age increases or other cost-saving measures have been applied).

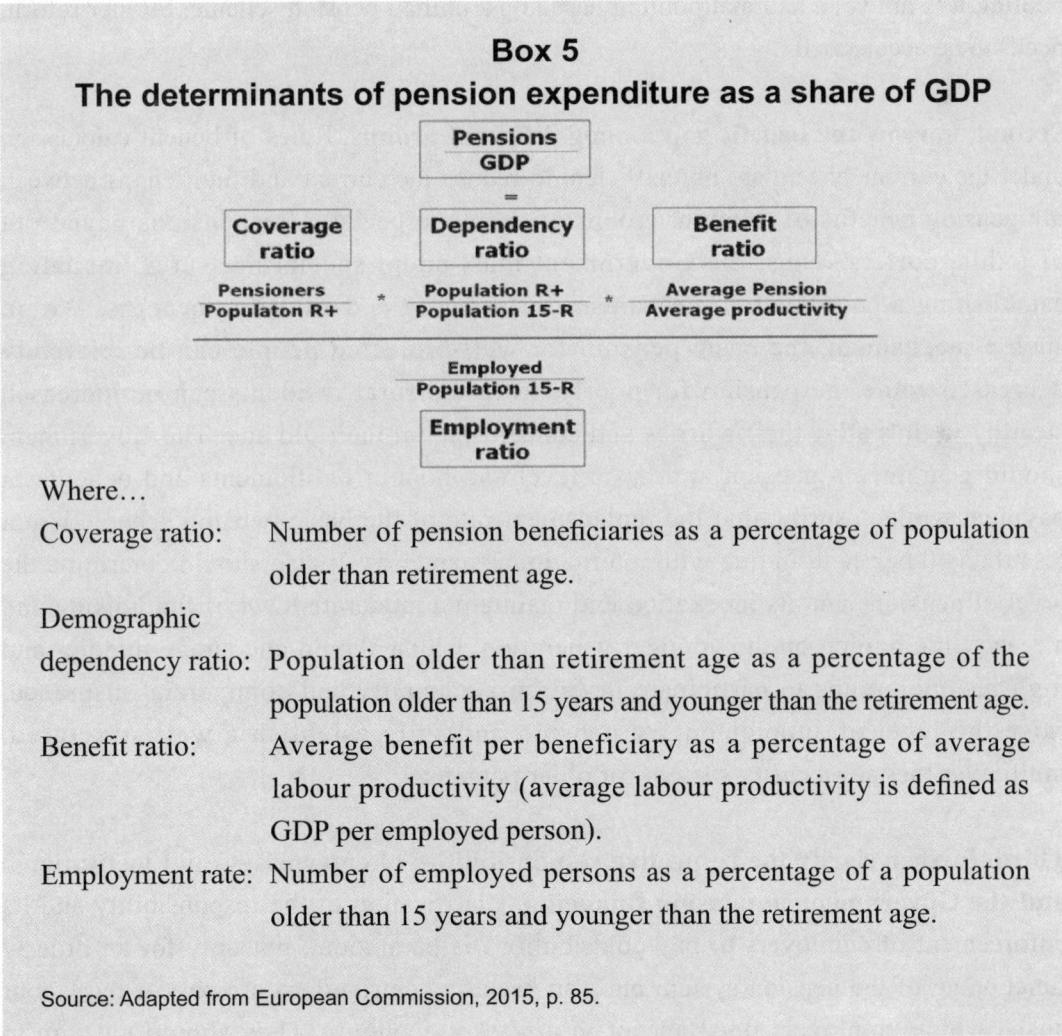

Box 5

The determinants of pension expenditure as a share of GDP

Where...

Coverage ratio: Number of pension beneficiaries as a percentage of population older than retirement age.

Demographic dependency ratio: Population older than retirement age as a percentage of the population older than 15 years and younger than the retirement age.

Benefit ratio: Average benefit per beneficiary as a percentage of average labour productivity (average labour productivity is defined as GDP per employed person).

Employment rate: Number of employed persons as a percentage of a population older than 15 years and younger than the retirement age.

Source: Adapted from European Commission, 2015, p. 85.

defined common contribution base, a common contribution rate as well as a unified rule for benefit calculation and rules governing the pay-out of pension entitlements. This would guarantee fair pension provision for all workers and thus create a level playing field for pension system stakeholders (employers and employees), including in their role as actors in the market economy. In 2017, the Government decided to establish a central adjustment system for basic pension funds of employees to enhance mutual-help and solidarity financing and to balance the payment burden among regions, some of which were in surplus while others were in deficit. Starting from 2018, the adjustment fund draws a portion (at least 3 per cent) from capital pools of provincial regions (provinces, autonomous regions and municipalities) that is then redistributed based on the number of pensioners in each provincial region. This first step is a bridging solution for national pooling-it is not yet a national pooling based on a unified pension scheme. Further reform needs to be accelerated.

Second, narrow the benefit gap among different groups. Rules of benefit calculation under the current system are not sufficient to reduce the current and future gaps between the pension benefits of different groups of people, especially for pensions payed out of public coffers. Thus, the Government must adopt special measures, including establishing a coordination mechanism for defining and adjusting benefits. Within such a mechanism, the basic pension for well-protected people can be relatively decreased while the pension for poorly protected rural residents can be increased steadily to thus allay their worries and concerns about their old age. The Government should guarantee a pension at a basic level and honour entitlements and benefits in payment while ensuring that the replacement rate of the basic pension scheme is not less than 40 per cent, in line with international standards. It also should determine the level of pensions and its indexation and maintain a moderate level of fundraising and a reasonable burden on the younger generation. China should encourage middle- and high-income groups to participate in enterprise annuity and commercial insurance, raise the level of supplementary pension and fully establish a well-structured, multilayer income security system for older persons.

Third, further clarify the respective responsibilities of enterprises (and institutions) and the Government in pension financing. Clarification of the responsibility and its enforcement of employers to pay contributions is paramount, not only for an orderly functioning of the pension system but also because contributions are part of the labour costs, which employers must accept in a market economy. They should not aim to

First, the current system is regionally segmented. This includes regionally unfair allocation of contribution and benefit burdens with respective implications for the financial situation of funds, of which some are in surplus and others in deficit. This has substantially reduced the pension system to local schemes, aggravated the social and economic imbalances among regions and undermined fair conditions for the competition among enterprises and among regions in the market economy (Zheng, 2013). The statutory pension system should be consistent across the country-the same policy should apply to all localities, with national pooling and a common contribution rate.

Second, there are huge gaps between different groups in terms of benefit levels. For instance, the pension for retirees in government departments and public institutions is generally two times higher than that of their counterparts in enterprises, while the pension for rural seniors is much lower than both-with a floor standard of CNY88 ($13 at the yearly average exchange rate for 2017) per month currently and a monthly average pension of CNY126.72 ($18.8) (NBS, 2018). The gaps in benefit levels are generally judged unfair and, unless rectified, will undermine the general public's sense of identity to the pension system at large.

Third, the problem of pension reform transition costs is unresolved. The well-known problem is that the current working-age generation must shoulder the double burden of contributing to their pension funds for future payments in addition to supporting pensioners with the old labour insurance. The reformed pension system introduced in 1995 is, by design, a combination of pay-as-you-go social pooling and fully funded individual accounts. However, the envisaged design of the system has failed to materialize because the fiscal costs of the transition were underestimated; as yet, no solution has been found for who bears how much of the transition costs. Indeed, employers contribute to social pooling accounts and employees into their own accounts but, given the regional segmentation, in some regions (north-eastern China, for example) employees' contributions are used for the immediate pay-out of current pensions, resulting in empty individual accounts. Whereas some other regions (Guangdong Province, for example) have a huge amount of surpluses. This reality adds up to the complexity of addressing the transition costs.

Solutions for these problems should pursue the following lines:
First, achieve national pooling of the pension system without further delay. The regional segmentation and its consequence can best be overcome through unification of the pension system across the country. The unified system would establish a uniformly

Both schemes also experienced growth in paid benefit levels (see figure 8 and Annex 2, table A5). Pension levels grew for 15 consecutive years. The monthly per capita fund expenditure of the basic pension scheme for employees increased from $69.13 in 2001 to $425.95 in 2017, while the monthly per capita fund expenditure of the basic pension for urban and rural residents rose from $5.96 in 2009 to $18.77 in 2017(NBS, 2018).

Figure 8   Average per capita fund expenditure under the basic old-age pension scheme, 2009-2017

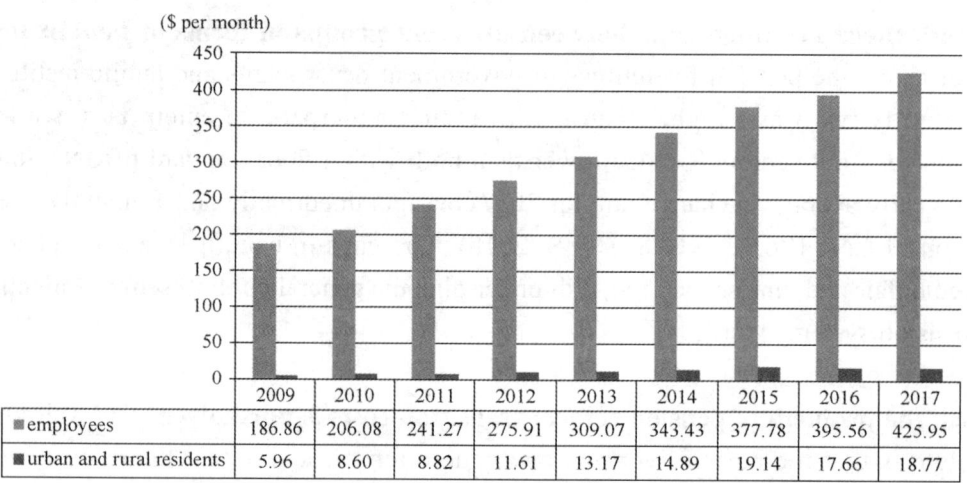

Note: (i) The per capita fund expenditure is used to estimate the per capita pension. Per capita fund expenditure = total annual fund expenditure / end-of-the-year number of pensioners. The fund expenditure includes pension payment, funeral subsidy, condolence payment, etc. Pension payments account for a tremendous share of the total fund expenditure.

(ii) Per capita pension provided under the residents scheme declined slightly in 2016. The reason is that a majority of the newly added pension recipients came from regions with relatively low level of pension, thus reducing the national average. As a matter of fact, per capita pension of all different regions saw a rise, rather than a decline.

Source: NBS, 2018 (*China Statistical Yearbook 2018*).

Problems and solutions

Like all pension systems around the world, China's pension system must be permanently adjusted to economic and demographic impacts and changes. In China's case, the specific leftovers of the reform process, as described here, are to be addressed as well.

Among the many problems confronting China's pension system, the following three are currently considered most pressing.

from a completely non-contributory scheme to a contributory model.

In 2018, a central adjustment system for basic pension funds of employees to be used inter-provincially was introduced as a step towards a nationally unified basic pension scheme for employees. Consequently, China achieved universalstatutory coverage of the basic pension, with the basic pension for urban employees applied to salaried employees and the rural and urban resident basic pensions applied to all other citizens.

Over the past two decades, public pension coverage was extended while the paid benefit levels kept growing steadily. In 2017, the number of old-age insurance (pension) participants reached nearly 915.5 million, whereas the number of pensioners (column 2 plus column 4 in Annex 2, table A2) hit 266.2 million.

From 1998 to 2017, the number of participants in the basic pension system for urban employees rose from 112.0 million to 402.9 million; the number of people covered by the basic pension system for urban and rural residents rose from nearly 80.3 million to nearly 512.6 million (see figure 7 and Annex 2, table A2).

Figure 7 Number of participants in basic old-age pension system and its changes, 1998-2017

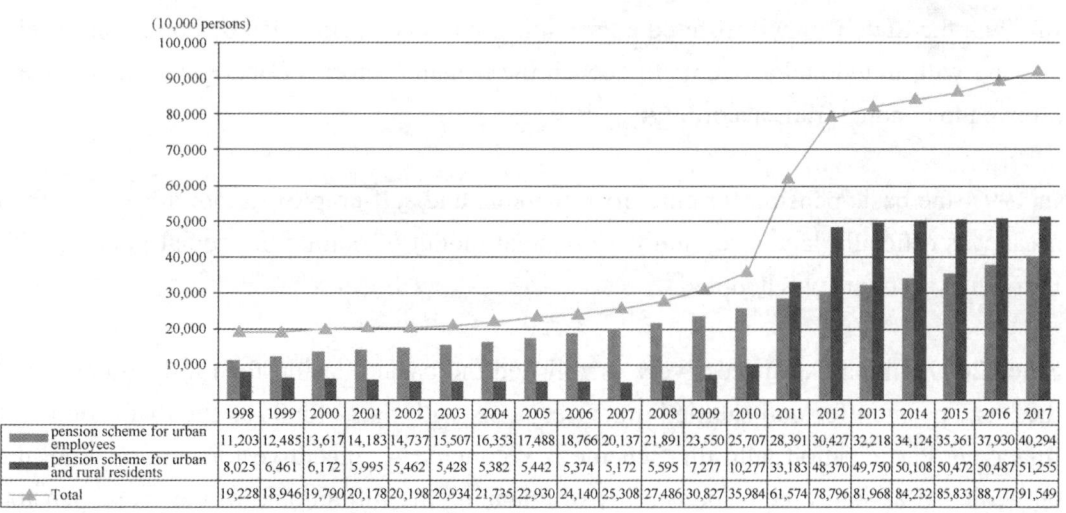

Source: NBS, 2018 (*China Statistical Yearbook 2018*).

China's social security consists of several schemes, with pension, health insurance, subsistence allowances, education benefits and housing benefits the mainstay and closely associated with its economic development. The following sections assesses the major social security schemes, with discussion on their evolution, problems and solutions.

Public pension

Evolution of the public pension

China's public pension system, created in 1951 and targeted at workers of the state-owned enterprises and collectively owned enterprises, was non-contributory. It held the State accountable and was organized at the enterprise level. The pension system for employees of government departments and public institutions was set up soon afterwards and followed similar principles.

In the mid-1980s, a few localities began exploring social pooling-based pension systems, as opposed to enterprise-based schemes.

In 1991, China embarked on the reform of the pension system for enterprise workers and turned its previous system into one jointly funded by the State, enterprises and individuals. Workers hence had to pay contributions. Since then, China has more generally changed its policy orientation towards contributory pensions.

In 1995, the State Council fostered contributory financing principles by combining social pooling with individual accounts to deepen the pension reform. Local governments were allowed to conduct trials accordingly.

In 1997, the basic pension for enterprise workers and self-employed individuals in urban areas was officially launched, and the financial model of combining social pooling with individual accounts was adopted.

Since 2009, China has successively established the basic pension for rural residents and the basic pension for non-salaried urban residents with fiscal funds as the main source of financing. Participation with this scheme is voluntary. As incentive for participation, the Government assumes the responsibility of financing the full amount of the social pension and partially subsidizing the contribution of insured persons.

In 2015, the employees of government departments and public institutions were incorporated into the coverage of the basic pension system, which means they shifted

2. Social insurance

(1) Old-age pension

(2) Health insurance

(3) Employment injury insurance

(4) Unemployment insurance

(5) Maternity insurance

(6) Long-term care insurance (trial)

3. Social welfare

(1) Social welfare for the elderly

(2) Social welfare for children

(3) Social welfare for women

(4) Social welfare for people with disabilities

(5) Educational benefits

(6) Housing benefits

4. Benefits for entitled groups

(1) Preferential treatment to servicemen and their families

(2) Pension for servicemen and their families

(3) Assistance to disabled servicemen

(4) Assistance to ex-servicemen

Note: (i) State Council Information Office:"China's social security and its policy (2004)",in *Bulletin of the State Council,* No. 32, 2004.This policy document states that China's social security system consists of social insurance, social welfare, benefits for entitled groups and housing benefits.

(ii) The Social Insurance Law of the People's Republic of China, adopted in 2010, provides for old-age pension, health insurance, employment injury insurance, unemployment insurance and maternity insurance as social insurance schemes. In 2017, the Government launched pilot schemes in 15 cities for long-term care insurance.

(iii) The Interim Regulations on Social Assistance promulgated by the State Council in 2014 explicitly stipulates eight social assistance schemes, including a minimum livelihood guarantee.

(iv) The Regulations on Pensions and Preferential Treatment for Servicemen, issued by the State Council in 2004, provides preferential treatment and pension for military personnel. The Regulations on Resettlement of Ex-Servicemen, promulgated by the State Council in 2011, guarantees appropriate reintegration ofveterans.

(v) Social welfare in China includes benefits in cash and in kind for older persons, children, women and people with disabilities; in academic discourse, housing benefits and educational benefits are also considered subject to social welfare policies.

towards enhancing people's well-being and quality of life but it helped close gaps in global social security coverage. The global coverage rate would be 50 per cent if China were excluded-it is 61 per cent with China.[1] It was not surprising that in 2016 the Chinese Government received the ISSA Award for Outstanding Achievements in Social Security for its unprecedented achievements in extending pensions, health insurance and other social protection schemes (ISSA, 2016). China's social security system has become a central instrument for the allocation of the fruits of the country's development for all (Zheng, 2016b).

Of course, other factors also (must) have contributed to these developments because China's social security system is still small in terms of its financial provisions (in international comparison) and thus its positive financial impacts on the economy can only be modest.[2] Nevertheless, it has been emancipating itself from a system that passively reacts to poverty and shifting to a system that proactively redistributing the fruits of economic development to persons in need while supporting the whole population.

Box 4
China's social security system: A comprehensive list of schemes

1. Social assistance

(1) Minimum livelihood guarantee and subsistence allowances (*dibao*)

(2) Disaster relief

(3) Medical assistance

(4) Education assistance

(5) Assistance to people living in extreme difficulty

(6) Housing assistance

(7) Employment assistance

(8) Temporary assistance

---

[1] See http://www.gov.cn/xinwen/2016-11/18/content_5134319.htm (accessed 10 Oct. 2018) [in Chinese].

[2] Even when fully developed, social security systems cannot be expected to rectify societies' unfair income and wealth distributions. For this to happen, support is required through adequate tax policies and, not the least, well-functioning effective labour market institutions and wage negotiation systems.

intensified its effort to extend its social security system, with the aim of reaching universal pension and health insurance coverage. Before 2009, nearly 250 million people were covered (including pensioners), representing about 23 per cent of the population aged 15 and older. Following a series of reforms in 2009, 2011, 2014 and 2015, an old-age pension scheme was established for the rural and urban populations (non-participants of the social insurance scheme), while the civil servants pension scheme was merged with the pension scheme for urban workers (ILO, 2014). Pensions under the newly established scheme consist of a social pension and an individual savings account pension. A similar structure applies to health insurance. The health insurance scheme for employees is financed by contributions from employers and insured persons, whereas the scheme for urban and rural residents is mainly financed by government subsidies, with individual contributions accounting for only one fourth to one fifth of the total fund revenue (see the next section for more details on these schemes).

The innovative policy design of the old-age pension and health insurance schemes and the direct responsibility assumed by the Government to provide for the pensions and health care of its residents constituted vital drivers of the rapid extension of pension and health insurance coverage.

In addition, a comprehensive social assistance system targeting low-income groups has taken shape, providing growing benefits to urban and rural families, which account for 10 per cent of the total population.[1] Social welfare schemes, including government-subsidized housing, older-person care services and social welfare services for people with disabilities and for children, have been reformed and improved (see box 4). An increasingly extensive social safety net has been built that not only defuses social risks resulting from market competition, natural disasters or human-made catastrophes but also improves social justice.

The rapid development of China's social security system not only greatly contributed

---

[1] Estimated with statistics for the number of (i) recipients of subsistence allowances (*dibao*), assistance to people living in extreme difficulty, temporary assistance, medical assistance, disaster relief released in the *Statistical Bulletin on Social Service Development 2016* (MCA, 2017); (ii) recipients of employment assistance released by the Ministry of Human Resources and Social Security; (iii) recipients of housing assistance released by the Ministry of Housing and Urban-Rural Development; and (iv) recipients of educational assistance released by the Ministry of Education. Double counting is avoided to the best of our knowledge.

could have given rise to huge social risk. Akin to the economic reform process, the social security system was progressively reformed, going through a transformative process:

- from a system of passive reaction to emerging socioeconomic needs to one that was able to take action on own initiative;
- from a bottom-up to a top-down approach to reform;
- from initial local trials and incremental system implementation towards overarching system design and full implementation nationwide, with provisions defined by the central Government; and
- from a system that had been serving, and was subject to, economic reform as a governance instrument towards a more independent system generally and more indirectly influencing, bolstering and promoting economic development.

During the 30 years of institutional re-organization, China's social security system also transformed from an institutional setting based on the State and work units (*danwei*) towards one that is independent of the work units. In the planned economy era, the functions of social security had been carried out by the work units, including a wide array of government departments, public institutions and state-owned enterprises, to which urban workers were attached. Welfare schemes, such as pensions, medical care and housing, organized and maintained by the work units, were subsidized by the Government. The schemes covered employees and their family members. Rural residents were attached to different organizations with distinctive boundaries at the grass-roots level, where the welfare benefits were delivered through a mutual distribution mechanism among collective members.

The Government was only in charge of affairs involving disaster relief and related poverty alleviation. The system was thus highly fragmented and segmented as it was fully arranged by work units with their respective boundaries. China's social security has thus experienced comprehensive transformation: from one that was the State's responsibility, fully arranged by work units, providing comprehensive protection yet fragmented and segmented and operating with distinctive boundaries in a planned economy to a system that is government led, in which enterprises and individuals share responsibilities and that covers the whole population, is socially organized and multilayered. The transformation from the State and work unit-based protection to the State and society-based protection (Zheng, 2008a) enabled China's social security system to access modern management techniques required for large-scale institutions serving large numbers of people.

In the aftermath of the global financial crisis that began in 2008, the Chinese Government

Government expects the country to have developed into a modern socialist nation that is prosperous, strong, democratic, culturally advanced and harmonious-when what President Xi Jinping defines as the "achievement of common prosperity for everyone" is basically reached (Xi, 2017).[1]

Figure 6   Engel's coefficient of urban and rural households in China

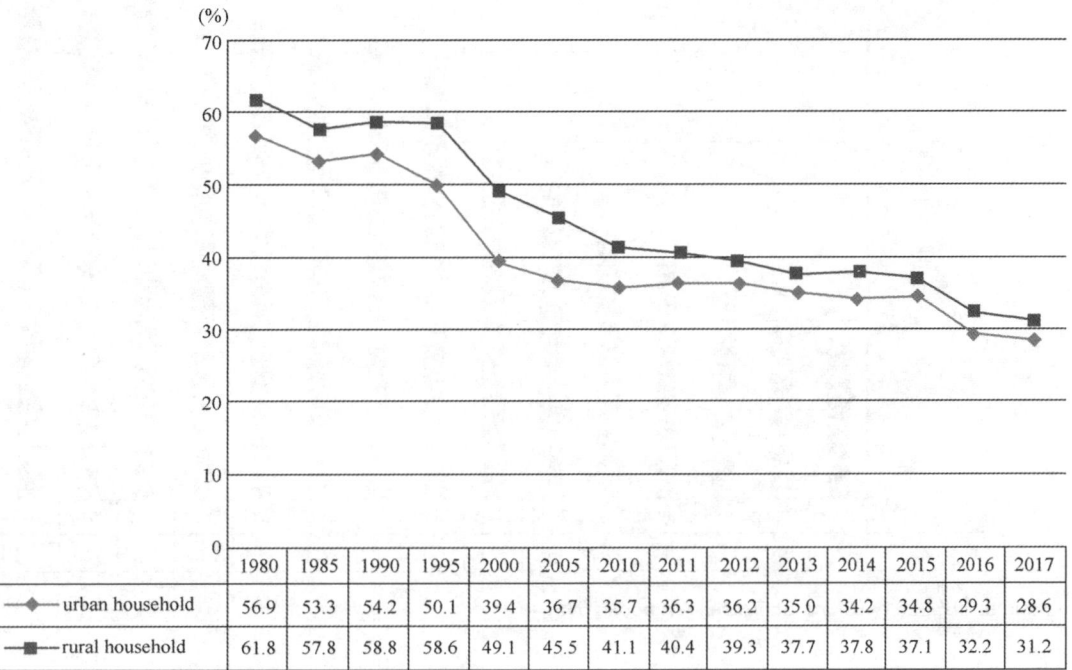

	1980	1985	1990	1995	2000	2005	2010	2011	2012	2013	2014	2015	2016	2017
urban household	56.9	53.3	54.2	50.1	39.4	36.7	35.7	36.3	36.2	35.0	34.2	34.8	29.3	28.6
rural household	61.8	57.8	58.8	58.6	49.1	45.5	41.1	40.4	39.3	37.7	37.8	37.1	32.2	31.2

Note: Engel's coefficient calculates the proportion of total private household expenditure spent on food. The rationale is that the less income a family or individual has, the greater will be the proportion of the expenditure on food.
Source: NBS (*Statistical Bulletin on National Economic and Social Development, various issues*).

3.1.2 China's achievements in social security reform and development

Triggered by the economic reforms, China's social security system had to undergo a comprehensive and profound overhaul beginning in the mid-1980s. This was intended to support the economic reform process but also to avoid overly radical changes, which

---

[1] See *People's Daily*: "Secure a decisive victory in building a moderately prosperous society in all respects and strive for the great success of socialism with Chinese characteristics for a new era" (Xi Jinping's report at 19th CPC National Congress), 28 Oct.

allocation of national resources continues to be based on the information provided by the *hukou* system. The resulting social and administrative problems continue to date and are elements to be addressed in the (near) future.

Figure 5 China's urbanization rate, 1978-2017

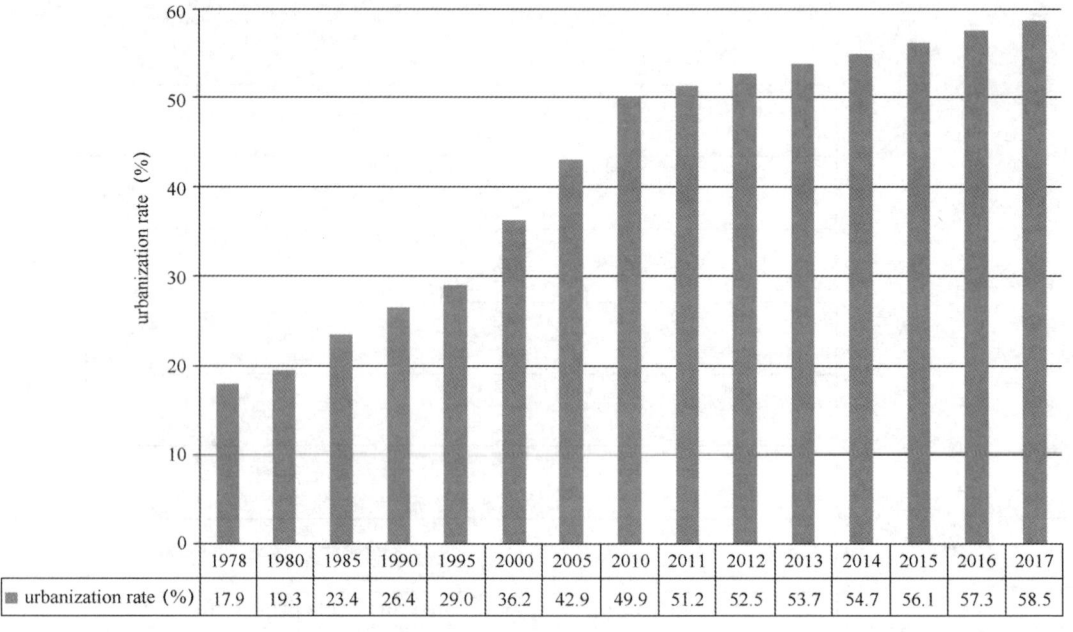

Source: NBS, 2018 (*China Statistical Yearbook 2018*).

Over the same period, China lifted a total of 660 million people out of poverty. Livelihoods improved significantly, as indicated by a declining Engels coefficient (see figure 6). Nonetheless, the vast majority of China's population has yet to reach high-income status. Although the rural poverty headcount ratio dropped from 10.2 per cent in 2012 to 1.7 per cent in 2018, nearly 16.6 million rural people still lived on income below the poverty line (CNY2,300 per person per year, at 2010 constant price) by the end of 2018 (National Bureau of Statistics, 2019).[1] The Government's goal is to eliminate regional and absolute poverty and thus build a moderately prosperous society in all respects by 2020 (CCCP, 2015).[2] By the mid-twenty-first century, when China celebrates its centenary, the

---

[1] NBS, http://www.stats.gov.cn/tjsj/zxfb/201902/t20190215_1649231.html.
[2] See Central Committee of the Communist Party: *13th Five-Year Plan for Economic and Social Development of the People's Republic of China (2016-2020)* (Beijing, 2015). Translated by Compilation and Translation Bureau, http://en.ndrc.gov.cn/newsrelease/201612/P020161207645765233498.pdf.

As figure 3 and figure 4 shows, the economy underwent a classical (and fast) transformation of its overall employment and industrial structures towards features typical of modern industrialized countries: The number of workers in the primary industries significantly reduced while the numbers of those working in the secondary (manufacturing, construction and others) and tertiary (services) industries accordingly increased. The relatively constant output share of the secondary sector, together with the employment numbers, indirectly points to the enormous productivity gains in this sector. The statistical stability of aggregate employment in the secondary sector camouflages the enormous changes that took place that were bolstered through focused social security reform as a result of modernization and marketization.

Figure 4 China's industrial transformation: Share of industry type as a percentage of GDP, 1978-2017

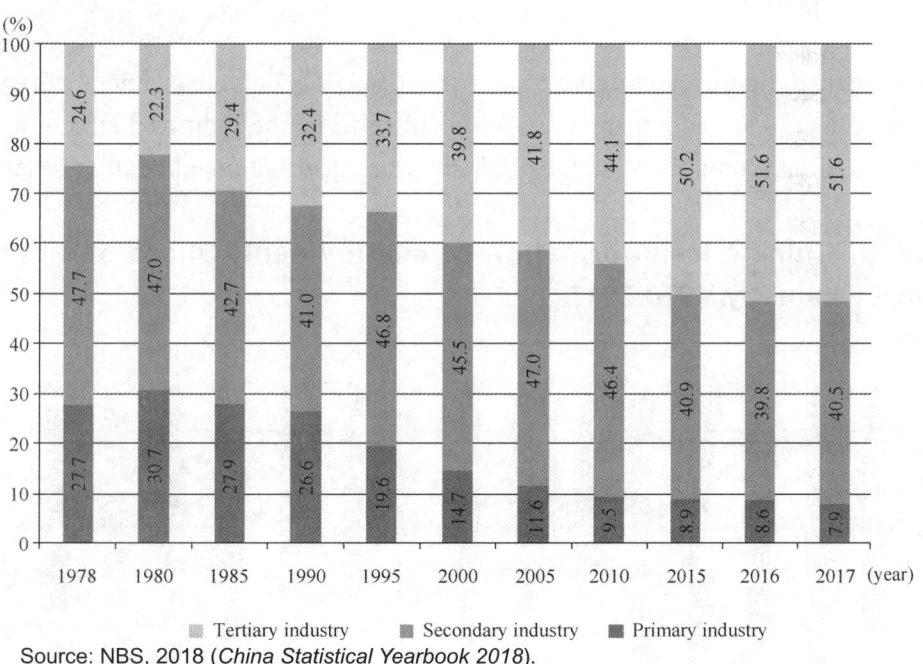

Source: NBS, 2018 (*China Statistical Yearbook 2018*).

The rapid urbanization (see figure 5) presented additional challenges to the country's social security system. Under the continued existence of the *hukou* system (administrative household registration), the large number of migrating workers were, by law, obliged to remain registered in their home village and town. As a consequence, they lost, de facto, health and social assistance coverage as well as schooling access for any accompanying children (which was provided in their home village and town). The regional and local

(c) Real growth rate of total GDP and per capita GDP

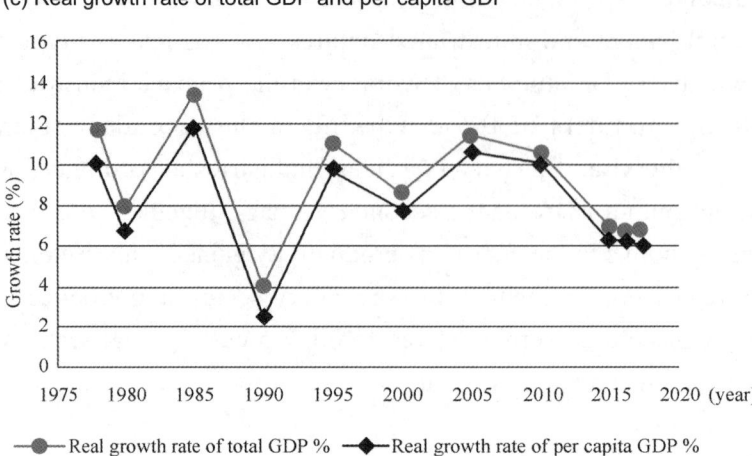

Source:(i) NBS, 2019. National data. Available at: http://data.stats.gov.cn/english/easyquery.htm?cn=C01 [Jan. 2019].
(ii) GDP data based on dollarsare calculated on the basis of yearly exchange rate averages (NBS, various years).

Figure 3, figure 4, figure 5 and figure 6 show that China's economic development over the past four decades was accompanied by profound shifts in the industrial structure, in the composition of the labour force, in the rural and urban distribution and in living standards.

Figure 3   China's transformation of employment: Share of employed people, by industry, 1978-2017

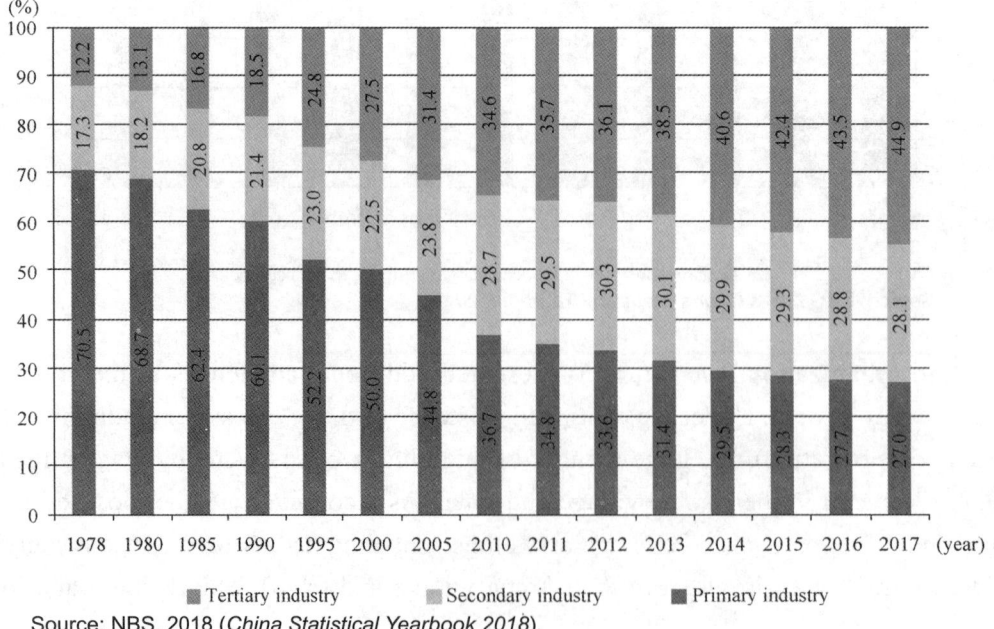

Source: NBS, 2018 (*China Statistical Yearbook 2018*).

wide gap between the more developed eastern regions and the less developed western areas.

Figure 2　Total GDP and GDP per capita for China, 1978-2017

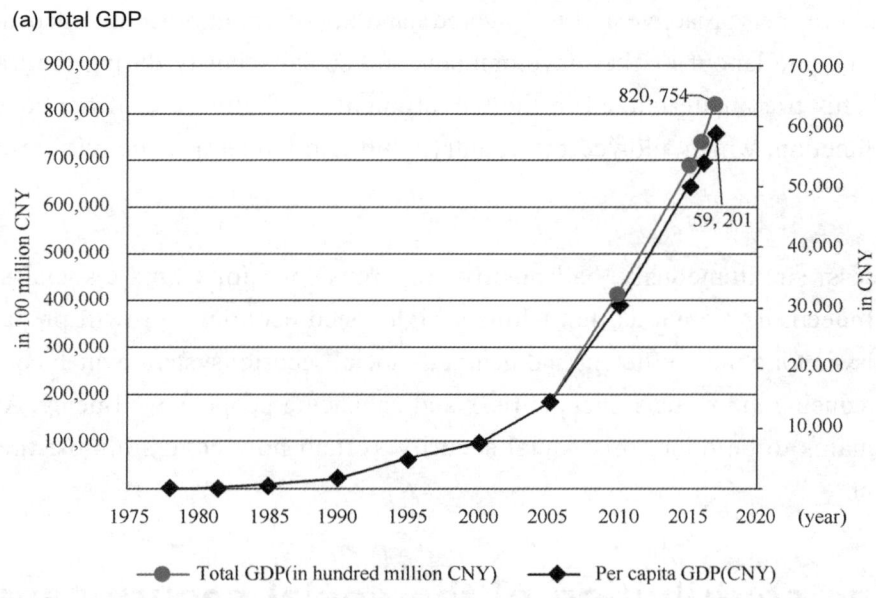

(a) Total GDP

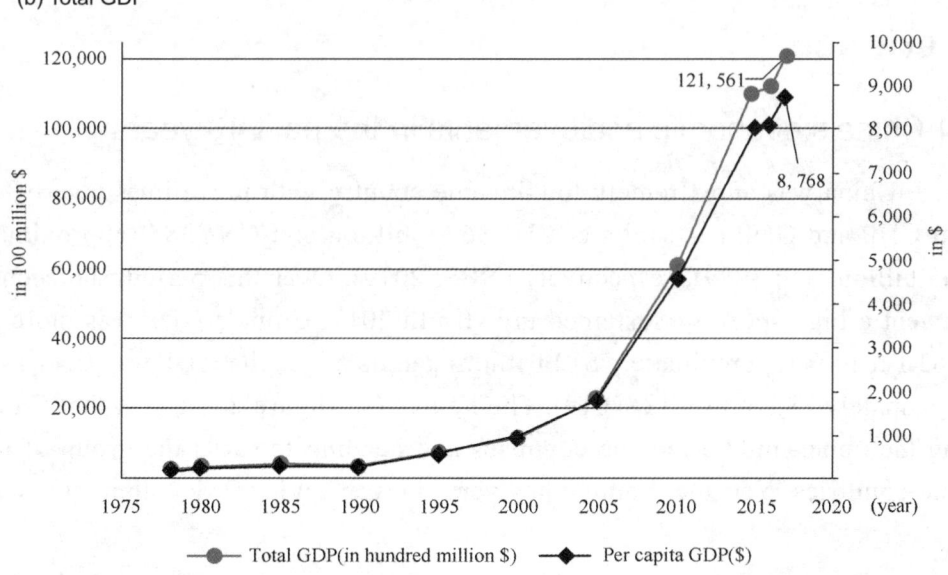

(b) Total GDP

production structures, abundance of labour and a determined policy of opening up to the world. One core reason has been the Government's fundamental trust in social security as an important governance instrument for managing the reform risks and improving people's well-being and its conviction of the positive relationship between unfolding social security and economic progress. In a nutshell, the Government trusted in a proper, proactive and foresighted handling of the intrinsic interdependencies of economic and labour market developments and social security during the transition process. This trust materialized in the Government's effective use of the core social security function, which allowed the country's hitherto hidden productivity reserves to surge.

The process, simultaneously, had positive repercussions for China's social security system. Indeed, it is obvious that China's high-speed economic growth prepared the material basis for a more efficient and generous social security system, which contributes towards reducing individuals' income risks and enhancing people's well-being. Although much remains to be done, this social security system now covers almost the whole population.

3.1 The contribution of the social security system to economic development: China's historical experience

3.1.1 China's economic achievements in the past 40 years

In 1978, China was an extremely low-income country with prevailing poverty, with a total GDP and GDP per capita at CNY367.9 billion and CNY385 (approximately $218.5 billion[1] and $229), respectively (NBS, 2019). Over this period, the economy underwent a high speed of sustained growth: In 2017, China's GDP was more than CNY82.1 trillion (approximately $12 trillion) and its per capita GDP was CNY59,210 (approximately $8,768) (NBS, 2019). The figures (see figure 2) suggest that China is among the upper-middle-income countries and heading towards the group of high-income countries. Yet, the country has very uneven regional development, with a

---

[1] The CNY-$ conversions are on basis of the yearly average exchange rates published by the National Bureau of Statistics of China. See http://data.stats.gov.cn/easyquery.htm?cn=C01&zb=A060J&sj=2017 (accessed 10 Oct 2018).

3. Social security and economic development: China

China has accomplished a remarkable feat in transforming itself from a low-income country to a major economic power in just over past decades. Since the onset of its transformation from a planned to a market economy in the 1980s, China's economy has experienced an impressive pace of growth. It is thus not surprising that its economy is the second-largest in the world, contributing around 31.5 per cent to global economic growth, compared with around 11.5 per cent by the United States and around 9 per cent by the euro area.[1]

China replaced its earlier highly centralized planned economy with a market economy, adapting itself to economic globalization. The approach adopted is generally considered a success: First, by allowing localities to make breakthroughs with existing national policies, replacing old practices with innovative ones through the implementation of pilots and then drawing lessons from those experiences and formulating new national policies that eventually came to full application nationwide. However, there was a significant risk of failure for both the economic as well as social reform because the transformation process required a change of the old system, which was characterized by vested interests and strong path dependencies.

During these decades of reform and development, the risk of failure significantly declined. The reasons are manifold, including political stability, broad markets, deep

---

[1] All figures are partially authors' estimates, based on the IMF October 2017 World Economic Outlook Database, http://www.imf.org/external/pubs/ft/weo/2017/02/weodata/download.aspx (accessed 10 Oct. 2018).

agreement on the importance of social security among multilateral organizations was reached. Even if there might not be agreement on the model and the levels of expenditure, institutions like the International Monetary Fund (IMF) or the World Bank have agreed, to a certain extent, on the importance of social security. For instance, the IMF Independent Evaluation Office stated in a report: "Over the past decade, the IMF has stepped up its attention to social protection as it has dealt with the aftermath of the global financial crisis and addressed concerns from the impact of food and fuel price shocks and broader stresses on low-income groups and the most vulnerable. Thus, the IMF has moved beyond its traditional fiscal-centric approach to recognize that social protection can also be macro-critical for broader reasons including social and political stability concerns" (IMF, 2017b). The World Bank Group and ILO-led Global Partnership for Universal Social Protection, launched in 2016, demonstrates the recognition by the World Bank of the importance of social protection to combat poverty and rising income inequality (World Bank and ILO, 2016).

societal problems, cannot, must not and will not be confined to low levels of protection, that is, only offering charity-type social assistance of giving a hand in times of trouble. Instead, if well maintained and managed, social security can reasonably be the governance instrument expected to bring about a state in which "a rising tide lifts all boats"(Zheng, 2018a).

As population ageing brings profound changes in demographic structures, family-based provisions (intra-family help and transfers) will inevitably continue fading away. Instead, social security expenditure, such as pensions, health care and long-term care, is bound to grow. This kind of rigid growth has been the norm of development practices in developed countries and has begun to manifest in developing countries with rapid growth, including China.

These observations must be clearly distinguished from countries' social expenditure ratios (see box 2 on the definition of social security) that increase and/or decline depending on the economic cycle. When economic development stagnates or even declines, this is usually combined with growing unemployment (implying more needy households). In economic booms, unemployment usually declines, rendering less public social support. Short-term cyclical developments might be superseded by the financial inertia of big existing systems, especially pensions and health systems that exert counter-cyclical financial stability. The complex interplay of the short-term developments and longer-term intrinsic inertia, in turn, directly affects the financial revenue of a country's public sector as well as the financing of social security and people's ability to pay for social welfare services. Such a mixed and thus complicatedsituation requires careful governance. Otherwise, unless ameliorating measures are taken, it can easily undermine the financial sustainability of social security. Thus, exploiting new sources of revenue and further optimizing the social security structure are policy measures that must be taken by countries to adapt to the future.

To sum up, there are *de facto* contradictions between the rigid growth of welfare and financial sustainability once a social security system takes its full shape. As a result, in addition to boosting efforts to strengthen and maintain the fairness of statutory social security systems, effective measures need to be adopted to mobilize market and public resources in the field of social security.

Particularly during the last global financial and economic crisis, a certain level of home-based business and intelligent monitoring, have made new working patterns and new forms of employment become the new normal for many persons. This not only directly affects the economic development and social governance patterns but also presents new challenges for social security systems. As employment flexibility and turnover keep increasing, employment venues and labour relations will metamorphose into new forms, in addition to the new social networks and ways of expressing demand (Zheng, 2017c).

But fears that labour will disappear are premature. Even under the new technological revolution, the nature of work and mechanisms for ensuring sufficient remuneration will remain, although working patterns will vary and how remuneration is received might change.

In the context of the new technologies and new forms of business, governments of all countries are exposed to the challenge of maintaining fair primary income distribution and to constantly optimize their social security system to ensure its effectiveness and fairness. One cannot expect social security to solve the problem of primary income distribution in practice. Instead, it is incumbent upon governments to emphasize the protection of labour rights, not only through fair wages but also by developing the adaptability of labour-capital relations as well as their social security system. These must be underpinned by stable industrial relations and profound changes in income, wealth distribution and societal structures to ensure that the welfare of workers is not compromised.

2.2.5 The paradox of rigid growth of welfare and financial sustainability

Social welfare is one of human being's fundamental rights as well as a major responsibility for governments to bear. International cross-country comparison and long-term historical development suggests that once social security is in place, it will develop over-proportionally with socioeconomic progress. This is attributed to modern societies' growing complexity and also to growing demands that can only be fulfilled by increasing the provision of public goods and services (Lindert, 2010; Wagner, 1876). It appears to be a universal law that social security programmes can only increase and have proven unlikely to be cut; benefit levels tend to be uplifted instead of lowered (notwithstanding that, in practice, individual programmes might be expanded or downsized, according to needs or be only temporarily in place or mismanaged). Because of these system-inherent upward drifts, social security, as one basic way of sharing the fruits of national development through institutional guarantees and as a prominent tool to solve certain are not necessarily negative, and therefore ageing should not at all be alarming. Despite its position as a super-aged country, Germany managed to maintain a vital and growing economy with a well-functioning social security system; however, the key to this lies also in Germany's silent changes in its production processes carried out in the 1990s (Bosch, 2017); this was combined with accommodating adjustments to its social security system, especially a sequence of substantial, mainly parametric old-age security reforms.

- China, as a fast-ageing country, has been economically successful while building up its social security system rapidly and enhancing its older persons' purchasing power. Despite mounting pressure of pension pay-outs and older person services, enhanced labour productivity and intelligent solutions credited to technological progress lay the economic and technical ground for tackling ageing-related challenges.

Population ageing adds risks but also opportunities, and governments should respond more actively to their country's ageing processes.

At the international level, possibilities should be explored to take the cost effects of ageing out of the international competition debate. If all countries accept the worldwide ageing reality and stop efforts at countering the implied cost effects, then ageing will cease to be an economic problem. It might still impact the structure of demand, but this is not a problem for social market economies, which will easily adapt.

2.2.4 The impact of the new technological revolution on traditional industries and the normalization of new business types

The process of globalization is accompanied by the widespread application of information technology and the Internet to the mode of production and employment as well as to people's daily routines. The further improvement and application of artificial intelligence will add to and revolutionize these ongoing developments. These achievements have created new centres of economic growth but have also resulted in changes in social relations, especially in labour relations, which brings about new problems to social security systems, including their administration.

In recent years, the emergence of a wide array of new sectors and businesses as a result of artificial intelligence and the Internet, coupled with the boom of e-commerce, has reached 14 per cent, and it is beyond 20 per cent in a super-aged society (WHO, 1982). Germany, Italy and Japan became "super-aged societies" in 2011, while more than 50 countries, including Sweden, Bulgaria, Greece, Spain, France, the United Kingdom, Canada, Belarus and Australia turned aged. The United States, the Russian Federation, China, Kazakhstan and many other countries remain ageing.

Continued demographic ageing has considerable direct impact on employment, consumption and industries as well as on overall economic development. It will also have lasting and profound influence on the structure, resource allocation and financial balance of social security systems. Pressure on pension payments and health system finance as well as on the provision of personal care services (and their financing) will continue to challenge societies in their search for solutions.[1] While demographic changes brought about by population ageing are posing great challenges to social security and economic development in both the short and long terms, improving social security systems to cope with population ageing has become a consensus among the international community.[2]

Social security systems for older persons have, in many cases, been adjusted towards a positive and supportive role to economic development. Two countries at different stages of development are outstanding in this respect:
- The impacts of an ageing population on economic development and social security

---

[1] It must be acknowledged, though, that the impact of population ageing on average health care cost levels is much less documented in international research than for pensions or old-age care costs.

[2] Given the profound impacts of demographic changes on economic and social development as early as the 1980s, the United Nations addressed the implications of population ageing. In 1982, the United Nations convened the First World Assembly on Ageing in Vienna and adopted theInternational Plan of Action on Ageing, which includes 62 recommendations. The United Nations Principles for Older Persons, adopted by the General Assembly in 1991, established five universal principles: independence, participation, care, self-fulfilment and dignity. In 2002, the United Nations convened the Second World Assembly on Ageing in Madrid to summarize the progress of action in countries over the past 20 years following the Vienna Conference; in conclusion, the Madrid Political Declaration and International Plan of Action on Ageing was adopted and calls for incorporating a positive view of ageing into national development frameworks. Since then, the issue of ageing appears on the UN agenda from time to time. The seventh Working Session of the Open-Ended Working Group on Ageing that took place at UN headquarters in New York in 2016 focused on such issues as the participation of NGOs in the work of ageing and measures to enhance the promotion and protection of the human rights and dignity of older persons.

symptomatic of unforeseeable intertwined effects of free trade and free flow of capital, coupled with growing labour mobility and less stabilizing social security, where economic fluctuations in one country inevitably affect others and possibly the whole world. In fact, the instability of the global economy is increasing, which poses emerging threats to economic security-and not only for developing countries.

Globalization has also upset previously well-balanced industrial relations, resulting in a "strong capital, weak labour" pattern worldwide (Zheng, 2002). The reason is because capital is allowed to float freely so as to find lower-paid (but still sufficiently productive) labour. Especially for developing countries, it would be a hard choice not to pursue the offered capital-induced development path. To minimize the related cost of labour, welfare measures must be taken that lead to better-balanced industrial relations and an equitable distribution of wages and profits.

The wide-ranging uncertainties of globalization have profound impacts on economic development and social security policy in many countries. Under intensified competition and increased risks, countries have the choice between a synchronized long-term development of their economies, together with the improvement of their general welfare, and unsustainable policies of short-term and volatile gains in prosperity at the expense of welfare. The principles of social security, with mutual help and organized solidarity as its foundation, can add stable expectations to the process of globalization and help to counterbalance and overcome the current disadvantageous position of labour. The current problem is to better implement social security to adapt to the socioeconomic dynamics and emerging new forms of business. The unfolding digital economy indeed poses new challenges to the social security system, such as giving rise to non-standard forms of employment. But the wide application of information technology lays technical ground for tackling these challenges.

2.2.3 Far-reaching influence of rapidly ageing populations on economies and societies

Today, the world has moved into an era in which its demographic structure is transforming, and the ageing process is accelerating and deepening. While this positive development constitutes social progress, it poses increasingly critical challenges to social security and economic development. According to the definitions of the World Health Organization, an ageing society is a society in which the percentage of persons aged 65 and older in the total population reaches 7 per cent. In an aged society, that population

One core misconception of the past few decades was to assume that income and wealth inequality would be reduced through automatic trickle-down effects that allow persons who are rich to profit over-proportionally from economic growth (which has been the case in many countries), which eventually also benefits persons who are poor. Consequently, to reduce investment in social welfare and curtail social security would do no harm but be compensated through such trickle-down conditions.

Under the influence of these ideas, social security is no longer regarded as an important goal of economic development in many countries, nor as an instrument to fix defects of the market or to promote sustainable and coordinated development of economies and societies. Even more, some economistic arguments incautiously attribute financial crises, debt crises and even political crises to welfare systems, thus covering up the institutional root cause of crisis-prone capitalism while exaggerating alleged negative effects of social security, which leads to the inability of recognizing the necessity to strengthen social security in processes of socioeconomic transformation.

Misunderstanding the principally positive mutual relationship between social security and economic development can have severe adverse consequences, such as the hampering of social justice and coordinated socioeconomic development. The international community and individual member States alike must keep an open mind to clarify these positive relationships, or other pressing global problems, like poverty, climate change, environmental pollution and population growth and migration, will have no or only little chance to be successfully tackled. In September 2015, the United Nations formally adopted the 17 Sustainable Development Goals on such issues as ending poverty, zero hunger, good health and well-being, quality education, gender equality and reduced inequalities (United Nations, 2015). The achievement of the goals implicitly requires well-established and fully functioning social security systems.

2.2.2 Uncertainties of globalization

For most countries, globalization has prominently shown its two sides: opportunity and challenge. Globalization can often be a process of economic growth and accumulating wealth, in which many people's livelihoods are improved. Such positive effects have manifested in developing countries, such as Brazil, India, China and South Africa.

Notwithstanding the positive effects, globalization has also intensified international competition and speculation. The sequence of numerous crises in recent decades is development.

Between the end of World War II and the mid-1970s, Keynesianism was prevalent to counter economic crises credited to market failures. Most countries promoted economic development and equally improved people's living standards by proactively implementing social security and employment policies. For many countries, this was the golden time of both economic expansion and social welfare extension.

In the 1970s and 1980s, however, such developments as two oil crises and the subsequent Eastern European upheaval and disorganization in the Soviet region constituted the historical background to the simultaneous success of neoliberalism and monetarism. The Washington Consensus of 1989 (Williamson, 2002) can be regarded as one mature manifestation of how to apply neoliberal concepts in practice. In the past 30 years, the global economy and the reform and development of social security in many countries have been profoundly influenced by this paradigm, which in its essence advocates free competition, liberalization, privatization and marketization while demanding to downsize the State to its minimal role of a "night watchman".[1]

Obviously, social security could not be left unaffected by these developments. Neoliberalism prioritizes economic growth over social protection, thus likely exerting undeniable negative impacts on the development of social policies in many countries. The Eastern European countries quite consistently adopted economic shock therapy (Klein, 2007), although it did not achieve the intended development results.[2] Latin America, as a pilot zone for implementation of the Washington Consensus, became the hardest-hit area as well as the area where the later emerging anti-neoliberalism reactions were fiercest. The gap between the rich and the poor widened extremely in many countries, and structural crises of societies became increasingly visible. The current situation in Europe and the United States, including the anti-globalization trends, rising social movements, extremism and populism, indicate people's growing sense of insecurity in a world that has maneuvered itself into a situation of increasing difficulty to maintain the core role of social security, which is to provide income security when needed. This adds difficulties to maintaining social peace.

---

[1] See https://definitions.uslegal.com/n/night-watchman-state/.
[2] Much of the later economic success of countries like Poland or Czech Republic can be attributed to the positive repercussions stemming from their EU membership.

World Bank). It was also through these influences that the traditional Western welfare state concept was suddenly challenged.

Some of these developments have been described and analysed in detail (Mueller, 1999). However, the greater bulk of the respective developments and influences, structurally and personally, are still to be uncovered by historians and other researchers.

2.2 Emerging challenges facing social security and economic development around the globe

Since the beginning of the twenty-first century, along with the accelerating globalization and thriving of the Internet, the global socioeconomic context has undergone tremendous changes that are gaining momentum in both depth and breadth and posing new challenges to the context of social security and economic development. The issue of how to tackle these challenges has constituted a major policy agenda with strategic significance for countries around the world to achieve their national development goals.

In this section, we depict five aspects considered critical to this policy agenda: (i) changing paradigmatic thought; (ii) uncertainties of globalization; (iii) the impacts of ageing; (iv) new technological revolution and the normalization of new business types; and (v) the paradox of rigid growth of welfare and financial sustainability.

2.2.1 Divergent development philosophies underlying the relationship between economic development and social security

In institutionalizing social security as a system, the underlying concepts and principles determine the quality of the design of the system and the latter determines the effectiveness of technical (parametric) solutions. Although this interaction may sometimes be reversed in practice, a ground rule for constructing a social security system is indeed that scientific concepts should dominate its design and appropriate system design should dominate the choice of techniques applied (Zheng, 2008b).

As the previous chapters have mentioned, the best policy choice changes over time, influencing the understanding of the interaction of social security and economy delivered through enterprises. Other than China, however, Eastern European and Central Asian countries were, as a result of the revolution, deprived of the governance means that would have helped transform state-owned enterprises towards market conditions in an organized and rational way. All of a sudden, enterprises and other institutions were exposed to radical market shocks and thus had to cease operations, temporarily or for good, or continued for some while only formally on a no-revenue basis, heavily subsidized out of rapidly ailing state coffers.

With collapsing enterprises, social security collapsed. Despite these dramatic changes and the most difficult financial and administrative circumstances in most countries, certain categories of benefits and services were steadily delivered. For example, pensions continued to be paid, and health services were maintained at minimal levels.It cannot be overappreciated how fast social security institutions, now made independent from earlier enterprises, were installed and regionalized to deliver social benefit payments. This process was accompanied by international financial support, such as by the World Bank, and by international and bilateral technical advice, not the least through twinning programmes that linked technocrats from Western social security institutions (mainly from Europe and the United States) with those from the East. This process was superseded by conceptual debates for best solutions between the World Bank and the ILO, between Sweden and France, between proponents of market economy solutions and those of social market economy solutions (among others).

The financial industry had a most influential role in promoting the privatization of social security. Not surprising, governments and civil societies, after just having overcome a state-run system, were curious and eager to enjoy the (promised) delights from market solutions. Only a few had an understanding of the time-consuming complexities of decent state administration (to be established) under market conditions based on private property rights, including the resulting legal and administrative obligations and chores of enterprises and the respective interlinkages with social security. The difficulties stemming from the simultaneous implementation of a new legal regime can explain why, by contrast, the Chinese transformation was more easily handled-China could concentrate on managing the structural change while no legal system change was necessary. The discussions and reforms that took place in the East after 1989 made their way into Western Europe's institutions, universities, civil societies and lobby groups, including through an East-West brain drain of young gifted people (for example, into EU institutions and the in which municipalities and local organizations should be given prime responsibility. Enhancing health care and social services at home (rather than in institutional facilities) should be a priority. Households should be supported in their engagement in preventive measures and mutual help that enable older persons to remain active as long as possible. Working conditions for care workers for frail older persons must be enhanced and their salaries increased.

2.1.6 Developments in Eastern Europe, Central Asia and other world regions after 1989

Social reforms have taken place in other regions of the world as well, although they are not or only cursorily introduced by this report. They are party to the overall global socioeconomic process but also have their own peculiarities. For example, some countries that had moved towards privatization of their public pension systems in the pre- and post-1990 period have begun re-reforming. Since 2000:

- Reforms in some Latin American countries have been judged failures (including by the World Bank), were annulled or declared counter-constitutional (Ecuador and Nicaragua), and the public pension systems were finally kept. Systems were partially or fully reinstituted in Argentina (2008), Bolivia (2010), Hungary (2010), Poland (2013), Bulgaria (2014) and Kazakhstan (2013).
- More countries are investigating into re-reforming: Chile, El Salvador and the Russian Federation. Whether these reversals improve the material situation of scheme members remains to be seen; many complex issues need to be addressed. In any case, these reactions clearly signal that societies have limits in accepting "de-solidarization".

The following briefly deals with the developments in Eastern Europe and Central Asia after 1989 as background explanation for why the paradigmatic changes of the (Western) welfare state concept after 1989 were successful.

The revolutionary developments in the former Soviet Union, including the states of the Council for Mutual Economic Assistance, placed social security under enormous stress. Collapsing capital stock, hyperinflation, massive unemployment and underemployment, wage arrears, inefficient and non-trusted state institutions (including lack of functioning statistics) and other detrimental developments made it enormously difficult (to continue) providing social security, especially to collect the required resources. The problems were augmented by the fact that under the Soviet system, as in China, most social security was the country's health infrastructure, investment in economical public (social) housing to stimulate birth rates and reduction of childcare and health care costs, especially for the generations in reproductive ages.

- To counter the detrimental implications for old age of the current labour market dualization, Japan is looking to improve public pension benefit levels without additional burden to the younger generation, which could be achieved through (i) coverage of employees with short working hours and of employees in microenterprises; (ii) voluntary extension of contribution years consistent with the extension of working years; and (iii) the full application of macroeconomic indexation so as to improve the benefit of future pension recipients. Whether such policy would be suitable for Japan remains a question for the time being, given the Government's fiscal constraints. In any case, there is urgent need in all countries to improve pension coverage for persons in precarious work; otherwise, system loyalty will be undermined.

- In Germany, changing pension finance would probably have (positive) implications on health financing, which could help to overcome the problem that, despite obligatory health coverage for all (since 2007 and 2009), Germany may have up to 1 per cent of its population left uninsured (Koschnitzke, 2015).[1] This situation could be tackled through an all-citizens health insurance, a reform that would leave private health insurance with a complementary role.

- Republican governments always pursue conservative policies-essentially no social policies (except for tax benefits). Whether the current administration finally dismantles the Patient Protection and Affordable Care Act (known as Obamacare), the attempts of which have been unsuccessful thus far, remained an open question at the time this report was written. From the point of view of the international community expertise, the intended policy goes in the wrong direction and stands in contrast to international recommendations and conventions.

How China fits into these developments is explored in greater detail in Chapter 3.

It is obvious that all countries covered in this report, including China, must seek to consolidate or enhance their policies in relation to long-term care for older persons,

---

[1] There are no official statistics on the non-insured; estimates draw information from contribution arrears and other indirect indicators.

community structures must adjust to situations in which the majority of residents are aged 65 or older.

- As in the United Kingdom, **childcare** is an issue in Germany, where every fifth to sixth child is currently considered living in poverty (Bertelsmann Stiftung, 2016). Direct state provision of a universal childcare service appears to be an effective way forward. A second option would be greater state subsidy of childcare provision, whereby delivery is left to the market. Either way, the exceptionally high costs of childcare require action. The same focus must be pursued in Japan.

The United Kingdom still suffers from the policy of de-industrialization of the 1980s in many of its former industrial heartlands. A rebooting of national insurance along the lines that Beveridge had intended could help all persons see just how much they benefit from what they are (and should be) asked to pay in. Mutatis mutandis, more honesty in respect of the costs of social security (but also its returns to societies) applies to all countries

- In Germany, as in France, building a universal layer into social security system appears overdue. It could be achieved in France by enlarging the safety nets and increasing the minimum benefits and in Germany by gradually giving up the principle of actuarial fairness in the public pension insurance and replacing it with a redistributive design (BMAS and BArch, 2016a; Scholz, 2009). In both countries, financing of social security should be sought through larger shares of taxation. Otherwise, income inequality among people will continue to grow with detrimental economic effects (Cingano, 2014) and undesirable social and political implications (see Nordic countries further on).

- Discussions in the Republic of Korea go in the same direction, where a general basic income for all has been proposed[1] in reaction to the strong trends of jobless growth, increased non-regular work and increasing youth unemployment. Because the country's social expenditure ratio, at 10 per cent, is still very low, this measure would be a most effective method to expand domestic demand. Due to the high fiscal costs involved, the discussions currently focus on (limited) demogrants, such as expanding the basic pension and establishing age-dependent social allowances, like child and youth benefits. Also under debate in the Republic of Korea are issues of improving

---

[1] Similar proposals were made in other countries, including Germany.

five countries included in this report-France, Germany, the United Kingdom and less so in Japan and the Republic of Korea (but still significant and which is nested in more general issues of rectifying the worldwide deteriorating distribution of income and wealth) to a set of required policies addressing the situation of (precarious) employment and unemployment, children and families, health care, pensions, care systems and housing. France, Germany and the United Kingdom suffer from large (or growing) sectors of sub-poverty-level wages, with immanent direct repercussions on social benefits. In other words, substantial wage increases are overdue, not the least of which is minimum wages.[1]

More specifically:
- In the United Kingdom as well as in Germany (probably also in the Nordic countries), the operation of the conditionality regime must be reviewed. Removing the penalizing elements of respective legislation is overdue. There is growing evidence that the increasingly harsh policy approach of recent years has denied many citizens their basic social rights and helped fuel the rise of low-paid and extremely insecure contracts.

- Urgent action is required to address the **high cost of housing** in the United Kingdom as well as in France, with the same problem now occurring, with some time lag, also in Germany. And in Germany, the massive privatization of public housing Since 1990s left municipalities with little means to counter market rent rates. Ultimately, this means a revert to policies that facilitate the construction of more social housing. Stronger regulation of private sector rent levels could be an option, too. Housing in Japan should also become an integral part of social policy. Especially given the changing household size and structures, housing, in conjunction with social security, should aim to support economically vulnerable families of any generation. In Japan,

---

[1] In this respect, France and Germany are intrinsically tied under the euro (while the United Kingdom can adjust its exchange rate, if so required). For instance, France cannot solve its too-low-wage-level problems without Germany's accommodation. If France, as has been suggested, pursues policies of enhanced wage increases, Germany will have to increase its wage levels even faster. Otherwise, Germany's competitiveness, compared with France, would be further strengthened, with additional pressure on France's employment (Flassbeck, 2017). Germany needs significant wage-level increases to ease the growing tensions in the euro area and to provide space for their own required increases of benefits and wage levels. Otherwise, Germany's export-led economic model will sooner or later fail.

New reforms and reform needs ahead (in the mid-2010s and beyond)

In some sense, the West's social security policy is currently at a crossroads: It appears that social security policy has been moved towards a position where it intrinsically serves exogenously defined business needs. Rules and incentives have been adjusted, such that persons often gain effective access to coverage only in the event of proven accommodating behaviour, including acquiescing to the efficiency requirements of an anonymous system that is mastered by economic command. Under this perspective, it is to be expected that people will be less and less willing to exert loyalty to a social security system that has lost much of its earlier emancipating approach, which had evolved up until the late 1970s or early 1980s (Bosch, 2015; Gauti, 2015; Grimshaw, 2015; Vaughan-Whitehead, 2015a). To regain public support, social policy must turn away from this auxiliary role of social security and take a more independent posture (again)-one that actively seeks to close the (national) inequality gaps that otherwise will continue to expand due to globalization.

This task, which can only be insufficiently sketched in passing, implies changing the academic, professional and public discourse about social security and its beneficiaries. Hope that this will happen might come from the role of the Nordic countriesover the past two decades, which had a prominent role in co-shaping the world's current social security paradigm. First, it must be admitted that the developments in the Nordic countries might sooner or later lead to legitimacy problems. An important part of this development is the ongoing change in paradigm from economic development for social security to social security for economic development. Where this will lead to in the Nordic countries is difficult to say. For the time being, one can see a change in the normative compass, away from collective concerns and towards more individual interest. As a small group of small nations (in international comparison) and despite their frequent taking on of a social role model, the Nordic countries have only limited choice to stem their welfare state policies against the big tides. That Sweden was successful in influencing international pension reforms in the past two decades and that Denmark influenced discussions surrounding labour market flexicurity (Auer, 2010) are positive signals.

At the same time, as the remainder of this section shows, all countries covered in this report have reason and ample room for reforming their social security systems to the better in practice. For instance, there is high potential to combine the required change of the social security narrative with tangible progress in reality. Concrete fields of social policy improvement range from the new (old, classical) wage issue which is prevalent in with the perception of long-term moderate growth, in conjunction with increased labour market flexibility. Respective measures were introduced after the global financial crisis, which increased the number of non-regular jobs and accelerated labour market dualization with increasingly visible detrimental effects on the Korean society's income and wealth distribution. The rapidly declining birth rates and the ageing of the population are now high on the agenda of public debate. These developments appear to have improved the society's perception of social security.

The **United States** finally took a bold step towards comprehensive health coverage (with the Patient Protection and Affordable Care Act introduced in 2010). Otherwise, no changes in the American social fabric has occurred. With the short interludes of the 1930s and 1960s, it appears to be outside the realm of US polity to use and instrumentalize social security measures for concerted action to enhance the society's overall (economic) well-being. Social tax expenditures continued accruing overwhelmingly to upper-income groups and thus increasing income inequality. The real minimum wage continued falling, and income inequality further increased due to the failure to invest evenly in education. The most important reason for both the rise over time in the Gini index and in the top 1 per cent income share has been workers' declining degree of unionization and the related loss of the bargaining power and political impact of labour unions, which is a development occurring around the globe.

It is difficult to judge whether the new paradigm of the competition state will continue to shape a new world order of social security. Countries that have adjusted their economies and social security systems to an export-led (trade surplus) model will sooner or later have to adapt, like China already has, to the reactions of those trade partners in deficit, with inevitable impacts on social security. In the next section, we address some possible new reforms and reform needs that, with good reason, can be seen ahead.

Over the past few years, Western societies have shown growing concern about the increasing role of social security serving business demands. This is because the hope that social security could be a redistributive tool to let people effectively participate in the economic gains from globalization has not come true, with no signal that it will occur in the future. Whether both strands of development will achieve critical mass to trigger momentum for change must, for the time being, remain an open question.

such that the system is now characterized by much greater heterogeneity than, say, 30 years ago-with a growing segmentation of social rights and, on average, decreasing real values of benefits, which contributed to replacing earlier labour-friendly trends with more inequality and poverty. Therefore, although France has not officially joined the new internationally dominant narrative, it has adjusted in a piecemeal approach to the international trends.

Japan experienced its economy stepping into stagnation. Social policy has since been dominated by fiscal constraints: The financial situation of the National Health Insurance, already worse than that of other employment-based schemes because of different age compositions and occupational backgrounds, was exacerbated by the upsurge of enrolment of marginalized persons with no regular employment. Therefore, health insurance (subsidized by public transfers for some schemes) was further rationalized:

- Co-payment was increased from 10 per cent to 20 per cent, and transfers to hospitals and clinics were reduced in an unprecedented manner in 2006.
- The basic pension scheme is in a similar financial situation; therefore, the national treasury's subsidy was increased in 2009.
- To cope with continued population ageing, a new health insurance scheme for older persons was introduced in 2008.
- Long-term care insurance, which had been introduced in 2000, was overhauled in 2005 to focus more on preventive care.
- Public pension insurance begun applying macroeconomic indexation.

Policies reacting to the issues associated with the declining birth rate remain high on Japan's political agenda. Childcare cash benefits and in-kind support to child-rearing families became top of the agenda of the social security policy. Under the impact of the 2008 financial crisis, the general public began to realize and accept the precarious employment conditions of the youth and young adults as a problem.

Policies that strengthen the financial and organizational bases of Japan's social security system have become inevitable. The Comprehensive Reform of Tax and Social Security Initiative also climbed to the top of the political agenda in the late 2000s.

The Republic of Korea has begun gradually altering its economic growth-first paradigm. The earlier high economic growth was acknowledged as unsustainable and replaced

In all three areas of social security, new rules trimmed administration for cost-efficiency purposes.

The reforms resulted in (inter alia) establishing a large low-wages sector with precarious working conditions: For persons remaining over long periods in this sector, a significant future old-age poverty risk evolved.

Macroeconomically, the same policy achieved a significant reduction of average labour unit costs vis-à-vis Germany's main European competitors (France and Italy, for example). An unprecedented triple surplus in the private household sector (with growing income inequalities), the enterprises and corporation sector and the government sector evolved, resulting in large and growing trade surpluses.[1]

Germany's corporatist social features functioned well between 2008 and 2010, in a coordinated tripartite effort of government, employers and trade unions, in making large-scale use of the Federal Employment Agency's appropriate instruments to counter the destabilizing macroeconomic effects of the global financial crisis. As a consequence, the social expenditure ratio increased in 2009 dynamically by 2.7 percentage points,[2] excellently proving social security's role as a macroeconomic income stabilizer. Later, the ratio gradually fell again as a result of economic recovery.

From 1993 to 2008, **France** maintained a relatively steady real social spending growth of around 2 per cent per annum, which is now generally considered also the economic long-term real growth rate of the country. Accordingly, the social protection to net national income ratio broadly stabilized; since the 2008 crisis, the economy has been stagnating, which explains the recent increase of the ratio. France did not pursue similar comprehensive reforms as in Germany and the United Kingdom. Nevertheless, the country gradually adapted its social security system to the needs of the national economy,

---

[1] For a country's economy, the following accounts-based macroeconomic equation always holds: private household sector balance + enterprises sector balance + state sector balance + balance vis-à-vis the rest of the world = 0. It follows that a national economy, like Germany's which is running a triple surplus, must run a trade surplus. Another implication is that investments (I) create savings (S), not the other way around-savings are no prerequisite for investments (Lindner, 2012).

[2] Official figures show an increase of 3.4 percentage points. But 0.7 percentage points of that increase are the technical result of incorporation of private health insurance into Germany's 2009 social budget due to changes in the social legislation.

moment, not the least because the consequences of the British exit from the European Union are difficult to judge.[1]

Germany took bold steps (in the early 2000s) in the marketization of its social security. The reform process concerned mainly the labour market, pensions and health insurance reforms[2]-echoing distantly the reforms undertaken in the United Kingdom in 1997 and after. In terms of labour market, reform measures included, among others, new rules stipulating that after the entitlement of employable persons to (strictly limited) earnings-related unemployment insurance benefits ceases, only (meagre) basic (flat) support is being offered. Recipients of basic support are no longer covered by statutory pension insurance, although they are still offered access to basic health services. Jobseekers see themselves commodified through legalized, highly flexible forms of labour contracts (Pusch, 2017; Amlinger, Bispinck and Schulten, 2016). Strong penalizing elements accompany the relation between the individual jobseeker and their case manager at the employment exchange (see the discussion on the United Kingdom); and the trade unions' role in bargaining tariff agreements has been significantly weakened.

With respect to pensions, new rules reduced the link of social security pensions with their economic source (their contributable wages) in favour of occupational and private pensions. Besides, the statutory retirement age was increased to 67 years in Germany, and the standard replacement rate legislated to fall by around one third (BMAS and BArch, 2016b).[3]

In terms of health insurance, social or private, new rules make coverage universal (obligatory for all). Since 2004, redundant (financially ailing) hospitals have closed, and many remaining hospitals have privatized in the name of efficiency.

---

[1] On 23 June 2016, the British people voted with a majority of almost 52 per cent of voters in favour of leaving the European Union. The formal exit process was initiated by the British Government on 29 Mar. 2017. A period of two years is stipulated in the European Treaty for the exit-process-during this period, the details of the exit consequences must be negotiated between the (remaining) EU Members and the United Kingdom. This period ends on 28 Mar. 2019. All parliaments of the remaining 27 EU Member States must agree to the results of those negotiations (within the stipulated two-year period).

[2] This policy of a third way had been inspired and to some extent politically coordinated by or with developments in the United Kingdom (Blair, 1999).

[3] Both measures to be completed by 2030; transition is on its way.

Since the beginning of this phase, the **United Kingdom**, after 1997, pursued a third-way agenda consisting of a supply-side approach to social policy aimed to boost human capital and the knowledge economy (with a time lag of a few years, this agenda inspired similar reforms in Germany, see below).

The social investment agenda placed strong emphasis on the development of active labour market policies offering innovative services and one-to-one discussions between jobseekers and personal advisors. Some of these new deals included sanction regimes for those not participating. Under these regimes, individual jobseekers were monitored in their obligation of active job search, with social security payments increasingly being made conditional and sanctioning becoming more commonplace. These and other changes also aimed to improve support for jobseekers through integration of job search support and benefit payment functions providing individualized one-stop service.

This policy of penalization through social security was combined with attempts to make work pay. A national minimum wage was introduced for the first time, and there was a significant increase in the use of in-work income top-ups to boost the incomes of persons in low-paid work.[1] In this respect, there was particular focus on families with children (eventually quite successfully) aiming to eliminate relative child poverty. In this period, social spending rose more quickly than across the OECD countries, with family-related spending rising from 2.1 per cent of GDP in 1997 to 4 per cent in 2010, accompanied by a marked spending increase in health. Economic performance was strong during 1997-2007, when unemployment dropped to around 5 per cent while inflation remained at a low of around 3 per cent for a prolonged period for the first time since the 1960s. Inequality remained high, but its growth was halted.

In the aftermath of the global financial crisis, growing public concerns over the state of the economy and public finances triggered ensuing (conservative-liberal and conservative) governments' responses to the social investment model and the global financial crisis. Instead of addressing the imperfections and possible detrimental aspects of the new labour market and anti-poverty policies, a kind of rollback took place to radical spending cuts, paralleled with further tightening of the punitive conditions of the system, the impacts of which are still in a process of unfolding. Firm conclusions would be premature at this

---

[1] In Germany also, a top-up scheme for low-paid workers was introduced, less generous though. A national minimum wage was introduced much later, where recent research indicates that it is partially still dysfunctional (Pusch, 2017).

A major (and internationally highly successful) ideological player during this period was the World Bank, which aggressively promoted the (highly sophisticated) Swedish pension model as an alternative for those countries that were not ready to follow the Chilean way (World Bank, 1994). The success of this policy was supported by the so-called Washington Consensus (Williamson, 2002; Mueller, 1999; see also section 2.1.6), the coincidental fall of the Berlin Wall and the resulting political turmoil, especially in the countries of the former Soviet Union, prompted governments to ignore reasonable arguments against immature social security marketization experiments (Hagemejer and Scholz, 2004). Since the international financial and economic crises of 2008-2010, social security policies have been further tightened through **fiscal austerity** in many countries.

As a result, the welfare state as it existed up to the mid-1990s (structurally and in its dynamics) has lost most of its earlier emancipating features, such that the descriptive use of the term "welfare state" appears no longer justified. Social security in the West less and less secures people on a solidarity basis but, rather, increasingly transfers risk to individuals and, thus, quite paradoxically, contributes towards people's insecurity (Judt, 2010).

In pre-empting the China-specific findings of this report, one can conclude that during the same period, a similar perception of social security was put into practice in China, where the impact vector took a direction different from the Western countries' trends. The similarity is to be seen in the fact that China, since the onset of its transformation process that began in the 1980s, has used social security as a governance tool explicitly serving the requirements of the country's intended modernization and economic growth process.[1] At the same time, the psychology for the population was probably very different: While social reforms in the West were usually imposing harsh conditionality and, in consequence, perceived as policies that erased former societal achievements, China's policy helped to unleash economic growth forces and (later) provided, for the first time, room to extend social security coverage to all. Indeed, reforms could be perceived by China's population as gaining simultaneously a combination of security and economic progress unknown before. These developments need to be assessed taking into consideration the different departure points, with the levels of social spending in the 1980s and social security development being extremely different between the West and China. This gap is, however, narrowing down.

---

[1] It would be interesting to explore whether an exchange of ideas took place at that time between, for example, Chinese and Nordic scholars.

Welfare state as investment (after the mid-1990s): From the welfare state to the competition state

After the fall of the Soviet system (around 1989), social security sceptics and proponents alike, in a sort of *alliance impie*, developed language explaining social security as an investment (into human productivity and the economy). In this period, the Nordic countries, somewhat paradoxically, became the superheroes in the world of social models.[1] This took place not so much because of their (continued) high social benefits, equality or low poverty levels but rather as illustrating the **changed logic of the social security and economic growth nexus,** whereby the welfare state was no longer the goal but a means to strengthen economic performance.

Some researchers labelled the new paradigm the "competition state", which, like in Germany and the United Kingdom, emerged in reaction to globalization. A new conventional wisdom emerged that social policy was a public investment that should strengthen economic growth and national competitiveness in world markets. Indeed, in the (classical) social security logic, economic development is a precondition for expanding social security. Here, the ultimate goals are social inclusion, no poverty, redistribution, equality and the creation of equal opportunities. In the (new) growth-competition-innovation logic, social security is instrumental to promoting the national economy. The Nordic welfare State started out as the first model (social security logic), but has over the past decades gradually transformed into the second (growth-competition-innovation logic). While institutions were formally left unchanged, their content changed: Social contingencies more and more shifted from solidarity financing onto individuals' shoulders; public social security spending was reduced (or even ceased) and replaced with voluntary or mandated individual private arrangements, with increased reliance on financial markets; and social security scheme members became customers rather than citizens with rights-based public benefits entitlements. It was around this time that the international community gradually replaced the earlier term of "social security" with "social protection", the former more perceived as comprising social insurance language and the requirements of the middle classes, while the latter more echoed safety-net language and addressing the poor.

---

[1] Paradoxically, their practice of interweaving social security with the economy had always been highly esteemed among left-leaning politicians and social security specialists but, due to being perceived as Nordic-specific, never achieved an international breakthrough.

Republic of Korea joined the group of countries aiming to take advantage of the labour productivity-enhancing effects of social security.

Towards the end of this period, the international social security debate, including in Europe and in China and promoted by the World Bank and the German financial industry, was massively influenced by the aggressive promotion of pension reform in Chile, which took place in the early 1980s (World Bank, 1994). This reform, which cannot be laid out in further detail in this report (but which has been extensively described and analysed in numerous publications, such as Gillion et al., 2000), incorporated all ingredients of the post-Keynesian state perception: minimal tax-financed social security provision by the State, with higher protection (for individuals who could afford it) provided through competing and profit-oriented private agencies, where financial risks were shifted from solidarity financing to individuals and employer obligations were minimized. The impact of this reform on the international debate and social policy developments, although often absent in national debates, cannot be overestimated because decision-makers in many countries, especially in Eastern Europe, felt highly attracted to its features.[1]

At the same time, the Western welfare States-most of them in a process of adapting to the ageing of their covered populations-saw themselves more generally confronted with dramatically changed positions in the world economy. The Soviet system of Eastern Europe had collapsed, and China had begun opening itself internationally. China's opening posed challenges as the country adapted fast to modern technology, expanded production enormously and seized opportunities to export at low prices to the open Western consumer markets. A protectionist reaction of the West was neither thought of in practice nor judged compliant with policies of decent international cooperation nor considered consistent with the market paradigm that had evolved in the West since the 1970s. The further retrenchment of the welfare state and the emergence of the notion of social security as investment in people (see the following section) can be seen as a potentially transitory reaction to China's opening, which could be argued will come to an end once its average labour costs have reached Western levels. One might argue, in a generalizing way and as is done in the context of contemporary Chinese social security policy (see Chapter 3), that conflicts between social security and economic requirements might be unavoidable in some periods, but that overall and measured over long periods, the relationship between the two is positive, with mutually reinforcing elements.

---

[1] The Chilean finance minister is now struggling with the late repercussions of the reform (see section 2.1.6).

And the minimum wage continued falling: From the late 1960s to 2010, the real minimum wage fell by about one third.

Japan shifted its fiscal policy towards austerity with the clear intention to avoid tax increases. Here, also, growing social expenditure was more and more considered unsustainable. To counter accelerating health care costs (resulting from the free medical care consultation policy instituted in 1973), fixed rate co-payments for older persons were introduced, paralleled by a new 10 per cent co-payment of the insured under the employment-based health insurance scheme. In the mid-1980s, fiscal adjustments aimed to equalize the various health insurance schemes' cost-burden in relation to their covered older persons.[1]

Also, to achieve better cost control (as well as to enhance equity among members), a unified first-tier (basic pension) was implemented in all public pension schemes.

In response to continued concerns about the ageing of the population, the Government initiated in the late 1980s policies in preparation for the aged society. A huge multiannual public investment programme (the Gold Plan) was launched to establish welfare services for older persons, such as day-care centres or nursing homes. The programme was financed by levying a 3 per cent consumption tax. It came to a preliminary completion in 2000, when a public long-term care insurance (presumably resting upon the results of the incomplete Gold Plan) was started. It appears that Japan is the only industrialized country with such a prominent focus on ageing in its social (health and services) policies.

The Republic of Korea continued concentrating on "employment first, redistribution second" policies, nevertheless, made national health insurance universal in 1988. In the same year, it implemented a general public pension scheme that became universal ten years later. The scheme was very conservative, however: It was partially funded and accumulated a huge reserve because initially only a few pensions were paid out. Additionally, the fund was only of minimal financial burden to the State because it was run as a social insurance system financed by employers and employees. The option was to keep a relatively low contribution rate, with also a low replacement rate. Generally, social expenditure is still at low levels. In its decision for (Bismarckian) social insurance, the

---

[1] Similar policies had been introduced in Germany and are being pursued. Cost containment in health appears to be a never-ending task for governments everywhere in the world.

in financing its social security system while replacing them with general tax revenue, private household fees for service and the like.¹ In other words, the expenditure ratio was kept at historical levels, but the financing regime was changed to support business competitiveness.

The **Nordic countries** survived the economic (oil price) crises of the 1970s and 1980s better than most other European welfare States. The high acceptance of the welfare state concept in the Nordic populations, together with its effective administration, contributed to the Nordic countries' high resilience against external shocks and major changes. Careful analysis of the interaction between social security and the economy, and labour markets especially, allowed them to prepare better for challenges in the future. In fact, in the world of social models, the Nordic countries were highly influential in preparing the contemporary paradigmatic understanding of social security as investment into people.

The **United States** pursued policies resulting in steeply rising inequality. Increases in social spending came mainly in the form of tax expenditures-tax deductions given for social ends. The ratio of social tax expenditures to ordinary federal social spending rose, from 5 per cent in 1975 to 30 per cent in 2010 (Faricy, 2015). These tax expenditures accrued overwhelmingly to upper-income groups and thus increased income inequality.[2,3] At the same time, education expenditure declined, from its high in 1970 (at 7.4 per cent) to a low of 5.2 per cent of GDP in the mid-1990s, where it stabilized (Stephens, 2019).

---

[1] Under the conditions of the European monetary system (allowing only little flexibility within a managed x-rate regime), this policy was also a lagged reaction to Germany's additional competitiveness as achieved through its preceding consolidation process Regrettably, social security has always been seen in the European Union as an instrumental variable of competition among Member States rather than a policy field requiring close coordination. The implications for people have become more visible under the euro, where x-rate adjustments are impossible.

[2] European Union Member States equally use the instrument of tax expenditure for social purposes. The European Union has decided not to include these anymore in its ESSPROS due to the difficulties of estimating the amount of tax foregone (see ESSPROS).

[3] In the same period in Germany, tax relief gained importance as an instrument in the field of family benefits, because the higher-income classes profit more from child-related tax deductions than families with low or no taxable income (who, instead, receive direct flat cash benefits per child). Proponents of this policy argued that it is in full compliance with fair and redistributive income tax rules; opponents argued that the same policy implies that children of high-income households are of a higher absolute value to the State than children of low-income households.

transfers and by containing benefits. The cost of social security was increasingly seen as the main cause for the rise of the unemployment rate, from 0.7 per cent at the beginning of the 1970s to 9 per cent by the decade's end (BMA, 2016). Social security coverage was still extended in some areas but generally an embargo on additional programmes was put in place while access to certain benefits was tightened. In 1989, just before German unification, the social expenditure ratio had dropped to 24.6 per cent, a low ratio at that time, due to temporarily accelerated GDP growth rates (and not as a result of overall benefit cuts) (BMAS, 2015).

Unified Germany(since 1990) briefly interrupted the process of social security consolidation during the short economic unification boom between 1990 and 1992: East German social benefit levels had to be increased significantly, and fast, to adjust them (partially) to increased price levels; economic echo-effects resulted in slightly higher adjustments also in West Germany (BMASand BArch, 2008; BMGand BArch, 2004). Together with an effective use of labour market instruments countering massive underemployment and unemployment in the East and the introduction of a newly introduced care insurance (1994), these policies lifted the country's overall social expenditure ratio in the 1990s to just only 1.5 percentage points above the (West Germany) ratio of the 1980s.[1]

France used social security in 1973 as a macroeconomic stabilizer and also as an indirect reaction to the Bundesbank's tight monetary policy of the time. The country's social security systems' capacities to function alike were increasingly questioned during subsequent years. As in Germany and the United Kingdom, social expenditure was increasingly seen as a problem for regaining dynamic economic growth rather than part of the solution. After the mid-1980s, the social expenditure ratio reached levels between 25 per cent and 30 per cent, which, under the given financial regime of labour-based contributions, were considered economically unsustainable. During this time, France, like Germany, resisted the United Kingdom's market radicalism, although it did not fully ignore it. In the 1990s, France began to significantly reduce the share of contributions

---

[1] Although politically unified as of October 1990, with subsequent fast extension of West Germany's social security legislation to the East, both former territories were administratively (and statistically) kept separate to allow for a rational adjustment of East German living conditions to those of the West. As was foreseeable, this transition process took social security broadly one generation; it has just now come to a (successful) halt.

and the Republic of Korea becoming outliers.

Interesting enough, during this period (mid 1980s-mid 1990s), China also cut welfare provisions in order to prepare and support economic structural reforms (see Chapter 3 for details).

The **United Kingdom** finally began ending the remains of its Beveridgean welfare state regime with the 1976 balance of payments crisis, high inflation and growing unemployment, to which the International Monetary Fund gave relief in return for a social adjustment programme.

After 1979, rolling back the State became the leitmotif of a radical neoliberal programme of free market-driven reforms, which looked to reverse the gradual move towards collectivism that had characterized the period from 1945 to 1975. The programme included high-profile privatization (including large parts of the social housing stock), the marketization of some public services and a push to reduce tax rates and the overall level of public spending.[1]

The social security focus was on cutting unemployment benefits to trigger incentives for taking up work.[2] The replacement rate of benefits for a single unemployed person (with average earnings) fell from 50 per cent in 1979 to just 25 per cent by 1983 (Hudson, 2016). These cuts came despite the rapidly rising and unprecedented post-World War II unemployment rate resulting from the escalating economic problems in the early years of the reform process.

This was one of the reasons that the social spending ratio, while initially around 8 percentage points lower than (West) Germany's of the time, continued growing.

West Germany, the economic heavyweight in the European Union, financially consolidated its social security schemes by increasing contribution rates and government

---

[1] As indicated before, the policy had been long before prepared ideologically, mainly through the works of August Hayek.
[2] An adapted version of this policy, including housing privatization and unemployment benefit cuts, was implemented in Germany a decade later. This is an interesting case and confirmation of the fact that social policies in Europe keep fertilizing each other, sometimes to the better, sometimes to the worse.

of sufficient size, at first contributed effectively to stabilizing aggregate domestic demand and individual expectations well into 1974 and 1975. However, most governments began postponing planned improvements until further notice.[1] The main psychological effect was that people's (and government's) belief in never-ending growth was broken and that the new Chicago School of thought, with its trust in the rationale of markets (at minimal State involvement), gained prominence.[2] In short, the neoliberal counter-revolution was looming.

Consolidation (retrenchment) of the welfare state (mid-1970s to mid-1990s)[3]

This phase began in the aftermath of the break-up of the Bretton Woods system (1971) and the first oil price crisis (1973), which, together, resulted in a major global economic recession. In Europe, the Deutsche mark became the new anchor currency to which European currencies were pegged and the German central bank pursued its (in-)famous price stability policy[4] with repercussions on the other European economies. The Keynesian consensus broke up and was gradually replaced with the new paradigm of monetarism (Friedman and Bordo, 2005). (Costly) unemployment increased and remained high, trade unions fell to defensive positions. Improvements of social security stalled. Together, these developments resulted in the year-long new phenomenon of stagflation (stagnating real growth and inflation). After the second oil price crisis (1981), the labour income share in GDP began falling in many countries, and financing social security became more difficult. With respect to welfare, governments significantly reduced expansionary plans and gradually began to reverse earlier social security and labour rights legislation, with Japan

---

[1,3] France is a prominent outlier in that respect. Significant improvements were made to social security schemes in the 1970s and up to the early 1980s. Cost-containment policies started to be implemented after 1983, not the least after the Bundesbank exerted its dominant influence in the European monetary system.

[2] The Chicago School had ideologically been prepared by August Hayek, an Austrian economist, of whom Milton Friedman (Chicago) was a student and follower. Hayek had been the long-standing antagonist to Keynes. While Keynesian economics was core condition for a successful welfare state, Hayek's economics relied on markets alone, allowing only for minimal social protection. Contemporary proposals of general minimum income are consistent with the Hayekian paradigm.

[4] According to federal law, guaranteeing price stability was the main task of the Deutsche Bundesbank (the German central bank). Whether the Bundesbank used the right indicators and policies to fulfil its task has been debated at length in the German as well as international literature. Suggestions to make low unemployment an equally important goal of the Bundesbank's policy never made it even close to realization (legislation).

1972, a child allowance was paid, and in 1973, older persons were given free access to medical care consultations. As well, Japan's labour relations were modernized through several laws.

Nevertheless and as a result of high post-war economic growth, the social expenditure ratio remained low, at less than 5 per cent, until the early 1970s-well below the levels of France or Germany, for example. As a result, Japan's macroeconomic supply-side and demand-side functions of social security could not unfold its growth-enhancing and stabilizing fiscal effects on the economy. However, social security functioned well by establishing social stability, which constituted the basis for Japan's sound economic growth after the war (Ono, 2019).

The Republic of Korea pursued socioeconomic policies under a paradigm of "compressed growth with equity" (this policy was maintained until the late 1980s), through which it achieved remarkable social equity, mainly at the level of primary income distribution-without major (redistributive) social security programmes. This unique historical experience contributed to a deep conviction in the Korean society of a predominantly negative interrelationship between economic growth and institutionalized social security, which was paraphrased as economic growth first, distribution second. The general policy orientation is that all societal resources should be invested only into economic growth because social spending would hinder economic development. Accordingly, the Government focused its social spending on education (which resembled features of the United States).

The Republic of Korea's Industrial Accident Compensation Insurance Act was implemented only in 1964, with low coverage at the time. A national health insurance was introduced in 1977, when the urban population had nearly reached 50 per cent of the total (the scheme became universal in 1988) (Kim, 2019). During this period, no public pension scheme had yet been introduced.

Not surprising, the social expenditure ratio was extremely low (at one-digit levels), when compared with other OECD countries.

At the end of this phase (1973), the oil price crisis hit. The psychological effects in the Western economies (including Japan and the Republic of Korea) were deeper than recessions retrospectively measured by statistical offices. Social security, where financially result of the disputes over costs that were a constant feature of the political debates and of funding issues that often produced compromises that diluted the Beveridge model, while Keynesian macroeconomic policy missed incorporating social protection into its theoretical reasoning and fiscal practice. As a result, successive governments used cheaper targeted benefits for economizing on social spending. Also, although in large parts financed out of employer and employee contributions, the British social security system never established a routine of formal assessment of the relationships between contributions paid and benefits received while, at the same time, many, if not all, privately managed (occupational) schemes for the middle classes were controlled by such techniques.[1]

As a consequence, even if spending was steadily growing,[2] the United Kingdom could only suboptimally harvest the macroeconomically stabilizing and productivity-enhancing functions of social security (in case it would have been implemented more in line with the applications in the other European countries), which most probably contributed to the failed macroeconomic stabilization later in the 1970s.

Japan had to first take on emergency measures to support its suffering population after World War II and then to re-establish its system from scratch, including administration. This included social assistance (completely reformed in 1950 and put under State responsibility) and the universalization of pension and health care coverage in the 1950s, which was achieved for both in 1961. Both schemes were based on social insurance principles, with the municipalities taking organizational responsibility for the National Health Insurance. In the 1960s, cash benefit levels were significantly improved for public pensions and for social assistance. Similar to Western Europe, legislation aimed to enhance social welfare for disadvantaged groups, such as intellectually challenged persons. Limitations on medical treatment were removed in Japan; as of

---

[1] Actuarial methods consist of applied mathematical techniques but are most influential in political debates because it is often assumed that they automatically guarantee financial fairness between those who pay and those who receive social benefits or between individually paid-in contributions and individually received annuities. The term actuarial fairness is, however, of a shimmering nature because fairness is multidimensional and must therefore be used with care. See Plamondon (2002) for an overview of actuarial methods used in practice.

[2] Social security and health care, respectively, amounted to 4.8 per cent and 3.3 per cent of GDP in 1950, 5.6 per cent and 3.1 per cent in 1960, 7.3 per cent and 3.5 per cent in 1970, and 9 per cent and 4.4 per cent in 1980.

increasing, hitting 26.3 per cent in 1975 (BMAS and BArch, 2017) in technical reaction to the economic recession in the aftermath of the first oil price crisis. The legal expansion was mainly driven by several extensions of social insurance coverage and other non-means-tested benefits. It was complemented (at the end of the 1960s) by a modern social assistance system that aimed at preventing poverty among the few persons not employed or having no other entitlements (see the Japan discussion further on) (Schroeder, 2019).

The **Nordic countries** initially showed relatively low public expenditure ratios, partly associated with the common criticism that extended social rights would hamper economic growth and generate idleness. This changed dramatically during the 1960s (mainly in Denmark and Sweden) through reforms that gradually introduced new social rights, included more people and legislated higher benefits and more state regulation. During this period, a revolution took place that resulted in the emergence of what is nowadays called the Nordic welfare state, which is characterized by: universalism (one system for everybody versus scattered systems, such as in Germany or the United Kingdom); social rights (based on citizenship in all EU countries); state regulation (in all EU countries, with variance); tax financing (a dominant principle other than in countries pursuing Bismarckian systems); a large public sector (other than in countries like Germany and United Kingdom); a local community approach (small room for variation); highly organized labour markets (more than in Germany and much more than in the United Kingdom) and a focus on redistribution and equality (class and gender, like in the British public health service; other than Germany, for example, where the focus is more on efficiency).

These features emerged under specific political constellations and through incremental change and a window of opportunity created by the economic growth of the 1960s. In the corresponding Nordic political debates, economic development was meant to secure the goals of inclusion, social security, equality and the opportunity for all citizens to live a better life (Petersen, 2019).

In the 1960s, the **United Kingdom** became an international exemplar in terms of welfare capitalism through social reforms that were inspired by the Beveridge report and implemented from 1945 to 1951. The country missed, however, the opportunity to move progressively forward towards a Nordic design. Instead, it appears the United Kingdom moved from a temporary welfare state leader to a more laggard position in the decades that followed. This early step off the general welfare bandwagon was mainly a for social policy. There is also agreement, however, that social security policy was no cause for hampering or limiting economic growth. The costs of social security were not the reason for the 1973 crisis-this conservative argument emerged only after the first oil price crisis.

Right after World War II, **France** began to create the General Scheme (Régime général), aiming to rapidly cover the entire population. It started as an occupational scheme limited to private sector employees, which is still the case today for pensions and unemployment benefits. Family benefits and health insurance now cover the whole population.

Social expenditure grew in line with the general economic trend, except during two periods (1949-1953 and 1961-1968) when paid cash benefits dynamically surpassed economic growth, while (much lower) health services continued growing gradually. Together, this explains the stepwise increase of France's social expenditure ratio, from initially less than 15 per cent of net national income to around 20 per cent by 1973 (Concialdi, 2019).

West Germany's immediate social post-war problem was to absorb a total of around 12 million refugees (at a total population of slightly more than 50 million) from the lost territories in the East and other displaced persons (BMAS and BArch, 2006). This was supported by social programmes (unemployment insurance and social assistance) and other measures, like temporary rationing of housing. But it was mainly solved by the buoyant recovery and investment process of the 1950s, which was supported through US aid: As with the other European countries, employment grew fast and unemployment rates declined rapidly in Germany. The system of collective bargaining enforced companies' organizational productivity. Labour rights were further strengthened through a system of workers' co-determination at the management level,[1] which also helped to integrate surplus labour.

Until around 1960, the social expenditure ratio (social expenditure as a percentage of GDP) in west Germany remained at less than 20 per cent.[2] Then it began continuously

---

[1] This feature of cooperation between labour and capital was actually triggered by the Western Allied Forces holding (West) Germany occupied after World War II. It took up ideas that had been intensely discussed for a short period in the United Kingdom after World War I but that had not been implemented (Rodgers, 1998).

[2] Consolidated time series statistics began only in 1960.

transfers and health care, only making leaps forward in the Great Depression and again in the 1960s but still lagging behind other industrial democracies. This pattern of social development could be one of the influencing factors for why the United States was a leader in the nineteenth and early twentieth centuries in economic development but lagged in growth levels after World War II.

The New Deal was a turning point for the American welfare state, but it was only short lived. On one hand, the Social Security Act (1935) provided basic pensions, unemployment and disability insurance, and social assistance was complemented with a federal minimum wage (1938). With these measures, the United States became, transitorily (during the Depression), a world leader in public social spending on the basis of work and relief. On the other hand, the Social Security Act's achievements were permanent while the work and relief schemes were allowed to lapse. Plans to complement the Social Security Act with comprehensive health care provision were unsuccessful. The administration only managed covering the aged (Medicare) and the poor (Medicaid) (1965).[1] In addition, the Great Society social programmes of the 1960s provided for poverty relief, established a preschool programme and greatly increased aid to education at all levels. In 1970, public spending on education in the United States was 7.4 per cent of GDP, second only to Canada (at 8.5 per cent) and tied with Sweden among the country members of the Organisation for Economic Co-operation and Development (OECD).

Thus, while the American expansionary social security policy came to a halt after World War II, it gained much momentum in Western Europe, which enjoyed high economic growth rates for 25 years, ending in 1973. One might argue, with some effort, that Europe's expansionary social policy contributed to the economic growth during this period (for example, the trade unions' working time and wage policy contributed to labour productivity and the system of co-determination eased dynamic structural change during growth). But there is wide agreement among scholars that this argument must be used with care because it can easily overstretch the perception of the significance of the role and impact of social security during this period.

In fact, it was predominantly investment, consumption and (partially) export-driven economic growth that offered, not the least through the increasing (non-adjusted) wage share in primary income, increasingly affluent middle-class conditions and opportunities

---

[1] It was not until the recent Patient Protection and Affordable Care Act was introduced (2010) that the United States approached comprehensive health coverage.

Implementation and expansion of the welfare state (post-1945 to mid-1970s)

This initial post-World War II phase of the welfare state was characterized by high economic growth, a fast decline of unemployment, strong wage increases and little resistance against income tax and social contribution rate increases. Labour rights were improved, and capital accepted social obligations. Social expenditure as well as social revenue ratios were initially low but increased as a result of redistributive legislation. Internationally, this policy was generously supported by the United States as provider of the anchor currency in a fixed exchange rate regime (Bretton Woods system) (DeLong, 2002) and, not the least, by wide consensus among state leaders of Keynesian macroeconomic policies (Samuelson, 1983). The political and (Keynesian) macroeconomic supporting role of the United States cannot be overestimated during this expansionary period of the welfare state. At the same time, in terms of concrete realization of social security, the United States remained modestly in the background.

Although widely alien to the United States' societal and economic constitution, the European States were free to keep significant numbers of structurally important enterprises in public ownership (France, Germany and the United Kingdom, for example). Trade unions had a significant role in the organization of the economies at large and in extending labour rights and working conditions specifically: Directly or indirectly, trade unions explicitly assumed a political role (next to political parties), often with direct influence on political decisions.

During the 1960s, Denmark and Sweden dramatically changed their societal fabric and went from being relative spending laggards to the top of the class. Japan followed suit (DeLong, 2002).

European countries began striving to maximize social security coverage (to leave no citizen behind), but this was never an explicit goal of social policy in the post-World War II **United States**. Accordingly, improvements in social security were limited. The United States had been a leader for the century and a half up to the mid-1970s in the development of social right to education[1] but a laggard in the development of social rights to income

---

[1] Education is not included as part of the welfare state in many early studies, but more recently, particularly after the European Union's turn to social investment, it has more often been included.

and dynamics (Vaughan-Whitehead, 2015a and 2015b). What remains of the welfare state is now predominantly understood as a means to support economic growth rather than a fruit to be harvested from positive economic development (Vaughan-Whitehead, 2015a). In adapting Hudson (2016), we distinguish in this section four trends (phases) of post-World War II development of the welfare state (also see Judt, 2010):

- implementation and expansion of the welfare state (post-1945 to mid-1970s);
- consolidotion (retrenchment)of the welfare state (mid-1970s to mid-1990s);
- welfare state as investment (after the mid-1990s);and
- new reforms and reform needs ahead(in the mid-2010s and beyond).

This section elaborates on those four phases, based on the detailed background reports covering Germany, the United Kingdom, France, the Nordic countries, the United States, Japan and the Republic of Korea. With respect to the four European cases, the narratives differ. This is not only a result of the different analytical views of the contributing authors but also because the European Union, from its beginnings,[1] deliberately excluded social security policy from its agenda of subject matters to be regulated by common rules and regulations.[2]

The four phased trends are evident in all cases covered in this section, with the Korean and US trends differing more while the Japanese situation differs less from the Europeans. China's commencing journey towards completing its socialist market economy with more comprehensive social security began in a phase in which most comparable countries conceptually pursued an approach of social security as investment-where the welfare state is expected to serve economic purposes. But, as we see from history, this is not the only possibility to interpret role and functions of the welfare state.

Under a global perspective, one might argue that the West is searching for a new, paradigmatically consolidated welfare state model, with China, in its reflecting on international typical models and their developments, is seen as joining that search. If things go right, the participants in the search process might find a new (old?) paradigm that not only satisfies, in a narrower sense, the social needs of people but also helps to stabilize future inherently volatile and imbalanced global economic developments (including trade relations).

---

[1] See the Treaty of Rome, 1956, https://eur-lex.europa.eu/legal-content/EN/TXT/?uri= CELEX:11957E/TXT (accessed 16 Feb. 2018).

[2] Keep in mind that many significant national differences in many regulatory and behavioural details remained undisclosed when grouping the European countries in this report.

Figure 1 Social protection programmes anchored in national legislation, by branch, from pre-1900 to post-2010

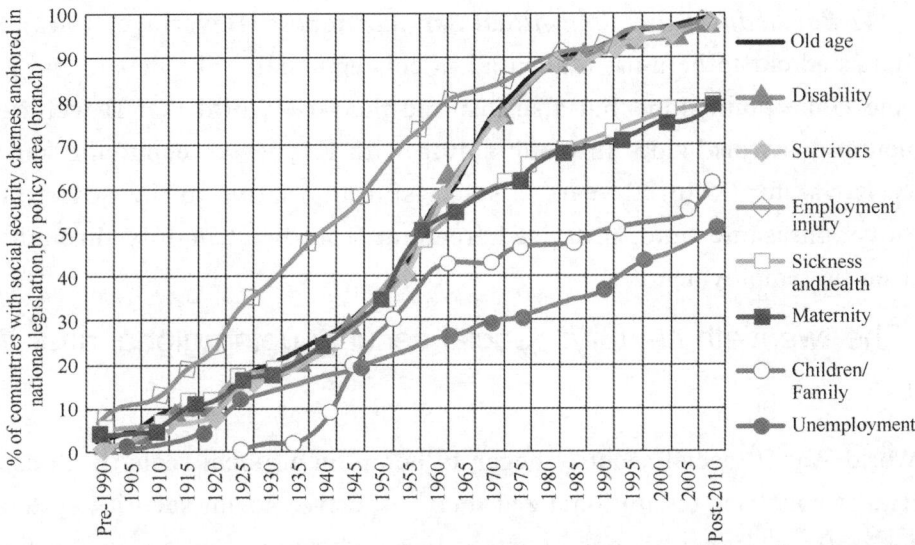

Source: ILO, 2017; based on ILO World Social Protection Database and ISSA and SSA: *Social Security Programs Throughout the World*.

Nor does figure 1 reflect to what extent social security covers people legally and/or materially. As a matter of fact, 4 billion people, or 55 per cent of the world's population, are not covered by any social security benefit, and only 29 per cent of the global population has access to comprehensive social security (ILO, 2017).

While these facts are not seriously challenged, the reasons for the still unsatisfactory implementation of social security globally can be seen in social policy's inevitable interaction with other policy fields and developments, of which some favour (while others disfavour) the extension of social security coverage.

2.1.5 The post-World War II developments in the West

In the West,[1] the welfare state, as a concept as well as in socioeconomic reality, experienced various phases, ranging from strong political support and expansion over what might be called consolidation to its crisis and marketization during the past two to three decades. Its European variants recently lost much of their earlier emancipating thrust

---

[1] The term "West" is understood as comprising mainly the group of countries that are OECD members but not only. Many countries that belonged to the East before the fall of the Soviet system are now considered part of the Western hemisphere.

When the US President Roosevelt added to the New Deal his famous four freedoms,[1] the United Kingdom could no longer hold back envisaging major social reforms. Commissioned by the Government, William Henry Beveridge (1879-1963) presented in his 1942 *Social Insurance and Allied Services* report (Beveridge, 1942), which not only turned out to be most influential in conceptualizing the debate and politics within the United Kingdom[2] but also inspired the post-World War II welfare state implementations worldwide. In combination with Keynesian economic and fiscal policies, it was for 25 to 30 years, a successful alternative to the Soviet system, which, over the same time, promised freedom from want mainly through state-guaranteed full employment.

2.1.4 The twentieth century: Social security going global after World War II

After World War II, social security began to boom on a global scale. Both capitalist and socialist countries institutionalized their respective social security system. The evolution of the welfare state and its interaction with people and economies has been extensively described in numerous books and articles with various viewpoints and where political, fiscal economic and social analyses dominated. The United Nations, especially the ILO, has increasingly dealt with issues of social security and massively expanded research, analysis and advocacy. The concept of social protection has metamorphosed into an integral part of most governments' general policy portfolio and thus near impossible to withdraw from (see figure 1). This does not imply that all people around the globe are covered by social security. Although impressive at first glance, it must be understood that figure 1 reflects the percentage of countries that have anchored social security of some sort in their national legislation-it does not reflect to what extent social security, as acknowledged in the legislation, has transformed materially into reality. It also does not distinguish schemes legislated to cover all populations from schemes covering (deliberately or not) only small groups of population.

---

[1] The four are freedom of speech, freedom of worship, freedom from want and freedom from fear.
[2] The 1942 Beveridge report is definitely a reference document for the welfare states that emerged after World War II in many countries of the West. Its ideas have recently regained international recognition and momentum.

but failed to complete the system with a similar health and unemployment insurance solution, which can be seen as the result of that competitive system fertilization. The Bismarckian solutions were, as in the United Kingdom, not especially popular after World War I. The arguments that won over the social insurance solution for pensions (in 1935) came from the German (heavy) industry's outstanding success in reducing the number of work accidents as a result of its **social work accident insurance** (Rodgers, 1998).

Apart from workers' (accidents) compensation schemes, incrementally implemented over time, US President Roosevelt's social security is the only state-run and nationwide social insurance solution in the United States worth mentioning. Social health insurance was hindered from flourishing as a result of heavy indecent lobbying of private insurance companies (which saw their business endangered).[1]

Between 1919 and 1939, the ILO issued 67 Conventions and 66 Recommendations.[2] Yet, in a context of re-emerging political competition and international mistrust, workers' social situations did not improve much globally. Only a few countries extended or formally completed their respective social security system, among them Germany (1927 with unemployment insurance) and France (1928 with health insurance).[3]

During those years of international consultancy, legislation and constitutional discussions and concerns between the European Continent, the United Kingdom and the United States, most British participants realized that the UK system was no attractive alternative to Bismarck. Persons in British society of the 1920s and 1930s who lived a modest life as a farmer or a member of the miserably paid working class were always at risk of falling into poverty when sickness, work accident, unemployment or disability at old-age hit.

---

[1] One can get a comprehensive understanding of President Obamas' (2009-2017) difficulties in implementing health coverage for all only by going back into the respective debates that took place in the United States before and after World War I.

[2] See http://www.ilo.org/dyn/normlex/en/f?p=1000:12000:::NO::: (accessed 23 Nov. 2016).

[3] France began implementing a modern social security system only from 1945 (Concialdi, 2019).

the founding of the ILO (ILO, 2016). Under the tight monetary conditions of the **gold standard**, it was not surprising that the issues of international competition required an international mechanism that allowed mediation on the effects of social security legislation on labour costs.

Even before World War I, European governments and American civil society had adopted laws and activities concerning labour-oriented social security (a detailed account is provided in Rodgers, 1998). Bismarckian approaches were aimed at, received fresh attention, got new momentum and/or were gradually applied also by Germany's Continental neighbours.[1]

At the same time, politicians and social protection activists in the United Kingdom considered Bismarck's state-run social insurance approach un-British (Rodgers, 1998). It turned out that state-organized social insurance (even when coming with self-governance) had no chance of implementation in the United Kingdom.[2]

While the United Kingdom's official reaction to Bismarck's legislation was clear-cut, the situation in the United States was less transparent. Much travelling of delegations between Germany and the United States took place to explore the applicability of the Bismarckian system to the United States or seek alternatives. What actually took place was a combination of hidden mutual-system fertilizations and simultaneous competitive search for best solutions, which have become part of normal international interaction, although the general public usually does not take much notice of it. To cut a long story short, the United States implemented social security system in 1935[3]

---

[1] Germany's neighbours had been impressed by Bismarck's system, not because of the legislation but because of its systemic, focused and modern approach; it was seen as excellent governance while it influenced ongoing and triggered new debates on social security in Europe and beyond.

[2] This stance was observed much later again: In the 1970s, a Labour government implemented a more thorough version of (the widely diluted Beveridgean) contribution-financed social insurance, but the system was closed a few years later by the Conservative government of Margaret Thatcher (1979-1990).

[3] The US Social Security Act (Act of 14 Aug. 1935) [H.R. 7260] was an act to provide for general welfare by establishing a system of federal old-age benefits and by enabling the states to make more adequate provision for aged persons, blind persons, dependant and crippled children, maternal and child welfare, public health and the administration of their unemployment compensation laws; to establish a Social Security Board; to raise revenue; and for other purposes (SSA, 2016).

Table 1 Years of initial social security legislation and economic development levels in selected OECD countries

	Country	Work accidents insurance	Health insurance	Pension insurance	Unemployment insurance	Family support	Country rank (by year of first social security legislation)	GDP per capita in the year of first social law of country	GDP per capita 1883 (year of first social law in Germany)
		Year					Index	International dollars	
	1	2	3	4	5	6	7	8	9
1	Australia	1902	1948	1908	1944	1941	15	3,823	4,475
2	Austria	1887	1888	1907	1920	1948	4	2,404	2,209
3	Belgium	1903	1894	1900	1920	1930	3	3,468	3,145
4	Canada	1930	1977	1927	1940	–	23	4,847	2,090
5	Denmark	1898	1892	1891	1907	1952	2	2,555	2,299
6	Finland	1895	1963	1937	1917	1948	17	1,492	1,230
7	France	1898	1928	1910	1905	1932	6	2,760	2,288
8	Germany	1884	1883	1889	1927	1954	1	2,143	2,143
9	Greece	1914	1922	1934	1945	1958	18	1,592	1,178
10	Iceland	1925	1936	1909	1936	1946	16	–	–
11	Ireland	1897	1911	1911	1911	1944	7	2,736	1,775
12	Italy	1898	1943	1919	1919	1937	13	1,672	1,568
13	Japan	1911	1927	1941	1947	1971	19	837	1,356
14	Luxembourg	1902	1901	1911	1921	1947	8	–	–
15	Netherlands	1901	1931	1919	1916	1939	12	3,440	3,305
16	New Zealand	1908	1938	1898	1930	1926	11	3,985	3,495
17	Norway	1895	1909	1936	1906	1946	10	1,872	1,588
18	Portugal	1913	1935	1935	1975	1942	20	1,250	1,008
19	Spain	1900	1942	1919	1919	1938	14	1,654	1,720
20	Sweden	1901	1891	1913	1934	1947	9	2,105	1,937
21	Switzerland	1918	1911	1946	1982	1952	21	4,378	2,396
22	United Kingdom	1897	1911	1908	1911	1945	5	4,264	3,643
23	United States	1930	1965	1935	1935	1935	22	6,213	3,008
24	Simple average	1903	1920	1918	1925	1945	–	2,949	2,249
25	Range	46	94	57	77	45	–	5,376	3,467
26	Maximum	1930	1977	1946	1982	1971	–	6,213	4,475
27	Minimum	1884	1883	1889	1905	1926	–	837	1,008

Note:
Column 1:   Selected OECD countries
Columns 8 & 9:   Internationally and historically comparable estimates (Maddison, 2003)
Line 25:   Difference of lines 26 and 27; indicates, for columns 2 to 6, the time range, in years that it took the selected countries to legislate.
Source: Adapted from Schmidt, 2005, p. 182 [original in German].

2.1.3 The twentieth century: Social security between the two great wars

A major step towards internationalization of social security was made in 1919 with also in Austria, France, Italy, Spain and other Continental countries.

From an international perspective, one can argue that it was only by chance that, among all industrializing countries of the time, it was Germany to first legislate modern social security. Nevertheless, it was (and still is in hindsight) impressive that the country, at that time by far not the most advanced economy, implemented a modern set of social laws within a short period of seven years. It took most countries several decades to accomplish something similar (see table 1). In the twentieth century, the design of that legislation was a successful blueprint for other countries to follow suit.

The details of Bismarck's social security legislation have been meticulously and widely documented by German and international research and are, therefore, not discussed here. They nicely illustrate, though, how modern social security policy occasionally was not driven by idealistic motives and how the final outcome of a policy process, once activated, might differ from initial intentions. This observation is not trivial. For Germany, the implemented system was designed such that its population and economy were able and ready to adapt to it most productively. This success story, however, is no guarantee that quasi copies of the same system by other countries, in usually other demographic and socioeconomic contexts, would lead to the same social and economic results.

In 1891, the Vatican published the first Social Encyclical,[1] which dealt with the conflictual relations between capital and labour, specifically with such topics as (institutionalized) bipartite cooperation among workers and employers and the social obligations resulting from property ownership. Meanwhile, the Holy See published eight Social Encyclicals[2] that covered additional topics, such as workers' codetermination in the management of enterprises, priorities of labour over capital and workers' right to organize in trade unions and a social market economy. The analyses and conclusions of these documents continue to influence public attitudes in relation to social security in predominantly Catholic countries (even if, regrettably, often not very successful in practice).[3]

---

[1] Rerum Novarum (see Leo XIII, 1891).
[2] In 1891, 1931, 1961, 1967, 1981, 1987, 1991 and 2009.
[3] There have always been close ties between the Holy See in Rome and German governments and civil society, not the least for financial reasons (Germany's rich Catholic parishes are traditionally major financial contributors to the budget of the Holy See). After all, until 1806 (end of the Napoleonic Wars), the German Empire was officially called the Holy Roman Empire.

as well as shared organizational structures of families and the State as a whole. While providing social security, the State also regulated family-based protection which was closely related to state welfare, and guided mutual help among neighbourhoods and work units' welfare provisions (Zheng, 2014a).

2.1.2 The nineteenth century, the United Kingdom, Germany and the Holy See

In 1834, the Old Poor Law of 1597 and 1601 were streamlined with England's evolving unrestricted market capitalism. The New Poor Law stipulated that no able-bodied person was to receive money or other help from the authorities except when an inmate of a workhouse. Together with the principle that conditions for workhouse inmates had to be worse than those of the poorest free labourer outside, this ruling often led to starvation.[1] The New Poor Law was unable to deal with the social consequences of locally and cyclically occurring unemployment (the new phenomenon of industrialization). Social security, so designed, not only failed in almost all respects of modern human rights but also fundamentally ran against minimum conditions of fostering labour productivity. As a result of the counterproductive but sustained 1834 legislation, the much later European trend towards capitalism with a human face took nearly a full century before it materialized.

The New Poor Law, one of the most significant UK laws of the time, equally influenced and reflected the country's socioeconomic structures well into the twentieth century. Its underlying laissez-faire philosophy was an intellectually deceiving and powerful governance instrument[2] and shaped the attitudes of UK citizens who migrated to the United States. This is one of the reasons why Germany's corporatist social insurance legislation of the 1880s had no success as a model in the United Kingdom and only partially so in the United States.

The nineteenth century debate on the European Continent, at its core, took a different direction from UK practice, not the least as a result of the continued influence of the Holy See, which, while carrying long-term memories of the old Roman law, preached and practised ecclesiastic charity and supported paternal attitudes not only in Germany but

---

[1] This principle is reflected in contemporary rules stipulating that social assistance must be significantly lower than the lowest paid wage; such rules are more questionable the more societies allow for near-poverty wage levels (precarious work).

[2] The idea of a social market economy had not yet gained prominence.

poverty relief, it was less so in the East.¹ Instead, certain obligations of individual income redistribution were developed in ancient times, whereby persons who were rich donated alimony to the ascetics and impoverished confreres in belief. The nobles and the rich households took responsibility for widows and orphans (Weber, 1991 [1920]). Confucianism(Confucius, 551-479 B.C.) is an impressive example of laying foundations of early contemplation in respect of addressing duty and commitment relative to the needs of social groups (Wang, 2017).

Confucius elaborated the famous concept of "universal harmony" for the ideal society, which still exerts its influence nowadays, nationally as well as internationally. It describes a situation in which "people provide for their own parents as well as other elders and raise their own children as well as those of others. Elders live their full span, adults exert their talents, children are nurtured, and the widowed, orphaned, childless as well as people with disabilities are all taken care of...Instead of being selfish, people are willing to devote themselves to public services. As a result, people feel secure enough to open their house doors" (Confucius, n.d.).²

Even though this ideal was developed around 2,500 years ago, early practices of China's social security can be rooted back to the Shang Dynasty (1600-1046 B.C.), during which a disaster relief system came hand in hand with the origination of the State with formal structures. Preferential treatment for soldiers, like in the Roman Empire, was documented in 1046 B.C. In 179 B.C., the Emperor of the Han Dynasty issued a decree stipulating that the State was obligated to provide support to older persons. During the Tang Dynasty (608-907 A.D.), a system of storage and reserve for emergencies was set up, and later, in the Song Dynasty (960-1279 A.D.), a highly developed social system and welfare institutions were established. Along socioeconomic developments and dynastic alterations, both format and substance of these systems underwent certain changes nevertheless, the State took responsibility.

Thus, ever since ancient times, social security has been regarded as an important part of public governance, embodying features of state paternalism and family-nation integration

---

¹ The terms "West" and "East" are used to signify the Western and Eastern hemispheres.
² The original text in Chinese is: "故人不独亲其亲，不独子其子，使老有所终，壮有所用，幼有所长，矜鳏寡孤独废疾者皆有所养。……力恶其不出于身也，不必为己。……故外户而不闭". See http://eh.net/encyclopedia/article/boyer.poor.laws.england Economic History Association (accessed 14 Dec. 2018).

the stories to tell become ever more detailed the more one aims to identify typical tracks of development. And the more one goes international, especially in recent years, the more one wants to distinguish between national, regional and international trends of social security implementation. The more one wants to reflect on international (United Nations and ILO) agreements, the more it is difficult to distinguish the various contemporary lines of social security thought, design and reality. This chapter pursues a narrative at varying levels of abstraction versus concreteness. Much of the content was influenced by background reports that were commissioned for this report. The China-specific results were cursorily taken into account but are dealt with at length in Chapter 3. This chapter, therefore, aims at comprehensiveness but also unavoidably must allow for omissions; for example, developments in India or within the Association of Southeast Asian Nations region[1] had to be left aside.

2.1.1 The distant past: Forerunners of and reasons for modern social security

One of the distant roots of modern social security is ancient Roman law; it constitutes a core base of paternalistic social security that emerged in the nineteenth century (Scholz, 2017; Bleicken, 2015; Manthe, 2011).

Another strand of thought is the European Poor Laws Tradition (Dixon, 1999).[2] The Poor Laws (1597 and 1601) summarized and consolidated various Continental and English legislation. Nowadays, it is considered the first post-medieval legislation consistently addressing the societal treatment of people who are poor. In contrast to Roman law tradition, the Poor Laws of England were more explicitly of a punitive nature to deter potential applicants rather than proactively provide them with help. The application nowadays is mainly understood as the result of labour shortages stemming from the Black Death's toll in the fourteenth century. The remains of such norms are active today, mainly in Anglo-American social security contexts but also increasingly visible in recent years in the middle and northern regions of the European Continent.

While the Roman law and the Western **institutionalized** (predominantly Catholic and protestant) Christian belief systems and the strong impetus of the Sermon of the Mount probably supported people's acceptance of **impersonalized institutions** providing

---

[1] The ILO is preparing a report on old-age income security in Asia, which comprises the ASEAN members and a few other Asian States. Publication will probably be in 2019. The report is expected to take up and deepen some of the issues of this report.

[2] See http://eh.net/encyclopedia/article/boyer.poor.laws.england Economic History Association (accessed 14 Dec. 2018).

2. Social security and economic development from an international perspective: Historical experiences and contemporary challenges

2.1 Historical experiences of social security and economic development around the globe

It is consensus among experts that the first modern comprehensive social security legislation emerged in Germany in the 1880s, mainly as political reaction to societal impacts of the first industrial revolution, based on the preceding century-long evolvements of socio-philosophical and religious thought and, not the least, in reaction to ruling elites' fears of upheavals similar to the French Revolution (1789-1799).

In the period before World War I, social security ideas and institutions spread over Europe and in the United States. Partial acceleration of that process took place during and immediately after World War I, with some boost in the 1920s and 1930s before culminating under US President Roosevelt's New Deal social security legislation (1935), together with the British Beveridge report (1942). After World War II inspired the unprecedented evolution of the welfare state, which became an instrument in international politics during the period of the so-called Cold War (1945-1989).

Although it is possible to identify historical social security trends after World War II,

The system needs adequate production to generate the taxable resources for redistribution but, strictly speaking, there is, from the individual's point of view, no need of formal or full employment as long as taxes can be collected independently from any employment[1] that would guarantee government ability to pay benefits. With these features, the Beveridgean system protects itself against the permanent requirement of maximizing productivity and employment to achieve universality (a duress that is immanent in Bismarck's system) and allows individuals to take decisions irrespective of material constraints. In other words, the system is potentially highly redistributive and reacts with the economy only on the demand side, whereas Bismarck's system, while far less redistributive, reacts also with the supply side.

It is the usual case that some countries have hybrid systems that combine Bismarckian and Beveridgean approaches. For example, in China, pensions provided by the scheme for rural and urban non-salaried residents consist of two components: a social pension entirely provided by the Government and an individual savings account pension financed through individual contributions and government subsidies. This scheme has traces of the Bismarckian and the Beveridgean models as well as elements of individual accounts from Singapore and Chile.

---

[1] Beveridge's political programme, being of a Keynesian nature, included full employment. However, technically speaking, his system does not need individuals to go through employment to receive benefits.

if wages are too low, the system is unable to avoid poverty. The longstanding success of the Bismarckian approach in developed countries (which does not mean that the implementation was always successful) can be explained as follows: It has a natural logic and is intuitively easy to understand; it can be pay-as-you-go or prefunded; multiple combinations are possible; it is possible to pay benefits without a prior contribution accumulation period (known as grandfathering); it can be technically adjusted to demographic and new economic developments; and it can be made intrinsically redistributive (to some extent) while not losing its economically supportive features.

The last point is important because the Bismarckian system operates well as long as socioeconomic and technological developments allow for a broad middle class. It comes to its limits and becomes socially dysfunctional when the middle class erodes (or remains too small, as is often the case in developing countries), with wages resulting in benefit levels insufficient to avoid poverty. In the case of too low wages, benefits will fall systematically below the poverty line and would need to be topped up systematically by social assistance.

The potential economic power of self-governed Bismarckian systems as a social governance instrument was last demonstrated during the 2008-10 financial and economic crises by some European countries (Austria, Belgium and Germany, for example), when they proactively used social security to prepare for the economic recovery. China, in its much longer and complex transformation process, also successfully applied Bismarckian elements (see Chapter 3).

We now turn to the issue of how Beveridge is nested into economic development. Beveridge proposed a system in which the State guarantees freedom from want for all through the following: All citizens pay (low) flat contributions (capitation tax); all citizens receive sufficient (adequate) cash (and services) in case of need; there is no means test; the State covers any emerging system deficit; and anyone wanting higher protection than freedom from want are referred to the private sector. It is important to understand that under Beveridge's proposal, finance and individual entitlement to benefits are independent of each other (this is the core difference to Bismarck). This implies that the level of benefits depends on a societal definition, which must be decided with every new government budget. Because the system, by design, guarantees freedom from want, no social assistance means testing is required.

with economies. From the point of view of **economic development,** we are interested in the question: How have certain traditions been functioning in reality? In the search for answers, we have made informed choices on options that best fit societies' economic preferences.

In addressing the issue of best choice more concretely, we restrict our analysis to two contemporary generic systems of delivery of social security: contribution-financed social insurance (Bismarckian) and tax-financed social transfer systems (Beveridgean).[1]

Otto von Bismarck launched a system that was later called by some analysts a "lucky strike of history" (Ritter, 2014), not the least because of its intrinsic economic features:

The State offers workers income replacement through social insurance in the event of certain contingencies occurring. Under this approach, workers (as well as employers and the government) contribute relative to their individual earnings, and benefits are defined relative to (prior) earnings. The system is completed by means-tested social assistance, which guarantees a minimum income at levels (just) preventing individuals from poverty. For a proper economic understanding of Bismarckian systems, it is paramount to realize that finance (revenue) and benefits are intrinsically interwoven. Through this specific feature of the system, workers have an interest to maximize productivity in order to maximize their wages and thus maximize benefits. If workers are unable to lift their wages above a certain minimal level, the earned benefits will be too low to avoid poverty. The system needs (formal) employment **to be administratively able** to pay benefits, and it needs **maximum employment** to emulate **universal coverage**.[2]

The requirement of maximum employment triggers the need for state-induced macroeconomic pro-growth policy that allows for wage levels, also at the bottom end of the income distribution, to earn sufficiently high social security benefits. Otherwise,

---

[1] With respect to the terms, refer to section 2.1. Strictly speaking, Beveridge's proposal was to finance the welfare state out of flat contributions, which can be regarded as equivalent to capitation or a tax.

[2] The term "maximum employment" needs to be specified: It means, in the Bismarckian context, that each and every individual must join the labour force, work and pay contributions; individuals not complying with this rule can receive benefits from the system (the system takes care of such persons), but these benefits are only derived from other system's participants rather than based on their direct legal entitlements.

system was introduced in a relatively stable growth period while the country's absolute income levels (per capita) were still significantly lower than its major neighbours and competitors (Maddison, 2016). China's recent transformation has been described as an approach in which economic, labour and social security measures are mutually reinforcing each other to the benefit of the overall population (see Chapter 3).

Although these conditions just described are usually broadly fulfilled in developed countries (with deep and wide capital stock and deep and wide production and labour markets), the same is, by definition, not the case in countries with large informal sectors and only small capital stock, small capital-based production and small formal labour markets-in developing countries. If the formal sector is too small, the production basis might actually turn out to be overstretched when attempting to finance social security for all. Deductions from labour income would thus need to be (prohibitively) high, so much that the remaining net income for the active workers would be insufficient to support their own decent living. Additional indirect taxation of goods and services would contribute to a worsening of workers' net income position. It would then be necessary to find other possibilities of financing (ILO, 2017).

Even though the possibilities of a quick, effective implementation of full-fledged social security in developing countries must be viewed with some scepticism,[1] the effective redistributive functioning has repeatedly been proven in most developed countries, mainly in Europe and Japan. In these countries, financially large and mostly well-governed social security systems were able to effectively unfold their demand-stabilizing function during economic crises. The last such functioning was observed during the global financial and economic crises of 2008-2010. In Europe, social security provided significant financial-income bolsters to the crisis-affected populations, even though it was not able to fully counterbalance the primary income effects of the economic downswing. The macroeconomic stabilizing effect was more pronounced the more emerging, temporary state deficits were politically accommodated and not reduced through austerity measures.

1.2.5 Social security design and economic performance

For the remainder of this chapter, we turn to the question of whether there are **social security traditions** that are preferential to others in terms of their impact on or interaction

---

[1] If one takes China as a benchmark country for a successful social security extension, it should not be forgotten that the process, which is not yet over, has thus far taken around three decades, or one generation.

labour income (labour costs)[1] is **inflexible** (in its level or amount and its composition (see box 3; United Nations et al., 2009). In such a situation, any additional social spending would have to be financed out of profits and would reduce profits, which, in turn, would trigger reactions aimed at reducing labour costs (labour income).

The situation is different if labour income is **flexible in its composition**. In this situation, social security can be financed out of labour income without negatively affecting profits [labour cost levels (amounts) remaining unchanged]. Parts of labour income can be set aside for current social security or, with pensions, the pay-out of labour income can be postponed until workers retire from the production process.[2] Many national laws treat earnings-based pensions like postponed wages. This is standard with social **insurance** solutions to social security pensions.

Financing social security out of labour income requires that the labour income net of those amounts tagged for social security (and the net of possibly other deductions from labour income) leave sufficient financial room for a decent living for workers during their time as a participant in the production process.[3]

This aspect is one of the core reasons why, according to international principles, the implementation and management of social security should be based on bipartite (or tripartite) principles-that they involve workers and employers. In economic reality, the introduction of social security might require compromises between the income interests of labour and capital because it probably, in the moment of implementation, negatively affects both labour income and profits. Such compromises are easiest to be achieved in growing economies, when the additional costs of social security are least felt. For the implementation of social security, the absolute level of national income at the time is less important than the dynamics of its growth, assuming that labour and capital equally participate in the benefits from growth.

For a historical example, we refer to Germany in the 1880s, when its social security

---

[1] The two terms indicate different viewpoints on the same subject. In accounting terms, labour income and labour costs are identical (United Nations et al., 2009).
[2] In this case, pensions can be understood as postponed payment of labour income.
[3] Not only mandated deductions from gross labour income determine workers consumption levels but also indirect tax on consumer goods and consumed services. For the sake of simplicity, we refrain here from a detailed discussion of this aspect.

> redistribution (often called "secondary income" or "secondary distribution"). Societies may also choose to redistribute nationally or internationally accumulated wealth, which - other than GDP - is no income flow but a stock (as a result of accumulated savings).
>
> For more information, see United Nations et al.: *System of National Accounts 2008* (New York, United Nations, 2009).

Production requires effective demand. Growing effective demand is a prerequisite for growing production (resulting in growing labour income and profits).

From an individual country perspective, **external** demand is one obvious source of this additional demand. Relying on external demand can be a temporary and transitionary option for countries, but logically, not all countries can rely on external demand because the sum total of the current account balances of all nations is equal to zero. It has been countries like China, Germany, Japan or Switzerland (among others and over periods of time) that traditionally relied on such external demand, while after World War II and to this day, it is mainly the United States that has created this demand by externally indebting itself. Creating additional demand domestically, through social security, would theoretically be easiest if the additional demand coming from social transfers would be for free-they would not affect the costs of production. Contemporary proposals to finance social benefits through "helicopter" money, or through a government's permanent deficit spending, can be regarded as attempts at insinuating that social security can be introduced free of cost. While these proposals might be helpful and possibly also applicable in the short run, to get the world economy out of its current austerity situation, they are here considered **inadequate** to finance social security in the longer run.

We hold that social security transfers must be financed out of current production, that they are a direct cost to the production process and thus can reduce profits or can change the composition of labour income. We provide explanation for this position further on. For simplicity, we assume that gross domestic product (GDP) is equivalent to national income, which is composed of labour income and capital income ("profits") (for details, see United Nations et al., 2009).

Obviously, in static analysis, any additional social security would reduce profits in case is not directly involved in the production-of-income process (workers who are bought out). Essentially, we argue, capital-based production at a certain stage of development depends on financial flows from persons who gain primary income from their direct involvement in production to persons who do not in order to maximize and maintain the production of goods and services for final consumption (to maximize profits)[1]. Social security is a convenient and practical way for societies to organize such a flow of funds.

> **Box 3**
> **What is primary income?**
>
> The term "primary income" signifies a core concept of the measurement of income that is produced by an economy (a society) within a certain period, such as one year, and that can be used for final consumption. Often, primary income is called gross domestic product (GDP). GDP is basically calculated as a balancing item:
>
> *total production minus intermediate consumption = value added (= GDP),*
> where intermediate consumption is that part of total output that must be channelled back into production to keep the process going.
>
> GDP can be regarded as a dual concept: While it is the result of production, GDP is equally a measure of an economy's total (monetary) income that emerges in parallel to production and that is allocated to workers in the form of primary labour income (workers' remuneration) and to the owners of capital (as profits). This allocation on the two production factors (labour and capital) is often called "primary income distribution". This income can be redistributed (via state institutions, including social security) and be used for private consumption, government consumption, for private and public capital formation (investments) and for exports (where imports must be subtracted to avoid double-counting).
>
> Value added (GDP or primary income) is the only source for a society's income

---

[1] For reasons of better readability, we simplify the argument. It is well understood that maximizing production can take place, and usually does, under preformulated policy conditions; this includes, in developed economies for example, maximizing free time (reducing working time as a result of maximized labour productivity).

society's acceptance, which, in turn, is an issue of political and societal practice.

Of course, an economy must be willing to internalize the related buy-out or buy-in costs, otherwise, this explanation for the existence of social security is not valid. It must be assumed that the productivity gains achieved through social security's functionality clearly outpace the related increases in production costs. This assumption would need to be put to the empirical test (which has not been done thus far). There are, however, good reasons to assume that the huge productivity differences between economies worldwide, at regional levels and within nations are highly correlated with accessibility to (more or less developed) social security systems and their application. On this basis, the hypothesis appears justified that, at least partially, those internationally observable differences in productivity levels relate to the existence of a social security system's ability (for better or for worse) to perform as a productivity enhancer.

Discussing the buy-out or buy-in function of social security is not only an academic undertaking. More important is that it reminds governments (and, generally, social policy analysts) that, worldwide, contemporary policies of containing or even reducing social spending may unintentionally face economic costs in terms of negative productivity effects. Indeed, it is justified to argue that all those countries that adopted neoliberal policies (see section 2.1) and adjusted their social security parameters to accommodate economic (business) requirements, simultaneously created either additional unemployment or large low-wage sectors with no or only low productivity. Given the insecurities of the coming technological changes and their potential impact on labour markets, governments would be well advised to consider the proactive and productivity-oriented use of the buy-out or buy-in function of social security.

Social security is a human right, but it is also a powerful governance tool for tackling a society's insecurities.

1.2.4 Social security as a redistributor of primary income

In the previous section, we developed an argument to explain social security as a necessary element of modern capital-based means of production mainly for the sake of the long-term survival of this core, constituting characteristic of modern societies. The point we address now is of a different nature: It looks at social security as a (necessary) tool for transferring income (in cash or in kind) to the population that

Child (cash) benefits usually support schooling and enhance the quality of future workforces and prevent child labour, which reduces enterprise productivity (except for pathological cases); **sickness benefits** allow workers to stay home instead of possibly transmitting diseases to the workplace; **hospitalization** is an extreme case whereby sickness-infused labour is bought out of the remaining healthy labour force (a similar argument holds for social occupational injury insurance and social care insurance); and in the case of **unemployment insurance**, the buy-out argument can almost be considered a tautology because unemployed labour is analytically identical with zero-productive labour (two sides of the same coin). In analogy, social security also can have an economic **buy-in function**. This is evident in those cases in which social programmes intend to increase the (productive) labour force, either directly or indirectly. For instance, in contemporary debates concerning the provision of (additional) kindergarten places for children, often the argument is used (next to others) that such policy provides additional space for female (mothers) employment and thus contributes to increasing labour market participation and economic growth.

Another example would be student grants or the subsidizing of homes for underprivileged university students, at least in those cases for which the availability of such grants or places allows them to study and to improve future labour productivity. Of course, the buy-out or buy-in argument for the economic roots of social protection only holds *cum grano salis*; other economic reasoning, depending on a society's history and value systems, may (and usually do) apply. This view on the economic impacts of social security is not only of a theoretical nature. As a matter of fact, it gained prominence over recent years in the **social policy practice** of many developed countries, whereby governments began adjusting their respective social security system to economic needs, such as by tightening people's accessibility to social benefits to counter the demographically induced decline of the labour force.

China can be taken as another example of how the buy-out function was successfully applied (see Chapter 3). In pursuing buy-out or buy-in policies, governments can easily make mistakes, resulting in suboptimal productivity: If too much labour force is bought out, then the remaining labour force may turn out less productive than before; if too much is bought in, then the same can happen. It is empirically difficult, if not impossible, to find the optimal size of the labour force-it depends on the economy's unknown production function. In other words, there is no objectively correct solution to applying social security's buy-out or buy-in function in the end. Its use can only be legitimized by

buy-in function and the resulting positive effects on labour productivity. Basically, the argument is that social security is a societal instrument that buys out of the production process unproductive labour (as well as buys productive labour into the process) to maintain or enhance productivity levels of the resulting (remaining) labour force[1].

The core of this argument dates back probably to pre-World War I discussions, among and with pro-pension activists (Rodgers, 1998) in the United States (around 30 years before a social pension system was introduced in that country). It was formalized in the 1990s using the mathematical tools of contemporary mainstream marginalism (Sala-i-martin, 1996).

The argument was initially developed solely with respect to pension systems. It is intuitively convincing to argue that there is a point in everyone's life from which personal (physical) productivity declines. It is a situation probably happening even earlier in terms of individual (workplace-related) "labour productivity" as a result of technological progress and/or deterioration of individual skills or declining health or other detrimental developments affecting individual productivity. Continuous training on the job, work routine and experience might help counterbalance such deterioration, but there are limits. Depending on a society's (the enterprises) production functions, it makes sense to expect that continued employment, in enterprises and administrations, of progressively unproductive labour and thus the growing productivity gap between older persons and younger employees, at some point, negatively affects a company's total productivity and reduces its competitiveness. From this view, an institution, such as the social pension insurance, that "takes over" (or "buys out") the increasingly unproductive older employees is a relief that can be interpreted as a productivity-enhancing institution, which, simultaneously, fulfils a social purpose in that it provides continuation of certain levels of income to those (now retired = bought-out) persons. This situation was obviously well understood by the Chinese Government when it made effective use of social security during its endeavours to expose state-owned enterprises to market conditions (see Chapter 3).

We hold that the argument can be generalized to practically all other social security institutions, whether they provide benefits in cash or in kind. For example:

---

[1] The authors of this report are aware that by forwarding this argument for social security they risk being (falsely) criticized as adhering to what has been called the Ricardian Vice (Kurz, 2017; Schumpeter, 1954). Yet, to the same extent as Ricardo's logical invention of the "comparative advantage" provides 200-year-old mainstream economics reason for promoting free and unrestrained international trade, the buy-in or buy-out argument might be similarly taken as offering a theoretical basis to social security.

contrary is core to the successful functioning of market economies. It also reduces individual willingness to save, while the contrary is necessary for economic growth. And it increases production costs and therefore reduces international competitiveness and has negative effects on a nation's balance of payments and stability of currency.

Many more such examples exist for social security regulations and benefits. They are typically based on partial analysis, whereby their content depends on implicit or explicit, strong or weak, behavioural and structural assumptions about individuals and economies. The crux with the items listed (including those not listed) is that they may indeed be true or false, depending on the underlying assumptions or empirical material against which those (partial) hypotheses have been tested in reality. From a theoretical analysis point of view, this is unsatisfying because it leaves the nesting of social security in economics as a science quite arbitrary and undecided and strengthens, rather than counters, observers' (and possibly political actors') impression that social security is alien to (rather than an integral element of) modern economies.[1]

One of the strongest arguments against the practice of such positive and negative listings is that they focus only on a limited socioeconomic reality (markets) while showing a tendency to ignore other, equally important and observable economic phenomena. One of the strongest arguments in favour of social security is, after all, that institutions of social security do exist, which the opponents to social security have no choice but to accept. Against all odds of pure economics, societies have obviously decided to implement such social institutions. One of the research questions to be explored by theoretical economics should therefore be: Why?

1.2.3 A positive argument for social security

The question, why does social security exist? can be transformed into, is it possible to spot "objective" conditions that are accessible to "pure" economic reasoning and logically imply the existence of social security in societies? Indeed, standard economic theory has developed one such argument, which we now explore. Under this reason, social security becomes an intrinsic element of economic theory through its **buy-out or**

---

[1] Where social security systems have already been implemented, the situation is different in terms of the macroeconomics of aggregate supply and demand, as well as macro- and microeconomic (personal) distribution issues.

appropriate jobs and thus facilitates labour force adjustments in case of structural economic and labour market changes.
- Social security institutions, more generally, including pension schemes and social assistance, and welfare-oriented institutions can be used as policy instruments to support people's acceptance of economic reforms.
- Health care and work safety schemes maintain and increase individual and collective labour productivity.
- Social security offers a practical societal mechanism to channel positive income effects of globalization to vulnerable persons.
- Social security guarantees equilibrium labour costs at levels lower than in its absence, in which (the latter case) workers, saving individually, would need higher labour income to achieve predefined lifetime income levels.
- Social security provides information to businesses on core variables of domestic competition. When self-governed, the institutionalized social dialogue helps to reduce economic rigidities.

Examples of the **economic cons to social security**:
- Unemployment and social assistance benefits function as benchmarks for workers' reservation wage (the wage level below which they will not be willing to work but prefer to receive an unemployment benefit). This constellation of wages expected and benefits offered increases production costs and hinders certain production from taking place. As a result, total national income falls behind its potential level and unemployment increases. More unemployment benefits must be paid and, thus, social security becomes a reason for itself.
- Pay-as-you-go pension schemes [with predefined standard retirement ages and standard benefit levels, for example, along the lines cited in the ILO Social Security (Minimum Standards) Convention, 1952 (No. 102)] provide incentives for early labour market exit. This constellation reduces the labour force, in comparison to a situation with no such predefined retirement age and benefit. Again, this reduces economic output and thus increases society's social costs in relation to its total available income.
- Sickness benefits reduce labour productivity because they facilitate workers' temporary exit from work without consequence to individual available income.
- Social security generally creates individual dependency on benefit transfers and reduces people's ability to live self-determined and self-confident lives; individuals are distracted from taking the risk of economic failure while the

very much depends on a solid understanding by policy-makers of the prevailing social security tradition or a mix of such traditions. Missing such understanding can easily result in non-achievement of expected reform results, of which many examples exist in modern history.

1.2.2 The pros and cons of social security

Standard microeconomic theory seeks to formulate conditions (the price and cost levels) that must be fulfilled to clear markets (the markets of goods and services and also labour markets). This approach stands in stark contrast to the Declaration of Philadelphia, which stipulates that labour is not a commodity (ILO, 1944). It usually also ignores social security's potential role in employment maximization, and implicitly (sometimes explicitly) characterizes social security as an obstacle to such market clearance. In other words, as long as full employment is a socioeconomic goal of society, social security is considered an undertaking that should be avoided rather than actively pursued.

The purist microeconomic approach is often criticized from within the economic academic professions but also from other specializations of societal research, such as sociology, the political sciences and psychology. Nevertheless, the approach shows stubborn resistance and thus maintains significance, often in "popularized" versions and in public debates dealing with the pros and cons of social security or, where social security institutions have already been implemented in historical practice, the approach indicates market-type reforms of such institutions.

Reflecting on this analytical and policy framework and very much in a Popperian scientific tradition (Popper, 1977; Frisby, 1972), the available literature includes lists of arguments in favour ("pros") of social security and against it ("cons"), as follows (adapted from Cichon et al., 2004). We paraphrase these arguments here without going into detail concerning their relevance.

Examples of **the economic pros to social security:**
- Social security stabilizes domestic demand and can help to reduce excessive savings by reducing the existential insecurity of people. It contributes to social peace and creates an environment for profitability and positive rates of return on private investments.
- Unemployment insurance provides unemployed individuals with time to seek out

The **welfare state** tradition, while supported by full-employment-oriented macroeconomic and macro-fiscal policy of a government, seeks to humanize capitalism through the pursuance of social stability and societal progress while aiming to remove the social sources of our distress (Sigmund Freud, quoted in Dixon, 1999).

The **marketization** tradition, by contrast, emphasizes and focuses on the virtues of the marketplace. This tradition believes in the Pareto principle[1] and that individuals are best judges of their own well-being; it holds that individuals are rational, desirous, calculating and self-interested, with individually known ordered sets of preferences.

The **general minimum income** tradition is a radical completion of neoliberal thought because it endows the State to provide minimal social income guarantees to its citizens while leaving any additional income security to the private sector. In most blueprints, the general minimum income tradition aims at two goals: (i) to remove the necessity of primary income production from individuals, such that they are free from the constraints of material want in their daily decisions while enabled to choose freely and voluntarily to work (or not); and/or (ii) to reduce administrative complexities by replacing social security institutions and their unavoidable interactions with minimal administrative units that register births and deaths.

These traditions implicitly or explicitly reflect specific prevailing economic paradigmatic thought, usually complemented with certain political ethics, with risk sharing having a more or less prominent role. In modern full-fledged social welfare states, we usually find many or even all of these traditions in parallel-we just might be calling them differently. If one understands economies as sets of interacting institutions, such as private households, enterprises and government entities, where economic development is a result of their dynamic interacting, then, obviously, interdependencies between social security and the economy occur because social institutions are economic actors intervening in the structure and behaviour of other such acting institutions. From this point of view, it is the role and art of economic policy to set external conditions such that institutions can pursue an optimal development path. How best to set such conditions in concrete (reform) situations

---

[1] The Pareto Principle is a term used in welfare economics. The weak Pareto Principle states that a group of individuals will prefer welfare situation B over A if all individuals have a higher utility in B than in A; the strong Pareto Principle holds that a group of individuals will prefer welfare situation B over A if at least one individual has a higher utility in B than in A, while no one in A is worse off.

1.2.1 Introduction to social security traditions

Social security is deeply rooted in a number of different traditions of thought, which have had different impact on social policy preferences and practices, as follows (adapted from Dixon, 1999).

The **European Poor Laws** tradition of 1597, 1601 and 1834[1] rest upon workhouse elements and are the ideological origin of the modern means-test practices (as opposed to unconditional benefits).

The **master-servant** tradition holds that when a person, who, on their own responsibility for their own profit, sets in motion agencies that create risk for others, should be civilly responsible for the consequences of what they do (Herbert Asquith, 1906, quoted in Dixon, 1999). It is a seemingly reasonable principle that has been all too often misused within enterprises to perpetuate employers' (the "master") superiority over workers (the "servants").

The **occupational provident fund** tradition, if kept as the sole instrument, falls short of modern society's social security requirements but nevertheless continues to attract the interest of policy-makers, especially as an option for an additional layer of income security.

The **(social) insurance** tradition, while resting upon principles of mutual help and actuarial fairness, was the dominant social security success story of the nineteenth and twentieth centuries, mainly in developed countries. It only recently lost some of its attraction among social security planners, especially in development economics.

The **Marxist-Leninist** tradition, by its formal design-strove for a welfare state scenario that appears to have had much overlap with a hybrid Bismarck-Beveridge concept. By contrast, however, it replaced individual with collective entitlement and macro-fiscal employment policy with work discipline, thereby aiming to enforce that daily social practice became directly equivalent to economic growth.

---

[1] In a strict sense, the Poor Laws originated in the United Kingdom; however, similar rules and practices were applied at the same time all over Europe. This is why we take the liberty of calling the Poor Laws **European**.

Annex 1 contains more detailed information as to how the European System of integrated Social Protection Statistics (ESSPROS) defines social security[1]; the reader will realize that the definition has significant linguistic problems when including private interventions, which implies that the borderline between the definition of publicly organized solidarity schemes and private arrangements is becoming increasingly blurred, not the least as a result of the worldwide trends over the past two to three decades of privatizing social risks.

While the above definition is mainstream, it might be interesting to note that the United Nations' System of National Accounts (SNA) (and the European Union's SNA) broadly covers the same needs and risks but includes education as another social need. Depending on the context, we also take education as a social need into account in this report.[2] Yet, continued payment of wages in the event of sickness is not included in the SNA as social spending; rather, it is part of the gross sum of wages and salaries. There are other differences in the methodologies that render it is important to clearly understand the statistical bases of social indicators used in public debate. For example, it is important to know, especially for international comparison, whether a social expenditure ratio was calculated on the basis of ESSPROS-type or SNA-style statistics. Even if the indicators calculated either way came to similar numerical results, they would still represent different content.

Source: Mainly ESSPROS, 2012; United Nations et al., 2009.

Within this report, the social security nomenclature and practice are interpreted and assessed within their economic function, despite any interventions that provide net gains economically, in cash or in kind, that are implemented by the State as prescribed by law. At the core of these interventions lie the schemes for pensions, health insurance, unemployment insurance, social assistance, educational benefits and housing benefits.

---

[1] Actually, ESSPROS uses the term "social protection" instead of "social security".
[2] There are pros and cons to including and excluding education as a need (rather than an investment) in definitions. Because this report is not about statistical methodologies or legal nomenclature but social policies, the adhering to an exact definition is no priority. An a priori understanding of the term social security should be sufficient for understanding the contents of this report.

Box 2
How to define social security and some implications

Many definitions of social security exist but not any one of them is definitive. Societies differ and change over time, and so does social security. Sometimes, definitions are relatively vague, using unspecific terminology; sometimes they are specific and detailed. Definitions may be static or take into account dynamic elements. There are numerous definitions between these benchmarks. Most experts would agree on some core elements and characteristics of social security, with a few grey areas of undecidedness that remain around the definition boundaries.

Here we briefly adapt and reflect on a definition that was mainly developed for statistical purposes by the European Union (ESSPROS, 2012) and that is nowadays used by the International Labour Organization and other institutions.

Social security, according to this definition, encompasses all interventions from public or private bodies intended to relieve households and individuals of the burden of a defined set of risks or needs, provided that there is neither a simultaneous reciprocal nor an individual arrangement involved (see Annex 1). The list of risks or needs is, by convention, as follows:

1. Sickness and health care
2. Disability
3. Old age
4. Survivors
5. Family and children
6. Unemployment
7. Housing
8. Social exclusion

The origin of this definition, still in use today as a core reference, is the nomenclature of the ILO Social Security (Minimum Standards) Convention, 1952 (No. 102), which enumerates nine branches that provide, on the basis of solidarity-based financing principles and as an individual legal entitlement, support to persons in the event of predefined contingencies occurring through medical care, sickness benefits, unemployment benefits, old-age benefits, employment injury benefits, family/children benefits, maternity benefits, invalidity benefits and survivor benefits. These benefits must comply with minimum standards (ILO, 1952).

The term "interventions" in the definition indicates that social security is not only considered a financial undertaking but that it might consist of certain social activities; accordingly, the definition separates in-kind from in-cash benefits.

Beijing to exchange views on the first draft of the main body of the report and on the country reports.

In September 2017, CAOSS, ILO and FES arranged the International Conference on Global Social Security and Economic Development at Nanjing University. Ideas were exchanged, and further views were collected from a wider audience. Shortly after, Zheng Gongcheng, Wolfgang Scholz, Nuno Cunha, Li Qingyi, He Wenjiong, Hua Ying, Lu Quan and Christoph Pohlmann organized a seminar in Nanjing to discuss the revised country reports and collect views on the further improvements of the main report. Between February and December 2018, the report benefited from further revision by the three collaborating organizations and was finalized by Zheng Gongcheng, Wolfgang Scholz and Hua Ying before its publication in English and Chinese.

1.2 Theoretical hypotheses on the interdependencies between social security and economic development

This section introduces the hypotheses that have been used in the literature to explain the interdependencies between social security and economic development. For consistency of argument, we first describe social security traditions that will later help to better understand the current status of interaction between social security and an economy as well as where we stand in contemporary discussions. Specifying these traditions will also help to better understand the situation of China, which has a prominent presence in this report. We then develop a productivity-oriented argument to explain the intrinsic economic reasons for the very existence of social security. The argument is adhoc but intuitively deceiving and therefore worth inclusion for the context of this report. We also explore the pros and cons of social security that have been developed over decades as a result of worldwide ups and downs of the economic (business) cycle and in reaction to the interplay between social security and exogenous or endogenous crises.

Box 1
Research process

This project was inspired by a fundamental consensus among the China Association of Social Security (CAOSS), the International Labour Organization (ILO) and Friedrich-Ebert-Stiftung (FES) that the current global economic development and social security systems are exposed to complex changes and challenges and that, more than ever, it is important to understand the relationships between them.

The report is the outcome of a research process that benefited from rich discussions, inputs and findings from several meetings, high-level conferences and seminars and several rounds of revisions. Between September and October 2015, the president of CAOSS met successively with the ILO senior social protection specialist and the secretary general of the International Social Security Association (ISSA) to discuss the research. As well at that time, the resident representative of the FES China's Beijing Representative Office expressed full support for the research project. They agreed on the importance to conduct an up-to-date piece of research on the relationship between social security and economic development in the modern world.

In September 2016, the CAOSS, the ILO and FES jointly hosted the launch meeting of the Global Social Security and Economic Development Project in Beijing. More than 20 experts and scholars from CAOSS, the ILO, FES, ISSA and from Demark, France, Germany, Japan, the Republic of Korea, the United Kingdom and the United States participated in the discussion. The conference participants agreed on the framework, developed key viewpoints, assigned tasks and agreed on timelines. Between September and December 2016, the authors of the seven country reports (on France, Germany, Japan, the Nordic countries, the Republic of Korea, the United Kingdom and the United States) submitted first drafts.

In May 2017, Zheng Gongcheng, Wolfgang Scholz, Nuno Cunha, Li Qingyi, He Wenjiong, Hua Ying, Lu Quan and Christoph Pohlmann organized a seminar in basis for a comprehensive and correct understanding of these relationships and then seek a path to the sustainable development of social security in the context of a new era. The research took a special focus on China's experience as well as several major countries with mature social security systems.

This report encompasses four parts:
1. Global social security and economic development: historical experiences and trends. This touched upon the relationship between social security and economic growth and the relationship between less investment in social security and economic crisis.
2. Theoretical explanation of the relationship between social security and economic development and the effects of different social security patterns on economic development.
3. The evolution of social security and economic development in selected countries, including policy measures to coordinate social security and economic development in the new economy dynamics.
4. Social security and economic development in China: historical experiences and current challenges and trends.

The significance of this report lies in its relevance to current worldwide transformations. This report intended to develop a rational understanding of the historic mission as well as contemporary responsibilities shouldered by social security in promoting the further development of human society. This report also sought to propose a model of social equity-oriented and sustainable social security that would cover the entire population, with adequate protection and clearly defined rights and responsibilities. Such a social security design should be immune to short-sighted solutions (Zheng, 2016a).

This report provides an up-to-date assessment of social security and economic development in China, Germany, the United Kingdom, France, Scandinavia, the United States, Japan and the Republic of Korea. It hopes to serve as an authoritative source to enhance the understanding of the evolution of China's social security system and its active role in the recent socioeconomic transformation in a comprehensive and objective manner.

The Chinese social security system, which provides stable and ever-growing social protection for a population of more than 1.3 billion persons and facilitates the policy of sustainable national economic development, offers useful insights for countries all over the world in their efforts to reshape their respective system.

assessment are still required.[1] Generally, it is fair to say that the global experiences of the past century show an overall positive relationship between the expansion of social security and economic development. International consensus among political and economic elites in this respect has, however, weakened over the past three decades. It has returned in recent years largely due to worldwide aggravated inequalities and their resulting harmful socioeconomic consequences to the process of globalization (see section 2.1).[2]

1.1.2 Research purpose and content

Social security and economic development are deeply intertwined, constituting elements of the same socioeconomic reality. They should thus not be put into undue contradicting positions so as to avoid the undesirable consequence of policy measures arising from misconceptions. Rather, social security and economic development are two sides of the same coin and should be analysed from a holistic perspective. It is imperative to explore and promote those constellations that have proven reasonable, reliable and productive in their guaranteeing positive interactions between social security and economic development, on the basis of clarifying the historical logic of and the relationship between the two. This does not imply to ignore or hide the unavoidable inherent conflicts between the very interests of enterprises and individuals' claims to be protected through socially organized security. Only transparently addressing such conflicts can solutions be found, which, depending on institutional specifications, may have more or less significant impacts on the productivity of an economy (see section 1.2.5).

Central to this report's research are the relationships between social security and economic development around the globe. The research set out to gain a scientific and theoretical

---

[1] Some economists have always argued that the welfare system is to blame for economic downturns or, even, more generally, for any restraints on people's productive forces. Others have argued, especially in the context of year-long detrimental developments, that inequality is a prominent trigger as well as driver of political and economic crises and therefore public expenditure and social protection can and should have an important role in propelling countries towards recovery (Cingano, 2014).

[2] Despite the divergence in the current global debate, institutions like the International Monetary Fund and the Organisation for Economic Co-Operation and Development are presenting research conclusions that point to the negative impact of inequality, that is, the weakening redistributive effects hamper both social justice and economic development (IMF, 2015; Cingano, 2014).

for all humankind repeatedly proposed by Chinese President Xi Jinping in recent years.[1]

History has proven that the dual goals of achieving economic growth and a stronger welfare system are inescapable in every country's economic and social development. The social insurance that emerged in Europe in the late nineteenth century helped to improve industrial relations and provided important impetus for the development of modern capitalism. The Social Security Act of 1935 in the United States not only saved the country from economic crisis but also effectively maintained its long-term prosperity. The United Kingdom's welfare state design in the 1940s strengthened consensus views on social solidarity, created jobs and thus was conducive to the transformation of economic growth patterns. The economic take-off in Japan and the Republic of Korea in the second half of the twentieth century was accompanied by the establishment of their respective social security system.

The more or less stringent application of market mechanisms to social security and the introduction of funded pension systems in the 1980s in some countries contributed to capital accumulation to a certain extent, although often with negative results in terms of its impact on the redistributive function of social security. The return of the public solidarity pension to strengthen elements of redistribution in such countries as Argentina and Hungary in the past decade repeatedly demonstrated that the reform towards individualization and marketization has weakened income distribution to the extent that political and social risks are huge. Since the beginning of the twenty-first century, China's social security has been developed in all classical dimensions, with similar policy approaches found in such countries as Brazil.

Despite the efforts to assess the relationship between social security and economic growth, the debates around different views are far from being concluded; additional evidence and

---

[1] The idea of building a community of shared future for all humankind advocated by Chinese President Xi Jinping is aligned with the United Nations values and echoes the Sustainable Development Goals. In November 2012, the concept of "a community of shared future for all humankind" was first proposed in the report of the 18th National Congress of the Communist Party of China. In the following years, Chinese President Xi Jinping mentioned and expounded the concept on various international and domestic occasions. China pursues shared development and advocates for building a community of shared future for all humankind, which is coherent with the global recent developments.

In the less developed countries and developed countries alike, the crisis directly or indirectly triggered further critical income and wealth splits between the few at the top of the income hierarchy and the many at its bottom. It resulted in hunger, migration, economic fragility and political instability, which have further weakened the regional economic basis and thus countries' ability to maintain and widen effective social security. Some countries with a well-established social security system have faced pressure to reduce welfare expenditure.[1] In 2016, a major austerity shock of expenditure contraction was initiated globally and is expected to last at least until 2020. In 2018, 124 countries, 81 of them developing countries expected to adjust expenditure, will hover around those levels until 2020 (ILO, 2017).

Some countries have moved in a different direction by introducing structural adaptations to their systems to revert previous reforms and reduce the risks of individualization and marketization of social security and to support the long-term social sustainability of their welfare system. In terms of the rapid development of both social security and an economy, China offers prime evidence (see Chapter 3), whereas most of the less and least developed countries in Southern Asia and Africa thus far maintain only narrowly defined social assistance policies and tax-funded benefits and/or run social insurance, though often with limited coverage. For instance, less than 30 per cent of the population is protected in most of the countries in Africa for which data are available (ILO, 2017).

With this backdrop, it is logical that developed countries need to continue helping those regions develop meaningful social security and help narrow the inequalities, including through the use of North-South transfers("North"refers to developed countries,"South"refers to less developed coutries). It must be stipulated that social security alone will not solve the problems of those developing countries: Without sound primary income distribution, which fairly allocates the fruits of national income generation to persons producing the income, the income basis will be too weak to finance social security.

Building a world in which no one is left behind and poverty is eradicated in all its forms and dimensions is the greatest global challenge and an indispensable requirement for sustainable development. It is also the core of the 2030 Agenda for Sustainable Economic Development. These principles are present in the concept of a community of shared future

---

[1] With respect to issues and use of terminology, see box 2 (definition of social security) and Annex 1.

1. Introduction

1.1 Research background

1.1.1 Background

The world is witnessing an era of deepening globalization. This irreversible and unstoppable momentum for change appears to be merging civilizations with diversified cultures, institutions and technology through comparison and identification. Together with the remarkable acceleration of industrialization, information technology and modernization, it has initiated realignments of global political and economic patterns and begun strengthening the possibility of global governance, with high potential to elevate human civilization to a new level. From these developments, the world is experiencing profound impacts while entering a period of deep social and economic reconstruction. The rapid development of China and other developing countries since the 1980s proves that globalization can have positive impact on the progress of human society. However, protectionist tendencies, widening income gaps in combination with growing poverty and the subsequent spreading of unease and unrest indicate that further globalization needs to be pursued with the principles of building a community of a shared future for all humankind and promoting social justice (Zheng, 2017b).

The subprime mortgage crisis of the United States in 2008 triggered the latest global economic downturn. All major economies have since been confronted with new challenges. The United States, Europe, Japan and emerging economies (such as Brazil, the Russian Federation, India and China) are experiencing slow economic growth and even stagnation or recession. In the aftermath of the 2008 crisis, a range of countries sought remedy through welfare retrenchment, though obviously unpopular, as part of a package of fiscal contraction commonly called "austerity".

Figure 7   Number of participants in basic old-age pension system and its changes, 1998-2017 82

Figure 8   Average per capita fund expenditure under the basic old-age pension scheme, 2009-2017 83

Figure 9   Per capita fund expenditure of the health insurance and its changes, 2000-2017 90

Figure 10   Poverty line and poverty headcount ratio in rural areas, 1998-2017 95

Figure 11   Average per capita fund expenditure of the basic old-age pension scheme for employees and its annual growth rate, 2005-2017 109

Figure 12   Accumulated balances of the basic old-age pension system fund, 1998-2017 110

Boxes

Box 1   Research process 06
Box 2   How to define social security and some implications 08
Box 3   What is primary income? 18
Box 4   China's social security system: A comprehensive list of schemes 79
Box 5   The determinants of pension expenditure as a share of GDP 86
Box 6   Poverty alleviation and development in rural China: Stronger measures to eliminate poverty 96
Box 7   Reform and development of China's housing benefits: Returning from de-welfare to social security 115

Tables Figures Boxes

Tables

Table 1   Years of initial social security legislation and economic development levels in selected OECD countries 30
Table 2   Numbers of participants in basic health insurance in China, 2006-2017 89
Table 3   Subsistence allowance scheme, 2000-2017 97
Table 4   Public budget expenditure in China, 2007-2017 123
Table 5   Structure of health care expenditure in China, 1978-2017 124
Table A1 China's total GDP and GDP per capita, 1978-2017 156
Table A2 Number of participants and pensioners of the basic old-age pension system in China, 1978-2017 157
Table A3 Accumulated balances of the basic old-age pension system fund in China, 1998-2017 158
Table A4 Number of basic old-age insurance participants in China, 1978-2017 159
Table A5 Average per capita fund expenditure under the basic old-age pension scheme in China, 2001-2017 160
Table A6 Poverty line and impoverished population and poverty headcount ratio in China's rural areas, 1985-2017 161

Figures

Figure 1   Social protection programmes anchored in national legislation, by branch, from pre-1900 to post-2010 34
Figure 2   Total GDP and GDP per capita for China, 1978-2017 72
Figure 3   China's transformation of employment: Share of employed people, by industry, 1978-2017 73
Figure 4   China's industrial transformation: Share of industry type as a percentage of GDP, 1978-2017 74
Figure 5   China's urbanization rate, 1978-2017 75
Figure 6   Engel's coefficient of urban and rural households in China 76

2.2.3 Far-reaching influence of rapidly ageing populations on economies and societies 64
2.2.4 The impact of the new technological revolution on traditional industries and the normalization of new business types..........66
2.2.5 The paradox of rigid growth of welfare and financial sustainability..........67

3. Social security and economic development: China 70
3.1 The contribution of the social security system to economic development: China's historical experience 71
  3.1.1 China's economic achievements in the past 40 years 71
  3.1.2 China's achievements in social security reform and development 76
  3.1.3 The contribution of social security to China's economic growth 103
  3.1.4 China's experience of the relationship between economic development and social security as guidelines for the future 121
3.2 Major socioeconomic challenges and policy recommendations 128
  3.2.1 Challenges confronting China 128
  3.2.2 Policy recommendations for the Government of China 133

4. Summary 140
4.1 Basic historical experience and theoretical consensus on the relationship between global economic development and social security 140
4.2 Conclusions and policy recommendations for countries 144

Annex 1. Definition of social security 150
Annex 2. Additional tables 156
References 162

Contents

1. Introduction 01
   1.1 Research background 01
      1.1.1 Background 01
      1.1.2 Research purpose and content 04
   1.2 Theoretical hypotheses on the interdependencies between social security
       and economic development...07
      1.2.1 Introduction to social security traditions 10
      1.2.2 The pros and cons of social security 12
      1.2.3 A positive argument for social security 14
      1.2.4 Social security as a redistributor of primary income 17
      1.2.5 Social security design and economic performance 21

**2. Social security and economic development from an international
perspective: Historical experiences and contemporary challenges** 25
   2.1 Historical experiences of social security and economic development around
       the globe..25
      2.1.1 The distant past: Forerunners of and reasons for modern social security.......26
      2.1.2 The nineteenth century, the United Kingdom, Germany and the Holy See....28
      2.1.3 The twentieth century: Social security between the two great wars...............30
      2.1.4 The twentieth century: Social security going global after World War II 33
      2.1.5 The post-World War II developments in the West 34
      2.1.6 Developments in Eastern Europe, Central Asia and other world regions
          after 1989...59
   2.2 Emerging challenges facing social security and economic development around
       the globe..61
      2.2.1 Divergent development philosophies underlying the relationship between
          economic development and social security 61
      2.2.2 Uncertainties of globalization..63

Abbreviations

ASEAN	Association of Southeast Asian Nations
CAOSS	China Association of Social Security, Beijing
CNY	Chinese yuan
ESSPROS	European System of Integrated Social Protection Statistics (manual)
EU	European Union
EUROSTAT	Statistical Office of the European Union
FES	Friedrich-Ebert-Stiftung
GDP	gross domestic product
ILO	International Labour Organization
ISSA	International Social Security Association
MHRSS	Ministry of Human Resources and Social Security of the People's Republic of China
OECD	Organisation for Economic Co-operation and Development
SNA	system of national accounts
UN	United Nations
US	United States

Note: All $ currencies are US dollars.

"Continent" and "continental" signify the European mainland without the United Kingdom and Ireland.

Nordic countries refer to Denmark, Finland, Iceland, Norway and Sweden and their associated territories.

About the authors

Zheng Gongcheng is a member of the Standing Committee of the National People's Congress of China, President of the China Association of Social Security and professor at Renmin University of China. He has long been devoted to research in social security, labour and employment. His research provides important theoretical support and references for China's social security reform and legislation.

Wolfgang Scholz is a senior consultant to the ILO and former social security advisor to the Social Security Department of the International Labour Office in Geneva. He has rich experience in social security planning at the national ministerial level and in social policy advice at the international (United Nations) level.

Declaration: *The responsibility for opinions expressed in articles, studies and other contributions rests solely with their authors, and publication does not constitute an endorsement by the International Labour Office of the opinions expressed in them, or of any products, processes or geographical designations mentioned.*

very positive direct and indirect productivity effects, while economic growth is central to enabling the expansion of social security. The long-term experiences of Germany, the United States and the United Kingdom as well as countries of high (social) expenditure, like the Nordic countries, reinforce that enhancing human capital accumulation and productivity, including, prominently, through social security, does not negatively affect economic development. The synchronized economic take-off and establishment of the social security systems in Japan and the Republic of Korea in the second half of the twentieth century point in the same direction.

It appears that in the contemporary world, there is no scientific evidence to attribute economic downturn to a well-managed welfare system. Not only does such misunderstanding impair the sound development of social security, it also hinders the pursuit of a positive way for economic growth.

This report explores and highlights such interlinkages in detail.

Particularly during the last global financial and economic crises, a certain level of agreement on the importance of social security among multilateral organizations was reached. Even if there might not be agreement on the model and the levels of expenditure, institutions like the International Monetary Fund (IMF) or the World Bank have agreed, to a certain extent, on the importance of social security. For instance, the IMF Independent Evaluation Office stated in a report: "Over the past decade, the IMF has stepped up its attention to social protection as it has dealt with the aftermath of the global financial crisis and addressed concerns from the impact of food and fuel price shocks and broader stresses on low-income groups and the most vulnerable. Thus, the IMF has moved beyond its traditional fiscal-centric approach to recognize that social protection can also be macro-critical for broader reasons including social and political stability concerns" (IMF, 2017b). The World Bank Group and ILO-led Global Partnership for Universal Social Protection, launched in 2016, demonstrates the recognition by the World Bank of the importance of social protection to combat poverty and rising income inequality (World Bank and ILO, 2016).

10. The construction of comprehensive and multilayered social security systems, which are in line with basic social security principles (as stipulated in ILO Conventions and Recommendations), is advisable for minimizing system failures during crises. To improve and maintain social security's function as a service, the workflows within and between social security agencies should be optimized and modernized, including with the help of information technology. This will fortify social security's attractiveness in relation to private competitors.

Both social security and economic development in the twenty-first century will require continued innovation and institutional modifications to keep pace with changing times, while social security, through its practice, must be the solid guarantee for its members and its beneficiaries. In this respect, the positive interaction between and joint progress of social security and economic development should be a guideline for all stakeholders, while dependency on immediate and immanent business interests should be avoided.

China's development over the past 30 years is not without flaw but still offers prime evidence of the positive synergy that can be achieved between social security and economic developments.

When well adapted to a country's societal and economic fabric, social security can have

- Neoliberal exaggerations of the past must be overcome (for example, labour rights must be re-strengthened) with re-fostering social security's implicit and explicit productivity effects.
- Labour remuneration must be increased. This includes taking the ageing-induced social security costs off the international competitiveness agenda to facilitate national anti-poverty policies.
- Income and wealth inequalities must be reduced (including through more redistributive elements in tax and social security legislation) to strengthen domestic demand, at the least.
- With the accelerated development of the digital economy, social security systems should enhance their adaptability, not only to guarantee the financial basis but also to cover (workers in) new forms of employment brought about by the digital economy.
- People must be provided with more equal access to quality education to ensure the constant improvement of human capital.
- Social security must be strengthened to respond to the continued growth of the world population, to environmental issues and other global challenges, like pollution, the shortage of fresh water and climate change.

In all these cases, social security cannot be the (sole) solution. Given its socioeconomic impact, it is an indispensable prerequisite for providing people (and governments) with the necessary time required to find trustable solutions (ILO, 2017).

9. Economic globalization and regional competition, population ageing, population movement, social structure changes, progress in science and information technology followed by new industries, non-standard forms of employment and lifestyle changes are presenting new challenges to economic and other developments and to social security around the globe.

These changes may have various impacts on social security but are far from affecting its principal resilience and effective capacity to maintain its economic and social roles. Because all countries must cope actively and steadily with the above challenges and changes, they will need to seek new balances in numerous policy fields. Social security should be used proactively in finding such solutions rather than being used as a narrow instrument for cost adjustments in international competition. Also, social security, because of its nature, should neither take the role of economic policies nor be held accountable for the failure of economic policies.

7. China's impressive role in contemporary debates on social security policy stems from it being regarded as an important example of how to use institutionalized social security (among others) to orchestrate institutional adjustments as a means to initiate dynamic growth policy. Indeed, in taking a comprehensive approach, China succeeded in pursuing a policy strategy in which economic reform and problem-focused social security overhaul mutually complemented each other. While social security reforms allowed the unleashing of economic growth, it, in turn, had positive repercussions on social security – in general, a virtuous cycle.

One deeper reason for the success of this policy was that it provided institutional guarantees to promises of sustained improvement of people's livelihoods (as a result of the reforms) not only in the future but immediately. Although China is in the middle of deepening its reforms towards an upgraded social security system, which requires further overarching redesign, the tremendous progress already achieved is a prime policy example for developing countries around the world of adhering to an effective combination of social security and economic development. From an international perspective, it is not so much the measures that impress (after all, the Chinese Government applied well-known instruments: pension benefits and health insurance nearly covering the whole population, supplemented with unemployment benefits and minimum income guarantees). Rather, it is the speed with which the instruments were institutionalized and made ready to serve.

8. Social security is an effective governance tool for countering negative crisis effects or, more generally, for fostering system transformation. These situations are, however, not the standard cases for which social security is to be designed, nor should social security be applied only in such circumstances. Rather, it should also be socially effective and economically productive under normal (non-crisis) conditions. Social security systems must be designed so that they function well under both normal and crisis conditions. For this to happen, a whole range of various aspects and tools are available. Understanding the socioeconomic functions of different social security programmes is requisite for their proper design and for maximizing, in practice, the positive social and economic functions of the different schemes. Nevertheless, it needs to be emphasized that social security should not be seen predominantly as a means to meet political or economic goals but as a crucial instrument to realize a decent life and human dignity.

With those realities in mind, the following social security challenges loom for many countries covered in this report (as well as many others not included):

necessary ingredient to development in the twenty-first century (Zheng, 2017a). China is a prominent example of adapting social security for a successful economic transformation and contributing to unleashing the country's long-retained growth potential. Yet, with a social expenditure ratio of around 13 per cent[1], China is still half way from Europe's relative social expenditure levels, and, despite remarkable progress made, its primary income distribution is still unfair.

Therefore, China should systematically further expand its social security system in line with the evolving economic capacities to prepare, at the very least, for the next economic crisis. China should pursue such policy also to maximize the likelihood of success in shifting its economy from an export-led to a domestically driven growth path. This policy requires fostering education and educational benefits, employment measures, housing policies and, most importantly, steady increases in wages, especially for low-income workers.

6. In many countries, including China, demographic ageing is seen as triggering social costs that hamper national economic development, including through negative effects on international competitiveness. Such concerns, however, appear to ignore that the populations of almost all world regions are ageing – and all regions are exposed to the expansion of the related costs. Therefore, international agreement should be sought (at least among the Group of Twenty countries) to take the unavoidable additional social costs that are induced through ageing off the international competition agenda. With such agreement at hand, all countries could much more effectively pursue social policies aimed at poverty alleviation, including avoiding old-age poverty, which otherwise will become a growing problem around the globe in the future.

---

[1] Authors' estimates based on *China Statistical Yearbook 2018*. In this calculation, the total spending on social security includes fiscal expenditures on social security, public health expenditure, public education expenditure and social insurance expenditure. Fiscal expenditures on social security includes expenditures on social assistance and government-subsidized housing, financial subsidies to social insurance programmes, allowances for people with disabilities and older persons, etc. Social insurance expenditure includes pay-outs of pension scheme, health insurance, employment injury insurance, unemployment insurance and maternity insurance. Public education expenditure includes compulsory education, early childhood education, education for people with disabilities, vocational education and subsidies for higher education. This figure is different from ILO (2017) estimates, which do not include health expenditures.

and enhance social security.[1] However, of the group of developing countries, particularly within the association of Brazil, the Russian Federation, India, China and South Africa (known as the BRICS), it was mainly China that could successfully grasp the opportunity of economic transformation, including through export-oriented trade policy, a process in which the application of significantly enhanced social security had a major supportive role.

Those (temporarily) fast-developing countries (mainly the BRICS), all took steps to improve social security with the intention of having their general populations participate in the fruits of globalization, which otherwise were expected to end in the hands of only a few. Through technical cooperation in social security and other engagements, the International Labour Organization (ILO) has reminded countries worldwide of the fundamental goal of economic development: to enhance people's welfare. The approval of ILO Recommendation No. 202 and adoption of the SDGs demonstrates that social security has become much more implicit in the international agenda, showing the existence of trends with different directions, which are the result of a complex dynamic between different players.

At the same time, a retrenchment of social security has been observed in Western countries, while space for social security increased in some regions (for instance, among member countries of the Association of Southeast Asian Nations, ASEAN), following the similar direction observed in China and the other BRICS.

5. Given this background, countries must find ways to reshape their welfare policies (including social security) as their societies continue (or return to) accepting the new realities of globalization. Western countries and some developing countries should reconsider their current austere social policy and seek to replace it with policies that strengthen income security and narrow down income disparity. It is consistent to counter people's increased insecurities with strengthened social security.

Generally, more proactive social security systems, which are self-adjustable and resilient to keep up with the times, and are able to constantly optimize themselves, should be a

---

[1] This statement must be read with care and needs more explanation that cannot be undertaken in this report: At the global level, trade-surplus countries need trade-deficit countries as counterparts because the global trade balance is, logically, zero. In other words: export-led strategies in the 1990s and after relied on the readiness of (mainly) the United States to run such deficits.

participation, income distribution and international trade, among others (Scholz, 2015). Concrete conclusions of the debate often rest upon the design of the social security system under consideration; for example, whether it is more of a Bismarckian or a Beveridgean or a hybrid system design.

Generally, conclusions appear accepted among specialists that Bismarckian systems are more productivity-oriented, whereas Beveridgean systems lean towards achieving societal equity. With socioeconomic developments evolving, combinations of characteristics of both designs tend to appear more frequently, and it is most likely that in the future, further system hybridization will take place.

3. In modern societies, social security is a structurally complex and financially comprehensive system, taking shares of between 25 per cent and more than 30 per cent of GDP. One third or more of social security revenue is sustained by a government (the public sector), with the system comprising schemes and programmes of income protection in cash and/or in kind, all of which accompany individuals through various stages of their life cycle.[1]

Despite its inherent stabilizing features, social security and its role in national economies underwent another phase of significant adjustment some 20 to 30 years ago, which can, in a nutshell, be attributed to the post-1989 international spread of the Washington Consensus (Williamson, 2002), the reform and opening up of China and the subsequent commencement of intensified competitive globalization.

In the West, many countries decided to manage the resulting challenges, including demographic ageing, fiscal indebtedness and the complex impacts on labour markets, through cost containment and, after the 2008 subprime crisis, through austerity. Short of accommodating economic and fiscal policy, the Western welfare state as a guiding concept has been on the retreat for several decades.

4. In principle, globalization offered a number of countries the opportunity to embark on temporary export-led, high-growth development strategies and to simultaneously develop

---

[1] In this paper, social security includes benefits for children and families, maternity, unemployment, employment injury, sickness, old-age, disability, survivors, health protection and education benefits.

many nations in continental Europe. While, at first, it emerged primarily as a governance mechanism for countering political or economic crises, social security later also helped foster system transformation. There was a recognition that social security can and should also be applied outside of crisis response. Indeed, in many countries it has proven itself a socially effective and economically productive policy tool under "normal" (non-crisis) conditions. Social security systems must therefore be designed so that they are trusted by their stakeholders and function well under both auspices.

For more than a century, well-governed social security reduced social contradictions, enhanced national identity, compensated for market failures and contributed to stabilizing, often even stimulating, economic growth. The growing attention to the importance of building social protection systems in middle- and low-income countries over the past two or three decades is the latest chapter of a century-long history of building social protection systems (ILO, 2017). China has been at the forefront of these latest developments. Today, most countries have in place social protection schemes anchored in national legislation; yet, in many cases, these schemes cover only a minority of their populations. Despite laudable progress, large gaps remain, mainly in parts of Asia and Africa (ILO, 2017).

With the founding of the United Nations, social security became a human right.[1] Hence, it is generally accepted that social security is not only a potentially effective anti-crisis governance tool to counter temporary negative income effects on people, but that it equally represents a body of human rights and entitlements. Rights and entitlements will easily lose their significance if not materially supported. Therefore, policies of joint social security and economic development must be given focused attention. In modern countries, both are mutually dependent cornerstones of political and socioeconomic practice and cannot be separated. Instead, much care must be taken with their complementing each other to achieve a maximum of positive interaction (Scholz, 2015).

2. The international debate on the effects of social security on economic growth is complex, and its results have not always been unanimously accepted. Overall, it is held that once a social security system of sufficient financial size is in place, it can affect production (gross domestic product) and employment, labour productivity, labour market

---

[1] The human right to social security is enshrined in the Universal Declaration of Human Rights (1948), the International Covenant on Economic, Social and Cultural Rights (1966) and in other major United Nations human rights instruments as well as ILO standards.

Executive summary

Since the subprime mortgage crisis of the United States in 2008, the global economy has been mired in difficulties, and social security[1] has become an increased focus of policy discussions and academic debates. How to interpret and properly handle the relationships between social security and economic development has also become a major issue of international and national debates.

The adoption of the Social Protection Floors Recommendation, 2012 (No. 202) by the International Labour Conference reaffirms that social security is a human right and urges all countries to develop their social security systems. In September 2015, 193 Member States of the United Nations formally adopted the 17 Sustainable Development Goals (SDGs) at the United Nations Sustainable Development Summit in New York.

This report generalizes theoretical considerations on the relationship between social security and economic development and analyses contemporary and future challenges to social security brought about by paradigmatic changes in economic thought and realities. While aiming to clarify possible misconceptions, the report summarizes the relationship between social security and economic development from a historical perspective and explores how synchronized development and positive interaction between the two can be achieved.

The following summarizes the report's main viewpoints.

1. Historically, social security has been important to the socioeconomic, macroeconomic and political development of diverse countries and regions, like the United States and

---

[1] The term "social security" used here has no significant difference with "social protection" as defined and commonly used by the ILO. In this report, both terms are used interchangeably according to the context.

ILO Regional Office for Asia and the Pacific; Li Qingyi, Programme Officer of the ILO Country Office for China and Mongolia; Christoph Pohlmann, former Resident Representative of the FES Beijing Representative Office; and Zhu Yukun, Senior Social Security Specialist, ISSA. Earlier versions of this report were also presented in various high-level conferences and seminars, and the authors would like to thank the participants for their comments and suggestions, including Athar Hussain, professor, London School of Economics; Francis Kessler, professor, University of Paris 1; Lin Mingang, professor, Nanjing University; Shen Jie, professor, Japan Women's University; and Hong Kyung-Zoon, professor, Sungkyunkwan University. The authors would also like to thank Tim De Meyer, former Director of the ILO Country Office for China and Mongolia who was involved throughout the research project as well as Christina Behrendt, Head of the Social Policy Unit at the Social Protection Department of the ILO and Sara Elder, Head of the Regional Economic and Social Analysis Unit and Senior Economist, ILO Regional Office for Asia and the Pacific, for their comments and feedback.

It should also be noted that Professor He Wenjiong and Dr Hua Ying not only participated in the writing of Section 3.1, but also were involved in discussions throughout the research process. In addition, by liaising with the authors of the country reports and translating the main report from Chinese into English and English into Chinese, Dr Hua Ying made a unique contribution to this report.

Acknowledgements

This report is the result of shared effort by the China Association of Social Security (CAOSS), the International Labour Organization (ILO) and Friedrich-Ebert-Stiftung (FES). The executive summary, section 1.1, section 2.2, Chapter 3 and Chapter 4 were written by Zheng Gongcheng, president of CAOSS and professor at Renmin University of China. Wolfgang Scholz, senior consultant to the ILO, was responsible for writing sections 1.2 and 2.1. He Wenjiong, professor at Zhejiang University and Hua Ying, Chinese Academy of Social Sciences, contributed to the writing of section 3.1. All other text is a result of joint efforts of Zheng Gongcheng, Wolfgang Scholz, Hua Ying.

Special thanks go to Hua Jianmin, Honorary President of the CAOSS, former state councillor and vice chairman of the standing committee of the eleventh National People's Congress, for his remarkable and insightful opinions presented at the project launch meeting. The authors are grateful for contributions to discussions received from Zhou Hong, former Director of the Institute of European Studies at Chinese Academy of Social Sciences; Shen Shuguang, professor, Sun Yat-sen University of China; Yang Lixiong, professor, Renmin University of China; and Lu Quan, associate professor at Renmin University of China. The authors are also very grateful for the contributions to discussions received from the authors of the country reports, including John D. Stephens, professor, University of North Carolina (USA); John Hudson, professor, University of York (UK); Wolfgang Schroeder, professor, State University of Kassel (Germany); Pierre Concialdi, researcher, Institute de Recherches Economiques et Sociales (France); Klaus Petersen, professor, University of Southern Denmark (Denmark); Taichi Ono, professor, National Graduate Institute for Policy Studies (Japan); and Kim Yeon-Myung, professor, Chung-Ang University (Republic of Korea).

For the valuable contributions to discussions and various versions of the report, the authors would also like to thank Nuno Cunha, Senior Social Protection Specialist, shaping each nation's economic development. Economic growth creates the material basis for adequate social security benefits, while social security systems contribute to stabilizing economies and often even stimulating economic growth. But despite the inherent stability function of social security, its relationship with and effect on economic growth are complex, and not without controversy. Different systems and schemes can have different effects in specific contexts. Unpacking the complexity of the interactions between social protection and economic growth, will help improve national systems and maximize positive synergies.

Today, most countries have put in place social protection systems that are anchored in national legislation, although in many cases, the schemes only cover a minority of the national population. Starting from the introduction of social security in Europe and moving to recent developments in emerging countries, most prominently in China, this Working Paper offers insights into global experiences of the past century that reflect an overall positive relationship between the expansion of social security and economic development.

This Working Paper provides an assessment of the relationship between social security and the economic development in China, the United States, the United Kingdom, Germany, France, the Nordic countries, Japan and the Republic of Korea. Further, it provides thorough insights on the evolution of China's social security system and its role in the country's recent socioeconomic transformation. Based on the Chinese experience, the Paper argues that, when well adapted to a country's societal and economic fabric, social security can have positive direct and indirect productivity effects and, vice versa, positive economic development can promote the progressive development of social security.

This Working Paper relies on a convergence of views between the China Association of Social Security, the ILO and FES that in the current context characterized by profound structural changes and global instability, social security is an indispensable part of sustainable development. Economic growth is meant to bring more benefits to people's livelihoods through adequate social security benefits, while social security systems have a positive role in promoting economic development.

We hope that this Working Paper will contribute to a better understanding of these complex relationships and shed the light on the importance of social security systems as an integral element of sustainable development and transformation processes.

Tomoko Nishimoto
Assistant Director-General and Regional Director
for Asia and the Pacific

Preface

This Working Paper is the result of a joint research project between the China Association of Social Security, the International Labour Organization (ILO) and the Friedrich-Ebert-Stiftung (FES). The China Association of Social Security is a national academic organization bringing together professionals and scholars of social security and related fields, with fairness, justice and shared benefits as its core values. It is devoted to promoting China's social security system and fostering global cooperation and exchanges in the field of social security. The ILO has a global mandate to promote social justice and advance opportunities for women and men to access decent and productive work. Through its tripartite structure involving the governments as well as workers' and employers' organisations of 187 states, the ILO adopts and promotes international labour standards and rights at work, universal and effective social protection systems and improved social dialogue on work-related issues. The FES is a German non-profit organization that promotes social justice, sustainable development and international cooperation.

As a part of the ILO Asia-Pacific Working Paper Series, this Working Paper focuses on the relationship between social security and economic development. It aims at sharing knowledge and stimulating the discussion on the development of social security systems around the globe, especially in developing countries.

Social security is widely recognized as a primary tool in reducing poverty and preventing vulnerability throughout individuals' life cycle. Additionally, the economic impact of effective social security has been proven positive in a variety of context, making it an irreplaceable institutional arrangement of any modern societies. Both the adoption of the ILO Social Protection Floors Recommendation, 2012 (No. 202) and the prominent role of social security in the 2030 Agenda for Sustainable Development reflect a consensus on the imperative of social security, as a matter of human rights and dignity.

Societies across the globe increasingly acknowledge that social security has a role in

Copyright © International Labour Organization [2019]

First published [2019]

Publications of the International Labour Office enjoy copyright under Protocol 2 of the Universal Copyright Convention. Nevertheless, short excerpts from them may be reproduced without authorization, on condition that the source is indicated. For rights of reproduction or translation, application should be made to ILO Publications (Rights and Licensing), International Labour Office, CH-1211 Geneva 22, Switzerland, or by email: rights@ilo.org. The International Labour Office welcomes such applications.

ISBN: 978-92-2-133727-0 (print); 978-92-2-133728-7(web pdf)

Libraries, institutions and other users registered with a reproduction rights organization may make copies in accordance with the licences issued to them for this purpose. Visit www.ifrro.org to find the reproduction rights organization in your country.

The designations employed in ILO publications, which are in conformity with United Nations practice, and the presentation of material therein do not imply the expression of any opinion whatsoever on the part of the International Labour Office concerning the legal status of any country, area or territory or of its authorities, or concerning the delimitation of its frontiers.

The responsibility for opinions expressed in signed articles, studies and other contributions rests solely with their authors, and publication does not constitute an endorsement by the International Labour Office of the opinions expressed in them.

Reference to names of firms and commercial products and processes does not imply their endorsement by the International Labour Office, and any failure to mention a particular firm, commercial product or process is not a sign of disapproval.

Information on ILO publications and digital products can be found at: www.ilo.org/publns.

GLOBAL SOCIAL SECURITY AND ECONOMIC DEVELOPMENT:
RETROSPECT AND PROSPECT

Zheng Gongcheng
Wolfgang Scholz

China Labor & Social Security Publishing House